Essentials of Electrical and Computer Engineering

Essentials of Electrical and Computer Engineering

SECOND EDITION

By

J. David Irwin—David V. Kerns, Jr.

SENIOR DIRECTOR	Don Fowley
EDITORIAL ASSISTANT	Molly Geisinger
SENIOR MANAGING EDITOR	Judy Howarth
PRODUCTION EDITOR	Umamaheswari Gnanamani
COVER PHOTO CREDIT	© Tanarch/Shutterstock; Courtesy of J. David Irwin and David V. Kerns, Jr.

This book was set in 9.5/12pt STIXTwoText by Straive™.

Founded in 1807, John Wiley & Sons, Inc. has been a valued source of knowledge and understanding for more than 200 years, helping people around the world meet their needs and fulfill their aspirations. Our company is built on a foundation of principles that include responsibility to the communities we serve and where we live and work. In 2008, we launched a Corporate Citizenship Initiative, a global effort to address the environmental, social, economic, and ethical challenges we face in our business. Among the issues we are addressing are carbon impact, paper specifications and procurement, ethical conduct within our business and among our vendors, and community and charitable support. For more information, please visit our website: www.wiley.com/go/citizenship.

ISBN: 9781119832829 (Print)
ISBN: 9781119832850 (EVAL)

Library of Congress Cataloging-in-Publication Data

Names: Irwin, J. David, 1939– author. | Kerns, David V., Jr., author.
Title: Essentials of electrical and computer engineering / by J. David
    Irwin, David V. Kerns.
Description: 2e. | Hoboken, NJ : Wiley, [2022] | Includes bibliographical
    references and index.
Identifiers: LCCN 2021054515 (print) | LCCN 2021054516 (ebook) | ISBN
    9781119832829 (paperback) | ISBN 9781119832843 (adobe pdf) | ISBN
    9781119832812 (epub) | ISBN 9781119832850 (eval)
Subjects: LCSH: Electrical engineering. | Computer engineering.
Classification: LCC TK146 .I79 2022 (print) | LCC TK146 (ebook) | DDC
    621.3—dc23/eng/20211123
LC record available at https://lccn.loc.gov/2021054515
LC ebook record available at https://lccn.loc.gov/2021054516

The inside back cover will contain printing identification and country of origin if omitted from this page. In addition, if the ISBN on the back cover differs from the ISBN on this page, the one on the back cover is correct.

SKY10031976_121421

Preface

This book is intended to serve as a text or guidebook for an introductory course or course sequence in electrical and computer engineering. It is unique in that it is concise, clear, and highly concentrated on the essential elements of understanding required for all engineering students and for successfully passing the electrical engineering portion of the Fundamentals of Engineering (FE) exam.

There is constant attention to providing a learning environment accessible to those with little or no electrical or computer engineering background. This is achieved through a large number of clear and concise explanations, worked examples, and homework problems crafted to illustrate key principles with a level of difficulty over a wide range. The optional use of MATLAB as a computing tool means that the study of the material can focus on the electrical engineering content, rather than linear algebra and differential equations. Furthermore, this mathematical solution technique is normally used by the students in their own curriculum to solve engineering problems.

The basic understanding and knowledge of electrical and computer engineering provided by this text will serve as a valuable reference for these fields as readers progress in their careers as practicing engineers. However, in the short term, this text is an important self-study aid as students prepare to take the FE exam.

The hallmark of the book is the manner in which complicated topics are made simple through a presentation that combines analogies, examples, and end-of-chapter problems. This text is student-oriented and aimed at presenting the topics in a way that is easy to grasp.

There are some special chapters and sections in the book that provide material not typically found in books that address the needs of non-ECE students and yet they are very important to the development of the student's understanding of the way in which the material is applied in their chosen field. For example, the chapter on instrumentation illustrates the manner in which the students must test and/or analyze their systems. Appendix D expands on how these measurements and other circuits can be made with modern integrated circuits. The in-depth look at the power system provides the student with an overview of the Power Grid and the manner in which the component elements work in concert to produce and deliver power. Modern electronic device technology is highlighted including its impact on society. The differences between power supply systems using silicon diodes and modern Schottky devices is explained; the biasing of LEDs of different colors for displays is illustrated as one of various applications of diodes.

There are multiple specific areas of interest that enhance the student's understanding of concepts that are not typically covered in most texts and yet are important topics that add much to the learning experience.

1. The Power System – an explanation of how the various components of the Grid work together to produce and deliver electric power.

2. Instrumentation – a close look at the manner in which electrical measurements support the analysis and development of engineering systems.

3. Integration of load line analysis with small-signal analysis – an analysis feature with wide application for enhancing the student's understanding of transistor and circuit operation and their options for analysis.

4. Modern electronic devices and their applications are presented in a manner useful for all majors, and at a level presuming no prior knowledge.

Finally, in both the classroom and self-study modes of learning via this text, there is considerable flexibility in the manner in which the material is covered. Once the basic circuits material is learned, there are several paths that can be used to learn necessary material or develop a strong course in these subjects.

ACKNOWLEDGMENTS

We gratefully acknowledge our wives, Edie Irwin and Sherra Kerns, for their patience and understanding as we worked to complete this project. In addition, there are two individuals who deserve special recognition. They are Ms. Elizabeth Devore and Dr. Daniel Geiger. They have contributed to this book by providing content as well as checking material for errors. We are most appreciative of their excellent support. We also acknowledge the suggestions and assistance by Mr. Keith Warren, P.E.

Contents

13   Electrical Measurements and Instrumentation   427

14   DC Machines   467

About the Authors

J. David Irwin is Professor and Department Head Emeritus in the Department of Electrical and Computer Engineering at Auburn University. He is the author or coauthor of 10 university-level textbooks, one of which is currently in the 12th edition and has been used both nationally and internationally for more than 35 years. He has served as President of two IEEE Technical Societies and Editor-in-Chief of the *IEEE Transactions on Industrial Electronics*. He served as a Series Editor for both CRC Press and the Academic Press and in those capacities oversaw the development of 23 books. He has served as both a member and chair of a host of IEEE technical committees and has been General Chair or Honorary Chair for a number of IEEE conferences throughout the world. He is a Life Fellow of the IEEE, and a Fellow of ASEE, AAAS, and NAI. He is the recipient of numerous education, professional, and technical awards including the IEEE's James H. Mulligan Jr. Education Medal. The IEEE industrial Electronics Society created the J. David Irwin Early Career award in recognition of the many contributions made to the development of young professionals and the award is given annually to outstanding IEEE members throughout the world.

David V. Kerns, Jr is the Founding Provost and Distinguished Professor of Electrical Engineering Emeritus at Olin College. Dr. Kerns led the development of the entire academic and student-life programs and introduced project-based, student-centered learning into all facets of the Olin College curriculum. He currently is Adjoint Professor of Electrical Engineering at Vanderbilt University, and previously served as the Electrical Engineering Department Chair, Associate Dean, and Distinguished Professor at Vanderbilt University. He also has served on the faculties of Florida State University, Auburn University, and Bucknell University, where he taught electrical engineering courses for over 25 years and has coauthored two electrical engineering textbooks. Dr. Kerns also served in industry at Bell Telephone Laboratories and as an entrepreneur in cofounding two successful electronic companies. He is a Fellow of the IEEE, served multiple terms as President of the IEEE Education Society, and served as Editor of the *IEEE Transactions on Education*. He has over 100 publications in the areas of microelectronics research, engineering education, and entrepreneurship. He has received numerous awards recognizing accomplishments in these areas. Dr. Kerns is recipient of the National Academy of Engineering's Bernard M. Gordon Prize in 2013 for Innovation in Engineering and Technology Education.

Introduction

CHAPTER 1

LEARNING OBJECTIVES

- To understand the system of units and standard prefixes used throughout the text

- To review the fundamental building blocks, e.g. charge, current, voltage, and power

- To learn the definition and symbols employed to describe the sources, both independent and dependent, that represent the forcing functions for electric circuits

- To present Tellegen's theorem and describe its usefulness in circuit analysis

---

To begin our study of electrical and computer engineering, we should first note that the units employed in this area of technology are not those used in the English system, i.e. feet, pounds, etc. Rather, we employ the International System of Units, which are composed of meter, kilogram, second, ampere, degree Kelvin, and candela. In addition, there are a standard set of prefixes that are employed in this technology, some of which have found their way into contemporary communication. The prefixes are

| FUNDAMENTAL |
| CONCEPTS |

$$\text{Kilo (k)} - 10^3$$
$$\text{Mega (M)} - 10^6$$
$$\text{Giga (G)} - 10^9$$
$$\text{Tera (T)} - 10^{12}$$
$$\text{Milli (m)} - 10^{-3}$$
$$\text{Micro (}\mu\text{)} - 10^{-6}$$
$$\text{Nano (n)} - 10^{-9}$$
$$\text{Pico (p)} - 10^{-12}$$

It is interesting to note that these prefixes are often used in conversation, e.g. an individual speaks of paying 25k for a car, indicating that the car costs $25,000, or stating that a company just sold for 100 Megabucks or $100 million. However, the importance of these prefixes in the current context is that they are continuously used throughout this text.

An understanding of the material in this book is typically predicated upon the fact that anyone reading this book has already taken the basic physics sequence offered at essentially every college and university where this book would be logically used. Therefore, we will provide simple and succinct discussions of the various quantities that are the fundamental building blocks in electrical and computer technology.

Electric *current* is a measure of how much charge is moved per unit of time, i.e. it is *charge* in motion, and this charge in motion results in transfer of energy. The mathematical expression for current is

$$i(t) = dq(t)/dt$$

where q is the charge in coulombs, t is the time in seconds, and i(t) is the current in amperes (A), and hence 1 ampere is equal to 1 coulomb per second. While current flow is caused by electron motion in metallic conductors, conventional current flow is the net rate of flow of positive charges. Therefore, throughout the book the convention we will adopt is that if a metal conductor, e.g. a wire, is conducting electrons to the left, then there is positive current to the right. Nevertheless, in all that follows think of current as the movement of positive charges.

It is interesting at this point to pause and mention two of the basic forms of current as well as the range of their values. The two common types of current are direct current (dc) and alternating current (ac), as shown in Figure 1.1a and b, respectively. Note that dc is independent of time, i.e. it is constant. dc is generated by batteries, such as those found in flashlights, automobiles, and a host of electronic equipment such as cell phones and iPads. In sharp contrast, ac current is the current used in the power grid and used to run all appliances and lights in the home. In the United States, it is a sine wave with a frequency of 60 Hz (60 cycles per second). The magnitude of these currents is enormous and ranges from pico amperes in nerve cells in the body to thousands of amperes in a lightning bolt, thus encompassing a range of some 15 orders of magnitude.

Current requires a path. Some type of pipeline must exist in order to facilitate the movement of charge. Without charge in motion, there is no current. It is the electric circuit that provides this path. We will learn later that it is not sufficient to specify only the magnitude of the current, we must also know the direction of the current. Furthermore, we use the convention that a positive current of 2 A flowing right to left is equivalent to −2 A flowing left to right. This symbolism is shown in Figure 1.2. This is a critical point worth mentioning even at this early stage in our discussion. The reason is simply this: when we solve for currents in a circuit, in general we will not know the direction of the current we seek, but will assume a direction and if the current value is negative, we know the current is simply flowing in the direction opposite to that assumed.

In contrast to current, which is charge in motion, the *voltage,* often referred to as potential, that exists between any two points in the circuit is defined as the difference in energy levels of a positive charge located at each of these points. In other words, if a positive charge is moved from one point to another, then the energy required is the difference in energy levels between the two points. Voltage in volts is measured in joules per coulomb, and 1 volt is the energy in joules that is necessary to move a charge of 1 coulomb from one point to another. This definition is defined mathematically as

$$v(t) = dw(t)/dq(t)$$

where v is the voltage in volts, w is the *energy* in joules, and q is the charge in coulombs.

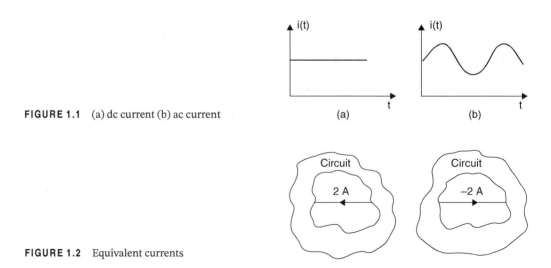

FIGURE 1.1 (a) dc current (b) ac current

FIGURE 1.2 Equivalent currents

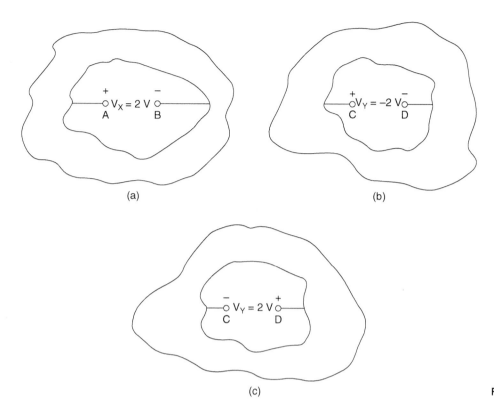

FIGURE 1.3 Voltage description

Much of what has been said for current applies to voltage as well. When describing current, we must specify both magnitude and direction. In a similar manner, when describing the voltage that exists between two points, we need to know which point is at the higher potential. In Figure 1.3a, the voltage V_x represents the voltage between points A and B, and the + and − signs define its reference direction. In this case, the voltage V_x is 2 V, and point A is at the higher potential. Thus, if a unit positive charge is moved from point B, through the circuit to point A, it will gain 2 J of energy, and if a unit positive charge is moved from point A through the circuit to point B, it will lose 2 J of energy. So point A is 2 V positive with respect to point B, and point B is 2 V negative with respect to point A.

As we indicated, if we change the direction of the current we change the sign, and the same rule applies with voltage. This concept is shown in Figure 1.3b and c. In Figure 1.3b, the voltage between points C and D is 2 V, and point D is at the higher potential. Figure 1.3c indicates that the voltage between points C and D is 2 V, and point D is at the higher potential. Note that Figure 1.3b and Figure 1.3c are equivalent and express exactly the same concept. Once again, both magnitude and direction must be specified, and if we reverse the direction, we change the sign.

Voltages, like currents, range from one end of the spectrum to the other. The voltage at the antenna of a cell phone may be in the microvolt range, while the magnitude of a lightning strike may be in millions of volts.

Recall that *power* is the time rate of change of energy and is therefore defined as

$$p(t) = dw(t)/dt$$

The relationship among voltage, current, and power is expressed by the equation

$$p(t) = dw(t)/dt = [dw(t)/dq(t)]\,[dq(t)/dt] = v(t)\,i(t)$$

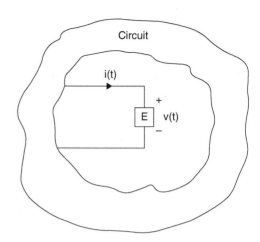

FIGURE 1.4 Circuit used to describe the passive sign convention

Thus, power can be expressed as the product of the voltage across the element and the current through it. Furthermore, the change in energy from time t_1 to t_2 can be determined by the equation

$$w(t) = \int_{t_1}^{t_2} v(t)\, i(t)\, dt$$

Clearly, it is important to know if the circuit element in question is supplying or absorbing power. A convention has been adopted to address this question. The *passive sign convention* for power is defined via the circuit in Figure 1.4. If the voltage across the element and the current through it are arranged as shown in the figure, i.e. the current enters the positive terminal, then the product of v(t) and i(t), together with their attendant signs, will generate both the magnitude of the power and specify if the element is absorbing or supplying power. If the resulting sign is positive, the element is absorbing power and if the sign is negative the element is supplying power.

Examples 1.1 and 1.2 illustrate the salient points of this discussion.

Example 1.1

Let us determine if the elements E1 and E2 in Figures 1.5 and 1.6, respectively, are absorbing or supplying power and how much.

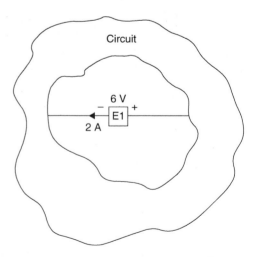

FIGURE 1.5 Circuit used in Example 1.1

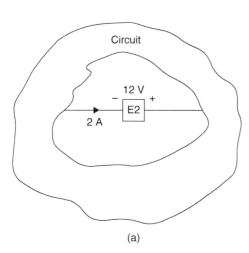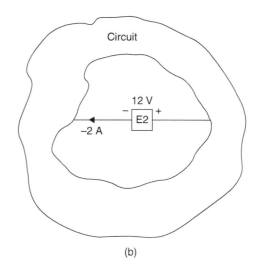

(a)   (b)

FIGURE 1.6   Circuit used in Example 1.1

First of all, note that Figure 1.5 is exactly the same as the configuration that defines the passive sign convention. The current enters the positive terminal of E1, and the equation for power is

$$P = (+6)(+2) = 12\ W$$

Since the result is positive, the element is absorbing power. An examination of Figure 1.6a indicates that the 2 A is leaving the positive terminal of E2, or equivalently −2 A is entering the positive terminal of E2 as shown in Figure 1.6b. Therefore, the power is

$$P = (+12)(-2) = -24\ W$$

and thus the negative sign indicates that element E2 is supplying power.

Example 1.2

Let us determine if element E1 in Figure 1.7a is absorbing or supplying power, and how much.

Recall that if we reverse the direction of the voltage or the current, we must change the sign. So Figure 1.7a can be changed to Figure 1.7b by reversing the direction of the current and changing the sign. Now the current enters the positive terminal of E1 and the equation for power is

$$P = (-6)(2) = -12\ W$$

and the negative sign indicates that 12 W is being supplied by E1. Likewise, we can reverse the voltage, as shown in Figure 1.7c, and then the equation for power is

$$P = (+6)(-2) = -12\ W$$

Therefore, once we place the circuit in question in the form of the passive sign convention, the result is not only the magnitude of the power but also the sign that indicates whether power is being supplied or absorbed.

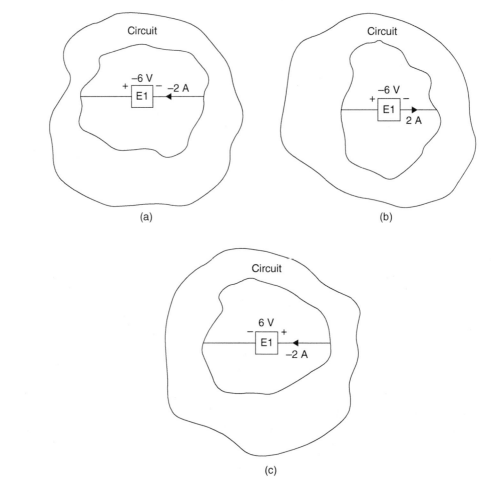

FIGURE 1.7 Circuits used in Example 1.2

SOURCES

Throughout this book, we will assume ideal circuit elements. As we progress in our understanding of the material, the differences between ideal and nonideal elements will become clearer. However, any discussion of these differences is premature at this point.

The circuit elements we will discuss here can be broadly classified as either *passive* or *active* elements. As one might expect, passive elements only absorb power. However, as we will demonstrate later in this book, some are capable of storing power. On the other hand, active elements can supply power.

Sources may be either voltage sources or current sources, and they may be either *independent* or *dependent*. An independent voltage source, shown in Figure 1.8a, produces a voltage v(t) between terminals A–B, where terminal A is v(t) volts positive with respect to terminal B. This source produces this voltage between these terminals independent of the current in the source.

The independent current source produces a current of i(t) from terminal B to terminal A (as the arrow indicates in Figure 1.8b), and this current is independent of the voltage across the current source.

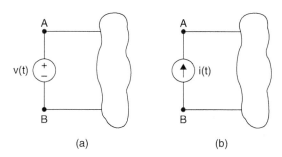

FIGURE 1.8   Circuits used to define sources

These independent sources typically supply power to a circuit, but there are circumstances when they actually absorb power, e.g. charging a battery.

In sharp contrast to independent sources that produce a voltage or current completely independent of anything else in the network, dependent sources generate a voltage or current that is dependent or controlled by some voltage or current at some other location in the circuit. The importance of these dependent sources stems from the fact that we model all active devices, e.g. transistors, with these elements. While independent sources are modeled with a circle, dependent sources are modeled with a diamond. The four different types of dependent sources are shown in Figure 1.9. There are voltage sources and current sources, and they can each be controlled by a voltage or a current.

A close examination of these circuits will indicate that coefficients a and d are dimensionless constants because we are transforming voltage to voltage and current to current. The constants b and c are not dimensionless since we are transforming voltage to current and vice versa. However, we must defer a discussion of these constants until later.

Before completing our discussion of sources, it is very important that the reader understand a couple of salient points concerning sources. With reference to Figure 1.8a, the voltage between the terminals A and B is $v(t)$ regardless of the current in the source. In fact, we can only calculate this current from the circuit components in the cloud, which represents the remainder of the circuit. Similarly, the current from B to A in the circuit in Figure 1.8b is $i(t)$ independent of the voltage across the current source. And once again, we will have to use the circuit components in the cloud to determine this voltage.

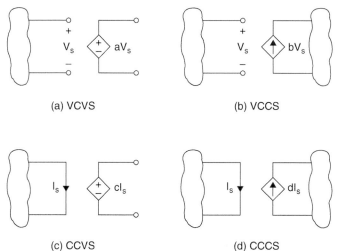

(a) VCVS

(b) VCCS

(c) CCVS

(d) CCCS

FIGURE 1.9   Dependent sources

Example 1.3

Two dependent source circuits are shown in Figure 1.10. Let us determine the outputs of each source.

Figure 1.10a is an illustration of a voltage-controlled voltage source (VCVS). The output voltage is

$$V_0 = 12\,V_S \text{ or } V_0 = 12 \times 2\,V = 24\,V$$

Similarly, Figure 1.10b is an illustration of a current-controlled current source (CCCS). The output current is

$$I_0 = 4\,I_S = 4 \times 2\,A = 8\,A$$

Note that both circuits are amplifiers. The voltage gain in the first circuit is 12 and the current gain in the second circuit is 4.

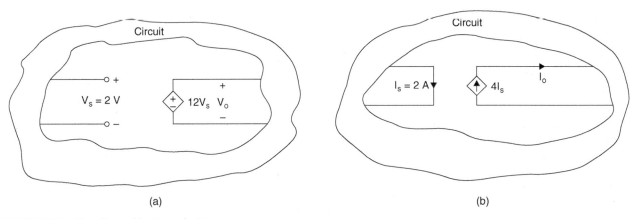

(a)   (b)

FIGURE 1.10   Circuits used in Example 1.3

TELLEGEN'S THEOREM

The law of *conservation of energy* is typically introduced in physics, and simply means that energy cannot be created or destroyed. Energy can, however, be transformed from one form to another, e.g. thermal energy to mechanical energy or mechanical energy to electrical energy. As indicated earlier, energy and power are related, and B. D. H. Tellegen formally proved that this concept is extended to electrical circuits, and thus the power supplied to an electrical network is exactly equal to that which is absorbed by the network.

We will find in the material ahead that many of the calculations performed on an electric circuit can be checked, i.e. currents and voltages in a circuit must satisfy certain laws. Tellegen's theorem provides an additional method for checking the results of an analysis since the power generated in the network must equal the power that is absorbed. Example 1.4 serves to illustrate this point.

Example 1.4

Consider the circuit in Figure 1.11. We wish to employ Tellegen's theorem to find the value of the voltage across the independent current source.

Note that the voltage and current are known for every element in the network with the exception of the voltage, V_x, across the independent current source. Therefore, we can identify the elements that are supplying power and the elements that are absorbing power.

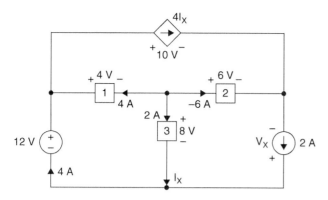

FIGURE 1.11 Circuit used in Example 1.4

The following elements are supplying power:

The 12 V independent voltage source is supplying power because a positive current of 4 A is leaving the positive terminal or equivalently −4 A is entering the positive terminal.

Element 1 is supplying power because a positive current of 4 A is leaving the positive terminal or equivalently −4 A is entering the positive terminal.

Element 2 is supplying power because a current of −6 A is entering the positive terminal.

The 2 A independent current source is supplying power because a positive current of −2 A is entering the positive terminal of the source.

The following elements are absorbing power:

The dependent current source, $4 I_x$, is absorbing power since the positive current is entering the positive terminal.

Element 3 is absorbing power because the positive current of 2 A is entering the positive terminal.

Summing the power for each individual element and setting the result to zero yield the equation

$$(12)(-4) + (4)(-4) + (6)(-6) + (V_x)(-2) + (10)(4 I_x) + (8)(2) = 0$$

However, note that $I_x = 2$ A, and therefore

$$-48 - 16 - 36 - 2V_x + 80 + 16 = 0$$

Solving for V_x yields

$$V_x = -2 \text{ V}$$

Since power must be conserved in a network, i.e. whatever is generated must be absorbed, the use of Tellegen's theorem provides a means to check the analysis results when determining a voltage, current, or power within a network. In the following chapter, we will learn other methods for calculating these quantities.

Problems

1.1 A dc source supplies 6×10^{20} electrons in 5 s to a load. How much current is supplied to the load? (The charge of an electron is 1.9×10^{-19} Coulombs).

1.2 One of the connecting wires in an electronic circuit has 4×10^{18} electrons flowing through it in 8 s. What is the current in the wire?

1.3 When starting an automobile, the battery delivers 125 A in a 2-s period. How many electrons emanate from the battery?

1.4 How many electrons are passing through a wire in 1 s if the current in the wire is 400 mA?

1.5 A power source supplies 2 J of energy in the process of transferring 0.333 coulombs of charge to a load. What is the voltage across the source?

1.6 A 12 V battery supplies 0.6 A to a light bulb for 20 min. How many electrons pass through the bulb during this period?

1.7 Determine the power delivered to the light bulb in Problem 1.6.

1.8 Calculate the amount of energy provided to the bulb in Problem 1.6.

1.9 During ignition, a 12 V car battery supplies 125 A in a 2-s period. How much energy does the battery supply?

1.10 Two batteries are connected as shown in Figure P1.10. Is battery A supplying power to battery B or vice versa?

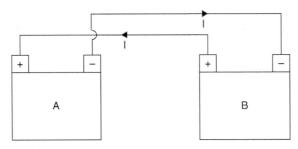

FIGURE P1.10

1.11 Determine whether the elements shown in Figure P1.11 are absorbing or supplying power.

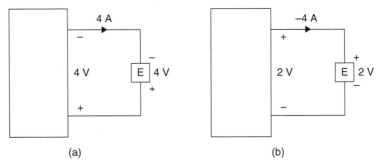

(a)   (b)

FIGURE P1.11

1.12   Determine the amount of power absorbed or supplied by the elements in Figure P1.12.

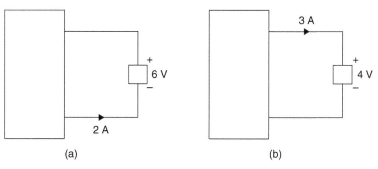

(a)   (b)

FIGURE P1.12

1.13   Determine the amount of power absorbed or supplied by the elements in Figure P1.13.

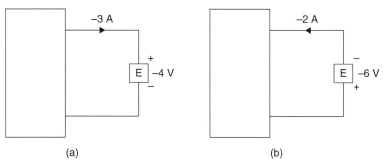

(a)   (b)

FIGURE P1.13

1.14   Determine whether the elements shown in Figure P1.14 are absorbing or supplying power.

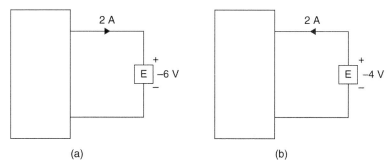

(a)   (b)

FIGURE P1.14

1.15 Determine the unknown voltages in the networks in Figure P1.15.

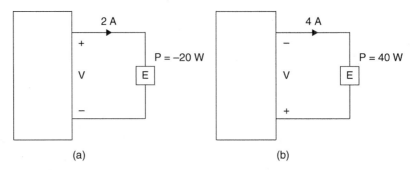

(a)

(b)

FIGURE P1.15

1.16 Determine the unknown voltages in the network in Figure P1.16.

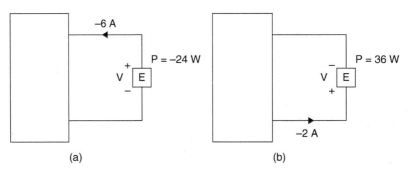

(a)

(b)

FIGURE P1.16

1.17 Determine the unknown currents in the circuits in Figure P1.17.

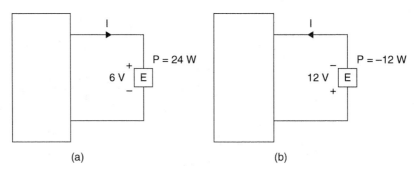

(a)

(b)

FIGURE P1.17

1.18   Determine the unknown currents in the circuits in Figure P1.18.

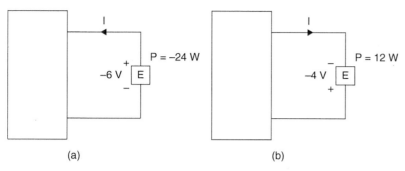

(a)   (b)

FIGURE P1.18

1.19   Determine if power is being absorbed or supplied by the elements in Figure P1.19.

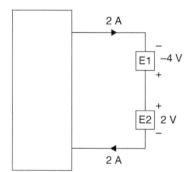

FIGURE P1.19

1.20   Determine if power is being absorbed or supplied by the elements in Figure P1.20.

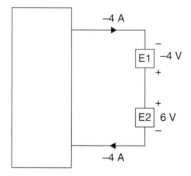

FIGURE P1.20

1.21 If element E1 in Figure P1.21 is absorbing 12 W, is element E2 absorbing or supplying power, and how much?

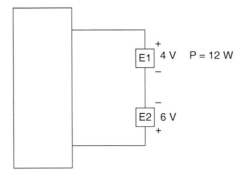

FIGURE P1.21

1.22 If element E2 in Figure P1.22 is supplying 24 W, is element E1 absorbing or supplying power, and how much?

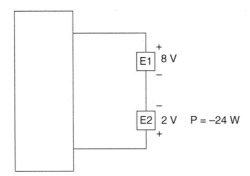

FIGURE P1.22

1.23 If element E1 in Figure P1.23 is absorbing 24 W, is element E2 absorbing or supplying power, and how much?

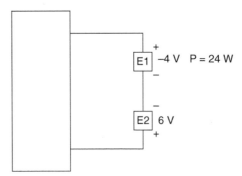

FIGURE P1.23

1.24 If element E2 in Figure P1.24 is supplying 36 W, is element E1 absorbing or supplying power, and how much?

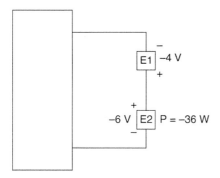

FIGURE P1.24

1.25 Determine the output voltage in the dependent source shown in Figure P1.25.

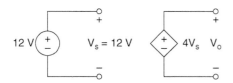

FIGURE P1.25

1.26 Determine the output voltage in the dependent source shown in Figure P1.26.

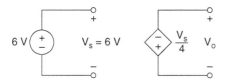

FIGURE P1.26

1.27 Determine the output current in the dependent source shown in Figure P1.27.

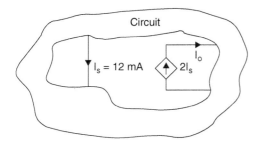

FIGURE P1.27

1.28 Determine the output current in the dependent source shown in Figure P1.28.

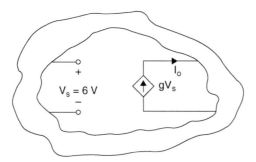

FIGURE P1.28

1.29 Determine the output voltage in the dependent source shown in Figure P1.29.

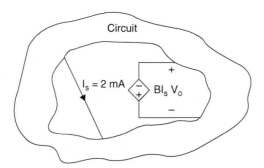

FIGURE P1.29

1.30 Find the power that is absorbed or supplied by the circuit elements in Figure P1.30.

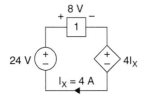

FIGURE P1.30

1.31 Determine the power that is absorbed or supplied by the circuit elements in Figure P1.31.

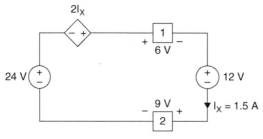

FIGURE P1.31

1.32   Use Tellegen's theorem to determine I_X in the network in Figure P1.32.

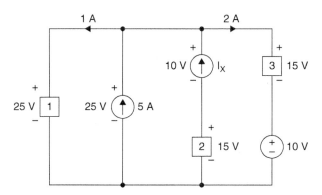

FIGURE P1.32

1.33   Determine the power absorbed or supplied by each element in the network in Figure P1.33 and verify that Tellegen's theorem is satisfied.

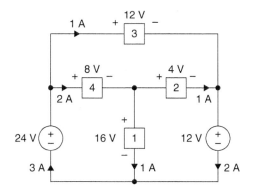

FIGURE P1.33

1.34   Use Tellegen's theorem to determine I_0 in the network in Figure P1.34.

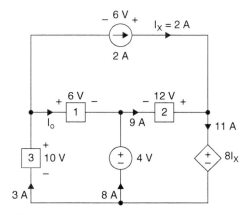

FIGURE P1.34

CHAPTER 2	# The Basic Laws of Circuit Analysis

LEARNING OBJECTIVES

- To learn the three basic laws that are universally applied in circuit analysis: Ohm's law, Kirchhoff's Current Law (KCL), and Kirchhoff's Voltage Law (KVL)

- To understand current division and voltage division

- To be able to simplify complicated resistor networks and reduce them to a single resistor

- To be able to analyze simple networks containing both independent and dependent sources

---

INTRODUCTION

In this chapter, the laws that form the basis of our discussion of circuit analysis are presented and demonstrated in a variety of examples. The examples employed are designed to address the salient features of these laws in an attempt to foster a quick understanding of these topics.

OHM'S LAW

The German physicist Georg Simon Ohm is credited with discovering the voltage/current relationship for resistance and thus the law is named for him. *Ohm's law simply states that the voltage across a resistance is directly proportional to the current flowing through it.* The voltage is measured in volts (V), the current is measured in amperes (A), and the resistance is measured in ohms (Ω). Resistors, as the elements are called, come in various sizes and are manufactured using a variety of techniques, e.g. carbon composition or wirewound, to name only two. Figure 2.1 shows a variety of resistors that range from small resistors that have a power rating of $\frac{1}{4}$ Watt to those with high power ratings. While these passive components find wide application in circuits, they are by no means the only format in which resistors are used today. At this point in time, resistors are manufactured directly on the substrate of integrated circuits and millions of them appear on a tiny integrated circuit chip.

The symbol that represents resistance is shown in Figure 2.2, and the mathematical equation that defines Ohm's law is the following:

$$v(t) = i(t) R, \text{ for } R > 0$$

where we assume that the resistors are linear devices and therefore the V–I relationship is linear too. *The polarity of the voltage and its relationship to the direction of the current are critical.* To ensure the reader does not miss this point, let's consider the network shown in Figure 2.3. A single point of interconnection within a larger network is singled out for examination. Let us determine the unknowns illustrated in the figure using Ohm's law. First, consider the unknown I_1. This current is into the positive terminal, and therefore the relationship for Ohm's law is

$$V = I_1 R$$
$$\text{or}$$
$$4 = I_1(4k)$$
$$I_1 = 2 \text{ mA}$$

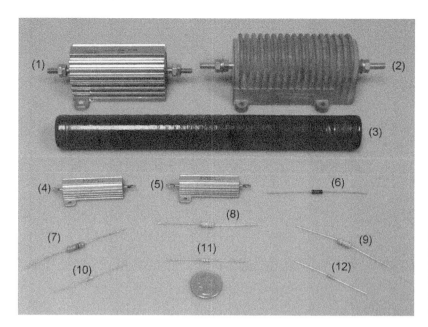

FIGURE 2.1 Some practical devices. (1), (2), and (3) are high-power resistors. (4) and (5) are high-wattage fixed resistors. (6) is a high-precision resistor. (7)–(12) are fixed resistors with different power ratings (Courtesy of Mark Nelms and Jo Ann Loden)

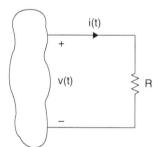

FIGURE 2.2 Symbol for resistance

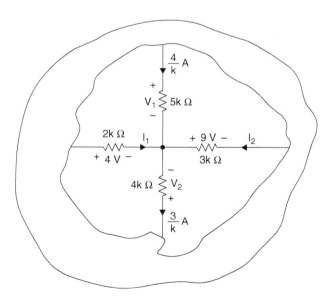

FIGURE 2.3 Circuit illustrating Ohm's Law

The voltage V_1 is obtained from the relationship

$$V_1 = IR$$

Since the current is into the positive terminal

$$V_1 = (4/k)(5k)$$
$$= 20 \text{ V}$$

The current I_2 is obtained from the relationship

$$-V = I_2 R$$

Since the current is in the opposite direction as specified by Ohm's law,

$$-9 = (I_2)(3k)$$
$$I_2 = -3 \text{ mA}$$

Ohm's law for the voltage V_2 is

$$V_2 = -I \, R$$

or

$$V_2 = (-3/k)(4k)$$
$$= -12 \text{ V}$$

One critical issue in the application of Ohm's law is the following. Ohm's law only applies when the voltage is *directly across* the resistor and the current is in the resistor. Ohm's law cannot be applied arbitrarily to a circuit containing multiple resistors.

Another quantity, directly related to resistance and one that also finds wide application in circuit analysis, is conductance. Conductance is defined as the reciprocal of resistance. The symbol for conductance is G and the units are Siemens, i.e.

$$G = 1/R$$

Hence 1 Siemen = 1 A/V, and the V–I relationship is

$$i(t) = v(t)G$$

The resistor is a passive element, that is, it does not generate any power; it simply absorbs power and dissipates it in the form of heat. The instantaneous power is

$$p(t) = v(t) \, i(t)$$

Note that power is a nonlinear relationship and by using Ohm's law can be expressed in the form $p(t) = i^2(t)R = v^2(t)/R$, measured in Watts.

Using conductance, the equations can be also expressed in the form $p(t) = i^2(t)/G = v^2(t)G$, measured in Watts.

Before proceeding with a number of examples illustrating the application of Ohm's law, we pause to examine two important values of R and G. First, $R = 0$ and thus $G =$ infinity. $R = 0$ is called a short circuit and

$$v(t) = i(t)0 = 0$$

In this case, the voltage is zero, while the current could be anything. Second, R = infinity and thus G = 0. R equal to infinity is called an open circuit and

$$i(t) = v(t)/\text{infinity} = 0$$

For an open circuit, the current is zero, while the voltage across the open terminals could be any value.

Now that we have discussed the basic concepts surrounding Ohm's law, let us look at several examples that will hopefully explain the various facets of this law.

Consider the circuit in Figure 2.4. The current circulating in the circuit is

$$I = V/R = 9/3k = 3 \text{ mA}$$

Example 2.1

The power absorbed by the resistor is

$$P = VI = (9)(3 \times 10^{-3}) = 27 \text{ mW}$$
$$= I^2R = (3 \times 10^{-3})^2(3k) = 27mW$$
$$= V^2/R = (9)^2/3k = 27mW$$

Clearly, we can calculate the power absorbed by the resistor in a variety of ways. In addition, we know that there must exist a power balance in the circuit, i.e. the power absorbed must be equal to the power supplied. The power supplied by the source is P = VI. Using the passive sign convention, the current into the source is −3 mA, and therefore the power at the source is −27 mW, indicating that power is being supplied by the source.

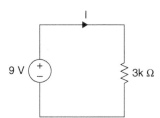

FIGURE 2.4   Circuit description for Example 2.1

Let us examine the network in Figure 2.5. The voltage of the source is

$$V = I/G = 3/0.25 = 12 \text{ V}$$

Example 2.2

The power absorbed by the conductance computed from any one of the following equations yields

$$P = I^2/G = V^2G = VI = 36 \text{ W}$$

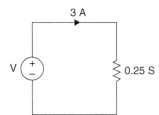

FIGURE 2.5   Circuit description for Example 2.2

| Example 2.3 | The power absorbed by the resistor in Figure 2.6 is 54 W. Let us determine the voltage and the current. We know that the power can be expressed as |

$$P = I^2R = V^2/R$$

Therefore, the voltage and current are

$$I = [54/6]^{1/2} \text{ and } V = [6 \times 54]^{1/2}$$

These equations yield values of $I = 3$ A and $V = 18$ V. Note that the directions of the voltage and current are specified in the circuit. However, the math will yield both positive and negative values for the two variables.

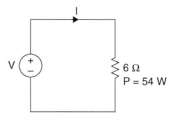

FIGURE 2.6   Circuit description for Example 2.3

| KIRCHHOFF'S LAWS | Thus far in our discussion of circuits we have dealt only with a single resistor and a single source. Kirchhoff's laws provide us with the tools we need to expand our capabilities to any network containing an interconnection of sources and resistors. We will assume that the interconnection mechanism is a wire that has zero resistance, i.e. a perfect conductor. |

In the application of Kirchhoff's laws, we will use several terms to explain these laws, and we need to define these terms now. The terms are **node, loop, mesh,** and **branch.** Consider the networks in Figure 2.7 a and b. However, it is important to note prior to defining these terms that the two circuits in Figure 2.7 are identical. Recall that the wires connecting the components are

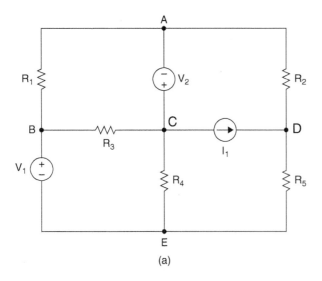
(a)

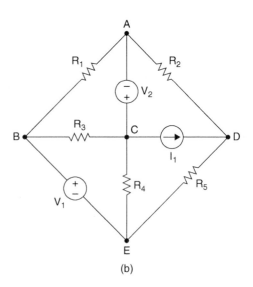
(b)

FIGURE 2.7   Diagram used to define circuit terms

perfect conductors and therefore we can shrink them to a single point since there is no resistance in the wires.

A node is nothing more than a point of interconnection of two or more elements. Therefore, the circuit has five nodes, labeled A through E because there are at least two components connected to each point. Note carefully that nodes A and E are comprised of a lot of wire, but because the wire is a perfect conductor, all the wire is still one node.

A loop is just any closed path through the network in which no node is traversed more than once. The following paths are examples of a loop: ACEBA and BCDEB. However, the path ACDECA is not a loop because the node C is encountered more than once. A mesh is defined as a loop that does not contain another loop. Meshes are typically identified as the "window panes," e.g. ADCA and CDEC. However, ADECA is not a mesh because it contains the two loops, CDEC and ADCA. Finally, a branch is any element connected between two nodes. The network in Figure 2.7 has eight branches.

At this point, we have the tools we need to examine two fundamental laws, named for the German scientist Gustav Robert Kirchhoff. The two laws are *Kirchhoff's current law (KCL)* and *Kirchhoff's voltage law (KVL)*. These two laws are simple to state, but extremely important in our discussion of circuit analysis. In addition, we will use them almost continuously in all the material that follows, and therefore it is important that we have a good understanding of their use.

KCL states that the algebraic sum of the currents entering a node is zero. Or equivalently, the algebraic sum of the currents leaving a node is zero. Or, KCL simply states that the currents entering a node must be equal to the currents leaving the node. Remember, current is charge in motion, so current is not sitting anywhere.

Let us reexamine the network in Figure 2.7 and assume some current directions in order to explain KCL. The network is redrawn in Figure 2.8 with assumed directions for the branch currents. We need to adopt a convention for defining the current directions. First, we will assume the currents leaving the node are positive and the currents entering the node are negative. Then KCL for node A is

$$-i_1(t) + i_2(t) - i_3(t) = 0$$

At this point note that if we multiplied the equation through by a minus sign (which, of course, would not change the equation), we would essentially be writing the equation with the opposite convention, i.e. the currents leaving the node are negative and the currents entering the node are positive.

Furthermore, the equation can be written as

$$i_1(t) + i_3(t) = i_2(t)$$

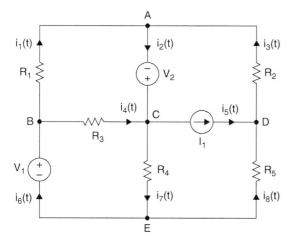

FIGURE 2.8 Circuit used to explain KCL

which simply states that the currents that enter the node must be equal to the currents that leave the node. Example 2.4 illustrates the application of KCL.

Example 2.4

Let us consider the stick diagram in Figure 2.9 that is a representation of the network in Figure 2.8. Several currents in the network are known. We need to use KCL to determine the unknown currents. Once again, we need to adopt a convention for applying KCL. We will assume the currents leaving the node are positive and the currents entering the node are negative. The opposite convention would be fine too. At node A, KCL is

$$-4 + 1 - I_3 = 0$$

At node B, KCL is
$$4 - 6 + I_4 = 0$$

At node C, KCL is

$$-1 - I_4 + 2 + I_7 = 0$$

At node D, KCL is

$$I_3 - 2 - I_8 = 0$$

And finally at node E, KCL is

$$6 - I_7 + I_8 = 0$$

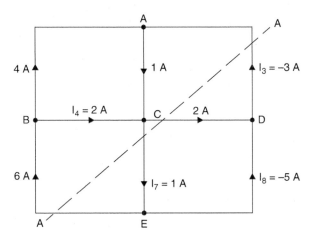

FIGURE 2.9 Stick diagram to describe KCL

Solving these equations for the unknown currents yields $I_3 = -3$ A, $I_4 = 2$ A, $I_7 = 1$ A, and $I_8 = -5$A. Note that although the currents I_3 and I_8 were assumed in one direction, the currents are actually going in the opposite direction. In general, we will not know the actual current direction, so we just assume one and if the actual current is flowing in the opposite direction to that assumed, we simply will end up with a negative sign. This process is the norm rather than the exception since we will normally not know the actual direction of the current. However, the solution will clearly identify the actual direction. One additional point is important here. Since current cannot sit on a node, it cannot sit on two nodes, three nodes, etc. and therefore when the circuit is cut into two complete pieces, KCL must be satisfied at the boundary of this cut. See for example the boundary A–A that slices the network into two pieces. KCL must be satisfied at this boundary, i.e. the currents flowing to the right must be equal to the currents flowing to the left across this slice, and indeed they do. If we assume the currents going left are positive and the currents going right are negative, then

$$+6 - I_7 - 2 + I_3 = 0$$

What we have demonstrated here is true in general. A final point of critical importance in the application of KCL is that *current is defined by two identifiers: magnitude and direction.* It is not sufficient to state that the current in a wire or circuit element is X. That answer would identify only the magnitude. We must also know the direction. How else could we possibly apply KCL?

Kirchhoff's second law, i.e. KVL, states that the algebraic sum of the voltages around any loop is zero. In a manner completely analogous to that used with KCL to identify whether currents were entering or leaving a node, *we must keep track of the voltage polarity as we traverse a loop.* Anyone who has replaced a battery in some electronic device knows that the terminals are marked + and −, and it makes a big difference if the terminals are reversed. In the application of KVL we traverse the loop and algebraically sum the increases (− to +) and decreases (+ to −) in energy level. So, here again, *as we apply KVL we must know magnitude and direction,* i.e. we need to know the magnitude of the voltage and we need to know if we are experiencing an increase or decrease in energy level in each circuit element as we traverse the loop. In a manner similar to that applied with KCL, we need to adopt a convention for the voltage. Let us do the following. We will assume that a rise in voltage in going from − to + will be considered negative and a decrease in voltage in going from + to − will be considered positive, i.e. as we traverse the network if we encounter a − sign first, there is an increase in energy level and if we encounter a + sign first, there is a decrease in energy level. Once again, we will find that if we multiply the resulting equations through by a minus sign, we will end up with the opposite convention.

In describing the voltage across some element in the network, we will use the equivalent forms shown in Figure 2.10. The plus and minus signs indicate the polarity of the voltage, i.e. which terminal is at the higher potential, and the arrow points toward the terminal of higher potential. In addition, the voltage V_{AB} means the voltage at point A with respect to point B. At this early point in our presentation of KVL, it is worthwhile to point out an issue that is often confusing to readers. When we are describing voltage in a network, we must refer to the reference point. For example, what is the voltage at the positive terminal of a 12 V battery? We don't have a clue – it means nothing. We do know, however, that the voltage at the positive terminal of a 12 V battery *with respect to the negative terminal* is 12 V. This is an important point, and the reader is cautioned to keep this in mind as we progress through our discussion of KVL.

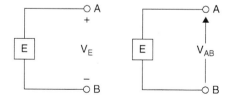

FIGURE 2.10 Equivalent forms that describe voltage

Example 2.5

Consider the network in Figure 2.11. We wish to find the value of the unknown source V_1. In addition, we want to find the voltages V_{AE} and V_{EC}, where V_{AE} is the voltage at point A with respect to point E and V_{EC} is the voltage at point E with respect to point C.

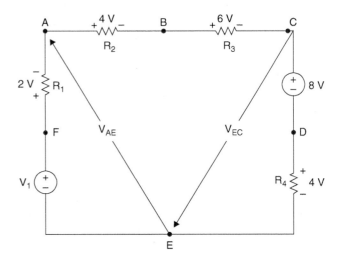

FIGURE 2.11   Circuit used in Example 2.5

In order to determine the unknown voltages, we apply KVL. We will traverse the circuit and algebraically add the increases and decreases in energy level. As indicted earlier, we can consider an increase in energy level as negative and a decrease in energy level as positive. Of course, the opposite convention is just as good. Starting at node E and traversing the circuit in a clockwise direction yields the KVL equation

$$-V_1 + 2 + 4 + 6 + 8 + 4 = 0$$

And thus, $V_1 = 24$ V. Now that we know all the voltages around the loop, we can find the remaining unknowns. We apply the same technique and simply include the unknown voltage in the loop. For example, we can determine V_{AE} using the loop EFAE. In this case,

$$-V_1 + 2 + V_{AE} = 0$$

And $V_{AE} = 22$ V. In a similar manner, V_{EC} can be computed using the path ECDE, which results in the equation

$$V_{EC} + 8 + 4 = 0$$

which yields $V_{EC} = -12$ V. Note that since the voltage is independent of the path, we could have used the path EABCE resulting in

$$-V_{AE} + 4 + 6 - V_{EC} = 0$$

which again yields a value for V_{EC} of -12 V.

SINGLE-LOOP CIRCUITS

At this point, we begin to apply the basic principles we have learned to simple circuits. The first circuit we will examine is a single loop. Let's examine the circuit in Figure 2.12a. This network has two independent sources and three resistors. We have assumed that the current is flowing in a clockwise direction. Is this assumption correct? We don't know, and we won't know until we solve the KVL equation that yields this current. However, if the solution produces a positive value

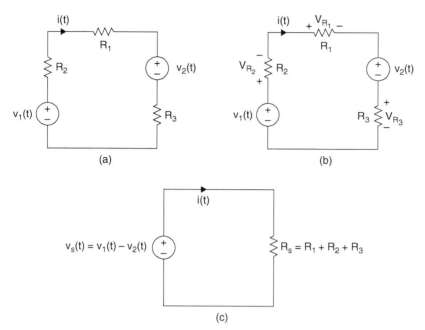

(a)

(b)

(c)

$v_s(t) = v_1(t) - v_2(t)$ $R_s = R_1 + R_2 + R_3$

FIGURE 2.12   A single-loop circuit

for the current, then our assumption was correct. If a negative value is obtained, we simply know that the current is flowing in the opposite direction.

In Figure 2.12b, we have shown voltages across the three resistors. These polarity assignments are made in conjunction with Ohm's law and based on the assumed direction of the current as shown in Figure 2.12b. For example, if we had assumed the current flowing in a counterclockwise direction, then the voltage across the resistor R_1 would be positive on the right and negative on the left – in accordance with Ohm's law.

Applying KVL to the network in Figure 2.12b yields the following:

$$-v_1(t) + v_{R2} + v_{R1} + v_2(t) + v_{R3} = 0$$

However, applying Ohm's law to this equation yields

$$-v_1(t) + i(t)\,R_2 + i(t)\,R_1 + v_2(t) + i(t)\,R_3 = 0$$

which can be written as

$$[R_1 + R_2 + R_3]\,i(t) = v_1(t) - v_2(t)$$

or

$$i(t)\,R_s = v_s(t)$$

where

$$R_s = R_1 + R_2 + R_3$$

and

$$v_s(t) = v_1(t) - v_2(t)$$

Now the current in the network can be calculated from the equation

$$i(t) = v_s(t)/R_s$$

Since this current is common to every element in the network, we can now calculate the voltage across every resistor. From the standpoint of calculating the current, note that the network in

Figure 2.12c is identical to that in Figure 2.12 a and b. In addition, two combinations demonstrated in this simple case are true in general, i.e. *resistors in series add*, and *voltage sources in series add algebraically*. One additional point is in order. If we had assumed the direction of the current to be in a counterclockwise direction, the resulting equation for the current would have yielded a value that is equal in magnitude but opposite in direction to that obtained above.

Example 2.6

Given the circuit in Figure 2.13, let us determine the current, I, the voltage V_x, and the power supplied or absorbed by each element.

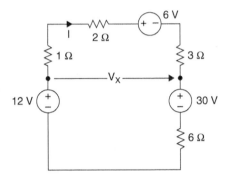

FIGURE 2.13   Circuit used in Example 2.6

KVL for the network is

$$-12 + 1I + 2I + 6 + 3I + 30 + 6I = 0$$

Or I = −2A, indicating that the assumed direction of the current is wrong and the current is actually flowing in a counterclockwise direction. No problem. As we indicated earlier, we will not always know the direction of the current, but the mathematics will tell us. Now in order to determine the voltage V_x, we simply apply KVL to a path in the circuit that includes this voltage, since we know all the other voltages because we now know the current, i.e. I = −2A. Let's write two equations, one for the top loop including V_x and one for the bottom loop including V_x. The two equations are

$$1I + 2I + 6 + 3I + V_x = 0$$

and

$$-12 - V_x + 30 + 6I = 0$$

In each case, we find that $V_x = 6$ V.

Resistors are passive elements, indicating that they do not generate any power, only absorb power, and do so in the form of heat. Therefore, the power dissipated by the resistors in the network is

$$P_R = I^2[1 + 2 + 3 + 6] = (-2)^2(12) = 48 \text{ W}$$

Let us examine each of the sources. Employing the passive sign convention, the power equation for the 12 V source is

$P_{12V} = VI = (12)(+2) = 24$ W. Power is absorbed, since positive current is entering the positive terminal.

For the two remaining sources,

$P_{6V} = VI = (6)(-2) = -12$ W. Power is supplied, since negative current is entering the positive terminal.

$P_{30V} = VI = (30)(-2) = -60$ W. Power is supplied, since negative current is entering the positive terminal.

Note the power balance that is exhibited, and the fact that the 12 V source is actually absorbing power.

Voltage division is a technique we will employ on numerous occasions in our study of circuit analysis. It is a very simple technique that indicates the manner in which a voltage divides between resistors in series. Consider the circuit in Figure 2.14. Applying KVL, yields the following equation:

$$v(t) = i(t)R_1 + i(t)R_2$$

and thus

$$i(t) = v(t)/(R_1 + R_2)$$

But

$$v_{R_1} = i(t)R_1 \text{ and } v_{R_2} = i(t)R_2$$

So,

$$v_{R_1} = [R_1/(R_1 + R_2)]\, v(t)$$
$$v_{R_2} = [R_2/(R_1 + R_2)]\, v(t)$$

These equations indicate that the source *v(t) divides between the two resistors in direct proportion to the total resistance $R_1 + R_2$.*

VOLTAGE DIVISION

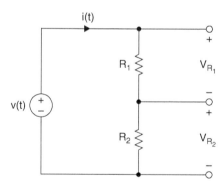

FIGURE 2.14   Circuit used to describe voltage division

Given the circuit in Figure 2.15, let us determine the voltages V_1 and V_2.
   Applying voltage division

$$V_1 = [2/(2 + 4 + 6)]\, 24 = 4 \text{ V}$$
$$V_2 = [(4 + 6)/(2 + 4 + 6)]\, 24 = 20 \text{ V}$$

And, of course, 4 V + 20 V is equal to the source voltage. We could also calculate the voltage across the 6 Ω resistor and find that it is 12 V. Note carefully, that voltage division is simply equivalent to calculating the current and then applying Ohm's law – it is just done in one step.

Example 2.7

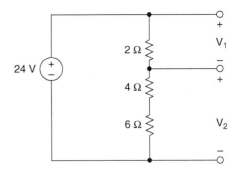

FIGURE 2.15 Circuit used in Example 2.7

Example 2.8

Let us apply voltage division to determine the voltage V_x in the network in Figure 2.16.

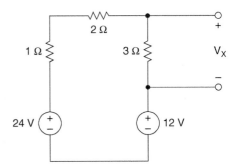

FIGURE 2.16 Circuit used in Example 2.8

The net sum of the voltages that causes a clockwise current is $24 - 12 = 12$ V. The sum of all the resistors in the network is $1 + 2 + 3 = 6 \, \Omega$. Therefore, the voltage across the 3 Ω resistor is

$$V_x = [3/6] \, 12 = 6 \text{ V}$$

KVL provides a quick check for this value. The KVL equation is

$$-24 + 1I + 2I + 3I + 12 = 0$$

which yields a current of 2 A, and $V_x = 3I = 6$ V.

SINGLE NODE-PAIR CIRCUITS

Consider the circuit shown in Figure 2.17a, known as a single node-pair circuit. In contrast to the single-loop circuit in which every element had the same current through it, every element in the single node-pair circuit has the same voltage across it, i.e. the loop current is common to all elements in the series circuit case, while the node voltage is common to all elements in this parallel configuration. While KVL and Ohm's law were employed to calculate the unknown quantities in the series circuit, KCL and Ohm's law will be employed to determine the unknown quantities in this parallel circuit. Note that there are only two nodes and the upper node is shown to be v(t) volts positive with respect to the lower node.

If we apply KCL to the upper node and assume that the currents entering the node are negative and the currents leaving the node are positive we obtain the equation

$$i_1(t) - i_A(t) + i_2(t) + i_B(t) + i_3(t) = 0$$

However,

$$i_j(t) = v(t)/R_j$$

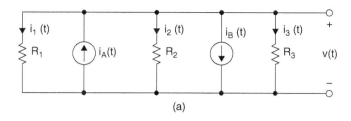

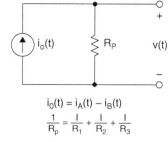

(a)

$i_0(t) = i_A(t) - i_B(t)$

$\dfrac{1}{R_p} = \dfrac{1}{R_1} + \dfrac{1}{R_2} + \dfrac{1}{R_3}$

FIGURE 2.17 Single node-pair circuits

(b)

and thus

$$[1/R_1 + 1/R_2 + 1/R_3]\, v(t) = i_A(t) - i_B(t)$$

or

$$[1/R_p]\, v(t) = i_0(t)$$

where

$$1/R_p = 1/R_1 + 1/R_2 + 1/R_3$$
$$i_0(t) = i_A(t) - i_B(t)$$

Note that the circuit in Figure 2.17b is equivalent to the circuit in Figure 2.17a when calculating the voltage v(t). Furthermore, when the passive elements are expressed as conductance, the equation

$$[1/R_1 + 1/R_2 + 1/R_3]\, v(t) = i_A(t) - i_B(t)$$

can be written as

$$\{G_1 + G_2 + G_3\}\, v(t) = i_A(t) - i_B(t) = i_0(t)$$

where $G_j = 1/R_j$.

What is demonstrated in this example is true in general. *Conductances add in parallel and current sources in parallel add algebraically.* In addition, if we have only two resistors, R_1 and R_2 connected in parallel, then their combination is derived from the expression

$$1/R_p = 1/R_1 + 1/R_2$$

and

$$R_p = (R_1)(R_2)/[R_1 + R_2]$$

The equivalent resistance of two resistors connected in parallel is equal to their product divided by their sum. Therefore, a 3 Ω resistor connected in parallel with a 6 Ω resistor could be replaced with one 2 Ω resistor.

Consider the circuit in Figure 2.18. Let us determine the voltage V_s, the current in each element, and the power supplied and absorbed in the network.

Assuming the currents leaving the node are positive and those entering the node are negative, KCL at the upper node yields

$$-12 + I_1 + I_2 + 6 + I_3 = 0$$

Example 2.9

Or

$$[1/4 + 1/6 + 1/12]V_s = 12 - 6$$
$$[3/12 + 2/12 + 1/12]V_s = 6$$

which yields $V_s = 12$ V. Then, $I_1 = 12/4 = 3$ A, $i_2 = 12/6 = 2$ A, and $i_3 = 12/12 = 1$ A. Note that 12 A is pumped into the node and 3 A + 2 A + 6 A + 1 A = 12 A is taken out, i.e. KCL is satisfied at the node. The power absorbed by the resistors can be calculated using either I^2R or V^2/R. Using the former equation yields

$$P_{4\Omega} = (3)^2(4) = 36 \text{ W}$$
$$p_{6\Omega} = (2)^2(6) = 24 \text{ W}$$
$$P_{12\Omega} = (1)^2(12) = 12 \text{ W}$$

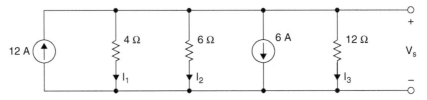

FIGURE 2.18 Circuit used in Example 2.9

The passive sign convention is used for the two sources, and the results are

$$P_{12A} = (12)(-12) = -144 \text{ W}$$
$$P_{6A} = (12)(6) = 72 \text{ W}$$

Note that there is indeed a power balance in the network, and the 6 A source is actually absorbing power rather than supplying it.

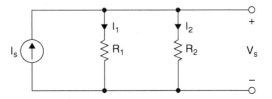

FIGURE 2.19 Circuit used to describe current division

CURRENT DIVISION

Current divides among parallel resistors in a manner similar to the way in which voltage divides among series resistors. Consider the network in Figure 2.19. KCL at the upper node yields

$$I_1 + I_2 = I_s$$

Or

$$[1/R_1 + 1/R_2] V_s = I_s$$

And thus

$$V_s = [(R_1)(R_2)/(R_1 + R_2)] I_s$$

But $I_1 = V_s/R_1$ and $I_2 = V_s/R_2$ so that

$$I_1 = [R_2/(R_1 + R_2)]I_s$$

and

$$I_2 = [R_1/(R_1 + R_2)]\, I_s$$

So, in the case of only two resistors connected in parallel, the current in one resistor is determined by multiplying the current incoming to the pair by the opposite resistor and dividing by the sum of the two resistors. If there are multiple resistors connected in parallel, then the current in the jth resistor is equal to the voltage across the entire combination of resistors, i.e. $(I_s)\,(R_p)$ divided by R_j or

$$I_j = (I_s)(R_p)/R_j$$

Example 2.10

Let us calculate the currents in the two resistors in Figure 2.20.

$$I_1 = [12/(6 + 12)](12) = 8\ \text{A}$$
$$I_2 = [6/(6 + 12)](12) = 4\ \text{A}$$

And note that $I_1 + I_2 = I_s$. In addition, the voltage V_s is

$$V_s = [(R_1)(R_2)/(R_1 + R_2)]\, I_s$$
$$= 48\ \text{V}$$

And then Ohm's law can be used to find $I_x = V_s/R_x$, where I_x is either I_1 or I_2.

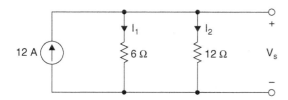

FIGURE 2.20   Circuit used in Example 2.10

RESISTOR COMBINATIONS

In our analysis thus far, we have shown that the equivalent resistance of any number of resistors connected in series is obtained by simply adding the resistors, and the equivalent resistance of any number of resistors connected in parallel is obtained by adding the conductance of each and then calculating the reciprocal of that total conductance.

$$R_s = R_1 + R_2 + \cdots + R_n$$

and

$$1/R_p = 1/R_1 + 1/R_2 + \cdots + 1/R_n$$

It is critically important to understand that in order for two resistors to be in series, they must both have the same current, and in order for two resistors to be in parallel, they must have the same voltage across them. Once these concepts are understood, and we are sure which resistors are in series and which resistors are in parallel, we can apply the two formulas to determine the manner in which to combine them. We will employ two examples to illustrate these points.

Example 2.11

We wish to find the equivalent resistance of the network in Figure 2.21a at the terminals A–B. Note carefully that the two 4 Ω resistors are in parallel and can be combined to yield a 2 Ω resistor, i.e.

$$1/R_p = 1/4 + 1/4 = 1/2$$
$$R_p = 2 \ \Omega$$

Or equivalently

$$R_p = (4)(4)/[4 + 4] = 2 \ \Omega$$

and the 12 Ω and 6 Ω resistor are also in parallel producing a 4 Ω resistor, i.e.

$$R_p = (6)(12)/[6 + 12] = 4 \ \Omega$$

By combining these resistors, we obtain the network in Figure 2.21b. Now, the 2 and 4 Ω resistors are in series yielding a 6 Ω resistor, which is in turn in parallel with the 18 Ω resistor producing a 4.5 Ω resistor, which when combined with the 2 Ω resistor yields a total resistance at the terminals A–B of 6.5 Ω.

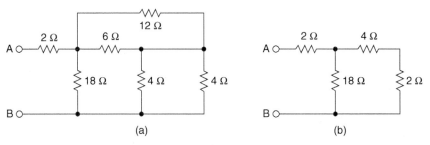

FIGURE 2.21 Circuit used in Example 2.11

Example 2.12

Consider the network in Figure 2.22a. Let us determine the equivalent resistance at the terminals A–B. This example indicates the importance of being able to recognize a node. The circuit connection points are labeled as C, D, E, and F. Since the connecting lines represent perfect conductors, note carefully that the points E and F are really the same node, and in that regard we note that the network in Figure 2.22b is equivalent to that in Figure 2.22a. Now in this format, the resistors that are in series and parallel are more obvious. The 6 and 3 Ω resistors are in parallel and combining that result with the 2 Ω resistor yields the network in Figure 2.22c. The 4 and 12 Ω resistors combine to produce a 3 Ω resistor, which when combined with the 1 Ω resistor yields a total resistance at the terminals A–B of 4 Ω.

As we continue to develop our understanding of the techniques employed to combine resistors in a network, consider the circuit shown in Figure 2.23. The reader who cannot find any resistors in series or parallel has already developed an understanding of this area, since there are no resistors connected in series or parallel! Are we unable to proceed then in determining the equivalent resistance of this network at the terminals A–B? No way. While our series and parallel combinations will not help with the network in its present form, we can transform a portion of the network to an equivalent architecture where they can be used. The technique we will employ is called the *delta to wye*, or *wye to delta, transformation*. If we isolate the top portion of the network in Figure 2.23 as shown in Figure 2.24a, we can show that this portion of the network can be replaced with an equivalent network as shown in Figure 2.24b. However, in order to perform this replacement, we have to ensure that the resistance seen at each corresponding pair of terminals is exactly the same. For example, in comparing the two networks in Figure 2.24, the

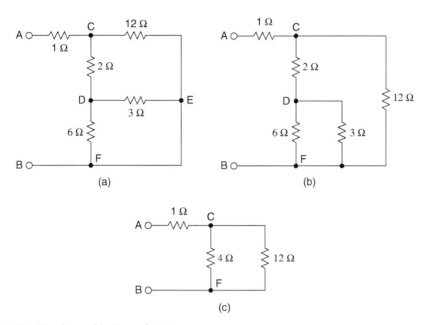

FIGURE 2.22   Circuits used in Example 2.12

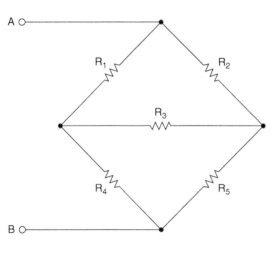

FIGURE 2.23   A circuit with no series or parallel combinations of resistors

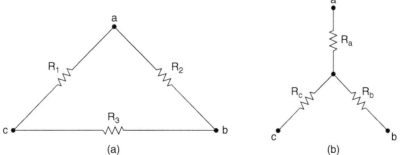

FIGURE 2.24   Circuits used to describe a delta to wye transformation

resistance at the terminals A–B in the network in Figure 2.24a must be identical to the resistance at the terminals A–B in Figure 2.24b, i.e. the parallel combination of R_1 with the series combination of R_2 and R_3, i.e.

$$R_2(R_1 + R_3)/(R_1 + R_2 + R_3)$$

must be equal to the series combination of R_a and R_b, i.e.

$$R_a + R_b$$

Note carefully that R_c is hanging open and not connected to anything. This equivalence in resistance must be true at each pair of terminals where the delta configuration was connected in the original circuit. If this is the case, the balance of the network cannot tell the difference when the delta configuration is replaced by the wye configuration. The equations for each set of terminals are listed as follows.

$$R_{ab} = R_a + R_b = \frac{R_2(R_1 + R_3)}{R_2 + R_1 + R_3}$$

$$R_{bc} = R_b + R_c = \frac{R_3(R_1 + R_2)}{R_3 + R_1 + R_2}$$

$$R_{ca} = R_c + R_a = \frac{R_1(R_2 + R_3)}{R_1 + R_2 + R_3}$$

Solving these equations yields the expressions for R_a, R_b, and R_c in terms of the original circuit parameters R_1, R_2, and R_3.

$$R_a = \frac{R_1 R_2}{R_1 + R_2 + R_3}$$

$$R_b = \frac{R_2 R_3}{R_1 + R_2 + R_3}$$

$$R_c = \frac{R_1 R_3}{R_1 + R_2 + R_3}$$

The formula is really easy to remember, since, for example, R_a is equal to the product of the two resistors connected at terminal a, R_1 and R_2, divided by the sum of all the resistors in the delta. This procedure applies at all terminals.

If we desired to transform a wye into a delta configuration, the equations could be solved to yield

$$R_1 = \frac{R_a R_b + R_b R_c + R_a R_c}{R_b}$$

$$R_2 = \frac{R_a R_b + R_b R_c + R_a R_c}{R_c}$$

$$R_3 = \frac{R_a R_b + R_b R_c + R_a R_c}{R_a}$$

Thus, within any network we can interchange a delta for a wye and vice versa at a set of three terminals in such a way that the remainder of the circuit is unchanged. There is a special case in which the resistors are all equal, i.e. $R_1 = R_2 = R_3$. In this case,

$$R_{wye} = (1/3)R_{delta}$$

Let us determine the equivalent resistance at the terminals A–B for the network in Figure 2.25a. First of all, the reader is encouraged to note that there are no resistors connected in series or parallel anywhere in the circuit. It is important to stop for a moment to be sure the reader understands this last statement. Remember, the acid test for two resistors to be in series is that they must both have the same current, and in order for two resistors to be in parallel, they must have the same voltage across them. Note that there are not two resistors in the circuit in Figure 2.25a that satisfy either condition.

Example 2.13

Note that the center portion of the network consists of two deltas back to back. Although we could transform either delta, i.e. ABC or BCD into a wye, we will perform this operation on the upper delta ABC. The resistor, R_A, is equal to

$$R_A = (18)(54)/[18 + 54 + 36] = 9\,\Omega$$

In a similar manner,

$$R_B = (18)(36)[18 + 54 + 36] = 6\,\Omega$$
$$R_C = (36)(54)/[18 + 54 + 36] = 18\,\Omega$$

This transformation results in the network shown in Figure 2.25b, where the nodes are labeled as shown in Figure 2.25a. Now we are in business, since the resistors in this latter circuit are either in series or parallel. The 6 and 2 Ω resistors combine to produce an 8 Ω resistor, which is in parallel with the series combination of the 18 and 6 Ω resistors, which yields 24 Ω. As shown in Figure 2.25c, 8Ω in parallel with 24 Ω produces an equivalent 6 Ω resistor. The 9 Ω

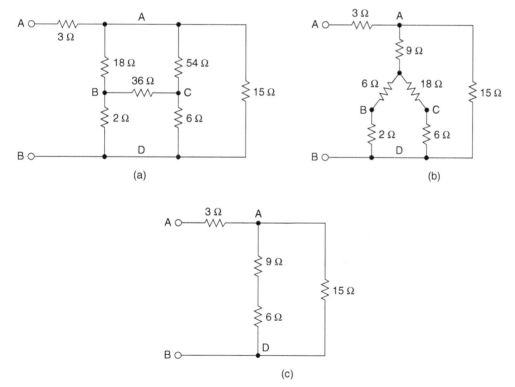

FIGURE 2.25 Circuit used in Example 2.13

resistor in series with the 6 Ω resistor produces a 15 Ω resistor, and the two equivalent 15 Ω resistors are in parallel yielding a 7.5 Ω resistor, which when combined with the 3 Ω resistor yields a total resistance at the terminals A–B of 10.5 Ω.

SIMPLE NETWORK ANALYSIS

We are now in a position to apply all that we have learned in the analysis of some simple networks containing a single independent source. The following examples have been carefully selected to illustrate the principles we have explained to this point.

Example 2.14

Consider the network shown in Figure 2.26a. We wish to determine the voltages and currents that are identified in this circuit. Note that if we can calculate the total resistance seen by the 12 V source, we can determine the current I_1, i.e. we replace all the resistors by one equivalent resistor and then simply apply Ohm's law. In calculating the equivalent resistance, we see that the 6 and 12 Ω resistors are in parallel and that combination is in series with the 8 Ω resistor, yielding a 12 Ω resistor as shown in Figure 2.26b. The 4 and 12 Ω resistors in Figure 2.26b are in parallel, and that combination is in series with the 3 Ω resistor for a total equivalent resistance, as seen by the 12 V source, of 6 Ω. Therefore, the current I_1 is

$$I_1 = 12/6$$
$$I_1 = 2\ A$$

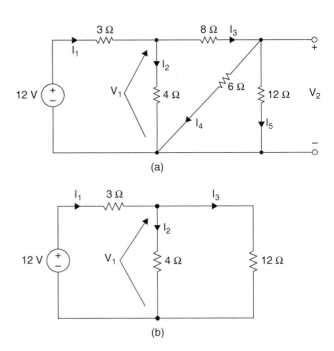

(a)

(b)

FIGURE 2.26 Circuit used in Example 2.14

At this point, we have several options as we proceed, and we will try to indicate the various ways in which we can proceed. Since we know I_1, V_1 can be calculated using KVL as

$$V_1 = 12 - 3I_1 = 6\ V$$

Note that since the 4 and 12 Ω resistors are in parallel, which yield a 3 Ω resistor, the circuit can be viewed as simply the 12 V source in series with two 3 Ω resistors, and we are interested in the voltage across the 3 Ω resistor, which resulted from the combination of the 4 and 12 Ω resistors. Therefore, voltage division can be applied to yield

$$V_1 = (12)(3)/(3+3) = 6 \text{ V}$$

Knowing V_1 permits us to calculate I_2 and I_3 from Ohm's law as $I_2 = V_1/4 = 1.5$ A and $I_3 = V_1/12 = 0.5$ A. We could also calculate I_2 and I_3 using current division.

$$I_2 = (I_1)(12)/(4+12) = 1.5 \text{ A}$$
$$I_3 + (I_1)(4)/(4+12) = 0.5 \text{ A}$$

To determine the remaining voltage and currents in Figure 2.26a, we first note that the 6 and 12 Ω resistors are in parallel and their combination produces an equivalent 4 Ω resistor. Then simply repeating the approach used to determine V_1, the voltage V_2 is determined by voltage division as

$$V_2 = (V_1)(4)/(4+8) = 2 \text{ V}$$

Therefore, the currents I_4 and I_5 are $I_4 = V_2/6 = 1/3$ A and $I_5 = V_2/12 = 1/6$ A. Or, we could have used current division

$$I_4 = (I_3)(12)/(6+12) = 1/3 \text{ A}$$
$$I_5 = (I_3)(6)/(6+12) = 1/6 \text{ A}$$

A quick check indicates that KCL is satisfied in that $I_1 = I_2 + I_4 + I_5$ and KVL is satisfied around any closed loop, e.g. consider the outer path in Figure 2.26a

$$-12 + 3I_1 + 8I_3 + 12I_5 = 0$$
$$-12 + (3)(2) + (8)(1/2) + (12)(1/6) = 0$$
$$0 = 0$$

Any network with a single source can be analyzed as indicated to determine any voltage, current, or power.

In order to help solidify an understanding of the manner in which Ohm's law, KVL, and KCL can be applied to analyze circuits, let us consider now an example in which we know a voltage or current somewhere in the network and have to work our way back to calculate the value of the source that caused that voltage of current.

Consider the network in Figure 2.27. Given that the current in the 3 Ω resistor is 2 A as shown, we want to find the value of the current source and the amount of power it supplies to the network.

Example 2.15

Using Ohm's law, we know that the voltage V_1 is equal to $(2)(3) = 6$ V. Hence, the current in the 6 Ω resistor is $I_1 = 1$ A. Then using KCL, $I_2 = 1 + 2 = 3$ A. Then applying KVL,

$$-V_s + 4\,I_2 + 2\,I_2 + V_1 = 0$$

the voltage V_s is then

$$V_s = I_2(2+4) + 6 = 24 \text{ V}$$

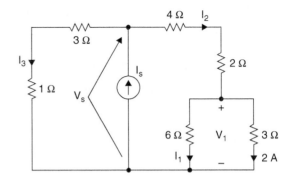

FIGURE 2.27   Circuit used in Example 2.15

Then, since the voltage V_s is directly across the series combination of the 1 and 3 Ω resistors, I_3 is

$$I_3 = V_s/(1 + 3) = 6A$$

As a result, KCL indicates the current source I_s is

$$I_s = I_2 + I_3 = 9 \text{ A}$$

The power supplied by the source is

$$P_s = (V_s)(I_s) = 216 \text{ W}$$

A quick check of the power absorbed by the resistors will demonstrate that the power supplied by the current source is equal to that absorbed by the resistors.

Example 2.16

Given the network in Figure 2.28a, let us determine the value of the voltage source V_s and the power absorbed or supplied to the network by this source.

The voltage across the 2 Ω resistor connected at node C is 4 V, and therefore the current in this resistor is 2 A top to bottom. Applying KCL at node C indicates that the current in the 3 Ω resistor is 4 A left to right. The voltage across the 3 Ω resistor, connected between nodes A and C, determined by Ohm's law is $(3)(4) = 12$ V positive on the left and negative on the right. V_s can now be determined by applying KVL to the outer loop, i.e.

$$-V_s + 12 + 4 = 0$$

or

$$V_s = 16 \text{ V}$$

The current in the 2 Ω resistor connected between nodes A and B can be determined by KVL, i.e.

$$-16 + 2I + 4 = 0$$

where I is assumed to be flowing left to right. Solving the equation yields

$$I = 6A$$

Applying KCL at node B indicates that the current in the 4 V source is $6 + 2 = 8$ A top to bottom.

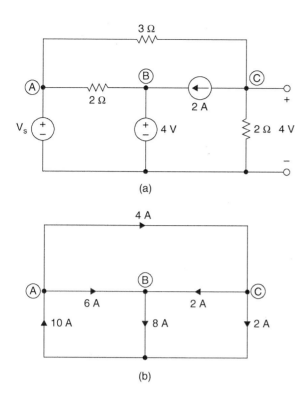

(a)

(b)

FIGURE 2.28   Circuit used in Example 2.16

KCL at node A indicates that the current in V_s, bottom to top, is equal to the current in the 2 and 3 Ω resistors, or $4 + 6 + 10$ A Therefore, using the passive sign convention, we find that

$$P_{vs} = (16)(-10) = -160 \text{ W}$$

The sign indicates that this source is supplying 160 W.

The stick diagram in Figure 2.28b illustrates that KCL is satisfied at every node.

In order to complete our discussion of simple circuit architectures and lay the groundwork for the analysis techniques that follow, we will now consider one additional feature in our analysis that will strengthen our repertoire going forward, i.e. circuits with dependent, or controlled, sources. The dependent sources, outlined in Chapter 1, are important because they are employed to model our electronic devices, as we will demonstrate later.

In sharp contrast to independent sources, the value of which is clearly defined and independent of any other circuit parameter, the value of a dependent source is unknown until the value of the controlling variable is known. In developing our analysis approach to circuits with these devices, we will simply write the KCL and KVL equations for the circuit, treating the dependent sources as though their values were known, and then determine the equation for the controlling variable. The following examples, one with a dependent voltage source and one with a dependent current source, will serve to illustrate our approach.

CIRCUITS WITH DEPENDENT SOURCES

Example 2.17

Consider the network in Figure 2.29, which contains a voltage-controlled voltage source. We wish to find the output voltage, V_0.

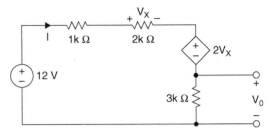

FIGURE 2.29 Circuit used in Example 2.17

The KVL equation for the network is

$$-12 + 1k\,I + 2k\,I + 2V_x + 3k\,I = 0$$

Note that we have treated the controlled source just like it was an independent source. Although this is a valid KVL equation, there are two unknowns in this single equation. Now, we look for the second equation that defines the controlling variable, V_x. V_x is equal to the voltage across the 2k Ω resistor. Using Ohm's law, and noting carefully the direction of the current, the defining equation for the controlling variable is

$$V_x = 2k\,I$$

If the voltage polarity had been defined in the opposite direction, the defining equation would be

$$V_x = -2k\,I$$

Substituting the equation for the dependent variable into the KVL equation yields an equation in which current is the only unknown.

$$-12 + 1k\,I + 2k\,I + 2(2k\,I) + 3k\,I = 0$$
$$10k\,I = 12$$
$$I = 1.2 \text{ mA}$$

Note that current is the variable common to all elements in the circuit, so once we know the current, we can determine every other unknown. Since $I = 1.2$ mA,

$$V_0 = 3k\,I = 3.6 \text{ V}$$

Example 2.18

Consider the circuit in Figure 2.30 containing a current-controlled current source. We wish to find the output voltage and the power absorbed by the 2k Ω resistor.

Noting the parallel structure in which the voltage V_s is across all elements (we can combine the series combination of the 1k and 2k Ω resistors for writing a KCL equation), the KCL equation at the top node is

$$-12/k + V_s/6k - 2I_x + V_s/(1k + 2k) = 0$$

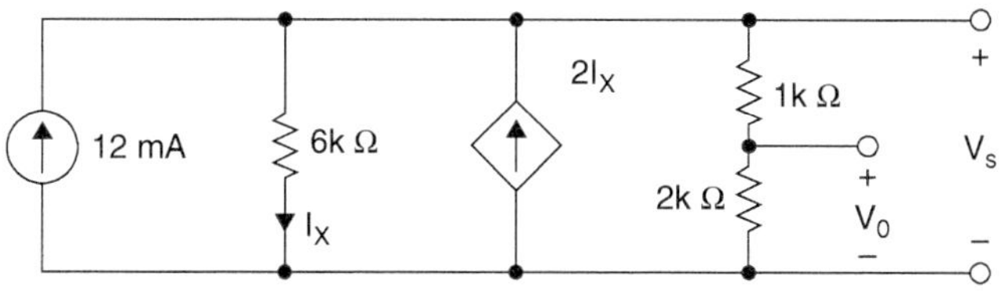

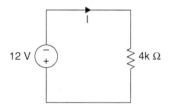

FIGURE 2.30   Circuit used in Example 2.18

If we now write the equation for the dependent variable, I_x, in terms of the voltage V_s, we will have one equation in the unknown V_s. The equation for I_x in terms of V_s is obtained using Ohm's law as

$$I_x = V_s/6k$$

Substituting this equation into the KCL equation

$$-12/k + V_s/6k - 2(V_s/6k) + V_s/(lk + 2k) = 0$$
$$V_s[1/6k - 2/6k + 1/3k] = 12/k$$
$$V_s[-2/12k + 4/12k] = 12/k$$
$$V_s[2/12k] = 12/k$$
$$V_s = 72 \text{ V}$$

Using a voltage divider,

$$V_0 = [2k/(1k + 2k)]72 = 48 \text{ V}$$

And the power dissipated in the 2k Ω resistor is

$$P = V_0{}^2/2k = 1152 \text{ mW}$$

2.1   Find I in the circuit in Figure P2.1.

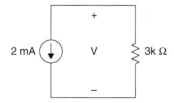

FIGURE P2.1

2.2   Find V in the network in Figure P2.2.

FIGURE P2.2

2.3 Given the circuit in Figure P2.3, find V_s if the power absorbed by the resistor is 16 mW.

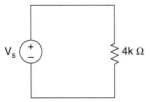

FIGURE P2.3

2.4 If the resistor in the circuit in Figure P2.4 absorbs 64 mW, find I_s.

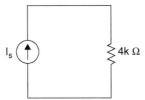

FIGURE P2.4

2.5 Find I and V_0 in the circuit in Figure P2.5.

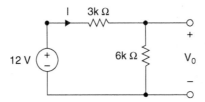

FIGURE P2.5

2.6 Find I, V_1, and V_2 in the circuit in Figure P2.6.

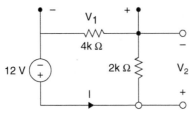

FIGURE P2.6

2.7   Find I, V_1, and V_2 in the network in Figure P2.7.

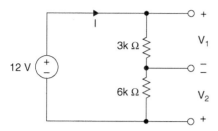

FIGURE P2.7

2.8   Find I and V_s in the network in Figure P2.8.

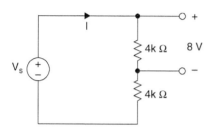

FIGURE P2.8

2.9   Find I and V_s in the circuit in Figure P2.9.

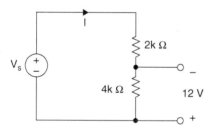

FIGURE P2.9

2.10   Find V_{CE} and the power absorbed by the lk Ω resistor in the circuit in Figure P2.10.

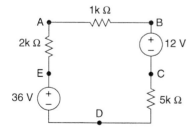

FIGURE P2.10

2.11 Find V_x in the network in Figure 2.11.

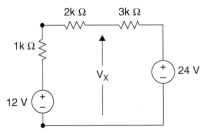

FIGURE P2.11

2.12 If the power absorbed by the 6k Ω resistor in the network in Figure P2.12 is 96 mW, find V_s.

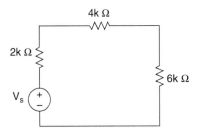

FIGURE P2.12

2.13 Find V_s and I_x in the circuit in Figure P2.13.

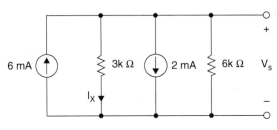

FIGURE P2.13

2.14 Find V_s and the power absorbed by the 4k Ω resistor in Figure P2.14.

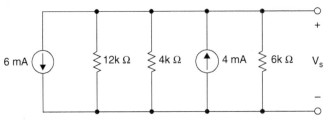

FIGURE P2.14

2.15 Find I_s in the network in Figure P2.15. In addition, determine whether the 2 mA source is absorbing or supplying power, and how much.

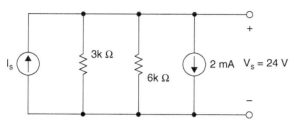

FIGURE P2.15

2.16 Find V_s and V_2 in the circuit in Figure P2.16.

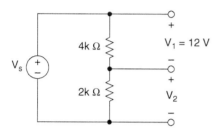

FIGURE P2.16

2.17 Find V_s and V_0 in the network in Figure 2.17 if the 4k Ω resistor absorbs 144 mW.

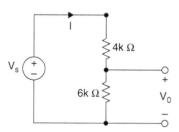

FIGURE P2.17

2.18 The source in the network in Figure P2.18 supplies 144 mW of power. Determine R.

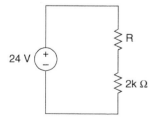

FIGURE P2.18

2.19 Determine the value of the resistor, R, in the network in Figure P2.19.

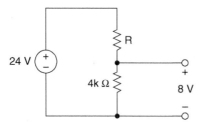

FIGURE P2.19

2.20 Use voltage division to determine V_0 in the network in Figure P2.20.

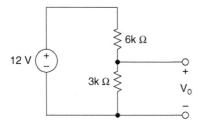

FIGURE P2.20

2.21 Use voltage division to find V_1 and V_2 in the circuit in Figure P2.21.

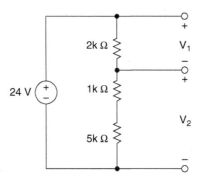

FIGURE P2.21

2.22 Find V_0, I_1, and I_2 in the network in Figure P2.22.

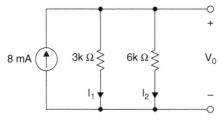

FIGURE P2.22

2.23 Find I_1 in the circuit in Figure P2.23.

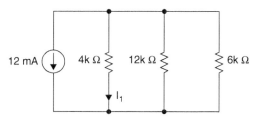

FIGURE P2.23

2.24 Find V_0 in the circuit in Figure P2.24.

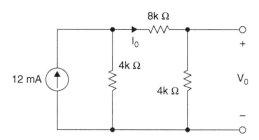

FIGURE P2.24

2.25 Find V_0 in the circuit in Figure P2.25.

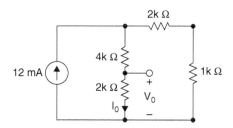

FIGURE P2.25

2.26 Find the resistance at the terminals A–B in the circuit in Figure P2.26.

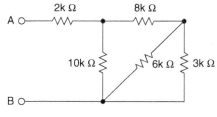

FIGURE P2.26

2.27 Find the resistance at the terminals A–B in the circuit in Figure P2.27.

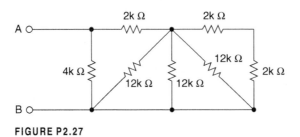

FIGURE P2.27

2.28 Find the resistance at the terminals A–B in the network in Figure P2.28.

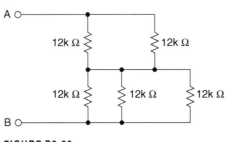

FIGURE P2.28

2.29 Find the resistance at the terminals A–B in the circuit in Figure P2.29.

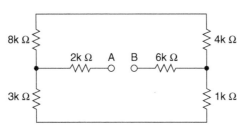

FIGURE P2.29

2.30 Determine the resistance at the terminals A–B in the circuit in Figure P2.30.

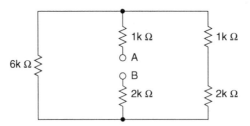

FIGURE P2.30

2.31 Find the resistance at the terminals A–B in the circuit in Figure P2.31.

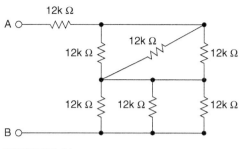

FIGURE P2.31

2.32 Determine the resistance at the terminals A–B in the circuit in Figure P2.32.

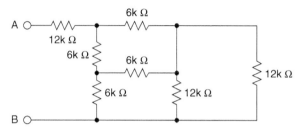

FIGURE P2.32

2.33 Find the resistance at the terminals A–B in the circuit in Figure P2.33.

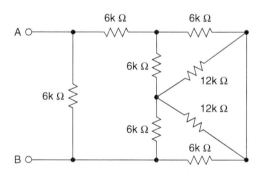

FIGURE P2.33

2.34 Find the resistance at the terminals A–B in the network in Figure P2.34.

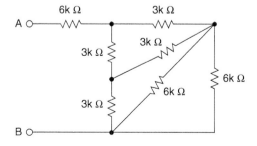

FIGURE P2.34

2.35 Determine the resistance at the terminals A–B in the circuit in Figure P2.35.

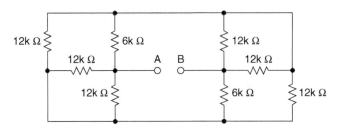

FIGURE P2.35

2.36 Given the circuit in Figure P2.36, determine V_s and the power absorbed by the 3k Ω resistor.

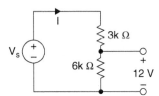

FIGURE P2.36

2.37 Find I_0 in the network in Figure P2.37.

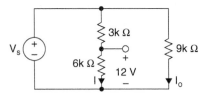

FIGURE P2.37

2.38 Find V_s and V_x in the circuit in Figure P2.38.

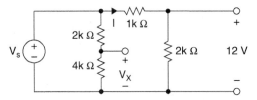

FIGURE P2.38

2.39 Find V_0 in the circuit in Figure P2.39.

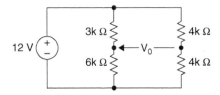

FIGURE P2.39

2.40 Find V_s and I_x in the network in Figure P2.40.

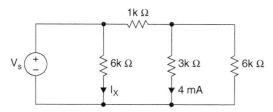

FIGURE P2.40

2.41 Find I_s and I_x in the network in Figure P2.41.

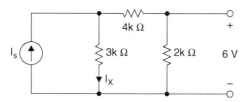

FIGURE P2.41

2.42 Determine the value of I_s in the network in Figure P2.42.

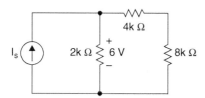

FIGURE P2.42

2.43 If the 8k Ω resistor in the network in Figure P2.43 absorbs 32 mW, find I_s and V_0.

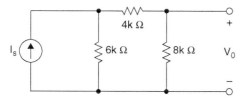

FIGURE P2.43

2.44 Find I_s and V_0 in the circuit in Figure P2.44.

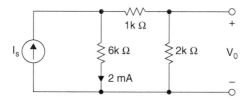

FIGURE P2.44

2.45 Find V_s in the circuit in Figure P2.45.

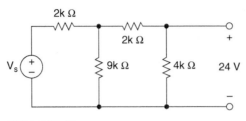

FIGURE P2.45

2.46 Determine V_s and V_0 in the circuit in Figure P2.46.

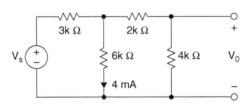

FIGURE P2.46

2.47 Find I_s in the circuit in Figure P2.47.

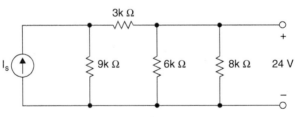

FIGURE P2.47

2.48 Determine I_s in the circuit in Figure P2.48.

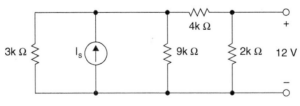

FIGURE P2.48

2.49 Find I_s and V_0 in the circuit in Figure P2.49.

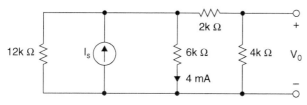

FIGURE P2.49

2.50 Determine the voltage V_0 in the circuit in Figure P2.50.

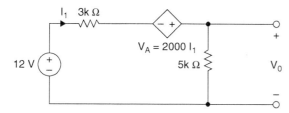

FIGURE P2.50

2.51 Find the voltage V_0 in the network in Figure P2.51.

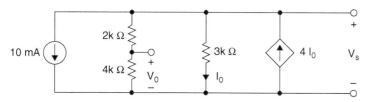

FIGURE P2.51

2.52 Find the value of the voltage V_0 in the circuit in Figure P2.52.

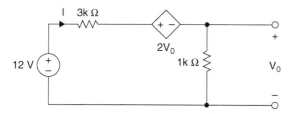

FIGURE P2.52

2.53 Find V_0 in the network in Figure P2.53.

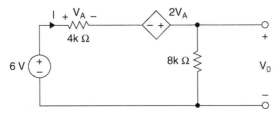

FIGURE P2.53

2.54 Find V_0 in the network in Figure P2.54.

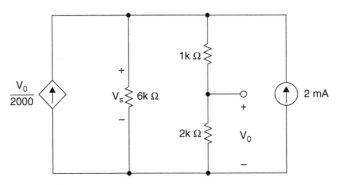

FIGURE P2.54

2.55 Find V_A in the network in Figure P2.55.

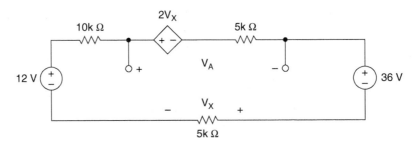

FIGURE P2.55

Circuit Analysis Techniques

CHAPTER 3

LEARNING OBJECTIVES

- To understand how to apply Ohm's law and Kirchhoff's laws to analyze circuits

- To be able to determine voltages and currents anywhere in the network using both nodal and loop analysis

- To be able to effectively apply both superposition and Thevenin's theorems in network analysis

- To understand and apply maximum power transfer

In this chapter, we present several techniques that find wide application in the analysis of electric circuits. These basic techniques will include those that represent, in essence, a sledgehammer approach to solving electric circuits as well as others that provide some actual insight into network performance.

Our first technique is called nodal analyses. In order to understand the power of this approach to circuit analysis, consider the network shown in Figure 3.1. Suppose for a moment that we somehow know that the voltages $V_1 = 6$ V and $V_2 = 4$ V, i.e. we know the voltage across the 3k Ω resistor and the voltage across the (4/3)k Ω resistor. We can now show that this knowledge is sufficient to determine the current in each element and, in turn, the voltage across each element. For example, since $V_1 = 6$ V, applying Ohm's law yields

| NODAL |
| ANALYSIS |

$$I_B = 6/3k = 2 \text{ mA}$$

Similarly, since $V_2 = 4$ V

$$I_D = 4/(4/3)k = 3 \text{ mA}$$

Now, the systematic application of KVL to the loops in the network yields the following equations:

$$-12 + (2k)I_A + V_1 = 0$$
$$-V_1 + (2k)I_C + V_2 = 0$$

and

$$-12 + (4k)I_E + V_2 = 0$$

which produces the unknown currents, $I_A = 3$ mA, $I_C = 1$ mA, and $I_E = 2$ mA. Note that KCL is satisfied at every node in the network, and KVL is satisfied around every loop. In addition, this information permits us to calculate the power absorbed or supplied by every element. So in essence, a knowledge of all the node voltages provides us with a complete analysis of the circuit.

As we indicated earlier in the book, the voltage must be referenced to some specific point. Recall that the voltage at the positive terminal of a 12 V battery means nothing. However, the voltage at the positive terminal with respect to the negative terminal is 12 V (i.e. the difference in potential between the two terminals is 12 V). So in performing a nodal analysis in which we will use KCL to determine node voltages in the circuit, it is logical that we select some reference point,

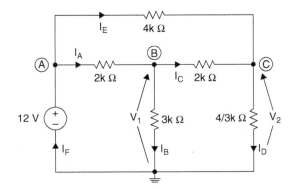

FIGURE 3.1   An example network

i.e. one node, in the circuit and we reference all node voltages in the network to that specific node. We typically call this node the ground node, assume it is at zero potential, and identify it with the ground symbol $\perp$.

At this point, let us revisit the network in Figure 3.1 to illustrate some salient features of our nodal analysis technique. Imagine now that we have labeled the node at the bottom of the network as the ground node. Since we are referencing all node voltages with respect to this ground node, we can state that the voltage $V_A = 12$ V, $V_B = 6$ V, and $V_C = 4$ V. In other words, when we identify the node voltage V_X, we mean the voltage at node X with respect to the reference, i.e. ground, node. However, it is important to note that the voltage at node A with respect to node B $(V_A - V_B)$ is 6 V, and the voltage at node B with respect to node C is 2 V. Similarly, the voltage at node C with respect to node A is -8 V $(4$ V $- 12$ V$)$. Since we will apply KCL in this analysis, it is important to remember that the branch currents are computed as follows:

$$I_B = (V_B - 0)/3k \text{ or } I_B = V_B/3k = 2 \text{ mA}$$

and

$$I_E = (V_A - V_c)/4k = (12 - 2)/4k = 2 \text{ mA}$$

Note that this last equation is nothing more than an application of KVL, i.e.

$$-V_A + 4k\,I_E + V_C = 0$$

If we examine the foregoing analysis in a more general fashion, the branch currents between any two nodes in the network can be determined using KVL when the node voltages are known. As illustrated in Figure 3.2, the branch currents I_1 and I_2 can be derived via KVL and expressed as follows:

$$-V_A + I_1 R_X + V_B = 0$$

or

$$I_1 = [V_A - V_B]/R_X$$

and

$$-V_B + I_2 R_X + V_A = 0$$

or

$$I_2 = [V_B - V_A]/R_X$$

These equations indicate that $I_1 = -I_2$ and $I_2 = -I_1$, as indicated in Figure 3.2.

Thus, a nodal analysis proceeds as follows. Given an N-node circuit, we first identify one node as the reference node and the voltages at every other node in the network are referenced to

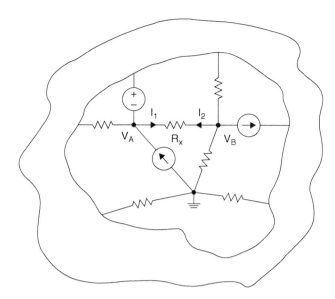

FIGURE 3.2   Determining the current in a resistor

this node. Having selected one node as the reference node, there will be N − 1 nodes remaining in the network and we need to determine the voltages at those nodes with respect to this reference node. The vehicle we will employ to determine these unknown node voltages is the application of KCL at these nodes, which will result in N − 1 KCL equations, and the solution of which will yield the N − 1 node voltages. Although any viable method can be used to solve the mathematical equations that result from our analysis, and modern scientific calculators are well equipped to do the job, throughout this book we will use a combination of matrices and MATLAB to derive our solutions. Because of the simplicity with which two linearly independent simultaneous equations can be solved using matrices, we will employ that technique in those cases and rely on MATLAB to help when we encounter three or more equations. Two linearly independent simultaneous equations can be written in the form

$$AV_1 + BV_2 = I_1$$
$$CV_1 + DV_2 = I_2$$

which can be written in matrix form as

$$\begin{bmatrix} A & B \\ C & D \end{bmatrix} \begin{bmatrix} V_1 \\ V_2 \end{bmatrix} = \begin{bmatrix} I_1 \\ I_2 \end{bmatrix}$$

and can be expressed in general as

$$\mathbf{GV} = \mathbf{I}$$

where G is a 2 × 2 matrix (2 rows and 2 columns) and V and I are 2 × 1 column vectors (2 rows and 1 column). Recall that matrix multiplication is a row-by-column operation, which in this case is a 2 × 2 matrix multiplied by a 2 × 1 vector to produce a 2 × 1 vector. The solution of this matrix equation is obtained by multiplying both sides of the equation by the inverse of the matrix **G,** which is $\mathbf{G^{-1}}$ yielding the equation

$$\mathbf{G^{-1}GV} = \mathbf{G^{-1}I}$$

However, $\mathbf{GG^{-1}}$ is the identity matrix, **I**. This operation is similar to multiplying a scalar by its inverse, i.e. $r^{-1}r = (1/r)(r) = 1$ and thus the solution to the matrix equation is

$$\mathbf{V} = \mathbf{G^{-1}I}$$

G^{-1} is equal the Adjoint (Adj) of the matrix divided by the determinant (Det), which in the case of a 2×2 matrix is simple to calculate.

$$G^{-1} = \text{Adj}(G)/\text{Det}$$

It is interesting that the modern scientific calculators take this same approach to solving simultaneous equations, and in MATLAB the solution of the equation

$$GV = I$$

is expressed as

$$V = \text{inv}(G)^*I$$

where inv(G) is the inverse of the matrix G, i.e. G^{-1}. We will defer any further discussion of these approaches to the solutions of actual circuits where the reader can clearly see the manner in which these operations lead to a circuit solution.

Our approach to this nodal analysis technique will be to begin with simple circuits and progress to those that are more complicated. Consider Example 3.1.

Example 3.1

We wish to find all unknown node voltages and branch currents in the network in Figure 3.3a.

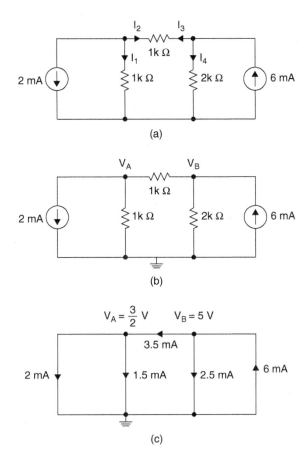

(a)

(b)

(c)

FIGURE 3.3 Circuit used in Example 3.1

The network is redrawn in Figure 3.3b to emphasize the two unknown node voltages V_A and V_B, as well as the reference node. In order to write the KCL equations, we must adopt a convention that specifies the direction of the currents, i.e. the currents entering or leaving the node. The following convention will be consistently employed:

Currents *entering* the node will be labeled with a *negative sign*.

Currents *leaving* the node will be labeled with a *positive sign*.

It is important to remember that the exact opposite convention could just as easily be adopted. This opposite convention would be equivalent to multiplying the equations in the original convention by a negative sign (and remember that an equation is not changed if every term in the equation is multiplied by a negative sign).

Applying KCL at the upper-left node yields the equation

$$2\,mA + I_1 + I_2 = 0$$
$$2/k + V_A/1k + [V_A - V_B]/1k = 0$$

Applying KCL at the upper-right node yields the equation

$$I_3 + I_4 - 6\,mA = 0$$
$$[V_B - V_A]/1k + V_B/1k - 6/k = 0$$

where we have written the 1 mA as 1/k and the branch currents are expressed as the difference in the voltage between the nodes divided by the resistance between them, and as we indicated earlier, this is simply an application of KVL.

If the two linearly independent KCL equations, in the two unknowns V_A and V_B, are multiplied through by k, the following results are obtained:

$$2V_A - V_B = -2$$
$$-V_A + (3/2)V_B = 6$$

At this point, we pause to remind the reader that these are just two linearly independent equations, which can be solved in a variety of ways, e.g. solve the first equation for V_A in terms of V_B, substitute this expression into the second equation where now the only unknown variable will be V_B, solve for V_B, and then substitute this value of V_B into either of the original equations where now V_A is the only unknown.

However, since a matrix solution is a very simple method for solving two linearly independent equations, and it provides the reader with a view of the manner in which MATLAB solves these equations, we will employ this approach here. The equations in matrix form are

$$\begin{bmatrix} 2 & -1 \\ -1 & 3/2 \end{bmatrix} \begin{bmatrix} V_A \\ V_B \end{bmatrix} = \begin{bmatrix} -2 \\ 6 \end{bmatrix}$$

The determinant of the matrix is obtained by the product of the terms on the main diagonal minus the product of the off-diagonal terms, i.e.

$$Det = (2)(3/2) - (-1)(-1)$$
$$= 2$$

And the Adjoint of the matrix is obtained by interchanging the terms on the main diagonal and changing the signs on the off-diagonal terms resulting in the following form.

$$\text{Adj }(\mathbf{G}) = \begin{bmatrix} 3/2 & 1 \\ 1 & 2 \end{bmatrix}$$

The solution is then

$$\mathbf{V} = (1/\text{Det}) \text{ Adj }(\mathbf{G})\mathbf{I}$$

$$= (1/2)\begin{bmatrix} 3/2 & 1 \\ 1 & 2 \end{bmatrix}\begin{bmatrix} -2 \\ 6 \end{bmatrix}$$

The row-by-column multiplication of the adjoint matrix, Adj $(\mathbf{G})$, by the column vector, $\mathbf{I}$, yields

$$V_A = (1/2)[(3/2)(-2) + (1)(6)]$$
$$= 3/2 \text{ V}$$
$$V_B = (1/2)[(1)(-2) + (2)(6)]$$
$$= 5 \text{ V}$$

The operation written in matrix form would be

$$\begin{bmatrix} V_A \\ V_B \end{bmatrix} = (1/2)\begin{bmatrix} 3/2 & 1 \\ 1 & 2 \end{bmatrix}\begin{bmatrix} -2 \\ 6 \end{bmatrix} = (1/2)\begin{bmatrix} (3/2)(-2) + (1)(6) \\ (1)(-2) + (2)(6) \end{bmatrix} = (1/2)\begin{bmatrix} 3 \\ 10 \end{bmatrix} = \begin{bmatrix} 3/2 \\ 5 \end{bmatrix}$$

indicating that $V_A = 3/2$ V and $V_B = 5$ V.

We now list the results on the stick diagram in Figure 3.3c to illustrate the complete solution showing the node voltages and branch currents. The current $I_1 = V_A/1k = 1.5$ mA, the current $I_4 = V_B/2k = 2.5$ mA, the current $I_2 = (V_A - V_B)/1k = -3.5$ mA, and the current $I_3 = (V_B - V_A)/1k = 3.5$ mA. Note that KCL is satisfied at every node. It is important to remember that when defining currents (and voltages) we need to know *both* magnitude and direction. How could we ever expect to apply KCL if we did not know the direction of the current as well as the magnitude?

Now let's consider a circuit that is slightly more complicated.

Example 3.2

Let's calculate all the voltages and currents in the network in Figure 3.4a.

There are four nodes, one of which is the reference node, indicating that three linearly independent simultaneous KCL equations will be required to determine the three unknown node voltages. We obtain these three equations by applying KCL at the nodes labeled V_1, V_2, and V_3.

Applying KCL by summing the currents that leave the three nodes results in the following equations:

Node labeled V_1: $-6/k + [V_1 - V_2]/2k + [V_1 - V_3]/1k = 0$

Node labeled V_2: $[V_2 - V_1]/2k + [V_2 - 0]/4k + [V_2 - V_3]/3k = 0$

Node labeled V_3: $[V_3 - V_1]/1k + [V_3 - V_2]/3k + 2/k = 0$

Simplifying the equations yields

$$V_1[1/2k + 1/k] - V_2[1/2k] - V_3[1/k] = 6/k$$
$$-V_1[1/2k] + V_2[1/2k + 1/4k + 1/3k] - V_3[1/3k] = 0$$
$$-V_1[1/k] - V_2[1/3k] + V_3[1/3k + 1/k] = -2/k$$

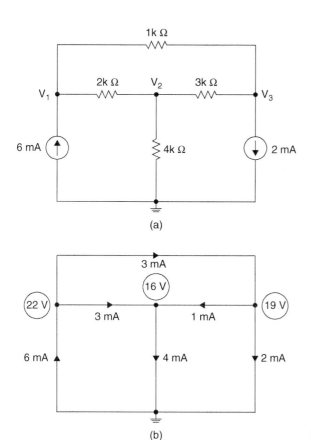

FIGURE 3.4   Circuit used in Example 3.2

Multiplying the equations through by k, and simplifying the coefficients yields

$$1.5 \, V_1 - 0.5 \, V_2 - 1 \, V_3 = 6$$
$$-0.5 \, V_1 + 1.083 \, V_2 - 0.333 \, V_3 = 0$$
$$-1 \, V_1 - 0.333 \, V_2 + 1.333 \, V_3 = -2$$

Solving these equations using either variable elimination or matrices is tedious; therefore we should employ a modern scientific calculator or MATLAB. The MATLAB solution consists of inputting the **G** matrix and the **I** vector and then requesting the solution $\mathbf{V} = \text{inv}(\mathbf{G})^*\mathbf{I}$. The **G** matrix is

$$\mathbf{G} = \begin{bmatrix} 1.5 & -0.5 & -1 \\ -0.5 & 1.083 & -0.333 \\ -1 & -0.333 & 1.333 \end{bmatrix}$$

The **I** vector is

$$\mathbf{I} = \begin{bmatrix} 6 \\ 0 \\ -2 \end{bmatrix}$$

At the MATLAB, prompt >> list the components of the G matrix one row at a time where the elements of the row are separated by spaces and the rows are separated by semicolons. The listing and solution are as follows:

$$>> G = [1.5 - 0.5 - 1; -0.5\ 1.083 - 0.333; -1 - 0.333\ 1.333]$$

$$G = \begin{matrix} 1.5000 & -0.5000 & -1.0000 \\ -0.5000 & 1.0830 & -0.3330 \\ -1.0000 & -0.3330 & 1.3330 \end{matrix}$$

$$>> I = [6;\ 0; -2]$$

$$I = \begin{matrix} 6 \\ 0 \\ -2 \end{matrix}$$

$$>> V = inv\ (G)^*I$$

$$V = \begin{matrix} 22.0010 \\ 16.0000 \\ 19.0015 \end{matrix}$$

The results indicate that $V_1 = 22.0100$ V, $V_2 = 16.0000$ V, and $V_3 = 19.0015$ V. These node voltages are labeled on the stick diagram in Figure 3.4b. The currents shown in the diagram are determined by applying Ohm's law, i.e. the voltage across the resistor divided by the resistance is equal to the current in that resistor. For example, the current – left to right – in the 2k Ω resistor is equal to the voltage across this resistor divided by this resistance, or

$$[V_1 - V_2]/2k = [22 - 16]/2k = 3\ mA$$

which, once again, is simply an application of KVL, i.e. $- V_1 + 2kI + V_2 = 0$, where we have assumed the direction of the current is from left to right. A quick check will indicate that KCL is satisfied at every node, which provides some assurance that the data entered into MATLAB program was correct.

Note that the only sources employed in the previous examples were current sources. As we indicated at the outset, we will now increase the complexity of our analysis by analyzing circuits that contain voltage sources as well as current sources. Although it would appear at this point that this introduction of voltage sources would complicate the solution, in a nodal analysis this is far from the case, as we will indicate in the material that follows.

Example 3.3

Let us determine the voltages and currents in the network in Figure 3.5a.

In our nodal analysis, the presence of a voltage source makes a huge difference. The reason is simply this: in a nodal analysis we are using KCL to determine the non-reference node voltages. However, we note that since both the 12 V source and the 4 V source are connected directly between the reference and the non-reference nodes labeled V_1 and V_3, these non-reference node voltages are actually known, i.e. $V_1 = 12$ V and $V_3 = -4$ V. Since the circuit contains four nodes,

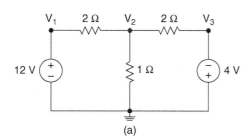 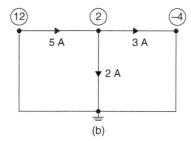

(a)   (b)

FIGURE 3.5 Circuit used in Example 3.3

three linearly independent equations are required to determine the non-reference node voltages, and in this case, two of the three equations are

$$V_1 = 12 \text{ V}$$
$$V_3 = -4 \text{ V}$$

As a result, V_2 is the only unknown node voltage. The KCL equation at the node labeled V_2 is

$$[V_2 - V_1]/2 + V_2/1 + [V_2 - V_3]/2 = 0$$

or

$$[V_2 - 12]/2 + V_2/1 + [V_2 - (-4)]/2 = 0$$

Solving for V_2 yields $V_2 = 2$ V. The voltages and currents are shown in the stick diagram in Figure 3.5b. Note that KCL is satisfied at every node.

Example 3.4

We wish to find the unknown node voltages and the branch currents in the network in Figure 3.6a.

First of all, note that this is a three-node network, and therefore two linearly independent KCL equations are required to determine the two non-reference node voltages labeled as V_1 and V_2, in Figure 3.6b. Since the 12 V source is not connected to the reference node, we do not know the voltage at either node V_1 or V_2. However, while we do not know either V_1 or V_2, we do know that the difference in voltage between them is 12 V, i.e. if we know V_1, then V_2 is $V_1 + 12$ and if we know V_2, then V_1 is $V_2 - 12$. Thus, the voltage between these two nodes is constrained to be 12 V. Remember that both V_1 and V_2 represent the voltage at those nodes with respect to the reference node. Therefore, the KVL equation for the circuit is

$$-V_1 - 12 + V_2 = 0$$

or

$$-V_1 + V_2 = 12$$

which is not only a constraint equation for the network, but one of the two linearly independent equations needed to find the node voltages. Therefore, we need only one additional equation. Recall, in Chapter 2, we demonstrated that KCL must not only be satisfied at a node but also at a boundary that divides the network into two complete pieces. In other words, the total current that enters a boundary must also exit the boundary because current is charge in motion and cannot sit still on a node or even a group of nodes. We employ that concept here and form a boundary around the voltage source as shown in Figure 3.6b. We call the voltage source and the two connecting

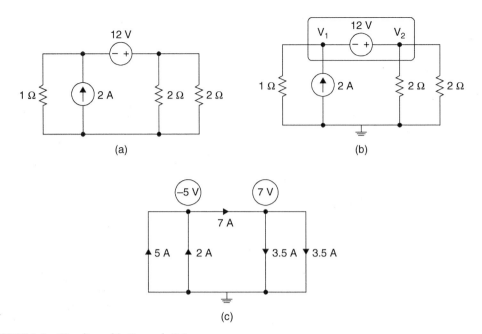

FIGURE 3.6   Circuit used in Example 3.4

nodes a supernode, and it is identified by the boundary that encompasses it. The second required KCL equation is obtained by summing the currents that leave the supernode. That equation is

$$V_1/1 - 2 + V_2/2 + V_2/2 = 0$$

Therefore, the two KCL equations needed to find the two unknown node voltages are

$$-V_1 + V_2 = 12$$
$$V_1 + V_2 = 2$$

Adding the equations yields

$$2V_2 = 14$$
$$V_2 = 7 \text{ V}$$

Substituting this value into either equation yields $V_1 = -5$ V. The stick diagram in Figure 3.6c indicates that KCL is satisfied at all the nodes.

Example 3.5

Let us determine all the node voltages and branch currents in the network in Figure 3.7a.

This is a four-node network, and hence three linearly independent KCL equations will be required to find the three non-reference node voltages labeled as V_1, V_2, and V_3 in Figure 3.7b. Since the 8 V source is connected directly between the node labeled V_2 and the reference node, we already know V_2, and it is 8 V. In addition, although we don't know either V_1 or V_3, we do know that their voltages are constrained by the 6 V source that is connected between them, i.e. if we know V_1, then $V_3 = V_1 - 6$ V and if we know V_3, then $V_1 = V_3 + 6$ V. Again we remind the reader that these equations are nothing more than an application of KVL around the outer loop.

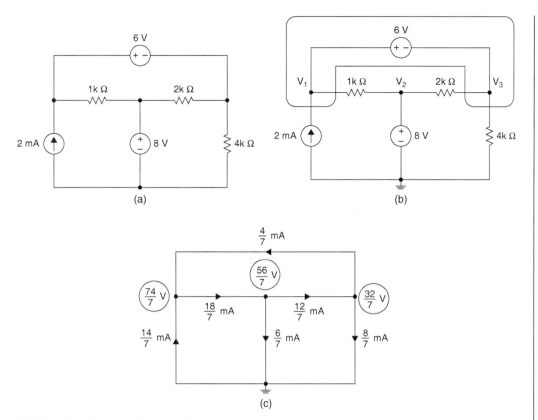

FIGURE 3.7   Circuit used in Example 3.5

Given the presence of the voltage sources, two of the three equations required to solve for the non-reference node voltages are

$$V_1 - V_3 = 6$$
$$V_2 = 8 \text{ V}$$

The third equation is the KCL equation at the boundary, i.e. the supernode.

$$-2/k + [V_1 - V_2]/2k + [V_3 - V_2]/2k + V_3/4k = 0$$

Substituting the two constraint equations into the latter equation and solving for V_3 yields

$$V_3 = 32/7 \text{ V}$$

And then V_1 is

$$V_1 = V_3 + 6$$
$$= 74/7 \text{ V}$$

For convenience in calculating the currents, we express V_2 as 56/7 V. These voltages, together with the branch currents, are shown in the stick diagram in Figure 3.7c. The branch currents in the resistors are determined by Ohm's law, i.e. the difference in voltage across the resistor divided by the resistance. Once the resistor currents are known, their values are used to calculate the currents in the voltage sources using KCL.

As indicated, the presence of voltage sources in the network actually simplifies the analysis. In addition, this technique can be used regardless of whether the source is an independent or dependent source, as will be demonstrated later in this chapter.

LOOP/MESH ANALYSIS

Recall that in a nodal analysis, KCL is employed to determine all the non-reference node voltages in the circuit. Once these node voltages are known, the current in any element in the network can be easily obtained via Ohm's law. In contrast, in a mesh/loop analysis, a set of mesh/loop currents for the network is defined, and KVL is employed to determine them. Once the current in every element is known, then Ohm's law can be used to determine any voltage in the network.

Although mathematical topology is the vehicle used in the general case (even for three-dimensional circuits) to determine both the number of nodal equations required to perform a nodal analysis and the number of equations necessary to perform a mesh/loop analysis in a network, our analysis will deal only with planar networks and thus we know that we can determine the number of linearly independent equations required to perform a mesh/loop analysis by simply counting the number of "window panes" in the network. Our approach to mesh/loop analysis will follow closely the manner in which nodal analysis was introduced, and the reader is encouraged to note the salient differences.

One additional issue we mention as a reminder is that a mesh is a loop that does not contain any other loops. Therefore, note in Example 3.6 that follows, the equations written to determine the currents in the network are actually mesh equations.

Example 3.6

Let us employ mesh analysis to determine all the currents and voltages in the network in Figure 3.8a.

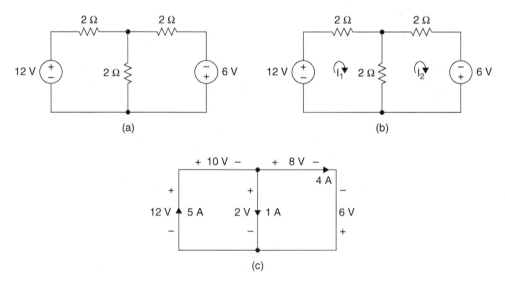

(a)

(b)

(c)

FIGURE 3.8 Circuit used in Example 3.6

First we define two mesh currents, I_1 and I_2, as shown in Figure 3.8b. Given the defined directions of the currents, Ohm's law can be used to determine the voltage across each resistor. Note carefully that the current in the 2 Ω resistor in the center of the network is either $I_1 - I_2$ going down or $I_2 - I_1$ going up. Let's assume that the current in the center resistor is going down, i.e. the current in this resistor is $I_1 - I_2$. The KVL equation for the mesh on the left is

$$-12 + 2I_1 + 2(I_1 - I_2) = 0$$

The KVL equation for the mesh on the right is

$$2I_2 - 6 - 2(I_1 - I_2) = 0$$

If instead of assuming the current in the center resistor was going down, we had written this second KVL equation assuming the current in the center resistor was going up, in which case the current would be $I_2 - I_1$, then the KVL equation would be

$$2I_2 - 6 + 2(I_2 - I_1) = 0$$

However, these two equations are identical. Therefore, when writing the equation for a particular mesh, we simply assume that the current in that mesh is positive and subtract the current in the opposite direction.

The two mesh equations for the circuit are then

$$4I_1 - 2I_2 = 12$$
$$-2I_1 + 4I_2 = 6$$

Since there are only two equations, matrix analysis will be used to solve them. The determinant is

$$\text{Det} = (4)(4) - (-2)(-2) = 12$$

The adjoint is

$$\text{Adj} = \begin{bmatrix} 4 & 2 \\ 2 & 4 \end{bmatrix}$$

Therefore,

$$\begin{bmatrix} I_1 \\ I_2 \end{bmatrix} = (1/12)\begin{bmatrix} 4 & 2 \\ 2 & 4 \end{bmatrix}\begin{bmatrix} 12 \\ 6 \end{bmatrix} = (1/12)\begin{bmatrix} (4)(12)+(2)(6) \\ (2)(12)+(4)(6) \end{bmatrix} = (1/12)\begin{bmatrix} 60 \\ 48 \end{bmatrix} = \begin{bmatrix} 5 \\ 4 \end{bmatrix}$$

Thus,

$$I_1 = 5\,A$$
$$I_2 = 4\,A$$

Using Ohm's law, the voltage across each element in the network is shown in Figure 3.8c. Note that KVL and KCL are satisfied in this circuit.

Just as the presence of a voltage source made nodal analysis easier, the presence of a current source makes mesh/loop analysis easier as Examples 3.7–3.10 indicate.

Example 3.7

Given the circuit in Figure 3.9a, let us determine all voltages and currents in this circuit.

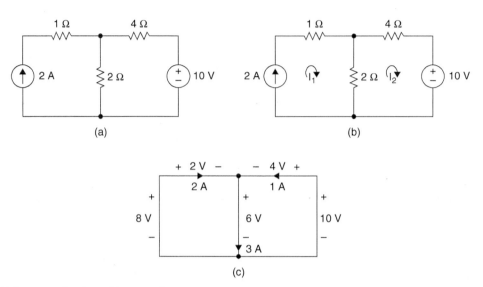

FIGURE 3.9   Circuit used in Example 3.7

The circuit is redrawn in Figure 3.9b with the mesh currents defined. Note that current I_1 is directly through the current source; therefore, I_1 must be equal to 2 A. We know that since there are two meshes, two KVL equations will be required to find the two mesh currents, and one of them is

$$I_1 = 2\ A$$

The remaining equation is KVL around the right mesh, which is

$$2[I_2 - I_1] + 4I_2 + 10 = 0$$

If the value of $I_1 = 2$ is substituted into this equation, the results are

$$I_2 = -1\ A$$

Figure 3.9c shows the results of the analysis, where the voltages across the resistors are determined via Ohm's law.

Example 3.8

We wish to find all the currents and voltages in the network in Figure 3.10a.

The circuit is redrawn in Figure 3.10b, where the mesh currents are defined. Note that in this case, there are two currents defined through the current source, and given the current directions, $I_1 - I_2 = 4$. This configuration is called a supermesh. Note the similarity of this situation with the supernode in a nodal analysis. The determination of the two mesh currents will require two linearly independent equations, and, in this case, one of them is

$$I_1 - I_2 = 4$$

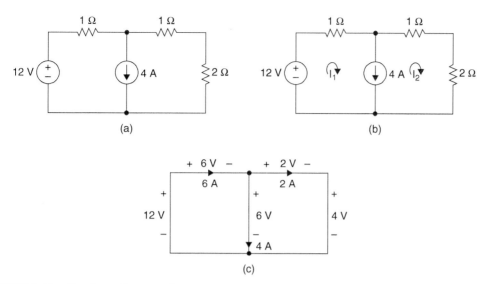

FIGURE 3.10   Circuit used in Example 3.8

The remaining equation is KVL around the outer loop, i.e.

$$-12 + 1I_1 + 1I_2 + 2I_2 = 0$$

Therefore, the two equations required to find the two mesh currents are

$$I_1 - I_2 = 4$$
$$I_1 + 3I_2 = 12$$

If we multiply the first equation by a minus sign (which does not change the equation), and add it to the second equation, we obtain

$$4I_2 = 8$$
$$I_2 = 2 \text{ A}$$

Substituting this value into either original equation yields

$$I_1 = 6 \text{ A}$$

Figure 3.10c illustrates the results of the analysis where the voltages are calculated using Ohm's law.

Once the basic principles are understood, we are in a position to examine more complicated networks where these principles are applied.

Let us use a mesh analysis to determine the output voltage, V_0, in the network in Figure 3.11.

The mesh currents have been defined in the circuit. Note that the currents I_1 and I_2 go directly through current sources. Therefore, $I_1 = -4$ mA and $I_2 = 2$ mA. Their values cannot be anything else because these currents are constrained in the branches where the sources exist. This is clearly a three-mesh circuit, indicating that three linearly independent equations will be necessary

Example 3.9

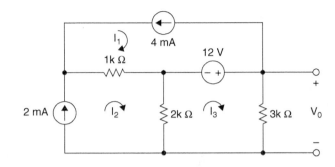

FIGURE 3.11 Circuit used in
Example 3.9

to determine the three currents; however, we already know two of the currents because of the presence of the current sources.

The equations necessary to solve the network are

$$I_1 = -4/k$$
$$I_2 = 2/k$$

and

$$2k(I_3 - I_2) - 12 + 3kI_3 = 0$$

Solving these equations yields $I_3 = 16/5$ mA and $V_0 = 48/5$ V.

Note that the current sources in the circuit in Figure 3.11 were located on the outer boundary such that only one of the mesh currents, as defined, went through them. Consider the more general case shown in Example 3.10.

Example 3.10

Given the circuit in Figure 3.12a, let us determine the voltage V_0.

Note that the 4 mA current source is not on an outer boundary; thus the use of mesh currents would indicate that more than one mesh current would be defined through this source, i.e. we have what is called a supermesh situation. However, the technique we will outline in this example will avoid dealing with the supermesh. If we define the currents I_1 and I_2 to be through the current sources, then

$$I_1 = 2 \text{ mA}$$
$$I_2 = -4 \text{ mA}$$

These are two of the linearly independent equations required to solve the circuit. Once again, we know that three linearly independent equations are needed to perform a mesh/loop analysis in this case. The technique for determining the remaining, i.e. third equation, is the following one. We open-circuit the current sources, which reveals one more loop as shown in Figure 3.12b, and KVL for this loop is the third required equation. When writing the KVL equation for this loop, we must remember that I_1 and I_2 are present in the components where they exist as shown in Figure 3.12a. This data is identified in Figure 3.12c. The third equation needed to solve the network is then

$$-12 + 3k(I_2 + I_3) + 2k(I_2 + I_3 - I_1) + Ik(I_3 - I_1) = 0$$

Substituting the values for I_1 and I_2 into this equation yields $I_3 = 19/3$ mA. Then the equation for V_0 is

$$V_0 = 3k(I_2 + I_3)$$
$$= 7 \text{ V}$$

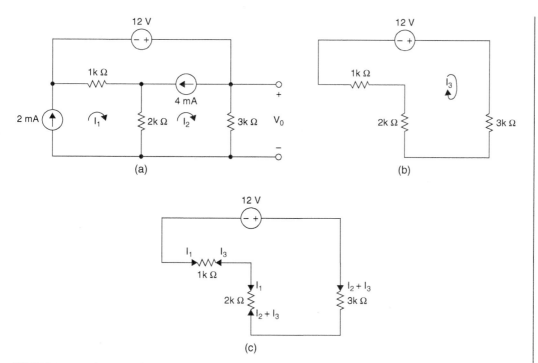

FIGURE 3.12   Circuit used in Example 3.10

This technique, demonstrated in the foregoing example, is valid in any network. The approach is simply to draw one current through each current source, and then the remaining equations consist of the KVL equations for the network that results from open-circuiting these current sources. *In writing these KVL equations, it is critically important to remember that the currents defined for the current sources are still present in the components where they exist in the original network.* The KVL equations for these loops, together with the equations for the current sources, will produce the necessary equations needed to solve for all currents in the network.

Now that we know two techniques for performing circuit analysis that are generally applicable, let's demonstrate that in specific cases, one technique may be much easier to use than the other. Some of the circuits we will analyze will contain dependent sources, which will further strengthen our knowledge of this subject.	**NODAL ANALYSIS VERSUS MESH/LOOP ANALYSIS**

Let us use both mesh analysis and nodal analysis to determine all the currents in the network in Figure 3.13a. The nodes have been labeled and the direction of the mesh currents is assigned. We could have assigned the direction of the currents in a different manner; however, in our discussions we will always assign the currents in a clockwise direction.	Example 3.11

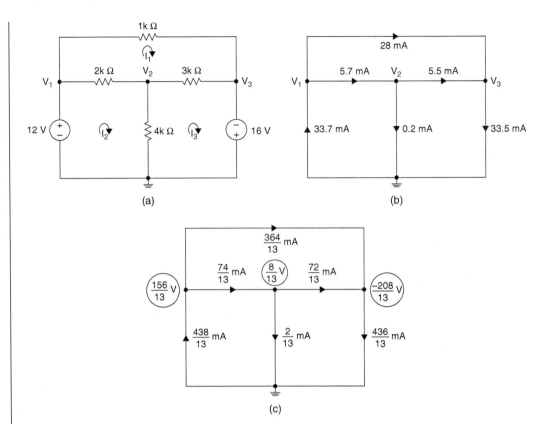

FIGURE 3.13 Circuit used in Example 3.11

The KVL equations for the three meshes are

$$+I_1 1k + (I_1 - I_3)3k + (I_1 - I_2)2k = 0$$
$$-12 + 2k(I_2 - I_1) + 4k(I_2 - I_3) = 0$$
$$4k(I_3 - I_2) + 3k(I_3 - I_2) - 16 = 0$$

Simplifying the equations and putting them in matrix form produces the matrix equation

$$\begin{bmatrix} 6k & -2k & -3k \\ -2k & 6k & -4k \\ -3k & -4k & 7k \end{bmatrix}\begin{bmatrix} I_1 \\ I_2 \\ I_3 \end{bmatrix} = \begin{bmatrix} 0 \\ 12 \\ 16 \end{bmatrix}$$

The MATLAB solution for these equations is outlined as follows:

```
>> R = [6000 – 2000 – 3000;  –2000 6000 – 4000; –3000 – 4000 7000]
```

$$R = \begin{matrix} 6000 & -2000 & -3000 \\ -2000 & 6000 & -4000 \\ -3000 & -4000 & 7000 \end{matrix}$$

```
>> V = [0; 12; 16]
```

$$V = \begin{matrix} 0 \\ 12 \\ 16 \end{matrix}$$

$$>> I = inv\ (R)^*V$$

$$I = \begin{matrix} 0.0280 \\ 0.0337 \\ 0.0335 \end{matrix}$$

The results are placed on the stick diagram in Figure 3.13b where the currents in each branch are shown. Knowing all the currents permits us to calculate all the voltages in the network. For example, the node voltage V_2 is

$$V_2 = (I_2 - I_3)4k = (-33.7/k - 33.5/k)4k = 0.8\ V$$

All other voltages in the network can be computed in a similar manner.

Let's now solve for all the currents and voltages in Figure 3.13a using nodal analysis. We note immediately that the node voltages V_1 and V_3 are known, i.e.

$$V_1 = 12\ V$$
$$V_3 = -16\ V$$

Furthermore, there are four nodes in the network; therefore, we need three linearly independent equations. The third equation is KCL at node V_2, i.e.

$$[V_2 - V_1]/2k + V_2/4k + [V_2 - V_3]/3k = 0$$

or

$$[V_2 - 12]/2k + V_2/4k + [V_2 - (-16)]/3k = 0$$

Solving this equation for V_2 yields

$$V_2 = (8/13)\ V$$

It is convenient to express 12 as 156/13 and 16 = 208/13. Then all the voltages and currents in the network can be displayed as shown in Figure 3.13c.

Note the simplicity of the nodal analysis compared with a mesh analysis. It is essentially a 3-to-1 complexity issue, since the nodal equation for V_2 could have been written with the known node voltages V_1 and V_2 included in the first equation. The reason for the difference is, of course, the presence of the voltage sources, i.e. we knew at the outset the value of two of the three node voltages.

Let us consider now two examples that are not only more complicated because of the number of components involved but the presence of a dependent source as well.

Let us find the current I_0 in the network in Figure 3.14a.

The number of voltage sources in the network, both independent and dependent, indicates that a nodal analysis will be the simplest means of attack. The node equations for the circuit are

$$V_2 = 12\ V$$
$$V_3 = -6\ V$$
$$V_1 - V_4 = 2\ V_X$$

Example 3.12

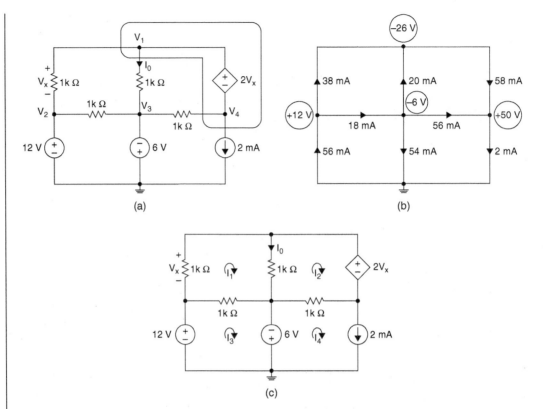

FIGURE 3.14 Circuit used in Example 3.12

And KCL at the supernode is

$$(V_1 - V_2)/1k + (V_1 - V_3)/1k + (V_4 - V_3)/1k + 2/k = 0$$

Finally, the equation that defines the controlling variable is

$$V_1 - V_2 = V_x$$

Combining the two equations for V_x to obtain an equation for V_4 in terms of V_1 and the known values for V_2 and V_3, and then substituting this value for V_4 into the KCL equation for the supernode yields

$$V_1 = -26 \text{ V}$$
$$V_4 = 50 \text{ V}$$

Then,

$$I_0 = (V_1 - V_3)/1k = -20 \text{ mA}$$

The results are shown in Figure 3.14b. Also shown in the circuit are the branch currents where Ohm's law has been used to compute the currents in the resistors and then KCL is applied to determine the currents in the voltage sources.

Now for purposes of comparison, let us use mesh analysis to determine the currents in this network. The mesh equations are shown defined in Figure 3.14c and listed below.

$$1k\,I_1 + 1k[I_1 - I_2] + 1k[I_1 - I_3] = 0$$
$$1k[I_2 - I_1] + 2V_X + 1k[I_2 - I_4] = 0$$
$$-12 + 1k\,[I_3 - I_1] - 6 = 0$$
$$I_4 = 2/k$$
$$V_X = -1k\ I_1$$

The equations can be written in matrix form as

$$
\begin{bmatrix}
1k & -1k & -1k & 0 \\
-3k & 2k & 0 & -1k \\
-1k & 0 & 1k & 0 \\
0 & 0 & 0 & 1
\end{bmatrix}
\begin{bmatrix}
I_1 \\ I_2 \\ I_3 \\ I_4
\end{bmatrix}
=
\begin{bmatrix}
0 \\ 0 \\ 18 \\ 2/k
\end{bmatrix}
$$

The MATLAB solution is then

```
>> R = [3000 – 1000 – 1000 0; –3000 2000 0 – 1000; –1000 0 1000 0; 0 0 0 1]
```

$$
R =
\begin{matrix}
3000 & -1000 & -1000 & 0 \\
-3000 & 2000 & 0 & -1000 \\
-1000 & 0 & 1000 & 0 \\
0 & 0 & 0 & 1
\end{matrix}
$$

```
>> V = [0; 0; 18; 0.002]
```

$$
V =
\begin{matrix}
0 \\
0 \\
18.0000 \\
0.0020
\end{matrix}
$$

```
>> I = inv (R)*V
```

$$
I =
\begin{matrix}
0.0380 \\
0.0580 \\
0.0560 \\
0.0020
\end{matrix}
$$

A quick check will indicate that the two methods have produced the same results, i.e.

$$I_0 = I_1 - I_2 = -20 \text{ mA}$$

Let us demonstrate that the power generated in the circuit in Figure 3.15a is equal to the power absorbed.

Example 3.13

Since there are more current sources than voltage sources, the use of a mesh analysis to determine all the currents and voltages will undoubtedly be the simplest approach. The mesh currents are shown in Figure 3.15a and the defining equations are

$$I_2 = 2\,I_X$$
$$I_3 = 6/k$$
$$I_4 = -2/k$$
$$1k\,I_1 + 12 + 1k(I_1 - I_3) = 0$$

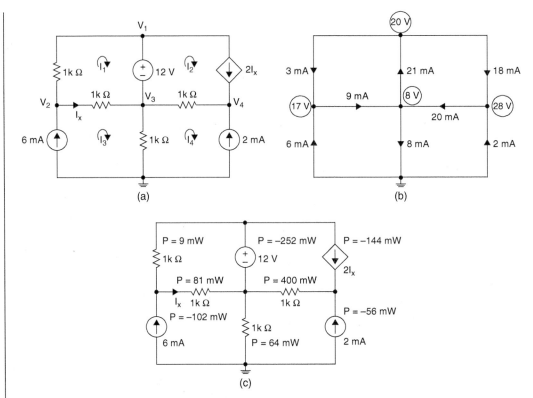

FIGURE 3.15 Circuit used in Example 3.13

And the equation for the controlling variable is

$$I_X = I_3 - I_1$$

Solving these equations yields

$$I_1 = -3\ mA$$
$$I_X = 9\ mA$$

The node voltages can then be computed as follows:

$$V_3 = (I_3 - I_4)1k = 8\,V$$
$$V_2 = 1kI_X + V_3 = 17\,V$$
$$V_1 = V_3 + 12 = 20\,V$$
$$V_4 = V_3 - (I_4 - I_2)1k = 28\,V$$

All the results are shown on the stick diagram in Figure 3.15b. The power absorbed or supplied by each element is shown in Figure 3.15c. Note that the passive sign convention has been employed so that power absorbed is positive and power supplied is negative, as indicated in the circuit diagram. The totals are listed as follows:

$$P_{ABS} = 9 + 81 + 400 + 64 = 554\ mW$$
$$P_{SUP} = 252 + 144 + 102 + 56 = 554\ mW$$

Although the nodal and mesh/loop analysis techniques are applicable and powerful, and can be used on any size network, they provide no information about the internal workings of the circuit. These two techniques generate an answer, and we have no clue about the manner in which the various sources contribute to this answer. We now consider an approach that does give us some insight into the operation of the network.

This analysis technique is based upon the *Principle of Superposition*, which is a property of any linear system, i.e. electrical, mechanical, etc. This principle states that given a linear circuit with multiple independent sources, the voltage or current at any point in the network is equal to the algebraic sum of the contributions of each source acting alone. In calculating the contribution of an individual source, the remaining sources in the network must be made zero. As we learned earlier, *we zero a voltage source by replacing it with a short circuit and we zero a current source by replacing it with an open circuit.* This principle can be applied to networks with any number of independent and dependent sources. In addition, it can be applied in the following manner. If the network contains sources, S_1, S_2, and S_3, then we can use each one individually or we can use S_1 and S_2 together and then S_3 or any other combination. We must use each source in any combination, but not more than once. Example 3.14 is designed to illustrate these issues.

SUPERPOSITION

Let us apply superposition to determine the voltage V_0 in the network in Figure 3.16a. Since the circuit contains three sources, we will independently determine the contribution of each source to the voltage V_0 and then algebraically add the results to determine V_0. Note that this approach will provide some specific information, i.e. what does each source contribute to the total answer.

Figure 3.16b is the network in which the 6 V source is acting alone. V_0' can be obtained using a simple voltage divider

$$V_0' = (-6)(6k)/(3k + 6k) = -4 \text{ V}$$

Figure 3.16c, which is redrawn in Figure 3.16d, illustrates the 24 V source acting alone. V_0'' can be obtained with another voltage divider:

$$V_0'' = (24)(3k)/(3k + 6k) = 8 \text{ V}$$

Figure 3.16e, which is redrawn in Figure 3.16f, illustrates the 2 mA source acting alone. In this case,

$$V_0''' = (2/k)(2k) = 4 \text{ V}$$

Then V_0 is the algebraic sum of the sources operating independently, i.e.

$$V_0 = V_0' + V_0'' + V_0'''$$
$$= -4 + 8 + 4 = 8 \text{ V}$$

We can quickly check this answer by applying nodal analysis (because there are more voltage sources than current sources). Using a supernode in the network in Figure 3.16a for the 24 V source, and noting that the node voltage at the top of the current source can be expressed as $V_0 - 24$, yields the KCL equation:

$$[V_0 - (-6)]/6k + [V_0 - 24 - (-6)]/6k - 2/k + V_0/6k = 0$$

The solution of which is $V_0 = 8$ V.

Example 3.14

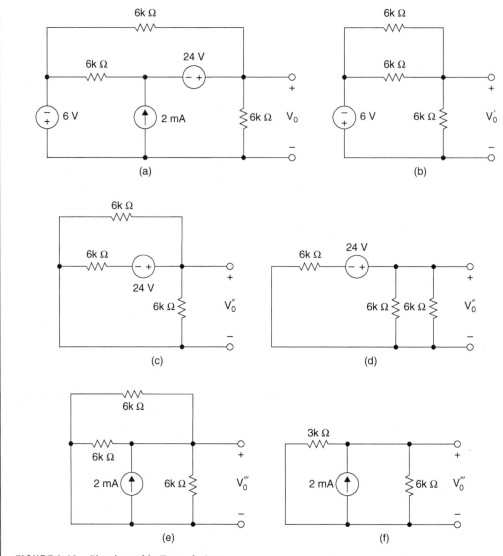

FIGURE 3.16 Circuit used in Example 3.14

THEVENIN'S THEOREM

This analysis technique, named for the French engineer M. L. Thevenin who developed this technique, is a very powerful method for analyzing circuits. Although this theorem is more useful than we will indicate with the circuits analyzed here, the reader interested in exploring the wide applications of this technique is referred to *Basic Engineering Circuit Analysis* by Irwin and Nelms.

Although Thevenin's theorem applies to any network, i.e. those containing both independent and dependent sources, in the analysis that follows we will apply this approach to the solution of circuits containing only independent sources and show how to use the technique without proof. Consider the network in Figure 3.17a and suppose that we split this network into two pieces, circuit B and some load, typically a resistor R_L, as shown in Figure 3.17b. Now Thevenin's theorem states that we can replace circuit B at the terminals A–B with a voltage source in series with a resistor, as shown in Figure 3.17c. The voltage V_{OC} is the open-circuit voltage at the terminals A–B, as shown in Figure 3.17d, and R_{TH} is the Thevenin equivalent resistance looking

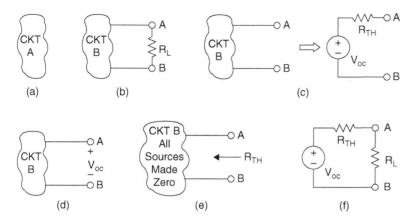

FIGURE 3.17   Circuits used to describe Thevenin's theorem

into the terminals A–B in Figure 3.17e with all sources in circuit B made zero. Finally, we reconnect the Thevenin equivalent for circuit B, which consists of the open-circuit voltage in series with the Thevenin equivalent resistance, to the load as shown in Figure 3.17f. In the general case, the theorem states that at a particular pair of terminals, we can replace the entire circuit, regardless of its size with one voltage source and one resistor. Wow! Examples 3.15 and 3.16 will serve to demonstrate the power of this technique.

Let's apply Thevenin's theorem to find the output voltage, V_0, in the circuit in Figure 3.18a.   **Example 3.15**

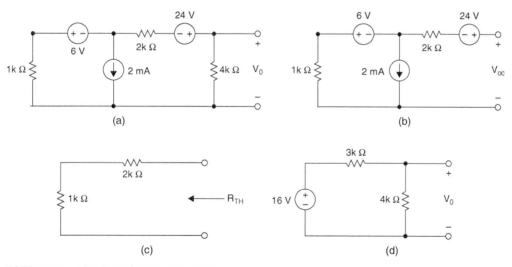

FIGURE 3.18   Circuit used in Example 3.15

We begin by breaking the network into two pieces. We can break the network anywhere we like; however, note that we should go beyond one loop, i.e. to the right of the current source, since if we break the network to the left of the current source we already have a Thevenin equivalent consisting of the 6 V source and 1k Ω resistor! We will let circuit B consist of all the elements except the 4k Ω resistor, as shown in Figure 3.18b. Note that there is no current in the 2k Ω resistor and, therefore, there is no voltage drop across it. In addition, 2 mA will circulate in the loop consisting of the 2 mA source, the 1k Ω resistor and the 6 V source. The voltage drop across the 1k Ω resistor will be 2 V, + to −, bottom to top. Now applying KVL to the outer loop yields the equation

$$(2/k)1k + 6 - 24 + V_{OC} = 0$$

or

$$V_{OC} = 16 \text{ V}$$

Now we need the Thevenin equivalent resistance at the open-circuit terminals where the 4k Ω resistor was connected. This resistance is found by looking back into the open terminals of the network with all sources made zero. Recall that we make a voltage source zero by replacing it with a short circuit and we make the current source zero by replacing it with an open circuit. The resulting network is shown in Figure 3.18c. Clearly, the Thevenin equivalent resistance is 3k Ω. Finally, we connect the Thevenin equivalent circuit back to the 4k Ω resistor as shown in Figure 3.18d. The voltage V_0 is then easily determined using a simple voltage divider as

$$V_0 = (16)[4k/(3k + 4k)] = 64/7 \text{ V}$$

Example 3.16 is a little more challenging, but it will also help solidify some of the concepts presented here for this new technique.

| Example 3.16 |

Let us determine the current I_0 in the network in Figure 3.19a using Thevenin's theorem.

We first break the network into two pieces, one is the 3k Ω resistor and the other is everything else, as shown in Figure 3.19b. For purposes of explanation, we have labeled two of the nodes A and B. Note that the current in the 2k Ω resistor has to be 2 mA, from top to bottom because it is in series with the 2 mA source. Therefore, the voltage drop across this resistor is 4 V as shown in Figure 3.19b. In addition, KCL at node B indicates that the current in the 1k Ω resistor is 2 mA, right to left, and hence the voltage drop across this resistor is as shown in Figure 3.19b. Given this data, note that we have a path around the network in which all the voltages are known except V_{OC}. This path is the 2k Ω resistor, the 1k Ω resistor, the 12 V source, and V_{OC}. KVL around this closed path is

$$-4 + 2 - 12 + V_{OC} = 0$$

or

$$V_{OC} = 14 \text{ V}$$

The Thevenin equivalent resistance is determined from the network in Figure 3.19c, and $R_{TH} = 3k$ Ω. Now connecting the Thevenin equivalent circuit, i.e. the 14 V source and 3k Ω resistor, to the 3k Ω resistor, which was originally connected to the terminals that were broken, yields the network in Figure. 3.19d. I_0 is clearly 14/6k = 7/3 mA. Although this result could be checked by any of the methods previously discussed, and a simple technique would be to apply mesh analysis because of the presence of the two current sources, the stick diagram in Figure 3.19e shows that KCL is satisfied at every node.

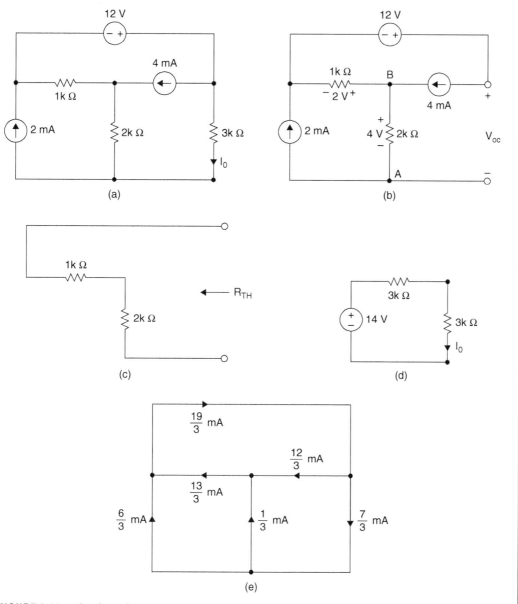

FIGURE 3.19 Circuit used in Example 3.16

Situations exist in circuit design where the selection of a load is predicated upon our ability to transfer maximum power to it. The determination of the specific load and the amount of power that can be transferred to it can be easily derived via Thevenin's theorem.

Consider the circuit in Figure 3.20. The power delivered to the load is

$$P_L = I^2 R_L = [V/(R + R_L)]^2 R_L$$

MAXIMUM POWER TRANSFER

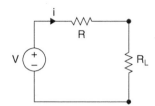

FIGURE 3.20   Circuit used to exchange maximum power transfer

The value of R_L that maximizes this equation can be determined by differentiating the equation with respect to R_L and setting the result to zero, i.e.

$$dP_L/dR_L = 0$$

The result of this operation is

$$R_L = R$$

In other words, for maximum power transfer to the load R_L, we simply set the value of R_L equal to the value of R. While we have employed a very simple circuit to derive this important result, we are able to do this because V and R could represent the Thevenin equivalent network for any circuit.

Let us demonstrate this technique with a couple of examples.

Example 3.17

Given the circuit in Figure 3.21a, let us determine the value of R_L for maximum power transfer and the amount of this maximum power.

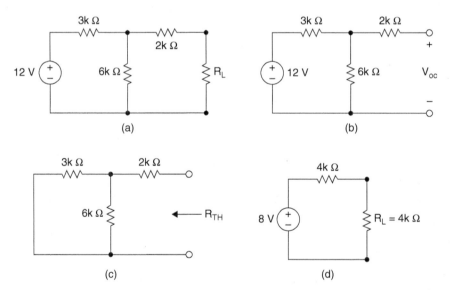

(a)

(b)

(c)

(d)

FIGURE 3.21   Circuits used to illustrate maximum power transfer

We first determine the Thevenin equivalent circuit for the network without the load attached as shown in Figure 3.21b. Since there is no current in the 2 Ω resistor, the open-circuit voltage can be calculated via a simple voltage divider, i.e.

$$V_{OC} = 12[6k/(3k + 6k)] = 8 \text{ V}$$

The Thevenin equivalent resistance is determined from the network in Figure 3.21c as

$$R_{TH} = (3k)(6k)/(3k + 6k) + 2k = 4k\ \Omega$$

Now the network in Figure 3.21a is represented by the circuit in Figure 3.20d. For maximum power transfer to the load, R_L must be chosen as 4k Ω. Then the maximum power transferred to this load is

$$P_{Lmax} = (12/8k)^2(4k) = 9\ mW$$

Let us determine the value of R_L for maximum power transfer and the amount of that power for the circuit in Figure 3.22a.

Example 3.18

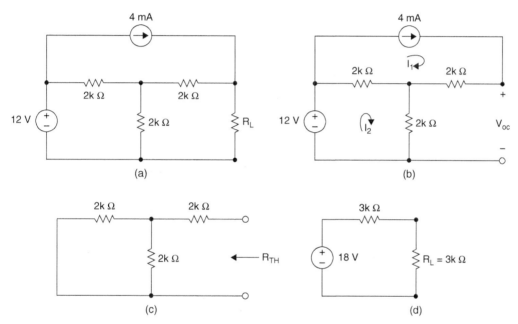

FIGURE 3.22   Circuit used in Example 3.18

The Thevenin equivalent circuit for the original network without the load resistor present is shown in Figure 3.22b. Although the open-circuit voltage could be determined in a number of different ways, we will simply use mesh analysis, with the currents as defined in Figure 3.22b. The equations are

$$I_1 = 4/k$$

$$-12 + 2k[I_2 - I_1] + 2k\ I_2 = 0$$

Substituting the first equation into the second and solving for I_2 yields

$$I_2 = 5/k\ A\ or\ 5\ mA$$

Then the open-circuit voltage

$$V_{OC} = 2k\ I_1 + 2k\ I_2$$
$$= 18\ V$$

R_{TH} is determined from the circuit in Figure 3.22c as

$$R_{TH} = (2k)(2k)/(2k + 2k) + 2k$$
$$= 3k\ \Omega$$

The network in Figure 3.22a can now be represented by the network in Figure 3.22d where the load resistor is set equal to the Thevenin equivalent resistance. The maximum power transferred to this load is then

$$P_{Lmax} = (18/6k)^2(3k)$$
$$= 27\ mW$$

Problems

3.1 Use nodal analysis to find I_0 in the network in Figure P3.1

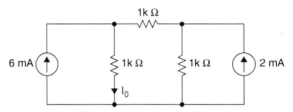

FIGURE P3.1

3.2 Use nodal analysis to find I_0 in the circuit in Figure P3.2

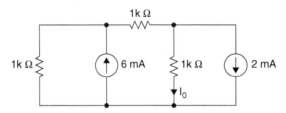

FIGURE P3.2

3.3 Find I_0 in the network in Figure P3.3 using nodal analysis.

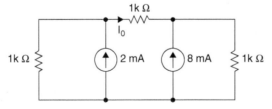

FIGURE P3.3

3.4 Find I_0 in the circuit in Figure P3.4 using nodal analysis.

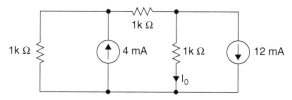

FIGURE P3.4

3.5 Determine the power absorbed or supplied by the two sources in the network in Figure P3.4.

3.6 Determine the power absorbed by the 2k Ω resistor in the circuit in Figure P3.6.

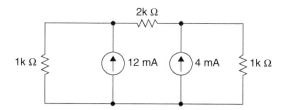

FIGURE P3.6

3.7 Find I_0 in the circuit in Figure P3.7 using nodal analysis.

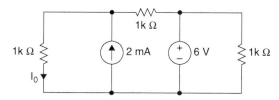

FIGURE P3.7

3.8 Find V_0 in the circuit in Figure P3.8 using nodal analysis.

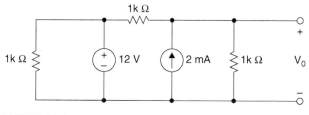

FIGURE P3.8

3.9 Use nodal analysis to find V_0 in the circuit in Figure 3.9.

3.10 Determine the power absorbed by the 1k Ω resistor in the network in Figure P3.9.

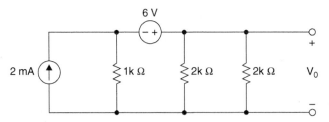

FIGURE P3.9

3.11 Determine the power generated by the 6 V source in the circuit in Figure P3.9.

3.12 Use nodal analysis to determine I_0 in the circuit in Figure P3.12.

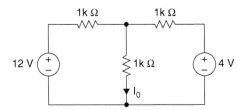

FIGURE P3.12

3.13 Find V_0 in the circuit in Figure P3.13.

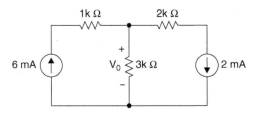

FIGURE P3.13

3.14 Determine the power absorbed by the 2k Ω resistor in the circuit in Figure P3.14.

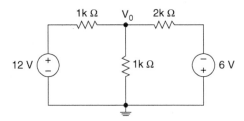

FIGURE P3.14

3.15 Use nodal analysis to find V_0 in the circuit in Figure P3.15.

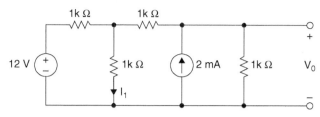

FIGURE P3.15

3.16 Find I_1 in the network in Figure P3.15.

3.17 Is power being supplied or absorbed by the current source in the network in Figure P3.15 and how much?

3.18 Use mesh analysis to find I_0 in the circuit in Figure P3.18.

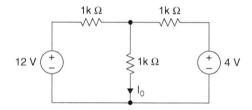

FIGURE P3.18

3.19 Use mesh analysis to solve Problem 3.14.

3.20 Use mesh analysis to determine V_X in the network in Figure P3.20.

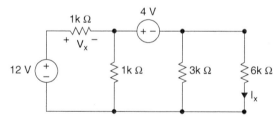

FIGURE P3.20

3.21 Find I_X in the network Figure P3.20.

3.22 Use loop analysis to determine V_0 in the network in Figure P3.22.

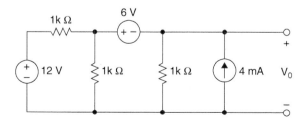

FIGURE P3.22

3.23 Solve Problem 3.22 using nodal analysis.

3.24 Determine if the 6 V source in the network in Figure P3.22 is supplying or absorbing power, and how much.

3.25 Determine if the current source in the network in Figure P3.22 is absorbing or supplying power, and how much.

3.26 Find I_X in the circuit in Figure P3.26 using nodal analysis.

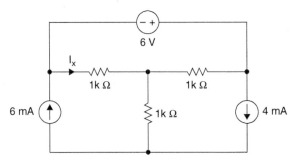

FIGURE P3.26

3.27 Use loop analysis to solve Problem 3.26.

3.28 Determine V_X in the network in Figure P3.28 using nodal analysis.

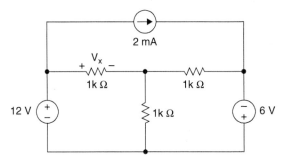

FIGURE P3.28

3.29 Use mesh analysis to solve Problem 3.28.

3.30 Use nodal analysis to find I_X in the circuit in Figure P3.30.

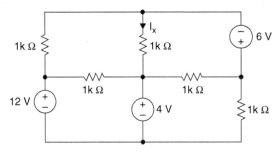

FIGURE P3.30

3.31 Use mesh analysis to solve Problem 3.30.

3.32 Find V_0 in the network in Figure P3.32 using nodal analysis and MATLAB.

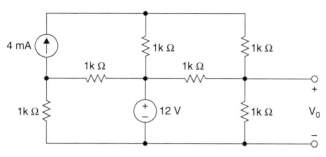

FIGURE P3.32

3.33 Use loop analysis and MATLAB to solve Problem 3.32.

3.34 Find V_0 in the circuit in Figure P3.34 using nodal analysis.

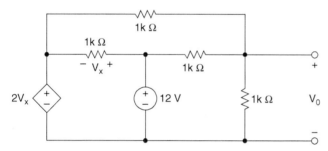

FIGURE P3.34

3.35 Is the controlled source in the network in Figure P3.34 absorbing or supplying power, and how much?

3.36 Use loop analysis to find V_0 in the circuit in Figure P3.36.

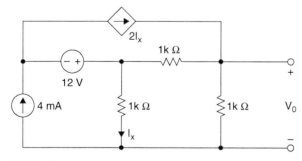

FIGURE P3.36

3.37 Is the 12 V source in the circuit in Figure P3.36 absorbing or supplying power, and how much?

3.38 Find I_0 in the network in Figure P3.1 using superposition.

3.39 Find V_0 in the circuit in Figure P3.8 using superposition.

3.40 Solve Problem 3.9 using superposition.

3.41 Find I_0 in the network in Figure P3.12 using superposition.

3.42 Use superposition to solve Problem 3.15.

3.43 Solve Problem 3.22 using superposition.

3.44 Find V_X in the network in Figure P3.28 using superposition.

3.45 Solve Problem 3.1 using Thevenin's theorem.

3.46 Find V_0 in the network in Figure P3.8 using Thevenin's theorem.

3.47 Solve Problem 3.9 using Thevenin's theorem.

3.48 Find I_0 in the circuit in Figure P3.12 using Thevenin's theorem.

3.49 Use Thevenin's theorem to solve Problem 3.15.

3.50 Find V_0 in the circuit in Figure P3.22 using Thevenin's theorem.

3.51 Solve Problem 3.28 using Thevenin's theorem.

3.52 Find R_L for maximum power transfer and the amount of power transferred in the network in Figure P3.52.

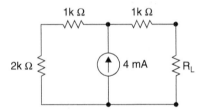

FIGURE P3.52

3.53 Determine the maximum power that can be transferred to the load in the network in Figure P3.53.

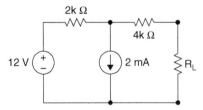

FIGURE P3.53

3.54 Find R_L for maximum power transfer and the amount of power transferred in the network in Figure P3.54.

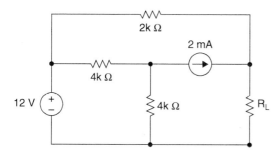

FIGURE P3.54

3.55 Determine the maximum power that can be transferred to the load in the network in Figure P3.55.

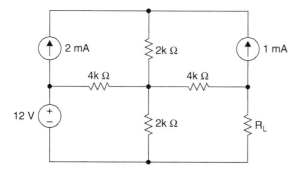

FIGURE P3.55

CHAPTER 4

Transient Analysis

LEARNING OBJECTIVES

- To understand the characteristics of capacitors and inductors
- To learn how to reduce a network of either capacitors or inductors to a single capacitor or inductor
- To understand the storage capability of these two elements
- To understand the concept of a time constant
- To solve first-order transient circuits
- To solve second-order transient circuits

INTRODUCTION

The term *transient analysis* implies that we will analyze a network during the time frame in which the network is in some sort of transitional behavior, i.e. voltages and currents change as a function of time. The impetus for the change in network behavior will be the opening or closing of a switch that will alter the network structure. In our analysis then we will examine various voltages and currents in a network following some sort of switch action.

If the network consisted of only sources and resistors, the opening or closing of a switch in the network would produce an immediate change and the transition to a different network would be instantaneous. Thus, the network must consist of a different set of circuit elements if the change in network performance will take place over time, and the two elements that produce this change are a capacitor and an inductor. Similar to the resistor, these elements are linear. In addition, their terminal characteristics are described by a linear differential equation, and from the standpoint of this chapter, they are capable of storing and releasing energy to the network following the opening or closing of a switch. Although these circuit components may contain some leakage resistance and thus are not ideal, we will assume ideal circuit elements in the following development.

STORAGE ELEMENTS

CAPACITORS

Most readers, no doubt, first encountered the capacitor and inductor in a physics course, under the topics "Electricity and Magnetism." Nevertheless, we will quickly review the salient features of these devices and then employ them in transient circuits.

The capacitor is a two-terminal device that employs the symbol shown in Figure 4.1. Capacitors range from small to large, as shown by the variety of capacitors in Figure 4.2. Their construction spans from microscopic elements on an integrated circuit chip to very large components when employed in electric power systems, and everything in between. Their values typically range from thousands of microfarads to picofarads, where the designation for the units, i.e. farads, originates with the English physicist Michael Faraday. As their symbol implies, they are typically constructed of two parallel conducting surfaces separated by a nonconducting material, and the charge on the capacitor is expressed as follows:

$$q(t) = C v(t)$$

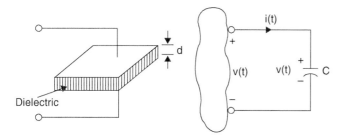

FIGURE 4.1 Capacitor configuration and symbol

FIGURE 4.2 Some typical capacitors (Courtesy of Mark Nelms and Jo Ann Loden)

where q(t) is the charge in coulombs, v(t) is the voltage in volts, and C is the capacitance in farads, and hence 1 farad = 1 coulomb/volt. However, the time rate of change of charge is current and therefore

$$i(t) = dq(t)/dt = C\, dv(t)/dt$$

Note that this equation defines the voltage–current relationship for a capacitor just as V = IR does for a resistor. If we integrate this equation over time, we obtain the equation

$$v(t) = \frac{1}{C}\int_{-\infty}^{t} i(x)\, dx$$

which can be expressed as

$$v(t) = \frac{1}{C}\int_{\infty}^{t_0} i(x)\, dx + \frac{1}{C}\int_{t_0}^{t} i(x)\, dx$$
$$= v(t_0) + \frac{1}{C}\int_{t_0}^{t} i(x)\, dx$$

where $v(t_0)$ is the initial voltage across the capacitor.

The energy stored in the capacitor can be obtained by integrating the power over time since power is the time rate of change of energy.

$$
\begin{aligned}
w_c(t) &= \int p(t)dt \\
&= \int_{-\infty}^{t} [v(x)] \left[C\frac{dv(x)}{dx} \right] dx \\
&= \frac{1}{2}Cv^2(t) \text{ joules}
\end{aligned}
$$

Since capacitors are typically manufactured in standard sizes, being able to combine them to generate the actual value of capacitance needed is important. If many capacitors are interconnected in series, then KVL can be used to show that their equivalent capacitance is

$$ 1/C_s = 1/C_1 + 1/C_2 + 1/C_3 + \cdots $$

And the equivalent capacitance of a number of capacitors interconnected in parallel can be shown via KCL to be

$$ C_p = C_1 + C_2 + C_3 + \cdots $$

These equations should look strangely familiar since they indicate that capacitors in series combine like resistors in parallel, and capacitors in parallel combine like resistors in series.

Example 4.1

Given the network in Figure 4.3a, let us determine the equivalent capacitance at the terminals A–B.

Using the same approach employed to determine the equivalent resistance at a pair of terminals, we can redraw the network as shown in Figure 4.3b, where the 4 and 12 µF capacitors are combined to produce a 3 µF capacitor, which, in turn, is in parallel with the 3 µF capacitor resulting

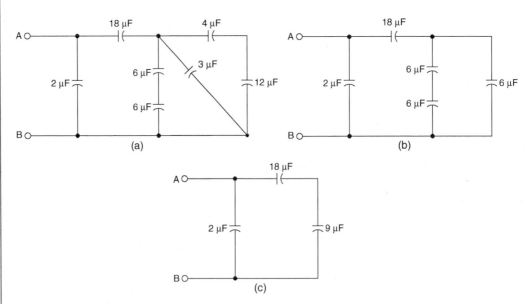

FIGURE 4.3 Circuits used in Example 4.1

in a 6 µF capacitor. Now, the two 6 µF capacitors in series can be combined to produce a 3 µF capacitor, which is in parallel with the other 6 µF capacitor, producing a 9 µF capacitor, as shown in Figure 4.3c. Finally, the 9 and 18 µF capacitors in series are combined to produce a 6 µF capacitor, which is in parallel with the 2 µF capacitor, yielding a capacitance of 8 µF at the terminals A–B.

INDUCTORS

The inductor is a two-terminal device that employs the symbol shown in Figure 4.4. Similar to capacitors, inductors come in a variety of different forms, as shown in Figure 4.5. We can actually construct a simple inductor by winding a conducting wire around some core material. This core material could range from some nonmagnetic material, e.g. air to a ferromagnetic material, e.g. iron. Inductors find wide application in electric equipment such as radios and TVs. In addition, they form the basis for the construction of high-power transformers, which are used to transform the voltage level in electric power transmission and distribution systems. Their values typically range from tens of henries to microhenries, where the designation for the unit, i.e. Henry, originates with the American inventor Joseph Henry, who discovered the voltage–current relationship for an inductor, i.e.

$$v(t) = L\, di(t)/dt$$

where L is measured in henries. As the equation implies, 1 henry is equal to 1 volt-s/ampere, and the voltage across the inductor is generated by a changing magnetic field and proportional to the time rate of change of the current that produced it.

The current in the inductor can be expressed as

$$i(t) = \frac{1}{L}\int_{-\infty}^{t} v(x)dx$$

$$i(t) = i(t_0) + \frac{1}{L}\int_{t_0}^{t} v(x)dx$$

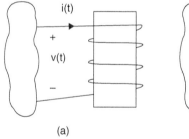
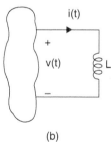

(a)   (b)

FIGURE 4.4   An inductor structure and the electrical symbol

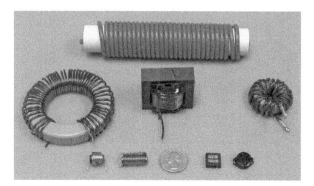

FIGURE 4.5   Some typical inductors (Courtesy of Mark Nelms and Jo Ann Loden)

And the power relationship for an inductor is

$$p(t) = v(t)i(t)$$

$$= \left[L\frac{di(t)}{dt} \right] i(t)$$

The energy stored in the magnetic field of the inductor is obtained by integrating the power to produce

$$w_L(t) = \int_{-\infty}^{t} \left[L\frac{di(x)}{dx} \right] i(x)dx$$

or

$$w_L(t) = \frac{1}{2}Li^2(t) \text{ joules}$$

Similar to resistors and capacitors, standard inductors can be combined to produce a desired value. KVL can be applied to show that inductors in series combine just like resistors in series and KCL can be employed to show that inductors in parallel combine just like resistors in parallel. Therefore,

$$L_s = L_1 + L_2 + L_3 + \cdots$$
$$1/L_p = 1/L_1 + 1/L_2 + 1/L_3 + \cdots$$

Example 4.2

Let's determine the equivalent inductance at the terminals A–B for the circuit in Figure 4.6a.

An examination of the network indicates that the 3 and 6 mH inductors are in parallel, and all of the 9 mH inductors are in parallel. The 3 and 6 mH inductors combine to produce a 2 mH

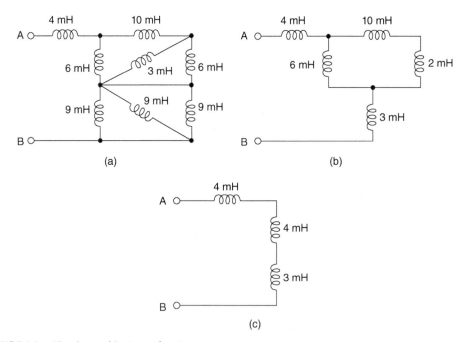

FIGURE 4.6 Circuits used in Example 4.2

inductor, and the three 9 mH inductors can be combined to produce a 3 mH inductor. These combinations result in the network shown in Figure 4.6b. Now, the 10 and 2 mH inductors are in series and their combination is in parallel with the 6 mH inductor yielding a 4 mH inductor, as shown in Figure 4.6c. Finally, the series combination results in an 11 mH inductor, which is the total inductance at the terminals A–B.

Before proceeding with our discussion of transient behavior, it is important to mention some characteristics of these storage elements that we will employ in our analysis. First of all, note the similarities of the equations that describe the voltage–current relationships for these two storage elements. In the equations for the capacitor, if we replace v with i and i with v and C with L, the result is the equations that describe the inductor.

CAPACITOR/ INDUCTOR CHARACTERISTICS

Now, consider once again the defining equations for these two elements.

$$i(t) = C\,dv(t)/dt \text{ and } v(t) = L\,di(t)/dt$$

Note that if a capacitor is present in a network and the voltage is constant, the current in the capacitor is zero and the capacitor looks like an open circuit. Similarly, if an inductor is present in a network and the current is constant, the voltage across the inductor is zero and the inductor looks like a short circuit. It can also be shown that the voltage across a capacitor or the current in an inductor cannot change instantly. These points are very important because they form the basis for our analysis of circuits, which contain a capacitor or inductor, and are interrupted by the closing or opening of a switch, thus changing the network structure.

We define first-order circuits as those that contain a single storage element, i.e. one capacitor or one inductor. In the analysis that follows, we will assume the network is in a steady state prior to a network interruption, i.e. the opening or closing of a switch at some time, which we will refer to as $t = 0$. After a significant period of time, which we will quantify, the network will again settle down and reach a steady-state condition. It is the network performance in this transient interval between these two steady-state network conditions that we will analyze.

FIRST-ORDER TRANSIENT CIRCUITS

We begin our analysis by examining the two networks shown in Figure 4.7. Applying KCL and summing the currents that leave the node A in the network in Figure 4.7c (Figure 4.7a with the switch closed) yields the equation

$$Cdv(t)/dt + [v(t) - V_s]/R = 0$$

or

$$dv(t)/dt + v(t)/RC = V_s/RC$$

Applying KVL to the network in Figure 4.7d (Figure 4.7b with the switch closed) yields the equation

$$-V_s + Ri(t) + Ldi(t)/dt = 0$$

or

$$di(t)/dt + (R/L)i(t) = V_s/L$$

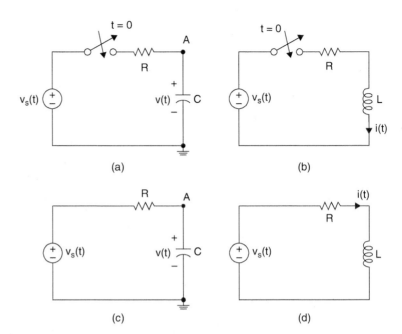

FIGURE 4.7 RC and RL networks

Note that both circuits are described by a first-order differential equation of the form $dx(t)/dt + ax(t) = F$.

Therefore, we will examine this equation carefully to see what it implies. Clearly, this is a first-order differential equation with constant coefficients. The *general solution* of this equation is of the form

$$x(t) = K_1 + K_2 e^{-t/\tau}$$

where K_1 is any solution of the original equation, referred to as the *particular integral solution, i.e. forced response,* and $K_2\, e^{-t/\tau}$ is the solution of the homogeneous equation

$$dx(t)/dt + ax(t) = 0$$

known as the *complementary solution, i.e. natural response.*

Note that the general solution for the voltage across the capacitor or the current in the inductor can be determined by calculating three constants, K_1, K_2, and τ. Let's examine for a moment these three constants. As indicated, K_1 *is called the steady-state solution,* i.e. the forced response, which is the value that remains after a long period of time. Note that as t approaches infinity, the exponential term goes to zero leaving only K_1. *The term $K_2\, e^{-t/\tau}$ is the natural response* of the network. τ *is called the time constant.* Note that this term controls the speed at which the second term goes to zero. For example, if τ is small, the exponential term will approach zero very quickly, and if τ is large, the exponential will slowly approach zero. In other words, a small time constant is a fast time constant, and a large time constant is a slow time constant. A comparison of these time constants is shown in Figure 4.8a. In addition, if $t = \tau$, i.e. one time constant, then

$$K_2 e^{-t/\tau} = K_2 e^{-1} = 0.368\, K_2$$

This means that in one time constant this function has decreased from K_2 to $0.368\, K_2$, or a drop of 63.2%. Furthermore, the function will drop by 63.2% in the following time constant, etc. For all practical purposes, the function will be essentially zero in five time constants, as shown in Figure 4.8b.

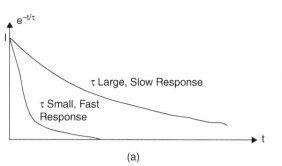

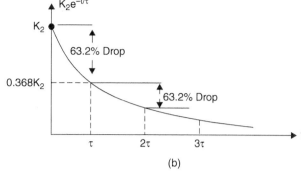

FIGURE 4.8   Properties of the time constant

Time constants vary widely depending upon the technology involved. For example, suppose that you are carrying a thermometer in your shirt pocket and you go from your air conditioned office where the temperature is about 70° F to an outside courtyard in your building during the summer when the outside temperature is 90° F. This change in temperature will cause the reading on the thermometer to begin to rise, and it may take a minute or two before the temperature on the thermometer reaches the outside temperature. If we plotted this temperature rise on a graph, the curve would rise slowly from 70° to 90°, and the shape of the curve is determined by the time constant of this operation. However, there are many other systems where the time constant is very fast, e.g. chemical, electronic, and hydraulic, to name a few.

Now that we understand the terms involved in a transient solution, let us revisit the network in Figure 4.7a.

Substituting the general solution into the differential equation that defines the voltage $v(t)$ yields

$$[-K_2/\tau]\, e^{-t/\tau} + K_1/RC + [K_2/RC]\, e^{-t/\tau} = V_s/RC$$

which can be written as

$$[-K_2/\tau + K_2/RC]\, e^{-t/\tau} + K_1/RC = V_s/RC$$

In order for the left-hand side of the equation to be equal to the right-hand side, the constant terms must be equal, implying that $K_1 = V_s$ and the two exponential terms on the left-hand side of the equation must add to zero.

This latter condition is satisfied if $\tau = RC$. Therefore, the solution of the differential equation is

$$v(t) = V_s + K_2 e^{-t/RC}$$

indicating that V_s is the steady-state solution and RC is the time constant. The remaining constant, K_2, is determined using the initial condition on the capacitor. Note carefully that $v(t)$ is the voltage across the capacitor and thus knowing the initial condition of this element permits us to find K_2. In this case, the initial voltage across the capacitor is zero because the circuit in Figure 4.7a has no source that provides a voltage across the capacitor until the switch is thrown. Therefore, at time zero, when the switch is thrown,

$$v(t) = v(0) = 0 = V_s + K_2$$

and $K_2 = -V_s$. Now, the final solution is then

$$v(t) = V_s - V_s e^{-t/RC}$$

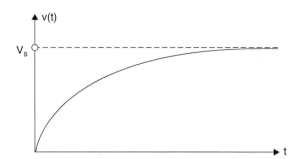

FIGURE 4.9 Plot of $v(t) = v_s - v_s e^{-t/RC}$

A plot of this function is shown in Figure 4.9. This plot shows that the voltage across the capacitor starts at zero and rises to a value of V_s. Note that the equation for $v(t)$ states the same thing. At $t = 0$, $v(t) = 0$ and at $t =$ infinity, $v(t) = V_s$. The speed at which the voltage rises from a value of zero to the final value of V_s is controlled by the time constant $\tau = RC$.

An identical analysis, performed on the network in Figure 4.7b, would yield the following equation for the current in the inductor:

$$i(t) = V_s/R - [V_s/R]e^{-(R/L)t}$$

This equation indicates that at $t = 0$, the current in the inductor is zero, and the current rises to a value of V_s/R, where the time constant controls the time to reach steady state, which for both the capacitive and inductive circuits is about five time constants, i.e. $t = 5\tau$ indicates $e^{-5\tau/\tau} = e^{-5}$ or 0.0067.

Let us now illustrate the manner a transient analysis is performed. However, before outlining the steps involved, let us review the critical issues that govern the approach:

1. The analysis, involving a single capacitor or a single inductor, results in a first-order differential equation, the solution of which is of the form $x(t) = K_1 + K_2 e^{-t/\tau}$. Therefore, the solution involves finding the constants K_1, K_2, and τ.

2. In a steady-state condition, either before the switch is thrown or five time constants after switch action, the capacitor voltage is constant and thus the current in the capacitor is zero, i.e. $i(t) = C\,dv(t)/dt$, so in essence the capacitor looks like an open circuit.

3. In a steady-state condition, either before the switch is thrown or five time constants after switch action, the inductor current is constant and thus the voltage across the inductor is zero, i.e. $v(t) = L\,di(t)/dt$, so in essence the inductor looks like a short circuit.

4. The analysis is performed to determine either the voltage across the capacitor or the current in the inductor. Once this value is known, then any other voltage or current in the network is determined from these values. The capacitor voltage and inductor current are often referred to as state variables, and they are similar to velocity and acceleration in mechanical systems.

The previous discussion outlines the issues involved in solving transient circuits via development and solution of a first-order differential equation. However, there is another method we can apply to obtain a solution to a transient problem that involves only circuit analysis. In an effort to provide as much explanation of the issues involved in performing a transient analysis as possible, we will solve the transient problems using both techniques in the hope that a comparison of the two approaches will provide additional insight.

The circuit analysis technique involves the determination of several quantities, the use of which provides the necessary data for calculating K_1, K_2, and τ.

Calculate the initial conditions

In steady state prior to switch action, replace the capacitor with an open circuit or the inductor with a short circuit. Calculate this initial voltage across the capacitor or the initial current in the inductor, i.e. $v_c(0-)$ or $i_L(0-)$. Then, with the switch in its new position, and a knowledge that these initial values cannot change instantaneously, replace the capacitor with a voltage source $v_c(0-)$ or the inductor with a current source $i_L(0-)$ and calculate the initial value, $x(0)$, where $x(0)$ is the initial value of the desired quantity, i.e. $v_0(t)$ or $i_0(t)$.

Calculate the final condition

With the switch in its final position and the capacitor replaced with an open circuit or the inductor replaced with a short circuit, determine the final value, $x(\infty)$, where $x(\infty)$ is the final value of the desired quantity, i.e. $v_0(t)$ or $i_0(t)$.

Calculate the network's time constant

The time constant, which is common to all voltages and currents in the circuit, is obtained by calculating the Thevenin equivalent resistance, R_{TH}, at the terminals of the storage element with all sources made zero, i.e. voltage sources replaced the short circuits and current sources replaced with open circuits. Then, the time constant $\tau = R_{TH}C$ for capacitive circuits and $\tau = L/R_{TH}$ for inductive circuits.

Assemble the calculations to generate the final solution

At this point, all the necessary information, $x(0)$, $x(\infty)$, and τ are known. Since the general solution is

$$x(t) = K_1 + K_2 e^{-t/\tau}$$

and

$$x(0) = K_1 + K_2$$
$$x(\infty) = K_1$$

Then, the final solution is

$$x(t) = x(0) + [x(0) - x(\infty)]\, e^{-t/\tau}$$

Note that in applying this approach, which is based purely upon circuit analysis, so far we have been evaluating circuits only containing capacitors or inductors (not both).

In the circuit analysis approach, we will take advantage of the results obtained in the differential equation method and employ them to short cut the presentation of the circuit analysis technique. Note carefully that in this latter method, we do not have to deal with a circuit containing a storage element, and, furthermore, this approach will generate the solution directly.

Examples 4.3–4.6 will apply both the differential equation and circuit analysis techniques to understand the behavior of a network under transient conditions.

The network in Figure 4.10a is in steady state prior to the switch moving from position 1 to position 2 at time $t = 0$. We want to find the output current, $i_0(t)$ for $t > 0$.

Example 4.3

(a) The differential equation technique

We already know the form of the solution, and our job here is to find the constants K_1, K_2, and τ. In steady state prior to switch action, the voltage is constant, the capacitor looks like

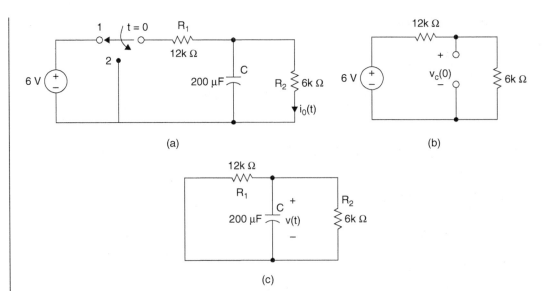

FIGURE 4.10 Circuit used in Example 4.3

an open circuit and thus the network reduces to that shown in Figure 4.10b. A simple voltage divider indicates that the initial capacitor voltage is

$$v_c(0) = (6)(6k)/(12k + 6k) = 2 \text{ V}$$

Now that we know the initial condition on the storage element, i.e. the capacitor, we now examine the circuit that results from throwing the switch, and that circuit is shown in Figure 4.10c. We now write the differential equation for the voltage across the capacitor. Recall, it is this voltage that we determine first, and we know its initial condition. KCL at the top node yields the equation

$$v(t)/R_1 + Cdv(t)/dt + v(t)/R_2 = 0$$

or

$$Cdv(t)/dt + (1/R_1 + 1/R_2)v(t) = 0$$

which, given the circuit parameters, reduces to

$$[200 \times 10^{-6}]dv(t)/dt + [1/6k + 1/12k]v(t) = 0$$
$$[200 \times 10^{-6}]dv(t)/dt + [1/4k]v(t) = 0$$
$$dv(t)/dt + v(t)/0.8 = 0$$

Although the general form of the solution of this equation is $K_1 + K_2 e^{-t/\tau}$, K_1 is zero because the forcing function, i.e. the 6 V source, has been switched out of the network, as shown in Figure 4.10c. Since there is no constant source of energy remaining in the network after the switch action, the initial capacitor voltage will be simply bled off through the resistors in accordance with the time constant. Thus, the solution is of the form

$$v(t) = K_2 e^{-t/\tau}$$

Substituting this form of the solution into the differential equation yields

$$d/dt[K_2 e^{-t/\tau}] + K_2 e^{-t/\tau}/0.8 = 0$$
$$-K_2/\tau + K_2 e^{-t/\tau}/0.8 = 0$$
$$K_2[-1/\tau + 1/0.8]\, e^{-t/\tau} = 0$$

or $\tau = 0.8$ s. And since $v(0) = 2$ V, $K_2 = 2$, and the final solution is

$$v(t) = 2e^{-t\backslash 0.8}\ \text{V}$$

Once the capacitor voltage is known, $i_0(t)$ can be easily determined as

$$I_0(t) = v(t)/6k = (1/3)e^{-t/0.8}\,\text{mA}$$

(b) The circuit analysis technique

In the differential equation approach, the initial condition on the capacitor was found using the circuit in Figure 4.10b as $v_c(0-) = 2$ V. Since this voltage cannot change in zero time, the capacitor is replaced with a voltage source of this magnitude, as shown in Figure 4.11a, and the initial value of the current $i_0(0)$ is seen to be

$$i_0(0) = 2/6k = 1/3\ \text{mA}$$

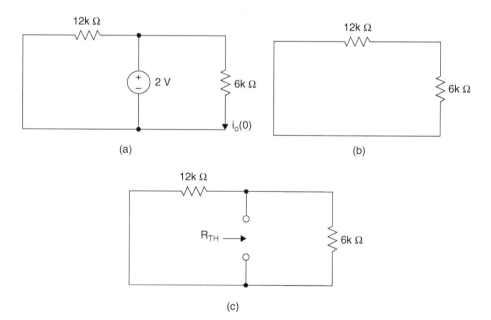

(a)

(b)

(c)

FIGURE 4.11   Additional circuits used in Example 4.3

After a period of five time constants, the capacitor looks like an open circuit, and since the forcing function has been switched out of the network, the network appears as shown in Figure 4.11b, and the final value of the output current is

$$i_0(\infty) = 0$$

The time constant, $R_{TH}C$, is determined from the Thevenin equivalent resistance at the terminals of the storage element as shown in Figure 4.11c. Since the two resistors are in parallel,

$$R_{TH} = (12k)(6k)/[12k + 6k] = 4k\ \Omega$$

Therefore, the time constant is

$$\tau = R_{TH}\ C = (4 \times 10^3)(200 \times 10^{-6}) = 0.8\ s$$

Now assembling the data for the solution,

$$K_1 + K_2 = i_o(0) = 1/3\ mA$$
$$K_1 = 0$$

Therefore,

$$K_2 = 1/3\ mA \ \ and \ \ \tau = 0.8\ s, \ so$$
$$i_o(t) = (1/3)\ e^{-t/0.8}\ mA$$

Example 4.4

Given the network in Figure 4.12a, let us find $i_o(t)$ for $t > 0$.

(a) The differential equation technique

Before we begin our analysis, we note one important difference between this network and the one in Figure 4.10a. Once the switch is thrown, the 6 V source and the 2k Ω resistor in series with this source are switched out of the network via the short circuit. However, the 12 V source remains in the network, providing a constant source of energy, and, therefore, we expect the solution to contain the constant term K_1.

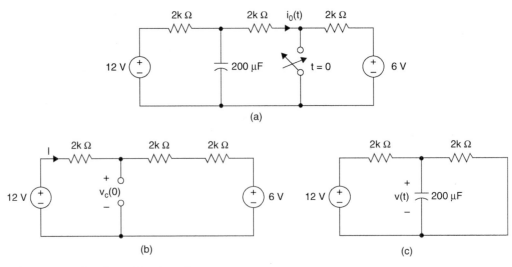

(a)

(b)   (c)

FIGURE 4.12   Circuits used in Example 4.4

The initial condition on the capacitor is determined from the circuit in Figure 4.12b where the capacitor has been replaced with an open circuit. The KVL equation for this loop in the steady-state condition prior to switch action is

$$-12 + 3k\ I + 2k\ I + 2k\ I + 6 = 0$$

or

$$I = (12 - 6)/(2k + 2k + 2k) = 1\ mA$$

Then,

$$v_c(0) = 12 - (1/k)\ 2k = 10\ V$$

The circuit for $t > 0$ is shown in Figure 4.12c. KCL at the node at the top of the capacitor is

$$(v(t) - 12)/2k + (200 \times 10^{-6})\ dv(t)/dt + v(t)/2k = 0$$
$$(200 \times 10^{-6})\ dv(t)/dt + v(t)[1/2k + 1/2k] = 12/2k$$

or

$$dv(t)/dt + v(t)/0.2 = 12/0.4$$

Substituting the general form of the solution into this equation yields

$$d/dt[K_1 + K_2\ e^{-t/\tau}] + (1/0.2)[K_1 + K_2\ e^{-t/\tau}] = 12/0.4$$
$$K_2[-1/\tau + 1/0.2]e^{-t/\tau} + K_1/0.2 = 12/0.4$$

equating like coefficients

$$K_1 = 6$$
$$\tau = 0.2\ s$$

Thus, the solution is

$$v(t) = 6 + K_2\ e^{-t/0.2}\ V$$

However, we know the value of $v(t)$ at time $t = 0$, i.e. the initial condition. So,

$$v(0) = 10 = 6 + K_2$$

And then $K_2 = 4$.
And then the general solution for $v(t)$ is

$$v(t) = 6 + 4\ e^{-t/0.2}\ V$$

Now that we know the voltage across the capacitor, we are in a position to find $i_0(t)$, which is simply

$$i_0(t) = v(t)/2K = 3 + 2\ e^{-t/0.2}\ mA$$

(b) The circuit analysis technique

In the differential equation approach, the initial condition on the capacitor was found using the circuit in Figure 4.12b as $v_c(0-) = 10\ V$. Since this voltage cannot change in zero time, the capacitor is replaced with a voltage source of this magnitude, as shown in Figure 4.13a, and the initial value of the current $i_0(0)$ is seen to be

$$i_0(0) = 10/2k = 5\text{ mA}$$

After a period of five time constants, the capacitor looks like an open circuit, and while the 6 V source has been switched out of the circuit, the 12 V source remains and the network appears as shown in Figure 4.13b, and the final value of the output current is

$$i_0(\infty) = 12/[2k + 2k]$$
$$= 3\text{ mA}$$

The time constant is determined by calculating the Thevenin equivalent resistance at the terminals of the storage element as shown in Figure 4.13c. Since the two resistors are in parallel,

$$R_{TH} = (2k)(2k)/[2k + 2k] = 1k\ \Omega$$

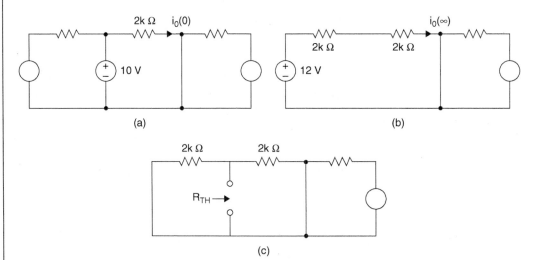

(a)   (b)

(c)

FIGURE 4.13 Additional circuits used in Example 4.4

Therefore, the time constant is

$$\tau = R_{TH}\ C = (1 \times 10^3)(200 \times 10^{-6}) = 0.2\text{ s}$$

Now assembling the data for the solution,

$$K_1 + K_2 = i_0(0) = 5\text{ mA}$$
$$K_1 = 3\text{ mA}$$

Therefore,
$K_2 = 2$ mA and $\tau = 0.2$ s and hence the solution is

$$i_0(t) = (3 + 2)\ e^{-t/0.2}\text{ mA}$$

Let us now examine two problems with inductors in the network.

Let us determine the voltage $v_0(t)$ for $t > 0$ in the network in Figure 4.14a.

Example 4.5

(a) The differential equation technique

The initial condition on the inductor is determined from the circuit in Figure 4.14b where the inductor has been replaced with a short circuit. The determination of $i_L(0)$ is a simple dc circuit problem, and at this point the reader knows several methods for determining this value, e.g. one node equation or two mesh equations. However, note that the total resistance seen by the voltage source is 1 Ω in series with the parallel combination of 3 Ω and the series combination of 2 Ω and 4 Ω, i.e.

Total resistance seen by the source is $1 + (3)(2 + 4)/[3 + 2 + 4] = 1 + (3)(6)/9 = 1 + 2 = 3\,\Omega$

Thus, the current emanating from the source is $12/3 = 4$ A. Using current division, we find that the initial current in the inductor is

$$i_L(0) = (4)(6)/(3 + 6) = 8/3\ \text{A}$$

The circuit for $t > 0$ is shown in Figure 4.14c. KVL around the loop in a counterclockwise direction is

$$3\,i(t) + 2\,di(t)/dt + 4\,i(t) + 2\,i(t) = 0$$

or

$$2\,di(t)/dt + 9\,i(t) = 0$$

which can be written in the form

$$di(t)/dt + i(t)/(2/9) = 0$$

Since the network in Figure 4.14c does not contain a forcing function, we know that $K_1 = 0$ and the form of the solution is

$$v(t) = K_2 e^{-t/\tau}$$

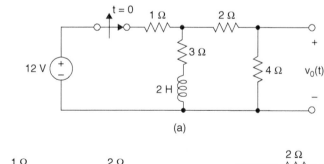

(a)

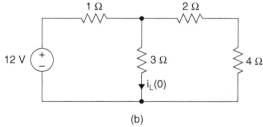

(b)

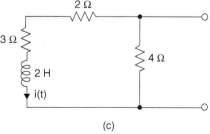

(c)

FIGURE 4.14   Circuits used in Example 4.5

Substituting this form of the solution into the differential equation yields

$$d/dt[K_2 e^{-t/\tau}] + [K_2 e^{-t/\tau}]/(2/9) = 0$$
$$K_2 e^{-t/\tau}[-1/\tau + 1/(2/9)] = 0$$

Therefore, $\tau = 2/9$ s. And since $i_L(0) = 8/3$ A, $K_2 = 8/3$ and the final solution is

$$i(t) = 8/3\, e^{-t/(2/9)}\,\text{A}$$

Now that the current in the inductor is known, $v_0(t)$ can be easily determined. Recall that the current in the circuit in Figure 4.14c is in a counterclockwise direction, and thus the output voltage is

$$v_0(t) = -i(t)4 = -(32/3)e^{-t/(2/9)}\ \text{V}$$

(b) The circuit analysis technique

In the differential equation approach, the initial condition on the inductor was found to be $i_0(0) = (8/3)$ A. Since this current cannot change in zero time, the inductor is replaced with a current source of this magnitude, as shown in Figure 4.15a, and the initial value of the voltage $v_0(0)$ is seen to be

$$v_0(0) = -4\,(8/3) = -32/3\ \text{V}$$

After a period of five time constants, the inductor looks like a short circuit, and since the forcing function has been switched out of the network, the network appears as shown in Figure 4.15b, and the final value of the output voltage, $v_0(0) = 0$.

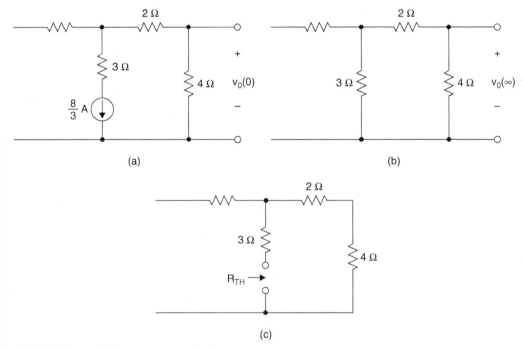

FIGURE 4.15 Additional circuits used in Example 4.5

The time constant is determined by calculating the Thevenin equivalent resistance at the terminals of the storage element as shown in Figure 4.15c. Since all the resistors are in series,

$$R_{TH} = 3 + 2 + 4 = 9\ \Omega$$

Therefore, the time constant is

$$\tau = L/R_{TH} = 2/9\ s$$

Now assembling the data for the solution,

$$K_1 + K_2 = v_0(0) = -32/3\ V$$
$$K_1 = 0$$

Therefore,

$$K_2 = -32/3\ \text{ and }\ \tau = 2/9\ s$$
$$\text{and}$$
$$v_0(t) = -32/3\ e^{-9t/2}\ V$$

Let us determine the voltage $v_0(t)$ for $t > 0$ in the network in Figure 4.16a.

Example 4.6

(a) The differential equation technique

We begin our analysis by first simplifying the network. Prior to the time the switch is thrown, i.e. $t < 0$, we can simplify the network by forming a Thevenin equivalent for the circuit to the left of the inductor, as shown in Figure 4.16b. The open-circuit voltage is determined as follows. The current I in the loop is obtained from the KVL equation

$$-36 + 2I + 2I + 12 = 0$$
$$\text{or}$$
$$I = (36 - 12)/(2 + 2) = 6\ A$$

Then the open-circuit voltage is

$$V_{OC} = 2I + 12 = 24\ V$$

The Thevenin equivalent resistance for this network is found from the circuit in Figure 4.16c as

$$R_{TH} = (2)(2)/(2 + 2) = 1\ \Omega$$

Thus, replacing the left loop in the network in Figure 4.16a with the Thevenin equivalent circuit, which consists of the 24 V source and the 1 Ω resistor, results in the network in Figure 4.16d where the inductor has been replaced with a short circuit in steady state. The initial value of the inductor current is

$$i_L(0) = 24/3 = 8\ A$$

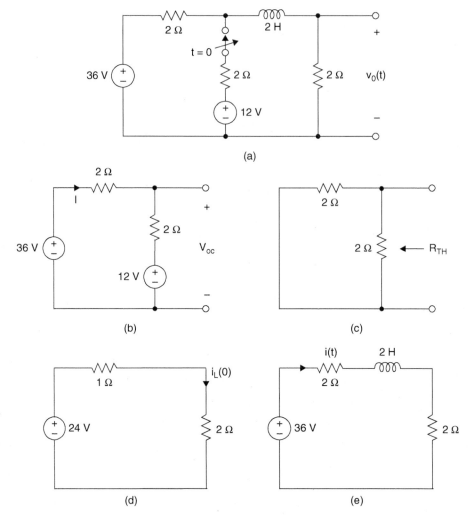

FIGURE 4.16 Circuits used in Example 4.6

Now that we know the initial inductor current, the circuit valid for $t > 0$ is shown in Figure 4.16e. The differential equation for the current in the inductor is obtained from the KVL equation

$$-36 + 2i(t) + 2di(t)/dt + 2i(t) = 0$$

or

$$2di(t)/dt + 4i(t) = 36$$

which can be written as

$$di(t)/dt + i(t)/(1/2) = 18$$

Substituting the general solution for a first-order differential equation into this equation and equating coefficients yields

$$d/dt[K_1 + K_2 e^{-t/\tau}] + 1/(1/2)[K_1 + K_2 e^{-t/\tau}] = 18$$
$$K_2 e^{-t/\tau}[-1/\tau + 1/(1/2)] + K_1/(1/2) = 18$$

Therefore,

$$K_1 = 9$$

$$\tau = {}^1\!/_2 \text{ s}$$

Then

$$i(t) = 9 + K_2 e^{-t/(1/2)} \text{A}$$

However, the initial condition on the inductor is $i(0) = 8$ A. Therefore,

$$i(0) = 9 + K_2$$

$$K_2 = -1$$

Therefore, the final solution for the current is

$$i(t) = 9 - 1e^{-t/(1/2)} \text{A}$$

Hence, the output voltage is

$$v_0(t) = 2i(t) = [18 - 2]\, e^{-2t} \text{V}$$

Once again we expect, and the final value confirms, that K_1 will not be zero because we have a forcing function, i.e. the 36 V source, remaining in the network and supplying energy to it after the switch has been thrown.

(b) The circuit analysis technique

In the differential equation approach, the initial condition on the inductor was found to be $i_0(0) = 8$ A. Since this current cannot change in zero time, the inductor is replaced with a current source of this magnitude, as shown in Figure 4.17a, and the initial value of the voltage $v_0(0)$ is seen to be

$$v_0(0) = (2)(8) = 16 \text{ V}$$

After a period of five time constants, the inductor looks like a short circuit, and while the 12 V source has been switched out of the circuit, the 36 V source remains, and the network appears as shown in Figure 4.17b. A simple voltage divider indicates that the final value of the output voltage is

$$v_0(\infty) = 18 \text{ V}$$

The time constant is determined by calculating the Thevenin equivalent resistance at the terminals of the storage element as shown in Figure 4.17c. Note that the resistance consists of two 2 Ω resistors in series:

$$R_{TH} = 2 + 2 = 4 \,\Omega$$

Therefore, the time constant is

$$\tau = L/R_{TH} = 2/4 = 1/2 \text{ s}$$

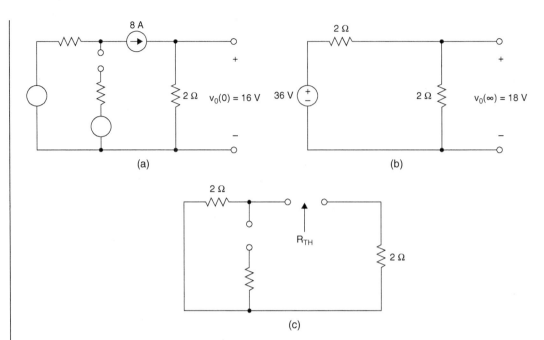

FIGURE 4.17 Additional circuits used in Example 4.6

Now assembling the data for the solution,

$$K_1 + K_2 = v_0(0) = 16 \text{ V}$$
$$K_1 = 18$$

Therefore,

$$K_2 = 6 \text{ and } \tau = 1/2 \text{ s}$$
$$\text{and}$$
$$v_0(t) = [18 - 2] e^{-2t} \text{ V}$$

The examples have demonstrated that when the energy sources are switched out of the network, the final solution, whether it is a voltage or current, is of the form $K_2 e^{-t/\tau}$, and if one or more energy sources remain in the circuit following the switch action, then the form of the final solution, $v_0(t)$ or $i_0(t)$, will be of the form $K_1 + K_2 e^{-t/\tau}$.

SECOND-ORDER TRANSIENT CIRCUITS

Up to this point, we have examined only circuits containing only a single capacitor or a single inductor or circuits containing more than one of these elements, which could be combined so that we are dealing with one equivalent storage element, i.e. C_{total} or L_{total}. Now we briefly examine the situation in which both the capacitor and inductor are simultaneously present in the network.

Two basic circuits are shown in Figure 4.18a and b. If we apply KCL to the network in Figure 4.18a, we obtain the equation

$$\frac{v}{R} + \frac{1}{L}\int_{t_0}^{t} v(x) \ dx + i_L(t_0) + C\frac{dv}{dt} = i_s(t)$$

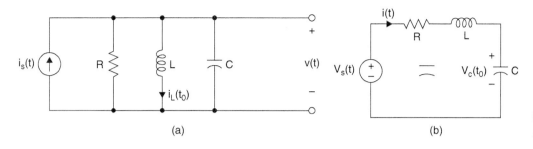

FIGURE 4.18   Parallel and series RLC circuits

If we now differentiate this equation with respect to time, we obtain the equation

$$C\frac{d^2v}{dt^2} + \frac{1}{R}\frac{dv}{dt} + \frac{v}{L} = \frac{di_s}{dt}$$

Writing the KVL equation for the network in Figure 4.18b and differentiating it with respect to time yields the equation

$$L\frac{d^2i}{dt^2} + R\frac{di}{dt} + \frac{i}{C} = \frac{dv_s}{dt}$$

Note that the KCL equation for the network in Figure 4.18a and the KVL equation for the network in Figure 4.18b both result in an equation of the general form

$$\frac{d^2x(t)}{dt^2} + a_1\frac{dx(t)}{dt} + a_2x(t) = f(t)$$

where the variable $x(t)$ represents either $v(t)$ or $i(t)$. Recall that in first-order circuits the solution of the complementary equation, i.e.

$$dx(t)/dt + ax(t) = 0$$

is $K_2e^{-t/\tau}$. In a similar situation, the homogeneous equation for the second-order differential equation is

$$\frac{d^2x(t)}{dt^2} + 2\xi\omega_0\frac{dx(t)}{dt} + \omega_0^2x(t) = 0$$

where $a_1 = 2\xi\omega_0$ and $a_2 = \omega_0^2$. These new constants have special significance as will be indicated in the following discussion. Note that the solution to this homogeneous equation must be a function whose first- and second-order derivatives have the same form so that the left-hand side of the homogeneous equation will become identically zero for all t. If we assume

$$x(t) = Ke^{st}$$

Then substituting this expression into the homogeneous equation and performing the derivatives yields

$$s^2Ke^{st} + 2\xi\omega_0sKe^{st} + \omega_0^2Ke^{st} = 0$$

Dividing both sides of the equation by Ke^{st} yields

$$s^2 + 2\xi\omega_0s + \omega_0^2 = 0$$

which is commonly referred to as the *characteristic equation*. The importance of this equation stems from the fact that the roots of this equation are the *natural frequencies* of the network, i.e. they control the unforced response of the network. By unforced response, we mean the response to an initial condition, e.g. a voltage on the capacitor or current in an inductor, rather than the response to a voltage or current source. ξ is the *exponential damping coefficient* and ω_0 is the network's *undamped natural frequency*.

Given the assumed solution of the form Ke^{st}, the roots of the characteristic equation, i.e. the natural frequencies of the network, are obtained by applying the quadratic formula to the characteristic equation to yield

$$s = \frac{-2\xi\omega_0 \pm \sqrt{4\xi^2\omega_0^2 - 4\omega_0^2}}{2}$$
$$= -\xi\omega_0 \pm \omega_0\sqrt{\xi^2 - 1}$$

Therefore, the two roots are

$$s_1 = -\xi\omega_0 + \omega_0\sqrt{\xi^2 - 1}$$
$$s_2 = -\xi\omega_0 - \omega_0\sqrt{\xi^2 - 1}$$

In general, then, the complementary solution of the equation

$$\frac{d^2x(t)}{dt^2} + 2\xi\omega_0\frac{dx(t)}{dt} + \omega_0^2 x(t) = 0$$

is of the form

$$x_c(t) = K_1 e^{s_1 t} + K_2 e^{s_2 t}$$

K_1 and K_2 are constants that can be evaluated via the initial conditions $x(0)$ and $dx(0)/dt$. For example, since

$$x(t) = K_1 e^{s_1 t} + K_2 e^{s_2 t}$$

then

$$x(0) = K_1 + K_2$$

and

$$\left.\frac{dx(t)}{dt}\right|_{t=0} = \frac{dx(0)}{dt} = s_1 K_1 + s_2 K_2$$

Hence, $x(0)$ and $dx(0)/dt$ produce two simultaneous equations, which when solved yield the constants K_1 and K_2.

The form of the solution of the homogeneous equation is dependent on the value ξ. For example, if $\xi > 1$, the roots of the characteristic equation, s_1 and s_2, also called the *natural frequencies* because they determine the natural (unforced) response of the network, are real and unequal; if $\xi < 1$, the roots are complex numbers; and finally, if $\xi = 1$, the roots are real and equal.

Let us now consider the three distinct forms of the unforced response—that is, the response due to an initial capacitor voltage or initial inductor current.

Case 1, $\xi > 1$ This case is commonly called *overdamped*. The natural frequencies s_1 and s_2 are real and unequal; therefore, the natural response of the network described by the second-order differential equation is of the form

$$x_C(t) = K_1 e^{-(\xi\omega_0 - \omega_0\sqrt{\xi^2-1})t} + K_2 e^{-(\xi\omega_0 + \omega_0\sqrt{\xi^2-1})t}$$

where K_1 and K_2 are found from the initial conditions. This indicates that the natural response is the sum of two decaying exponentials.

Case 2, $\xi < 1$ This case is called *underdamped*. Since $\xi < 1$, the roots of the characteristic equation can be written as

$$s_1 = -\xi\omega_0 + j\omega_0\sqrt{1-\xi^2} = -\sigma + j\omega_d$$
$$s_2 = -\xi\omega_0 - j\omega_0\sqrt{1-\xi^2} = -\sigma - j\omega_d$$

where $j = \sqrt{-1}$, $\sigma = \xi\omega_0$, and $\omega_d = \omega_0\sqrt{1-\xi^2}$. Thus, the natural frequencies are complex numbers (briefly discussed in the Appendix). Then, the natural response is of the form

$$x_c(t) = e^{-\xi\omega_0 t}\left(A_1\cos\omega_0\sqrt{1-\xi^2}t + A_2\sin\omega_0\sqrt{1-\xi^2}t\right)$$

where A_1 and A_2, like K_1 and K_2, are constants, which are evaluated using the initial conditions $x(0)$ and $dx(0)/dt$. This illustrates that the natural response is an exponentially damped oscillatory response.

Case 3, $\xi = 1$ This case, called *critically damped*, results in

$$s_1 = s_2 = -\xi\omega_0$$

In the case where the characteristic equation has repeated roots, the general solution is of the form

$$x_c(t) = B_1 e^{-\xi\omega_0 t} + B_2 t e^{-\xi\omega_0 t}$$

where B_1 and B_2 are constants derived from the initial conditions.

Given an initial value $x_c(0) = 1$, the responses shown in Figure 4.19 illustrate the natural response for each of the three cases outlined above. Note that in the *overdamped* case, the response is a decaying exponential. The response decays as fast as possible without overshoot in the *critically damped case*. The *underdamped* response is an exponentially damped sinusoid in which the rate of decay is dependent upon the damping factor.

As a general rule, the analysis of second-order circuits is performed as follows:

1. Develop the differential equation that describes the circuit and variable of interest, i.e. $v(t)$ or $i(t)$.

2. Determine the characteristic equation for the circuit.

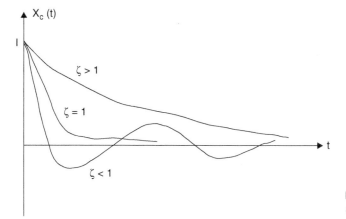

FIGURE 4.19   Response for different damping ratios

3. Compute the roots of the characteristic equation, which are dependent upon the damping ratio, to determine if the response is overdamped, critically damped, or underdamped.

4. Use the initial conditions on the storage elements to calculate the unknown coefficients in the response equation.

Let us now examine a circuit that has been chosen to illustrate the concepts that are employed in the analysis of second-order circuits.

Example 4.7

Let us examine the network in Figure 4.20 and determine the voltage v(t) for t > 0. The initial conditions in the network are $v_c(0) = 2$ V and L(0) = +2 A. We will determine the network response for three values of the resistor, i.e. (a) R = 2/5 Ω, (b) R = 1/2 Ω, and (c) R = 1 Ω.

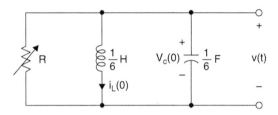

FIGURE 4.20 A second-order circuit

The differential equation that describes the voltage v(t), i.e. the voltage across the capacitor, for this parallel circuit with no forcing function is shown to be

$$C d^2v(t)/dt^2 + (1/R)dv(t)/dt + v(t)/L = 0$$

or

$$d^2v(t)/dt^2 + (1/RC)dv(t)/dt + v(t)/LC = 0$$

(a) R = 2/5 Ω In this case, the characteristic equation is

$$s^2 + (1/RC)s + (1/LC) = 0$$
$$s^2 + 15s + 36 = 0$$

Comparing this expression with the general form of the characteristic equation indicates that

$$2\xi\omega_0 = 15 \text{ and } \omega_0^2 = 36$$

therefore $\omega_0 = 6$ and $\xi = 1.25 > 1$. Since $\xi > 1$, this case is overdamped and the roots are real and unequal. The characteristic equation can be factored to yield

$$(s + 3)(s + 12) = 0$$

and therefore the roots are $s_1 = -3$ and $s_2 = -12$. The equation for the voltage v(t) is then

$$v(t) = K_1 e^{-3t} + K_2 e^{-12t}$$

Since v(0) = 2, then

$$v(0) = 2 = K_1 + K_2$$

KCL at the top node in the circuit is

$$C\frac{dv(t)}{dt} + \frac{v(t)}{R} + i_L(t) = 0$$

and

$$\frac{dv(0)}{dt} = -\frac{v(0)}{RC} - \frac{i_L(0)}{C}$$
$$= -30 - 12$$
$$= -42$$

In addition,

$$\frac{dv(t)}{dt} = -3K_1e^{-3t} - 12K_2e^{-12t}$$
$$\frac{dv(0)}{dt} = -3K_1 - 12K_2 = -42$$

Therefore, the two equations that yield the constants K_1 and K_2 are

$$K_1 + K_2 = 2$$
$$3K_1 + 12K_2 = 42$$

Multiplying the first equation by −3 and adding it to the second equation yields $K_2 = 4$. Substituting this value for K_2 into either equation results in $K_1 = -2$. Hence, v(t) for t > 0 is given by the expression

$$v(t) = -2e^{-3t} + 4e^{-12t} \text{ V} \qquad t > 0$$

(b) R = 1/2 Ω. In this case, the characteristic equation is

$$s^2 + (1/RC)\, s + (1/LC) = 0$$
$$s^2 + 12s + 36 = 0$$

Comparing this expression with the general form of the characteristic equation indicates that

$$2\xi\omega_0 = 12 \text{ and } \omega_0^2 = 36$$

therefore $\omega_0 = 6$ and $\xi = 1$. Since $\xi = 1$, this case is critically damped and the roots are real and equal.

The characteristic equation can be factored to yield

$$(s + 6)(s + 6) = 0$$

And the roots are $s_1 = -6$ and $s_2 = -6$. The equation for the voltage v(t) is then

$$v(t) = K_1e^{-6t} + K_2te^{-6t}$$

Evaluating this equation at the initial condition $v(0) = 2$ yields

$$2 = K_1 + 0$$
$$K_1 = 2$$

Once again,

$$\frac{dv(0)}{dt} = -\frac{v(0)}{RC} - \frac{i_L(0)}{C}$$
$$= -24 - 12$$
$$= -36$$

However, in this case

$$\frac{dv(t)}{dt} = -6K_1 e^{-6t} + K_2 e^{-6t} - 6K_2 t e^{-6t}$$
$$\frac{dv(0)}{dt} = -6K_1 + K_2$$
$$-36 = -12 + K_2$$
$$K_2 = -24$$

And then the equation for the network response $v(t)$ for $t > 0$ is

$$v(t) = 2e^{-6t} - 24te^{-6t} \text{ V}, \qquad t > 0$$

(c) $R = 1 \ \Omega$. The characteristic equation is then

$$s^2 + (1/RC)s + (1/LC) = 0$$
$$s^2 + 6s + 36 = 0$$

Comparing this expression with the general form of the characteristic equation indicates that

$$2\xi\omega_0 = 6 \text{ and } \omega_0^2 = 36$$

therefore $\omega_0 = 6$ and $\xi = 1/2$. Since $\xi = 1/2$, this case is underdamped and the roots are complex conjugates. The characteristic equation can be factored using the quadratic formula

$$s_1, s_2 = \left\{ -6 \pm [6^2 - 4\,(1)(36)]^{1/2} \right\} /2$$
$$= -6 \pm [-108]^{1/2}/2$$
$$= -3 \pm [-27]^{1/2}$$
$$= \left(-3 + j3\sqrt{3} \right)\left(-3 - j3\sqrt{3} \right)$$

and the roots are $s_1 = -3 - j\,3\sqrt{3}$ and $s_2 = -3 + j\,3\sqrt{3}$.
The equation for the voltage is then

$$v(t) = K_1 e^{-3t} \cos 3\sqrt{3}t + K_2 e^{-3t} \sin 3\sqrt{3}t$$

Evaluating this equation at the initial condition $v(0) = 2$ yields a value of $K_1 = 2$. Once again

$$\frac{dv(0)}{dt} = \frac{-v(0)}{RC} - \frac{i(0)}{C}$$

$$= -12 - 12$$

$$= -24$$

$$\frac{dv(t)}{dt} = -3K_1 e^{-3t} \cos 3\sqrt{3}t - 3\sqrt{3}K_1 e^{-3t} \sin 3\sqrt{3}t$$
$$- 3K_2 e^{-3t} \sin 3\sqrt{3}t + 3\sqrt{3}K_2 e^{-3t} \cos 3\sqrt{3}t$$

And since

$$\frac{dv(0)}{dt} = -3K_1, + 3\sqrt{3}K_2$$

then

$$\frac{dv(0)}{dt} = -24 = -3K_1, + 3\sqrt{3}K_2$$

And since $K_1 = 2$

$$-24 = -6 + 3\sqrt{3}K_2$$
$$K_2 = -\frac{6}{\sqrt{3}}$$

Thus, the equation for $v(t)$ is

$$v(t) = 2e^{-3t} \cos 3\sqrt{3}t - \frac{6}{\sqrt{3}} e^{-3t} \sin 3\sqrt{3}t \ \text{V}, \qquad t > 0$$

Let us now consider an example with a constant forcing function.

We wish to determine the equation for $v(t)$ for $t > 0$ in the network in Figure 4.21.   **Example 4.8**

The circuit parameters are given in the figure, and the following initial conditions are assumed: $v_c(0) = 0$ and $i_L(0) = 0$.

For $t > 0$, the KVL equation for the network is

$$R\,i(t) + L\frac{di(t)}{dt} + v(t) = 12$$

where

$$i(t) = C\frac{dv(t)}{dt}$$

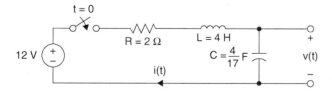

FIGURE 4.21   A series RLC circuit

Combining these two equations yields

$$RC\frac{dv(t)}{dt} + LC\frac{d^2v(t)}{dt^2} + v(t) = 12$$

or

$$\frac{d^2v(t)}{dt^2} + \frac{R}{L}\frac{dv(t)}{dt} + \frac{1}{LC}v(t) = \frac{12}{LC}$$

which, given the network parameters, is

$$\frac{d^2v(t)}{dt^2} + \frac{1}{2}\frac{dv(t)}{dt} + \frac{17}{16}v(t) = \frac{51}{4}$$

The characteristic equation is

$$s^2 + \frac{1}{2}s + \frac{17}{16} = 0$$

and the roots are

$$s_1 s_2 = \frac{-\frac{1}{2} \pm \sqrt{\left(\frac{1}{2}\right)^2 - 4\left(\frac{17}{16}\right)}}{2}$$

$$= \frac{-\frac{1}{2} \pm \sqrt{\frac{1}{4} - \frac{17}{4}}}{2}$$

$$= \frac{-\frac{1}{2} \pm \sqrt{-4}}{2}$$

$$= -\frac{1}{4} \pm j1$$

Since the roots are complex, the circuit is underdamped. In addition, a constant forcing function is present, that is, the 12 V source. Hence, the solution will be of the form

$$v(t) = K_1 e^{-\frac{1}{4}} \cos t + K_2 e^{-\frac{1}{4}} \sin t + K_3$$

Once again, we recall that in the steady state, the inductor looks like a short circuit and the capacitor looks like an open circuit. Therefore,

$$v(\infty) = v_c(\infty) = 12 = K_3$$

Thus

$$v(t) = K_1 e^{-\frac{1}{4}} \cos t + K_2 e^{-\frac{1}{4}} \sin t + 12$$

In addition,

$$v(0) = v_c(0) = 0 = K_1 + 12$$

or

$$K_1 = -12$$

then

$$v(t) = -12e^{-1/4} \cos t + K_2 e^{-1/4} \sin t + 12$$

The initial condition on the inductor can be employed using the expression

$$i(t) = C\frac{dv(t)}{dt}$$

Therefore,

$$\frac{dv(t)}{dt} = 3e^{-1/4} \cos t + 12e^{-1/4} \sin t - \frac{K_2}{4}e^{-1/4} \sin t + K_2 e^{-1/4} \cos t$$

$$= [3 + K_2]e^{-1/4} \cos t + \left[12 - \frac{K_2}{4}\right] e^{-1/4} \sin t$$

Then

$$i(0) = C\frac{dv(0)}{dt} = 0 = 3 + K_2$$
$$K_2 = -3$$

As a result

$$v(t) = -12e^{-1/4} \cos t - 3e^{-1/4} \sin t + 12$$

Note that this equation satisfies the initial condition $v(0) = 0$. In addition, as $t \to \infty$ (the steady-state condition), the inductor acts like a short circuit and the capacitor acts like an open circuit so that 12 V appears at the output. The equation also satisfies this final condition, that is, $v(\infty) = 12$ V.

Problems

4.1   Find the capacitance at the terminals A–B in the network in Figure P4.1. All capacitors are 12 μF.

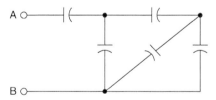

FIGURE P4.1

4.2   Determine the total capacitance at the terminals A–B in the circuit in Figure P4.2. All capacitors are 6 μF.

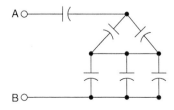

FIGURE P4.2

4.3 Find the capacitance at the terminals A–B in the circuit in Figure P4.3. All capacitors are 12 μF.

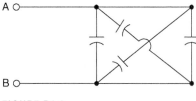

FIGURE P4.3

4.4 Determine the capacitance at the terminals A–B in the network in Figure P4.4.

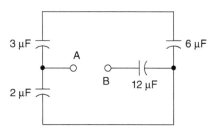

FIGURE P4.4

4.5 Find the capacitance at the terminals A–B in the circuit in Figure P4.5. All capacitors are 12 μF.

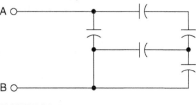

FIGURE P4.5

4.6 Determine the capacitance at the terminals A–B in the circuit in Figure P4.6.

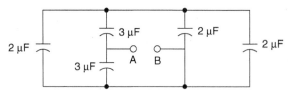

FIGURE P4.6

4.7 Show how to connect three 12 μF capacitors to obtain a capacitance of 8 μF.

4.8   Find the inductance at the terminals A–B in the network in Figure P4.8.

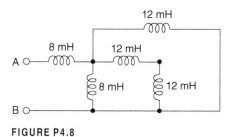

FIGURE P4.8

4.9   Determine the inductance at the terminals A–B in the circuit in Figure P4.9.

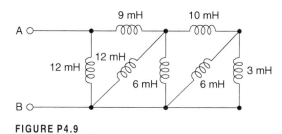

FIGURE P4.9

4.10   Find the inductance at the terminals A–B in the network in Figure P4.10. All inductors are 12 mH.

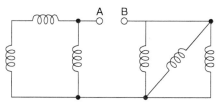

FIGURE P4.10

4.11   Determine the inductance at the terminals A–B in the circuit in Figure P4.11.

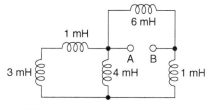

FIGURE P4.11

4.12 Compute the total inductance at the terminals A–B in the circuit in Figure P4.12.

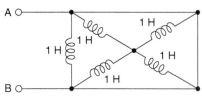

FIGURE P4.12

4.13 Find the inductance at the terminals A–B in the network in Figure P4.13. All inductors are 12 mH.

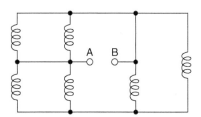

FIGURE P4.13

4.14 Determine the inductance at the terminals A–B in the circuit in Figure P4.14. All inductors are 6 mH.

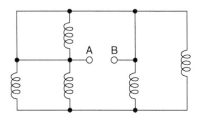

FIGURE P4.14

4.15 Show how to connect four 12 mH inductors to obtain a value of 16 mH.

4.16 Find $v_0(t)$ for $t > 0$ in the circuit in Figure P4.16.

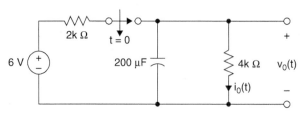

FIGURE P4.16

4.17 Find $i_0(t)$ for $t > 0$ in the circuit in Figure P4.16.

4.18 Find $v_0(t)$ for $t > 0$ in the circuit in Figure P4.18.

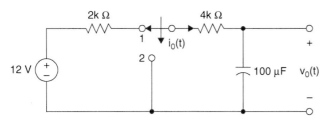

FIGURE P4.18

4.19 Find $i_0(t)$ for $t > 0$ in the circuit in Figure P4.18.

4.20 Find $v_0(t)$ for $t > 0$ in the circuit in Figure P4.20.

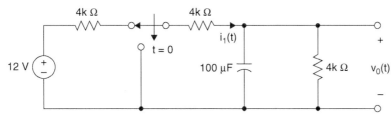

FIGURE P4.20

4.21 Find $i_1(t)$ for $t > 0$ in the circuit in Figure P4.20.

4.22 Find $i_0(t)$ for $t > 0$ in the circuit in Figure P4.22.

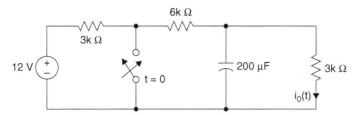

FIGURE P4.22

4.23 Find $v_0(t)$ for $t > 0$ in the circuit in Figure P4.23.

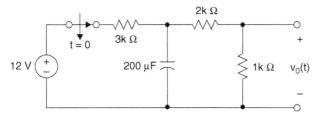

FIGURE P4.23

4.24   Find $v_0(t)$ for t > 0 in the circuit in Figure P4.24.

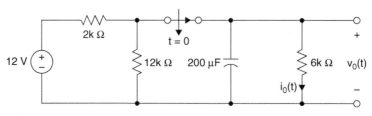

FIGURE P4.24

4.25   Find $i_0(t)$ for t > 0 in the circuit in Figure P4.24.

4.26   Find $v_0(t)$ for t > 0 in the circuit in Figure P4.26.

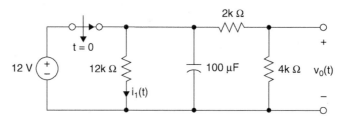

FIGURE P4.26

4.27   Find $i_1(t)$ for t > 0 in the circuit in Figure P4.26.

4.28   Find $i_1(t)$ and $i_2(t)$ for t > 0 in the circuit in Figure P4.28.

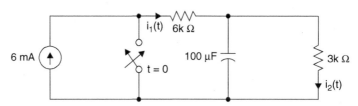

FIGURE P4.28

4.29   Find $i_1(t)$ and $v_0(t)$ for t > 0 in the circuit in Figure P4.29.

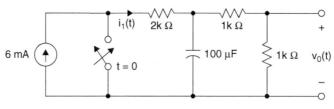

FIGURE P4.29

4.30   Find $i_0(t)$ for $t > 0$ in the circuit in Figure P4.30.

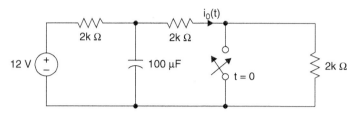

FIGURE P4.30

4.31   Find $v(t)$ for $t > 0$ in the circuit in Figure P4.31.

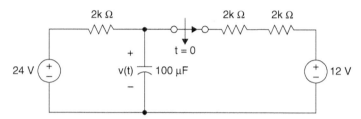

FIGURE P4.31

4.32   Find $v(t)$ for $t > 0$ in the circuit in Figure P4.32.

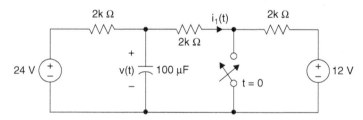

FIGURE P4.32

4.33   Find $i_1(t)$ for $t > 0$ in the circuit in Figure P4.32.

4.34   Find $v_c(t)$ for $t > 0$ in the circuit in Figure P4.34.

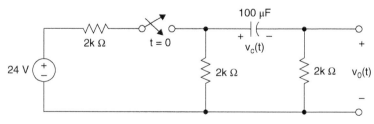

FIGURE P4.34

4.35 Find $v_0(t)$ for t > 0 in the circuit in Figure P4.34.

4.36 Find $i_L(t)$ for t > 0 in the circuit in Figure P4.36.

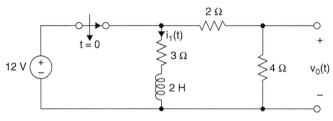

FIGURE P4.36

4.37 Find $v_0(t)$ for t > 0 in the circuit in Figure P4.36.

4.38 Find $v_0(t)$ for t > 0 in the circuit in Figure P4.38.

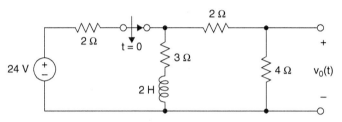

FIGURE P4.38

4.39 Find $v_0(t)$ for t > 0 in the circuit in Figure P4.39.

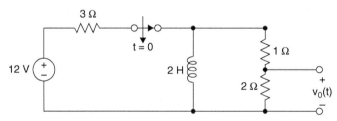

FIGURE P4.39

4.40 Find $v_0(t)$ for t > 0 in the circuit in Figure P4.40.

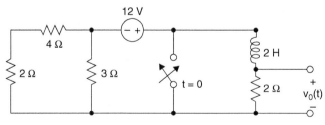

FIGURE P4.40

4.41   Find $v_0(t)$ for $t > 0$ in the circuit in Figure P4.41.

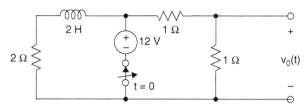

FIGURE P4.41

4.42   Find $i_0(t)$ for $t > 0$ in the circuit in Figure P4.42.

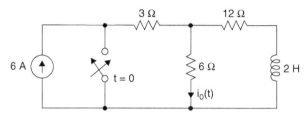

FIGURE P4.42

4.43   Find $v_0(t)$ for $t > 0$ in the circuit in Figure P4.43.

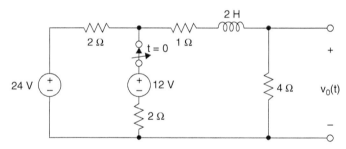

FIGURE P4.43

4.44   Find $v_0(t)$ for $t > 0$ in the circuit in Figure P4.44.

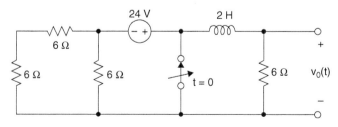

FIGURE P4.44

4.45 Find $v_0(t)$ for $t > 0$ in the circuit in Figure P4.45.

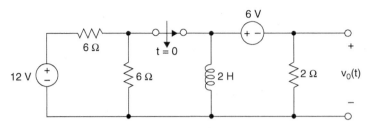

FIGURE P4.45

4.46 Determine the type of damping exhibited by the network in Figure P4.46 if $R = \frac{1}{2}\,\Omega$, $C = \frac{1}{4}$ F, and $L = \frac{1}{4}$ H.

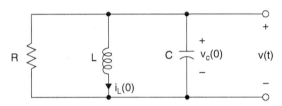

FIGURE P4.46

4.47 Determine the type of damping exhibited by the network in Figure P4.46 if $R = 1/5\,\Omega$, $C = 1/3$ F, and $L = 1/18$ H.

4.48 Determine the type of damping exhibited by the network in Figure P4.46 if $R = 1\,\Omega$, $C = 1/4$ F, and $L = 4/5$ H.

4.49 Determine the type of damping exhibited by the network in Figure P4.49 if $R = 3\,\Omega$, $C = 1/50$ F, and $L = 2$ H.

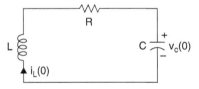

FIGURE P4.49

4.50 Determine the type of damping exhibited by the network in Figure P4.49 if $R = 2\,\Omega$, $C = 1/6$ F, and $L = 1/6$ H.

4.51 Determine the type of damping exhibited by the network in Figure P4.49 if $R = 3\,\Omega$, $C = 1/6$ F, and $L = 1/3$ H.

4.52 Find v(t) for t > 0 in the network in Figure P4.52 if the initial conditions on the network are $i_L(0) = 1$ A and $v_c(0) = 12$ V.

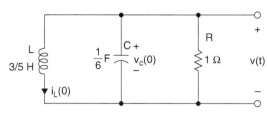

FIGURE P4.52

4.53 Find v(t) for t > 0 in the network in Figure P4.52 if the initial conditions on the network are $i_L(0) = 2$ A and $v_c(0) = 6$ V and the circuit parameters are R = 1 Ω, C = 1/3 F, and L = 3/2 H.

4.54 Find i(t) for t > 0 in the network in Figure P4.54 if the initial conditions on the network are $i_L(0) = 2$ A and $v_c(0) = 4$ V.

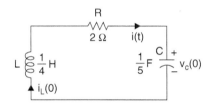

FIGURE P4.54

4.55 Find $v_c(t)$ for t > 0 in the network in Figure P4.54 if the initial conditions on the network are $i_L(0) = -1$ A and $v_c(0) = -2$ V and the circuit parameters are R = 3 Ω, C = 1/4 F, and L = 1/2 H.

4.56 Consider the network in Figure P4.56. The circuit parameters are R = 2 Ω, L = 5 H, C = 1/5 F, $i_L(0) = -1$ A, and $v_c(0) = 4$ V. We wish to determine the equation for the voltage v(t).

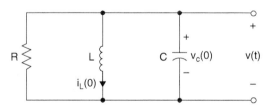

FIGURE P4.56

4.57 The series RLC circuit shown in Figure P4.57 has the following parameters: C = 0.04 F, L = 1 H, R = 6 Ω, $i_L(0) = 4$A, and $v_c(0) = -4$V. Find the equation for the current i(t).

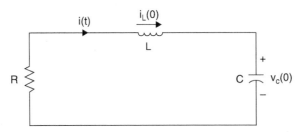

FIGURE P4.57

4.58 For the underdamped circuit shown in Figure P4.58, determine the voltage v(t) if the initial conditions on the storage elements are $i_L(0) = 1$ A and $v_c(0) = 10$ V.

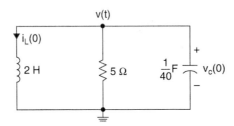

FIGURE P4.58

4.59 Determine the equation for the current i(t), t = 0, in the circuit shown in Figure P4.59. All initial conditions are zero.

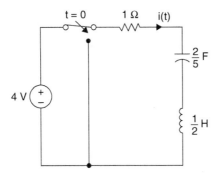

FIGURE P4.59

4.60 In the circuit shown in Figure P4.60, find v(t), t = 0. All initial conditions are zero.

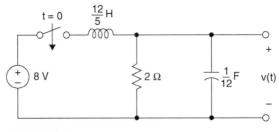

FIGURE P4.60

AC Steady-State Analysis

CHAPTER 5

LEARNING OBJECTIVES

- To understand the ac forcing function
- To be able to determine the network response to a sinusoidal signal
- To understand the phasor concept and its use in ac steady-state analysis
- To learn the concepts of impedance and admittance
- To be able to apply all the analysis procedures to ac sinusoidal steady-state circuits

Thus far in our study of circuit analysis, we have analyzed circuits in which the forcing function is a constant, i.e. dc value, and we have examined circuits in which a sudden change in the network has occurred as a result of opening or closing a switch to interrupt the network and in the process change its architecture. This latter analysis is called a transient analysis, and it generally consists of two components, one that is constant and independent of time and another that represents the natural response of the network and exponentially decays with time.

In this chapter, we learn to analyze networks in which the forcing function is an alternating current, i.e. the source outputs are sinusoidal in nature and appear as a sine or cosine wave. This steady-state analysis ignores the transient behavior, which will, of course, vanish with time.

The importance of this material stems from the fact that alternating current is the dominant waveform of the power industry, e.g. it is present at the power outlets in homes. In the United States, the waveform has a frequency of 60 cycles per second, called Hertz (Hz), while in other parts of the world, the frequency is 50 Hz. This ac waveform can be easily generated with rotating electric machines; it can be stepped up or down with a device known as a transformer and when configured properly can provide smooth power delivery from generator to destination. We will demonstrate all these features when we study electric power later in the book.

In trigonometry, we learned that a cosine function could be written in the form

$$x(t) = X_M \cos(\omega t)$$

THE AC FORCING FUNCTION

where X_M is the amplitude or maximum value of the function, ω is the angular or radian frequency, and ωt is the argument. This cosine waveform is plotted in Figure 5.1 as a function of the two arguments, ωt and t. This waveform is periodic and repeats every period, i.e. 2π radians in Figure 5.1a and T in Figure 5.1b. This means that $x(t) = x(t + nT)$ for $n = 1, 2, 3, \ldots$ and thus one period later in time, the function has the same identical value.

The frequency (in Hertz) of the waveform is related to the period by the expression

$$f = 1/T$$

where T is the period of the waveform in seconds. In addition, as shown in Figure 5.1a

$$T = 2\pi$$

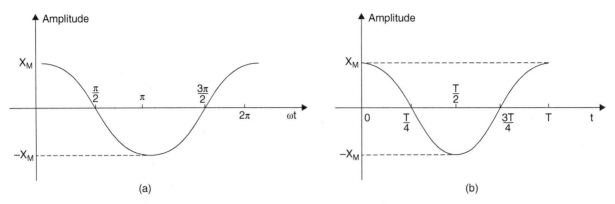

FIGURE 5.1 Cosine waves

and therefore the relationship among radian frequency in radians per second, frequency in Hertz, i.e. cycles per second and the period of the waveform in seconds is

$$\omega = (2\pi)/T = 2\pi f$$

A more general representation of the cosine wave is the form

$$x(t) = X_M \cos[\omega t + \theta]$$

where θ is referred to as the *phase angle* of the waveform. The significance of this phase angle is demonstrated in Figure 5.2 where the waveforms with and without a phase angle are shown. Note that the waveform $X_M \cos[\omega t + \theta]$ occurs θ radians earlier in time than the waveform $X_M \cos(\omega t)$. Or, said another way, the waveform $X_M \cos[\omega t + \theta]$ *leads* the waveform $X_M \cos(\omega t)$ by θ radians, and, correspondingly, the waveform $X_M \cos(\omega t)$ *lags* the waveform $X_M \cos[\omega t + \theta]$ by θ radians. In the general case, if

$$x_1(t) = X_M \cos[\omega t + \theta]$$
$$x_2(t) = X_N \cos[\omega t + \phi]$$

then $x_1(t)$ leads $x_2(t)$ by $(\theta - \phi)$ radians and $x_2(t)$ lags $x_1(t)$ by $(\theta - \phi)$ radians. In either case, the two functions are out of phase with each other. However, if $\theta = \phi$, the waveforms are said

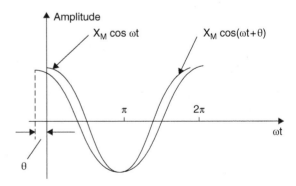

FIGURE 5.2 Phase angle illustration

to be in phase. These comparisons only make sense when comparing two functions of the same frequency.

Note that the phase angles in the two waveforms are in radians, since ωt is in radians, i.e. ω is in radians per second and t is in seconds, so ωt is in radians, which then matches the units of the phase angles. However, as will be demonstrated in the material that follows, it is most convenient to express the phase angle in degrees. Therefore, we will use the fact that 2π radians corresponds to 360°, so the argument in an expression such as $x(t) = X_M\cos[\omega t + \theta]$ is always expressed in degrees. In addition, a minus sign corresponds to + or $-180°$, so $-\cos \omega t = \cos[\omega t \pm 180°]$.

In the following analyses, we will assume that the network's forcing functions consist of voltage and current sources that can be expressed in the form $V_M\cos[\omega t + \theta]$ or $I_M\cos[\omega t + \theta]$. Although we have centered our discussion on a cosine function, we could just have easily used a sine function since the two functions are related as follows:

$$\cos t = \sin(\omega t + 90°)$$
$$\sin t = \cos(\omega t - 90°)$$

As these equations, and the waveforms shown in Figure 5.3, indicate, the cosine wave leads the sine wave by 90° and the sine wave lags the cosine wave by 90°.

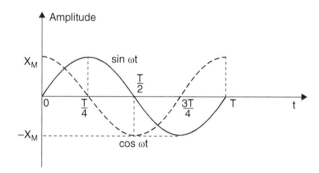

FIGURE 5.3   Sine and cosine wave comparison

Given the two voltages $v_1(t) = 6\cos[2513.3t + 20°]$ V and $v_2(t) = -4\sin[2513.3t + 60°]$ V, let us determine the frequency of the sources in Hertz and the phase angle between them.

Since $\omega = 2\pi f$, $f = 2513.3/(2\pi) = 400$ Hz. In order to determine the phase angle between the two voltages, we must express the voltages, of the same frequency, as either sine or cosine functions. $v_2(t)$ can be expressed as

$$v_2(t) = -4\sin[2513.3t + 60°] \text{ V}$$
$$= -4\cos[2513.3t - 30°] \text{ V}$$
$$= 4\cos[2513.3t + 150°] \text{ V} = 4\cos[2513.3t - 210°] \text{ V}$$

Therefore, $v_1(t)$ leads $v_2(t)$ by $20° - 150° = -130°$, and $v_2(t)$ lags $v_1(t)$ by $-130°$.

Example 5.1

THE NETWORK RESPONSE TO SINUSOIDAL FORCING FUNCTIONS

We found earlier that when we applied a dc source to a linear network all the currents and voltages in the network were constant, i.e. dc. It would be impossible to satisfy KVL and KCL in a network if the currents and voltages resulting from a constant source were not constant. In a similar manner, when we apply a sinusoidal source, e.g. a voltage source of the form $v(t) = V_M \cos[\omega t + \theta]$ V to a network, we would expect the currents in the circuit to be of the form $i(t) = I_M \cos[\omega t + \phi]$ A. In other words, when the sources in the network are of the same frequency, the resulting currents and voltages anywhere in the linear network will be of the same frequency and the only unknowns are the magnitudes and phase angles.

Consider for example the network in Figure 5.4. This is a simple series circuit consisting of a sinusoidal voltage source $v_S(t) = V_M \cos \omega t$ V, one resistor and one inductor. Note that if the inductor were a resistor, so the series circuit consisted of a voltage source and two resistors, the problem of finding the current would be trivial. However, in this case KVL yields

$$-V_M \cos \omega t + Ri(t) + Ldi(t)/dt = 0$$

which results in the differential equation

$$Ldi(t)/dt + Ri(t) = V_M \cos \omega t$$

the solution of which is the current $i(t)$. Since the voltage source is a cosine function and the circuit is linear, we expect the current to be a cosine function with the same frequency. Therefore, the current must be of the form

$$i(t) = I_M \cos[\omega t + \theta]$$

Note that the current is completely defined by two terms, i.e. the magnitude I_M and the phase angle θ.

At this point, recall that in our transient analysis we knew the form of the solution, and so we substituted this form into the differential equation and equated like coefficients to determine the unknown constants, which produced a solution. If we perform that same operation in this situation, we will obtain

$$I_M = V_M/[R^2 + \omega^2 L^2]^{1/2}$$

and

$$\theta = -\tan^{-1}\omega L/R$$

Substituting these results into the general form of the solution

$$i(t) = I_M \cos[\omega t + \theta]$$

yields

$$i(t) = \{V_M/[R^2 + \omega^2 L^2]^{1/2}\}\{\cos[\omega t - \tan^{-1}\omega L/R]\} \text{ A}$$

While the mathematical manipulations required to arrive at this solution are straightforward, they do consume about a page of algebraic manipulations (the reader interested in the

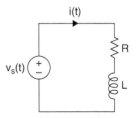

FIGURE 5.4 A simple RL circuit

details of this derivation are referred to chapter 8 in *Basic Engineering Circuit Analysis,* 12e). It is interesting to pause at this point and ask the following question. If this simple circuit required a page or two of algebra to arrive at a solution, what must be required for a much more complex circuit like some of those addressed in the analysis of dc circuits? Thank God there is a straight-forward approach, and it involves establishing a relationship between sinusoidal time functions and complex numbers. The actual process can be simply stated as follows.

- We begin with a problem in the time domain involving sinusoidal time functions where a differential equation must be solved to determine an unknown current or voltage.

- We use a correspondence between sinusoidal time functions and complex numbers to transform the problem from the time domain to what is called the frequency domain.

- We solve the problem in this frequency domain using complex algebra.

- We then transform this solution in the frequency domain back to the time domain.

As we will demonstrate in the material that follows, this process of transforming the problem from the time domain to the frequency domain, solving it in the frequency domain, and then transforming the solution back to the time domain allows us to employ all the techniques we have learned in dc circuit analysis to solve ac circuit problems. The only difference is that all of our mathematical manipulations are performed in complex algebra.

The correspondence that is established between sinusoidal time functions and complex numbers employs Euler's equation:

$$e^{j\omega t} = \cos \omega t + j \sin \omega t$$

where $\cos \omega t$ is the real part of this complex function and $\sin \omega t$ is the imaginary part of the complex function, and note that j is used to represent $\sqrt{-1}$, i.e. the imaginary operator. Given this relationship, let us now assume that instead of applying the source $v(t) = V_M \cos \omega t$, we apply $v(t) = V_M e^{j\omega t}$, which can, of course, be expressed as

$$v(t) = V_M[\cos \omega t + j \sin \omega t]$$

Note that although $V_M e^{j\omega t}$ is a non realizable source, both the real and imaginary parts of this function are physically realizable, i.e. we can build electronic equipment to generate these sinusoidal functions. Since the network is linear, the principle of superposition applies and the current response of the network to this voltage can be expressed as

$$i(t) = I_M \cos[\omega t + \phi] + jI_M \sin[\omega t + \phi]$$

where $I_M \cos[\omega t + \phi]$ is the response of the network to $V_M \cos \omega t$ and $I_M \sin[\omega t + \phi]$ is the response to $V_M \sin \omega t$. However, this response can be written via Euler's equation as

$$i(t) = I_M e^{j(\omega t + \phi)}$$

What does all this mean? It simply means the following. Instead of applying a voltage of the form $V_M \cos \omega t$, we will apply the voltage $V_M e^{j\omega t}$. The current response will be of the form $I_M e^{j(\omega t + \phi)}$. However, since we want the response to $V_M \cos \omega t$, we will simply take the real part of this current response, which is $I_M \cos[\omega t + \phi]$. Note carefully that since the circuit is linear, the frequency of all voltages and currents in the network will be the same. Therefore, *our solution consists of two items, I_M and ϕ, i.e. the magnitude and phase* of the current. Furthermore, we can express the current in the following form:

$$i(t) = I_M \cos[\omega t + \phi] = \text{Re}[I_M e^{j(\omega t + \phi)}] = \text{Re}[I_M e^{j\phi} e^{j\omega t}]$$

The term $I_M e^{j\phi}$ defines the magnitude and phase angle, which is precisely the desired result of the analysis, i.e. the two unknowns that define the current. This quantity is called a *phasor*, and *it is a complex number, representing a sinusoidal time-varying function, that defines the function's magnitude, I_M, and phase, ϕ,* measured with respect to a cosine function.

As illustrated in the appendix on complex numbers, the phasor can be written in multiple forms. In particular, we will use the polar representation, i.e. $\mathbf{I} = I_M \angle \theta$, where we adopt the convention that phasors are shown in **bold type** to distinguish them from a magnitude.

Now when we employ the phasor representation, we are transforming the time-domain problem into the frequency domain, and in this domain the voltage applied to the network is $v(t) = \mathbf{V}e^{j\omega t}$ and the current response will be $i(t) = \mathbf{I}e^{j\omega t}$, where the phasors $\mathbf{V}$ and $\mathbf{I}$ represent the magnitude and phase angle information.

To demonstrate the power of this phasor analysis, let us examine once again the RL circuit in Figure 5.4. The KVL equation for the network is

$$Ld(\mathbf{I}e^{j\omega t})/dt + R\mathbf{I}e^{j\omega t} = \mathbf{V}e^{j\omega t}$$

where the voltage and current phasors represent the magnitude and phase information, i.e. $\mathbf{V} = V_M \angle \theta$ and $\mathbf{I} = I_M \angle \phi$. Performing the indicated derivative and dividing the entire equation by the factor $e^{j\omega t}$ yields the phasor equation

$$j\omega L\mathbf{I} + R\mathbf{I} = \mathbf{V}$$

Therefore, the phasor current is

$$\mathbf{I} = \mathbf{V}/(R + j\omega L)$$

As shown in Appendix A, the complex number $(R + j\omega L)$, which is in rectangular form, can be expressed in polar form as a magnitude and phase angle:

$$R + j\omega L = [R^2 + \omega^2 L^2]^{1/2} \angle \tan^{-1}\omega L/R$$

Hence, the phasor current is

$$\mathbf{I} = V_M/[R^2 + \omega^2 L^2]^{1/2} \angle -\tan^{-1}\omega L/R$$

This function represents the solution for the current in the frequency domain. Then, transforming this result back to the time domain yields the desired current

$$i(t) = \{V_M/[R^2 + \omega^2 L^2]^{1/2}\}\{\cos[\omega t - \tan^{-1}\omega L/R]\}$$

which is the same answer that is obtained by solving the differential equation via a page of algebra. As the following analyses will demonstrate, the phasor analysis is performed exactly like a dc analysis, but the additions, subtractions, multiplications, and divisions required to obtain a solution are all done in complex numbers, and in order to facilitate this process, the ability to change a complex number from rectangular form to polar form and vice versa is essential.

Before proceeding let us summarize what we have done here. We started by writing a differential equation in the time domain for the current in the RL circuit. Rather than solve the differential equation in the time domain for the current $i(t)$, we transformed this differential equation into an algebraic equation in the frequency domain containing phasors that represent the current and voltage. We then solved for the unknown phasor current, which consisted of a magnitude and phase, using complex numbers in the frequency domain. Then the phasor current was simply transformed back to the time domain to yield the current i(t), using the correspondence between the two domains, i.e.

Time domain	Frequency domain
$I_M\cos(\omega t \pm \theta)$	$I_M\angle\pm\theta$

Although the analysis in the frequency domain requires the solution of algebraic equations with complex coefficients, the process is much simpler than solving a set of differential equations. Furthermore, we can take advantage of the powerful solution techniques such as MATLAB in obtaining a solution. One last point on this subject—we have measured the phase angle with respect to a cosine function; however, the relationship between the sine and cosine waves is well known.

In order to effectively apply phasor analysis, we must define the phasor relationship between voltage and current for each of the passive circuit elements. In the case of a resistor, the voltage/current relationship is v(t) = Ri(t). So, if the voltage is expressed in the form $v(t) = V_M e^{j(\omega t+\theta)}$ and the current is expressed in the form $i(t) = I_M e^{j(\omega t+\phi)}$, then

$$V_M e^{j(\omega t+\theta)} = RI_M e^{j(\omega t+\phi)}$$

PHASOR RELATIONSHIPS FOR THE RLC CIRCUIT COMPONENTS

This equation can be expressed in phasor form as

$$\mathbf{V} = R\mathbf{I}$$

where $\mathbf{V} = V_M\angle\theta$ and $\mathbf{I} = I_M\angle\phi$. In addition, note that $V_M = RI_M$ and $\theta = \phi$. Since θ is equal to ϕ, the current and voltage have the same phase angle and thus are in phase.

Using an identical approach illustrates that while the time-domain V–I relationship for an inductor is

$$v(t) = Ldi(t)/dt$$

The phasor relationship is

$$\mathbf{V} = j\omega L\mathbf{I}$$

and since the imaginary operator $j = \sqrt{-1} = 1\angle 90°$ in an inductor the voltage leads the current by 90° or the current lags the voltage by 90°.

Similarly, the time-domain V–I relationship for a capacitor is

$$i(t) = Cdv(t)/dt$$

and thus the phasor relationship is

$$\mathbf{I} = j\omega C\mathbf{V}$$

indicating that the current in a capacitor leads the voltage by 90°, or equivalently the voltage lags the current by 90°.

The voltage–current relationships for the three passive elements are summarized in Figure 5.5, where the time-domain and frequency-domain information is displayed. The relationship in the frequency domain employs what is commonly known as a phasor diagram, which graphically displays the relationship among the phasors. However, note that both the time domain and the frequency domain indicate that if the passive element is a resistor, the voltage and current are in phase; if the element is an inductor, the voltage leads the current or

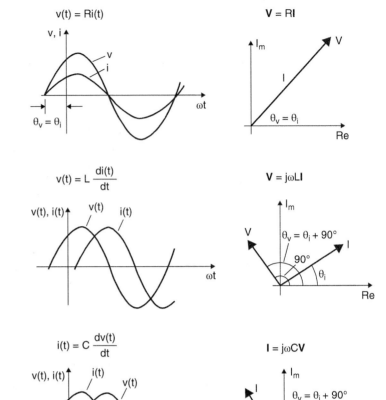

$$v(t) = Ri(t) \qquad \mathbf{V} = R\mathbf{I}$$

$$v(t) = L\frac{di(t)}{dt} \qquad \mathbf{V} = j\omega L\mathbf{I}$$

$$i(t) = C\frac{dv(t)}{dt} \qquad \mathbf{I} = j\omega C\mathbf{V}$$

FIGURE 5.5 Time-domain/ frequency-domain relationships

the current lags the voltage by 90°; and in the case of a capacitor the current leads the voltage or the voltage lags the current by 90°.

Using an approach similar to that applied in the dc case, we can show that both *KVL and KCL are valid in the frequency domain so that the algebraic sum of the voltages around any loop is equal to zero and the algebraic sum of the currents at any node must be zero.*

IMPEDANCE AND ADMITTANCE

Like resistance, the impedance, **Z**, at the two terminals of an element as shown in Figure 5.6, is defined as the ratio of the phasor voltage to the phasor current in accordance with the passive sign convention:

$$\mathbf{Z} = \mathbf{V}/\mathbf{I}$$

This equation can be expressed in the form

$$\mathbf{Z} = V_M\angle\theta_v/I_M\angle\theta_i = (V_M/I_M)\angle\theta_v - \theta_i = Z\angle\theta_z$$
$$Z\angle\theta_z = V_M\angle\theta_v/ I_M\angle\theta_i = V_M/I_M\angle\theta_v - \theta_i = R + jX$$
$$\theta_z = \tan^{-1}\frac{X}{R}$$

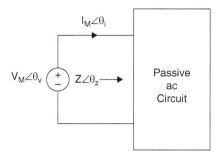

FIGURE 5.6   General impedance relationship

Since **Z** is the ratio of voltage to current, the units of **Z** are Ohms. In addition, note that *the angle of the impedance is always equal to the angle between the voltage and the current.*

Note that **Z** is frequency dependent, since in general the circuit contains capacitors and inductors and their values are dependent on frequency. Therefore, to indicate this dependence, we can express **Z** as

$$\mathbf{Z}(j\omega) = R(\omega) + jX(\omega)$$

where $R(\omega)$ is the real or resistive component and $X(\omega)$ is the imaginary or reactive component. While R and X are real functions of frequency, **Z** *is a complex number. However, it is not a phasor.* Remember that phasors are representations of time-varying sinusoidal functions, and **Z** has no meaning in the time domain.

The following equations are a summary of the relationships that exist among the terms discussed here.

$$Z\angle\theta_z = V_M\angle\theta_v / I_M\angle\theta_I = V_M/I_M\angle\theta_v - \theta_I = R + jX$$

and

$$Z = [R^2 + X^2]^{1/2}$$
$$\theta_z = \tan^{-1}X/R$$
$$R = Z\cos\theta_z$$
$$X = Z\sin\theta_z$$

The relationship among these quantities is shown in Figure 5.7. The impedance of the individual passive elements is

$$\mathbf{Z_R} = R, \mathbf{Z_L} = j\omega L, \text{ and } \mathbf{Z_c} = 1/j\omega C$$

Since KVL and KCL are both applicable in the frequency domain, their application will demonstrate that impedances can be combined in the same manner as that established for resistors, i.e. *the equivalent impedance of a number of impedances connected in series is*

$$\mathbf{Z_s} = \mathbf{Z_1} + \mathbf{Z_2} + \mathbf{Z_3} + \cdots$$

And *the equivalent impedance of a number of impedances connected in parallel is*

$$1/\mathbf{Z_p} = 1/\mathbf{Z_1} + 1/\mathbf{Z_2} + 1/\mathbf{Z_3} + \cdots$$

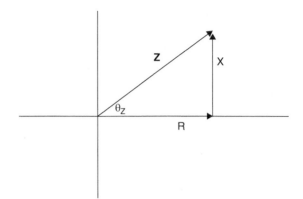

FIGURE 5.7   The relationship among **Z**, X, and R

| Example 5.2 |

Let us revisit the RL circuit in Figure 5.4 and use it as a vehicle to demonstrate some of the concepts we have described above. The parameters for the network are as follows: $v_s(t) = 12\cos(377t + 60°)$ V, R = 4 Ω, and L = 7.958 mH. We wish to determine the current i(t) and draw a phasor diagram that illustrates the phasor relationship of the current and voltages in the network.

The network in the time domain is shown in Figure 5.8a. Note that $\omega = 377$ rad/s and thus the impedance of the inductor is $\mathbf{Z_L} = j(377)(0.007958) = j3$ Ω. The time-domain network is transformed into the frequency domain in Figure 5.8b. We can now apply KVL to the network to determine the current.

$$-12\angle 60° + 4\mathbf{I} + j3\mathbf{I} = 0$$

Hence,

$$\mathbf{I} = 12\angle 60°/(4 + j3) = 12\angle 60°/5\angle 36.9° = 2.4\angle 23.1° \text{ A}$$

Then,

$$\mathbf{V_R} = 4\mathbf{I} = 9.6\angle 23.1° \text{ V}$$

$$\mathbf{V_L} = j3\mathbf{I} = (3\angle 90°)(2.4\angle 23.1°) = 7.2\angle 113.1° \text{ V}$$

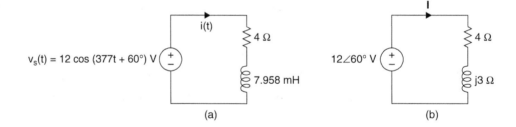

(a)   (b)

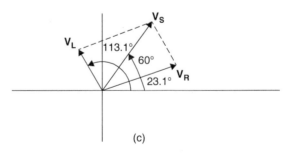

(c)

FIGURE 5.8   Network for Example 5.2

The phasor diagram for the network is shown in Figure 5.8c. Note that the voltage across the inductor leads the current by 90°, and the phasor addition of the voltage across the resistor and the voltage across the inductor yields the source voltage. In addition, now that the network current has been calculated in the frequency domain, the final step is to transform this current back to the time domain. Since

$$\mathbf{I} = 2.4\angle 23.10 \text{ A}$$

$$i(t) = 2.4\cos(377t + 23.1°) \text{ A}$$

Although the complex algebra involved in a phasor analysis is not trivial, the approach is definitely superior to a differential equation solution, and the phasor analysis becomes even more valuable as the complexity of the network increases.

Let's determine the impedance at the terminals A–B for the network in Figure 5.9a at a frequency of 60 Hz.

Example 5.3

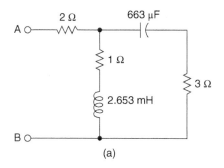
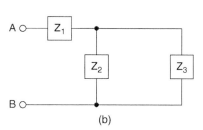

(a)   (b)

FIGURE 5.9   Circuit used in Example 5.3

Since the frequency is 60 Hz, the radian frequency, $\omega = 2\pi 60 = 377 \text{ rad/s}$. The impedance of the capacitor is then

$$\mathbf{Z_c} = 1/j\omega C = 1/j\,[(377)(663 \times 10^{-6})] = 1/j(0.25) = -j4 \text{ } \Omega$$

and

$$\mathbf{Z_L} = j\omega L = j[(377)(2.653 \times 10^{-3})] = j1 \text{ } \Omega$$

Given this data, the circuit is redrawn in Figure 5.9b, where

$$\mathbf{Z_1} = 2 \text{ } \Omega$$
$$\mathbf{Z_2} = 1 + j1 \text{ } \Omega$$
$$\mathbf{Z_3} = 3 - j4 \text{ } \Omega$$

The impedance $\mathbf{Z_{AB}}$ is equal to $\mathbf{Z_1}$ plus the parallel combination of $\mathbf{Z_2}$ and $\mathbf{Z_3}$. The parallel combination is

$$\mathbf{Z_2 Z_3}/(\mathbf{Z_2} + \mathbf{Z_3}) = (1 + j1)(3 - j4)/[1 + j1 + 3 - j4]$$
$$= (7 - j1)/(4 - j3)$$
$$= (7.07\angle -8.13°)/(5.00\angle -36.87°)$$
$$= 1.414\angle 28.74° \text{ } \Omega$$

and then

$$\mathbf{Z_{AB}} = \mathbf{Z_1} + 1.414\angle 28.74° = 2 + 1.24 + j0.68 = 3.24 + j0.68 \text{ } \Omega$$

At this point, it is appropriate to define another term that is useful in ac circuit analysis, and that is admittance. Admittance is the reciprocal of impedance; thus

$$\mathbf{Y} = 1/\mathbf{Z} = \mathbf{I}/\mathbf{V}$$

Similar to impedance, admittance is a complex number, and the unit of admittance is Siemens (S).

$$\mathbf{Y} = Y_M \angle \theta_y = G + jB$$

where G is the familiar conductance and B is called susceptance. Since $\mathbf{Z}$ and $\mathbf{Y}$ are related, their components are also related. For example,

$$\mathbf{Y} = 1/\mathbf{Z}$$

$$G + jB = \frac{1}{R + jX}$$

$$= \frac{R - jX}{R^2 + X^2}$$

Therefore

$$G = \frac{R}{R^2 + X^2} \quad B = \frac{-X}{R^2 + X^2}$$

And

$$R = \frac{G}{G^2 + B^2}$$

$$X = \frac{-B}{G^2 + B^2}$$

It is important to note that, in general, neither R and G nor X and B are reciprocals of each other. Finally, the relationships that somewhat mirror those for impedance are

$$\mathbf{Y}_R = \frac{1}{R} = G$$

$$\mathbf{Y}_L = \frac{1}{j\omega L} = \frac{1}{\omega L} \angle -90°$$

$$\mathbf{Y}_C = j\omega C = \omega C \angle +90°$$

And the rules for combining admittances in series and parallel are

$$\mathbf{Y}_P = \mathbf{Y}_1 + \mathbf{Y}_2 + \cdots + \mathbf{Y}_n$$

$$\frac{1}{\mathbf{Y}_S} = \frac{1}{\mathbf{Y}_1} + \frac{1}{\mathbf{Y}_2} + \cdots + \frac{1}{\mathbf{Y}_n}$$

Example 5.4

Let us employ admittance to determine the impedance at the terminals A–B of the network in Figure 5.9.

Since $\mathbf{Z}_2$ and $\mathbf{Z}_3$ are in parallel, we can add their admittances. First, we compute the admittances of the individual components as follows:

$$\mathbf{Y}_2 = 1/(1 + j1) = 0.5 - j0.5 \text{ S}$$

$$\mathbf{Y}_3 = 1/(3 - j4) = 0.12 + j0.16 \text{ S}$$

Then

$$\mathbf{Y}_{23} = \mathbf{Y}_2 + \mathbf{Y}_3 = 0.62 - j0.34 = 0.707\angle{-}28.74° \text{ S}$$

and

$$\mathbf{Z}_{23} = 1/\mathbf{Y}_{23} = 1.414\angle 28.74° = 1.24 + j0.68 \ \Omega$$

Finally,

$$\mathbf{Z}_{AB} = \mathbf{Z}_1 + \mathbf{Z}_{23} = 3.24 + j0.68 \ \Omega$$

The final issue to address in the combination of impedances is the delta-to-wye/wye-to-delta transformations. Since the combination rules that apply for resistance apply also for impedance, the process is straightforward and mimics the operations in the dc case. Therefore, with reference to Figure 5.10,

$$\mathbf{Z}_a = \frac{\mathbf{Z}_1\mathbf{Z}_2}{\mathbf{Z}_1 + \mathbf{Z}_2 + \mathbf{Z}_3}$$

$$\mathbf{Z}_b = \frac{\mathbf{Z}_1\mathbf{Z}_3}{\mathbf{Z}_1 + \mathbf{Z}_2 + \mathbf{Z}_3}$$

$$\mathbf{Z}_c = \frac{\mathbf{Z}_2\mathbf{Z}_3}{\mathbf{Z}_1 + \mathbf{Z}_2 + \mathbf{Z}_3}$$

and

$$\mathbf{Z}_1 = \frac{\mathbf{Z}_a\mathbf{Z}_b + \mathbf{Z}_b\mathbf{Z}_c + \mathbf{Z}_c\mathbf{Z}_a}{\mathbf{Z}_c}$$

$$\mathbf{Z}_2 = \frac{\mathbf{Z}_a\mathbf{Z}_b + \mathbf{Z}_b\mathbf{Z}_c + \mathbf{Z}_c\mathbf{Z}_a}{\mathbf{Z}_b}$$

$$\mathbf{Z}_3 = \frac{\mathbf{Z}_a\mathbf{Z}_b + \mathbf{Z}_b\mathbf{Z}_c + \mathbf{Z}_c\mathbf{Z}_a}{\mathbf{Z}_a}$$

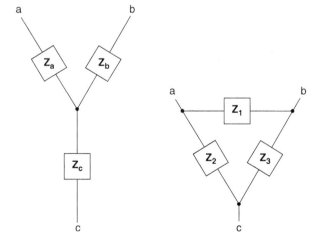

FIGURE 5.10   Delta–wye connected circuits

Let us determine the impedance at the terminals A–B in the circuit in Figure 5.11a.

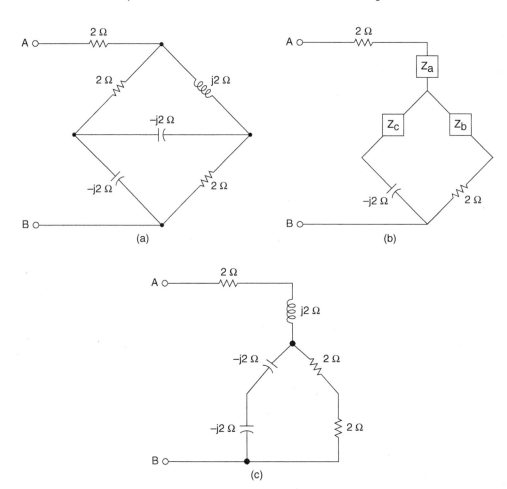

FIGURE 5.11 Circuits used in Example 5.5

The circuit consists of two back-to-back deltas. In our approach to this problem, we will transform the top delta as shown in Figure 5.11b.

$$\mathbf{Z_a} = (2)(j2)/[2 + j2 - j2] = j2 \ \Omega$$
$$\mathbf{Z_b} = (j2)(-j2)/[2 + j2 - j2] = 2 \ \Omega$$
$$\mathbf{Z_c} = (2)(-j2)/[2 + j2 - j2] = -j2 \ \Omega$$

The resulting circuit is shown in Figure 5.11c. The impedance $\mathbf{Z_{AB}}$ is then

$$\mathbf{Z_{AB}} = 2 + j2 + (4)(-j4)/[4 - j4]$$
$$= 2 + j2 + 16\angle-90°/5.66\angle-45°$$
$$= 4 \ \Omega$$

We are now in a position to attack any ac circuit problem. The following material will provide examples that are similar to those employed in the dc case, where the analysis is essentially the same, with the notable exception that all the mathematics is performed using complex algebra.

Examples 5.6–5.11 will serve to illustrate that all the techniques we learned for analyzing dc circuits apply to ac circuits as well.

Let us determine all the voltages and currents in the circuit in Figure 5.12a.

Example 5.6

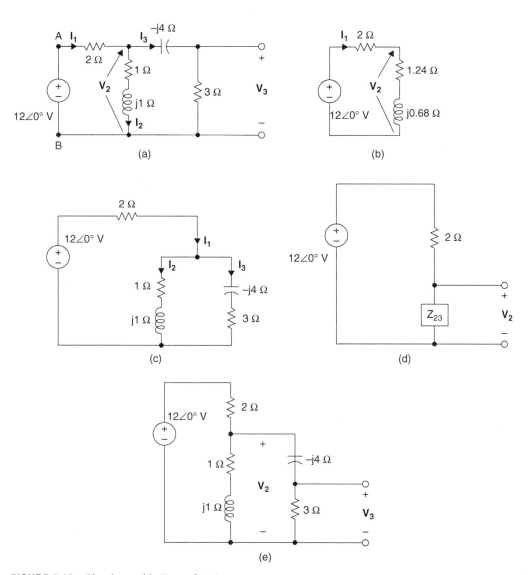

FIGURE 5.12   Circuits used in Example 5.6

Although we can approach this problem in many ways, we will begin our analysis by following the first technique we examined in the dc case, i.e. we will find the total impedance seen by the source, use Ohm's law to find the source current, I_1, and then proceed to find the remaining unknown voltages, V_2 and V_3, and currents, I_2 and I_3, using Ohm's law, KCL, and KVL.

First of all, recognize that this network is the same as that in Example 5.3, shown in Figure 5.9, with a $12\angle0°$ V source attached. We will use some of the data previously calculated for this network in the following analysis.

Recall that the total impedance at the terminals of the source was found to be $\mathbf{Z}_{AB} = 2 + \mathbf{Z}_{23} = 2 + 1.24 + j0.68 = 3.31\angle11.85°$ Ω, as shown in Figure 5.12b. Therefore,

$$\mathbf{I}_1 = 12\angle0°/[3.31\angle11.85°] = 3.62\angle-11.85°\text{ A}$$

Then, applying KVL to the loop in the equivalent circuit in Figure 5.12b yields

$$-12\angle0° + 2\mathbf{I}_1 + \mathbf{V}_2 = 0$$

or

$$\mathbf{V}_2 = 12\angle0° - 2(3.62\angle-11.85°)$$
$$= 5.13\angle16.9°\text{ V}$$

Knowing $\mathbf{V}_2$, we can calculate $\mathbf{I}_2$ and $\mathbf{I}_3$ as shown in Figure 5.12a as

$$\mathbf{I}_2 = \mathbf{V}_2/(1+j1) = 3.63\angle-28.1°\text{ A}$$
$$\mathbf{I}_3 = \mathbf{V}_2/(3-j4) = 1.03\angle70°\text{ A}$$

A quick check will show that $\mathbf{I}_2 + \mathbf{I}_3 = \mathbf{I}_1$. Knowing $\mathbf{I}_3$, the voltage $\mathbf{V}_3$ can be determined as

$$\mathbf{V}_3 = 3\mathbf{I}_3 = 3.09\angle70°\text{ V}$$

Although we have now found all the currents and voltages in the circuit, it is instructive to show that we could have determined $\mathbf{I}_2$ and $\mathbf{I}_3$ using current division, and we could have found $\mathbf{V}_2$ and $\mathbf{V}_3$ using voltage division. With reference to the equivalent circuit in Figure 5.12c, the current $\mathbf{I}_1$ splits as follows:

$$\mathbf{I}_2 = \mathbf{I}_1(3-j4)/[1+j1+3-j4] = 3.63\angle-28.1°\text{ A}$$
$$\mathbf{I}_3 = \mathbf{I}_1(1+j1)/[1+j1+3-j4] = 1.03\angle70°\text{ A}$$

Consider now the equivalent circuit in Figure 5.12d, where $\mathbf{Z}_{23}$ represents the equivalent impedance as indicated in Figure 5.9.

$$\mathbf{V}_2 = 12\angle0°\ \mathbf{Z}_{23}/[2+\mathbf{Z}_{23}] = (12\angle0°)(1.414\angle28.74°)/[2+1.414\angle28.74°] = 5.13\angle16.9°\text{ V}$$

Knowing $\mathbf{V}_2$, voltage division can be applied a second time to yield $\mathbf{V}_3$, as shown in Figure 5.12e.
$$\mathbf{V}_3 = \mathbf{V}_2(3)/[3-j4] = 3.09\angle70°\text{ V}$$

It is interesting to note that the voltage $\mathbf{V}_3$ could have been calculated by applying voltage division twice and the process would never have required the calculation of any current!

Example 5.7 is essentially the reverse of the previous example in that we are given the output voltage and asked to find the value of the source voltage that would generate this output.

Given that the value of the output voltage in the network in Figure 5.13a is $V_0 = 6\angle0°$ V, let us determine the value of the source voltage.

Example 5.7

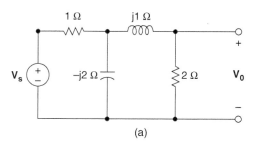
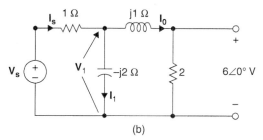

(a)   (b)

FIGURE 5.13   Circuit used in Example 5.7

The network is redrawn in Figure 5.13b in order to label all currents and voltages required for our analysis. Since the voltage across the 2 Ω resistor is $6\angle0°$ V, Ohm's law indicates the current I_0 is

$$I_0 = 6\angle0°/2 = 3\angle0° \text{ A}$$

Then KVL can be used to determine the voltage V_1 as

$$V_1 = j1(3\angle0°) + 6\angle0° = 6 + j3 \text{ V}$$

Using Ohm's law, I_1 is then

$$I_1 = V_1/-j2 = -1.5 + j3 \text{ A}$$

Now knowing I_1 and I_0 we can use KCL to determine I_S

$$I_S = -1.5 + j3 + 3 = 1.5 + j3 \text{ A}$$

And finally

$$V_S = (1)(I_S) + V_1 = 7.5 + j6 = 9.61\angle38.66° \text{ V}$$

Given the network in Figure 5.14a, we wish to calculate the output voltage, V_0, using (a) nodal analysis, (b) loop analysis, (c) superposition, and (d) Thevenin's theorem.

Example 5.8

(a) The network is redrawn in Figure 5.14b to illustrate the supernode. Note there are three nodes; therefore, we need two linearly independent equations to determine the two unknown node voltages V_1 and V_0. The constraint equation for the supernode obtained via the KVL equation

$$-V_1 - 12\angle0° + V_0 = 0$$

is

$$V_1 = V_0 - 12\angle0°$$

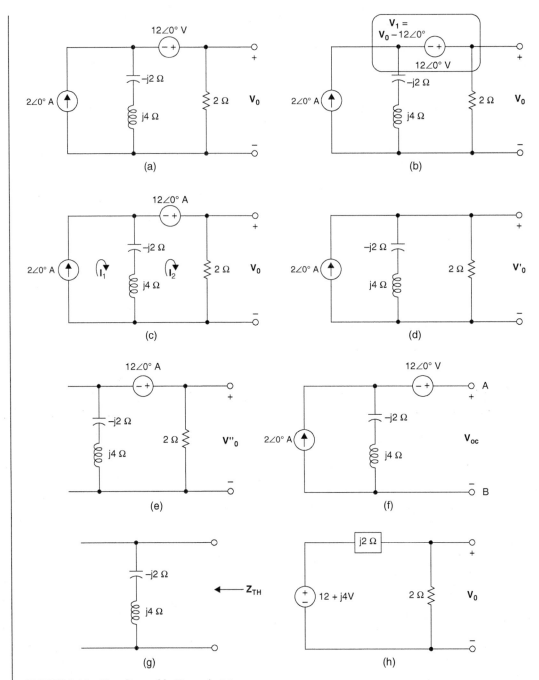

FIGURE 5.14 Circuits used in Example 5.8

which is one of our two linearly independent equations. The remaining equation is obtained by applying KCL at the supernode and summing the currents that leave this node:

$$-2\angle 0° + V_1/(j4 - j2) + V_0/2 = 0$$

Combining the equations yields

$$-2\angle 0° + [V_0 - 12\angle 0°]/(j2) + V_0/2 = 0$$

Solving this equation for V_0 yields

$$V_0(1 - j1) = 4 - j12$$

And finally

$$V_0 = 8.94\angle - 25.57° \text{ V}$$

(b) The circuit in Figure 5.14c illustrates the mesh currents selected for analysis. There are two window panes; therefore we need two linearly independent equations to determine the two mesh currents. Since the current I_1 is chosen to go directly through the current source, one of our equations is $I_1 = 2\angle 0°$. The KVL equation for the remaining loop is

$$(I_2 - I_1)(j4 - j2) - 12\angle 0° + 2I_2 = 0$$

then

$$(I_2 - 2\angle 0°)(j2) - 12\angle 0° + 2I_2 = 0$$

Combining terms yields

$$(2 + j2)I_2 = 12 + j4$$

And then

$$I_2 = 4.47\angle -26.57° \text{ A}$$

And since $V_0 = 2I_2$,

$$V_0 = 8.94\angle -26.57° \text{ V}$$

(c) In applying superposition, we determine the contribution of each source operating independently and then algebraically add the results to obtain V_0. The circuit in Figure 5.14d will yield the current source's contribution to V_0, which we label as V_0'. Note that the voltage source has been made zero by replacing it with a short circuit. V_0' is simply the voltage across the parallel passive elements, i.e.

$$V_0' = (2\angle 0°)[(2)(j2)/(2 + j2)] = j8/(2 + j2) \text{ V}$$

The circuit in Figure 5.14e will yield the voltage source's contribution to V_0, which we will call V_0''. Because the circuit is a single loop with one source, we can apply voltage division as follows:

$$V_0'' = (12\angle 0°)[2/(2 + j4 - j2)] = 24/(2 + j2) \text{ V}$$

Now $V_0 = V_0' + V_0''$ and therefore

$$V_0 = (24 + j8)/(2 + j2) = 8.94\angle -26.57° \text{ V}$$

(d) In applying Thevenin's theorem, we will break the network into two parts, one is the 2 Ω resistor and the other is the remaining elements in the circuit. We will form the Thevenin equivalent circuit for the network in Figure 5.14f by replacing it with a voltage source equal to the open-circuit voltage at the terminals A–B in series with the Thevenin equivalent impedance obtained by calculating the impedance seen looking into the terminals A–B with all sources made zero. Note that the only path for the current is through the impedance, and then applying KVL to the right loop yields

$$-2\angle 0°(j4 - j2) - 12\angle 0° + \mathbf{V}_{OC} = 0$$

And thus

$$\mathbf{V}_{OC} = 12 + j4 \text{ V}$$

The Thevenin equivalent impedance is obtained from the network in Figure 5.14g as

$$\mathbf{Z}_{TH} = j2 \text{ } \Omega$$

Now, replacing the network in Figure 5.14f with the Thevenin equivalent network and reconnecting the 2 Ω resistor yields the circuit in Figure 5.14h. The voltage $\mathbf{V}_0$ is easily determined using a voltage divider as

$$\mathbf{V}_0 = (12 + j4)[2/(2 + j2)] = 8.94\angle -26.57° \text{ V}$$

Example 5.9

Let us determine all the node voltages in the network in Figure 5.15a.

Since we are interested in the node voltages, we will use nodal analysis. The network is redrawn in Figure 5.15b to illustrate the presence of a supernode and the dependence of the controlled voltage source. The equations for $\mathbf{V}_1$, $\mathbf{V}_2$, and the dependent source are as follows:

$$(\mathbf{V}_1 - \mathbf{V}_2)/1 + 2\angle 0° + (\mathbf{V}_1 - 6\angle 0°)/1 + (\mathbf{V}_1 - 6\angle 0° - 2\mathbf{V}_X)/-j = 0$$
$$(\mathbf{V}_2 - \mathbf{V}_1)/l + (\mathbf{V}_2 - 2\mathbf{V}_X)/1 + \mathbf{V}_2/l = 0$$
$$\mathbf{V}_X = \mathbf{V}_1 - \mathbf{V}_2$$

Combining the equations yields

$$(2 - j)\mathbf{V}_1 + (-1 + j2)\mathbf{V}_2 = 4 + j6$$
$$-3\mathbf{V}_1 + 5\mathbf{V}_2 = 0$$

In matrix form, the equations are

$$\begin{bmatrix} (2 - j) & (-1 + j2) \\ -3 & 5 \end{bmatrix} \begin{bmatrix} \mathbf{V}_1 \\ \mathbf{V}_2 \end{bmatrix} = \begin{bmatrix} 4 + j6 \\ 0 \end{bmatrix}$$

The determinant is

$$\text{Delta} = (2 - j)(5) - (-3)(-1 + j2)$$
$$= 10 - j5 - 3 + j6$$
$$= 7 + j$$

Then

$$\begin{bmatrix} \mathbf{V}_1 \\ \mathbf{V}_2 \end{bmatrix} = 1/(7 + j) \begin{bmatrix} 5 & 1 - j2 \\ 3 & 2 - j \end{bmatrix} \begin{bmatrix} 4 + j6 \\ 0 \end{bmatrix} = 1/(7 + j) \begin{bmatrix} 20 + j30 \\ 12 + j18 \end{bmatrix}$$

And therefore,

$$\mathbf{V}_1 = [(20 + j30)/(7 + j)]$$
$$\mathbf{V}_2 = [(12 + 18)/(7 + j)]$$

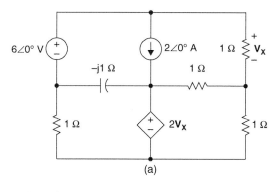

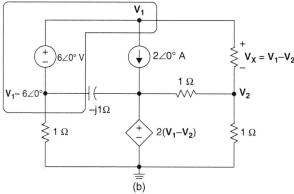

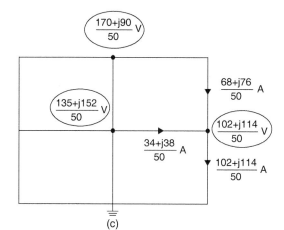

FIGURE 5.15   Circuit used in Example 5.9

Rationalizing, these expressions yield

$$\mathbf{V}_1 = [(20 + j30)/(7 + j)][(7 - j)/(7 - j)]$$
$$= (170 + j190)/50 \text{ V}$$
$$\mathbf{V}_2 = [(12 + 18)/(7 + j)][(7 - j)/(7 - j)]$$
$$= (102 + j114)/50 \text{ V}$$

The unknown node voltage that is part of the supernode is

$$\mathbf{V}_1 - 6\angle0° = (-130 + j190)/50 \text{ V}$$

The controlling variable for the dependent source is

$$\mathbf{V_x} = \mathbf{V_1} - \mathbf{V_2}$$
$$= (170 + j190)/50 - (102 + j114)/50$$
$$= (68 + j76)/50 \text{ V}$$

Therefore, the dependent source voltage is

$$2\mathbf{V_x} = (136 + j152)/50 \text{ V}$$

The stick diagram, shown in Figure 5.15c, indicates that KCL is satisfied at the node labeled $\mathbf{V_2}$, providing us with some confidence that our solution is correct. By carrying the fractions through the analysis, rather than converting into decimals, accuracy in the calculations is assured.

Example 5.10

Let us use loop analysis to determine all the loop currents in the network in Figure 5.15a.

The network is redrawn in Figure 5.16a to illustrate the selection of the loop currents. Note that we have drawn the current $\mathbf{I_1}$ directly through the current source, and, therefore, one of our four linearly independent equations is $\mathbf{I_1} = 2\angle0°$. The remaining loop equations are

$$-6 + 1\mathbf{I_2} + 1\mathbf{I_2} - 1\mathbf{I_4} - j(\mathbf{I_2} + \mathbf{I_1} - \mathbf{I_3}) = 0$$
$$\mathbf{I_3} - j(\mathbf{I_3} - \mathbf{I_1} - \mathbf{I_2}) + 2\mathbf{V_x} = 0$$
$$-2\mathbf{V_x} + 1\mathbf{I_4} - 1\mathbf{I_2} + 1\mathbf{I_4} = 0$$
$$\mathbf{V_x} = 1\mathbf{I_2}$$

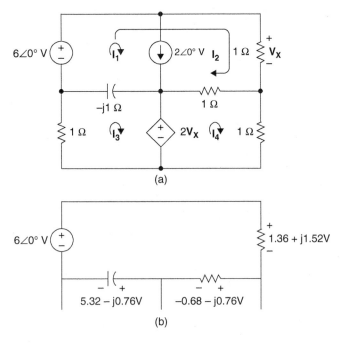

(a)

FIGURE 5.16   Circuit used in Example 5.10

(b)

Combining the equations yields

$$(2 - j)I_2 + jI_3 - I_4 = 6 + j2$$
$$(2 + j)I_2 + (1 - j)I_3 = -j2$$
$$-3I_2 + 2I_4 = 0$$

In matrix form, the equations are

$$\begin{bmatrix} 2-j & j & -1 \\ 2+j & 1-j & 0 \\ -3 & 0 & 2 \end{bmatrix} \begin{bmatrix} I_2 \\ I_3 \\ I_4 \end{bmatrix} = \begin{bmatrix} 6+j2 \\ -j2 \\ 0 \end{bmatrix}$$

Because of the complexity of these equations, we will employ MATLAB to generate a solution.

The MATLAB printout for these equations is as follows.

```
>> R = [2 - i i - 1; 2 + i 1 - i 0; -3 0 2]

        2.0000 - 1.0000i         0 + 1.0000i     -1.0000
R =     2.0000 + 1.0000i    1.0000 - 1.0000i           0
       -3.0000                            0      2.0000

>> V = [6 + i * 2; -i * 2; 0]

        6.0000 + 2.0000i
V =          0 - 2.0000i
                      0

>> I = inv(R) * V

        1.3600 + 1.5200i
I =     2.6000 - 3.8000i
        2.0400 + 2.2800i
```

The diagram, shown in Figure 5.16b, displays a loop in the network in Figure 5.16a, which is employed to check KVL. Note that the current flowing right to left in the $-j1\ \Omega$ capacitor is $I_1 - I_3$ and the current in the $1\ \Omega$ resistor between loop 1 and loop 4, right to left, is $I_2 - I_4$. Therefore, the KVL equation for this loop is

$$-6\angle 0° + 1I_2 + 1(I_2 - I_4) - j1\,(I_1 - I_3) = 0$$
$$-6 + 1.36 + j1.52 + 1(1.36 + j1.52 - 2.04 - j2.28) - j(2 - 2.6 + j3.8) = 0$$
$$0 = 0$$

Thus, KVL is satisfied; since this loop involves every loop current, we believe the solution obtained is correct.

Let us use Thevenin's theorem to determine the voltage V_0 in the network in Figure 5.17a.   **Example 5.11**

First, we break the network into two pieces, one of which is the resistor that produces the output voltage, and the other is the remaining portion of the network, which is shown in Figure 5.17b. Although the open-circuit voltage, V_{OC}, can be determined in a variety of ways, we will use loop analysis because the presence of the current source will make this process easier.

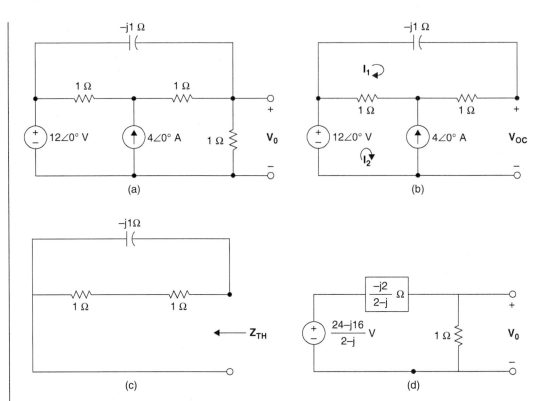

FIGURE 5.17   Circuits used in Example 5.11

The two KVL equations for the network are

$$-jI_1 + 1I_1 + 1(I_1 - I_2) = 0$$
$$I_2 = -4$$

Substituting the second equation into the first yields

$$I_1 = -4/(2 - j) \text{ A}$$

Now that I_1 is known, the KVL equation for the outer loop is

$$-12 - j[-4/(2 - j)] + V_{OC} = 0$$

Then

$$V_{OC} = 12 + j[-4/(2 - j)]$$
$$= (24 - j16)/(2 - j) \text{ V}$$

The Thevenin equivalent impedance is determined from the circuit in Figure 5.17c, which is equivalent to the network in Figure 5.17b with the sources made zero. Therefore, Z_{TH} is the parallel combination of the capacitor and an equivalent 2 Ω resistor, i.e.

$$Z_{TH} = (2)(-j)/(2 - j)$$
$$= -j2/(2 - j) \text{ Ω}$$

The Thevenin equivalent circuit with the load resistor reattached is shown in Figure 5.17d. The voltage V_0 can be determined via a simple voltage divider as

$$V_0 = (V_{OC})(1)/(1 + Z_{TH})$$
$$= [(24 - j16)/(2 - j)]/[1 - j2/(2 - j)]$$
$$= (24 - j16)/(2 - j3)$$

Rationalizing this fraction

$$V_0 = [(24 - j16)/(2 - j3)][(2 + j3)/(2 + j3)]$$
$$= (96 + j40)/13$$
$$= 7.38 + 3.08 \text{ V}$$

5.1 Determine the frequency of the two voltages and the phase angle between them.

$$v_1(t) = 6\cos[2513.3t - 60°] \text{ V}$$
$$v_2(t) = 12\cos[2513.3t + 20°] \text{ V}$$

5.2 Determine the frequency of the two voltages and the phase angle between them.

$$v_1(t) = 12\sin[628.3t - 60°] \text{ V}$$
$$v_2(t) = 6\cos[628.3t - 40°] \text{ V}$$

5.3 Find i(t) in the network in Figure P5.3.

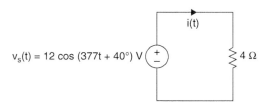

$v_s(t) = 12 \cos (377t + 40°)$ V

i(t)

4 Ω

FIGURE P5.3

5.4 Find the voltage V_S in the circuit in Figure P5.4.

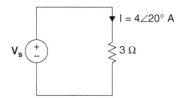

$I = 4\angle20°$ A

V_s

3 Ω

FIGURE P5.4

5.5 Find i(t) in the circuit in Figure P5.5.

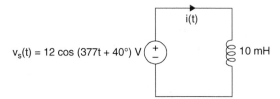

$v_s(t) = 12 \cos (377t + 40°)$ V

i(t)

10 mH

FIGURE P5.5

5.6 Determine i(t) in the network in Figure P5.6.

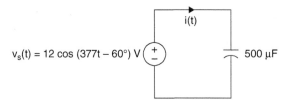

$v_s(t) = 12 \cos (377t - 60°)$ V

i(t)

500 μF

FIGURE P5.6

5.7 In the circuit in Figure P5.7, find $\mathbf{Z_{AB}}$ at a frequency of 60 Hz.

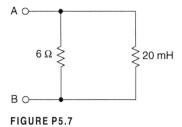

A

6 Ω   20 mH

B

FIGURE P5.7

5.8 Given the circuit in Figure P5.8, determine the impedance $\mathbf{Z_{AB}}$ at a frequency of 60 Hz.

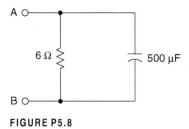

A

6 Ω   500 μF

B

FIGURE P5.8

5.9   Find $\mathbf{Z_{AB}}$ at 60 Hz for the network in Figure P5.9.

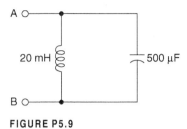

A

20 mH

500 μF

B

FIGURE P5.9

5.10   Determine the admittance at the terminals A–B for the network in Figure P5.10.

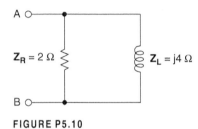

A

$\mathbf{Z_R} = 2\ \Omega$

$\mathbf{Z_L} = j4\ \Omega$

B

FIGURE P5.10

5.11   Determine the admittance at the terminals A–B for the network in Figure P5.11.

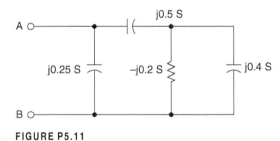

j0.5 S

A

j0.25 S

−j0.2 S

j0.4 S

B

FIGURE P5.11

5.12   Given the circuit in Figure P5.12, find the impedance $\mathbf{Z_{AB}}$.

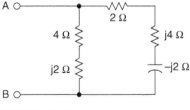

A

2 Ω

4 Ω

j4 Ω

j2 Ω

−j2 Ω

B

FIGURE P5.12

5.13 Given the circuit in Figure P5.13, find the impedance $\mathbf{Z}_{AB}$.

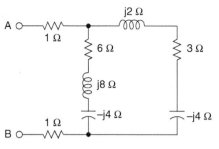

FIGURE P5.13

5.14 Find the impedance at the terminals A–B for the circuit in Figure P5.14.

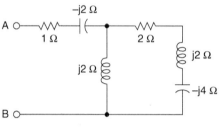

FIGURE P5.14

5.15 Find the impedance at the terminals A–B for the circuit in Figure P5.15.

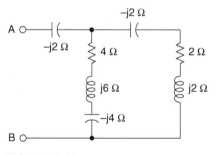

FIGURE P5.15

5.16 Find the impedance at the terminals A–B for the circuit in Figure P5.16.

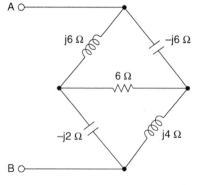

FIGURE P5.16

5.17 Find the impedance at the terminals A–B for the circuit in Figure P5.17.

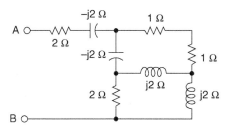

FIGURE P5.17

5.18 Determine the impedance at the terminals of the network in Figure P5.18 if the frequency is 60 Hz.

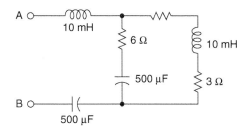

FIGURE P5.18

5.19 Calculate the impedance at the terminals of the circuit in Figure P5.19.

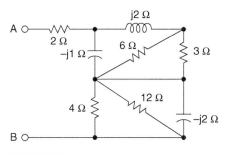

FIGURE P5.19

5.20 Find V_0 in the network in Figure P5.20.

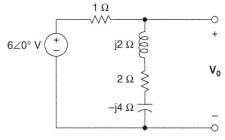

FIGURE P5.20

5.21 Find V_0 in the network in Figure P5.21.

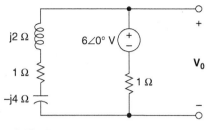

FIGURE P5.21

5.22 Find I_0 in the network in Figure P5.22.

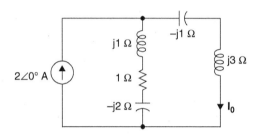

FIGURE P5.22

5.23 Find I_0 in the network in Figure P5.23.

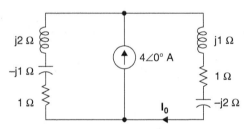

FIGURE P5.23

5.24 Find **I** in the network in Figure P5.24.

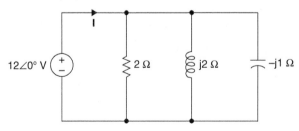

FIGURE P5.24

5.25   Find **I** in the network in Figure P5.25.

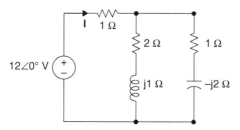

FIGURE P5.25

5.26   Calculate all the voltages in the circuit in Figure P5.26 and draw a phasor diagram illustrating their relationship to one another.

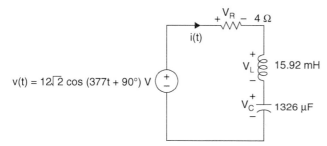

FIGURE P5.26

5.27   Draw a phasor diagram for the voltages and current in the network in Figure P5.27

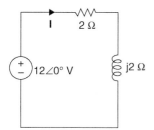

FIGURE P5.27

5.28   Draw a phasor diagram for the voltage and currents in the network in Figure P5.28.

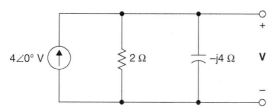

FIGURE P5.28

5.29 Given the circuit in Figure P5.29, find $i_0(t)$ and $v_0(t)$ if $v_S(t) = 120 \cos 5000t$ V.

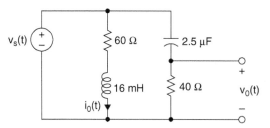

FIGURE P5.29

5.30 Find all the currents and voltages in the network in Figure P5.30. Then draw a phasor diagram to show that $I = I_1 + I_2$ and $V_1 + V_2 = V_3$.

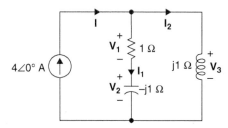

FIGURE P5.30

5.31 Find all the currents and the output voltage in the network in Figure P5.31. Then sketch a phasor diagram for the currents.

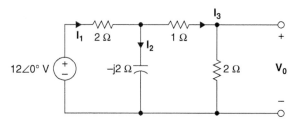

FIGURE P5.31

5.32 Find the current I_0 in the network in Figure P5.32.

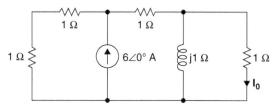

FIGURE P5.32

5.33   Find the current voltage $\mathbf{V_s}$ in the network in Figure P5.33.

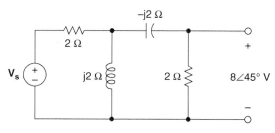

FIGURE P5.33

5.34   Use nodal analysis to find $\mathbf{I_0}$ in the network in Figure P5.34.

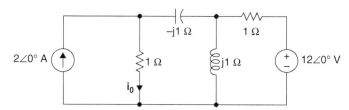

FIGURE P5.34

5.35   Use loop analysis to find $\mathbf{I_0}$ in the network in Figure P5.34.

5.36   Determine the voltage $\mathbf{V_0}$ in the circuit in Figure P5.36 using nodal analysis.

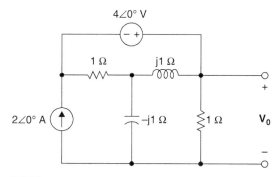

FIGURE P5.36

5.37   Determine the voltage $\mathbf{V_o}$ in the circuit in Figure P5.36 using mesh analysis.

5.38   Determine the voltage $\mathbf{V_o}$ in the circuit in Figure P5.36 using superposition.

5.39   Determine the voltage $\mathbf{V_o}$ in the circuit in Figure P5.36 using Thevenin's theorem.

5.40   Determine the current $\mathbf{I_0}$ in the circuit in Figure P5.34 using superposition.

5.41   Determine the current $\mathbf{I_0}$ in the circuit in Figure P5.34 using Thevenin's theorem.

5.42 Find $\mathbf{V_0}$ in the circuit in Figure P5.42 using nodal analysis. Check your answers using MATLAB.

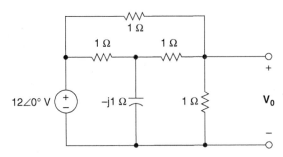

FIGURE P5.42

5.43 Determine the voltage $\mathbf{V_0}$ in the circuit in Figure P5.43 using nodal analysis.

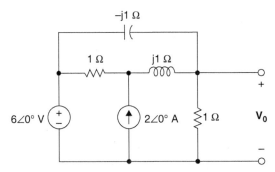

FIGURE P5.43

5.44 Determine the voltage $\mathbf{V_0}$ in the circuit in Figure P5.43 using loop analysis.

5.45 Determine the voltage $\mathbf{V_0}$ in the circuit in Figure P5.43 using superposition.

5.46 Determine the voltage $\mathbf{V_0}$ in the circuit in Figure P5.43 using Thevenin's theorem.

5.47 Determine the voltage $\mathbf{V_0}$ in the circuit in Figure P5.47 using nodal analysis.

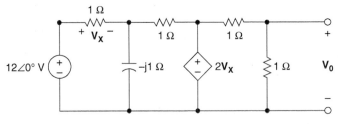

FIGURE P5.47

5.48   Determine the voltage V_0 in the circuit in Figure P5.48 using loop analysis.

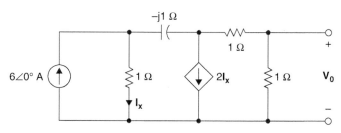

FIGURE P5.48

5.49   Given the network in Figure P5.49, use MATLAB to determine the current I_0 and the voltage V_0.

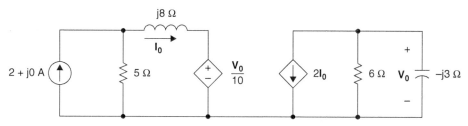

FIGURE P5.49

5.50   Use MATLAB to find the equivalent impedance, Z_S, seen by the source V_S in the circuit in Figure P5.50.

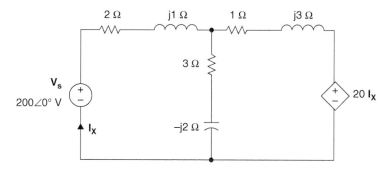

FIGURE P5.50

CHAPTER 6

Variable-frequency Network Characteristics

LEARNING OBJECTIVES

- To understand the concept of sinusoidal frequency response
- To learn the basics of passive filters, including low pass, high pass, bandpass, and band elimination
- To understand the importance of resonance and be able to analyze resonant circuits, both series and parallel

In our analysis of circuits thus far, we first learned how to analyze circuits in which the sources, whether current or voltage, were all dc. Next, we considered the manner in which circuits, which contained a storage element, i.e. a capacitor or inductor, would react to a sudden change in the network caused by opening or closing a switch. Then, we analyzed circuits in which the forcing functions were all sinusoidal and the frequency of the sources was fixed at the frequency of the U.S. power grid, i.e. an alternating current of 60 Hz or 377 rad/s. In each case, we learned that Ohm's law, KCL, and KVL applied. At this point, we will consider the manner in which a network reacts when the variable is frequency, i.e. rather than having a fixed frequency, as was the case in ac steady-state analyses, how do the network characteristics change when frequency changes?

In the previous analyses, we found that the resistor's impedance is independent of the frequency at which the network is forced, i.e. a 5 Ω resistor has a resistance of 5 Ω regardless of the frequency. However, both the inductor and capacitor impedances are frequency dependent. Therefore, if the frequency of the sources in the network changes, so do the values of $\mathbf{Z_L}$ and $\mathbf{Z_C}$. Therefore, it would at least appear that changes in network frequency could have a dramatic effect on the performance of the network. The following material will demonstrate just how the network characteristics change when frequency changes.

SINUSOIDAL FREQUENCY RESPONSE

Many networks are specifically designed to operate at a single frequency, e.g. those connected to the U.S. power grid operate continuously at a frequency of 60 Hz. In contrast, the tuning circuits within a radio receiver operate across a wide range of frequencies in order to access radio stations across the AM or FM frequency bands.

For a moment, let us examine the impedances of both the inductor and capacitor. Since

$$\mathbf{Z_L} = j\omega L = \omega L \angle 90°$$

we see that although the phase is constant at 90°, the magnitude of the impedance is directly proportional to frequency. In fact, the magnitude is zero at dc, indicating that the inductor looks like a short circuit at dc—a fact we employed earlier in our study of transient analysis. In a similar manner, the impedance of the capacitor is

$$\mathbf{Z_C} = 1/j\omega C = 1/\omega C \angle -90°$$

In this case, the phase is constant at $-90°$, and the magnitude of the impedance is inversely proportional to frequency. Note that the magnitude is infinite at dc, indicating that the capacitor looks like an open circuit at dc, which again is a fact we employed to our advantage in transient analysis.

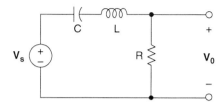

FIGURE 6.1   A series RLC circuit

In order to illustrate the frequency dependence of variables within the network, consider the circuit in Figure 6.1. Using a simple voltage divider, the V_0 (jω) can be written as

$$\frac{\mathbf{V_0}}{\mathbf{V_S}}(j\omega) = \frac{R}{R + j\omega L + \dfrac{1}{j\omega C}}$$

Or

$$\frac{\mathbf{V_0}}{\mathbf{V_S}}(j\omega) = \frac{(j\omega)\dfrac{R}{L}}{(j\omega)^2 + (j\omega)\dfrac{R}{L} + \dfrac{1}{LC}}$$

Note that for every value of ω, the *transfer function*, i.e. the ratio of output to input, has both a magnitude and a phase. For example, if the network parameters R, L, and C are given, then a specific value of frequency will yield a complex number consisting of a magnitude and a phase, which can be expressed in the general form as

$$\frac{\mathbf{V_0}}{\mathbf{V_S}}(j\omega) = |\mathbf{H}(j\omega)| \angle\phi(j\omega)$$

Example 6.1 will illustrate the manner in which network characteristics change as the frequency is varied over some range of values.

For the network in Figure 6.1, let us assume the circuit parameters are R = 12k Ω, L = 100 mH, and C = 278 nF. Given these values for the network parameters, let us determine the transfer function, i.e. the voltage gain, and plot this function as frequency is varied from 0 to 10^7 rad/s.

As indicated earlier, the transfer function, which relates the output to the input, is given by the expression

$$\frac{\mathbf{V_0}}{\mathbf{V_S}}(j\omega) = \frac{(j\omega)\dfrac{R}{L}}{(j\omega)^2 + (j\omega)\dfrac{R}{L} + \dfrac{1}{LC}}$$

Substituting the values for R, L, and C into this expression yields

$$\frac{\mathbf{V_0}}{\mathbf{V_S}}(j\omega) = \frac{120{,}000j\omega}{(j\omega)^2 + 120{,}000j\omega + (36)10^6}$$

From this expression, we are able to calculate the magnitude and phase of this transfer function for every value of ω. For example, if $\omega = 1000$ rad/s, then

$$\frac{\mathbf{V_0}}{\mathbf{V_s}}(\text{j } 1000) = \frac{120 \times 10^6 \text{ j}}{(\text{j } 1000)^2 + 120 \times 10^6 \text{ j} + 36 \times 10^6}$$

$$= 0.96 \ \angle 16.26°$$

Note that for each new value of the frequency, the transfer function may produce a different magnitude and phase. If we sweep the frequency over the range from 0 to 10^7 rad/s, as shown in the magnitude and phase plots in Figure 6.2, we obtain what is typically called the *frequency response* of the network. Given these two graphs, a vertical line through the two graphs at the same frequency will yield the magnitude and phase of the transfer function at that specific frequency. In addition, the plots provide a quick look at how this network will respond to changes as the frequency is varied across the *frequency spectrum*.

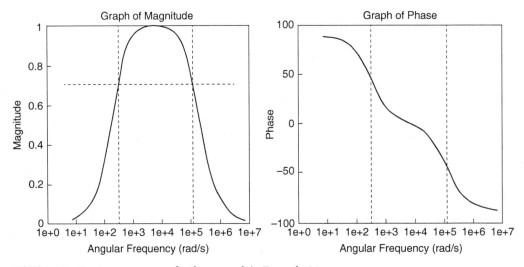

FIGURE 6.2 Frequency response for the network in Example 6.1

As the magnitude and phase plots indicate, at low frequencies the magnitude is zero, rises to a maximum, is flat over the center frequency range, and then decreases to zero at high frequencies. The phase starts at +90° at low frequencies and methodically decreases to −90° at high frequencies.

In general, the network's response to some input is called a *network function*, or a transfer function, and is the ratio of the response of the network to the particular input function. There are actually four types of transfer functions, generally labeled as $\mathbf{H}(\text{j}\omega)$ and they are

$$\mathbf{G_V}(\text{j}\omega) = \frac{\mathbf{V_0}}{\mathbf{V_s}}(\text{j}\omega)$$

$$\mathbf{G_I}(\text{j}\omega) = \frac{\mathbf{I_0}}{\mathbf{I_s}}(\text{j}\omega)$$

$$\mathbf{Z}(j\omega) = \frac{V_0}{I_s}(j\omega)$$

$$\mathbf{Y}(j\omega) = \frac{I_0}{V_s}(j\omega)$$

And as indicated in the previous example, all these transfer functions are of the form

$$\mathbf{H}(j\omega) = |\mathbf{H}(j\omega)| \angle \phi\,(j\omega)$$

Let us express the following function in the general form of the transfer function as a combination of magnitude and phase.

Example 6.2

$$\mathbf{H}(j\omega) = \frac{10(j\omega + 1)}{(2 + j\omega)(3 + j\omega)}$$

First of all, the function is placed in the following form:

$$\mathbf{H}(j\omega) = \frac{\dfrac{10}{6}(1 + j\omega)}{\left(1 + \dfrac{j\omega}{2}\right)\left(1 + \dfrac{j\omega}{3}\right)}$$

And then the magnitude is expressed as

$$|\mathbf{H}(j\omega)| = \frac{\dfrac{10}{6}\sqrt{1 + \omega^2}}{\sqrt{1 + \left(\dfrac{\omega}{2}\right)^2}\sqrt{1 + \left(\dfrac{\omega}{3}\right)^2}}$$

And the phase is

$$\phi(j\omega) = \tan^{-1}\frac{\omega}{1} - \tan^{-1}\frac{\omega}{2} - \tan^{-1}\frac{\omega}{3}$$

As the previous analysis indicates, a transfer function can be expressed in general as the ratio of two polynomials:

$$\mathbf{H}(j\omega) = \frac{a_n(j\omega)^n + a_{n-1}(j\omega)^{n-1} + \cdots + a_0}{b_m(j\omega)^m + b_{m-1}(j\omega)^{m-1} + \cdots + b_0}$$

Since the values of the circuit parameters are real numbers, the coefficients of the polynomials are also real numbers. In factored form, the equation can be expressed as

$$\mathbf{H}(j\omega) = \frac{K(j\omega - z_1)(j\omega - z_2)\dots}{(j\omega - p_1)(j\omega - p_2)\dots}$$

In this form, K is a constant, the numerator has m roots and the denominator has n roots. The roots of the numerator are called *zeros*, since if $j\omega = z_1, z_2, \dots$, the entire function will be zero. The roots of the denominator are called *poles* and if $j\omega = p_1, p_2, \dots$, the entire function becomes infinite. The roots of the polynomials may be complex; however, since the polynomial coefficients are real numbers, complex roots will occur in complex conjugate pairs of the form $-a - jb$ and $-a + jb$. Note that the transfer function in Example 6.2 has one zero at $j\omega = -1$ and two poles, one at $j\omega = -2$ and one at $j\omega = -3$.

This format is important for many reasons. For example, the performance of any dynamic system is governed by the poles of the system's transfer function. We have already gotten a glimpse of this relationship when we examined second-order transient circuits and found that the response could be overdamped, underdamped, or critically damped depending upon the network's poles, i.e. were they real and unequal, real and equal or complex conjugates.

Let us now demonstrate the importance of understanding the manner in which frequency impacts network performance.

PASSIVE FILTER NETWORKS

As the word *filter* implies, filter networks are used to pass signals in a specific frequency range and reject signals outside that range. If the networks are passive, they are constructed with R, L, and C components, i.e. there are no active devices present, such as transistors. Filters find wide application in electronic systems. For example, the human ear can hear frequencies in the range of 50–15,000 Hz. However, voice is typically transmitted in the 0–4000 Hz range. Therefore, noise that is present in the hearing range but not part of the conversation must be removed in order to prevent the message from being distorted.

Filter networks are typically classified into four types: *low pass, high pass, bandpass*, and *band elimination* or *band rejection*. When the filter is designed to eliminate one specific frequency, it is normally called a *notch*. The names by which the filters are identified describe the properties of the filter, e.g. a low-pass filter is designed to pass low frequencies and reject high frequencies, a high-pass filter passes high-frequency signal components and rejects low frequencies, etc.

LOW-PASS FILTERS

The circuit shown in Figure 6.3 is a simple example of a low-pass filter. Using a simple voltage divider, the filter output can be expressed as

$$\mathbf{V_0}(j\omega) = \left[\frac{\frac{1}{j\omega C}}{R + \frac{1}{j\omega C}} \right] \mathbf{V_S}(j\omega)$$

or as a voltage transfer function

$$\mathbf{G_V}(j\omega) = \frac{1}{1 + j\omega RC}$$

where the magnitude and phase of the transfer function are

$$|\mathbf{G_V}(j\omega)| = \frac{1}{\sqrt{1 + (\omega RC)^2}}$$

$$\phi(j\omega) = -\tan^{-1}\frac{\omega RC}{1}$$

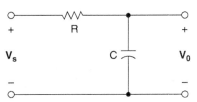

FIGURE 6.3   A simple low-pass filter

where we have simply used the fact that a complex number of the form a + jb has a magnitude of $[a^2 + b^2]^{1/2}$ and a phase of $\tan^{-1} b/a$.

The frequency at which $\omega = 1/RC$ is called the *break frequency* or the *half-power frequency*. At this frequency,

$$|\mathbf{G_V}(j\omega)| = \frac{1}{\sqrt{1+1}} = \frac{1}{\sqrt{2}}$$

and

$$\phi(j\omega) = -\tan^{-1} 1 = -45°$$

This half-power frequency designation refers to the fact that if the voltage or current is $1/\sqrt{2}$ of its maximum value, then the power, derived by squaring either term, is one half of the maximum value.

The magnitude characteristic for the low-pass filter is shown in Figure 6.4. Note that the low-frequency signal components are essentially passed right through the filter, i.e. the transfer function is essentially 1. However, the high-frequency signal components are attenuated and thus essentially blocked from reaching the output, and furthermore at very high frequencies the transfer function is essentially 0. The viable range of the filter is from $\omega = 0$ to $\omega = 1/RC$, and this range is called the *bandwidth* or *pass band* of the filter.

HIGH-PASS FILTERS

A simple high-pass filter is shown in Figure 6.5. Note the resemblance between the low-pass and high-pass filter architectures. The operation of this filter can once again be explained by noting the impedance of the capacitor at both low and high frequencies. At high frequencies, the impedance of the capacitor is very small, and thus it tends to provide a short-circuit path for high-frequency components in the signal as they transverse the filter. However, at low frequencies, the capacitor's impedance is very high thus blocking low frequencies from reaching the output.

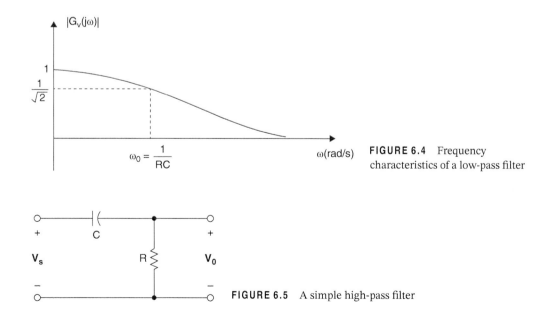

FIGURE 6.4 Frequency characteristics of a low-pass filter

FIGURE 6.5 A simple high-pass filter

Once again, a simple voltage divider can be used to determine the transfer function for this filter.

$$\mathbf{G_V}(j\omega) = \frac{j\omega RC}{1 + j\omega RC}$$

And the magnitude and phase are

$$|\mathbf{G_V}(j\omega)| = \frac{\omega RC}{\sqrt{1 + (\omega RC)^2}}$$

$$\phi(j\omega) = 90° - \tan^{-1}\frac{\omega RC}{1}$$

The frequency characteristic for this filter is shown in Figure 6.6. In this case, the filter passes all frequencies above $\omega = 1/RC$ and rejects the frequencies below this value. Thus, the bandwidth of the high-pass filter extends from $\omega = 1/RC$ to infinity.

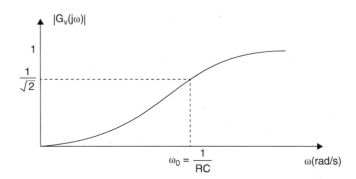

FIGURE 6.6   Frequency characteristic of a high-pass filter

BANDPASS FILTERS

A simple bandpass filter configuration is shown in Figure 6.7. The transfer function for this filter is

$$\mathbf{G_V}(j\omega) = \frac{R}{R + j\omega L + \dfrac{1}{j\omega C}}$$

which can be expressed as

$$\mathbf{G_V}(j\omega) = \frac{j\omega CR}{(\omega^2 LC - 1) + j\omega CR}$$

And then the magnitude of this function is

$$|\mathbf{G_V}(j\omega)| = \frac{\omega RC}{\sqrt{(\omega RC)^2 + (\omega^2 LC - 1)^2}}$$

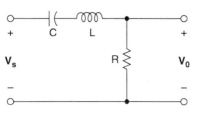

FIGURE 6.7   A simple bandpass filter

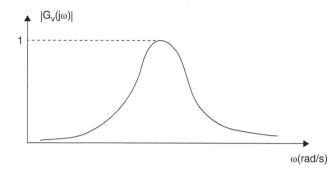

FIGURE 6.8 Frequency characteristic of a simple bandpass filter

There are several important points that can be gleaned from this expression. First, when $\omega^2 LC - 1 = 0$, the magnitude is 1. At the two ends of the frequency spectrum, i.e. $\omega = 0$ and $\omega = \infty$, the magnitude is 0. In the mid-band range, it can be shown that $(\omega LC)^2$ is much larger than $(\omega^2 LC - 1)$ and therefore $\mathbf{G_V}(j\omega)$ is approximately equal to 1. As a result, the frequency characteristic will be of the form shown in Figure 6.8.

Although we will not wade through the algebra (anyone interested will find it in *Basic Engineering Circuit Analysis, 12e*), it is straightforward but tedious to demonstrate that the equation

$$\frac{d|\mathbf{G_V}(j\omega)|}{d\omega} = 0$$

yields the peak, or center frequency, of the filter as

$$\omega_0 = \frac{1}{\sqrt{LC}}$$

The shape of the frequency characteristic indicates that there are two half-power frequencies that can be obtained from the equation

$$\mathbf{G_V}(j\omega) = \frac{1}{\sqrt{2}}$$

or equivalently

$$\frac{\omega RC}{\sqrt{(\omega RC)^2 + (\omega^2 LC - 1)^2}} = \frac{1}{\sqrt{2}}$$

Simplifying the algebra yields a quadratic equation in ω, and the two positive roots are ω_{LO} and ω_{HI},

$$\omega_{LO} = \frac{-\dfrac{R}{L} + \sqrt{\left(\dfrac{R}{L}\right)^2 + 4\omega_0^2}}{2}$$

$$\omega_{HI} = \frac{+\dfrac{R}{L} + \sqrt{\left(\dfrac{R}{L}\right)^2 + 4\omega_0^2}}{2}$$

The range between the half-power points is the bandwidth of the filter

$$BW = \omega_{HI} - \omega_{LO}$$
$$= \frac{R}{L}$$

Figure 6.9 illustrates the filter shape as well as the critical parameters that define the filter characteristics.

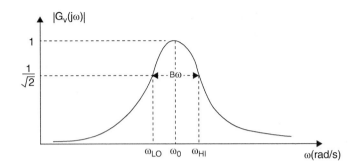

FIGURE 6.9 Illustration of the important frequencies in a bandpass filter

BAND ELIMINATION/REJECTION FILTERS

The band rejection filter, as the name implies, is employed to eliminate a range of frequencies. When the range consists of a single frequency, the filter is often called a notch. Two simple forms of this filter are shown in Figure 6.10, and the frequency characteristics are illustrated in Figure 6.11. The impedance of the parallel combination of inductor and capacitor, typically referred to as a tank circuit, in the filter in Figure 6.10a is

$$\mathbf{Z}_{LC} = \frac{(j\omega L)\left(\dfrac{1}{j\omega C}\right)}{(j\omega L) + \dfrac{1}{j\omega C}}$$

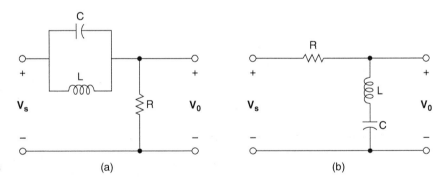

FIGURE 6.10 Simple band rejection filters

(a)   (b)

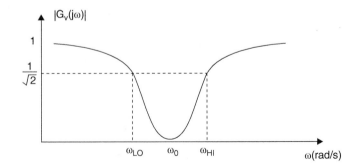

FIGURE 6.11 Frequency characteristics of a simple band rejection filter

or

$$\mathbf{Z}_{LC} = \frac{j\omega L}{-\omega^2 LC + 1}$$

Note that at the frequency $\omega^2 = 1/LC$, the impedance of this parallel combination is infinite, thus blocking any signal components at this frequency. In a similar manner, at the frequency $\omega^2 = 1/LC$, the impedance of the series combination of the inductor and capacitor is 0, thus effectively shorting any signal at this frequency from reaching the output.

The following examples will address the many salient features of these four types of passive filters.

Using a 10 μF capacitor, let us design a low-pass filter with a half-power frequency of $\omega_0 = 2$ kHz.   **Example 6.3**

Since

$$\omega_0 = \frac{1}{RC}$$

then

$$R = \frac{1}{\omega_0 C}$$

and

$$R = \frac{1}{(2\pi)(2000)(10 \times 10^{-6})}$$
$$= 8 \ \Omega$$

The filter is shown in Figure 6.12.

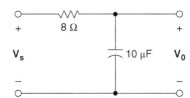

FIGURE 6.12   A low-pass filter design

Using the 10 μF capacitor in Example 6.3, let us design a high-pass filter with a half-power   **Example 6.4**
frequency of $\omega_0 = 20$ kHz.

Once again,

$$R = \frac{1}{\omega_0 C}$$
$$= \frac{1}{(2\pi)(20 \times 10^3)(10 \times 10^{-6})}$$
$$= 0.8 \ \Omega$$

And the filter is shown in Figure 6.13.

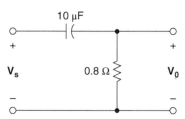

FIGURE 6.13 A high-pass filter design

Example 6.5

Let us once again employ the 10 μF capacitor to design a bandpass filter with a center frequency of 20 kHz and a bandwidth of 1 kHz.

At the center frequency

$$\omega_0 = \frac{1}{\sqrt{LC}}$$

or

$$L = \frac{1}{(2\pi)(20 \times 10^3)(10 \times 10^{-6})}$$
$$= 6.33 \,\mu\text{H}$$

The bandwidth is then

$$BW = \frac{R}{L}$$

And hence,

$$R = (2\pi \times 10^3)(6.33 \times 10^{-6})$$
$$= 0.039 \ \Omega$$

The resulting filter is shown in Figure 6.14.

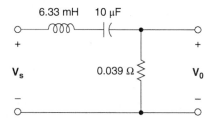

FIGURE 6.14 A bandpass filter design

Example 6.6

Given the bandpass filter in Figure 6.15, let us determine the center frequency, the two half-power frequencies, and the bandwidth.

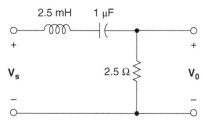

FIGURE 6.15 A bandpass filter

The center frequency is

$$\omega_0 = \frac{1}{\sqrt{LC}}$$

$$= \frac{1}{\sqrt{(3.5 \times 10^{-3})(1 \times 10^{-6})}}$$

$$= 20\,k\,rad/s$$

The lower half-power frequency is

$$\omega_{LO} = \frac{-\left(\dfrac{2.5}{2.5 \times 10^{-3}}\right) + \sqrt{\left(\dfrac{2.5}{2.5 \times 10^{-3}}\right)^2 + 4(20 \times 10^3)^2}}{2}$$

$$= \frac{-1000 + \sqrt{10^6 + 16 \times 10^8}}{2}$$

$$= \frac{-1000 + 40,000}{2}$$

$$= 19.5\,k\,rad/s$$

Thus, the upper half-power frequency is

$$\omega_{HI} = \frac{1000 + 40,000}{2}$$

$$= 20.5\,k\,rad/s$$

Finally, the bandwidth is

$$BW = \omega_{HI} - \omega_{LO}$$

$$= 1\,k\,rad/s$$

which, of course, could also be obtained via the expression

$$BW = \frac{R}{L}$$

A telephone transmission system suffers from 60 Hz caused by nearby power utility lines. Let us use the network in Figure 6.16 to design a simple notch filter to eliminate the 60 Hz interference.

Example 6.7

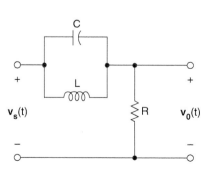

FIGURE 6.16   A notch filter design

Since we want a center frequency of 60 Hz or 377 rad/s,

$$\frac{1}{\sqrt{LC}} = 377 \text{ rad/s}$$

If we select a capacitor value of C = 100 μF, then

$$\frac{1}{\sqrt{(L)(10^{-4})}} = 377$$

and

$$L = 70.3 \text{ mH}$$

To demonstrate the effectiveness of the filter, let the input voltage consist of a 60 Hz sinusoid and a 1000 Hz sinusoid of the form

$$v_s(t) = 1 \sin[(2\pi)60t] + 0.2 \sin[(2\pi)1000t] \text{ V}$$

The input and output waveforms are both shown in Figure 6.17.

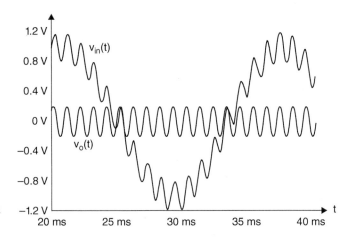

FIGURE 6.17 The effect of a notch filter to reduce 60 Hz interference

RESONANCE

Resonance is an extremely important topic, and ignoring it in the design of physical systems can result in devastating consequences. Unfortunately, the engineers who designed the Tacoma Narrows Bridge across Puget Sound in the State of Washington learned this lesson the hard way. The bridge was opened to traffic on July 1, 1940. At the time, it was one of the longest suspension bridges in the nation. Just four months later on November 7, 1940, the wind coming in from the Pacific began to excite the body bending modes of the bridge, and the bridge began to sway back and forth as shown in Figure 6.18. This gigantic structure swaying in the wind was nicknamed Galloping Gertie. For hours, the wind continued to blow across the bridge, and the deflections continued to increase until they became so large that the bridge collapsed, as shown in Figure 6.19. The engineering community saw this as a wakeup call and essentially any structure that was designed following this disaster was built with resonance in mind.

FIGURE 6.18   Tacoma Narrows
Bridge on the verge of collapse (AP
Photo). Everett Collection
Historical / Alamy Stock Photo

FIGURE 6.19   Tacoma Narrows
Bridge as it collapsed on November
7, 1940 (AP Photo/nap)

We would, of course, be remiss if we did not acknowledge the beneficial properties of resonance. For example, musical instruments and medical diagnostic tools such as magnetic resonance imaging (MRI) systems, to name only two.

Prior to the ubiquitous use of digital computers, analog computers were used to model physical systems and study the effects of such things as resonance. In this modeling environment, an electric circuit became the analog of the mechanical system and was used to study the effects created by changes in parameters. For example, it was much easier to adjust the value of a variable resistor in the analog circuit than to change the mechanical system's coefficient of friction. By accurately modeling systems in the design phase, engineers were able to not only determine the potential problems with resonance but also design the systems to avoid them.

The fact that there is a dual relationship between mechanical systems and electrical systems, i.e. we can model mechanical systems with electric circuits, would seem to indicate that resonance could also be a problem in electrical circuits. Potential problems do exist, and in what follows we illustrate the manner in which they may be encountered.

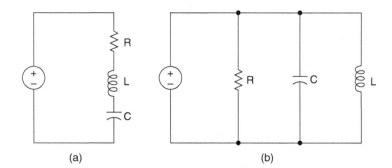

FIGURE 6.20 Series and parallel RLC circuits

(a) (b)

Consider the two networks in Figure 6.20. Note that the impedance of the series circuit is

$$\mathbf{Z}(j\omega) = R + j\omega L + \frac{1}{j\omega C} = R + j\left(\omega L - \frac{1}{\omega C}\right)$$

The admittance of the parallel circuit is

$$\mathbf{Y}(j\omega) = \frac{1}{R} + j\omega L + \frac{1}{j\omega C} = G + j\left(\omega C - \frac{1}{\omega L}\right)$$

The imaginary terms in both equations will be zero if

$$\omega L = \frac{1}{\omega C}$$

And the value of ω that satisfies this condition is

$$\omega_0 = \frac{1}{\sqrt{LC}}$$

Therefore,

$$\mathbf{Z}(j\omega_0) = R$$
$$\mathbf{Y}(j\omega_0) = G$$

The equations indicate that there is clearly a similarity between series and parallel resonance. We first consider the former and then the latter.

SERIES RESONANCE

In the series circuit, at the resonant frequency the voltage and current are in phase, the phase angle of the impedance is zero, the impedance is a minimum, and for any given voltage the current is a maximum. Furthermore, the impedance is capacitive at low frequencies and inductive at high frequencies.

A very important term, commonly employed in the study of resonance, is what is known as the quality factor, Q. Q is *defined* as

$$Q = \omega_0 L / R$$

And since at resonance

$$\omega_0^2 = 1/LC$$

an alternative expression is

$$Q = 1/\omega_0 CR$$

Example 6.8 illustrates the use of this factor.

Given the circuit in Figure 6.21, let us determine the voltage across each circuit element when the voltage source is operating at the resonant frequency of the network.

Example 6.8

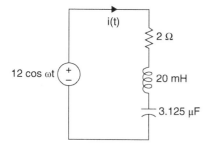

FIGURE 6.21   Circuit used in Example 6.8

The resonant frequency of the circuit is

$$\omega_0 = \frac{1}{\sqrt{LC}}$$

$$= \frac{1}{\sqrt{(20 \times 10^{-3})(3.125 \times 10^{-6})}}$$

$$= 4000 \ \text{rad/s}$$

Recall that at this frequency the impedance of the reactive components cancel each other, i.e. $\mathbf{Z_L} + \mathbf{Z_C} = 0$. As a result, the current is

$$\mathbf{I} = \frac{12\angle 0°}{2}$$

$$= 6\angle 0° \ \text{A}$$

Now that the current in every element is known, the voltage across each circuit element can be found.

$$\mathbf{V_R} = \mathbf{I}R = (6\angle 0°)(2)$$

$$= 12\angle 0° \ \text{V}$$

$$\mathbf{V_L} = j\omega_0 L\mathbf{I} = j\,4000(20 \times 10^{-3})(6\angle 0°)$$

$$= 480\angle 90° \ \text{V}$$

$$\mathbf{V_C} = \frac{\mathbf{I}}{j\omega_0 C} = \frac{6\angle 0°}{j\,4000(3.125 \times 10^{-6})}$$

$$= 480\angle -90° \ \text{V}$$

Wow! Look at those numbers again. Although the input voltage for the circuit, which contained only passive elements, is 12 V, the magnitude of the voltages across the reactive elements is a whopping 480 V, i.e. it is up by a factor of 40! Note also that the voltages across the reactive elements are 180° out of phase. This phenomenon is a result of the circuit operating at its resonant frequency.

An understanding of the role that Q plays in circuits operating in resonance shows us what to expect in situations such as this. In resonance, the voltage across the inductor is

$$\mathbf{V_L} = j\omega_0 L\mathbf{I}$$

The magnitude of the voltage is

$$|\mathbf{V_L}| = \omega_0 L|\mathbf{I}|$$
$$= \frac{\omega_0 L}{R}|\mathbf{IR}|$$
$$= Q|\mathbf{V_s}|$$

In a similar manner, the voltage across the capacitor is

$$|\mathbf{V_c}| = \frac{|\mathbf{I}|}{\omega_0 C}$$
$$= \frac{|\mathbf{V_s}|}{\omega_0 CR}$$
$$= Q|\mathbf{V_s}|$$

These equations indicate that the voltages across the reactive elements, although 180° out of phase, will rise by a factor of Q times the input voltage. Therefore, in dealing with high Q circuits operating in resonance, caution is advised.

For the network in Figure 6.21, the Q is

$$Q = \frac{\omega_0 L}{R}$$
$$= \frac{(4060)(20 \times 10^{-3})}{2}$$
$$= 40$$

which verifies the fact that the magnitude of the voltages across the reactive elements is $Q\mathbf{V_S}$.

The network Q is also important in that it is an indication of just how selective the network is. For example, note that circuit in Figure 6.21 has the same architecture as a bandpass filter. As a result, the bandwidth of this network is

$$BW = \omega_{HI} - \omega_{LO}$$
$$= \frac{R}{L}$$

However, multiplying both numerator and denominator by ω_0 and employing the definition for Q, the bandwidth can be expressed as

$$BW = \frac{R\omega_0}{L\omega_0}$$
$$= \frac{\omega_0}{Q}$$

indicating the bandwidth is inversely proportional to Q. Therefore, the higher the Q, the more selective the circuit, as shown in Figure 6.22.

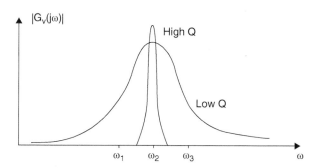

FIGURE 6.22   The effect of Q selectively

Imagine for a moment that a signal containing frequency components at frequencies ω_1, ω_2, and ω_3, as shown in Figure 6.22, is passed through a network, but only the signal components at frequency ω_2 are desired at the output, i.e. the frequencies ω_1 and ω_3 should be filtered out. Note that the high Q circuit is selective enough to pass only the signal components at frequency ω_2, while the low Q circuit's bandwidth is so large that all the frequencies will pass and the information at frequency ω_2 will be distorted.

Resonance is a fascinating phenomenon and the circuit in resonance exhibits some interesting characteristics. For example, there is a continuous exchange of energy between the magnetic field of the inductor and the electric field of the capacitor, i.e. the inductor absorbs energy as fast as it is released by the capacitor, and vice versa.

Given the network in Figure 6.23, let us determine the value of resistor so that the bandwidth of the circuit is (a) $0.1\omega_0$ and (b) $0.01\omega_0$.

Example 6.9

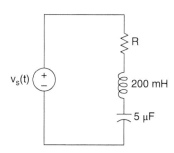

FIGURE 6.23   Circuit used in Example 6.9

The center frequency for the network is

$$\omega_0 = \frac{1}{\sqrt{(200 \times 10^{-3})(5 \times 10^{-6})}}$$
$$= 1000 \ \text{rad/s}$$

(a) If the bandwidth is to be $0.1\omega_0$, or 100 rad/s, then

$$100 = \frac{R}{L}$$
$$R = (100)(200 \times 10^{-3})$$

and

$$R = 20\ \Omega$$

(b) If the bandwidth is to be $0.01\omega_0$, or 10 rad/s, then

$$10 = \frac{R}{L}$$
$$R = (10)(200 \times 10^{-3})$$

and

$$R = 2\ \Omega$$

The results of this example are true in general, i.e. a high Q series circuit requires a small value of R.

Example 6.10

Given the network in Figure 6.24 let us determine ω_0, and the value for Q for the two conditions (a) R = 50 Ω and (b) R = 1 Ω. In addition, let us plot the frequency response for each case in order to compare their selectivity.

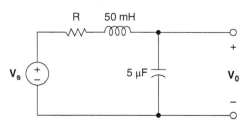

FIGURE 6.24 Circuit used in Example 6.10

The network parameters yield

$$\omega_0 = \frac{1}{\sqrt{LC}}$$
$$= \frac{1}{\sqrt{(5)(10^{-2})(5)(10^{-6})}}$$
$$= 2000\ \text{rad/s}$$

(a) If R = 50 Ω, then

$$Q = \frac{\omega_0 L}{R}$$
$$= \frac{(2000)(0.05)}{50}$$
$$= 2$$

The transfer function for this case is

$$\frac{\mathbf{V_o}}{\mathbf{V_s}} = \frac{1}{2.5 \times 10^{-7}(j\omega)^2 + 5 \times 10^{-6}(j\omega) + 1}$$

(b) If R = 1 Ω, then

$$Q = \frac{\omega_0 L}{R}$$
$$= \frac{(2000)(0.05)}{1}$$
$$= 100$$

And the transfer function for this case is

$$\frac{\mathbf{V_o}}{\mathbf{V_s}} = \frac{1}{2.5 \times 10^{-7}(j\omega)^2 + 2.5 \times 10^{-4}(j\omega) + 1}$$

The magnitude and phase plots for the case where Q = 2 are shown in Figure 6.25, and the same plots for the case in which Q = 100 are shown in Figure 6.26. Note the vast difference in the values of Q and the effect that these values have on the network's selectivity.

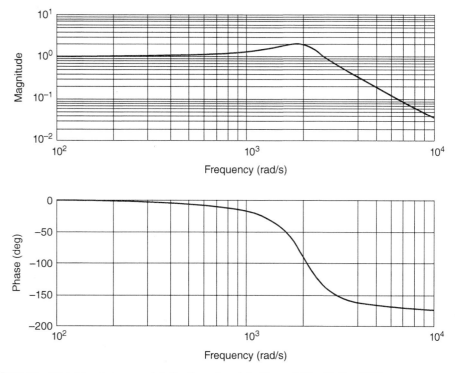

FIGURE 6.25   Frequency response plots for the network in Figure 6.24 with R = 50 Ω

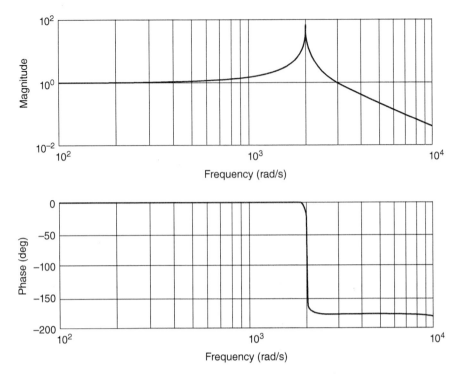

FIGURE 6.26   Frequency response plots for the network in Figure 6.24 with R = 1 Ω

PARALLEL RESONANCE

As we begin our discussion of parallel resonance recall that the impedance of a series RLC circuit is of the same form as the admittance of a parallel RLC circuit. Given the network in Figure 6.27, the equation for the source current is

$$\mathbf{I_S} = \left[G + j\omega C + \frac{1}{j\omega L} \right] \mathbf{V_S}$$

$$= \left[G + j\left(\omega C - \frac{1}{\omega L} \right) \right] \mathbf{V_S}$$

And at resonance the equation for the current is

$$\mathbf{I_S} = G\mathbf{V_S}$$

where $\mathbf{I_C}$ and $\mathbf{I_L}$ are equal in magnitude and 180° out of phase with each other.

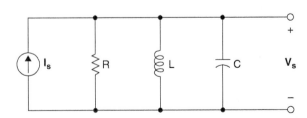

FIGURE 6.27   A parallel RLC circuit

It is instructive to compare the equations for both Q and the bandwidth for this parallel circuit with those of the series circuit. The transfer function relating the output voltage to the input current is

$$\frac{\mathbf{V}_o}{\mathbf{I}_S} = \frac{1}{Y_T}$$

or

$$\left|\frac{\mathbf{V}_o}{\mathbf{I}_S}\right| = \frac{1}{\sqrt{\left(\frac{1}{R}\right)^2 + \left(\omega C - \frac{1}{\omega L}\right)^2}}$$

where

$$\omega_0 = \frac{1}{\sqrt{LC}}$$

At the frequency ω_0, the transfer function is reduced to

$$\left|\frac{\mathbf{V}_o}{\mathbf{I}_S}\right| = R$$

Now recall that at the half-power frequencies the magnitude of the transfer characteristic is equal to $1/\sqrt{2}$ of its maximum value. Therefore, in the parallel RLC circuit, the positive values of ω that satisfy the equation

$$\frac{1}{\sqrt{\left(\frac{1}{R}\right)^2 + \left(\omega C - \frac{1}{\omega L}\right)^2}} = \frac{R}{\sqrt{2}}$$

will yield the values of ω_{LO} and ω_{HI}. The solution of this equation yields the two half-power frequencies

$$\omega_{LO} = \frac{-1}{2RC} + \sqrt{\left(\frac{1}{2RC}\right)^2 + \frac{1}{LC}}$$

$$\omega_{HI} = \frac{1}{2RC} + \sqrt{\left(\frac{1}{2RC}\right)^2 + \frac{1}{LC}}$$

Since the difference between these two frequencies is the bandwidth of the circuit, the expression for the bandwidth is

$$BW = \omega_{HI} - \omega_{LO}$$
$$= \frac{1}{RC}$$

In addition, the relationship between the circuit's bandwidth and the Q of the circuit is

$$BW = \frac{\omega_0}{Q}$$

Therefore, Q can be expressed in any one of the equivalent forms:

$$Q = \frac{\omega_0}{\text{BW}}$$
$$= \omega_0 CR$$
$$= \frac{R}{\omega_0 L}$$
$$= R\sqrt{\frac{C}{L}}$$

A comparison of the critical parameters for both the series and parallel RLC circuits is shown in Table 6.1.

Table 6.1   Series/Parallel RLC Circuits

Parameter	Series RLC circuit	Parallel RLC circuit
ω_0	$1/\sqrt{LC}$	$1/\sqrt{LC}$
Bandwidth	R/L	$1/RC$
Q	$\dfrac{1}{R}\sqrt{\dfrac{L}{C}}$	$R\sqrt{C/L}$

Continuing our comparative analysis between the series and parallel circuits, let us demonstrate that in addition to the voltage rise by a factor of Q across the reactive elements in the series case, there is an equivalent rise in current in the reactive components in the parallel circuit. At resonance

$$\left|\frac{\mathbf{V_o}}{\mathbf{I_S}}\right| = R$$

Then the inductor current is

$$|\mathbf{I_L}| = \left|\frac{\mathbf{I_S}R}{j\omega_0 L}\right|$$
$$= \frac{R}{\omega_0 L}|\mathbf{I_S}|$$
$$= Q|\mathbf{I_S}|$$

And a similar development will yield the equation

$$|\mathbf{I_C}| = Q|\mathbf{I_S}|$$

Example 6.11

Given the circuit in Figure 6.28, let us determine (a) the resonant frequency, (b) the half-power frequencies, (c) the bandwidth, (d) the Q of the network, and (e) all the currents when the circuit is operating at the resonant frequency.

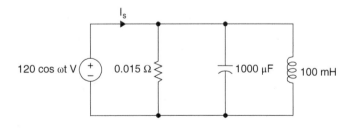

FIGURE 6.28   Circuit used in Example 6.11

(a) The resonant frequency is

$$\omega_0 = \frac{1}{\sqrt{(1000 \times 10^{-6})(100 \times 10^{-3})}}$$
$$= 100 \text{ rad/s}$$

(b) The half-power frequencies are

$$\omega_{LO} = \frac{-1}{2RC} + \sqrt{\left(\frac{1}{2RC}\right)^2 + \frac{1}{LC}}$$
$$= -5 + 100.125$$
$$= 95.125 \text{ rad/s}$$
$$\omega_{HI} = 5 + 100.125$$
$$= 105.125 \text{ rad/s}$$

(c) The bandwidth of the circuit is

$$BW = \omega_{HI} - \omega_{LO}$$
$$= 10 \text{ rad/s}$$

In addition, recall that

$$BW = \frac{1}{RC} = \frac{G}{C}$$
$$= 10 \text{ rad/s}$$

(d) The quality factor is defined by several equations, one of which is

$$Q = \omega_0 CR = \frac{\omega_0 C}{G}$$
$$= 10$$

(e) The currents at the resonant frequency are

$$I_G = (0.01)(120\angle 0°)$$
$$= 1.2\angle 0° \text{ A}$$
$$I_C = j(100)(1000 \times 10^{-6})(120\angle 0°)$$
$$= 12\angle 90° \text{ A}$$
$$I_L = \frac{-j\, 120\angle 0°}{(100)(100 \times 10^{-3})}$$
$$= 12\angle -90° \text{ A}$$

Note that

$$I_S = I_G + I_C + I_L$$

Although the circuit equations confirm it, we know in advance that the magnitude of current in the reactive components will be more than the input current I_S by a factor of Q, i.e.

$$|I_L| = |I_C| = Q|I_S| = 12A$$

Example 6.12

The antenna of an FM radio picks up stations across the entire FM frequency range—approximately 87.5–108 MHz. The radio's circuitry must have the capability to first reject all of the stations except the one that the listener wants to hear and then to boost the minute antenna signal. A tuned amplifier incorporating parallel resonance can perform both tasks simultaneously.

The network in Figure 6.29 is a circuit model for the single-stage tuned transistor amplifier with the parallel RLC circuit connected to the output of the transistor. Let us determine (a) the transfer function $V_0(j\omega)/V_A(j\omega)$, where $V_A(j\omega)$ is the antenna voltage, and (b) the value of the capacitor for maximum gain at 91.1 MHz.

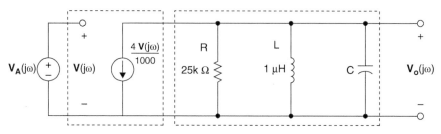

FIGURE 6.29   A parallel resonant tuned amplifier

(a) The output of the circuit is given by the equation

$$V_0(j\omega) = \frac{-4V_A(j\omega)}{1000} Z_{total}$$

where Z_{total} represents the parallel combination of the passive circuit elements. However, since the circuit elements are all in parallel, we will find Y_{total} and use the fact that

$$Z_{total} = 1/Y_{total}$$

Combining the elements in parallel yields

$$\begin{aligned} Y_{total} &= \frac{1}{R} + \frac{1}{j\omega L} + j\omega C \\ &= \frac{j\omega L + R + (j\omega)^2 RLC}{j\omega LR} \end{aligned}$$

Therefore, Z_{total} is

$$\begin{aligned} Z_{total} &= \frac{j\omega LR}{R + j\omega L + (j\omega)^2 RLC} \\ &= \frac{j\omega/C}{(j\omega)^2 + \dfrac{j\omega}{RC} + \dfrac{1}{LC}} \end{aligned}$$

Hence, the transfer function is

$$\frac{V_0(j\omega)}{V_A(j\omega)} = \frac{-4}{1000} \left[\frac{j\omega/C}{(j\omega)^2 + \dfrac{j\omega}{RC} + \dfrac{1}{LC}} \right]$$

(b) The parallel resonant network is essentially a bandpass filter, and thus the maximum value will occur at the center frequency, i.e.

$$\omega_0 = \frac{1}{\sqrt{LC}}$$

Then, for a center frequency of 91.1 MHz,

$$2\pi(91.1 \times 10^6) = \frac{1}{\sqrt{LC}}$$

Given the inductor value of 1 µH, the value of C is then

$$C = 3.05 \ \text{pF}$$

The frequency response of the circuit is shown in Figure 6.30.

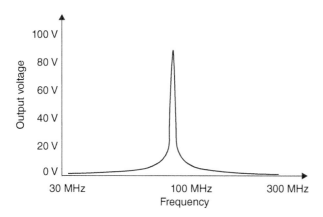

FIGURE 6.30   A Bode plot for the network in Figure 6.29

Consider the simplified block diagram of an AM radio shown in Figure 6.31a. We will model this network with the circuit shown in Figure 6.31b where we have modeled the antenna current I_a as a current source. The tank circuit is placed between the current source and input stage of the radio, which has been modeled by its Thevenin equivalent resistance R_i assumed to be 1 kΩ. We wish to select values for the tank circuit so that a station broadcasting at 1000 kHz will not be "picked up" when the radio is tuned to a signal at 1200 kHz.

Example 6.13

The impedance of the tank circuit is

$$\mathbf{Z_T}(j\omega) = \frac{j\omega L / j\omega C}{j\omega L + \dfrac{1}{j\omega C}}$$

$$= \frac{j\omega L}{-\omega^2 LC + 1}$$

The output current of the filter is then

$$\mathbf{I_o} = \mathbf{I_a}\frac{\mathbf{Z_T}}{\mathbf{Z_T} + \mathbf{R_i}}$$

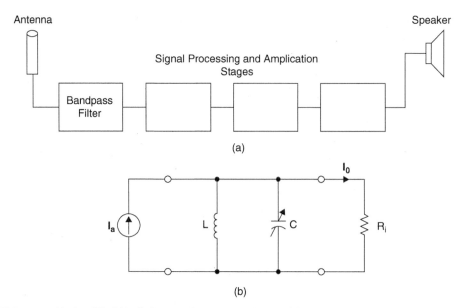

Antenna

Speaker

Signal Processing and Amplication
Stages

Bandpass
Filter

(a)

(b)

FIGURE 6.31 (a) Simplified block diagram for an AM radio and (b) a simple circuit used to model the radio's performance

and

$$\frac{I_o}{I_a} = \frac{\dfrac{j\omega L}{-\omega^2 LC + 1}}{\dfrac{j\omega L}{-\omega^2 LC + 1} + R_i}$$

which can be expressed as

$$\frac{I_o}{I_a} = \frac{\dfrac{j\omega}{R_i C}}{-\omega^2 + \dfrac{j\omega}{R_i C} + \dfrac{1}{LC}}$$

The center frequency of the filter and bandwidth expressed in rad/s are

$$\omega_0 = \frac{1}{LC}$$

$$BW = \frac{1}{R_i C}$$

or in Hertz, the variables are

$$f_o = \frac{1}{2\pi \sqrt{LC}}$$

$$BW = \frac{1}{2\pi R_i C}$$

Assuming the radio is tuned to 1200 kHz and assuming an inductor value of 100 μH, the value of the capacitor at 1200 kHz is derived from the expression

$$f_o = \frac{1}{2\pi \sqrt{LC}}$$

or, solving for C yields

$$C = \frac{1}{(2\pi f_o)^2 L}$$

$$= \frac{1}{[(2\pi)(12)(10^2)(10^3)]^2(10^{-4})}$$

$$= 176\,pF$$

The bandwidth of the tank circuit is then

$$BW = \frac{1}{2\pi R_i C}$$

$$= \frac{1}{(2\pi)(4000)(176)(10^{-12})}$$

$$= 226\ kHz$$

and the Q of the circuit is

$$Q = \frac{\omega_0}{BW}$$

$$= \frac{1200}{22.6}$$

$$= 5.3$$

If we now substitute all the component values into the transfer function expression, we obtain

$$\frac{I_o}{I_a}(f) = \frac{j(8.92)(10^6)f}{-39.48f^2 + j(8.92)(10^6)f + (56.82)(10^{12})}$$

A magnitude plot of this characteristic is shown Figure 6.32. Clearly, a station operating at l000 kHz will be picked up by the radio when tuned to 1200 kHz.

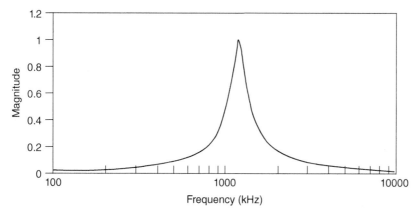

FIGURE 6.32   A plot of a bandpass filter with a center frequency of 1200 kHz and a bandwidth of 226 kHz

Since the bandwidth is inversely proportional to the capacitance, let us increase the capacitance value by a factor of 10 and decrease the inductor value by the same amount, thus maintaining the center frequency. Under this condition C = 1.76 nF and L = 10 μH. The new bandwidth and Q will be 22.6 kHz and 53, respectively. Obviously, this is a much more selective circuit. The transfer characteristic in this case is

$$\frac{I_o}{I_a}(f) = \frac{j(0.8925)(10^6)f}{-39.48f^2 + j(0.8925)(10^6)f + (56.82)(10^{12})}$$

A plot of this new characteristic is shown, together with the one in Figure 6.32 for comparison, in Figure 6.33. In this latter case, the station operating at 1000 kHz will have little, if any, impact when the radio is tuned to 1200 kHz.

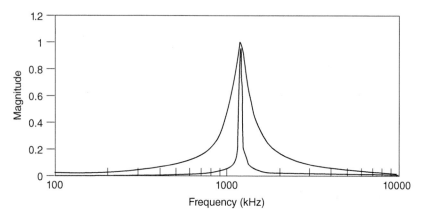

FIGURE 6.33   A plot of the bandpass filter with a center frequency of 1200 kHz and a bandwidth of 22.6 kHz

---

Problems

6.1 Determine the voltage transfer function for the network in Figure P6.1 and the poles and zeros of this function.

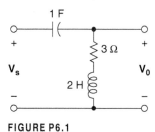

FIGURE P6.1

6.2 Determine the voltage transfer function for the network in Figure P6.2 and the poles and zeros of this function.

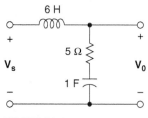

FIGURE P6.2

6.3   Calculate the half-power frequency for the circuit in Figure P6.3.

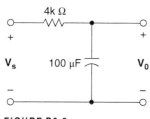

FIGURE P6.3

6.4   A low-pass filter has the following elements: R = 2 k Ω and C = 100 µF. Determine the half-power frequency.

6.5   A low-pass filter has the following parameters: R = 10 kΩ and C = 50 µF. (a) Determine the half-power frequency and (b) the impact on the half-power frequency if the resistor value is doubled.

6.6   Given the RC low-pass filter in Figure P6.6, determine the half-power frequency. What is the impact on the half-power frequency if the value of the capacitor is decreased by a factor of 10?

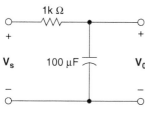

FIGURE P6.6

6.7   If a 10 µF capacitor is available, design a low-pass filter with a break frequency of 100 Hz.

6.8   Given a 100k Ω resistor, design a low-pass filter that has a break frequency of 1000 Hz.

6.9   If a high-pass filter is needed with a cutoff frequency of 120 rad/s, and a 5k Ω resistor is available, determine the value of the capacitance required.

6.10   Given the high-pass filter shown in Figure P6.10, determine the break frequency of the filter.

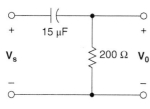

FIGURE P6.10

6.11 The high-pass filter in Figure P6.11 must have a cutoff frequency of 1200 rad/s. Find the value of R to satisfy this requirement.

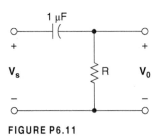

FIGURE P6.11

6.12 Calculate the value of C in the circuit in Figure P6.12 that will produce a high-pass filter with a cutoff frequency of 1000 Hz.

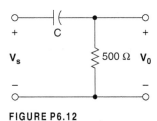

FIGURE P6.12

6.13 Determine the center frequency and the bandwidth of the bandpass filter in Figure P6.13.

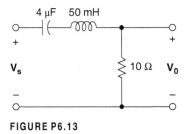

FIGURE P6.13

6.14 Determine the center frequency and the bandwidth of the bandpass filter in Figure P6.14.

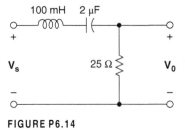

FIGURE P6.14

6.15 Determine the center frequency of the bandpass filter in Figure P6.15, and the value of R to produce a bandwidth of 50 rad/s.

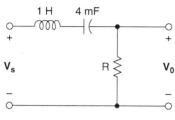

FIGURE P6.15

6.16 Given a 10 μF capacitor, design a bandpass filter with a center frequency of 40 k rad/s and a bandwidth of 2 k rad/s.

6.17 Given a 1 μF capacitor, design a bandpass filter with a center frequency of 10 k rad/s and a bandwidth of 1 k rad/s.

6.18 Given the bandpass filter shown in Figure P6.18, determine the values for L and R that will produce a center frequency of 20 k rad/s and a BW = 500 rad/s.

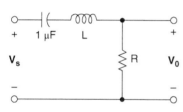

FIGURE P6.18

6.19 Determine the cutoff frequencies for the bandpass filter in Problem 6.18.

6.20 Determine the resonant frequency of the circuit in Figure P6.20.

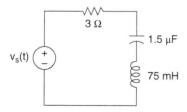

FIGURE P6.20

6.21 A series RLC circuit has the following parameters: R = 2 Ω, L = 100 mH, and C = 2 μF. Calculate the network's resonant frequency.

6.22 A series RLC contains a variable capacitor as shown in Figure P6.22. Calculate the value of C that will produce a resonant frequency of 1800 rad/s.

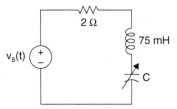

FIGURE P6.22

6.23 Given the series RLC circuit in Figure P6.23, determine the value of L that will produce a resonant frequency of 1400 rad/s.

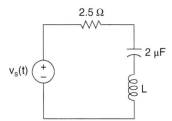

FIGURE P6.23

6.24 The network in Figure P6.24 is operating at the resonant frequency. Determine the Q of the network and the magnitude of the voltage across the inductor.

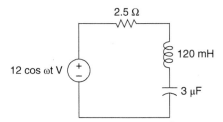

FIGURE P6.24

6.25 Given the circuit in Figure P6.25, calculate the half-power frequencies and the bandwidth.

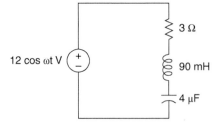

FIGURE P6.25

6.26 A series RLC circuit has the following parameters: R = 3.2 Ω, L = 50 mH, and C = 5 μF. Find (a) the circuit's resonant frequency, (b) the Q, and (c) the voltage across the capacitor at resonance if the forcing function for the network is a source $v_S(t) = 10 \cos \omega t$ **V**.

6.27 A series RLC circuit is operating at resonance. The forcing function is 12∠0° **V**, L = 36 mH, C = 1.2 μF and R is unknown. If the value of the voltage across the inductor has a maximum value of 180 **V**, determine the value of R.

6.28 If the parameters for the RLC circuit shown in Figure P6.28 are ω_0 = 5000 rad/s and Q = 30, determine the unknown circuit parameters.

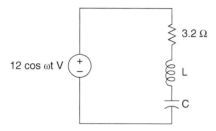

FIGURE P6.28

6.29 Given the RLC circuit shown in Figure P6.29, find the values for L and C so that the network will have a resonant frequency of 80 kHz and a bandwidth of 2 kHz.

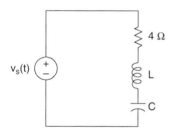

FIGURE P6.29

6.30 Determine the values for L and C in a series RLC circuit that contains a 4.4 Ω resistor. The desired bandwidth is 5 kHz and the resonant frequency is 64 kHz.

6.31 Given the network in Figure P6.31, determine the magnitude of the current in the resistor at the resonant frequency of the circuit.

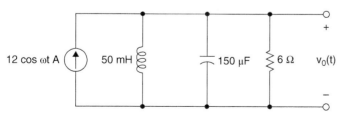

FIGURE P6.31

6.32 Determine the resonant frequency and the magnitude of the voltage across the elements in the network in Figure P6.32 at resonance.

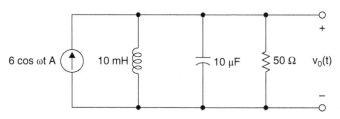

6 cos ωt A   10 mH   10 μF   50 Ω $v_0(t)$

FIGURE P6.32

6.33 Calculate the Q and the bandwidth of the circuit in Figure P6.33.

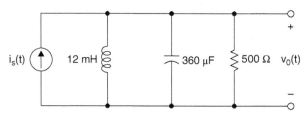

$i_s(t)$ 12 mH   360 μF   500 Ω $v_0(t)$

FIGURE P6.33

6.34 If the value of R in the Problem 6.33 is changed from 500 to 50 Ω, i.e. reduced by a factor of 10, determine the effect on Q and the bandwidth.

6.35 Determine the values for L and C and the resonant frequency of the network in Figure P6.35 if the network has a Q of 100 and a bandwidth of 1000 rad/s.

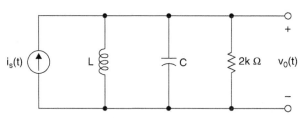

$i_s(t)$ L   C   2k Ω $v_0(t)$

FIGURE P6.35

6.36 The network in Figure P6.36 has a Q of 60 and a bandwidth of 400 rad/s. Determine the resonant frequency and the values of the circuit parameters L and C.

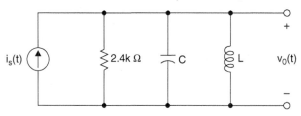

$i_s(t)$ 2.4k Ω   C   L $v_0(t)$

FIGURE P6.36

6.37 Determine the resonant frequency and the values of the circuit parameters in the network in Figure P6.37 if the network has a Q of 50 and a bandwidth of 200 rad/s.

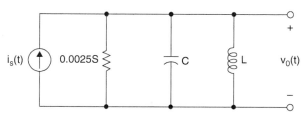

FIGURE P6.37

6.38 Given the circuit in Figure P6.38, find the bandwidth, Q, resonant frequency, and the half-power frequencies.

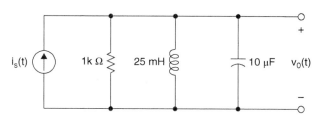

FIGURE P6.38

6.39 Calculate the resonant frequency, the Q, the bandwidth, and the half-power frequencies for the circuit in Figure P6.39.

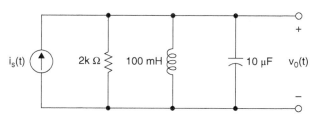

FIGURE P6.39

CHAPTER 7

Single-phase Steady-state Power Analysis

LEARNING OBJECTIVES

- To understand instantaneous and average power in ac circuits

- To be able to determine the maximum average power transfer in ac circuits

- To understand rms values and be able to calculate the rms value of an arbitrary periodic waveform

- To understand the relationship among real power, reactive power, and complex power

- To be able to raise the power factor in an ac circuit

In this chapter, we begin our study of electric power, and we start with the analysis of single-phase circuits. Although we have used the passive sign convention to aid us in determining if an element in the circuit was absorbing or supplying power in our earlier work, we will now expand our knowledge of this area and explore the many ramifications of this important topic.

Electric power plays a fundamental and important role in the lives of everyone. Only a moment's reflection is necessary to determine the critical impact electric power plays in our lives on a 24-hour timetable. If this important role is not obvious, then think about what you would have to do differently if there was no electric power. Yikes!

INSTANTANEOUS POWER

Given the circuit in Figure 7.1, we learned earlier that power for this network is equal to the product of the voltage and the current. Therefore, if

$$v(t) = V_M \cos [\omega t + \theta_v] \text{ V}$$
$$i(t) = I_M \cos [\omega t + \theta_i] \text{ A}$$

then the instantaneous power, i.e. the power at any instant of time is

$$p(t) = v(t)i(t)$$
$$= V_M I_M \cos(\omega t + \theta_v) \cos(\omega t + \theta_i)$$

There is a popular trigonometric identity that we will use more than once in our discussions of electric power that can be used to an advantage here, and the identity is

$$\cos \phi_1 \cos \phi_2 = 1/2[\cos(\phi_1 - \phi_2) + \cos(\phi_1 + \phi_2)]$$

Then instantaneous power can be expressed in the form

$$p(t) = \frac{V_M I_M}{2}[\cos(\theta_v - \theta_i) + \cos(2\omega t + \theta_v + \theta_i)]$$

Note that the instantaneous power is composed of two terms. The first term is clearly independent of time, i.e. a constant. The second term, like the voltage and current, is a cosine wave, but the frequency of this term is twice the frequency of the voltage or current. This indicates that the power is shifted by a constant value and pulsating at twice the frequency of the voltage or current in the circuit. A simple example will illustrate this phenomenon.

Suppose the values for the elements in Figure 7.1 are the following: $\mathbf{V} = 12\angle 30°$ V and the impedance is $\mathbf{Z} = 3\angle 10°$ Ω. We wish to determine the expression for the instantaneous power.

Example 7.1

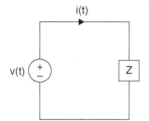

FIGURE 7.1   A simple ac network

The current is

$$\mathbf{I} = 12\angle 30°/3\angle 10° = 4\angle 20° \text{ A}$$

And then since the voltage and current are

$$v(t) = 12 \ \cos \ [\omega t + 30°] \text{ V}$$
$$i(t) = 4 \ \cos \ [\omega t + 20°] \text{ A}$$

The instantaneous power is

$$p(t) = [(12)(4)/2] \ \cos \ 10° + [(12)(4)/2] \ \cos \ [2\omega t + 50°] \text{ W}$$
$$= 23.64 + 24 \ \cos \ [2\omega t + 50°] \text{ W}$$

A plot of this power, together with the voltage and current, is shown in Figure 7.2.

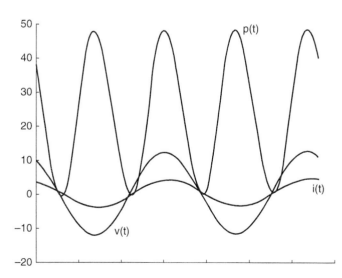

FIGURE 7.2   A plot of v(t), i(t), and p(t) for Example 7.1

AVERAGE POWER

We have seen in the previous section that the instantaneous power is a periodic waveform pulsating at twice the frequency of the voltage or current. We can determine the average value of this periodic waveform, and any other as well, by integrating the waveform over a complete period and dividing by the period. Thus, the average power is

$$P = \frac{1}{T} \int_{t_0}^{t_0+T} p(t)dt$$

$$= \frac{1}{T} \int_{t_0}^{t_0+T} V_M I_M \cos(\omega t + \theta_v) \cos(\omega t + \theta_i)dt$$

where t_0 is any time along the wave and T is the period of the voltage or current, i.e. $T = 2\pi/\omega$. Once again, using the popular trigonometric identity, we can express the average power as

$$P = \frac{1}{T} \int_{t_0}^{t_0+T} \frac{V_M I_M}{2} [\cos(\theta_v - \theta_i) + \cos(2\omega t + \theta_v + \theta_i)]dt$$

Before we grab our book of integral tables to evaluate this equation, it pays to take a moment to look at exactly what we are dealing with here. Note that the first term is independent of time, i.e. it is a constant with respect to time. We know that if we integrate a constant over a period of time and divide by the period, we obtain the constant. The second term is a cosine wave, and we know that if we integrate a cosine wave over a complete period we obtain the average value, which is, of course, zero, i.e. there is as much area above the line as there is below the line! Hence, the average power is

$$P = (1/2)V_M I_M \cos(\theta_v - \theta_i)$$

This is a really a simple result. However, the situation is actually less complicated than even this equation would indicate. Recall that $\theta_v - \theta_i = \theta_z$. Therefore, in a purely resistive circuit, $\theta_v = \theta_i$, and hence

$$P_{ave} = (\tfrac{1}{2}) V_M I_M$$

Employing Ohm's law, this equation can also be expressed in the following equivalent forms:

$$P_{ave} = (\tfrac{1}{2}) V^2/R = (\tfrac{1}{2}) I^2 R$$

Furthermore, if the circuit is purely reactive, $\theta_v - \theta_i = 90°$ and hence

$$P_{ave} = 0$$

In other words, the reactive elements in a network do not absorb any average power, and all the average power generated in the circuit will be absorbed by the resistors (and possibly one or more of the sources in the network, depending upon their values). Example 7.2 illustrates the salient features of this discussion.

Example 7.2

Consider the circuit in Figure 7.3a. We wish to show that the total average power supplied to the network is absorbed by the network's elements.

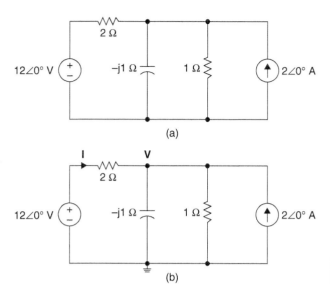

FIGURE 7.3   Circuit used in Example 7.2

The circuit in Figure 7.3b defines the variables **V** and **I**. The node equation for the unknown node voltage, **V**, is

$$\frac{V - 12\angle 0°}{2} + \frac{V}{-j} + \frac{V}{1} - 2\angle 0° = 0$$

$$\left[\frac{3 + j2}{2}\right] V = 8$$

$$V = 3.7 - j\,2.46 \ \ V$$

$$= 4.44\angle -33.62° \ V$$

Then the current, **I**, is

$$I = \frac{12 - 4.44\angle -33.62°}{2}$$

$$= 4.33\angle +16.51° \ A$$

We now have the information needed to compute the power absorbed or supplied by all the elements in the network since we now know the voltage across each element or the current through them.

The power generated by the 12∠0° V source is

$$P_{12\angle 0°} = \frac{1}{2} \,(12)(4.33) \ \cos(0 - 16.51°) = 24.92 \ W$$

Note carefully that the current is leaving the positive terminal of the source and the answer we have obtained is positive, i.e. power is being supplied.

Similarly, the power generated by the 2∠0° A source is

$$P_{2\angle 0°} = \frac{1}{2} \,(4.64)(2) \ \cos(-33.62° - 0°) = 3.7 \ W$$

Once again, the current is leaving the positive terminal of this source and the answer we obtained is positive. Therefore, the total power supplied to the network is

$$P_{supplied} = 24.92 + 3.7 = 28.62 \ W$$

The resistors in the network only absorb power, in the form of heat. The power absorbed by the 2 Ω resistor can be calculated via any one of the following equations:

$$P_{2\Omega} = \frac{1}{2}(I)^2 R = \frac{1}{2} (4.33)^2(2) = 18.75 \text{ W}$$

or

$$P_{2\Omega} = \frac{1}{2}(V_R)^2/2 = \frac{1}{2} \frac{(8.66)^2}{2} = 18.75 \text{ W}$$

or

$$P_{2\Omega} = \frac{1}{2} (V_R)(I_R) \cos(\theta_V - \theta_I)$$

$$= \frac{1}{2} (8.66)(4.33) \cos(16.5° - 16.5°)$$

$$= 18.75 \text{ W}$$

And the power absorbed by the 1 Ω resistor is

$$P_{1\Omega} = \frac{1}{2} \frac{(4.44)^2}{1} = 9.86 \text{ W}$$

Therefore, the total power absorbed is

$$P_{2\Omega} + P_{1\Omega} = P_{abs} = 18.75 + 9.86 = 28.6 \text{ W}$$

And we have a power balance in the circuit since the total power supplied to the network is being absorbed – by the resistors in this case.

Example 7.3

Given the network in Figure 7.4a, let us determine the power supplied to the network and the power absorbed by each of the network elements.

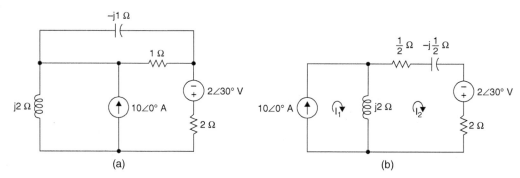

(a) (b)

FIGURE 7.4 Circuit used in Example 7.3

The parallel combination of the 1 Ω resistor and the –j1 Ω capacitor is

$$Z_p = (1)(-j1)/(1 - j1) = -j1/(1 - j1)$$

We can rationalize this function by multiplying both the numerator and denominator by $1 + j1$:

$$Z_p = [-j1/(1 - j1)] [(1 + j1)/(1 + j1)]$$
$$= (1 - j)/2$$
$$= 1/2 - j1/2 \ \Omega$$

The circuit is now redrawn as shown in Figure 7.4b. Although the network in Figure 7.4a could be analyzed directly, the modification to the equivalent network in Figure 7.4b was done not only to simplify the analysis but to illustrate the simplification procedure.

KVL for the right loop yields the equation

$$(I_2 - I_1)\,j2 + I_1(1/2 - j1/2) - 2\angle 30° + I_1(2) = 0$$
$$\text{where } I_1 = 10\angle 0° \text{ A rms}$$

Solving these equations for I_2 yields

$$I_2 = 7.23\angle 54.3° \text{ A rms}$$

The voltage across the current source is identical to that across the inductor, i.e.

$$\mathbf{V_{cs}} = j2(I_1 - I_2)$$
$$= j2(10\angle 0° - 7.23\angle 54.3°)$$
$$= 16.5\angle 44.6° \text{ V}$$

Now consider the power absorbed or supplied by each element. In the case of the current source, positive current is emanating from the positive terminal of the source, and thus this element is supplying power. The amount of power is

$$P_{cs} = (1/2)(16.5)(10)\ \cos[44.6° - 0°]$$
$$= 58.74 \text{ W}$$

In addition, positive current is leaving the positive terminal of the voltage source, and thus this element is supplying

$$P_{vs} = (1/2)(2)(7.23)\ \cos[30° - 54.3°]$$
$$= 6.59 \text{ W}$$

Since the passive elements do not generate, i.e. supply, any power, the total power supplied to the network is

$$P_{total} = 58.74 + 6.59$$
$$= 65.33 \text{ W}$$

It is important to stop at this point to note that if we had reversed the voltage or current at each source to comply with the manner in which to apply the passive sign convention, the calculation of power for each source would have been negative, indicating that the source was not absorbing power, but rather supplying power to the circuit.

As we have indicated, the reactive elements, capacitor and inductor, absorb no average power. Therefore, the power supplied to the circuit must be completely absorbed by the resistors. The 1/2 Ω resistor and the 2 Ω resistor have the same current and thus are in series. Hence, the power absorbed by the resistance in the circuit is

$$P_R = (1/2)(7.23)^2(2.5)$$
$$= 65.34 \text{ W}$$

Indicating that the power supplied to the circuit is absorbed by the resistance elements in the network.

MAXIMUM AVERAGE POWER TRANSFER

In our study of dc circuits, we addressed the issue of maximum power transfer to a resistive load, R_L. Our approach to that problem involved representing the network, exclusive of the load, by a Thevenin equivalent circuit. Then we set the load resistor R_L equal to the Thevenin equivalent resistance, R_{TH}, to achieve maximum power transfer to this load.

In ac circuits, where the circuit consists of impedances, we want to determine the value of the load impedance for maximum average power transfer. The problem in essence reduces to selecting the value of $\mathbf{Z_L}$ in the network in Figure 7.5 for maximum average power to this load, where once again we have represented the entire circuit, exclusive of the load impedance, by its Thevenin equivalent circuit. In this case, the impedances in this network are of the form

$$\mathbf{Z_{TH}} = R_{TH} + j\,X_{TH}$$
$$\mathbf{Z_L} = R_L + j\,X_L$$

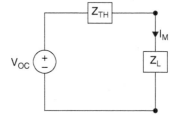

FIGURE 7.5 Thevenin equivalent circuit used in determining maximum average power transfer

The mathematical development that derives the proper selection of $\mathbf{Z_L}$ for maximum average power transfer can be found in *Basic Engineering Circuit Analysis, 12e*. However, it would appear reasonable that the current in the network in Figure 7.5 would have to be as large as possible, and since $(X_{TH} + X_L)$ absorbs no real power and any nonzero value of $(X_{TH} + X_L)$ will reduce the value of the current, maximum average power transfer is obtained when

$$\mathbf{Z_L} = R_L + j\,X_L = R_{TH} - j\,X_{TH}$$

In other words, to achieve maximum average power transfer to a load $\mathbf{Z_L}$, we set the load impedance equal to the complex conjugate of the Thevenin equivalent impedance, i.e. $\mathbf{Z_L} = \mathbf{Z_{TH}}^*$

$$R_L = R_{TH}$$

and

$$X_L = -X_{TH}$$

And then the maximum average power transferred to the load is

$$P_{max} = (½)\, I^2{}_M R_L$$

Example 7.4	We wish to find the $\mathbf{Z_L}$ for maximum average power transfer in the network in Figure 7.6a and the value of the maximum average power transferred.

The Thevenin equivalent circuit for the network, exclusive of the load, is shown in Figure 7.6b, where the mesh currents have been labeled. Since $\mathbf{I_2} = -4\angle 0°$ A rms, the KVL equation for loop 1 can be written as

$$1\mathbf{I_1} + 6\angle 0° + 1(\mathbf{I_1} + 4\angle 0°) = 0$$

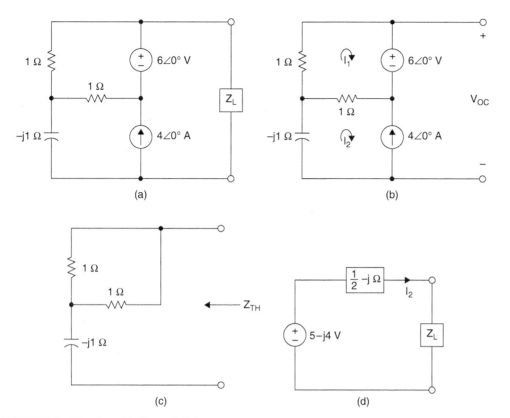

FIGURE 7.6   Circuit used in Example 7.4

which yields $I_1 = -5\angle0°$ A rms. Then the following KVL equation will yield the open-circuit voltage, V_{oc}.

$$-jI_2 + 1I_2 - 1I_1 - 6\angle0° + V_{oc} = 0$$
$$\text{And } V_{oc} = 5 - j4 \text{ V} = 6.4\angle{-38.66°} \text{ V}$$

The Thevenin equivalent impedance is obtained from the circuit in Figure 7.6c as $Z_{TH} = \dfrac{1}{2} - j1$ Ω, and therefore $Z_L = \dfrac{1}{2} + j1$ Ω as shown in Figure 7.6d. The maximum average power transfer can now be obtained as follows.

$$I_L = \frac{5 - j4}{\dfrac{1}{2} - j + \dfrac{1}{2} + j}$$
$$= 6.4\angle{-38.66°} \text{ A rms}$$

Then

$$P_L = \frac{1}{2}I_M^2 R$$
$$= \frac{1}{2}(6.4)^2(1/2)$$
$$= 10.25 \text{ W}$$

RMS VALUES

To begin this discussion, recall that the average power absorbed by a resistor is I^2R if the source is dc, and it is $\frac{1}{2}I_M^2R$ if the source is ac or sinusoidal. While these two types of sources are clearly very important, in circuit analysis we encounter a wide variety of sources, e.g. square waves, saw-tooth waves, and many others. Knowing that we can expect to encounter a wide spectrum of waveforms, it would certainly be advantageous to have a method by which we could compare the effectiveness of different sources in supplying power to a resistive load. Thus, we define what we call the effective value of a periodic current as the equivalent constant value that will deliver the same average power to a resistor, i.e.

$$P_{eff} = I_{eff}^2 R$$

The average power delivered to a resistor by a periodic current, $i(t)$, is

$$P = \frac{1}{T}\int_{t_0}^{t_0+T} i^2(t)R \, dt$$

If we equate these two expressions for average power, we will obtain the equation

$$I_{eff} = \sqrt{\frac{1}{T}\int_{t_0}^{t_0+T} i^2(t) \, dt}$$

We note that this effective value is calculated by first determining the *square* of the current, then determining the *mean* value, and finally evaluating the square *root*. Therefore, this calculation is called *root-mean-square* or rms. Thus, I_{eff} is labeled I_{rms}.

Example 7.5

The current waveform, shown in Figure 7.7, is flowing through a 10 Ω resistor. Let us determine the average power delivered to the resistor.

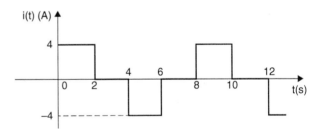

FIGURE 7.7 Waveform used in Example 7.5

Note that the waveform has different values within the different time intervals, 2–4 s, 4–6 s, etc. First, we must examine the waveform to determine the period of the curve. The point at which the waveform begins to repeat, i.e. the period, is 8 s. Within this period, the waveform has the following values within the specified time intervals.

$$
\begin{aligned}
i(t) &= 4 & 0 < t < 2\,\text{s} \\
&= 0 & 2 < t < 4\,\text{s} \\
&= -4 & 4 < t < 6\,\text{s} \\
&= 0 & 6 < 8\,\text{s}
\end{aligned}
$$

The rms value of the current is then derived from the expression

$$I_{rms} = \sqrt{\frac{1}{8}\left(\int_0^2 (4)^2 dt + \int_4^6 (-4)^2 dt\right)}$$

$$= \sqrt{\frac{1}{8}(16t|_0^2 + 16t|_4^6)}$$

$$= \sqrt{\frac{1}{8}(32 + 96 - 64)}$$

$$= \sqrt{\frac{1}{8}(64)}$$

$$= \sqrt{8}$$

The average power absorbed by the resistor is then

$$P_{10\Omega} = (\sqrt{8})^2(10)$$

$$= 80 \text{ W}$$

The current source supplying power to the 4 Ω resistor in the circuit in Figure 7.8a is given by the waveform shown in Figure 7.8b. Let us determine the average power absorbed by the resistor.

Example 7.6

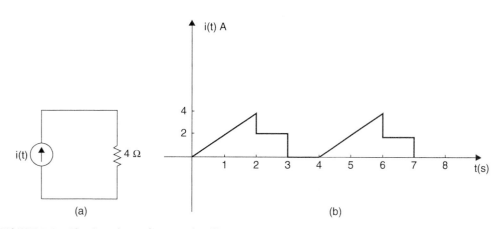

(a)   (b)

FIGURE 7.8   Circuit and waveform used to illustrate an rms value

Since the waveform has different values in different time intervals, we must first determine the equation of the waveform within the waveform's period. The period of this current waveform is 4 s, since it begins to repeat at that time. Within the three separate intervals, the equation for the current is

$$\begin{aligned} i(t) &= 2t & 0 < t \le 2 \text{ s} \\ &= 2 & 2 < t \le 3 \text{ s} \\ &= 0 & 3 < t \le 4 \text{ s} \end{aligned}$$

Then the rms value of the current is computed from the expression

$$I_{rms} = \sqrt{\frac{1}{4} \left(\int_0^2 (2t)^2 dt + | \int_2^3 2^2 dt \right)}$$

$$= \sqrt{\frac{1}{4} \left(\frac{4t^3}{3} |_0^2 + 4t|_2^3 \right)}$$

$$= \sqrt{\frac{1}{4}(10.67 + 4)}$$

$$= 1.92 \text{ A}$$

The average power absorbed by the resistor is then

$$P_{ave} = I^2 \text{ rms } R$$

$$= (1.92)^2(4) = 14.75 \text{ W}$$

Example 7.7

Because of its importance in our analysis of electric power, let us find the rms value of a cosine wave of the form $i(t) = I_M \cos [\omega t - \theta]$.

The rms value is obtained via the expression

$$I_{rms} = \sqrt{\left[\frac{1}{T} \int_0^T I_M^2 \cos^2(\omega t - \theta) dt \right]}$$

By employing the trigonometric identity

$$\cos^2 \phi = 1/2 + 1/2 \cos 2\phi$$

The equation for the rms current becomes

$$I_{rms} = I_M \sqrt{\left[\frac{\omega}{2\pi} \int_0^{2\pi/\omega} \left[1/2 + 1/2 \cos (2\omega t - 2\theta) \right] dt \right]}$$

Once again, prior to reaching for our book of integral tables, we note that the mean or average value of a cosine wave is zero, and thus the rms value is reduced to

$$I_{rms} = I_M \sqrt{\left[\frac{\omega}{2\pi} \int_0^{2\pi/\omega} \frac{1}{2} dt \right]}$$

$$= I_M \sqrt{\left[\frac{\omega}{2\pi} \left(\frac{t}{2} \right) \int_0^{2\pi/\omega} \right]} = \frac{I_M}{\sqrt{2}}$$

This equation demonstrates that the rms value of a cosine wave, i.e. a sinusoid, is equal to the peak value divided by $\sqrt{2}$, and, therefore, a sinusoidal current of maximum value I_M will supply the same average power to a resistor as a dc current with a value of $I_M/\sqrt{2}$.

In view of the result obtained in this example, it is important to note that the equation for average power can be written as

$$P_{ave} = (V_M/\sqrt{2})(I_M/\sqrt{2}) \cos [\theta_v - \theta_i]$$

or

$$P_{ave} = V_{rms}\, I_{rms}\, \cos\,[\theta_v - \theta_i]$$

Then the power absorbed by a resistor can be expressed in the forms

$$P_{ave} = I_{rms}^2\, R = V_{rms}^2/R$$

Note that when the current and voltage are in rms, these equations for power mimic the dc case.

POWER FACTOR

This very important quantity is defined as the ratio of the average power (P) to the apparent power $(V_{rms}\, I_{rms})$, i.e.

$$PF = P/(V_{rms}\, I_{rms}) = \cos\,[\theta_v - \theta_i]$$

where the units for average power are watts and the units for apparent power are volt-amperes, or kVA, since the power industry is typically dealing with high power. Clearly, the term $\cos\,[\theta_v - \theta_i]$ is dimensionless, and so the units for average power and apparent power are different in order to distinguish two quantities that result from a product of V and I.

Note that

$$PF = \cos\,[\theta_v - \theta_i] = \cos\,\theta_{ZL}$$

In other words, this power factor angle, $\theta_v - \theta_i$, is the angle of the load impedance. The range of the power factor is from 1, which corresponds to a purely resistive load in which $\theta_v - \theta_i = 0°$, to 0, which corresponds to a purely reactive load in which $\theta_v - \theta_i = \pm 90°$. A combination of R, L, and C elements could, of course, produce a unity power factor if the resulting impedances combine to produce a zero phase angle, i.e. the +j and −j terms cancel.

It is important to identify the network elements that produce the range of power factor angles from −90° to 0° and from 0° to +90°. A load that is an equivalent RC combination will have a phase angle in the range from −90° to 0°, and a load that is an equivalent RL combination will have a phase angle in the range from 0° to +90°. However, since $\cos\,[\theta] = \cos\,[-\theta]$, we need a way to distinguish between, for example, an angle of −45° and an angle of +45° since the $\cos\,[45°] = \cos\,[-45°]$. In order to make this distinction, we state that the power factor is either leading or lagging, and this designation refers the current with respect to the voltage. In an RC circuit, the current leads the voltage, and, therefore, an RC load has a leading power factor. In an RL circuit, the current lags the voltage, and, therefore, an RL load has a lagging power factor. Therefore, the load $Z_L = 1 - j1\ \Omega$ has a power factor of $\cos\,[-45°] = 0.707$ leading, and the load $Z_L = 1 + j1\ \Omega$ has a power factor of $\cos\,[+45°] = 0.707$ lagging.

Example 7.8 demonstrates the fundamental role that the power factor plays in the delivery of power to our businesses and residences.

Example 7.8

The circuit in Figure 7.9 represents an industrial load that is supplied by the power company along a transmission line with a total resistance of 0.1 Ω. The plant consumes 100 kW at a power factor of 0.66 lagging on a 480 V_{rms} 60 Hz line. Let us determine the power that must be supplied by the power company under the present conditions and also if a way could be found to change the power factor to 0.92 lagging.

Under the current conditions, the magnitude of the rms line current is

$$I_{rms} = P_L/(PF)(V_{rms}) = 100k/(0.66)(480) = 315.66\ A\ rms$$

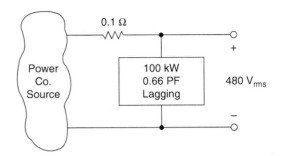

FIGURE 7.9 Circuit used to explain power factor

Then the power that must be supplied by the power company is equal to the power consumed by the load plus the line losses, i.e.

$$P_{source} = 100k + (315.66)^2(0.1)$$
$$= 109.96 \text{ kW}$$

However, if the PF is changed to 0.92 lagging, then the current is

$$I_{rms} = 100k/(0.92)(480) = 226.45 \text{ A rms}$$

And the power that must be supplied is

$$P_{source} = 100k + (226.45)^2(0.1)$$
$$= 105.13 \text{ kW}$$

Note carefully that a simple change in the power factor has saved 109.96 − 105.13 = 4.83 kW. This is not a trivial amount. The analysis indicates the effect of raising the power factor is to reduce the current. The line losses are related to the square of the current, and, thus, the line losses that benefit no one have been reduced. Clearly, power companies do not want industrial loads operating at low power factors, and they will take steps to raise them so they are not losing any more energy in the line than is unavoidable.

Now that we know there is a mechanism that has the potential to dramatically improve the delivery of power to a load, let us describe the procedure for accomplishing this feat. However, before we do this, we need to introduce a topic that will not only aid us in this analysis but help us better understand the topic of electric power.

COMPLEX POWER

Complex power is defined by the equation

$$\mathbf{S} = \mathbf{V_{rms}} \, \mathbf{I_{rms}^*}$$

where $\mathbf{I_{rms}^*}$ is the complex conjugate of $\mathbf{I_{rms}}$, i.e. if $\mathbf{I_{rms}} = I_{rms} \angle \theta$, then $\mathbf{I_{rms}^*} = I_{rms} \angle -\theta$. Hence, the complex power can be expressed as

$$\begin{aligned}
\mathbf{S} &= V_{rms} \, I_{rms} \angle \theta_v - \theta_i \\
&= V_{rms} \, I_{rms} \, \cos[\theta_v - \theta_i] + j \, V_{rms} \, I_{rms} \, \sin[\theta_v - \theta_i] \\
&= P + jQ
\end{aligned}$$

where P is the average, i.e. real, power, Q is the reactive, i.e. quadrature, power, and $\theta_v - \theta_i$ is the angle of the impedance, θ_z. In summary,

$$\mathbf{S} = S\angle\theta_v - \theta_i = P + jQ$$

and

$$\mathbf{S} = S\angle\theta_s$$

$\mathbf{S}$ = complex power measured in volt-amperes (VA)

S = apparent power measured in volt-amperes (VA)

P = real or average power measured in watts (W)

Q = reactive or quadrature power measured in volt-amperes reactive (VAR)

$\theta_s = \theta_v - \theta_i$ = power factor angle

The complex power can also be expressed in the following form:

$$\mathbf{S} = \mathbf{V}_{rms}\ \mathbf{I}^*_{rms} = I_{rms}\ \mathbf{Z}\ \mathbf{I}^*_{rms} = I^2_{rms}\ \mathbf{Z} = \mathbf{V}_{rms}[\mathbf{V}_{rms}/\mathbf{Z}]^* = V^2_{rms}/\mathbf{Z}^*$$

In an attempt to solidify the relationships among all these power quantities, it is helpful to view them on what is called the power triangle shown in Figure 7.10. This visual picture illustrates a number of critical points. First of all, recall that $\theta_v - \theta_i = \theta_z$, i.e. the power factor angle is the angle of the load impedance. In addition, if the load is inductive, i.e. of the form $R + jX$, then Q is positive, the power factor is lagging and $\mathbf{S}$ is in the first quadrant. If the load is capacitive, i.e. of the form $R - jX$, then Q is negative, the power factor is leading and $\mathbf{S}$ is in the fourth quadrant. Finally, if the load is resistive, Q is zero, the power factor is unity, and the complex power lies along the positive real axis. In addition, note that Q is the reactive power absorbed by the reactive elements just as P is the real power absorbed by the resistors. We will now demonstrate the use of these quantities.

Let us first demonstrate the use of these quantities in a circuit, and then apply them in the analysis of a power system.

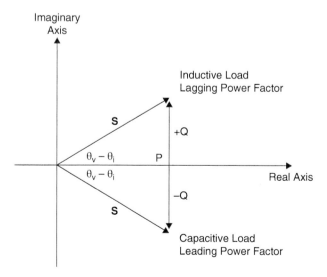

FIGURE 7.10   The power triangle

Example 7.9

Let us revisit Example 7.3 with the network in Figure 7.4, and determine the complex power delivered by the sources and use this information to calculate the average power supplied. In addition, let us determine the complex power of each element, and illustrate that a complex power balance exists. The following data were obtained in Example 7.3.

$$\mathbf{V_{cs}} = 16.5\angle 44.6° \text{ V} = [16.5/\sqrt{2}]\angle 44.6° \text{ V}_{rms}$$
$$\mathbf{I_{cs}} = 10\angle 0° \text{ A} = (10/\sqrt{2})\angle 0° \text{ A rms}$$
$$\mathbf{V_{vs}} = 2\angle 30° \text{ V} = (2/\sqrt{2}\angle 30° \text{ V}_{rms}$$
$$\mathbf{I_{vs}} = 7.23\angle 54.3° \text{ V} = [7.23/\sqrt{2}]\angle 54.3° \text{ V}_{rms}$$

All the data are shown in Figure 7.11. Once again, since the positive current is leaving the positive terminal of the source, both sources are supplying power. The amount of power can be computed using complex power, i.e.

$$\mathbf{S_{cs}} = \mathbf{V_{cs}} \text{ rms } \mathbf{I_{cs}} \text{ rms}^*$$
$$= (16.5/2) [10/\sqrt{2}]\angle 44.6°$$
$$= 82.5\angle 44.6° \text{ VA}$$

and

$$\mathbf{S_{vs}} = \mathbf{V_{vs}} \text{ rms } \mathbf{I_{vs}} \text{ rms}^*$$
$$= [2/\sqrt{2}] [7.23/\sqrt{2}]\angle 30° - 54.3°$$
$$= 7.23\angle -24.3° \text{ VA}$$

The average power delivered by the sources is obtained from the real part of the complex power, i.e.

$$P_{cs} = \text{Re } (\mathbf{S_{cs}})$$
$$= 82.5 \cos (44.6°)$$
$$= 58.73 \text{ W}$$

and

$$P_{vs} = \text{Re } (\mathbf{S_{vs}})$$
$$= 7.23 \cos (-24.3°)$$
$$= 6.59 \text{ W}$$

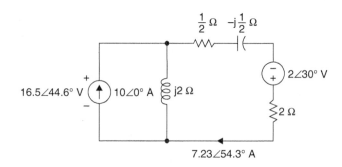

FIGURE 7.11 Circuit used in Example 7.9

Therefore, the total average power delivered to the circuit is

$$P_{total} = P_{cs} + P_{vs}$$
$$= 65.32 \text{ W}$$

The total complex power supplied is

$$\mathbf{S_{TS}} = 82.5\angle 44.6° + 7.23\angle -24.3°$$
$$= 58.74 + j57.93 + 6.58 - j2.96$$
$$= 65.32 + j55 \text{ VA}$$

Note that the total resistance in the circuit is $R_T = 2 + 1/2 = 2.5 \ \Omega$. Therefore, the complex power absorbed is the sum of the following.

$$\mathbf{S_R} = (I_{rms})^2 R_T$$
$$= [7.23/2]^2 (2.5)$$
$$= 65.32 \text{ W}$$
$$\mathbf{S_L} = (V_{rms})^2 / \mathbf{Z_L}^*$$
$$= [16.5/2]^2 / (-j2)$$
$$= j68.06 \text{ VAR}$$
$$\mathbf{S_C} = (I_{rms})^2 \mathbf{Z_C}$$
$$= [7.23/2]^2 (-j1/2)$$
$$= -j13.06 \text{ VAR}$$

and, therefore,

$$\mathbf{S_{TA}} = 65.32 + j68.06 - j13.06$$
$$= 65.32 + j55 \text{ VA}$$

As demonstrated earlier, the power factor for an inductive circuit is lagging because the current lags the voltage. The power factor is leading in a capacitive circuit because the current is leading the voltage. This information is shown in Figure 7.10, and demonstrated by the fact that

$$\theta_v - \theta_i = \theta_z$$

and θ_z is positive in an inductive circuit $(R + jX)$ and negative in a capacitive circuit $(R - jX)$. Hence, a positive power factor angle results from a lagging power factor, and a negative power factor angle is produced by a leading power factor.

An industrial plant is connected to the power company's source through a transmission line with a total impedance of 0.1 Ω. The line voltage at the plant is $480\angle 0°$ V_{rms}, and the plant consumes 100 kW at 0.74 power factor lagging. We wish to determine the magnitude of the source voltage and power factor at the source.

Example 7.10

The problem is modeled by the circuit shown in Figure 7.12a. Since $PF = \cos [\theta_v - \theta_i]$, then

$$[\theta_v - \theta_i] = \cos^{-1}(0.74) = 42.27°$$

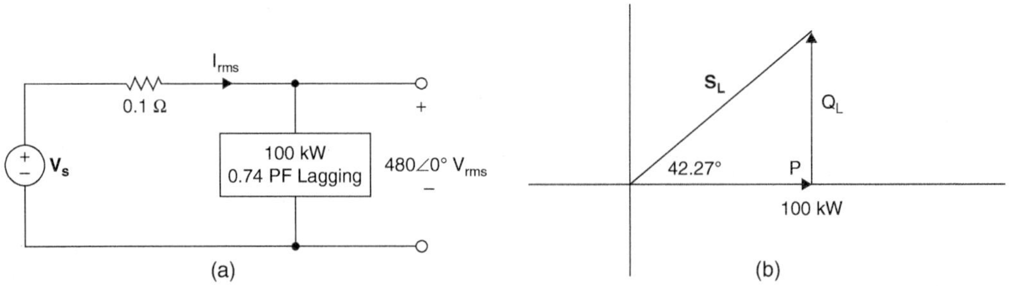

FIGURE 7.12 Circuit and power diagram for Example 7.10

Therefore, the power triangle is shown in Figure 7.12b. Now the value of Q_L can be determined from the equation

$$\tan 42.27° = Q_L/100k$$

$$Q_L = 90897.3 \text{ VAR}$$

Then

$$\mathbf{S_L} = P_L + jQ_L = 100{,}000 + j90897.3 = 135{,}138\angle42.27° \text{ VA}$$

The magnitude of the line current can now be determined from the apparent power at the load, i.e.

$$I_{rms} = S_L/V_{rms} = 135{,}138/480 = 281.54 \text{ A rms}$$

Now that we know the line current, we can compute the line losses as

$$P_{line} = (281.54)^2(0.1) = 7926.5 \text{ W}$$

The source must supply both the load power and the power absorbed in the line; hence

$$P_S = P_L + P_{line} = 100{,}000 + 7926.5 = 107{,}926.5 \text{ W}$$

The complex power at the source is then

$$\mathbf{S_S} = P_S + jQ_S = P_S + jQ_L = 107{,}926.5 + j90897.3 = 141{,}104.4\angle40.1° \text{ VA}$$

The magnitude of the source voltage is

$$V_S = S_S/I_{rms} = 141{,}104.4/281.54 = 501.2 \text{ V}_{rms}$$

The power factor at the source is

$$PF_S = \cos 40.1° = 0.765 \text{ lagging}$$

Example 7.11

The power source in the network in Figure 7.13 supplies two loads connected on a $220\angle0°$ V_{rms} line.

Load 1: 40 kW, 0.76 PF lagging

Load 2: 20 kW at unity PF

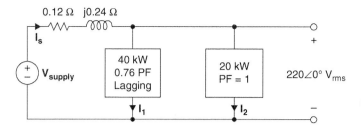

FIGURE 7.13   Circuit used in Example 7.11

We wish to determine the source voltage and the PF of the source.

Recall that the power factor is defined as

$$PF = P/[(V_{rms})(I_{rms})]$$

or

$$I_{rms} = P/[(V_{rms})(PF)]$$

Also recall that since the power factor is lagging, the circuit is inductive and the current lags the voltage. Therefore, the phase angle of current is negative. Substituting the given data into the equations yields the magnitude of the current.

$$I_1 = 40{,}000/[(220)(0.76)]$$
$$= 239.23 \text{ A rms}$$
$$\theta_1 = \cos^{-1}(0.76)$$
$$= 40.54°$$

The phase angle of the voltage is 0°, the power factor is lagging; hence the phasor current is

$$I_1 = 239.23\angle{-40.54°} \text{ A rms}$$

Similarly,

$$I_2 = 20{,}000/[(220)(1)]$$
$$= 90.91 \text{ A rms}$$

and

$$I_2 = 90.91\angle 0° \text{ A rms}$$

Since the power factor is unity, $\theta_i = \theta_v$.

The load currents are

$$I_1 = 40{,}000/(220)(0.76) = 239.23 \text{ and } \cos^{-1}(0.76) = -40.54° \ (\theta_i \text{ lags } \theta_v) \text{ and thus}$$
$$I_1 = 239.23\angle{-40.54°} \text{ A rms}$$

and

$$I_2 = 20{,}000/(220)(1) = 90.91\angle 0° \text{ A rms}$$

The source current is then

$$I_s = I_1 + I_2 = 239.23\angle{-40.54°} + 90.91\angle 10°$$
$$= 272.7 - j155.5$$
$$= 313.92\angle{-29.69°} \text{ A rms}$$

The source voltage is then

$$\mathbf{V_s} = [313.92\angle-29.69°][0.12 + j0.24] + 220\angle0°$$
$$= 84.13\angle33.74° + 220$$
$$= 289.96 + j46.73$$
$$= 293.7\angle9.16°\ V_{rms}$$

And the power factor at the source is

$$PF_S = \cos[9.16° - (-29.69°)] = \cos 38.85° = 0.78\ \text{lagging}$$

Now that we have discussed some of the salient features of complex power, let us employ this material to demonstrate the mechanisms involved in raising the power factor.

POWER FACTOR CORRECTION

Industrial loads typically consist of induction motors, fans, etc. and thus these loads usually have a lagging power factor. We found in Example 7.8 that by raising a low power factor we could achieve a real savings in delivering power, which translates into money. Furthermore, since the cost of machinery is typically high, it would be better if the correction mechanism was economical. As we will demonstrate, the "fix" is fairly simple and we will accomplish it with a capacitor.

Consider the circuit in Figure 7.14a where we have placed a capacitor across the load. The power triangle for the load is shown in Figure 7.14b and

$$\mathbf{S_{old}} = P_{old} + jQ_{old}$$

However, this condition illustrates a poor, i.e. low, power factor. Note carefully that a power factor closer to 1 would mean that the original phase angle must be reduced since PF is equal to the cosine of the angle. In Example 7.8, a PF of 0.66 corresponds to an angle of 48.7°, while a PF of 0.92 corresponds to a phase angle of 23.07°. Therefore, we want to add negative Q, which when added to Q_{old} will result in the proper phase angle corresponding to the new desired power factor.

Recall that one of the equations for complex power is

$$\mathbf{S} = V_{rms}^2/\mathbf{Z^*}$$

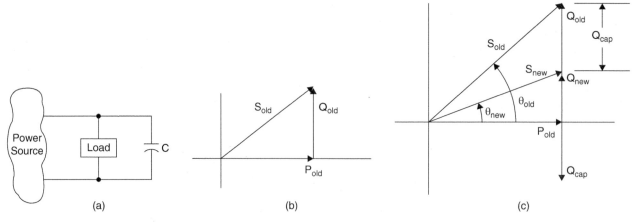

FIGURE 7.14   Diagrams used to explain power factor correction

The capacitor is purely reactive, i.e. P = 0, and its impedance is

$$\mathbf{Z} = 1/j\,\omega C$$

Therefore, $\mathbf{S_{cap}}$ is

$$\mathbf{S_{cap}} = V_{rms}^2/(1/j\,\omega C)^* = -j\,\omega C V_{rms}^2 = jQ_{cap}$$

and therefore,

$$Q_{cap} = -\omega\, C V_{rms}^2$$

   In other words, the capacitor provides only negative Q. If we now combine the negative Q provided by the capacitor with the load Q, i.e. Q_{old}, then the new Q, i.e. Q_{new}, which corresponds to the new desired power factor can be obtained as shown in Figure 7.14c. The initial data provided consists of the following: the industrial load consumes P_L at an old PF_{old} from a line voltage of V_L at 60 Hz. The old PF must be raised to a new power factor, PF_{new}. Therefore, the step-by-step procedure for power factor correction is performed in the following manner with reference to Figure 7.14.

1. The old power factor can be employed to determine the old power factor angle, i.e. $\theta_{old} = \cos^{-1}(PF_{old})$.

2. Using P_L and the power factor angle, Q_{old} can be determined via the tangent function as $Q_{old} = P_L \tan(\theta_{old})$.

3. The old, i.e. initial, value of the complex power is now known as $\mathbf{S_{old}} = P_L + j\,Q_{old}$.

4. The new, i.e. desired, power factor can be used to determine the new power factor angle, i.e. $\theta_{new} = \cos^{-1}(PF_{new})$.

5. Using P_L and the new power factor angle, Q_{new} can be determined via the tangent function as $Q_{new} = P_L \tan(\theta_{new})$.

6. The new, i.e. desired, value of the complex power is now known as $\mathbf{S_{new}} = P_L + jQ_{new}$.

7. The change in complex power affects only the reactive component, i.e. P_L is the same. Thus, the difference between $\mathbf{S_{new}}$ and $\mathbf{S_{old}}$ is caused by the addition of the capacitor, i.e. $\mathbf{S_{cap}}$. Therefore, $\mathbf{S_{new}} - \mathbf{S_{old}} = (P_L + jQ_{old}) - (P_L + jQ_{new}) = jQ_{cap}$ and this value will be negative, as shown in Figure 7.14c.

8. Since $\mathbf{Q_{cap}} = -\omega C V_{rms}^2$, the required value of the capacitor needed to raise the power factor is $C = Q_{cap}/\omega V_{rms}^2$.

Let's revisit the problem in Example 7.8 and determine the value of the capacitor, which when placed in parallel with the load will produce the desired power factor of 0.92 lagging.   **Example 7.12**
   The following analysis is performed with reference to the diagram in Figure 7.15.

$$\theta_{old} = \cos^{-1}(PF_{old}) = \cos^{-1}(0.66) = 48.7°$$
$$Q_{old} = (100k)\tan 48.7° = 113{,}800 \text{ VAR}$$
$$\theta_{new} = \cos^{-1}(PF_{new}) = \cos^{-1}(0.92) = 23.07°$$
$$Q_{new} = (100k)\tan 23.07° = 42{,}600 \text{ VAR}$$
$$Q_{cap} = Q_{new} - Q_{old} = j42{,}600 - j113{,}800 = -j71{,}200 \text{ VAR}$$
$$-j71{,}200 = -j377C(480)^2$$

Solving for C yields a value of 820 µF for the capacitor.

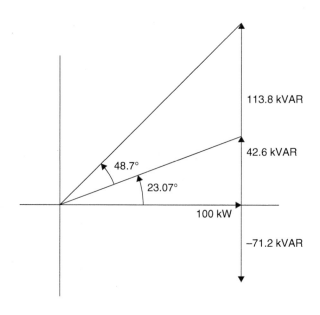

FIGURE 7.15 Power diagram for Example 7.12

Problems

7.1 In the network in Figure P7.1, determine the equation for the current and the instantaneous power as a function of time.

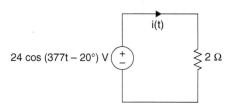

FIGURE P7.1

7.2 Given the network in Figure P7.2, find the equation for the voltage and the instantaneous power as a function of time.

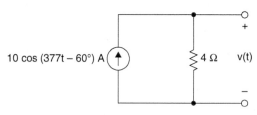

FIGURE P7.2

7.3   Determine the equations for the current and the instantaneous power as a function of time for the network in Figure P7.3.

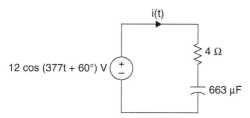

FIGURE P7.3

7.4   Given the network in Figure P7.4, find the equation for the voltage and the instantaneous power as a function of time.

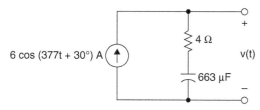

FIGURE P7.4

7.5   Determine the equations for the current and the instantaneous power as a function of time for the network in Figure P7.5.

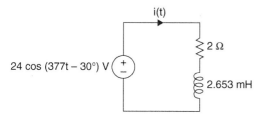

FIGURE P7.5

7.6   Given the network in Figure P7.6, find the equation for the voltage and the instantaneous power as a function of time.

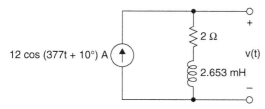

FIGURE P7.6

7.7 Determine the total average power supplied to the network in Figure P7.7.

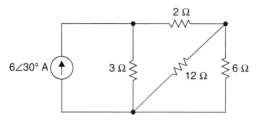

FIGURE P7.7

7.8 Determine the total average power absorbed by the network in Figure P7.8.

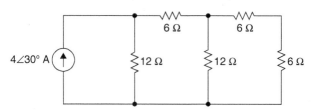

FIGURE P7.8

7.9 Find the total average power supplied to the network in Figure P7.9.

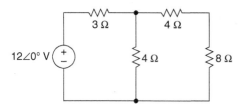

FIGURE P7.9

7.10 Determine the total average power absorbed by the $3\,\Omega$ resistor in the network in Figure P7.10.

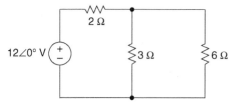

FIGURE P7.10

7.11 Determine the total average power absorbed by the 3 Ω resistor in the network in Figure P7.11.

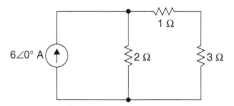

FIGURE P7.11

7.12 Find the total average power supplied to the network in Figure P7.12.

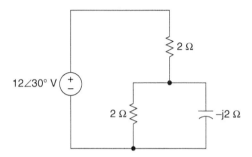

FIGURE P7.12

7.13 Determine the total average power supplied to the network in Figure P7.13.

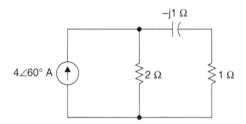

FIGURE P7.13

7.14 Calculate the average power absorbed by the 2 Ω resistor in the circuit in Figure P7.13.

7.15 Calculate the average power absorbed by the 1 Ω resistor in the circuit in Figure P7.13.

7.16 Determine the total average power supplied to the network in Figure P7.16.

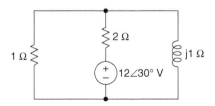

FIGURE P7.16

7.17 Calculate the average power absorbed by the 1 Ω resistor in the circuit in Figure P7.16.

7.18 Find the average power absorbed by the 2 Ω resistor in the circuit in Figure P7.16.

7.19 Determine the total average power supplied to the network in Figure P7.19. In addition, determine the amount of average power absorbed by each of the resistors in the network.

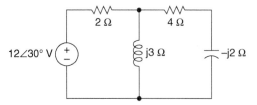

FIGURE P7.19

7.20 Determine the total average power supplied to the network in Figure P7.20. In addition, determine the amount of average power absorbed by each of the resistors in the network.

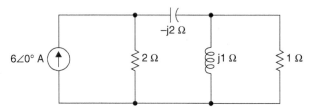

FIGURE P7.20

7.21 Determine the total average power supplied to the network in Figure P7.21. In addition, determine the amount of average power absorbed by each of the resistors in the network.

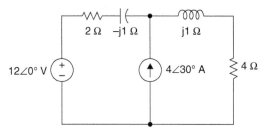

FIGURE P7.21

7.22 Determine the total average power supplied to the network in Figure P7.22. In addition, determine the amount of average power absorbed by each of the resistors in the network.

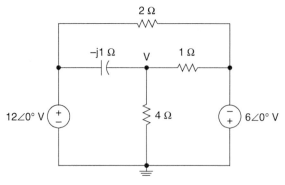

FIGURE P7.22

7.23   Given the circuit in Figure P7.23, determine the Z_L for maximum average power transfer and the value of the power transferred.

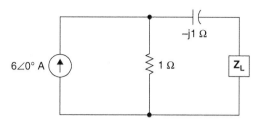

FIGURE P7.23

7.24   Given the circuit in Figure P7.24, determine the Z_L for maximum average power transfer and the value of the power transferred.

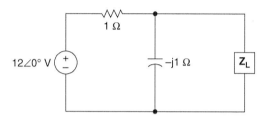

FIGURE P7.24

7.25   For the network in Figure P7.25, determine the Z_L for maximum average power transfer and the value of the power transferred.

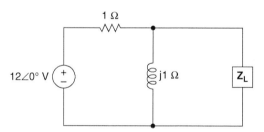

FIGURE P7.25

7.26   Given the circuit in Figure P7.26, determine the Z_L for maximum average power transfer and the value of the power transferred.

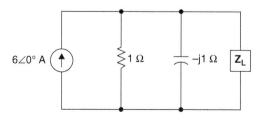

FIGURE P7.26

7.27 For the network in Figure P7.27, determine the Z_L for maximum average power transfer and the value of the power transferred.

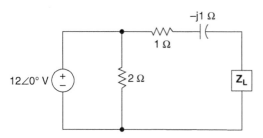

FIGURE P7.27

7.28 Given the circuit in Figure P7.28, determine the Z_L for maximum average power transfer and the value of the power transferred

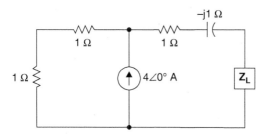

FIGURE P7.28

7.29 For the network in Figure P7.29, determine the Z_L for maximum average power transfer and the value of the power transferred.

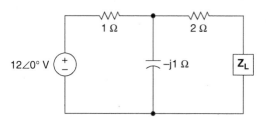

FIGURE P7.29

7.30 Given the circuit in Figure P7.30, determine the Z_L for maximum average power transfer and the value of the power transferred.

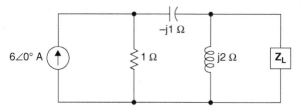

FIGURE P7.30

7.31 Given the circuit in Figure P7.31, determine the $\mathbf{Z_L}$ for maximum average power transfer
and the value of the power transferred.

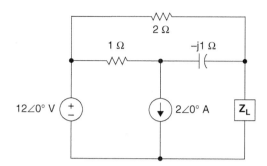

FIGURE P7.31

7.32 Determine the rms value of the waveform shown in Figure P7.32.

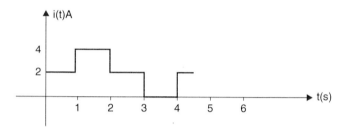

FIGURE P7.32

7.33 Calculate the rms value of the waveform shown in Figure P7.33.

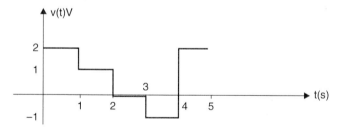

FIGURE P7.33

7.34 Determine the rms value of the waveform shown in Figure P7.34.

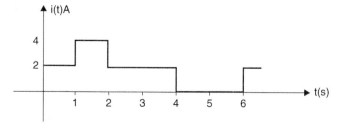

FIGURE P7.34

7.35 The current waveform shown in Figure P7.35 exists in a 5 Ω resistor. Calculate the average power absorbed by the resistor.

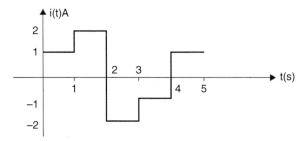

FIGURE P7.35

7.36 The current waveform shown in Figure P7.36 exists in a 4 Ω resistor. Calculate the average power absorbed by the resistor.

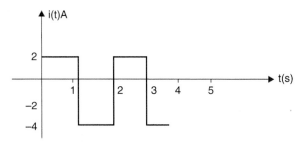

FIGURE P7.36

7.37 The current waveform shown in Figure P7.37 exists in a 6 Ω resistor. Calculate the average power absorbed by the resistor.

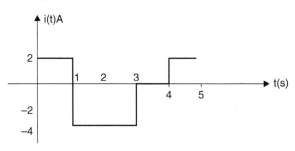

FIGURE P7.37

7.38 The current waveform shown in Figure P7.38 exists in a 2 Ω resistor. Determine the average power absorbed by the resistor.

v(t) V
2
-2
-4
-6
1
2
3
4
5
t(s)

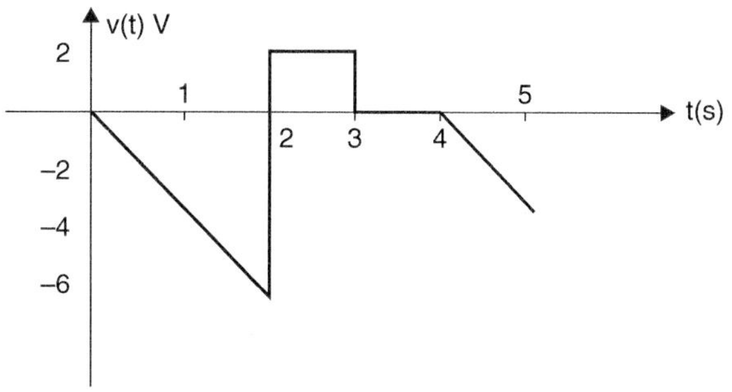

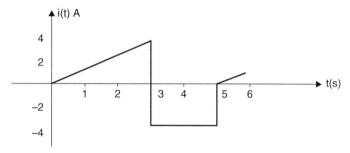

FIGURE P7.38

7.39 The current waveform shown in Figure P7.39 exists in a 4 Ω resistor. Calculate the average power absorbed by the resistor.

i(t) A
4
2
-2
-4
1
2
3
4
5
6
t(s)

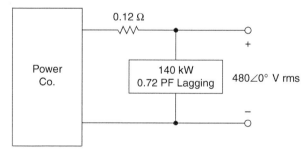

FIGURE P7.39

7.40 Calculate the power supplied to the network in Figure P7.40.

Power Co.
0.12 Ω
140 kW
0.72 PF Lagging
+
480∠0° V rms
–

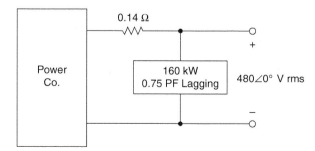

FIGURE P7.40

7.41 Determine the power supplied to the network in Figure P7.41.

Power Co.
0.14 Ω
160 kW
0.75 PF Lagging
+
480∠0° V rms
–

FIGURE P7.41

7.42 Determine the power that must be supplied to the network in Figure P 7.42, (a) under the conditions shown in the figure, and (b) if the power factor is changed to 0.92 lagging.

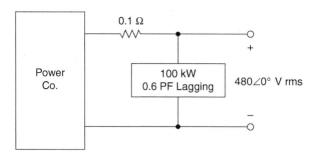

FIGURE P7.42

7.43 An industrial plant operates under the following conditions: the load is 40 kW, the line voltage is $220\angle 0°$ V_{rms} at 60 Hz, the power factor is 0.72 lagging, and the line resistance is 0.16 Ω. Determine the savings in kilowatts if the power factor is changed to 0.9 lagging.

7.44 An industrial plant operates under the following conditions: the load is 120 kW, the line voltage is $480\angle 0°$ V_{rms} at 60 Hz, the power factor is 0.84 lagging, and the line impedance is $0.1 + j0.2$ Ω. Determine the power factor at the source.

7.45 An industrial plant operates under the following conditions: the load is 180 kW, the line voltage is $480\angle 0°$ V_{rms} at 60 Hz, the power factor is 0.9 lagging, and the line impedance is $0.1 + j0.1$ Ω. Determine the power factor at the source.

7.46 Given the circuit in Figure P7.46, determine the line voltage and power factor at the source.

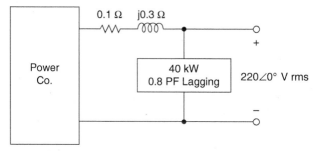

FIGURE P7.46

7.47 An industrial plant operates under the following conditions: the load is 36 kW, the line voltage is $220\angle 0°$ V_{rms} at 60 Hz, the power factor is 0.84 lagging, and the line impedance is $0.1 + j0.2$ Ω. Determine the line voltage and power factor at the source.

7.48   Given the circuit in Figure P7.48, determine the line voltage and power factor at the source.

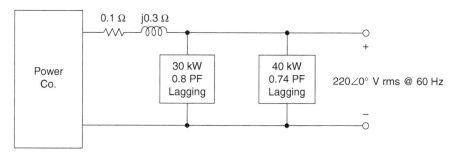

FIGURE P7.48

7.49   An industrial plant operates under the following conditions: the load is 40 kW, the line voltage is $220\angle0°$ V_{rms} at 60 Hz, and the power factor is 0.8 lagging. Determine the value of the capacitance, which when placed in parallel with the load will raise the power factor to 0.9 lagging.

7.50   An industrial plant operates under the following conditions: the load is 96 kW, the line voltage is $480\angle0°$ V_{rms} at 60 Hz, and the power factor is 0.69 lagging. Determine the value of the capacitance, which when placed in parallel with the load will raise the power factor to 0.9 lagging.

7.51   An industrial plant operates under the following conditions: the load is 110 kW, the line voltage is $480\angle0°$ V_{rms} at 60 Hz, and the power factor is 0.76 lagging. Determine the value of the capacitance, which when placed in parallel with the load will raise the power factor to 0.9 lagging.

7.52   An industrial plant operates under the following conditions: the load is 72 kW, the line voltage is $220\angle0°$ V_{rms} at 60 Hz, and the power factor is 0.68 lagging. Determine the value of the capacitance, which when placed in parallel with the load will raise the power factor to 0.9 lagging.

7.53   An industrial plant operates under the following conditions: the load is 80 kW, the line voltage is $220\angle0°$ V_{rms} at 60 Hz, and the power factor is 0.65 lagging. If 3000 μF of capacitance is placed in parallel with the load, determine the new power factor.

7.54   An industrial plant operates under the following conditions: the load is 60 kW, the line voltage is $220\angle0°$ V_{rms} at 60 Hz, and the power factor is 0.7 lagging. If 2500 μF of capacitance is placed in parallel with the load, determine the new power factor.

CHAPTER 8

The Electric Power System

LEARNING OBJECTIVES

- To understand the structure of the electric power system and the interconnection of its various components

- To understand magnetic circuits and their relationship to electric circuits

- To understand mutual inductance and its role in transformers

- To learn to calculate voltages and currents in various transformer circuits, including the ideal transformer

- To learn how to analyze three-phase circuits and calculate three-phase power

THE ELECTRIC POWER SYSTEM STRUCTURE

The electric power system is composed of a number of components, but a high-level examination of the system illustrates that it can be generally characterized by the following functions: *Generation* produces the power, *transformation* steps the voltage from a low level to a high level for long-haul transmission, *transmission* carries the power to the area where it will be used, *transformation* steps the voltage down from the high level to a lower level where it can be used by the customer, and *distribution* distributes the power to the end-point users. An overview of the system is shown in Figure 8.1.

The power systems that are interconnected throughout the country comprise the electric power grid or simply the *grid*. Thus, the electric power grid is an interconnected network of power plants, substations, transformers, and the attendant infrastructure required to deliver electric power from the utility companies that produce it to the various consumers that use it in a wide variety of applications ranging from simple households to large complex industrial plants. So, while most people think of the grid as simply the transmission system, it is actually a set of synchronized power stations connected by transmission facilities and managed by control centers. It is a constantly evolving optimization system with the aim of achieving high levels of system reliability, quality, and security.

The current focus of this system is the development of what is called the *smart grid*. This smart grid is characterized by a set of initiatives that generally speaking improve system operations, facilitate maintenance, and optimize planning by automating operations and ensuring that the grid components are able to communicate with each other when needed. For example, one of the initiatives that are currently in vogue is smart storage technology that helps integrate renewable energy, such as wind and solar, which are not always available, into the power grid by controlling the supply, storing the excess, and then distributing it in an efficient manner. The smart grid is a marvelous mixture of innovative products and services operating under intelligent control, communication, and monitoring and working in conjunction with self-healing technologies in order to better serve the existing customer base as well as the one expected in the future.

Let us now examine each of the major components of the electric power system.

GENERATION

Electric power begins at the generating station. At these stations, the source of power is typically coal, natural gas, hydro, or nuclear. Today, a limited amount of solar, wind, geothermal, and

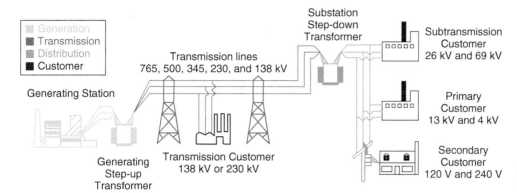

FIGURE 8.1   Overview of the electric power system

biomass also provide an alternative energy source in many areas of the country. Somewhat new to the mix are wave generators, and the U.S. Navy is testing these devices in the ocean off Hawaii as an alternative source of power for their bases.

Two typical generating plants are shown in Figure 8.2a and b. The former is a hydro plant in which the fall of the water is used to drive a turbine, which in turn drives the generator. The second plant is a fossil fuel plant in which fuel and air are added to a boiler, which produces steam from water. This steam drives the turbine, which in turn drives the generator. Prominently displayed are the cooling towers, which extract heat from the system primarily through evaporation.

A simplified version of the fossil generation cycle is shown in Figure 8.3, and the typical fuel and air flow paths are shown in Figure 8.4. Condensers, e.g. the cooling towers shown in Figure 8.2b, are used to recover water from the steam and close the loop. In a nuclear plant, it is the reactor that provides the power used to generate steam.

At the typical generating plant in the United States, the generators will produce a 60 Hz three-phase alternating current voltage. The voltage depends upon the generators, but will typically range from about 13.8 to 25 kV. The generators are designed to produce this voltage in a three-phase set. We will demonstrate in the material that follows that the reason for generating

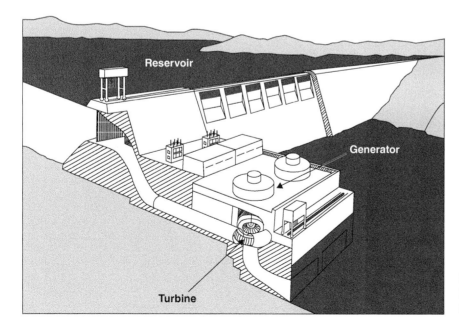

FIGURE 8.2a   Diagram of a hydroelectric-generating facility (courtesy of Southern Company)

FIGURE 8.2b   A fossil fuel generation plant

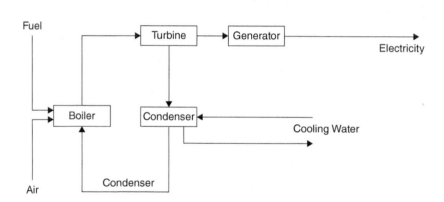

FIGURE 8.3   Air fossil fuel generation cycle

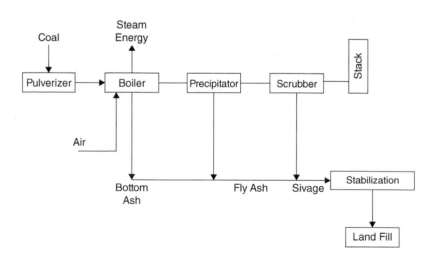

FIGURE 8.4   Fuel air flow in fossil generation

in three phase is that this set achieves smooth power delivery and does not pulsate as is the case in single-phase power.

TRANSFORMATION – LOW VOLTAGE TO HIGH VOLTAGE

In order to achieve efficient power delivery, the voltage produced by generators must be raised for transmission. Recall that power is essentially the product of voltage and current, and so we can transmit power at high voltage and low current or vice versa. The primary difference between these two alternatives is the line losses, i.e. if the current is very high, the resistance of the lines will cause high I^2R losses. In order to minimize these line losses, the voltage must be stepped up from the generator output voltage to the transmission line voltage, e.g. 230 kV or 500 kV are typical. The device that raises the generator output voltage to the transmission line level is a power transformer, an example of which is shown in Figure 8.5. The operational characteristics of this component will be presented later in this chapter.

TRANSMISSION

Once the voltage is raised to transmission level, it is carried across the country via high-voltage transmission lines, and it is almost impossible to travel any distance and not encounter one of them overhead. Figure 8.6 illustrates one such structure.

The three-phase power conductors are hanging on insulators, and at the top of each power pole, there is a wire that runs on top of the power conductors. These wires are used to provide about 60 degrees of coverage for lightning protection.

TRANSFORMATION—HIGH VOLTAGE TO LOW VOLTAGE

Once the power arrives in the local area, the high voltage must be stepped down so that it can be distributed and used. This process typically takes place at the substations within a local area. At these substations, the transformers step the voltage down from 230 kV or 500 kV to 115 kV and then again to a voltage in the 10–20 kV range. For example, Figures 8.7 and 8.8 show photos of transformers that step the voltage down from 230 to 115 kV and from 115 to 12 kV, respectively. Now the power is ready for distribution.

FIGURE 8.5 Step-up voltage transformer (Алексей Кравчук/ Adobe Stock)

FIGURE 8.6 High-voltage transmission line

FIGURE 8.7 A step down transformer
(Suprachai/Adobe Stock)

DISTRIBUTION

The last stage in the delivery of electric power is distribution. Distribution takes place at two levels: primary and secondary. The primary distribution takes place at, e.g. a 12 kV level, and only large consumers are fed directly from these lines. Power at this level is also distributed to neighborhoods, using either an overhead transformer, as shown in Figure 8.9, or underground

FIGURE 8.8   115 kV to 12 kV transformer (Алексей Кравчук/ Adobe Stock)

FIGURE 8.9   Overhead distribution transformer, i.e. pole pig

FIGURE 8.10
Underground distribution transformer

facilities using a transformer mounted on a pad, typically on lot lines, as shown in Figure 8.10. In the neighborhood, the power arrives at a transformer, such as the one shown in Figure 8.9, where the 12 kV is reduced to 240/120 V and sent to multiple homes via service drops. The 240 V is used in homes for big appliances, e.g. air conditioners and stoves that require relatively large amounts of power, and the lower voltage is used for lights and small appliances.

It is also important to note that along the lines in the distribution area there are fuses, i.e. cutouts, like the ones shown in Figure 8.11, that are designed to pop out and break the circuit in the event of trouble on the line, e.g. a lightning strike. It is important to remember that these circuit breakers, like the ground fault interrupters (GFIs) that are employed, for example, in the bathrooms in a home, are designed to protect the equipment – they are not designed to protect you.

MAGNETIC CIRCUIT FUNDAMENTALS

Magnetic circuits play a key role in electrical technology, primarily because they are a fundamental component in transformers and electric machines, i.e. motors and generators. The energy transfer mechanism within the magnetic circuit is the magnetic flux, or simply flux.

Most of us have used magnets to post notes on metal filing cabinets, refrigerators, and all sorts of similar objects. While the effect of the magnet is clear, what is really going on here? Regardless of the actual structure of the magnet, the operation is shown in Figure 8.12. Note the device has a north pole and a south pole, and flux that emanates at the north pole is returned via the south pole in a closed-loop fashion. The units of flux are Webers, named for the German physicist Wilhelm Weber. The earth itself has flux lines, which extend from the north pole to the south pole and a compass, used for navigation, employs a needle that aligns itself with these flux lines, thus providing the reference direction for travelers.

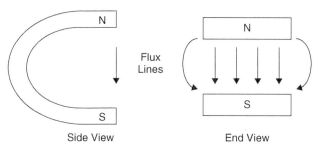

Side View   End View   **FIGURE 8.12**   Magnetic flux lines

Consider for a moment the bar magnet with the cross-sectional area, A, as shown in Figure 8.13. If we assume the flux, φ, is uniformly distributed over this cross-sectional area, then the flux density, B, in Webers/m^2 is

$$B = \phi/A$$

This unit Webers/m^2 is also known simply as Tesla, named for Nikola Tesla, another one of the original giants of this industry. As we will indicate in the material that follows, this flux will pass through anything from air to steel, e.g. the flux is in air in the earth's magnetic field as shown in Figure 8.14. As one might imagine, the flux density in air is much smaller than that of a ferromagnetic material such as iron or steel, i.e. air essentially provides more resistance than does a material such as steel. In fact, the magnetic flux density in steel is hundreds or thousands of times greater than that of air, i.e. ferromagnetic materials essentially grease the path for the flux, providing little resistance, and as a result the density is very high.

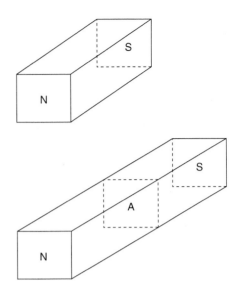

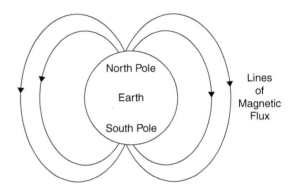

FIGURE 8.13 Cross-sectional area for a bar magnet

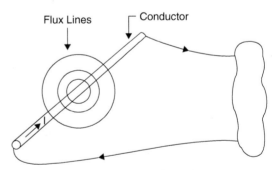

FIGURE 8.14 The earth's lines of magnetic flux

FIGURE 8.15 Flux lines around a current-carrying conductor

We learned in basic physics, when studying Faraday's law, that a magnetic field is created by a current flowing through a conductor, as shown in Figure 8.15. The flux lines encircle the conductor and become less dense as the distance from the conductor increases. What is known as the right-hand rule states that if the thumb of the right hand extends in the direction of positive current flow, then the fingers on the right hand in wrapping around the conductor indicate the direction of the flux. Two problems, which were solved long ago, serve to indicate the effects of this flux. Land telephone lines are typically bundled in 50 pair cables, and the cables run from the handset to the telephone company's central office where the communication is switched to its destination. So there may be 50 telephone conversations in progress in a single cable. In the early years you could hear another phone conversation taking place in the background while you were talking. This crosstalk resulted from magnetic flux linking the two circuits as well as parasitic capacitance. In addition, it was not uncommon in the past for a car radio to buzz when driving down the highway under high-voltage lines, which resulted from the radio entering the flux field of the high-voltage lines running overhead.

GENERATORS

There are two critical concepts that govern the operation of power generation equipment. (1) A voltage is induced in a coil of wire by a changing magnetic environment, i.e. if a coil is moved through a magnetic field or the magnetic field is changing in some manner relative to the coil, and (2) a force will be produced on a current-carrying conductor immersed in a magnetic field. These two fundamental concepts are employed in the operation of electric machines.

An electric machine is a device that can be operated in either direction and in any mode, i.e. as a motor or a generator. If the input to the device is mechanical energy, the output is electrical energy. If the input is electrical energy, the output is mechanical energy. In the former case, the machine operates as a generator, while in the latter case, the machine operates as a motor.

The grid is dominated by machines that generate alternating current, and these machines are sometimes referred to as alternators. The machine consists of a stator and rotor, as shown in Figure 8.16. As the name implies, the stator is the stationary portion of the machine, and the rotor is mounted on a shaft connected to a prime mover, e.g. a turbine. The armature, which can reside on either the stator or rotor, is the electric-current carrying component. The magnetic field within the machine is provided by magnets that are mounted on the stator or rotor. In electric power plants, the equipment is large, as shown in Figure 8.17.

While the ac machines may be either induction machines or synchronous machines, the synchronous generators are the primary source of energy in modern power generation. The output frequency of the voltage is directly related to the generator's exact rotational speed. Since frequency stability is extremely important on the grid, the issues involved in connecting other sources, e.g. solar, as shown in Figure 8.18, or wind, as shown in Figure 8.19, must be evaluated with this stability requirement as a primary concern.

FIGURE 8.16   Internal view of an ac machine

FIGURE 8.17 A large ac machine

FIGURE 8.18 A solar farm

The machine's operational characteristics are explained in more detail in Chapters 14 and 15. However, it is instructive to indicate at this point the key principles that underline the manner in which the machine produces power. While modern versions of these machines may employ different architectures, a simple version of the basic principles helps provide a fundamental understanding of the process involved. The ac generators use mechanical power, e.g. a turbine, to rotate a conductor in the form of a loop within a fixed magnetic field, which results in current being induced in the conductor in accordance with Faraday's law. Spinning the loop in a constant magnetic field at a constant speed generates a sine wave, and since 1 cycle/s corresponds to 1 revolution/s and 60 revolutions/s equals 60 cycles/s, which is 60 Hz, the loop would have to spin 60 times/s so that the output current matches that of the US power grid. Although we have outlined the process with a single loop, the generators used in power plants employ a huge number of coils, wrapped around a ferromagnetic material. Since Faraday's law states that each loop will produce the same electromotive force, the use of more coils generates more output power.

FIGURE 8.19   Wind turbines

ELECTRIC/MAGNETIC CIRCUIT ANALOGY

At this point it is instructive to indicate that there is an analogous relationship between magnetic circuits and electric circuits. Consider, for example, the magnetic circuit shown in Figure 8.20. The current-carrying coil has N turns, the current in the coil is I, and the core is a ferromagnetic material. Using the right-hand rule, we see that the current causes a flux to be established, and while there may be some leakage, the vast majority of the flux will be confined to the core. It is both the current and the number of turns of the coil that provide the force to push the flux around this magnetic circuit. So, what is known as the *magnetomotive force* (mmf), f, is

$$f = NI$$

where N is the number of turns and I is the current in amperes. This driving mechanism, measured in ampere-turns, is analogous to a voltage source in an electric circuit, and the flux, measured in Webers, is analogous to the current in an electric circuit.

The ferromagnetic material can saturate, i.e. increases in NI will not produce a corresponding increase in flux. So we will assume that the magnetic circuit, like the electric circuits we have been analyzing, is operating in the linear range.

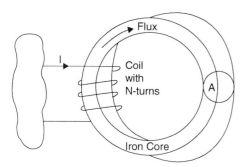

FIGURE 8.20   Flux confined to an iron core

The magnetic resistance that impedes the flow of flux is called *reluctance* and is defined by the equation

$$R = \frac{f}{\phi}$$

where the units of reluctance are ampere-turns/Weber. Note that this equation is often referred to as Ohm's law for magnetic circuits because of the similarity existing between it and its counterpart in electric circuits. The reluctance of materials varies from low-reluctance materials such as iron and steel to high-reluctance materials such as air, wood, and plastic.

MUTUAL INDUCTANCE

In the attempt of presenting the material in a simple and straightforward manner, we will assume the magnetic circuits are operating in the linear range and we are dealing with ideal elements, i.e. we will ignore such things as the resistance of the conductors or any stray capacitance between them.

An analysis of mutual inductance is based upon two fundamental laws: Ampere's law and Faraday's law. Ampere's law states that the current in a conductor will produce a magnetic field, as shown in Figure 8.15.

Then, if this magnetic field is time-varying, Faraday's law states that if this field links an electric circuit, it will produce a voltage in this linked circuit similar to the crosstalk problem discussed earlier. While these forces are always at work, they become a dominant issue when the conductors are in close proximity.

The mathematical development that describes mutual inductance is based upon these two fundamental laws and proceeds as follows. As indicated in Figure 8.17a, the flux linkage, symbol for lambda, for the coil and its relationship to current are defined by the following equations:

$$\lambda = N\phi$$
$$\lambda = Li$$

where the constant of proportionality between flux linkage and current is inductance. Therefore, the flux is related to current by the expression

$$\phi = \frac{L}{N}i$$

However, the voltage induced in the coil is related to the time rate of change of the flux linkage in accordance with Faraday's law and thus

$$v(t) = \frac{d\lambda}{dt}$$

Since we assume the inductance to be constant, the voltage is

$$v(t) = L\frac{di(t)}{dt}$$

which we recognize as Ohm's law for an inductor with the equivalent circuit shown in Figure 8.21a.

As indicated in Figure 8.21b, the flux extends beyond the immediate area of the coil. So, if we now move another coil into close proximity with this coil, we produce the circuit in Figure 8.22 in which the flux in coil 1 links with coil 2. Although there is no current in coil 2, a voltage v_2 will be induced in this coil via the flux linkage in accordance with Faraday's law. Since this circuit

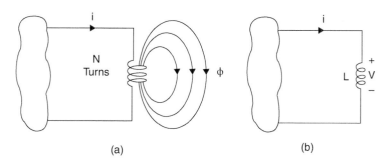

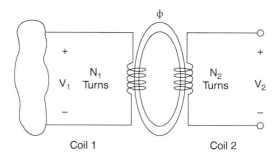

FIGURE 8.21 The current/flux linkage relationship for an inductor

(a)   (b)

FIGURE 8.22 Flux in coil 1 Links coil 2

contains more than one coil, we must be careful to note that L_1 is the inductance of coil 1, and to avoid any confusion with the labeling, we refer to this inductance as self-inductance. The voltage induced in coil 2 by the flux linkage is

$$v_2 = \frac{d\lambda_2}{dt} = \frac{d}{dt}(N_2\phi) = \frac{d}{dt}\left(N_2\left(\frac{L_1}{N_1}i_1\right)\right) = \frac{N_2}{N_1}L_1\frac{di_1}{dt} = L_{21}\frac{di_1}{dt}$$

And like v_1, this voltage is directly related to the time rate of change of the current i_1. Thus, the two coils are "magnetically coupled" and the quantity L_{21} is called the *mutual inductance* and measured in henrys.

In this analysis thus far, we first analyzed a single coil, and then we added another coil that linked with the first. Now we step the analysis up another notch to consider the circuit in Figure 8.23 in which the second coil is connected to a circuit and contains a current i_2. It is important to note the directions of the currents as well as that of each coil. In this case, the flux is dependent on both i_1 and i_2, and the flux linkages for each coil are

$$\lambda_1 = L_1 i_1 + L_{12} i_2$$
$$\lambda_2 = L_{21} i_1 + L_2 i_2$$

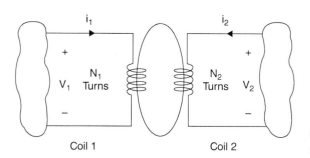

FIGURE 8.23 Flux linking two energized coils

And therefore by applying Faraday's law, we obtain

$$v_1 = \frac{d\lambda_1}{dt} = L_1 \frac{di_1}{dt} + L_{12} \frac{di_2}{dt}$$

$$v_2 = \frac{d\lambda_2}{dt} = L_{21} \frac{di_1}{dt} + L_2 \frac{di_2}{dt}$$

which in the linear case, where $L_{12} = L_{21} = M$, can be written as

$$v_1(t) = L_1 \frac{di_1}{dt} + M \frac{di_2}{dt}$$

$$v_2(t) = L_2 \frac{di_2}{dt} + M \frac{di_1}{dt}$$

When two coils are linked, the physical geometry is important, i.e. are the fluxes created by each coil adding or subtracting? The answer to this question is clearly important. Therefore, we must have some mechanism to answer this question, and it is what is known as the *dot convention* (the dot denotes which terminal is positive where the current enters). In the application of this convention, dots are placed on the coils and if the currents are either entering or leaving both dotted terminals, the mutual fluxes produced by the currents will add. However, if one current enters the dot and the other one leaves the dot, the mutual fluxes produced by the currents will subtract.

In sinusoidal steady-state circuit analysis, the equations can be written in the frequency domain for a phasor analysis as follows:

$$\mathbf{V_1} = j\omega L_1 \mathbf{I_1} + j\omega M \mathbf{I_2}$$
$$\mathbf{V_2} = j\omega L_2 \mathbf{I_2} + j\omega M \mathbf{I_1}$$

Thus, the transition from the physical configuration to the time domain and then to the frequency domain is shown in Figure 8.24. Given the circuit format in Figure 8.24c, it is much easier to write mesh equations to analyze this circuit than nodal equations and that will be the tack we take here. Examples 8.1 and 8.2 demonstrate the analysis approach to circuits containing coupled coils.

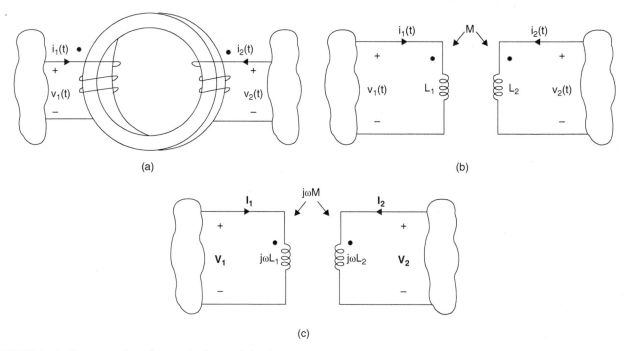

FIGURE 8.24 Representation of magnetically coupled coils

Let us determine the voltage V_0 in the network in Figure 8.25.

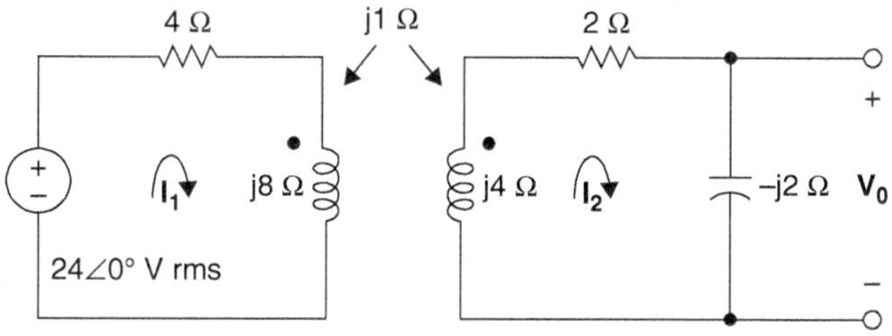

Example 8.1

FIGURE 8.25   Circuit used in Example 8.1

Given the directions of the currents shown in the circuit, the KVL equations for the network are

$$-24\angle0° + 4\,I_1 + j8\,I_1 - j1\,I_2 = 0$$
$$-j1\,I_1 + j4\,I_2 + 2\,I_2 - j2\,I_2 = 0$$

Note that the mutual term is negative since I_1 is into the dot and the current I_2 is out of the dot. Rearranging the terms yields the following:

$$(4 + j8)I_1 - j1\,I_2 = 24\angle0°$$
$$-j1\,I_1 + (2 + j2)I_2 = 0$$

In matrix form, the equations are

$$\begin{bmatrix} 4 + j8 & -j1 \\ -j1 & 2 + j2 \end{bmatrix} \begin{bmatrix} I_1 \\ I_2 \end{bmatrix} = \begin{bmatrix} 24\angle0° \\ 0 \end{bmatrix}$$

The determinant is

$$\Delta = (4 + j8)(2 + j2) - (-j1)(-j1)$$
$$= 8 + j16 + j8 - 16 + 1$$
$$= -7 + j24$$

The currents can then be obtained from the equation

$$\begin{bmatrix} I_1 \\ I_2 \end{bmatrix} = [1/(-7 + j24)] \begin{bmatrix} 2 + j2 & j1 \\ j1 & 4 + j8 \end{bmatrix} \begin{bmatrix} 24\angle0° \\ 0 \end{bmatrix}$$

Solving for I_2 yields

$$I_2 = (j1)(24)/[-7 + j24]$$

Rationalizing this equation yields

$$I_2 = [24j/(-7 + j24)][(-7 - j24)/(-7 - j24)]$$
$$= (-j168 + 576)/(49 + 576)$$
$$= 0.9216 - j0.2688 \text{ A rms}$$

or

$$I_2 = 0.96\angle-16.26° \text{ A rms}$$

And then

$$V_0 = -j2\,I_2 = 1.92\angle106.26° \text{ V rms}$$

Example 8.2

Given the circuit shown in Figure 8.26, let us determine the impedance, Z_{in}, seen by the source, i.e. the input impedance of the network.

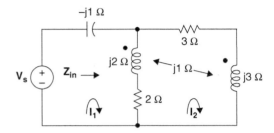

FIGURE 8.26 Circuit used in Example 8.2

The KVL equations, given the current directions, are listed as follows:

$$-V_S - j1\,I_1 + j2(I_1 - I_2) + j1\,I_2 + 2(I_1 - I_2) = 0$$
$$2(I_2 - I_1) + j2(I_2 - I_1) - j1\,I_2 + 3\,I_2 + j3\,I_2 - j1(I_2 - I_1) = 0$$

Before proceeding to a solution, let's pause to examine the critical terms in these equations. In the first equation, the current $I_1 - I_2$ is into the dot on the $j2\,\Omega$ inductor and the current I_2 is into the dot on the $j3\,\Omega$ inductor and thus the mutual term $j1I_2$ is positive. In the second equation, the current $I_2 - I_1$ is out of the dot on the $j2\,\Omega$ inductor and the current I_2 is into the dot on the $j3\,\Omega$ inductor, resulting in $j1I_2$ being negative. Then the current I_2 in the $j3\,\Omega$ inductor is into the dot and the current $I_2 - I_1$ is out of the dot on the $j2\,\Omega$ inductor, resulting in a term $j1(I_2 - I_1)$ that is negative.

The KVL equations can be reduced to

$$(2 + j)I_1 - (2 + j)I_2 = V_S$$
$$-(2 + j)I_1 + (5 + j3)I_2 = 0$$

In matrix form, the equations are

$$\begin{bmatrix} 2 + j & -(2 + j) \\ -(2 + j) & 5 + j3 \end{bmatrix} \begin{bmatrix} I_1 \\ I_2 \end{bmatrix} = \begin{bmatrix} V_S \\ 0 \end{bmatrix}$$

The determinant is

$$\Delta = (2 + j)(5 + j3) - (2 + j)^2$$
$$= 10 + j5 + j6 - 3 - (4 + j4 - 1)$$
$$= 4 + j7$$

The currents can be obtained from the equation

$$\begin{bmatrix} I_1 \\ I_2 \end{bmatrix} = [1/(4 + j7)] \begin{bmatrix} 5 + j3 & 2 + j \\ 2 + j & 2 + j \end{bmatrix} \begin{bmatrix} V_S \\ 0 \end{bmatrix}$$

Solving for the current I_1 yields

$$I_1 = (5 + j3)V_S/(4 + j7)$$

Rationalizing this equation yields

$$\begin{aligned}
\mathbf{I_1} &= \mathbf{V_S}[(5+j3)/(4+j7)][(4-j7)/(4-j7)] \\
&= \mathbf{V_S}[(20+j12-j35+21)/(16+49)] \\
&= \mathbf{V_S}[(41-j23)/65] \\
&= (0.631-j\,0.354)\mathbf{V_S} \\
&= [0.723\angle-29.3°]\mathbf{V_S}
\end{aligned}$$

And then

$$\mathbf{Z_{in}} = \mathbf{V_S}/\mathbf{I_1} = 1.38\angle29.3°\ \Omega$$

One additional quantity that plays a role in magnetically coupled circuits is what is called the coefficient of coupling, i.e. a measure of how tightly the coils are coupled. This quantity, k, is a measure of how much flux in one coil is linked to the other. If k = 1, then 100% of the flux emanating from one coil is linked to the other coil. This coefficient is defined as

$$k = M/\sqrt{L_1 L_2}$$

The range of this coefficient is $0 \le k \le 1$, and therefore the range of M is $0 \le M \le \sqrt{L_1 L_2}$.

IDEAL TRANSFORMERS

An ideal transformer is a special device with the following properties: the reactance of the coils approaches infinity, i.e. L_1, L_2, and $M \to \infty$, the coefficient of coupling is unity, i.e. k = 1 and the primary and secondary coils are lossless, i.e. the coil resistance is zero.

In the ideal case, the magnetic flux links all the turns of both the primary and secondary coils as shown in Figure 8.27. Therefore,

$$\frac{V_1}{V_2} = \frac{N_1\dfrac{d\phi}{dt}}{N_2\dfrac{d\phi}{dt}}$$

And hence

$$V_1 = N_1\frac{d\phi}{dt}$$

$$V_2 = N_2\frac{d\phi}{dt}$$

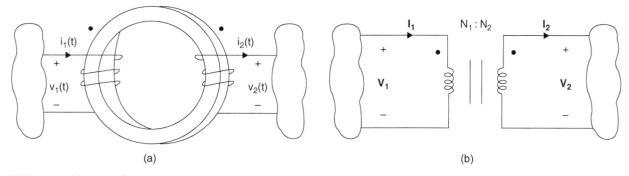

(a)   (b)

FIGURE 8.27   Ideal transformer representations

or simply stated

$$V_1 N_2 = V_2 N_1$$

Furthermore, since the transformer is lossless, the power into the device must be equal to the output power, and hence

$$V_1 I_1 = V_2 I_2$$

Using the fact that $V_1 = (N_1/N_2)V_2$ yields the relationship for the currents, i.e.

$$I_1 N_1 = I_2 N_2$$

If we now use phasor voltages and currents, the input/output relationships are

$$\mathbf{V_2}/\mathbf{V_1} = N_2/N_1$$
$$\mathbf{I_2}/\mathbf{I_1} = N_1/N_2$$

The turn's ratio indicates the type of transformation. If $N_2/N_1 > 1$, then the output (secondary) voltage is greater than the input (primary) voltage, and this indicates a step-up transformer. If $N_2/N_1 < 1$, then the output is less than the input, resulting in a step-down transformer. Finally, if $N_2/N_1 = 1$, the output and input are equal, and the transformer simply provides isolation between the primary and secondary circuits.

When writing the circuit equations for an ideal transformer, it is best to simply force the circuit variables to match those shown in Figure 8.27 by negating the necessary currents and voltages.

Since the transformer is lossless, we would expect that the complex power at the primary would be equal to that at the secondary, i.e.

$$\mathbf{S_1} = \mathbf{V_1}\mathbf{I^*_1} = \mathbf{V_2}\mathbf{I^*_2} = \mathbf{S_2}$$

With reference to Figure 8.28, we see that the input impedance of an ideal transformer with load $\mathbf{Z_L}$ is

$$\mathbf{Z_{in}} = \mathbf{V_1}/\mathbf{I_1}$$

and since

$$\mathbf{Z_L} = \mathbf{V_2}/\mathbf{I_2} = [(N_2/N_1)\mathbf{V_1}]/[(N_1/N_2)\mathbf{I_1}]$$
$$= (N_2/N_1)^2[\mathbf{V_1}/\mathbf{I_1}]$$
$$= (N_2/N_1)^2\mathbf{Z_{in}}$$

and then

$$\mathbf{Z_{in}} = \mathbf{Z_L}/(N_2/N_1)^2$$

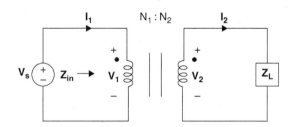

FIGURE 8.28 Transformer circuit used to demonstrate input impedance

This analysis indicates that we can reflect an impedance in the secondary back to the primary, and this impedance is a function of the turn's ratio. Examples 8.3 and 8.4 serve to indicate the manner in which these ideal transformers are treated in a network analysis.

Example 8.3

Let us determine the impedance seen by the source in the circuit in Figure 8.29a.

The turn's ratio in this circuit is $N_2/N_1 = 1/2$, and thus the reflected impedance of the secondary into the primary is

$$\mathbf{Z}_{RF} = \mathbf{Z}_L/(N_2/N_1)^2 = (2+j4)/(1/2)^2 = 8+j16 \ \Omega$$

Hence from the perspective of the source, the circuit is reduced to that shown in Figure 8.29b, and the total impedance seen by the source is

$$\mathbf{Z}_{total} = 4 - j2 + 8 + j16 = 12 + j14 \ \Omega$$

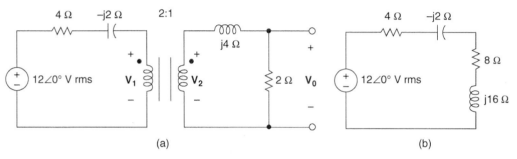

FIGURE 8.29   Circuits used in Example 8.3

Example 8.4

We wish to find the output voltage, $\mathbf{V}_0$, in the network in Figure 8.30.

FIGURE 8.30   Circuit used in Example 8.4

Given the direction of the currents and the reference direction for the voltages, the equations relating input to output are

$$\mathbf{V}_1 = -(N_1/N_2)\mathbf{V}_2$$

and

$$\mathbf{I}_1 = -(N_2/N_1)\mathbf{I}_2$$

The reflected impedance, $\mathbf{Z_{RF}}$, of the secondary into the primary is

$$\mathbf{Z_{RF}} = \mathbf{Z_1}/(N_2/N_1)^2$$
$$= (j2 + 1 - j1)/(1/2)^2$$
$$= 4 + j4 \ \Omega$$

and thus $\mathbf{Z_{total}}$ is

$$\mathbf{Z_{total}} = 2 - j1 + 4 + j4 = 6 + j3 \ \Omega$$

Then the current $\mathbf{I_1}$ is

$$\mathbf{I_1} = 12\angle 0° / (6 + j3) = 1.79\angle{-26.56°} \text{ A rms}$$

And then the current in the secondary is

$$\mathbf{I_2} = -\left(\frac{N_1}{N_2}\right)\mathbf{I_1}$$
$$= -3.58\angle{-26.56°} \text{ A rms}$$

Finally, the output voltage is

$$\mathbf{V_0} = (1 - j1)\mathbf{I_2} = 5.06\angle 108.44° \text{ V rms}$$

We could also attack the problem by transforming the voltage rather than the current. For example,

$$\mathbf{V_1} = \mathbf{I_1}\ \mathbf{Z_{RF}} = (1.79\angle{-26.56°})(4 + j4) = 10.12\angle 18.44° \text{ V rms}$$

Then the voltage at the secondary of the transformer is

$$\mathbf{V_2} = -(N_2/N_1)\mathbf{V_1}$$
$$= 5.06\angle{-161.56°} \text{ V rms}$$

A simple voltage divider will produce the output voltage

$$\mathbf{V_0} = \mathbf{V_2}[(1 - j1)/(j2 + 1 - j1)] = (5.06\angle 198.44°)(1\angle{-90°})$$
$$= 5.06\angle 108.44° \text{ V rms}$$

THREE-PHASE CIRCUITS

Circuits connected in three phase are an integral part of the power system. One need only to recall that when looking at the electric power lines overhead, there are always three lines either in a horizontal configuration or stacked vertically. Since the electric connections in our homes and offices for lights and small appliances are single phase, it is only natural to wonder why is power transmitted in three phase. We can answer this question by examining the simple three-phase network shown in Figure 8.31a. If the three sinusoidal voltages are of the same magnitude and 120° out of phase, they are referred to as a balanced set, as indicated in the phasor diagram in Figure 8.31b. Then, if the load is such that the resulting currents are also balanced, then we have a three-phase balanced circuit.

In the time domain, the balanced voltages are expressed as

$$v_{an}(t) = V_M \cos \omega t \text{ V}$$
$$v_{bn}(t) = V_M \cos(\omega t - 120°) \text{ V}$$
$$v_{cn}(t) = V_M \cos(\omega t - 240°) \text{ V}$$

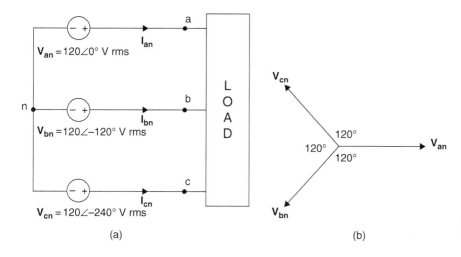

FIGURE 8.31 Balanced three-phase voltages

Then if the load is balanced, the resulting currents are

$$i_a(t) = I_M \cos(\omega t - \theta) \text{ A}$$
$$i_b(t) = I_M \cos(\omega t - \theta - 120°) \text{ A}$$
$$i_c(t) = I_M \cos(\omega t - \theta - 240°) \text{ A}$$

The instantaneous power produced by this system is

$$
\begin{aligned}
p(t) &= p_a(t) + p_b(t) + p_c(t) \\
&= V_M I_M [\cos\omega t \cos(\omega t - \theta) + \cos(\omega t - 120°)\cos(\omega t - \theta - 120°) \\
&\quad + \cos(\omega t - 240°)\cos(\omega t - \theta - 240°)]
\end{aligned}
$$

There are two trigonometric identities that can be applied to simplify this equation:

$$\cos\alpha\cos\beta = \frac{1}{2}[\cos(\alpha - \beta) + \cos(\alpha + \beta)]$$
$$\cos\phi + \cos(\phi - 120°) + \cos(\phi + 120°) = 0$$

Using these two identities, the expression for instantaneous power is reduced to

$$p(t) = 3\frac{V_M I_M}{2}\cos\theta \text{ W}$$

Now we see why we deliver power in a three-phase configuration. Note that the instantaneous power is NOT changing with time, i.e. it is constant. Recall that in the single-phase case the instantaneous power is pulsating at twice the frequency of the voltage and current. The smooth power delivery achieved in three phase is advantageous and economical because it results in less wear on the system components.

The sequence of voltages shown in Figure 8.31b is referred to as an abc or positive phase sequence. This balanced set of voltages has the property that

$$\mathbf{V}_{an} + \mathbf{V}_{bn} + \mathbf{V}_{cn} = 0$$

If the load is balanced so that the line currents are also balanced, then the load can be connected in only two possible configurations: wye (Y) or delta (Δ). These two load configurations are shown in Figure 8.32a and b, respectively.

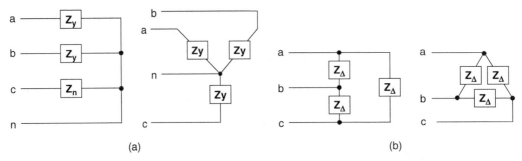

FIGURE 8.32 Balanced Y and Δ connections

THE BALANCED WYE–WYE CONNECTION

A balanced wye–wye circuit is shown in Figure 8.33. As shown in the figure, V_P is the magnitude of the phase voltage for each phase. The line-to-line voltage, i.e. the voltage from one line to another, can be obtained from KVL. The voltage from line a to line b is

$$\mathbf{V_{ab}} = \mathbf{V_{an}} - \mathbf{V_{bn}} = V_P\angle 0° - V_P\angle -120° = \sqrt{3}V_P\angle 30°$$

This equation can also be seen graphically using phasor addition as shown in Figure 8.34. Because of the balanced conditions, the other line voltages are $\mathbf{V_{bc}} = \sqrt{3}V_P\angle -90°$ and $\mathbf{V_{ca}} = \sqrt{3}V_P\angle -210°$. It is interesting to note that the current in the neutral line is

$$\mathbf{I_n} = \mathbf{I_a} + \mathbf{I_b} + \mathbf{I_c} = 0$$

which is, of course, a direct result of the balanced condition. Since there is no current in this line, it makes no difference what, if anything, is in this line. As a result, it is convenient to treat it as an short circuit. In addition, the balanced condition provides one other important feature. Note that there is a direct path from each phase to the load, through the neutral line and back. Therefore, we can analyze the a-phase and then the results are shifted by −120° and −240° to obtain the results for the two remaining phases.

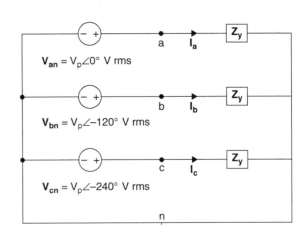

FIGURE 8.33 A balanced Y–Y circuit

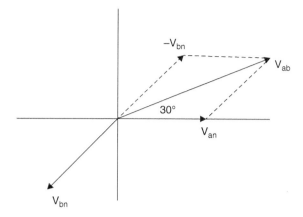

FIGURE 8.34   Phasor calculation of $\mathbf{V}_{ab}$

Given the balanced three-phase system shown in Figure 8.35a, let us determine the line currents and the load voltages.

As indicated, because the circuit is balanced, we need to analyze only the a-phase and then shift the results by −120° and −240° to obtain the results for the b- and c-phases. The circuit for the a-phase is shown in Figure 8.35b. The line current is

$$\mathbf{I_a} = 120\angle 0°/(12 + j8) = 8.32\angle -33.69° \text{ A rms}$$

Therefore, $\mathbf{I_b}$ = 8.32∠−153.69° A rms and $\mathbf{I_a}$ = 8.32∠−273.69° A rms. The load voltage is then

$$\mathbf{V_{AN}} = \mathbf{I_a Z_L} = (8.32\angle -33.69°)/(10 + j6) = 97.01\angle -2.73° \text{ V rms}$$

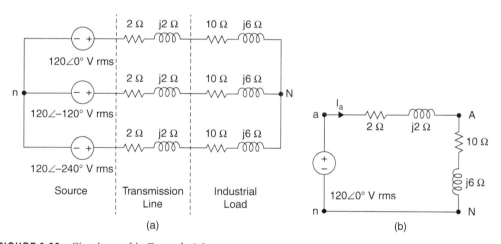

FIGURE 8.35   Circuits used in Example 8.5

And then $\mathbf{V_{BN}}$ = 97.01∠−122.73° V rms and $\mathbf{V_{CN}}$ = 97.01∠−242.73° V rms. In these three-phase analyses, we adopt the convention that lowercase letters represent the source and upper-case letters represent the load.

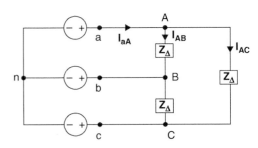

FIGURE 8.36 A balanced Y–Δ connection

THE BALANCED WYE–DELTA CONNECTION

A balanced wye–delta connection is shown in Figure 8.36. Assuming no line impedance, note that it is the line voltage that is directly across the load, whereas in the wye–wye system the phase voltage is directly across the load. KCL can be applied to determine the relationship between the phase currents in the delta and line currents. For example, at node A in the circuit in Figure 8.36,

$$\mathbf{I}_{aA} = \mathbf{I}_{AB} + \mathbf{I}_{AC} = \mathbf{I}_{AB} - \mathbf{I}_{CA}$$

Using a mathematical development similar to the one that led to the relationship between phase voltages and line voltages in the wye–wye case, we can show that if $\mathbf{I}_{AB}$ in the delta is $I_p\angle\theta$, then the line current $\mathbf{I}_{aA} = \sqrt{3}\,I_p\angle\theta - 30°$ A rms.

| Example 8.6 | Given the wye–delta configuration in Figure 8.37a, let us determine the line currents and the phase currents in the delta. |

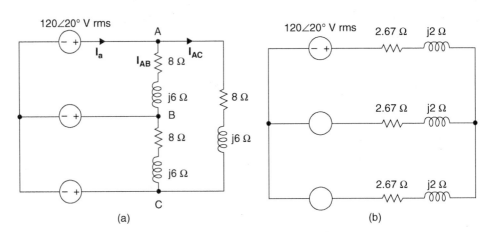

(a)   (b)

FIGURE 8.37 Circuits used in Example 8.6

Since $\mathbf{V}_{an} = 120\angle 20°$ V rms, $\mathbf{V}_{ab} = 120\sqrt{3}\angle 50°$ V rms, and since there is no line impedance, the phase-current $\mathbf{I}_{AB}$ is

$$\mathbf{I}_{AB} = 120\sqrt{3}\angle 50°/(8 + j6) = 20.78\angle 13.13° \text{ A rms}$$

Then $I_{BC} = 20.78\angle-106.87°$ A rms and $I_{CA} = 20.78\angle-226.87°$ A rms. Then KCL at node A yields the line current I_{aA}

$$I_{aA} = I_{AB} + I_{AC} = I_{AB} - I_{CA}$$
$$= 20.78\angle13.13° - 20.78\angle-226.87°$$
$$= 36\angle-16.87° \text{ A rms}$$

As a result, $I_{bB} = 36\angle-136.87°$ A rms and $I_{cC} = 36\angle-256.87°$ A rms.

Note that if we were only interested in the line currents, we could simply apply the delta-to-wye transformation to the load to obtain the network in Figure 8.37b, where we have used the fact that

$$Z_Y = 1/3 \ Z_\Delta = 2.666 + j2 \ \Omega.$$

Then, the line current, I_{aA} would be

$$I_{aA} = 120\angle20°/(2.6666 + j2) = 36\angle-16.87° \text{ A rms}$$

Although not as popular, the source can be connected in delta. If that is the case, then the phase voltage is the line voltage, and if $V_{ab} = V_L\angle\theta°$ then $V_{an} = (V_L/\sqrt{3})\angle\theta - 30°$ and the remaining voltages are obtained by shifting these voltages by $-120°$ and $-240°$.

THREE-PHASE POWER

Regardless of the configuration, i.e. is the circuit connected in wye or delta, the complex power for one phase of the three-phase system is

$$\mathbf{S_1} = V_P I_P \angle\theta_z$$

where we recall that θ_z is the phase angle of the load impedance in each phase. While this equation is certainly valid, keep in mind that it is the line voltage and line current that are accessible for making measurements. Therefore, we want to express the complex power for the three-phase circuit in terms of these two quantities.

For the wye-connected load, the line current is the phase current, i.e. $I_P = I_L$. The phase voltage, which is not available, is related to the line voltage, which is available, by the equation $V_P = V_L/\sqrt{3}$. Therefore, the complex power for a single phase in the wye-connected case is

$$\mathbf{S_1} = V_P I_P \angle\theta_z$$
$$= (V_L/\sqrt{3})I_L\angle\theta_z$$

For the delta-connected load, the phase voltage is the line voltage, i.e. $V_P = V_L$. The phase current, which is not available, is related to the line current, which is available, by the equation $I_P = I_L/\sqrt{3}$. Therefore, the complex power for a single phase in the delta-connected case is

$$\mathbf{S_1} = V_P I_P \angle\theta_z$$
$$= V_L(I_L/\sqrt{3})\angle\theta_z$$

Therefore, the complex power for a single phase of a three-phase system, regardless of whether the connection is wye or delta is

$$\mathbf{S_1} = (V_L I_L)\sqrt{3}\angle\theta_z$$

Then the total three-phase complex power is

$$\mathbf{S_3} = \sqrt{3}V_L I_L \angle \theta_z$$
$$= \sqrt{3}V_L I_L [\cos \angle \theta_z + j\sin \angle \theta_z]$$

and therefore

$$|\mathbf{S_3}| = \sqrt{3}V_L I_L.$$

Example 8.7

Two small industries are co-located and their power is fed from a three-phase balanced 60 Hz source with a line voltage of 480 V rms. The two loads are rated as follows:

Load 1: 20 kVA at 0.72 PF lagging

Load 2: 15 kVA at 0.8 PF lagging

We wish to determine the line current necessary to feed the loads and the power factor of the combined load.

The complex power for each of the loads is

$$\mathbf{S_1} = 20\,k\angle\cos^{-1}0.72 = 20\,k\angle43.95° = (14.4 + j13.88)\text{ kVA}$$
$$\mathbf{S_2} = 15\,k\angle\cos^{-1}0.8 = 15\,k\angle36.87° = (12 + j9)\text{ kVA}$$

The total complex power is then

$$\mathbf{S_T} = (26.4 + j22.88)\text{ kVA}$$
$$= 34{,}935\text{ VA or } 34.935\text{ kVA}$$

The line current that feeds the two loads is

$$I_L = 34{,}395/\sqrt{3}(480)$$
$$= 42.02\text{ A rms}$$

and the combined power factor is

$$PF_{load} = \cos 40.91° = 0.76 \text{ lagging}$$

Problems

8.1 Write the KVL equations necessary to solve for the two mesh currents in the network in Figure P8.1.

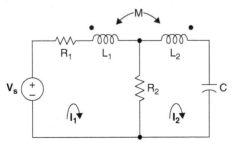

FIGURE P8.1

8.2   Write the KVL equations necessary to solve for the two mesh currents in the network in Figure P8.2.

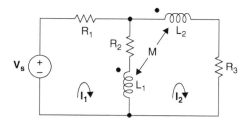

FIGURE P8.2

8.3   Find the voltage, V_0, in the circuit in Figure P8.3.

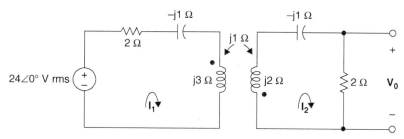

FIGURE P8.3

8.4   Determine the voltage, V_0, in the circuit in Figure P8.4.

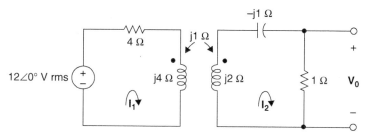

FIGURE P8.4

8.5   Determine the voltage, V_0, in the circuit in Figure P8.5.

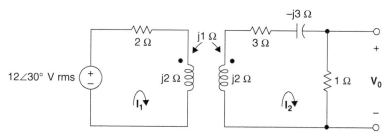

FIGURE P8.5

8.6 Calculate the voltage, V_0, in the circuit in Figure P8.6.

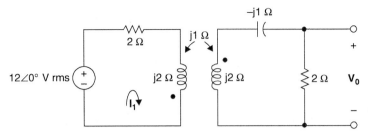

FIGURE P8.6

8.7 Calculate the current I_1 and the voltage, V_0, in the circuit in Figure P8.7.

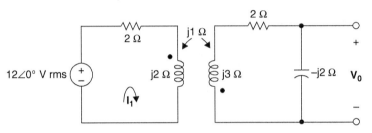

FIGURE P8.7

8.8 Determine the voltage, V_0, in the circuit in Figure P8.8.

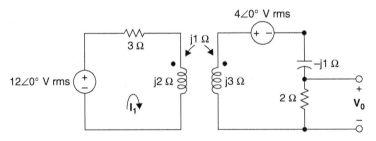

FIGURE P8.8

8.9 Calculate the voltage, V_0, in the circuit in Figure P8.9.

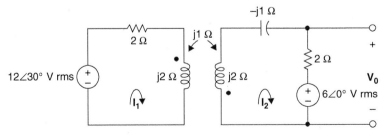

FIGURE P8.9

8.10 Determine the voltage, $\mathbf{V_0}$, in the circuit in Figure P8.10.

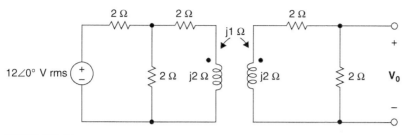

FIGURE P8.10

8.11 Determine the voltage, $\mathbf{V_0}$, in the circuit in Figure P8.11.

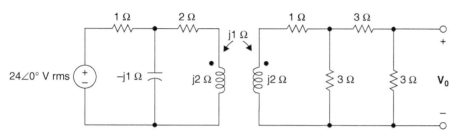

FIGURE P8.11

8.12 Calculate the voltage, $\mathbf{V_X}$, in the circuit in Figure P8.12.

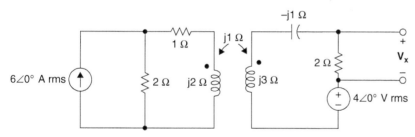

FIGURE P8.12

8.13 Determine the voltage, $\mathbf{V_0}$, in the circuit in Figure P8.13.

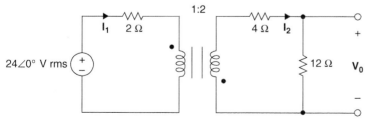

FIGURE P8.13

8.14 Calculate the voltage, $\mathbf{V_0}$, in the circuit in Figure P8.14.

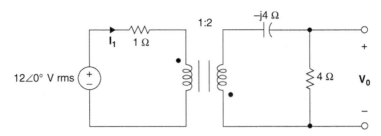

FIGURE P8.14

8.15 Determine the voltage, $\mathbf{V_0}$, in the circuit in Figure P8.15.

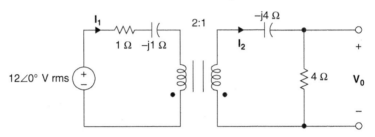

FIGURE P8.15

8.16 Calculate the voltage, $\mathbf{V_0}$, in the circuit in Figure P8.16.

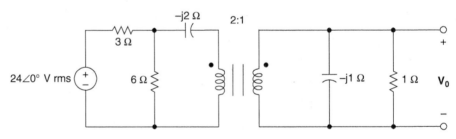

FIGURE P8.16

8.17 Determine the voltage, $\mathbf{V_0}$, in the circuit in Figure P8.17.

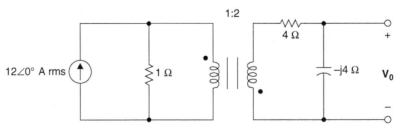

FIGURE P8.17

8.18   Calculate the voltage, $\mathbf{V_0}$, in the circuit in Figure P8.18.

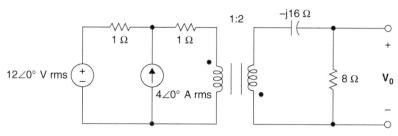

FIGURE P8.18

8.19   Determine the input impedance, $\mathbf{Z_{in}}$, as seen by the source in the circuit in Figure P8.19.

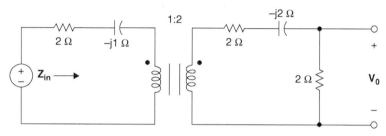

FIGURE P8.19

8.20   Calculate the input impedance, $\mathbf{Z_{in}}$, as seen by the source in the circuit in Figure P8.20.

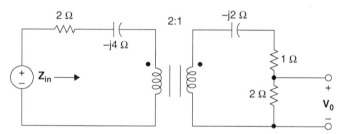

FIGURE P8.20

8.21   Determine the input impedance, $\mathbf{Z_{in}}$, in the circuit in Figure P8.21.

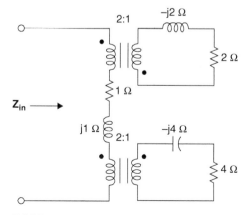

FIGURE P8.21

8.22 In the network in Figure P8.22, $I_1 = 6\angle 0°$. Determine the value of the output voltage, V_0.

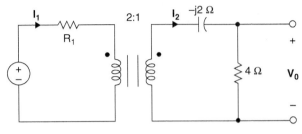

FIGURE P8.22

8.23 Find V_1 in the circuit in Figure P8.23.

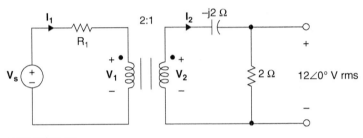

FIGURE P8.23

8.24 Find V_S in the circuit in Figure P8.24.

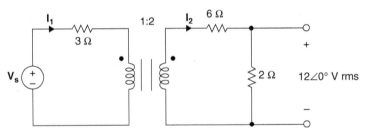

FIGURE P8.24

8.25 Calculate V_S in the circuit in Figure P8.25.

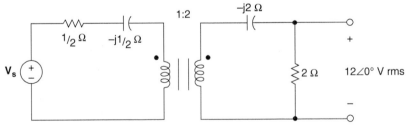

FIGURE P8.25

8.26 In an abc-phase sequence balanced Y-connected source, $\mathbf{V_{an}} = 120\angle60°$ V rms. Determine the line voltages.

8.27 In an abc-phase sequence balanced Y-connected source, $\mathbf{V_{ab}} = 208\angle10°$ V rms. Determine the phase voltages.

8.28 An abc-phase sequence balanced Y-connected source in which $\mathbf{V_{an}} = 120\angle0°$ V rms is connected to a balanced Y-connected load with a per-phase impedance of $40 + j30$ Ω. Determine the line currents.

8.29 An abc-phase sequence balanced Y-connected source is known to have a line voltage of $\mathbf{V_{bc}} = 240\angle-20°$. Determine the phase voltages of the source.

8.30 An abc-phase sequence balanced Y-connected source has a line voltage of 140 V rms. If $\mathbf{Z_{line}} = 2$ Ω, $\mathbf{Z_{load}} = 40 + j30$ Ω, and the phase angle of $\mathbf{V_{an}}$ is $\angle0°$, determine the load voltages.

8.31 Given the network in Figure P8.31, consisting of an abc-phase sequence balanced source, determine the line currents and load voltages.

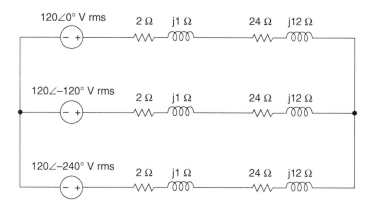

FIGURE P8.31

8.32 A balanced load consists of balanced wye in parallel with a balanced delta. If the per-phase impedance of the wye is $4 + j3$ Ω and the per-phase impedance of the delta is $18 + j\,12$ Ω, determine (a) the equivalent wye load and (b) the equivalent delta load.

8.33 An abc-phase sequence balanced Y-connected source is known to have a phase voltage of $\mathbf{V_{an}} = 180\angle30°$ V rms. The load is a balanced wye in parallel with a balanced delta. The per-phase impedance of the wye is $12 + j9$ Ω and the per-phase impedance of the delta is $30 + j\,12$ Ω. Determine the line currents when the load is converted to an equivalent wye.

8.34 Repeat Problem 8.33 if the load is converted to an equivalent delta.

8.35 In a balanced wye–delta system, if the load current $\mathbf{I_{AB}} = 30\angle60°$ A rms, determine all the line currents.

8.36 In a balanced wye–delta system, the per-phase impedance of the delta is $24 + j\,12$ Ω. If the line voltage is $\mathbf{V_{ab}} = 208\angle30°$ V rms, determine the line currents.

8.37 In a balanced wye–delta system, the source is an abc-phase sequence of voltages in which $\mathbf{V_{an}} = 120\angle30°$ V rms. The load consists of a balanced wye in parallel with a balanced delta.

The per-phase impedance of the wye is $4 + j2$ Ω and the per-phase impedance of the delta is $12 + j9$ Ω. Determine the line currents.

8.38 Determine the line currents in Problem 8.37 if $\mathbf{V_{ab}} = 90\angle{-50°}$ V rms.

8.39 A balanced three-phase wye–wye system consists of two loads:

Load 1: 4.8 kVA at 0.9 power factor lagging
Load 2: 3.0 kVA at 0.8 power factor lagging

If the line voltage is 208 V rms, determine the magnitude of the line current.

8.40 A balanced three-phase wye–wye system consists of three loads:

Load 1: 24 kVA at 0.9 power factor lagging
Load 2: 16 kVA at 0.72 power factor lagging
Load 3: 12 kW at unity power factor

If the line voltage is 480 V rms, determine the magnitude of the line current.

Diodes, Semiconductors and Applications

LEARNING OBJECTIVES

- To review the breadth of electronics in modern society
- To learn what a diode is and its basic characteristics
- To understand properties of a semiconductor and how a p–n junction diode works
- To learn the characteristics of the ideal diode model
- To learn how to analyze circuits containing diodes

- To understand the operation of REAL diodes, and the diode equation
- To understand light emitting diodes (LEDs) and how to bias them in applications
- To understand Schottky diodes and applications
- To understand load line analysis for a diode or other nonlinear circuit element

---

While in the distant past, electronics was a subject that was primarily of interest to those working in the field, today this subject is commonplace in normal discourse. The reason for this stems from the fact that it impacts our lives on a minute-by-minute basis through cell phones, TVs, and all manner of other electronic components, such as digital watches, Bluetooth headphones, drones, GPS devices, and all the instrumentation in the laboratories of almost every field. Furthermore, the size of the components has been drastically reduced. At present, a modern cell phone is capable of replacing a whole host of devices – it is a phone, a calendar, a camera, a GPS, a calculator, a watch, an Internet connection to mail, and a world of information and on-and-on. In addition, there are a staggering number of apps that can be added to your smartphone to do any number of tasks.

It is modern electronics that has made all of this possible. Most circuits are no longer constructed of individual electronic components. Instead, the electronics is integrated on a chip of silicon, for example, to produce the density that is now commonplace in electronic circuits. Electronic circuits have shrunk to the point that we can now put billions of electronic devices per square inch on a single circuit. The size of the components also means that a typical circuit does not draw much power, and therefore these circuits can be powered by 5 V or less, and operate at low power densities compared to the circuits of only a few decades ago.

> **INTRODUCTION TO MODERN ELECTRONICS**

A *diode* is a two-terminal electronic device that conducts current if a voltage source is applied in one direction, and refuses to conduct significant current when the voltage is applied with the opposite polarity.

A diode with a voltage applied so that the diode is conducting a current is said to be *forward biased;* a diode with a voltage applied in the opposite direction such that no current flows is said to be *reverse biased.*

> **THE DIODE AND ITS BASIC CHARACTERISTICS**

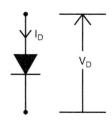

FIGURE 9.1   Diode symbol and current and voltage designations

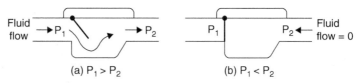

(a) $P_1 > P_2$ (b) $P_1 < P_2$

FIGURE 9.2   (a) Fluid passes through from left to right – valve forced open: $P_1 > P_2$; (b) No fluid flows from right to left – valve forced closed: $P_1 < P_2$

The schematic symbol for the diode is shown in Figure 9.1. The direction of the "arrow" contained in the symbol indicates the direction of positive current flow that is allowed, in this case top to bottom. Current will not flow in the opposite direction.

The fundamental characteristics of a diode can be illustrated by an analogous fluid system component – a valve that allows fluid to flow only in one direction. Usually, these valves are called "check" valves or "flapper" valves. Such valves allow flow in one direction, but close and stop fluid flow if the fluid attempts to move in the other direction, as illustrated in Figure 9.2a and b.

INTRODUCTION TO SEMI-CONDUCTORS

Modern electronic devices are constructed of solid-state materials called semiconductors and powered by dc batteries or an ac source, e.g. the wall socket, which also employ a device to convert the ac power into dc. The semiconductor material employed to construct the electronic devices can be made as either n-type or p-type, and since the majority of electronic devices are constructed of silicon, we will confine our initial discussion to this type of semiconductor material even though the principles used in our discussion could be generally applied to other semiconductor materials.

Pure silicon is an insulator and will not conduct current because the pure silicon lattice structure is neutral in total charge, i.e. there is a balance between the positive charge contributed by protons in each silicon nucleus and the negative charge resulting from electrons surrounding the nuclei. However, we know that current requires charge in motion. Therefore, something must be done to the silicon so that it can more easily conduct, and that process is called *doping*. Doping is simply a process of adding small, precise amounts of another element, i.e. an impurity, in the periodic table adjacent to silicon. The doping candidates are shown in Figure 9.3 where a small portion of the periodic table is displayed. These dopants are classified as either *donor* or *acceptor* impurities. Donor impurities are used to create n-type silicon; acceptor impurities create p-type silicon.

A typical n-type donor impurity is *phosphorus*. When this element is added to the silicon lattice, it produces a free electron that can be easily moved when a voltage is applied to the material, thus producing a current. Electrons are then the majority charge carrier and holes are the minority charge carrier. The more doping, the more electrons and hence the more conductive (lower resistance) the material becomes; since the electrons have a negative charge, the material is called n-type.

A typical acceptor impurity is *boron*. When this element is added to the silicon lattice, it leaves an electron missing, equivalent to a free positive charge. In essence, the free positive charge

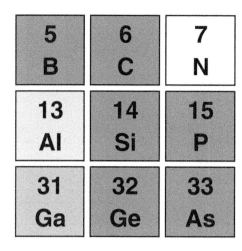

FIGURE 9.3   A subset of the periodic table

signifies the absence of an electron, and this is called a hole. In this case, holes are the majority charge carrier and electrons are the minority charge carrier. Holes behave like positively charged particles, so this material is p-type and their movement through the lattice creates hole conduction. As a result, it is the excess holes and electrons that conduct current in semiconductor devices.

Because of their thermal energy, holes and electrons are in constant motion in a material; however, the motion is random and there is no net motion in any direction. There are two mechanisms that cause these charged particles to move in a particular direction and thus create current, and they are *drift* and *diffusion*.

Drift is created by applying a voltage across the material. Although the motion may not be direct, a net excess of holes will drift to the negative terminal and electrons will drift to the positive terminal. Diffusion current, on the other hand, occurs because particles in random motion will eventually move from areas of high concentration to areas of low concentration. A typical example of this activity is smoke emanating from a stack and subsequently diffusing into the atmosphere. This same thing happens in a semiconductor material. Suppose that there is a high concentration of electrons at one end of a piece of the material. Over time, this high concentration of electrons will diffuse throughout the remainder of the material, creating a small current until the concentration equalizes throughout the material. This same argument applies to hole diffusion as well.

Let us now show how these fundamental actions in semiconductors can be used to create electronic components.

HOW A p–n JUNCTION DIODE WORKS

If we bring together p-type and n-type materials as shown in Figure 9.4a, we can create a p–n junction diode. If the n-type portion of the junction contains numerous free electrons and the p-type portion has an abundance of free holes, then the high concentration of electrons will diffuse into the p-type material where their initial concentration is low, and the high concentration of holes in the p-type material will diffuse into the area of low concentration within the n-type material. This process is short-lived, however, since the movement of an electron leaves in its wake a positive charge bound to the nucleus of the impurity atom in the n-type material, and a similar situation will take place on the other side of the junction, resulting in a buildup of charge layers, as indicated in Figure 9.4b. These charge layers are depleted of carriers; therefore, this region is known as the *depletion region*. Because this area is depleted of mobile carriers, it creates a region of balance and acts as a barrier for further diffusion. As the charge separation forms in the depletion region, this separation creates an electric field that extends from the positively charged area of the

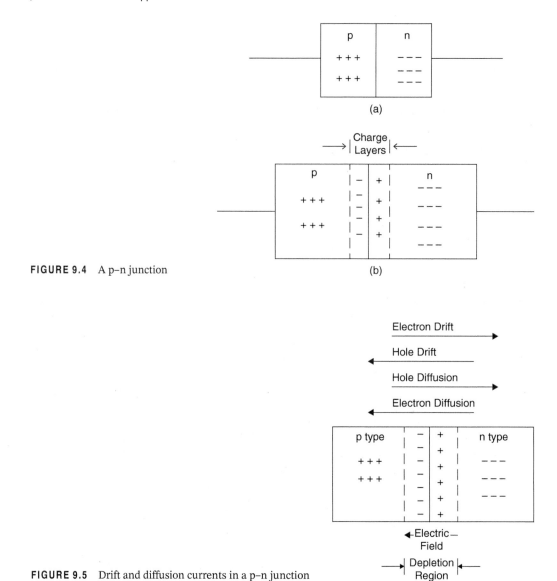

FIGURE 9.4 A p–n junction

FIGURE 9.5 Drift and diffusion currents in a p–n junction

n-type material to the negatively charged area of the p-type material, as shown in Figure 9.5. Also displayed in the figure are the drift and diffusion currents across the depletion region, and equilibrium is established when the average net drift current and the average net diffusion current offset each other.

The charge separation in the depletion region establishes a potential barrier across this region. However, the height of the barrier, i.e. the width of the depletion region, can be changed via an external voltage source. Consider, for example, the two cases illustrated in Figure 9.6 where a voltage source is applied to the p–n junction. In Figure 9.6a, the p–n junction is said to be forward biased, the depletion region is narrowed, the potential barrier is lowered, carriers can easily diffuse across the barrier, and the diode will conduct current. In Figure 9.6b, the p–n junction is said to be reverse biased, the depletion region is increased, the potential barrier is increased, fewer carriers can cross the barrier, and there is little or no current.

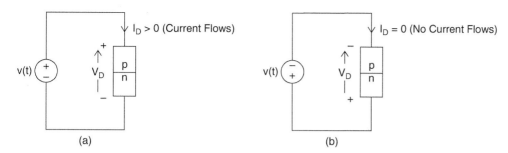

FIGURE 9.6   Forward- and reverse-biased p–n junctions

THE IDEAL DIODE MODEL

Although there are a number of models that describe the characteristics and operation of a diode, including the piecewise linear model and the diode equation model, we will confine our discussion here to the simplest model that relates the dc voltage across the diode to the current through it. In the case of the ideal diode, the diode is a two-terminal, nonlinear device that passes current without any resistance in one direction and blocks the current with infinite resistance in the opposite direction. While this model does not give perfectly accurate results when used in analyzing circuits, it does provide generally an excellent estimate of the actual results.

The actual diode structure and the symbolic representation of the model are repeated in Figure 9.7 where the p-type material is called the anode and the n-type material is referred to as the cathode. The V–I curve for the ideal diode is shown in Figure 9.8. This curve is a graphical display of the diode's operation in which a voltage applied to the diode, positive at the anode and negative at the cathode, will cause infinite current to flow since the diode has zero resistance in this forward-biased direction. Correspondingly, in the reverse-biased direction, a negative voltage applied in the same manner results in zero current because the device has infinite resistance in

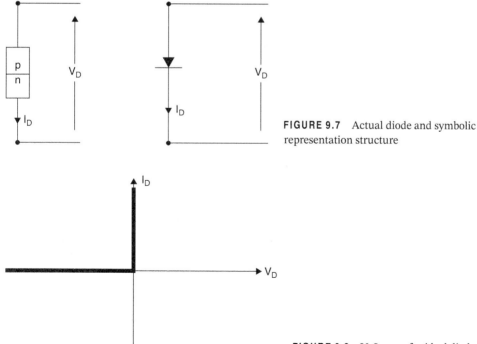

FIGURE 9.7   Actual diode and symbolic representation structure

FIGURE 9.8   V–I curve for ideal diode

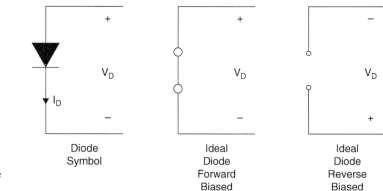

FIGURE 9.9 Ideal diode and circuit models

this situation. Because the diode has zero resistance in one direction and infinite resistance in the other, the diode acts essentially as a voltage-controlled switch, as indicated in Figure 9.9.

While we have described the operation of the diode in isolation using the ideal model, the real issue is how do we describe the diode when it is in a circuit. The problem then becomes one of determining the voltage polarity the network is trying to place on the terminals of the diode. One way to do this is to replace the diode with a small test resistor and determine if the voltage across this resistance is such that the diode would be forward or reverse biased. If the voltage across the test resistor is such that it would forward bias a diode in its place, then the resistor should be replaced with a short circuit. Conversely, if the voltage across the test resistor is such that it would reverse bias a diode in its place, then the resistor should be replaced with an open circuit. An alternative approach, which amounts to the same thing, is to determine the direction that the network tries to push positive current through the diode.

Example 9.1

Consider the network shown in Figure 9.10a containing two diodes, D_1 and D_2. We wish to determine the power supplied by the 12 V dc source.

The network is redrawn in Figure 9.10b where the diodes have been replaced with 1 Ω resistors; these test resistors are very small in relation to the other resistors in the circuit. Combining the two parallel paths yields the circuit in Figure 9.10c. The voltage across the parallel paths, i.e. V_0, can be obtained using a simple voltage divider.

$$V_0 = (12)(1000.5)/[2000 + 1000.5] = 4.0013 \text{ V}$$

As shown in Figure 9.10d, this voltage would attempt to force current down through the two parallel paths. Under this condition, D_1 is forward biased (conducting) and D_2 is reverse biased (nonconducting). Therefore, the network reduces to that shown in Figure 9.10e, in which the right branch is disconnected. The source current and power are calculated as

$$I_s = 12/4k = 3 \text{ mA and } P_s = V_s I_s = (12 \text{ V})(3 \text{ mA}) = 36 \text{ mW}$$

The actual output voltage V_0

$$V_0 = 12 \ (2k \ \Omega)/(4k \ \Omega) = 6 \text{ V}$$

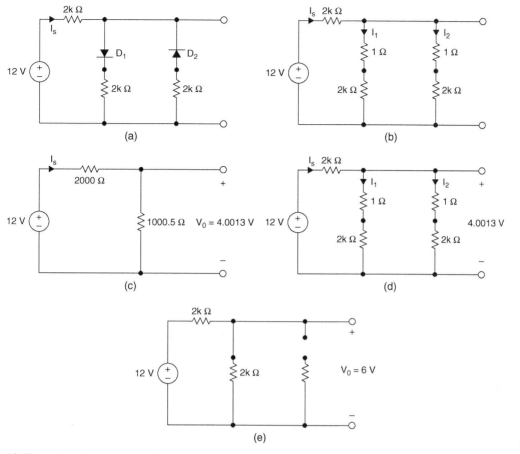

FIGURE 9.10   Circuits used in Example 9.1

There are a number of important applications where diodes play a fundamental role, such as a rectifier, a device that converts an ac power source to dc. These circuits are used in power supplies for a whole host of devices and systems, e.g. radios, TVs, computers and virtually every electronic device that operate from ac voltage supplied by the power grid. Electronic circuits in general require dc to operate; therefore the two primary choices are (1) batteries that supply dc voltage directly, or (2) taking ac from the power grid and rectifying it to create dc.

Other applications for diodes include clippers, clampers, and a variety of wave-shaping circuits.

Rectifier circuits generally use one or more diodes to covert an ac voltage into a pulsating dc voltage. Generally, there are two versions of rectifiers: (1) half-wave and (2) full-wave. The voltage pulsations are then followed by a frequency-selective, low-pass, filter circuit to smooth out the pulsations. Often a resistor and capacitor (or a combination of Rs and Cs) serve this function. The combination of a rectifier and a filter is called a *power supply*. Power supplies can accept ac voltage, for example from a wall-socket, and convert it into a dc voltage appropriate for the operation of complex electronic circuits.

RECTIFIER CIRCUITS AND POWER SUPPLIES

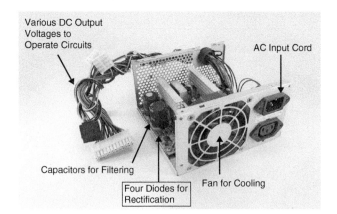

FIGURE 9.11 Typical power supply for PC (computer) (Kom_Pornnarong/Shutterstock)

Figure 9.11 shows an image of a typical power supply used in a PC. There is a socket for the ac cord to be attached to a wall socket, four diodes in a circuit for rectification (converting the ac into dc), capacitors for filtering out the pulsations in dc voltage from the rectifier, and output cables to connect the dc to the various electronic circuits in the computer. The details of these circuits are explained in the following sections.

HALF-WAVE RECTIFIER CIRCUITS

Real semiconductor diodes present a small but appreciable voltage drop in the forward direction (about 0.6 V for silicon) and permit a finite current to flow in the reverse direction. For most calculations, the reverse current flow is negligibly small and the forward voltage drop can be neglected with little error. Real diodes are discussed later in the chapter.

A practical circuit for *half-wave rectification* is shown in Figure 9.12a. A *transformer* supplied from 120-V, 60-Hz house current provides the desired operating voltage, which is applied to a series combination of diode and load resistance R_L. (The transformer, consisting of two multi-turn coils wound on a common iron core, provides a voltage "step-down" in direct proportion to the turn ratio.) For approximate analysis, the actual diode is represented by an ideal diode: the internal resistance of the transformer is neglected. For $v(t) = V_m \sin(\omega t)$, the resulting voltage $v(t)$ and $v_{R_L}(t)$ are shown in Figure 9.12b and c.

$$v_{R_L}(t) = V_m \sin(\omega t) \qquad \text{for} \qquad 0 < \omega t \leq \pi$$
$$v_{R_L}(t) = 0 \qquad\qquad \text{for} \qquad \pi < \omega t \leq 2\pi$$

$$V_{dc} = \frac{1}{2\pi} \int_0^{2\pi} v_{R_L} \, d(\omega t) = \frac{1}{2\pi} \int_0^{\pi} V_m \sin \omega t \, d(\omega t) + 0$$

$$V_{dc} = \frac{1}{2\pi} V_m [-\cos \omega t]_0^{\pi} = \frac{V_m}{\pi}$$

where V_{dc} is the average dc voltage. Note that for half-wave rectification the voltage pulsations are separated and the average dc voltage is about $1/3$ of V_m.

Note that the average current is

$$I_{dc} = \frac{V_{dc}}{R_L} = \frac{V_m}{R_L \pi}$$

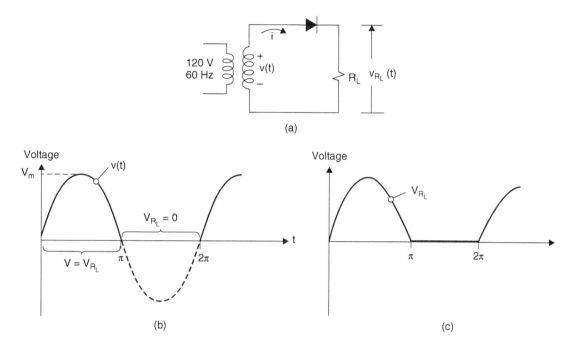

FIGURE 9.12   (a) Half-wave rectifier; Voltage waveforms of (b) v(t) and (c) $v_{R_L}(t)$

Assume a transformer is used to transform an input of 120 V ac rms to 15 V ac, at f = 60 Hz. If a half-wave rectifier is used, what is the average dc output voltage and the value of ω?

$$V = V_m \sin \omega t = (15)\sqrt{2}\ \sin(2\pi\ 60)t$$
$$= 21 \sin 377\ t$$
$$V_{dc} = \frac{V_m}{\pi} = \frac{21}{\pi} = 6.68\ V$$
$$\omega = 2\pi f = 377$$

Example 9.2

FULL-WAVE RECTIFIER CIRCUITS

The full-wave rectifier (often called a full-wave bridge rectifier) is the most common rectifier circuit because it uses the power from both the positive·and the negative excursions of the sinusoidal voltage input.

This circuit shown in Figure 9.13a operates as follows. The transformer output voltage is sinusoidal, as shown in Figure 9.13b, and as this voltage periodically alternates between positive and negative half cycles, pairs of the four diodes alternate between forward- and reverse-biased states. On the positive half cycle of the sine wave, point A is more positive than point B, diode D_1 is forward biased and thus supplies current to the load as shown in Figure 9.14a. This current returns through diode D_2, which is also forward biased; diodes D_3 and D_4 are reverse biased and therefore not conducting.

On the negative half cycle, point B is more positive than point A, diode D_3 is forward biased and supplies current to the load as shown in Figure 9.14b. This current returns through diode D_4, which is also forward biased. Diodes D_1 and D_2 are reverse biased and therefore not conducting. Note, as indicated in Figure 9.15, the current in the load is always in the same direction on each half cycle.

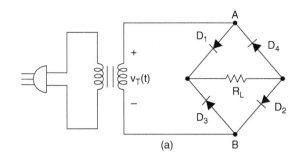

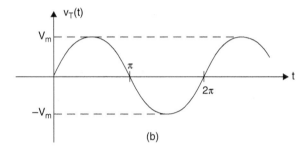

FIGURE 9.13 Full-wave bridge rectifier (a) circuit and (b) input waveform, $v_T(t) = V_m \sin(\omega t)$

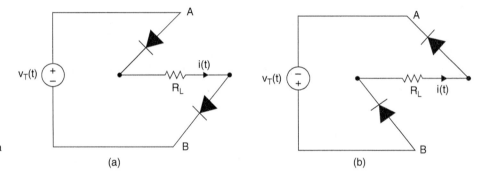

FIGURE 9.14 Current direction in rectifier during each half cycle

Figure 9.15a shows the original sine wave, $v_T(t) = V_m \sin(\omega t)$ and Figure 9.15b displays the rectified wave. Using techniques we have discussed earlier, we can show that the dc value of the rectified wave is

$V_{dc} = 2V_m/\pi$ as the following analysis demonstrates.

The dc value of the output of the full-wave rectifier circuit can be determined from the equation

$$V_{dc} = \frac{1}{T} \int_0^T V_T(t)dt$$

where the period is $T = \frac{\pi}{2}$ and $v_T(t)$ is a sine wave in this period. Therefore,

$$V_{DC} = \frac{1}{T} \int_0^T V_m \sin(\omega t)dt$$

$$= \frac{V_m}{\pi/2} \left[-\cos x \int_0^{\pi/2} \right]$$

$$= \frac{2V_m}{\pi}$$

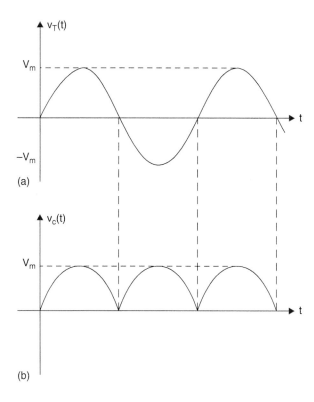

FIGURE 9.15   Original and full-wave
rectified sine waves

(a)

(b)

As expected, this is twice the value of the half-wave rectifier, since there are twice as many pulses per unit time.

If the input of the full-wave rectifier is an ac voltage of 24 V rms, determine the dc output voltage of the rectifier.

Since the voltage is 24 V rms, then the maximum value would be $V_m = 24\sqrt{2}$ V. Then

$$V_{dc} = (2)(24\sqrt{2})/\pi$$
$$= 21.6 \text{ V}$$

Example 9.3

The waveform shown in Figure 9.15b is clearly not a dc level. However, if we connect a low-pass filter between the rectifier and the load, as shown in Figure 9.16a, the filter will smooth the output to produce the waveform shown in Figure 9.16b. The rectifier output charges the capacitor, which tends to hold the voltage between charging cycles. Although the voltage drops slightly between charging cycles, the output is a good approximation to a dc-level voltage. The voltage between charging cycles reduces exponentially according to the equivalent RC time constant of the filter.

A variation of the full-wave bridge rectifier is shown in Figure 9.17. This circuit uses a center-tapped transformer and two diodes. The transformer provides both isolation, i.e. no direct connection from input to output, and scaling using the transformer's turns ratio. The voltage across each half of the transformer's secondary is $v_T(t)$, and during the positive half-cycle D_1 conducts and D_2 is reverse biased. This situation is reversed on the negative half cycle, but in each case the output current is in the same direction, resulting in a full-wave rectified output.

**POWER SUPPLY
FILTERS**

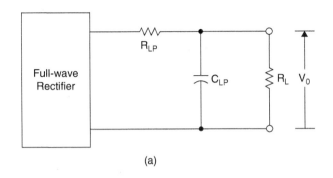

(a)

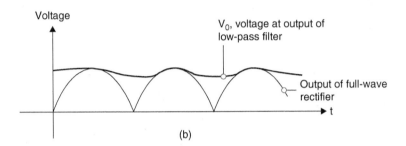

(b)

FIGURE 9.16 Smoothing a rectified wave with a low-pass filter

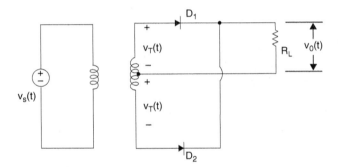

FIGURE 9.17 A full wave rectifier with a center-tap transformer and two diodes

CLIPPING AND CLAMPING CIRCUITS

While power supply circuits employ diodes as we have indicated, there are a number of other applications where these devices play a fundamental role. Two such applications are clipper and clamper circuits.

A simple *clipper circuit* is shown in Figure 9.18a. Assume that the input voltage $v_s(t)$ is a sinusoidal waveform and the voltage V_C is a dc voltage. Note that as long as the input voltage is less than V_C, the diode will be reverse biased and appears as an open circuit, i.e. point A is at a

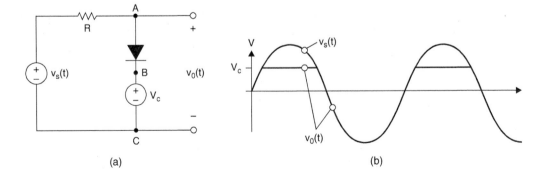

FIGURE 9.18 (a) A simple clipper circuit; (b) Output voltage of circuit in Figure 9.18a

(a)

(b)

lower voltage than point B. $v_s(t)$ is connected to the output via the resistor, R, which passes no current since the diode looks like an open circuit. However, when the input voltage exceeds V_C, then the diode will be forward biased, appears as a short circuit and V_C is connected directly to the output, which effectively clips the output voltage at a level equal to V_C. This is shown in Figure 9.18b.

The circuit in Figure 9.19a has the capability to independently clip both the positive and negative excursions of the input voltage. The positive values of the signal are clipped any time the signal exceeds 5 V, and the negative values of the input will be clipped whenever the signal exceeds negative 2.5 V. Therefore, with the input square wave, $v_s(t)$, shown in Figure 9.19b, the output voltage is shown in Figure 9.19c.

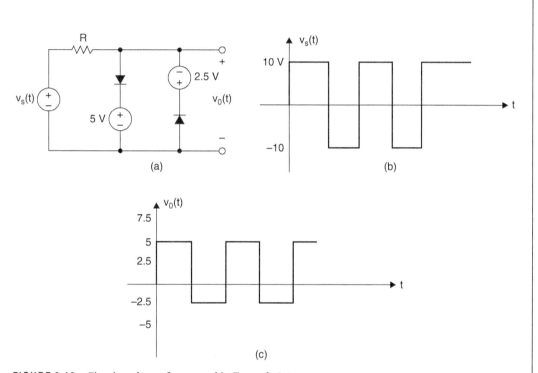

FIGURE 9.19   Circuit and waveforms used in Example 9.4

CLAMPER CIRCUITS

A *clamper circuit* is shown in Figure 9.20. This circuit, also known as a level shifter, simply reproduces the input signal, but shifts the dc level, or average value, up or down. An explanation of the circuit's operation is given as follows. Suppose the input signal is a sine wave $V_c \sin \omega t$. On the first positive half cycle, the diode will conduct and the capacitor will charge to the maximum value of $v_c(t)$, its amplitude V_c. The capacitor holds this charge when the input signal goes negative, which will reverse bias the diode and shut off the current. The charged capacitor then acts essentially as a voltage source of value V_c. The KVL equation for this one-loop circuit is

$$v_0(t) = v_s(t) - V_c$$

Thus, the output is simply a reproduction of the input shifted by V_c.

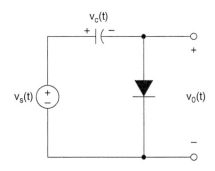

FIGURE 9.20   A simple clamper circuit

Example 9.5

Suppose the input to the clamper circuit in Figure 9.20 is the voltage shown in Figure 9.21a. Let us determine the waveform for the output of the clamper.

The output of the clamper circuit will be

$v_0(t) = v_s(t) - 2$, and, therefore, the clamper output is shown in Figure 9.21b.

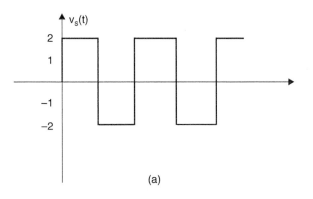

(a)

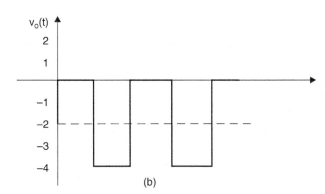

(b)

FIGURE 9.21   Waveforms used in Example 9.5

REAL SILICON DIODES

Up to this point we have assumed ideal diodes that have the V–I plot as shown in Figure 9.8.

Real diodes approximately follow an exponential relationship between voltage and current given by the "diode equation":

$$I_D = I_o \left(e^{\frac{qV_D}{kT}} - 1 \right)$$

In this equation, V_D is the externally applied voltage across the diode, I_D is the current through the diode, q is the electron charge, T is temperature in degrees Kelvin, k is Boltzmann's constant, and I_o is called the *reverse saturation current* and equals a constant that depends on the properties of the diode. At room temperature, the constants

$$\frac{q}{kT} \cong 39 \text{ or } \frac{kT}{q} = 0.026 \text{ V}$$

If a V–I curve is plotted on a linear scale, there is a voltage level *in forward bias* ($V_D > 0$) at which the current starts to become non-negligible. This voltage is defined as the "turn-on" voltage, V_{TO}, and is the amount of forward bias voltage that must be applied to get significant current to flow. Although somewhat a qualitative definition, it is often defined as the voltage at which the current reaches a particular low value for the application. The turn-on voltage differs in diodes of different materials, structures, and sizes.

For example, a typical silicon diode of normal size has a turn-on voltage of about 0.6 V. An example of the plot of current versus voltage of a silicon diode is shown in Figure 9.22.

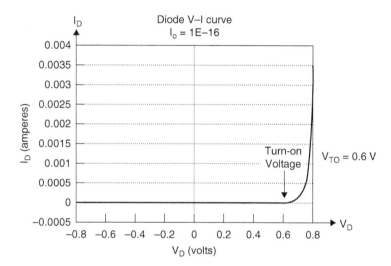

FIGURE 9.22   Plot of the diode equation for $I_o = 1 \times 10^{-16}$ A

Because the current depends exponentially on the voltage, *never* connect a diode across a voltage supply; very small changes in voltage can cause very large changes in current. To properly bias a diode, the diode should be placed in a circuit that limits and controls the current through the diode. Generally, this can be accomplished simply by putting a current-limiting resistor in series with the diode. See Example 9.6.

A silicon diode is forward biased, and the current must be limited to 10 mA. The voltage source is a dc source with a value of 10 V (Figure 9.23). What value resistor must be utilized to appropriately limit the current?

The voltage drop across the silicon diode is assumed to be 0.6 V. Therefore, by Ohm's law, a resistor of value R should be placed in series to limit the current to 10 mA.

$$R = (10 - 0.6)/10 \text{ mA} = 9.4/(10 \times 10^{-3}) = 940 \ \Omega$$

Example 9.6

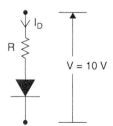

FIGURE 9.23   Circuit for Example 9.6

Example 9.7

A silicon diode is forward biased and the current must be limited to 10 mA. The applied voltage source is an ac source with a value of 10 V rms. What value of resistor must be utilized to appropriately limit the current?

10 V rms has a peak voltage of V_{peak}

$V_{peak} = 1.41(10) = 14.1$. The voltage drop across the diode is the turn-on voltage, 0.6 V.

Therefore,

$$R = (14.1 - 0.6)/10\ mA = 1350\ \Omega$$

Since nonideal diodes require a minimum voltage, V_{TO} (the turn-on) to conduct current, a useful circuit model to include this voltage drop is shown in Figure 9.24.

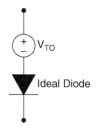

FIGURE 9.24 Circuit model of silicon diode with $V_{TO} = 0.6$ V

The V_{TO} of a diode depends on various factors, primarily the materials from which it's made, as illustrated in the next section.

The diode circuits previously presented in this chapter can be solved with more accuracy using the circuit model of Figure 9.24. Several examples are given below.

Example 9.8

Consider the half-wave rectifier circuit of Figure 9.12, using a silicon diode with $V_{TO} = 0.7$ V. If $v(t) = 3\sin(\omega t)$, plot the voltage across the load resistor, $v_{RL}(t)$ (Figure 9.25). The input voltage must reach 0.7 V before the diode begins to conduct; hence the delay before the $v_{RL}(t)$ begins to rise; when the peak of 3 V is reached at the input, the output peak is reduced by the voltage drop of 0.7 V, making the peak in $v_{RL}(t)$ 2.3 V.

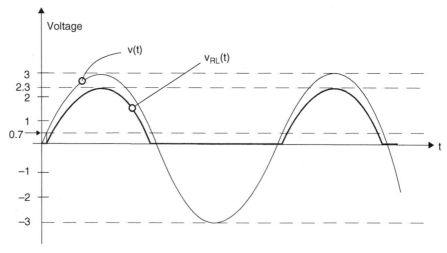

FIGURE 9.25 Waveform plotted from Example 9.8

Example 9.9

Consider the clipper circuit of Figure 9.18a. Draw the output voltage, $v_o(t)$, assuming the diode has a value of $V_{TO} = 0.7$ V. Further assume $v_s(t) = 4\sin(\omega t)$ and $V_C = 1$ V. In the original illustration, shown in Figure 9.18b, the output waveform would look a sine wave, but truncated at $V_C = 1$ V. If now we consider the voltage required to cause the diode to conduct, V_{TO}, by using the circuit model of Figure 9.24 inserted into the clipper circuit shown in Figure 9.26a, we obtain the waveform of Figure 9.26b.

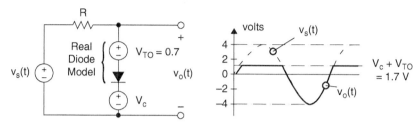

FIGURE 9.26   (a) Circuit model from Example 9.9 and (b) the resulting output waveform

Special-purpose diodes include light emitting diodes (LEDs), Schottky diodes, Zener diodes, etc. This section provides a brief description of these devices and how they can be used in applications.

LEDs and Schottky diodes, like silicon diodes, are designed to operate (conduct current) in forward bias ($V_D > 0$). Table 9.1 shows the turn-on voltage (V_{TO}) for these various diodes.

LIGHT EMITTING DIODES (LEDS)

Light emitting diodes or LEDs have become common as indicator lights in control panels, light generators of various colors for displays, traffic lights, and a host of applications. Modern LEDs are available in a variety of colors, at modest prices. Searching on the internet will disclose many sources for purchasing single color LEDs or multiple color LEDs in the same package.

Forward biasing a diode allows electrons and holes to diffuse and recombine, releasing energy. Silicon is an indirect bandgap material and this energy is generally released into lattice vibrations. There are direct bandgap materials that allow the direct transition of an electron from the conduction band to the valence band, and release light; the energy difference of the bandgap determines the energy of the photons released and hence their color. Such special materials include gallium arsenide, gallium nitride, and many more.

In order to properly bias a single LED, the same approach as that previously discussed for silicon should be used. The current allowed by the circuit must be less than the maximum current specification for the particular LED being used. For a standard 5-mm-diameter LED, the maximum current is usually in the 15–20 mA range, so basing at 10 mA is good for those applications.

Table 9.1   Approximate Turn-on Voltages of Various Diodes

Diode type	Approximate turn-on voltage, V_{TO}
Schottky diodes	0.3 V
Silicon diodes	0.6 V
LEDs (red, yellow, and green)	2 V
LEDs (blue and white)	4 V

Example 9.10

There is a system with a 5 V power supply available and it is desired to switch on and off a red LED. What value of resistor is required in series with the LED?

$$R = (5 - 2)/10 \text{ mA} = 300 \ \Omega$$

SCHOTTKY DIODES

Schottky diodes are created by a metal–semiconductor junction. The metal serves as the p-side of the junction and the semiconductor is generally n-type. The advantage of Schottky junctions are their low turn-on voltage of the range of $V_{TO} = 0.3$ V. Their application is particularly valuable in power supply circuits; as with less voltage drop, there is less power dissipated in the diode, and power circuits can be made more efficient. There are a variety of Schottky diodes on the market and generally specified to carry high currents.

Schottky diodes conduct under forward bias; therefore, all the problems at the end of the chapter can be reworked assuming Schottky diodes with different results.

INTRODUCTION TO LOAD LINE ANALYSIS

In this section, an introduction to load line analysis will be presented. Load line analysis is a graphical process and useful in the cases where a circuit contains a nonlinear component, like a diode or transistor combined with linear elements such as resistors.

Load line analysis will be used extensively in the biasing and analysis of transistors, so if this section is not completely clear to the reader, *please refer to Appendix B for a more in-depth discussion of load line analysis.*

First, to use load line analysis, one must have the V–I characteristics of a nonlinear element, either measured, from a data sheet or otherwise determined.

Load line analysis superimposes the V–I characteristics of the nonlinear device over the known characteristics of the linear device, usually a resistance that follows Ohm's law. This is most commonly accomplished by determining on the x- and y-axes the value where the linear element characteristics intersect the axes, as illustrated in the following Example 9.11.

Example 9.11

Assume a silicon diode has the V–I characteristics shown in Figure 9.27a and is placed in the circuit shown in Figure 9.27b.

Next we wish to determine where the linear resistor intersects each axis. This can be done in several ways.

In one method, assume the nonlinear device (the diode) is a short; therefore, $I_D = V_1/R = 1.5 \text{ V}/500 \ \Omega = 3$ mA; mark that spot on the current axis of the V–I curve (where $V_D = 0$); this is illustrated in Figure 9.27c.

Next assume the nonlinear element is an open circuit ($I_D = 0$); therefore, $V_D = V_1 = 1.5$ V; mark that spot on the voltage axis of the V–I curve.

Since the resistor is a linear element, draw a straight line connecting these two points. The point at which this line intersects the curve of the nonlinear element is called the quiescent point or Q-point. This is where the circuit will come to a stable bias situation. In this example, this occurs at a current I_D of 1.8 mA, and the voltage across the diode, V_D is 0.6 V. This entire process is shown in Figure 9.27c.

A second method, which is essentially equivalent, is to write the loop equation for the circuit:

$$V_D = V_1 - I_D R$$

Then take the extremes of $I_D = 0$ and $V_D = 0$, and the same result will be obtained.

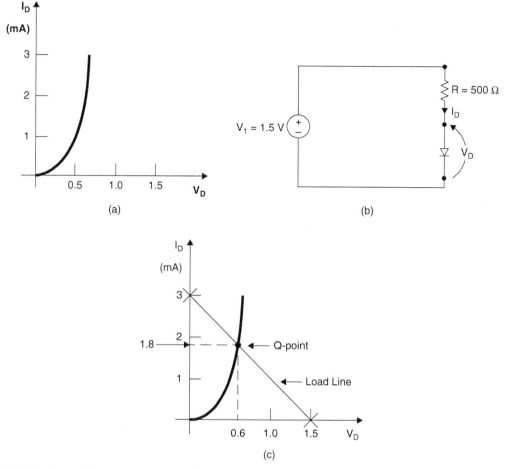

FIGURE 9.27   (a) V–I characteristics of silicon diode of Example 9.11; (b) Circuit of Example 9.11; (c) Load line intersecting V–I diode characteristics to determine operating point called Q-point

Assume diodes in the following problems are ideal, unless otherwise specified.

9.1   Find I in the networks in Figure P9.1.

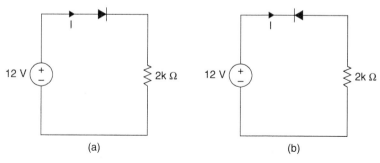

FIGURE P9.1

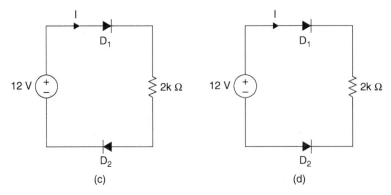

(c)   (d)

FIGURE P9.1 (*Continued*)

9.2 Determine the source current, I, in the circuit in Figure P9.2.

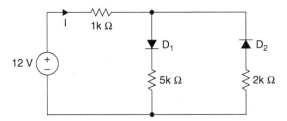

FIGURE P9.2

9.3 Given the circuit in Figure P9.3 calculate the value of I if (a) V_s = 12 V and (b) V_s = −12 V.

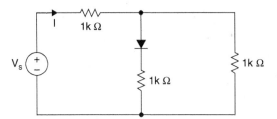

FIGURE P9.3

9.4 Assuming an ideal diode, in the circuit of Figure P9.4, (a) what is the voltage across R_2? and (b) what is the current through D?

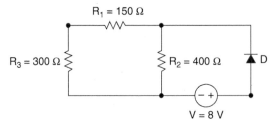

FIGURE P9.4

9.5 Calculate the current through R_1 in Figure P9.5, if
  (a) $V = 4$ V
  (b) $V = 8$ V
  (c) $V = -8$ V

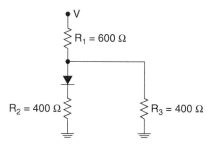

FIGURE P9.5

9.6 Plot V_o as a function of V_i from 0 to 10 V in the circuit of Figure P9.6.

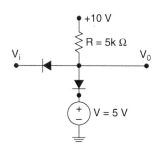

FIGURE P9.6

9.7 In the network of Figure P9.7, what is the current through R_1 when
  (a) $V = 10$ V?
  (b) $V = -10$ V?

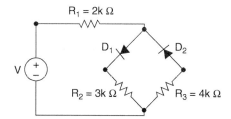

FIGURE P9.7

9.8 Sketch the V–I characteristics of each of the circuits in Figure P9.8 assuming
  (a) the diodes are ideal;
  (b) the diodes are silicon with $V_{TO} = 0.6$ V.

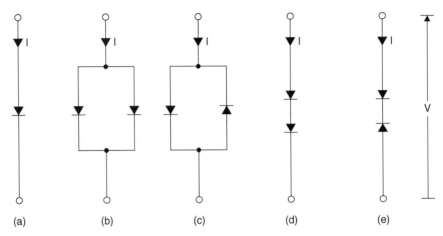

(a)   (b)   (c)   (d)   (e)

FIGURE P9.8

9.9 In the network in Figure P9.9, assuming ideal diodes, calculate the current through (a) D_1, (b) D_2, and (c) V, the source.

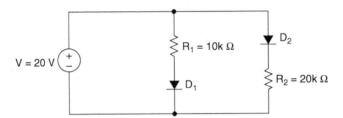

FIGURE P9.9

9.10 Find V_0 in the network in Figure P9.10, assuming silicon diodes with $V_{TO} = 0.7$ V.

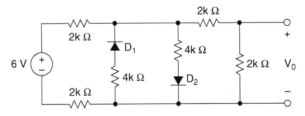

FIGURE P9.10

9.11 Calculate I_0 in the circuit in Figure P9.11 if (a) $V_s = 12$ V and (b) $V_s = -6$ V, assuming ideal diodes.

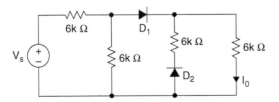

FIGURE P9.11

9.12 In the circuit in Figure P9.12 find V_0 if (a) $V_s = 12$ V and (b) $V_s = -12$ V.

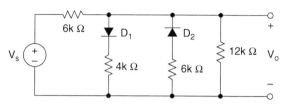

FIGURE P9.12

9.13 Find I_1 and I_2 in the network in Figure P9.13, assuming an ideal diode.

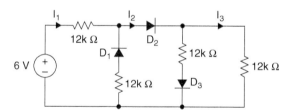

FIGURE P9.13

9.14 Determine the currents, I_1, I_2, and I_3 in the network in Figure P9.14.
    (a) Assume ideal diodes.
    (b) Assume silicon diodes with $V_{TO} = 0.6$ V.

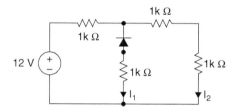

FIGURE P9.14

9.15 Calculate the current I in the circuit in Figure P9.15 if (a) $V_s = 12$ V and (b) $V_s = -12$ V, assuming ideal diodes.

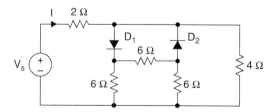

FIGURE P9.15

9.16 Find the current I in the circuit in Figure P9.16 if (a) $V_s = 12$ V and (b) $V_s = -12$ V, assuming ideal diodes.

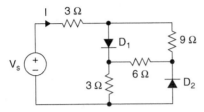

FIGURE P9.16

9.17 The input to the half-wave rectifier in Figure P9.17a is shown in Figure P9.17b. Draw the output waveform for the voltage $v_0(t)$.
(a) Assume ideal diode.
(b) Assume the diode is silicon with $V_{TO} = 0.7$ V.

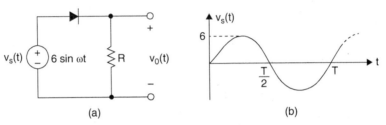

FIGURE P9.17

9.18 Calculate the dc level of the output voltage in Problem 9.17.

9.19 Sketch the output voltage $v_0(t)$, for the circuit shown in Figure P.9.19 for $0 \leq t \leq 10$ ms, where $v_i(t)$ is given in the figure. Assume an ideal diode.

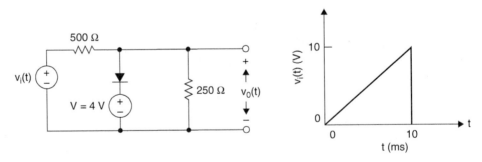

FIGURE P9.19

9.20 Consider the periodic triangular voltage waveform shown in Figure P9.20. (a) What is the average dc value, V_{dc}, of this wave? (b) If this wave is "half-wave" rectified, plot the voltage versus time and determine the dc value. (c) If this wave is "full-wave" rectified, plot the voltage versus time and calculate the dc value.

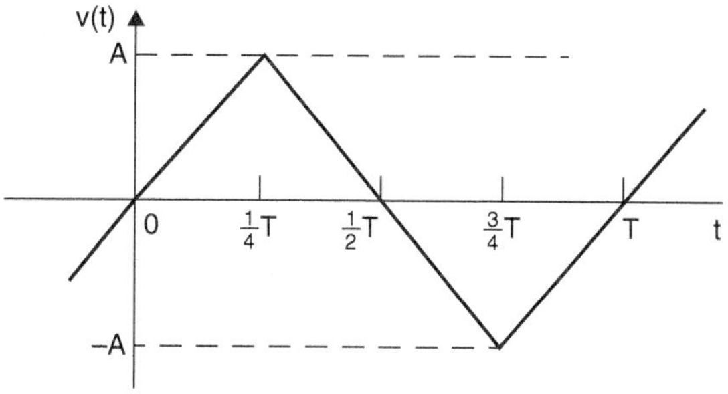

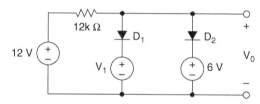

FIGURE P9.20

9.21 Find V_0 in the circuit in Figure P9.21 when (a) $V_1 = 2$ V and (b) $V_1 = 8$ V.
(a) Assume ideal diodes.
(b) Assume a silicon diode with $V_{TO} = 0.7$ V.
(c) Assume a Schottky diode with $V_{TO} = 0.3$ V.

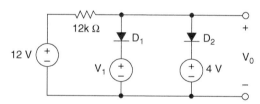

FIGURE P9.21

9.22 Given the circuit in Figure P9.22, plot the voltage V_0 as V_1 varies from 0 to 12 V. Assume ideal diodes.

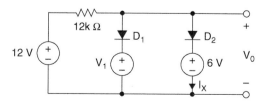

FIGURE P9.22

9.23 For the circuit in Figure P9.23, (a) plot V_0 as V_1 varies from 0 to 12 V, (b) find I_X if $V_1 = 3$ V, and (c) find I_X if $V_1 = 8$ V.
Assume ideal diodes.

FIGURE P9.23

9.24 Determine the currents I_1 and I_2 if (a) $V_s = 2$ V and (b) $V_s = 12$ V for the network in Figure P9.24.
(a) Assume an ideal diode.
(b) Assume a silicon diode with $V_{TO} = 0.7$ V.

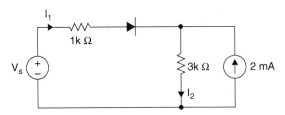

FIGURE P9.24

9.25 Find the current I_D in the circuit in Figure P9.25.

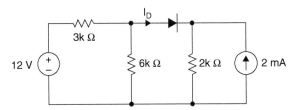

FIGURE P9.25

9.26 In the circuit in Figure P9.26, the source is $v_s(t) = 12 \sin 377t$ V rms. (a) Sketch the output voltage $v_0(t)$ and (b) determine the dc level of the output voltage.

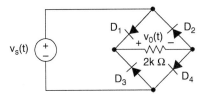

FIGURE P9.26

9.27 The input of the full-wave rectifier circuit in Figure P9.27 is $v_S(t) = 24 \sin 377t$ V rms. Sketch the output waveform and label all critical values.

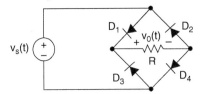

FIGURE P9.27

9.28 Given the full-wave rectifier circuit in Figure P9.28, (a) sketch the output waveform and label all critical values and (b) determine the dc level of the output voltage. Assume the total voltage across the secondary of the transformer is $2v_s(t)$, where $v_s(t) = 12 \sin 377t$ and R_L is 500 Ω.

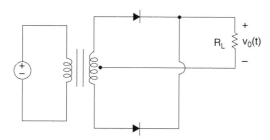

FIGURE P9.28

9.29 Determine the output waveform for the network in Figure P9.29.

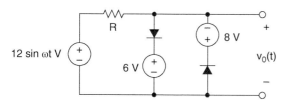

FIGURE P9.29

9.30 Calculate the waveform for the voltage $v_0(t)$ in the circuit in Figure P9.30.

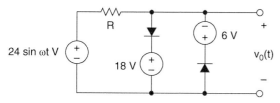

FIGURE P9.30

9.31 Determine the output waveform for the network in Figure P9.31.

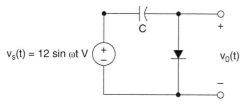

FIGURE P9.31

9.32 Calculate the waveform for the voltage $v_0(t)$ in the circuit in Figure P9.32.

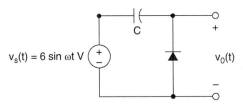

FIGURE P9.32

9.33 In Figure P9.33, assume $v_1(t) = 10\sin(\omega t)$ V, $\omega = 377$, and $V_a = 4$ V. Plot $v_1(t)$, $v_c(t)$, the voltage across the capacitor, and $v_0(t)$ on the same time axis. (Assume ideal diode.)

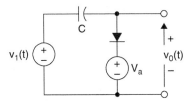

FIGURE P9.33

9.34 Repeat Problem 9.33 with $V_a = -3$ V.

9.35 A red LED is connected in the following circuit. (a) How much current flows when the switch is open? (b) How much current flows when the switch is closed?

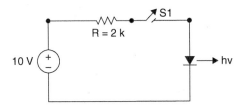

FIGURE P9.35

9.36 A green LED conducts 5 mA when connected in series with a resistor to a 12 V dc voltage source. (a) Draw the schematic drawing of this circuit. (b) What is the value of the resistor? Two red LEDs are connected in the following circuit in Figure P9.36. (a) How much current flows through the resistor, R? (b) What is the disadvantage of this circuit? (c) Using two resistors, design a better circuit for lighting the two LEDs.

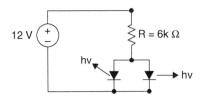

FIGURE P9.36

9.37 A Schottky diode is forward biased by a 12 V dc source in series with a 3k Ω resistor. (a) How much current flows through the diode? (b) If the polarity of the source is reversed, how much current flows through the diode?

9.38 A silicon diode is placed in the circuit of P9.38a; the diode has the V–I curve shown in Figure P9.38b. Solve for the Q-point using load line analysis. Show all calculations and plots.

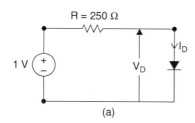

(a)

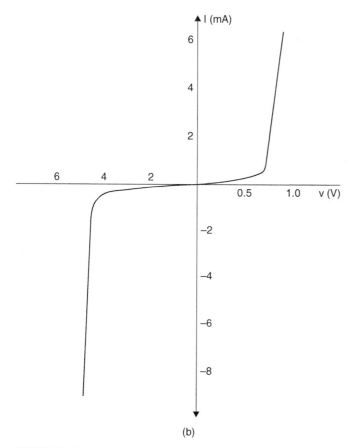

(b)

FIGURE P9.38

9.39 The diode in Figure P9.39a has V–I characteristics shown in Figure P9.39b. Use a graphical method to solve for the diode current and voltage in this circuit. Plot the load line on the same graph as the diode curve and clearly identify the Q-point.

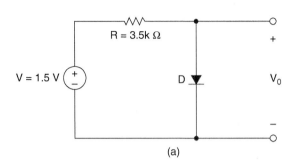

(a)

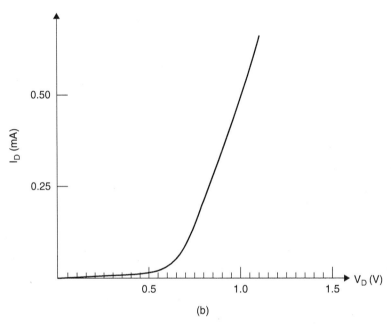

(b)

FIGURE P9.39

9.40 Repeat problem Figure P9.39 if
(a) R = 3.0k Ω
(b) R = 2.5k Ω

9.41 Briefly describe the difference between a photodiode and a light emitting diode (LED).

9.42 Given the circuit in Figure P9.42a, determine the voltage across the diode and the current in the circuit if the diode characteristic is represented by the graph in Figure P9.42b.

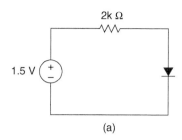

(a)

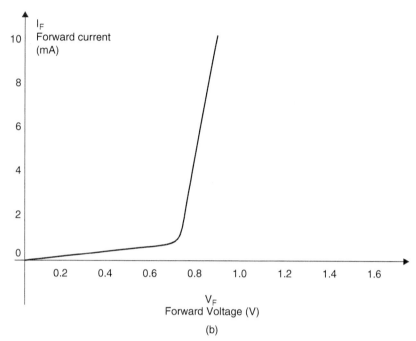

(b)

FIGURE P9.42

9.43   Given the circuit in Figure P9.43, determine the load voltage and load current (through the 400 Ω resistor on the right) in the circuit if the diode characteristic is represented by the graph in Figure P9.42b.

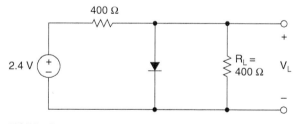

FIGURE P9.43

CHAPTER 10

Operational Amplifiers and Applications

LEARNING OBJECTIVES

- To understand the characteristics of operational amplifiers and differential amplifiers

- To understand the operation of the ideal op-amp model

- To be able to recognize and analyze fundamental op-amp circuits

- To understand the application of op-amps in the development of low-pass, high-pass, and bandpass filters

- To be able to understand the use of op-amps to construct differentiator and integrator circuits

- To understand multistage amplifier circuits

- To be able to use op-amps in instrumentation and laboratory measurements and in industrial applications.

INTRODUCTION

The operational amplifier, or op amp as it is commonly known, is a fundamental component in analog electronic systems. Although it can be used in a variety of applications, it is widely used in instrumentation and measurement systems.

An actual circuit diagram for a commercial op amp is the 741 Op Amp shown in Figure 10.1. Also shown in the figure are the pin connections for a dual in-line package, or DIP, which supports its connection with other electronic components. Even a cursory examination of the circuit schematic for the op amp indicates that this is not a trivial network. It is typically constructed as an integrated circuit and may be purchased as a single device, in a DIP that contains several op amps or in a "surface mount" package. These elements are not only powerful devices in analog circuit design but are also inexpensive – less than a dollar for a chip in a package.

Even after wading through the chapters in this book and developing a knowledge of transistors and their applications, the circuit diagram in Figure 10.1 may appear formidable. However, as sophisticated as it appears, it is really nothing more than a high-quality linear voltage amplifier. The details of how this circuit is designed are beyond the scope of this book, but follows basic principles described here.

A linear voltage amplifier is an electronic circuit that produces an output voltage signal that is an exact copy or replica of the input voltage signal, except the output is increased in amplitude (magnitude) by a factor, A_v, called the voltage gain. This is illustrated in Figure 10.2 and by the following equation. Note that in Figure 10.2, $A_v = 2$.

$$v_o = A_v v_i$$

In practice, op amps have significantly higher gains, A_v, than that illustrated, like 10,000 or 100,000 or more.

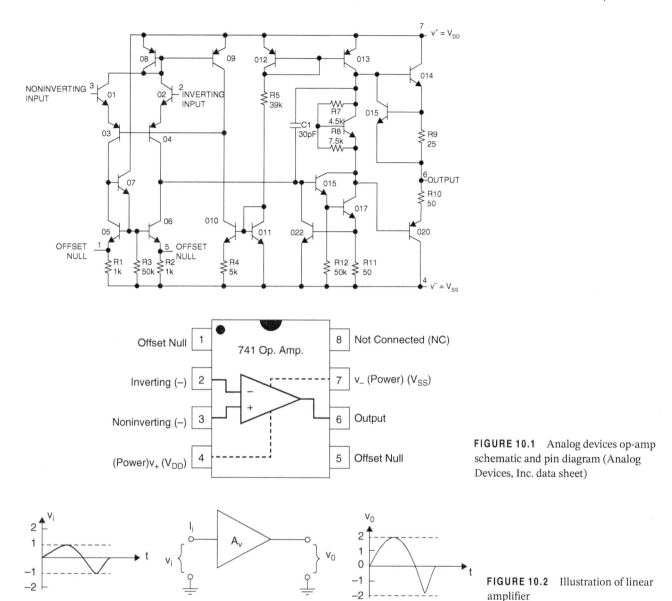

FIGURE 10.1 Analog devices op-amp schematic and pin diagram (Analog Devices, Inc. data sheet)

FIGURE 10.2 Illustration of linear amplifier

A differential amplifier has two inputs, generally labeled as v_+ and v_-, the noninverting and the inverting inputs, respectively; and there is one output, v_o. The output voltage is related to the *difference* in voltage between the two inputs. Power is supplied to the device via the two dc voltage sources, V_{DD} and V_{SS}, which are typically balanced, e.g. plus and minus 1.5–15 V. The output voltage of the amplifier is linear, i.e. not saturated, as long as it is within these limits. See Figure 10.3.

The differential amplifier circuit can be represented by the circuit model shown in Figure 10.4. In this circuit, V_{TH} and R_{TH} represent the Thevenin equivalent for the input circuit and R_L represents the load. The input voltage of the differential amplifier is v_{in}, which is equal to the differential input voltage, i.e. $v_{in} = (v_+ - v_-)$, R_{in} and R_o represent the input and output resistance of the amplifier, respectively, and A_v is the voltage gain of the amplifier.

DIFFERENTIAL AMPLIFIERS

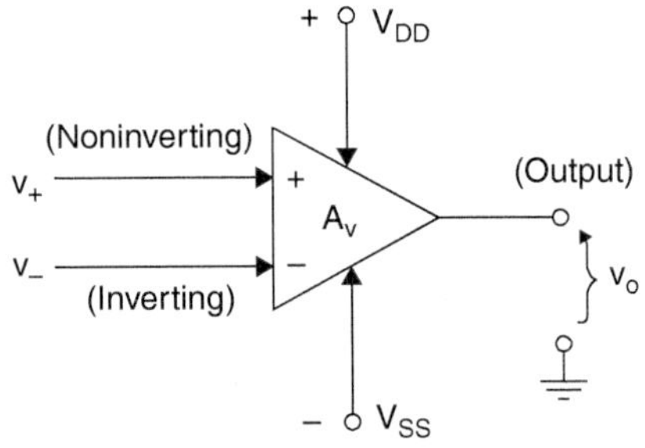

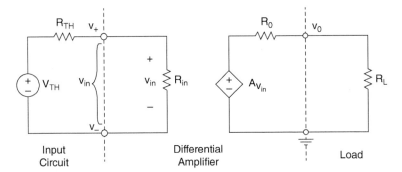

FIGURE 10.3   Op-amp symbol with dc supply voltages

FIGURE 10.4   Operational amplifier equivalent circuit with input circuit and load attached

Input Circuit

Differential Amplifier

Load

An operational amplifier, or op amp, is a differential amplifier designed such that the R_{in} and A are made as high as possible, and R_o is made as low as possible.

THE IDEAL OP AMP

Although it is not possible to realize an ideal op amp, modern op amps are very close, and the model employed to describe its performance can be used as an excellent approximation to understand its use in basic circuits. The ideal op amp has the following characteristics: R_{in} is infinite, R_o is zero, and A_v is infinite. An examination of the data sheets for some typical op amps manufactured by companies such as Texas Instruments indicates values of $R_{in} = 1\ M\Omega$, $R_o = 20\ \Omega$, and $A_v = 100{,}000$. This A_v is known as the open-circuit or open-loop gain, and although it is not infinite in practical circuits it is really quite large. The circuit model for the ideal op amp therefore reduces to that shown in Figure 10.5, where A_v is the open-loop gain.

In order to understand the term closed-loop gain, consider the standard block diagram for a feedback amplifier shown in Figure 10.6. This is a classic closed-loop diagram in which a portion of the output is fed back to the "−" input, and it is this feedback that provides control. If this feedback connection is disconnected, then the system is open loop and the gain from the input to output would be A_v. However, with the feedback path, which closes the loop, through the feedback network with a gain of B, the system equations can be derived.

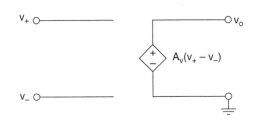

FIGURE 10.5   Equivalent circuit of ideal op amp

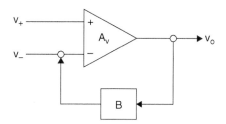

FIGURE 10.6   Op amp with feedback circuit

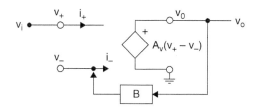

FIGURE 10.7   Circuit model of ideal op amp with feedback

A circuit drawing of the op-amp model with feedback is shown in Figure 10.7. From this figure, v_i (the input to the circuit) is equal to v_+ (the input to the op amp) since they are directly connected.

Therefore,

$$v_i = v_+$$

$v_o = A_v(v_+ - v_-)$ and $v_- = v_o B$

Therefore, $v_o = A_v v_+ - A_v B\, v_o$ or $v_o(1 + A_v B) = A_v v_+$

The inverse of the *closed-loop gain* is

$$\frac{v_+}{v_o} = \frac{v_i}{v_o} = \frac{1 + A_v B}{A_v} = \frac{1}{A_v} + B$$

$$\lim_{A_v \to \infty} \frac{v_i}{v_o} = B \text{ or the closed-loop gain } \frac{v_o}{v_i} = \frac{1}{B} = A_F$$

where we define A_F as the closed-loop gain

$$\boxed{A_F = \frac{v_o}{v_i} = \frac{1}{B}}$$

Note the amazing result that the gain of the *circuit* (the closed-loop gain), which we will call A_F, does not depend on the gain of the op amp (as long as it is very high), but rather depends only on the gain of the feedback circuit.

Also, since $v_- = B v_o$ and $v_o = A v_+ - A v_-$, then,

$$v_-(1 + A_v B) = v_+ A_v B$$

$$v_- \left(\frac{1}{A_v} + B \right) = v_+ B$$

$$\lim_{A_v \to \infty} v_- B = v_+ B$$

or

$$\boxed{v_- = v_+}$$

This says that the feedback drives or holds the v_- node at the same voltage as the voltage at v_+.

Therefore, in order to analyze most op-amp circuits with negative feedback, there are only *three* things that one needs to know. The following three rules (assuming the op amp has a high gain) are worth remembering:

1. The current into the inputs of the op amp are zero. Or $i_+ = i_- = 0$.

2. The negative feedback makes v_- the same as v_+. Or $v_- = v_+$.

3. v_o is bounded by the power supply voltages. Or v_o is limited between V_{SS} and V_{DD}. (Note: In practical circuits the output voltage may be limited to voltages slightly less than the supply voltages, but this is generally small and ignored.)

BASIC OPERATIONAL AMPLIFIER CONFIGURATIONS

Although op amps are used in a variety of circuits to perform a whole host of applications, there are several standard circuits, and we will examine them first. Note carefully that our analyses will involve the application of the fundamental rules for an ideal op amp, and the feedback path will be connected to the negative op-amp input terminal.

THE NONINVERTING OP AMP

When two resistors are connected to provide the feedback path shown in Figure 10.8, the result is a noninverting op amp. In this case, the overall, or *closed-loop*, gain is

$$A_F = v_o / v_i$$

Applying the three fundamental rules we note that $v_i = v_+ = v_-$, and v_- is equal to the voltage across the resistor R_1. Since $i_+ = i_- = 0$, there is no current into the negative input terminal of the op amp, and, therefore, v_- is related to the output voltage through a voltage divider, i.e.

$$v_i = v_- = v_o \left(\frac{R_1}{R_1 + R_2} \right)$$

and thus the closed-loop voltage gain is

$$A_F = \frac{v_o}{v_i} = \left(1 + \frac{R_2}{R_1} \right) \text{ for } v_o \text{ within the limits of the power supply.}$$

Note that since the gain is positive, the signal was not inverted. In addition, the closed-loop gain is dependent only on the feedback path, as we have indicated earlier. Finally, as a prelude to our next op-amp configuration, note that if the resistor R_2 is zero, the gain of this noninverting op-amp circuit is 1.

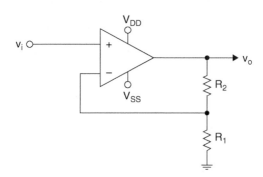

FIGURE 10.8 Noninverting op-amp circuit

The output of an electronic flow-rate transducer (used for example to monitor the flow rate of water in a pipe) has a maximum value of 12 mV corresponding to maximum flow rate. If the op-amp circuit shown in Figure 10.9 is used to amplify the signal to a maximum of 6 V for measurement purposes, determine the value of R_1 needed for this application.

Example 10.1

The closed-loop gain of this circuit, A_F, is

$$\frac{v_o}{v_i} = 6/(12)(10^{-3}) = 500$$

Therefore,

$$500 = 1 + \frac{R_1}{1000}$$

Solving for R_1 yields

$$R_1 = 490k\ \Omega$$

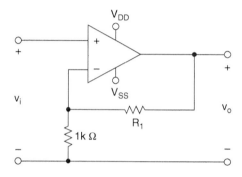

FIGURE 10.9   Circuit used in Example 10.1

THE UNITY-GAIN BUFFER

Consider now the op-amp configuration shown in Figure 10.10. Note that this circuit is a special case of the noninverting circuit in which R_2 is zero, and, thus, the output is connected directly to the noninverting input terminal of the op amp. The resistor R_1 has no impact in this situation and thus is simply eliminated from the circuit. Applying the fundamental rule

$$v_i = v_+ = v_- = v_o$$

and therefore

$$A_F = \frac{v_o}{v_i} = 1$$

The first question that typically comes to mind is this: if the gain is unity why bother to use an op amp – just connect the input directly to the output! However, there is a good reason to use this circuit for certain applications.

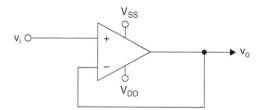

FIGURE 10.10   Unity gain buffer circuit

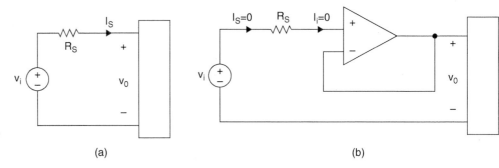

FIGURE 10.11 The effect of a unity-gain buffer

(a)   (b)

Consider the networks in Figure 10.11a, the voltage v_o is

$$v_o = v_i - i_s R_s$$

However, in the network in Figure 10.11b, $v_o = v_i$ and there is no input current. The op amp has provided some isolation and eliminated the loading effect of the input resistance of the next stage. One of the most important uses of this circuit is that of an impedance converter in which the input voltage from a high-impedance source is converted into an equivalent voltage at a low output impedance.

THE INVERTING OP AMP

The inverting op-amp circuit is shown in Figure 10.12. In this case, the noninverting terminal is connected to ground, or zero volts, i.e. $v_+ = 0$ V, and thus $v_- = 0$ V. Therefore, the input current is

$$i_i = \frac{(v_i - 0)}{R_1}$$

Likewise, the feedback current is

$$i_{FB} = \frac{(v_o - 0)}{R_2}$$

Since the current into the op-amp inverting terminal is zero, i.e. $i_- = 0$, $i_1 + i_{FB} = 0$. Thus,

$$\frac{v_i}{R_1} + \frac{v_o}{R_2} = 0$$

and then

$$A_F = v_o/v_i = -R_2/R_1$$

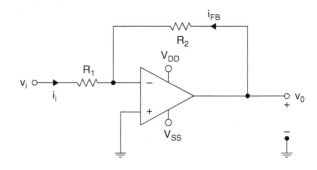

FIGURE 10.12 Inverting op-amp circuit

Note that the voltage has been inverted as indicated by the negative sign, i.e. the polarity of the output voltage is the opposite of the input voltage, and the closed-loop gain, A_F, is set by the *ratio* of two resistor values.

Given the op-amp configuration shown in Figure 10.12, let us calculate the gain, the output voltage, and the source current. Assume $R_2 = 360k$, $R_1 = 60k$, and $v_i = 2$ V.

The gain of this circuit is

$$A_F = -360k\ \Omega / 60k\ \Omega = -6$$

The output voltage is then

$v_0 = A_F\ v_1 = -12$ V (Assume the supply voltages, V_{DD} and V_{SS}, exceed ± 12 V.)

Since $v_+ = v_- = 0$, the input current is

$$i_i = v_i / 60k\ \Omega = 33.33\ mA$$

THE DIFFERENCE AMPLIFIER OR DIFFERENTIAL AMPLIFIER

The network in Figure 10.13 is a differential amplifier in that it amplifies the difference between the two inputs, v_1 and v_2. Application of the fundamental rule, i.e. $v_+ = v_-$, indicates that

$$v_+ = v_- = v_2 \left(\frac{R_2}{R_1 + R_2} \right)$$

Since the current into the op-amp input terminals must be zero, KCL at the negative input terminal yields

$$\frac{(v_1 - v_-)}{R_1} + \frac{(v_0 - v_-)}{R_2} = 0$$

Combining these two equations yields the result

$$v_0 = - \left(\frac{R_2}{R_1} \right) [v_1 - v_2]$$

This circuit is very useful in a variety of instrumentation applications where it is necessary to measure the difference between two small voltages. One example is the output of a Wheatstone bridge to measure strain in solid materials. Note that any interference signal that is common on both lines is canceled while the desired signal is amplified. This ability to reject common-mode

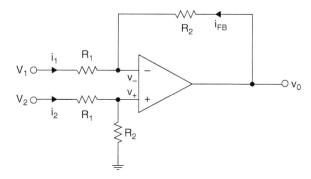

FIGURE 10.13 A differential op-amp circuit

signals is measured by what is known as the common-mode rejection ratio or CMRR. The higher the common-mode rejection ratio, the greater the ability of the circuit to extract the desired signal from background noise.

Example 10.3

Given the network in Figure 10.14, let us determine the input current i_1 and the output voltage v_0.

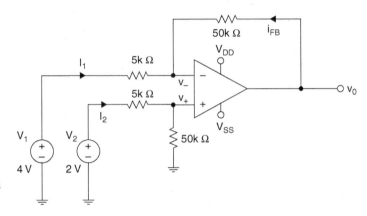

FIGURE 10.14 Circuit used in Example 10.3

To begin, we employ a voltage divider to determine v_+ as

$$v_+ = 2\left(\frac{50k\,\Omega}{55k\,\Omega}\right) = 1.82\ V$$

Applying KVL to the outer loop yields

$$-v_1 + 5k\Omega i_1 - 50k\Omega i_{FB} + v_0 = 0$$

Since $i_1 = -i_{FB}$,

$$-4 + 55k\Omega i_1 + v_0 = 0$$

And since $v_- = v_+ = 1.82\ V$

$$I_1 = \frac{(4 - 1.82)}{5k\Omega} = 437\ mA$$

Then

$$V_0 = -4 + 55k\Omega i_1 = -20\ V$$

A quick comparison with the equation

$$V_0 = -\frac{R_2}{R_1}[V_1 - V_2] = -20\ V$$

which confirms our analysis.

   (Note: The above assumes the op amp will operate with power supply voltages down to −20 V.)

THE SUMMING OP AMP

The summing op-amp circuit is similar to that of the inverting op-amp circuit with one fundamental difference; it has multiple inputs. The circuit for this configuration is shown in Figure 10.15, and the output voltage is a function of the sum, or addition, of the input voltages.

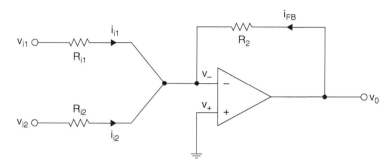

FIGURE 10.15 A summing op-amp circuit

The analysis of this circuit is performed in a manner similar to that used with the inverting op amp. Since $v_+ = v_- = 0$, the input currents are

$$i_{i1} = \frac{v_{i1}}{R_{i1}}$$

$$i_{i2} = \frac{v_{i2}}{R_{i2}}$$

and the feedback current is

$$i_{FB} = \frac{v_0}{R_2}$$

Since $i_- = 0$, KCL at the negative input terminal is

$$i_{i1} + i_{i2} + i_{FB} = 0$$

Making the appropriate substitutions and solving for v_0 yields

$$v_0 = -\left[\frac{R_2}{R_{i1}}v_{i1} + \frac{R_2}{R_{i2}}v_{i2}\right]$$

Note that the effect of each input is weighted by the ratio of the feedback resistor to that input's resistor, and, therefore, the effect of each input voltage is controlled by this ratio. Like the inverting op-amp configuration, the signals have been inverted, and it is straightforward to extend the analysis to a configuration with more inputs.

We wish to find the value of R in the op-amp circuit shown in Figure 10.16.

The equation for the summing op amp, employing the values of the various parameters in the network, is

$$-12 = -\left(\frac{2R}{4k\,\Omega} + \frac{4R}{8k\,\Omega}\right)$$

Example 10.4

Solving this equation for R yields the value

$$R = 12k\,\Omega$$

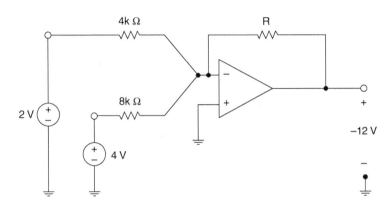

FIGURE 10.16 Circuit used in Example 10.4

CURRENT-TO-VOLTAGE CONVERTER

There are some applications for which a circuit is needed that will transform an input current to an output voltage. To accomplish this, a simple op-amp circuit can be used with a resistor in the feedback path, as shown in Figure 10.17.

The input current i_i cannot flow into the op amp since its input resistance is infinite; therefore, this current flows entirely through R_F. Hence

$$i_i = -i_f$$

The voltage at v_- is zero, and, therefore,

$$v_o = -i_i R_F$$

It is impossible to refer to the "voltage gain" or "current gain" of this circuit because the input is a current and the output is a voltage. The parameter that describes how much the output voltage changes for a given change in input current is the *transresistance*. *Trans* means the voltage and current are not measured at the same place. The transresistance is $-R_F$. This is often expressed as the inverse of transresistance or transconductance.

One such use of this type of circuit is in an electronic illumination (light) intensity meter. Photodiodes are devices that generate an output current approximately proportional to the incident radiation, such as light, on them. If a photodiode is connected to the input of a *current-to-voltage converter* circuit, the output voltage will be proportional to incident light intensity.

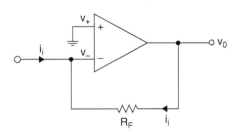

FIGURE 10.17 Current-to-voltage converter circuit

A photodiode designed for visible light has a sensitivity of 25 µA per milliwatt of incident radiation. If this diode is used in the light meter circuit in Figure 10.18, calculate the value of R_F needed to make the magnitude of the output voltage equal 4 V when the incident radiation deposits 50 mW at the photodiode detector.

Example 10.5

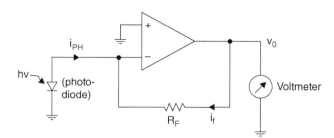

FIGURE 10.18   Circuit used in Example 10.5

The detector photodiode produces 25 µA per milliwatt of radiation; therefore, at 50 mW, it produces

$$i_{PH} = (50)(25 \times 10^{-6}) = 1.25 \text{ mA}$$

In order to produce a magnitude of 4 V at the output of the circuit,

$$R_F = \frac{4}{1.25 \times 10^{-3}} = 3.2\text{k } \Omega$$

The photodiode produces positive current flow from the anode, and, therefore, in this circuit, positive current flows inward and opposite to the assumed direction of i_f. Therefore, in operation, the output voltage goes more negative as light intensity increases, reaching −4 V with 50 mW of incident radiation. The photodiode could be reversed end-for-end, and the output voltage would go positive with increasing light intensity.

THE INTEGRATOR

In the circuit of Figure 10.19, a capacitor is placed in the feedback position of an inverting op-amp circuit. This circuit will provide an output voltage proportional to the integral of the input voltage. To illustrate this fact, we again assume an ideal op amp, and v_- is made zero by the feedback. Then

$$i_f = C\frac{dv_o}{dt};$$
$$i_i = \frac{v_i}{R_i};$$
$$i_f = -i_i$$

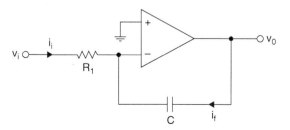

FIGURE 10.19   Op-amp integrator circuit

Combining these equations leads to the expression

$$\frac{v_i}{R_1} = -C\frac{dv_o}{dt}$$

Solving this equation for v_o yields

$$v_o = -\frac{1}{R_1 C}\int_0^t v_i\ dt + v_o(0)$$

The term $v_o(0)$ is the output voltage at time zero resulting from any initial charge on the capacitor.

Example 10.6

An *integrator circuit* of the type shown in Figure 10.19 has the following component values: $C = 100\ \mu F$ and $R_1 = 30k\ \Omega$. If the voltage, v_i, at the input of this circuit is given by the plot shown in Figure 10.20a, derive an expression for, and construct a plot of, the output voltage, v_o. Assume $v_o(0) = 0$.

$$v_o(t) = -\frac{1}{3}2t \quad \text{for } 0 < t < 2\ s$$

At $t = 2$ s, $v_o(2) = -1.33$ V.
   For the next interval,

$$v_o(t) = -\frac{1}{3}[-4(t-2)] - 1.33 \quad \text{for } 2 < t < 3\ s$$

A plot of the output voltage is given in Figure 10.20b.

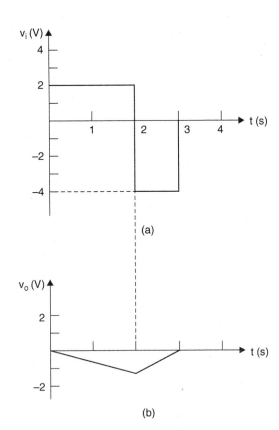

FIGURE 10.20   Integrator (a) input voltage and (b) output voltage

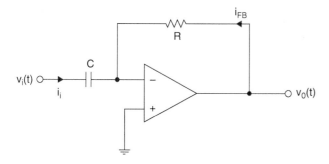

FIGURE 10.21   Op-amp differentiator circuit

THE DIFFERENTIATOR

The op-amp differentiator circuit is shown in Figure 10.21. Since $v_+ = v_- = 0$ and $i_- = 0$, $i_1 + i_{FB} = 0$, or

$$C \frac{dv_i(t)}{dt} + \frac{v_0(t)}{R} = 0$$

And therefore

$$v_0(t) = -RC \frac{dv_i(t)}{dt}$$

    The equation indicates that the output of this circuit is proportional to the derivative of the input. Although useful, this circuit is not very popular because it tends to emphasize the high-frequency components of the input signal, resulting in a noisy operation. The differentiator circuit is used, for example, at the input of some electric guitar amplifiers to create a buzzing distorted sound.

The differentiator circuit in Figure 10.21 has the following parameters: $R = 2k\ \Omega$ and $C = 1\ \mu F$. If the input to the circuit is that shown in Figure I0.22a, let us determine the output waveform. | **Example 10.7**
    The output of the differentiator is

$$v_0(t) = -RC \frac{dv_i(t)}{dt}$$

which, given the circuit parameters, reduces to

$$v_0(t) = -0.002 \frac{dv_i(t)}{dt}$$

In the time interval from 0 to 8 ms, $v_i(t) = (6/8)(10^3)t$, and, therefore, in this interval

$$v_0(t) = -2(10^{-3})(0.75)(10^3) = -1.5\ V$$

and in the time interval from 8 to 10 ms, $v_i(t) = 50 - (6/2)(10^3)t$, and, therefore, in this time interval

$$v_0(t) = -2(10^{-3})(-3)(10^3) = 6\ V$$

and the waveform for the differentiator output is shown in Figure 10.22b.

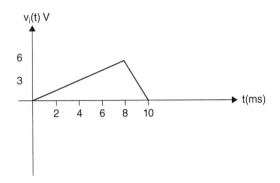

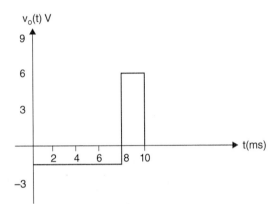

FIGURE 10.22 (a) Input voltage $v_i(t)$, and (b) output voltage $v_o(t)$ in Example 10.7

APPLICATION CIRCUITS WITH FREQUENCY DEPENDENCE (FILTERS)

There are numerous ways in which op amps are employed in a wide variety of frequency-dependent applications. Let us first consider their use in active filters. To simplify our discussion, let us once again review the gain of the network in Figure 10.23, where the input and feedback circuits are shown as impedances. Compare by analogy this circuit with Figure 10.12.

$$\mathbf{V}_i(j\omega)/\mathbf{Z}_i + \mathbf{V}_0(j\omega)/\mathbf{Z}_{FB} = 0$$

and, therefore,

$$\mathbf{V}_0(j\omega)/\mathbf{V}_i(j\omega) = -\mathbf{Z}_{FB}/\mathbf{Z}_i$$

$$\mathbf{A}_F(j\omega) = \frac{\mathbf{V}_0(j\omega)}{\mathbf{V}_i(j\omega)} = -\frac{\mathbf{Z}_{FB}}{\mathbf{Z}_i}(j\omega)$$

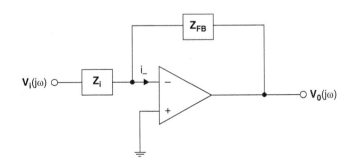

FIGURE 10.23 A generalized feedback amplifier circuit (with input and feedback elements expressed as impedances)

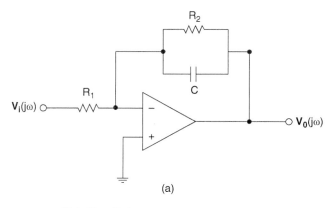

(a)

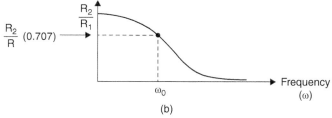

(b)

FIGURE 10.24   A low-pass filter showing the magnitude of gain versus frequency characteristic

LOW-PASS FILTERS

Let us examine the circuit in Figure 10.24a and determine the gain of this network. Following the analogy, this configuration is the same as that in Figure 10.12 under the following conditions:

$$R_i = Z_i$$

$$R_2 \Rightarrow Z_{FB} = \frac{R_2\left(\dfrac{1}{j\omega C}\right)}{\left(R_2 + \dfrac{1}{j\omega C}\right)} = \frac{R_2}{(1 + j\omega R_2 C)}$$

Therefore, the gain $\mathbf{A_F}(j\omega)$ is

$$\mathbf{A_F}(j\omega) = \frac{\mathbf{V_0}(j\omega)}{\mathbf{V_i}(j\omega)} = -\frac{R_2}{R_1}\left(\frac{1}{1 + j\omega R_2 C}\right)$$

The similarity between this equation and that of the passive low-pass filter is obvious, the difference being a gain factor of $-R_2/R_1$ (see Figures 6.3 and 6.4). Thus, with an op amp there is greater flexibility but the same cutoff frequency $\omega_0 = 1/R_2 C$. The frequency characteristic is shown in Figure 10.24b.

We wish to determine the circuit parameters for a low-pass filter that has a gain magnitude of 60, an input resistance of 2 kΩ, and a cutoff frequency of 1 kHz.

Since $v_+ = v_- = 0$, R_1 will be equal to $R_{in} = 2$k Ω, and since the gain is 60,

$R_2/R_1 = 60$ at low frequency

$$R_2 = 120\text{k }\Omega$$

and

$$C = 1/\omega R_2 = 1/(6283)(120\text{k}\Omega) = 1.33 \text{ nF}$$

Example 10.8

HIGH-PASS FILTERS

The high-pass filter configuration is shown in Figure 10.25a. Once again we can use the following expression:

$$A_F(j\omega) = \frac{V_0(j\omega)}{V_i(j\omega)} = \frac{-Z_{FB}}{Z_i}(j\omega)$$

And in this case

$$Z_i = R_1 + 1/j\omega C$$

$$Z_{FB} = R_2$$

resulting in a transfer function (voltage gain as a function of frequency) for the closed-loop gain of

$$A_F(j\omega) = -R_2 \frac{j\omega C}{[1 + j\omega R_1 C]}$$

The frequency response of this filter is shown in Figure 10.25b with a cutoff frequency (rad/s) of $\omega_0 = 1/R_1 C$. Compare this result with that presented in Figures 6.5 and 6.6.

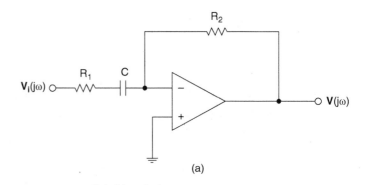

(a)

Gain Magnitude

(b)

FIGURE 10.25 A high-pass filter showing magnitude of gain versus frequency characteristic

---

| Example 10.9 | We wish to determine the two resistors in the network for a high-pass filter that has a passband gain magnitude of 10 and a cutoff frequency of 10 kHz, given a capacitor of 20 nF. |

Given the cutoff frequency and the capacitor value, we can determine the value of R_1 from the equation

$$10 \text{ kHz} = \frac{2\pi}{R_1 C}$$

$$\omega_0 = \frac{1}{R_1 C}$$

$$f_0 = \frac{\omega_0}{2\pi} = \frac{1}{2\pi R_1 C}$$

Therefore,

$$R_1 = 5k\,\Omega$$

$$R_1 = \frac{1}{f_0 2\pi\, C} = \frac{1}{2\pi(10^7)(20 \times 10^{-9})}$$

At high frequency, the passband gain is R_2/R_1 and hence $R_2 = 50k\,\Omega$.

BANDPASS FILTERS

A simple active bandpass filter is shown in Figure 10.26a. Note that the configuration suggests that it is essentially a combination of a high-pass filter and a low-pass filter. In this case,

$$Z_i = R_1 + 1/j\omega C_1$$

$$Z_{FB} = \frac{R_2\left(\dfrac{1}{j\omega C}\right)}{\left(R_2 + \dfrac{1}{j\omega C}\right)} = \frac{R_2}{(1 + j\omega R_2 C)}$$

Therefore, the closed-loop gain of this structure is

$$A_F(j\omega) = \frac{V_0(j\omega)}{V_i(j\omega)} = -R_2 \frac{j\omega C_1}{(1 + j\omega R_1 C_1)(1 + j\omega R_2 C_2)}$$

The frequency response of this filter is shown in Figure 10.26b. The low-frequency cutoff is at $\omega_{LO} = 1/R_2 C_2$ and the high-frequency cutoff is at $\omega_{HI} = 1/R_1 C_1$. Compare this result with the passive bandpass filter shown in Figure 6.9.

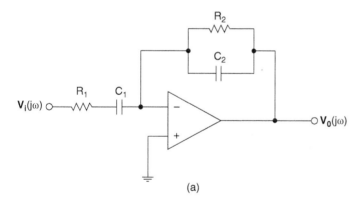

(a)

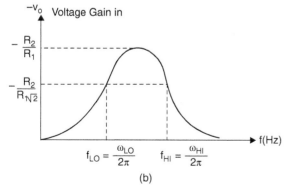

(b)

FIGURE 10.26   A bandpass filter and its frequency characteristic

Example 10.10

Suppose we are given two 50k Ω resistors and wish to determine the capacitor values that will produce a passband across the audio range from about 20 Hz to 20 kHz, as shown in Figure 10.27. Recall the corner frequency ω_o (in rad/s) of an RC filter is

$$\omega_o = \frac{1}{RC} \text{ and } f_0 = \frac{\omega_o}{2\pi} \text{ Hz}$$

With reference to the network in Figure 10.26, the capacitor value needed to fix the low-frequency cutoff, f_{LO} at 20 Hz is

$$C_2 = 1/[50(10^3)(2\pi)(20)]$$
$$C_2 = 159 \text{ nF}$$

The capacitor value needed for the high-frequency cutoff f_{HI} at 20 kHz is

$$C_1 = 1/[50(10^3)(2\pi)(20)(10^3)]$$
$$C_1 = 159 \text{ pF}$$

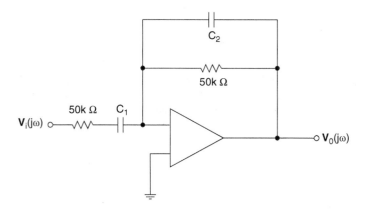

FIGURE 10.27 Circuit used in Example 10.10

MULTISTAGE AMPLIFIER CIRCUITS

In many situations, the performance needed cannot be obtained with one op amp. In most cases where more gain is required than can be achieved with a single stage, multistage amplifiers can be utilized.

The gain of a circuit with multiple stages is the product of the gain of the individual stages; therefore, if n stages are connected serially, the total circuit gain $A_F(\text{total}) = A_1 A_2 \ldots A_n$.

Example 10.11

Calculate the total voltage gain of the following circuit of Figure 10.28.

(a) What is the voltage gain of the entire circuit?

(b) If the power supplies used are as given below, what is the maximum input voltage that can be applied without distortion (clipping) at the output?

$$V_{DD} = +15 \text{ V and } V_{SS} = -15 \text{ V}$$

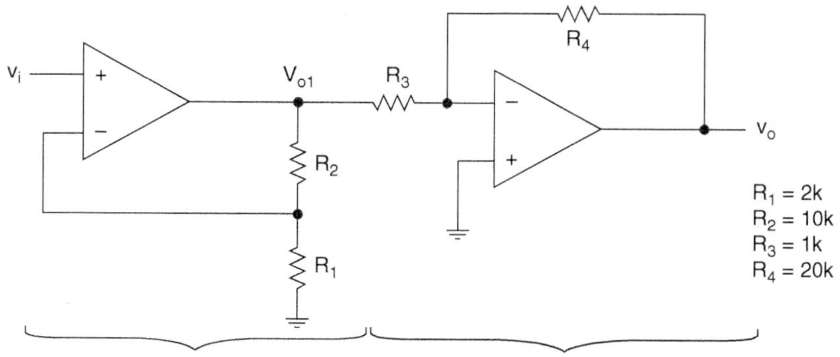

FIGURE 10.28   Circuit for Example 10.11

(a) This is a two-stage amplifier, so the total voltage gain, A_{FT}, is

$$A_{FT} = A_{F1}\, A_{F2}$$

The first stage is a noninverting amplifier configuration; therefore,

$$A_{F1} = \frac{v_o}{v_i} = 1 + \frac{10k\,\Omega}{2k\,\Omega} = 6$$

The second state is an inverting amplifier circuit; therefore,

$$A_{F2} = -\frac{R_4}{R_3} = -\frac{20k\,\Omega}{1k} = -20$$

Therefore, the total gain A_{FT} is

$$A_{FT} = A_{F1}\, A_{F2} = (6)(-20) = -120$$

(b) Since the supply voltages are $+$ and -15 V, the output of both op amps must remain within these voltage boundaries. (An amplifier cannot produce more output voltage than the voltage supply powering it.) The maximum input voltage, v_{in}, without saturating the *first* stage output (v_{o1}) is:

$$\frac{15}{6} = 2.5 \text{ V}$$

If this voltage is applied to the *second stage*, v_o is calculated to be $(2.5)(-20) = -50$ V. Since this is not allowed (the magnitude of the output exceeds 15 V), we must limit v_{in} to

$$v_{in}(\text{max}) = \frac{15}{A_{FT}} = \frac{15}{-120} = -0.125 \text{ V}$$

Note: If V_{DD} and V_{SS} are not given in a particular problem, assume they do not limit the output voltage.

Problems

10.1   The dc supplies for a noninverting op amp are $V_{DD} = 6$ V and $V_{SS} = 0$ V. The range of the input signal is from 0.1 to 0.4 V. Calculate the largest possible closed-loop gain that will permit a linear amplifier operation.

10.2 Find V_0 in the circuit in Figure P10.2.

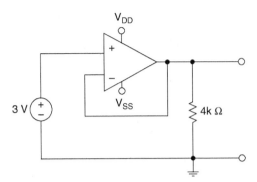

FIGURE P10.2

10.3 Determine the value of R in the network in Figure P10.3 that will produce a gain of at least 51. Assume the supply voltages will not limit the output.

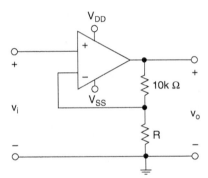

FIGURE P10.3

10.4 Determine the value of R_2 in the network in Figure P10.4 that will produce a gain of at least 41.

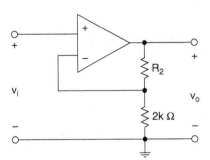

FIGURE P10.4

10.5 Calculate the value of I_0 in the circuit in Figure P10.5.

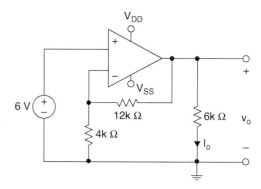

FIGURE P10.5

10.6 Compute the output voltage in the circuit in Figure P10.6.

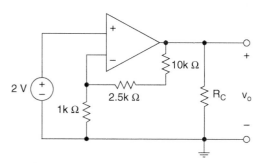

FIGURE P10.6

10.7 Calculate the amount of power dissipated in the network in Figure P10.7 excluding power used by op amp.

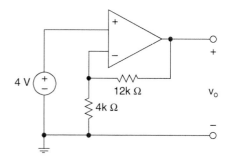

FIGURE P10.7

10.8 Determine the maximum value of R so that the power dissipation in the network in Figure P10.8 is less than 100 mW.

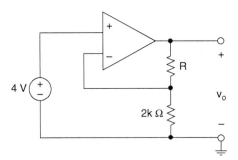

FIGURE P10.8

10.9 Determine the value of R in the network in Figure P10.9.

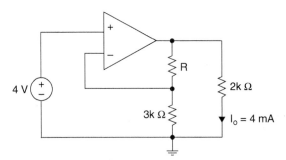

FIGURE P10.9

10.10 Determine the voltage gain for the circuit in Figure P10.10.

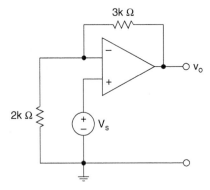

FIGURE P10.10

10.11 Determine the output voltage if $V_S = 2.4$ V in the circuit in Problem 10.10.

10.12   Find V_0 in the circuit in Figure P10.12.

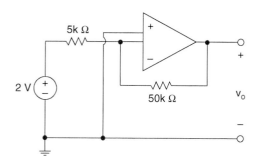

FIGURE P10.12

10.13   In the circuit of Figure P10.13, (a) determine the output voltage, V_0, (b) the current I_0, (c) the input current I_i, and (d) the voltage gain, A_F, of this circuit.

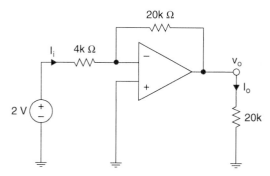

FIGURE P10.13

10.14   Find the value of R that will produce a closed-loop gain of −10 in the circuit in Figure P10.14.

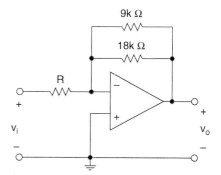

FIGURE P10.14

10.15 Find the value of R_2 that will produce a closed-loop gain of 6 in the circuit in Figure P10.15.

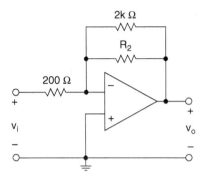

FIGURE P10.15

10.16 Find the values of R_1 and R_2 in the network in Figure P10.16 that will produce an output of the form $V_0 = -6\,V_1 - 2\,V_2$.

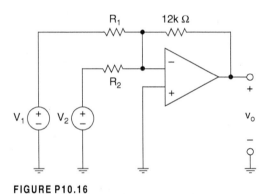

FIGURE P10.16

10.17 Can five 2k Ω resistors be employed to build an op-amp circuit that will realize the function $V_0 = -2\,V_1 - V_2$? If so, how?

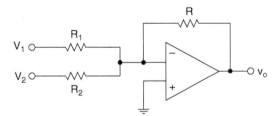

FIGURE P10.17

10.18 Given ten 1k Ω resistors, can a summing op-amp circuit be configured that will generate the function $V_0 = -[4\,V_1 + 2\,V_2]$? If so, how?

10.19 Select values for R_1 and R_2 that will realize the function $V_0 = -[4\,V_1 + 10\,V_2]$ in the circuit in Figure P10.19.

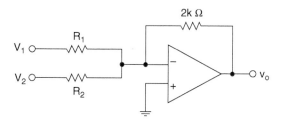

FIGURE P10.19

10.20 Determine the value of V_0 in the circuit in Figure P10.20.

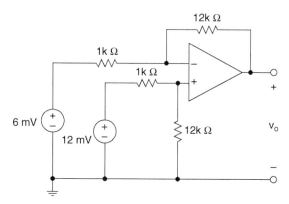

FIGURE P10.20

10.21 Find V_0 in the circuit in Figure P10.21.

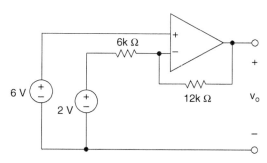

FIGURE P10.21

10.22 A circuit with an ideal op amp is shown in Figure P10.22a; let $C = 180\,\mu F$ and $R = 5k\,\Omega$. (a) Plot the input waveform, v_i, versus time, for the output, v_0, shown in Figure P10.22b.

(b) If the input is connected to a constant voltage, V_1, show that the output is the solution of the following equation:

$$C\frac{dv_o(t)}{dt} + \frac{V_1}{R} = 0$$

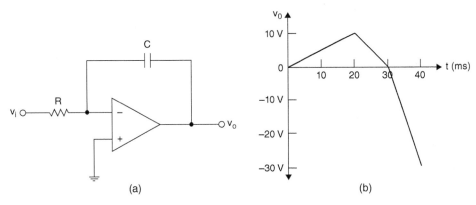

(a)   (b)

FIGURE P10.22

10.23 Using a summing amplifier, construct a circuit that will provide an output voltage that is the sum of three input signals, $v_1(t)$, $v_2(t)$, and $v_3(t)$, inverted (with a negative sign). Following the topology of the circuit in Figure 10.16, let $R_2 = 10k\ \Omega$, and find the appropriate values for R_{1A}, R_{1B}, and R_{1C}.

10.24 Given the circuit in Figure P10.24, carefully plot the input and output voltage if the input voltage is defined as follows (time is in seconds and the output is 0 at t = 0).

From t = 0 to t = 1, the input is at +1 V.
From t = 1 to t = 3, the input is at −0.5 V.
From t = 3 to t = 5, the input is at +0.5 V.

Assume $R_1 = 4k\ \Omega$, $C = 20\ \mu F$, and an ideal op amp.

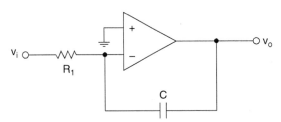

FIGURE P10.24

10.25 The input voltage for the network in Figure P10.25a is shown in Figure P10.25b. Calculate the output voltage waveform.

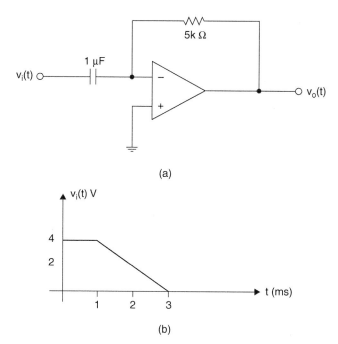

(a)

(b)

FIGURE P10.25

10.26   Given the input voltage for the network in Figure 10.26a, calculate the output voltage waveform.

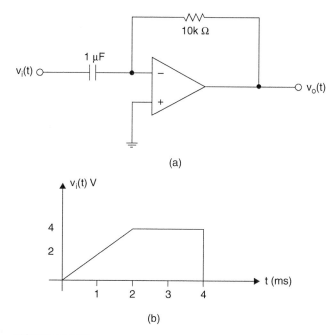

(a)

(b)

FIGURE P10.26

10.27 Given the network in Figure P10.27a and the input voltage shown in Figure P10.27b, determine the waveform of the output voltage if $v_i(t) = 0$ at $t = 0$.

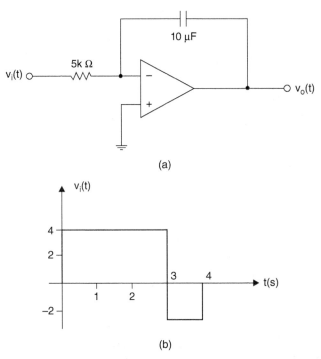

(a)

(b)

FIGURE P10.27

10.28 Given the network in Figure P10.28a and the input voltage shown in Figure P10.28b, determine the waveform of the output voltage if $v_i(t) = 0$ at $t = 0$.

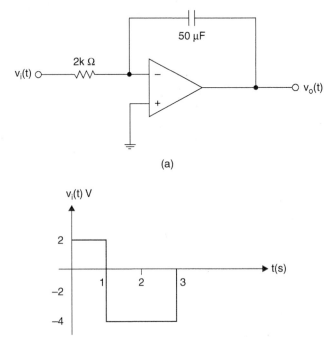

(a)

(b)

FIGURE P10.28

10.29   Determine the low-frequency closed-loop gain and the cutoff frequency for the filter in Figure P10.29.

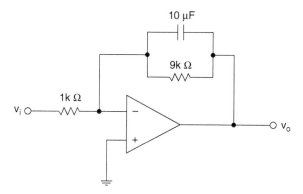

FIGURE P10.29

10.30   Given the circuit in Figure P10.30, sketch the magnitude of the closed-loop gain and label all critical values.

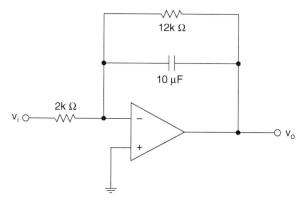

FIGURE P10.30

10.31   Determine the maximum closed-loop gain and the bandwidth of the circuit in Problem 10.30.

10.32   Given the circuit in Figure P10.32, sketch the magnitude of the closed-loop gain and label all critical values.

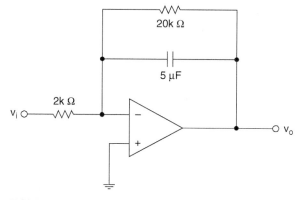

FIGURE P10.32

10.33 Determine the maximum closed-loop gain and the bandwidth of the circuit in Problem 10.32.

10.34 Determine the high-frequency gain and the cutoff frequency for the filter in Figure P10.34.

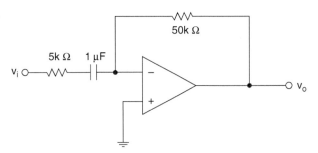

FIGURE P10.34

10.35 Given the circuit in Figure P10.35, sketch the magnitude of the closed-loop gain and label all critical values.

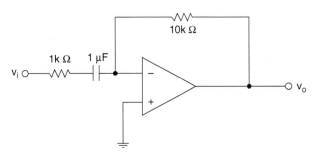

FIGURE P10.35

10.36 Given the circuit in Figure P10.36, sketch the magnitude of the closed-loop gain and label all critical values.

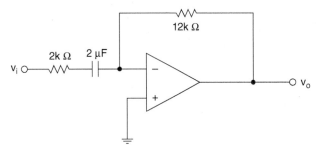

FIGURE P10.36

10.37 Determine the cutoff frequencies and sketch the magnitude of the closed-loop gain for the network in Figure P10.37.

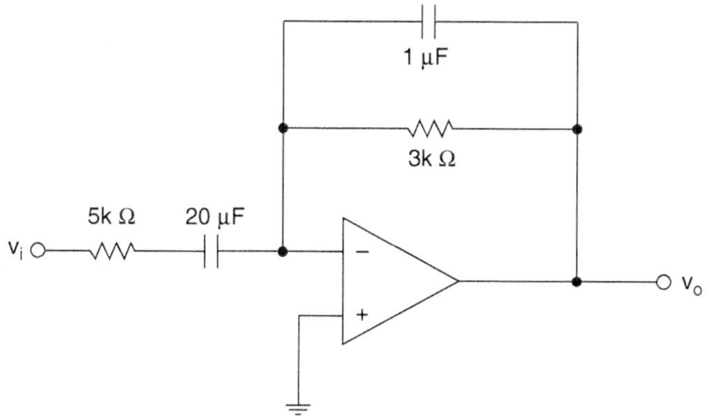

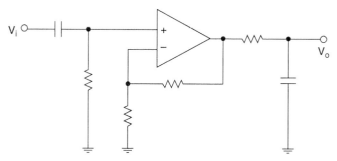

FIGURE P10.37

10.38 Determine the bandwidth of the network in Problem 10.37.

10.39 Determine the cutoff frequencies and sketch the magnitude of the closed-loop gain for the network in Figure P10.39.

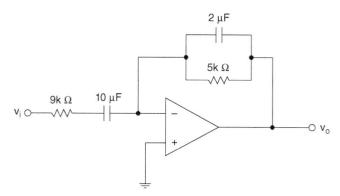

FIGURE P10.39

10.40 Determine the bandwidth of the network in Problem 10.39.

10.41 Identify the type of filter shown in Figure P10.41 and explain your answer.

FIGURE P10.41

10.42 Determine the equation for the output voltage of the network in Figure P10.42.

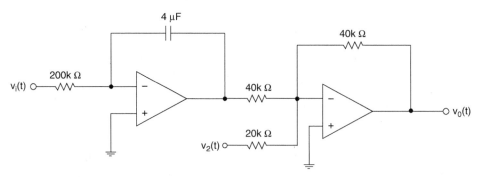

FIGURE P10.42

10.43 The circuit of Figure P10.43 is an electronic radiation detector. The photodiode has a sensitivity of $10\ \mu A/mW$ of incident radiation. If the voltmeter reads 8 V, determine the power being deposited by the radiation.

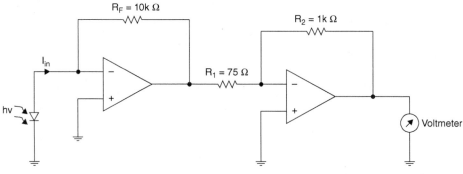

FIGURE P10.43

Analog Electronics

CHAPTER 11

LEARNING OBJECTIVES

- To recognize the impact on society of transistors and integrated circuits

- To gain an understanding of the basics of analog signals and circuits

- To Develop an Understanding of how MOS transistors operate

- To Learn to analyze MOS analog circuits

- To understand large-signal analysis with load lines, integrated with small signal analysis.

- To understand how the junction bipolar (BJT) transistor operates

- To gain understanding of biasing and operation of BJT circuits

- To be able to perform load line analysis and small signal analysis of BJT circuits

- To understand the basic operation of transistor amplifiers and their characteristics

---

INTRODUCTION

Electronic circuits or systems are classified into two major types, depending on the signal type they process:

1. Analog circuits

2. Digital circuits

Some, perhaps many, complex chips or circuits have elements of each, but they are fundamentally different, and we discuss analog electronics in this chapter and digital functions in Chapter 12.

A voltage or current that, in some manner, is varied over time in order to encode and transmit information is called a *signal*. Typically, signals are termed either *analog* if they vary continuously with time or *digital* if they switch between discrete levels. In a digital signal, there are typically two such levels, a "high" level and a "low" level, which are arbitrarily termed a "1" and a "0," respectively. The information conveyed by the single presentation of a high or low is called a *bit*. In the analog signal in Figure 11.1a, the amplitude of the signal represents the information at every point in time. For the digital signal in Figure 11.1b, the information is conveyed by the presence or absence of a pulse.

Since digital systems operate using 1s and 0s, the data in these signals is encoded in the *binary number system*. Therefore, prior to a detailed study of digital systems, a review of the binary system and basic logic will be presented in Chapter 12.

TRANSISTORS

The heart of both types of systems is transistors. Therefore, discussion of transistors is of critical importance.

A transistor is typically a three-terminal semiconductor device that is used to amplify signals or operate as a high-speed electronic switch. Transistors are a fundamental component in modern electronic systems, and their impact on our daily lives is absolutely staggering. They affect our lives in a meaningful way from the time we get out of bed until we return, and even while we are asleep. In homes, they are used in such things as clocks, radios, TVs, computers, phones

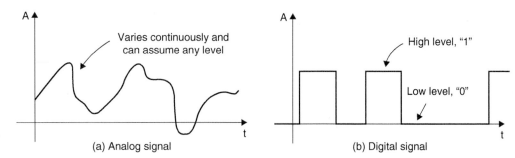

FIGURE 11.1 (a) Analog signal (b) Digital signal

(a) Analog signal

(b) Digital signal

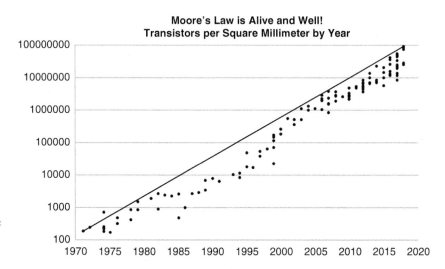

FIGURE 11.2 Transistors per square millimeter by year, 1971–2018. Logarithmic scale. Data from Wikipedia; chart by Eric Martin (From PREDICT)

and appliances such as ovens, refrigerators/freezers, air conditioners, and home security systems. Because of their usefulness in myriad applications, they must be one of the most important inventions in modern times.

Transistors are normally interconnected in large quantities with resistors, capacitors, and diodes to form an integrated circuit (IC). ICs continue to become more complex and more densely populated. For example, the feature size of a transistor is down to approximately 14 nm at the time of this writing. As we can easily glean from the graph in Figure 11.2, the density of transistors continues to increase exponentially with time, and the graph in Figure 11.2 depicts this statement of Moore's law. Gordon Moore, a co-founder of Intel Corporation, stated in the mid-1960s that the number of transistors per unit area on ICs would approximately double every year. The actual data indicates that this doubling phenomenon has actually been about 18 months, but we must marvel at the prescience of this modern electronics pioneer. Given the length of time spanned by the graph, we cannot help being impressed by the fact that in 2021 chips of an unfathomable 3 billion transistors are being produced! ... and this density increase has continued since at approximately the same rate.

An individual transistor and an IC packaged in a 40-pin dual inline pack (DIP) are shown in Figure 11.3.

The various sizes of the transistor packages (housings) shown in Figure 11.3a in general relate to their requirement for dissipation of heat. The larger package at the top is a typical "power transistor," used for high current and/or voltage devices, and the smaller ones for lower currents.

There are two primary types of transistors, which operate by very different physical mechanisms:

1. Field-effect transistors (FETs)

2. Bipolar junction transistors (BJTs)

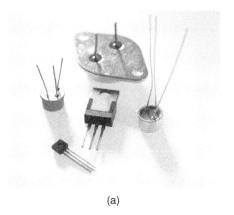

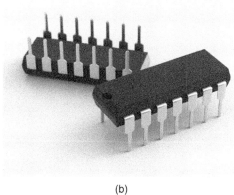

(a)

(b)

FIGURE 11.3 (a) Single transistor in a variety of packages (TEK IMAGE/Getty Images) (b) IC AT89C51-24PC 8-bit MCU CISC 40-pin DIP (Atmel Microchip) (Paket/Getty Images)

In all cases, the goal of a transistor is to control a current through the device (from essentially zero to some maximum value) by the application of a control signal. The three terminals referred to earlier generally consist of one terminal for the current "in"; a second for the current "out"; and the important third terminal for the application of a signal to control the flow of current from "in" to "out." As you will see, an FET controls the current through it by the input *voltage*; a BJT controls the current through it by input *current*.

In today's electronics, the FET dominates, and the MOSFET is the most common version, which stands for "metal–oxide–semiconductor," reflecting the original structure of these types of devices. In modern devices, some materials have changed, but the name stuck. Because of its extreme importance in modern analog circuits and particularly digital ICs, we first examine the MOSFET.

In general, these devices are used to either amplify a signal when used in analog circuits or when used in digital circuits they act as an electronically controlled switch.

The most commonly employed field effect transistor (FET) is the metal–oxide–semiconductor, or MOSFET. These devices can also be subdivided into either n-channel or p-channel, and each of these subcategories can be further divided into enhancement mode or depletion mode. Because of its most common use, *we will concentrate our discussion on the n-channel enhancement mode device.* We examine a MOSFET device in more detail as a switching device when we address digital electronics in the next chapter.

A MOSFET is a three-terminal device consisting of a source (S), a gate (G), and a drain (D). There is also a body (B) terminal connected to the substrate that is often connected to the source terminal or the most negative voltage in the circuit to maintain electrical isolation between transistors (i.e. the source–body and drain–body junctions are maintained at reverse bias to electrically isolate this transistor from other devices on the same chip). The structure of the device is shown in Figure 11.4 in cross section. The body, i.e. the substrate, is composed of p-type material, while the source and drain are made of n-type material. A thin layer of silicon dioxide, an insulator, covers the gap between the source and drain, and the gate is an electrically conducting layer placed over the insulating oxide spanning the gap between the source and drain.

Figure 11.5a shows a three-dimensional drawing of a planar, n-channel enhancement mode MOSFET shown in a cross-sectional view in Figure 11.4. The type (n-channel or p-channel) is always the opposite of the type of the bulk or body as will be explained later (bulk and body are used interchangeably). Note that the distance between the source and the drain is labeled L and is often termed the gate length; this is a critical dimension in a MOSFET. Note the thin layer called "oxide" is typically silicon dioxide or other insulating layer, and is the gate dielectric; finally,

> **METAL–OXIDE–SEMICONDUCTOR FIELD-EFFECT TRANSISTOR (MOSFET)**

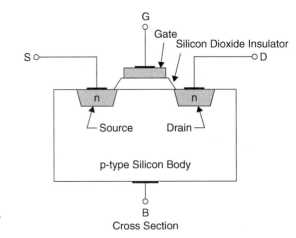

FIGURE 11.4 Cross-sectional view of planar, n-channel enhancement mode MOSFET

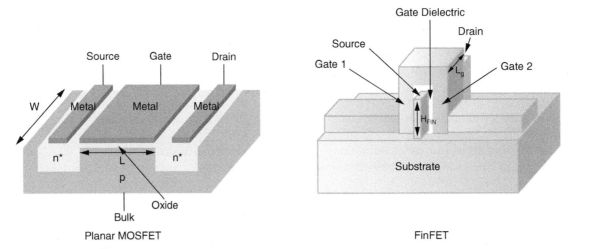

FIGURE 11.5 (a) Three-dimensional representations of a planar MOSFET and (b) FinFET – a modern MOSFET type structure with greatly reduced area on a chip (Source: MKS Instruments Website)

the gate is a conductive layer over the gate dielectric. Currently, the gate is often not metal, but polysilicon (poly) doped so that it will conduct. The region directly under the gate oxide in the body is where a "channel" will be electronically formed when voltages are applied.

Figure 11.5b is presented here simply to indicate that much of the continued increase in transistor density on a chip in recent years is the result of creative new structures, in addition to reduction of lateral dimensions of devices on a chip. The planar device (Figure 11.5a) is still in use; however, in order to produce MOSFET devices that consume less surface area on the chip, the vertical dimension is used. An example, first introduced in the early 2000s, is the FinFET, which is a MOSFET that has the semiconductor from the source to drain turned on its side, as a vertical slab, and the gate is wrapped around the gate dielectric and the semiconductor slab.

The schematic symbol for the n-channel enhancement mode MOSFET is generally represented by the symbol in Figure 11.6a, b, or c.

p-Channel devices have the same symbols with the direction of the arrows in the symbol reversed.

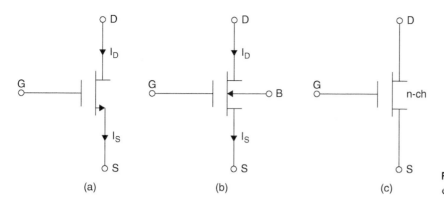

FIGURE 11.6   Symbols for n-channel enhancement mode MOSFETs

MOSFET DEVICE OPERATION

In Figure 11.7a, the $V_{GS} = 0$ (the terminals are shorted). In this situation, electrons at the source cannot cross the gap to the drain, even if V_{DS} increases. The drain current, I_D, remains zero, and the device is in *cutoff* mode. The circuit path from the source to drain appears as "back-to-back" diodes, a circuit combination that will not pass the current in either direction.

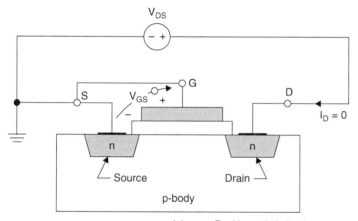

(a)   For $V_{GS} = 0$, I_D is always zero, regardless of V_{DS}.

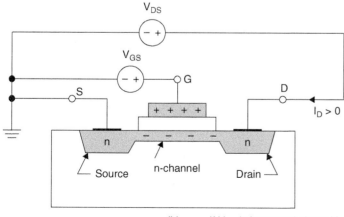

(b)   If V_{GS} is increased above V_T, I_D flows, assuming V_{DS} is not zero.

FIGURE 11.7   The operation of an n-channel enhancement mode MOSFET

Figure 11.7b shows the effect of increasing V_{GS} above a critical value known as the *threshold voltage*, V_T. If the gate is made sufficiently positive, then enough electrons are attracted to the silicon surface under the gate oxide to temporarily invert the surface body from p-type to n-type. This inversion layer, or n-*channel*, between the source and drain allows electrons to flow through a single n-type region from the source to drain and thus current flows. The current $I_D > 0$, and the device is conducting either in the *linear* or *saturation* mode, terms that are defined in the following sections "Output Characteristic Curves" and "Operational Modes."

The larger V_{GS} is made above V_T, the higher the drain current I_D. Note there is never any current into the gate since it is connected to a terminal over an insulator.

The same circuit shown in Figure 11.7b is replicated in Figure 11.8 using standard circuit symbols. This circuit can be used to generate a set of output characteristic curves for the device under test.

THE OUTPUT CHARACTERISTIC CURVES

The output characteristic curves can be generated via the circuit shown in Figure 11.8. The family of curves is generated by fixing a value for V_{GS}, sweeping V_{DS} throughout its range of values while recording the value of I_D. The process is repeated for all relevant values of V_{GS}, resulting in an entire family of output curves.

An example of a set of characteristic curves for an n-channel enhancement mode MOSFET is shown in Figure 11.9. These curves are a plot of the drain current, I_D, as a function of the drain-to-source voltage, V_{DS}, as the gate-to-source voltage, V_{GS}, is varied. It is important to note that the smallest value of V_{GS} is V_T since no drain current flows when V_{GS} is below this threshold voltage.

OPERATIONAL MODES

The output characteristic curves for the device identify three modes of operation as shown in Figure 11.9. In the ohmic mode, the curves are essentially upward sloping lines through the origin reminiscent of a resistor characteristic. In the saturation mode, the drain current, I_D, remains essentially constant as the drain-to-source voltage, V_{DS}, increases. Interestingly, in this region of operation, it is the gate voltage that controls the drain current. Finally, the cutoff mode is defined by the area below the $V_{GS} = V_T$ curve, where the drain current is zero. V_T is the threshold voltage and for any $V_{GS} < V_T, I_D = 0$

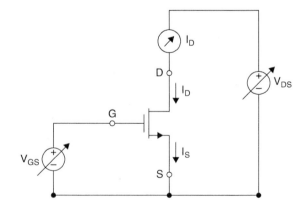

FIGURE 11.8 Circuit for generating output characteristic curves for n-channel enhancement mode MOSFET

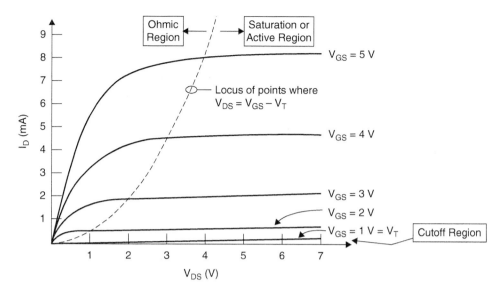

FIGURE 11.9 Example of a set of output characteristic curves for a specific n-channel enhancement mode MOSFET

Therefore in review:

In the *ohmic* region

$$V_{DS} < V_{GS} - V_T$$

In the *saturation* or *active* region

$$V_{DS} > V_{GS} - V_T$$

In the *cutoff* region

$$V_{GS} < V_T$$

Thus, the boundary line that separates the ohmic and saturation regions is defined by the following equation:

$$V_{DS} = V_{GS} - V_T$$

Figure 11.9 shows the output curves of a *particular* transistor, in this case with $V_T = 1$ V and an active or saturation region that is almost flat. MOSFET characteristics can vary greatly, and modern devices have V_T well under 1 V. A *general* set of MOSFET output curves is shown in Figure 11.10.

MOSFET BIASING TECHNIQUES

A typical biasing circuit for an n-channel enhancement mode MOSFET is shown in Figure 11.11a.

The transistor output characteristic curves of Figure 11.10 are reproduced in Figure 11.11b, with the load line for the circuit added.

The load line is defined by two points, i.e. the intercepts on the vertical and horizontal axes. The vertical axis intercept is the point at which $V_{DS} = 0$ calculated by assuming a short circuit exists between the drain and source terminals. The value of I_D under this condition is $I_D = V_{DD}/R_D$. The horizontal intercept occurs where I_D is zero and the drain-to-source junction is open circuited. This value is $V_{DS} = V_{DD}$. The load line is drawn on the graph in Figure 11.11b.

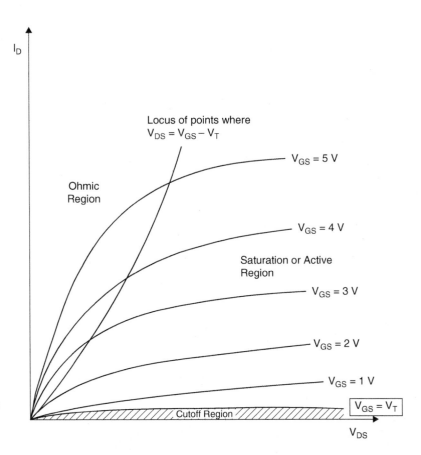

FIGURE 11.10 General MOSFET output characteristic curves and three modes (or regions) of operation: ohmic, saturation or active, and cutoff regions

The Q-point (unperturbed bias point) along the load line is set by the gate voltage V_{GS} and is typically positioned to be in the middle of the curves. This value of V_{GS} is selected by the voltage divider circuit consisting of V_{DD} and R_1 and R_2, i.e.

$$V_{GS} = V_{DD} \left(\frac{R_2}{R_1 + R_2} \right)$$

where we have used the fact that there is no dc current into the gate. Note that a gate current of zero also implies that $I_D = I_S$. The Q-point is the intersection of the load line and the appropriate V_{GS} curve.

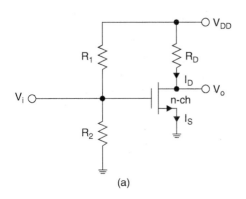

FIGURE 11.11 (a) Bias circuit for MOSFET (b) Output characteristic curves for an n-channel enhancement mode MOSFET

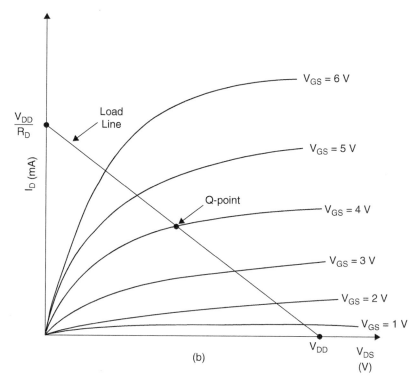

(b)

FIGURE 11.11   (*Continued*)

Let us determine the Q-point for the circuit shown in Figure 11.11a, if $R_D = 2.4k\ \Omega$, $R_1 = 12k\ \Omega$, and $R_2 = 6k\ \Omega$, assuming the transistor has the output curves of Figure 11.12, and $V_{DD} = 12$ V.

Example 11.1

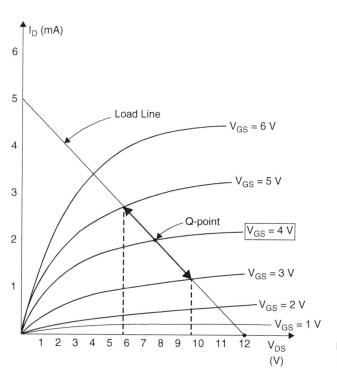

FIGURE 11.12   Output characteristic curves for Example 11.1

The load line is superimposed on the transistor curves in Figure 11.12. It is determined by the intercepts on the horizontal and vertical axes. If $I_D = 0$, then $V_{DS} = V_{DD} = 12$ V (the intercept on the horizontal axis); and if $V_{DS} = 0$, $I_D = V_{DD}/R_D = 12$ V$/2.4$k $\Omega = 5.0$ mA (the intercept on the vertical axis). A line between these points is the dc load line and is also drawn in Figure 11.12.

The gate voltage, V_{GS}, is determined by the voltage divider circuit consisting of V_{DD}, R_1, and R_2. In this case,

$$V_{GS} = 12 \left(\frac{6 \text{k} \, \Omega}{6 \text{k} \, \Omega + 12 \text{k} \, \Omega} \right) = 4 \text{ V}$$

The Q-point is then located along the load line at the intersection with the $V_{GS} = 4$ V curve. As the graph indicates, the Q-point is at $V_{GS} = 4$ V, $I_D = 2$ mA, and $V_{DS} = 7.2$ V.

One can easily see how this circuit can function as an amplifier; as the $v_i = V_{GS}$ swings up 1 V (to 5 V) and down 1 V (to 3 V), the output voltage, V_{DS}, swings from 5.5 to 9.25 V, or a difference of 3.75 V. Therefore, the input is replicated at the output but increased by a factor of:

$$\text{The magnitude of the voltage gain} = \frac{v_o}{v_i} = \frac{3.75}{2} = 1.9$$

Also note that the output signal is inverted from that of the input. As the input swings to a more positive voltage, the output swings negatively. Therefore, this circuit not only amplifies the signal, it also inverts the signal. So this circuit is often termed an "inverter," and this inversion is signified by the sign of the gain. The voltage gain is properly stated as $A_v = \frac{v_o}{v_i} = -1.9$.

Example 11.2

The network shown in Figure 11.13a is an enhancement mode n-channel device biased similarly to Example 11.1, but with a source resistor, R_S, added. The output characteristic curves for the transistor used in this circuit are provided in Figure 11.13b. There is a design requirement that the Q-point be placed near the middle of the load line; therefore we choose to place the Q-point to fall on the $V_{GS} = 2$ V curve.

The approximate middle of the $V_{GS} = 2$ V curve is $I_D = 2$ mA. The gate voltage is then determined by the voltage divider consisting of V_{DD}, R_1, and R_2:

$$V_G = 9 \left(\frac{3 \text{k} \, \Omega}{6 \text{k} \, \Omega + 3 \text{k} \, \Omega} \right) = 3 \text{ V}$$

The voltage across R_S is

$$V_S = V_G - V_{GS} = 3 - 2 = 1 \text{ V}$$

Then R_S is

$$R_S = \frac{V_S}{I_D} = \frac{1 \text{ V}}{2 \text{ mA}} = 500 \, \Omega$$

(b) Since $R_D + R_S = 2$k Ω, the load line intercept on the vertical axis is

$$I_D = \frac{9}{2 \text{k} \, \Omega} = 4.5 \text{ mA}$$

The results are shown in Figure 11.14 and the Q-point is $V_{DS} = 5$ V, $I_D = 2$ mA, and $V_{GS} = 2$ V.

The load line thus created is often termed the dc load line and is used in determining the Q-point. In this example, the dc load line has a slope of $(1/2000)$.

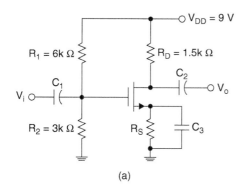

(a)

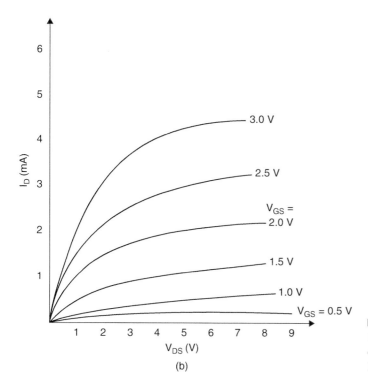

(b)

FIGURE 11.13 (a) Circuit for Example 11.2 (b) Output characteristic curves for MOSFET in Example 11.2

The capacitors in circuits of this type are used to block dc voltages and are of a value that their reactance is low and can be considered by ac signals as shorts. Therefore, R_S and R_D will figure into the dc biasing of the MOSFET, but capacitor C_3 will effectively short R_S for any ac signal applied at V_i. Similarly, the input capacitor C_1 allows the dc voltage level at the input to be at any constant voltage, but the input signal (variations in V_i) passes through C_1 to the gate.

With C_3 effectively shorting R_S for ac signals, we can introduce the concept of an *ac load line*. As shown in Figure 11.14, the ac load line is only determined by R_D; the ac load line is the track that current–voltage variations follow with an ac input, which, in this circuit, are ac variations in V_{GS} about the Q-point. The ac load line is centered on the Q-point, but has a slope given by the following equation:

$$\text{ac load line slope} = \frac{1}{R_D}$$

since R_S is effectively shorted (zero volts across it) to ac signals.

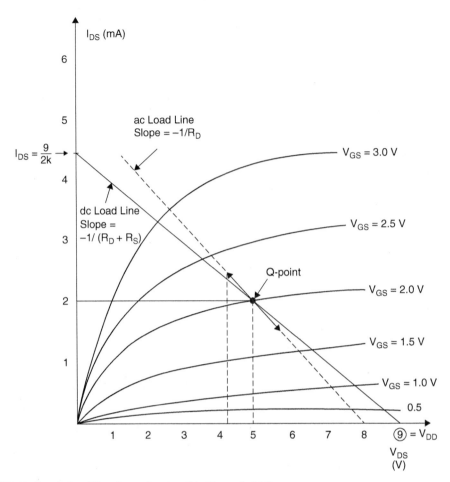

FIGURE 11.14 dc Load line drawn for circuit in Example 11.2

As illustrated in Figure 11.14, input signal variations (with R_s shorted to ac signals) are variations in V_{GS}. The output is the resulting variations in V_{DS}. Following the ac load line, if V_{GS} swings from 1.75 to 2.25 V (a difference of 0.5 V), the output, V_{DS}, swings from 4.3 to 5.6 V (a difference of 1.3 V).

Therefore, the ac voltage gain $A_v = \dfrac{v_o}{v_i} = \dfrac{-1.3}{0.5} = -2.6$.

This approach is sometimes useful for large ac signal inputs.

In general, the response of the circuit to ac signals is determined by small-signal analysis in which a circuit model of the transistor and its surrounding circuitry is created, as will be explained in the next section.

SMALL-SIGNAL ANALYSIS OF MOSFET CIRCUITS

In this section, we develop small-signal models that permit us to examine the response of the n-channel enhancement mode common source MOSFET amplifier (and other circuits) to small-signal variations around the Q-point. Once again, we assume that the amplifier is operating in the mid-band frequency range and the signal variations about the Q-point are small. The blocking capacitors and bypass capacitors, which are open circuits to dc, are considered to be ac short circuits, as well as are independent dc voltage sources. In addition, the input impedance of the MOSFET is essentially infinite. Under these conditions, the models are simple and typically composed of only dependent sources and resistors.

As we pursue an appropriate model for the n-channel enhancement mode common source MOSFET, recall several key points from our previous discussion. The input is voltage from the gate to source and the output is current from the drain to source (electrons from source to drain), and the characteristic curves indicate that the drain current, I_D, is changed little by changes in the drain-to-source voltage, V_{DS}, and is primarily controlled by the gate to source voltage, V_{GS}.

The small-signal model for the common source device reflects these facts, as shown in Figure 11.15a, where the parameter, g_m, is the transconductance of the device and g_o is the output conductance. These two parameters are estimated with the help of the output characteristic curves shown in Figure 11.15b. g_m is equal to the change in I_D divided by the change in V_{GS} at the Q-point, i.e. with V_{DS} constant. Thus,

$$g_m = \frac{\Delta I_{D1}}{\Delta V_{GS}} \text{ with } V_{DS} \text{ constant}$$

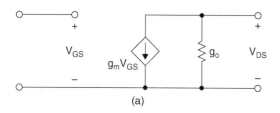

(a)

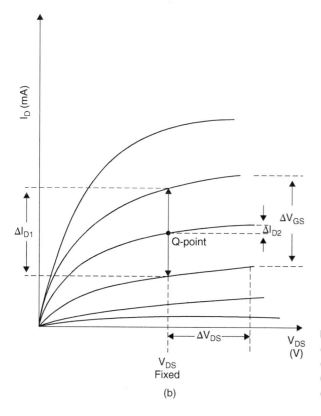

(b)

FIGURE 11.15 (a) Small-signal equivalent circuit for an n-channel enhancement mode MOSFET (b) Output characteristic curves used to determine g_m and g_o

and

$$g_o = \frac{\Delta\, I_{D2}}{\Delta\, V_{GS}} \text{ at the Q-point}$$

Although the output characteristic curves in the active region are almost horizontal, they do have a slight positive slope. While the current I_D is primarily dependent on V_{GS}, there are small changes in I_D caused by changes in V_{DS}. This phenomenon (often called output resistance or conductance) is modeled by the presence of g_o in the model.

Example 11.3

Given a MOSFET operating at the Q-point on the output characteristic curves shown in Figure 11.16, let us determine the small-signal parameters g_m and g_o.

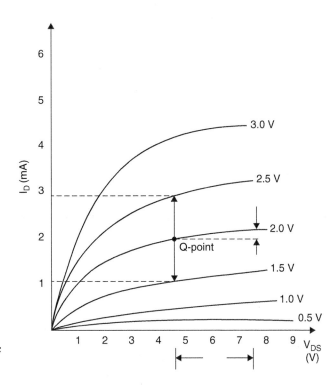

FIGURE 11.16 Output characteristic curves used in Example 11.3

The value of g_m estimated from the curves at the Q-point is

$$g_m = \frac{(2.95 - 1.05)(10^{-3})}{(2.5 - 1.5)} = 1.9 \text{ mS}$$

and

$$g_o = \frac{(2.2 - 2.0)(10^{-3})}{(7.66 - 4.66)} = 67 \text{ }\mu\text{S}$$

The small-signal gain for the common source n-channel MOSFET amplifier, shown in Figure 11.17a, can be determined using the model shown in Figure 11.17b. All independent dc

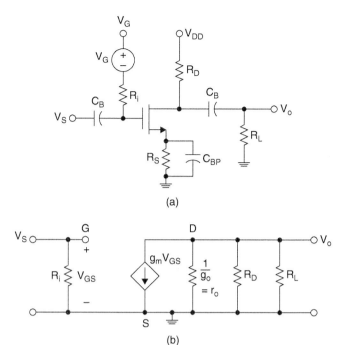

(a)

(b)

FIGURE 11.17   Common source amplifier and small-signal model

sources are considered ac short circuits. In addition, the amplifier is assumed to be operating in the mid-band frequency range, where the blocking and bypass capacitors are also ac short circuits. Thus, employing the small-signal representation for the device yields the small-signal equivalent circuit shown in Figure 11.17b. The *equivalent total load is the parallel combination of r_o, R_D, and R_1*, called R_{Ltotal} where we have used the fact that $r_o = 1/g_o$. The voltage gain of the amplifier is then

$$A_v = \frac{v_o}{v_s} = \frac{-g_m V_{GS} R_{Ltotal}}{V_{GS}} \qquad \text{where } R_{Ltotal} = r_o||R_D||R_L$$

Since $r_o = \dfrac{1}{g_o}$ is very high, $R_{Total} = R_D||R_L$.

$$A_v = -g_m R_{Ltotal}$$

In the circuit of Figure 11.17a, the input resistance is simply R_i. In addition to the amplifier voltage gain, there are two additional parameters that are often of interest, e.g. when cascading stages of amplification. The two parameters are the input and output resistance of the amplifier. With reference to the amplifier in Figure 11.18, the input resistance is the total resistance seen looking into the amplifier's input terminals, i.e. R_1 in parallel with R_2 as shown. The output resistance is the total resistance seen looking back into the amplifier's output terminals, i.e. r_o in parallel with R_D as shown in Figure 11.18a. In addition, the voltage divider composed of R_I and R_2 eliminates the need for a separate voltage source, V_G.

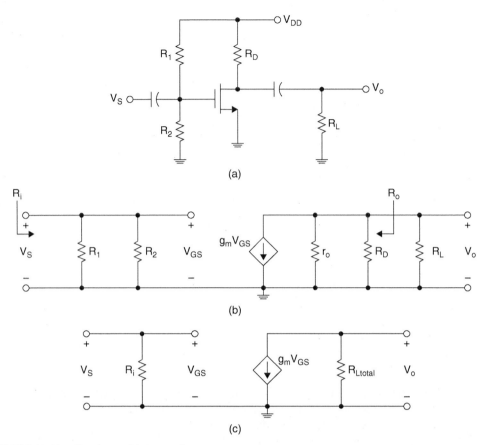

FIGURE 11.18 Circuits used in Example 11.4

Example 11.4

A common source amplifier with an n-channel enhancement mode MOSFET is shown in Figure 11.18a. It is assumed that the amplifier is operating in the mid-band frequency range, and the device parameters are $g_m = 2$ mS and $g_o = 50$ μS. The remaining circuit parameters are $R_1 = 12$k Ω, $R_D = 2$k Ω, $R_D = 1.6$k Ω, and $R_L = 10$k Ω. We wish to determine (a) the small-signal equivalent circuit, (b) the small-signal voltage gain, and (c) the input and output resistances of the amplifier.

(a) The small-signal equivalent circuit is shown in Figure 11.18b, where we have used the fact that the dc source acts as an ac short to ground and the capacitors are ac short circuits.

(b) Combining the resistors that are in parallel at both the input and output yields the equivalent circuit shown in Figure 11.18c, where R_i is equal to R_1 in parallel with R_2 and R_{Ltotal} is the parallel combination of r_o, R_D, and R_L. The network parameters yield the following values:

$$R_i = 1.71\text{k }\Omega$$
$$R_{Ltotal} = 1.29\text{k }\Omega$$

and therefore

$$A_v = -g_m R_{Ltotal}$$
$$= -(2)(10^{-3})(1.29)(10^3)$$
$$= -2.58$$

(c) The input resistance is $R_i = 1.71$k Ω as indicated above, and the output resistance, R_o, is

$$R_o = r_o || R_D = 1.48\text{k }\Omega$$

A common source amplifier with an n-channel enhancement mode MOSFET is shown in Figure 11.19a, and the output characteristic curves for the device are shown in Figure 11.19b. It is assumed that the amplifier is operating in the mid-band frequency range. Let us determine the voltage gain of this amplifier.

Example 11.5

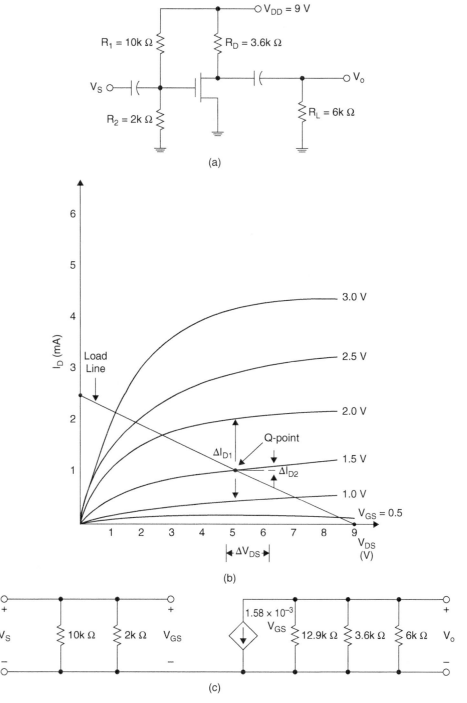

FIGURE 11.19   (a) Circuit used in Example 11.5; (b) Output characteristic curves; (c) Small-signal equivalent circuit

To determine the gain of this amplifier, we need to first determine the critical parameters that define the operation of the device. Since the drain current is primarily determined by the gate-to-source voltage, we must first determine V_{GS}.

$$V_G = 9\left(\frac{2k}{10k+2k}\right) = 1.5 \text{ V}$$

and

$$V_{GS} = V_G - V_S$$

Since the source is tied to ground, $V_S = 0$ and hence $V_{GS} = 1.5$ V. Therefore, the Q-point will lie along this curve. Although the value of I_D varies along this curve, a load line analysis confirms the Q-point is

$$I_D = 1.1 \text{ mA and } V_{DS} = 5 \text{ V.}$$

Alternatively, the value of V_{DS} is

$$V_{DS} = V_{DD} - I_D R_D - V_S$$
$$= 9 - (1.1/k)(3.6/k) - 0$$
$$= 5.04 \text{ V}$$

Thus, the Q-point is located at the point approximated by the values $I_D = 1.1$ mA, $V_{GS} = 1.5$ V, and $V_{DS} = 5.04$ V. At this point, shown in Figure 11.19b, g_m is approximately

$$g_m = \frac{(2.02 - 0.44)(10^{-3})}{(2-1)} = 1.58 \text{ mS}$$

and

$$g_o = \frac{(1.2 - 1.1)(10^{-3})}{(6.33 - 5.04)} = 77.5 \text{ } \mu\text{S}$$

and r_o is

$$r_o = 1/g_o = 12.9 \text{k}\Omega$$

Now that all the device parameters are known, the small-signal equivalent circuit is shown in Figure 11.19c. R_{Ltotal} is a parallel combination of resistors at the output, i.e.

$$R_{Ltotal} = 12.9k \,||3.6k||6k = 1.92k \text{ }\Omega$$

Therefore, the voltage gain of the circuit is

$$A_v = -(1.58)(10^{-3})(1.92)(10^3)$$
$$= -3.03$$

BIPOLAR JUNCTION TRANSISTORS

As mentioned earlier in the chapter, there are two major types of transistors. The MOSFET was just discussed. The second major type is the bipolar junction transistor (BJT). BJTs operate on an entirely different physical mechanism from that of MOSFETs. The three terminals of a BJT are the emitter, base, and collector.

The manner in which BJTs are configured in a network, i.e. common base, common collector, or common emitter, will depend upon a number of factors associated with a particular application, such as the gain required, the impedance at the input or output terminals. However, in the material that follows, we focus our discussion on what may be the most popular structure and configuration, i.e. an npn BJT connected in a common emitter configuration. In this configuration, the input signal is applied at the base, the output is taken at the collector, and the emitter is grounded.

Recall a MOSFET controls the current through the device by the input *voltage* (V_{GS}), while a BJT controls the current through the device by the input base *current* (I_B).

BJT STRUCTURE

The structure of a BJT consists of essentially two p–n junction diodes fabricated very close to each other so that they share a common region. Therefore, a BJT is a three-layer sandwich of alternating semiconductor material types. There are two possible variations, the *pnp transistor* and the *npn transistor*. Shown in Figure 11.20 is a simplified drawing of an npn transistor and its circuit symbol. In the following text, we focus on the npn transistor since it is more common. pnp circuit analysis can be done, if needed, by symmetry.

In modern silicon planar processing, bipolar transistors are generally fabricated with the emitter on top of the collector with a thin base between, as illustrated in Figure 11.21.

The primary carrier flow is downward from the emitter to collector through the base in the area labeled "active transistor region." The lateral part of the structure serves only to make electrical connections from the surface to the layers in the vertical transistor structure.

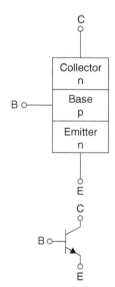

FIGURE 11.20   npn transistor structure and symbol

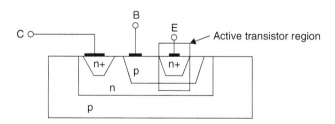

FIGURE 11.21   Cross section of a planar npn BJT

BJT DEVICE OPERATION

In this section, we first discuss how a BJT operates in the *active operational mode*, or in the active region. This is the most common mode for analog circuits such as amplifiers, signal conditioners, filters.

Since there are two p–n junctions in a BJT, and each can be forward or reverse biased, there are four bias possibilities.

To achieve the *active operational mode*:

(a) The emitter junction is forward biased.

(b) The collector junction is reverse biased.

From a previous study in Chapter 9, recall that:

(a) *Forward bias* implies that the p region is biased more than about 0.7 V more than the n region and current flows.

(b) *Reverse bias* implies that the n region is more positive than the p region, and no current flows.

Therefore, for the active mode:

The voltage across the emitter junction (from base to emitter), V_{BE} > about 0.7 V.

The voltage across the collector junction (from collector to base) V_{CB} > 0 V.

Under the conditions above, one might predict that emitter to base current would be flowing, but since the collector junction is reverse biased, no collector current, I_C, would flow; this would be wrong. Why? The reason is: The junctions are coupled. The magic of BJT operation is that the base is made very thin, and the forward-biased emitter junction injects electrons into the base. BUT, because the base is very thin and lightly doped, most of the electrons survive diffusion through the base and cross into the collector – even though the collector junction is reverse biased. There is essentially no collector current I_C resulting from the collector acting as a diode; I_C is constituted almost entirely by electrons arriving from the emitter. This is illustrated in Figure 11.22.

In Figure 11.22, the width of the arrows shows the magnitude of electron current flow. For the reasons stated above, only a small portion of the electrons constituting emitter current recombine in the base, and create through recombination the base current. Modern BJTs are very efficient and normally the percentage of electrons that survive the trip to the collector is well

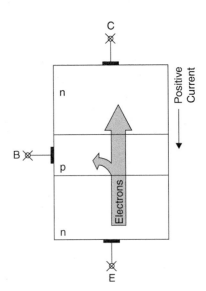

FIGURE 11.22 npn BJT electron carrier flow

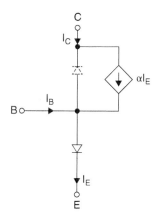

FIGURE 11.23   BJT circuit model in the active mode

over 95%. The fraction of carriers that enter the collector from the emitter is termed alpha (α), the forward current transfer ratio, and is always less than unity. BJTs typically have αs in the range of 0.97–0.99 and higher, but always less than 1.

We are now prepared to construct a circuit model of a BJT in the active mode, as shown in Figure 11.23. This model shows that between the base and emitter is a p–n junction diode. The diode between the base and collector is reverse biased and shown in the dotted outline, because it is not conducting. This diode can be ignored in the model. The important addition is a dependent current source to model the collector current with a magnitude of αI_E, representing the electron current flow surviving from the emitter.

This model gives us the equation for I_C as a function I_E.

$$I_C = \alpha\, I_E \text{ where } \alpha = \left.\frac{I_C}{I_E}\right|_{\text{active region}}$$

Since we are interested in the common emitter circuit configuration, the input would be at the base and output at the collector. Some simple algebra can lead us to another version of the common emitter circuit model.

Kirchhoff's current law gives

$$I_E = I_B + I_C$$

From the above discussion, it can inferred that the collector current (I_C) is always slightly smaller than the emitter current (I_E), and the base current (I_B) is significantly smaller than either.

Therefore,

$$I_C = \alpha(I_B + I_C)$$

and

$$I_C(1 - \alpha) = \alpha I_B$$

Hence

$$\left.\frac{I_C}{I_B}\right|_{\text{active region}} = \frac{\alpha}{1 - \alpha} = \beta$$

The parameter β is defined as the *common emitter current gain* and is a key transistor parameter for analyzing BJT circuits. From the results above, a common emitter circuit model is shown in Figure 11.24, with the value of the dependent current source at the collector as βI_B.

When operating within the *active region*, the npn BJT acts as a current amplifier; a small current into the base produces a large collector current.

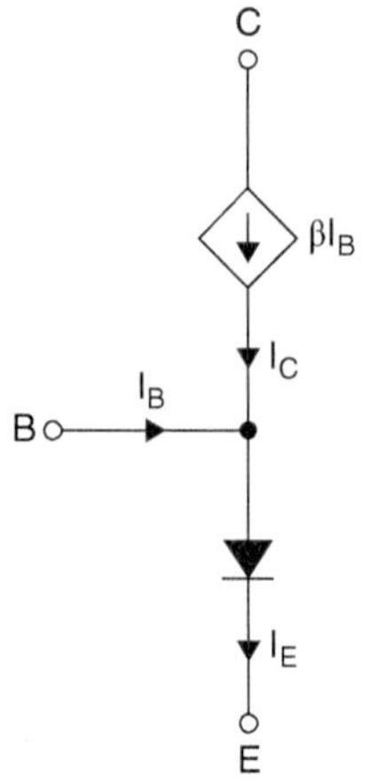

FIGURE 11.24 A BJT common emitter equivalent circuit

For example, if $\alpha = 0.99$, then a quick calculation reveals $\beta = 99$. In other words, the value of I_C is 99 times the value of the input current I_B.

Another important observation is that if the BJT remains biased in the active mode, the collector p–n junction is reverse biased, and, therefore, I_C is independent of the applied collector voltage. The current I_C only depends on the value of the input current I_B. (Real BJTs show a slight increase in I_C with increasing V_{CE} but it is small; we will analyze this later in the section on small-signal analysis.) Also, we reiterate that to initiate current flow through the device V_{BE} must be sufficient for the emitter junction to be forward biased; we are assuming this to be 0.7 V for silicon, unless stated otherwise.

This section has dealt with the BJT in the *active mode* as used in analog circuits. Looking ahead, if both junctions are forward biased, the device is in *saturation* – different meaning from that used in MOSFETs – and the BJT appears as a closed switch between the emitter and collector; and if both junctions are reverse biased, the device is in *cutoff* and appears as an open switch between the collector and emitter. This situation is useful as an electronic switch, as in digital applications, or a circuit as simple as turning an LED on or off. These two conditions, saturation and cutoff, occur at the two extremes of the load line when analyzing the active mode.

THE OUTPUT CHARACTERISTIC CURVES FOR BJTS

The data sheet for a transistor typically contains a family of curves that represent the voltage–current characteristics over a wide range of values. A typical set of output characteristic curves is shown in Figure 11.25. These curves can be generated using the circuit shown in Figure 11.26; in this network, the base current is fixed and the collector current I_C is recorded as the collector-to-emitter voltage is swept from zero to its maximum value.

The output characteristic curves display three significant regions. The *active region*, where the collector current is almost constant for a specific value of base current, occupies the majority of the graph, and it is this region where the transistor operates when biased to function as an amplifier. In the *cutoff mode*, I_C is approximately zero, i.e. the collector to emitter appears as an open circuit, or an open switch. The cutoff region is located where $I_B = 0$ and runs along the horizontal axis. A BJT biased in the *saturation mode* results in a V_{CE} very close to zero and it conducts as a closed switch. The current through the device is determined by the external circuitry and not the device itself. The method for biasing a BJT in saturation involves additional considerations and will be discussed later.

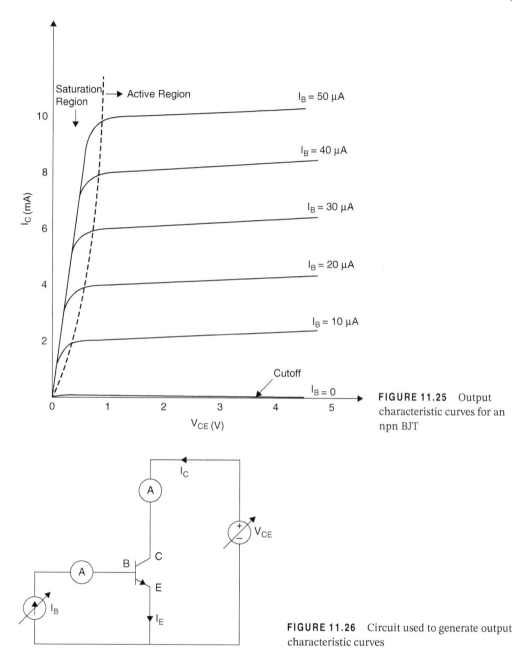

FIGURE 11.25 Output characteristic curves for an npn BJT

FIGURE 11.26 Circuit used to generate output characteristic curves

The load line can be determined via the network in Figure 11.27a and is defined by two points, i.e. the lines intercept on the horizontal and vertical axes, as shown in Figure 11.27b. The intercept on the vertical axis is the point where $V_{CE} = 0$, i.e. a short circuit exists between the collector and emitter terminals. The value of I_C is then V_C/R_C or in general the total resistance in the collector to emitter path from source to ground. The horizontal intercept is the point where $I_C = 0$, i.e. the collector to emitter junction is an open circuit. This value is typically the supply voltage as indicated. The operating point or Q-point lies along this line and is determined by the intersection of the load line with the particular I_B curve.

Example 11.6 illustrates the way the operating point (or Q-point) can be calculated.

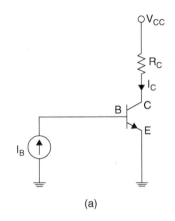

(a)

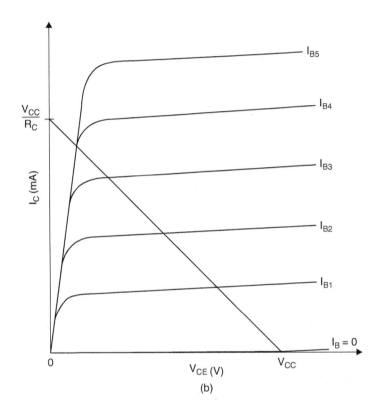

FIGURE 11.27 Common emitter circuit (a) and (b) load line calculation

(b)

Example 11.6

The output characteristic curves for a transistor are shown in Figure 11.28a. If this device is used in the circuit in Figure 11.28b, we wish to determine the Q-point for the transistor and the value of β at the Q-point.

The capacitors block dc in both directions, and, therefore, the circuit can be redrawn as shown in Figure 11.28c. Note that when $I_C = 0$, $V_{CE} = 6$ V, and when $V_{CE} = 0$, $I_C = 6/1.2\text{k }\Omega = 5$ mA. Given these results, the load line can be constructed as shown in Figure 11.28a. Using the fact that the base-to-emitter voltage $V_{BE} = 0.7$ V, KCL for the base-to-emitter circuit is

$$-6 + 265\text{k }\Omega\, I_B + 0.7 = 0$$

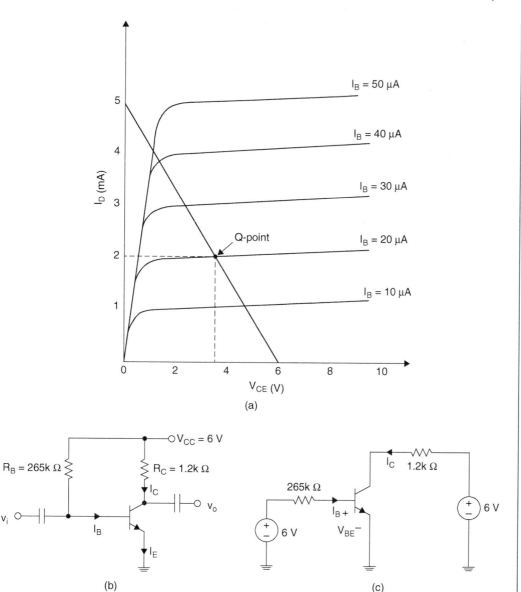

FIGURE 11.28 (a) Output characteristic curves for BJT in Example 11.6; (b) and (c) Circuits used in dc bias calculations in Example 11.6

Yielding a base current of $I_B = 20\ \mu A$. The intersection of the $I_B = 20\ \mu A$ curve and the load line defines the operating point. Note that at this point, $V_{CE} = 3.6$ V and $I_C = 2$ mA. Thus, the Q-point for the transistor in this circuit is $I_B = 20\ \mu A$, $I_C = 2$ mA, and $V_{CE} = 3.6$ V.

The value of β at the Q-point can be estimated by using a vertical line through the Q-point and measuring the change in I_C with respect to I_B:

$$\beta = \frac{(3\ mA - 1\ mA)}{(30\ \mu A - 10\ \mu A)} = 100$$

It should be noted that β may vary from one transistor to the next (of the same type) and also depends on other factors such as temperature. Therefore, the biasing circuit used in this example is not recommended in general because it forces a known I_B. Since $I_C = \beta I_B$, the Q-point is dependent on β. For example, if another transistor had a set of output curves with the horizontal lines showing half the spacing, $\beta = 50$ and I_C would be halved. A bias circuit that avoids this problem is shown in the next section.

BJT BIASING TECHNIQUES

The following dc biasing technique avoids the problems of β variations just described. This circuit establishes a known voltage across a resistor in the emitter leg of the circuit (in this case R_E), which establishes the emitter current I_E. Since I_C is approximately I_E, the Q-point becomes relatively independent of β.

The circuit employed in this approach is shown in Figure 11.29a. The circuit is redrawn in Figure 11.29b. Forming a Thevenin equivalent of the left portion of the network yields the network in Figure 11.29c, where

$$V_{OC} = V_{CC}\left(\frac{R_2}{R_1 + R_2}\right)$$

$$R_{TH} = R_1 || R_2 = \frac{R_1 R_2}{R_1 + R_2}$$

The KVL equation for the base–emitter circuit is

$$-V_{TH} + I_B R_{TH} + V_{BE} + I_E R_E = 0$$

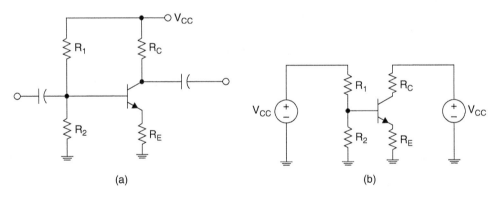

(a)

(b)

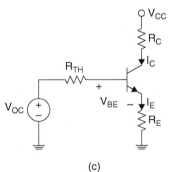

(c)

FIGURE 11.29 Circuits used in BJT bias calculations

Recall that the current gain from the base to collector is given by the expression

$$I_C = \beta I_B$$

And KVL for the device is

$$I_E = I_C + I_B$$
$$= (\beta + 1)I_B$$

Therefore,

$$-V_{OC} + I_B R_{TH} + V_{BE} + I_B(\beta + 1) R_E = 0$$

And

$$I_B = \frac{(V_{OC} - V_{BE})}{[R_{TH} + (\beta + 1) R_E]}$$

Then

$$I_C = \beta I_B$$

KVL for the collector–emitter loop is

$$-V_{CC} + R_C I_C + V_{CE} + I_E R_E = 0$$

and

$$V_{CE} = V_{CC} - R_C I_C - (\beta + 1)I_B R_E$$

The combination V_{CE}, I_B, and I_C defines the Q-point.

The cutoff and active regions of a BJT's output curves are easily identified. The active region is the important region for processing analog signals.

Saturation of a BJT requires special consideration. Saturation is achieved when both the emitter and the collector junctions are forward biased. The emitter junction is always forward biased except in cutoff. As seen in the active mode, if the emitter junction is forward biased, the base is 0.7 V more positive than the emitter; if the collector junction is forward biased, the collector must be 0.7 V more negative than the emitter. This implies that the voltage across the device is approximately zero and the device acts as a closed switch.

Note that as the base current increases, the collector current increases by a factor of β. As the collector current increases, collector voltage drops. The saturation mode can be achieved by "overdriving" the base current to the point that the collector current reduces the collector voltage to 0.7 V more negative than the base voltage. In saturation, the collector current is determined by the external circuitry, and the ratio of I_C to I_B in this case is always less than β of the device. This ratio is termed the *forced* β.

Example 11.7

For the transistor in the network shown in Figure 11.30a, $\beta = 100$; let us determine the Q-point.

The Thevenin equivalent for the input circuit is determined from the networks in Figure 11.30b, and c. The Thevenin equivalent voltage is

$$V_{OC} = 9 \left(\frac{30k\ \Omega}{30k\ \Omega + 60k\ \Omega} \right) = 3\ V$$

And the Thevenin equivalent resistance is

$$R_{TH} = \frac{(30k\ \Omega)(60k\ \Omega)}{30k\ \Omega + 60k\ \Omega} = 20k\ \Omega$$

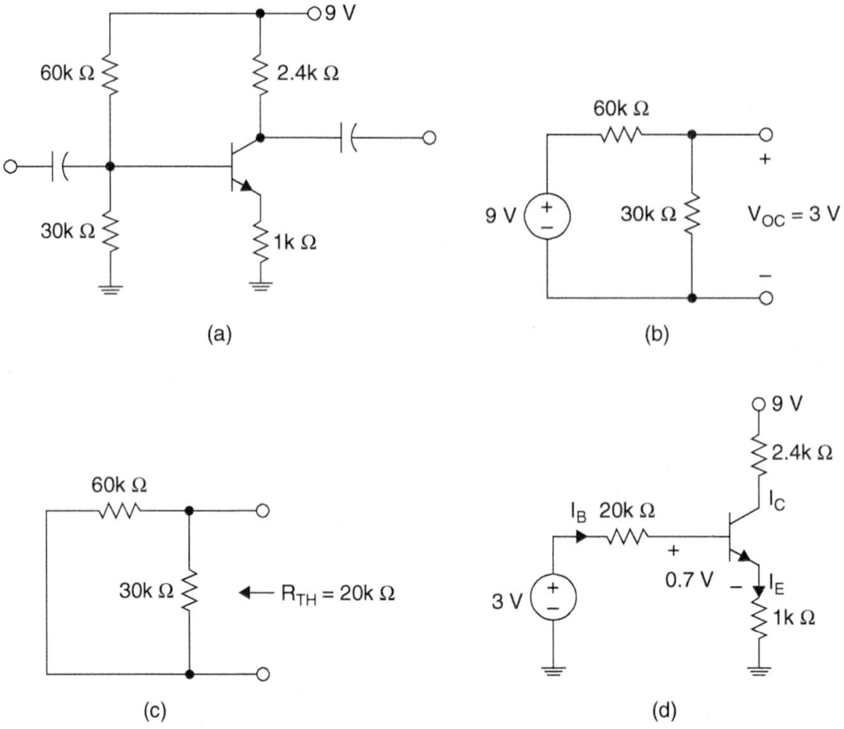

FIGURE 11.30 Circuits used in Example 11.7

The equivalent circuit for the original network is shown in Figure 11.30d. Using $V_{BE} = 0.7$ V, KVL for the base–emitter loop is

$$-3 + 20\text{k }\Omega\, I_B + 0.7 + (101)\, 1\text{k }\Omega\, I_B = 0$$

Solving the equation for I_B yields

$$I_B = 19\ \mu A$$

Then

$$I_C = \beta I_B = 1.9\text{ mA}$$
$$V_{CE} = 9 - (2.4\text{k }\Omega)(1.9 \times 10^{-3}) - (101)(19 \times 10^{-6})(1\text{k }\Omega)$$
$$= 2.52\text{ V}$$

Thus, the Q-point is defined by $V_{CE} = 2.52$ V, $I_C = 1.9$ mA, and $I_B = 19\ \mu A$.

Also, as this example indicates, I_B is much smaller than I_C and I_E, and since $I_E = I_C + I_B$, an approximation can be made by assuming that $I_E = I_C$. We will use this approach and compare the results with this more detailed analysis in the next example.

As illustrated in the previous discussion of MOSFETs, if the BJT output characteristic curves are available, one could use the load line analysis to determine the Q-point. If a bypass capacitor is placed across the 1k resistor, one could then construct an ac load line, and determine the large signal gain of the circuit from the analysis of the curves. This process exactly follows the steps utilized in Example 11.2 for a MOSFET.

Example 11.8

We wish to use the approximation ($I_E = I_C$) to solve the problem in the previous example. In this shortcut approach, the equation for the base–emitter circuit is

$$-V_{OC} = R_{TH}\left(\frac{-I_C}{\beta}\right) + 0.7 + R_E I_C = 0$$

or

$$-3 + 200\, I_C + 0.7 + 1000\, I_C = 0$$

Solving for I_C yields

$$I_C = 1.92\ \text{mA}$$

and

$$I_B = I_C/\beta = 1.92\ \mu\text{A}$$

Finally,

$$V_{CE} = 9 - (2.4k)(1.92 \times 10^{-3})(3.4 \times 10^3)$$
$$= 2.47\ \text{V}$$

A comparison of these results with those of the previous example shows that this shortcut approach is not only quick but also reasonably accurate, assuming β is reasonably high.

SMALL-SIGNAL ANALYSIS

In small-signal analysis, we will develop models that permit us to examine the response of the transistor amplifier to small-signal variations around the Q-point. Just as we employed a simple model for the MOSFET, we will treat the npn common emitter transistor configuration in a similar manner.

The normal frequency response of an amplifier is shown in Figure 11.31. The mid-band range is that portion that exists between the two half-power points. For audio, this range extends from about 50 Hz–20 kHz. Since most amplifiers are designed to operate in the mid-band frequency range, we will make that assumption here. These operating stipulations allow us to simplify the analysis. For example, given these signal characteristics, the blocking and by-pass capacitors can be considered ac short circuits, i.e. in this frequency range their impedance is

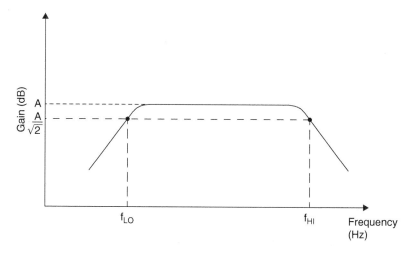

FIGURE 11.31 Amplifier frequency response

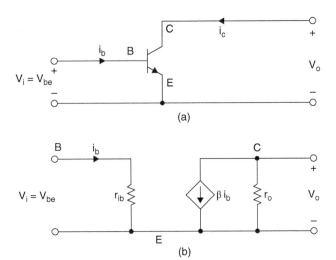

FIGURE 11.32 Common emitter BJT and its small-signal equivalent circuit

very low, stray capacitance can be considered ac open circuits since their impedance is high, and all nonlinearities will be ignored. Under these conditions, the models are simple and typically composed of only dependent sources and resistors.

The small-signal model for the npn BJT configuration is shown in Figure 11.32. The current gain is β, and the output resistance is r_o, which is typically high and often ignored. The base-to-emitter diode, shown in Figure 11.32a is represented in 11.32b as a small-signal resistance. This resistance is referred to as r_{ib}, and represents the small-signal resistance of the forward-biased base-to-emitter diode, i.e. the input resistance of the transistor at the base terminal. Although r_{ib} is a function of the diode current, the electronic charge, the temperature in degrees Kelvin, and Boltzmann's constant, the value at room temperature is normally approximated by the expression

$$r_{ib} = \frac{0.026}{I_B}$$

where I_B is, of course, the dc base current.

Our model indicates that the input is from base to emitter and the output is from collector to emitter. The output characteristic curves shown earlier indicate that the collector current, I_C, is changed little by changes in the collector-to-emitter voltage, V_{CE}, and is primarily controlled by the base current, I_B.

The small-signal model for the common emitter device reflects these facts, as shown in Figure 11.32b, where the parameter, β, is the current gain of the device and r_o is the output resistance. These two parameters can be approximated with the help of the output characteristic curves shown in Figure 11.33. β is equal to the change in I_C divided by the change in I_B at the Q-point, i.e. with V_{CE} constant. Thus,

$$\beta = \frac{\Delta I_{C1}}{\Delta I_B} \quad \text{with } V_{CE} \text{ constant}$$

and

$$g_o = \frac{\Delta I_{C2}}{\Delta V_{CE}} \quad \text{at the Q-point}$$

and

$$r_o = \frac{1}{g_o}$$

A similar model was employed for the n-channel enhancement mode MOSFET. Although I_C is primarily controlled by I_B, there are small changes in I_C caused by changes in V_{CE} and the parameter r_o is present in the model to represent this phenomenon.

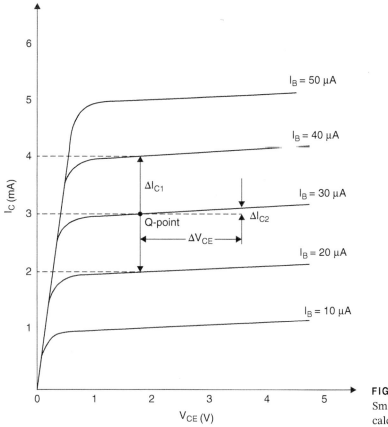

FIGURE 11.33
Small-signal parameter
calculations

Assuming that the output characteristic curves for a common emitter device are shown in Figure 11.33, and that the device is operating at the Q-point indicated, we wish to determine the approximate values for β and r_o.

Example 11.9

The value of β is calculated by the change in the collector current that occurs as a result of a change in the base current. As indicated in Figure 11.33,

$$\beta = \frac{(4.05 - 2.05)(10^{-3})}{(40 - 20)(10^{-6})} = 100$$

g_o is determined by the change in the collector current that occurs as a result of a change in the collector-to-emitter voltage at the Q-point:

$$g_o = \frac{(3.15 - 3.05)(10^{-3})}{(3.6 - 1.9)} = 5.9 \times 10^{-5}\ \Omega$$

and, therefore,

$$r_o = \frac{1}{g_o} = 16.95\text{k}\ \Omega$$

Note: The current changes are often small and hard to estimate; the author had the benefit of a higher resolution plot; in practice one can make these measurements accurately with a particular device and obtain reasonably accurate results.

Example 11.10	If an npn transistor, connected in a common emitter configuration, has a measured collector current of 3.6 mA and the β of the transistor is 200, let us determine the value of r_{ib}.

The required value of I_B can be obtained from the equation

$$I_B = \frac{I_C}{\beta} = \frac{(3.6 \times 10^{-3})}{200} = 18 \, \mu A$$

Then, r_{ib} is

$$r_{ib} = \frac{0.026}{18 \times 10^{-6}} = 1.44k \, \Omega$$

Let us now consider a couple of examples that will illustrate how the model is employed to determine the small-signal gain for the npn common emitter configuration.

Example 11.11	Given the npn common emitter amplifier circuit in Figure 11.34a, we wish to determine (a) the Q-point and (b) small-signal gain. The transistor has a β of 160, r_o can be ignored, and $V_{BE} = 0.7$ V.

The Thevenin equivalent circuit at the base of the transistor is determined as shown in Figure 11.34b. The open circuit voltage, V_{OC}, is

$$V_{OC} = 12 \left(\frac{90k}{90k + 180k} \right) = 4 \, V$$

And R_{TH} is

$$R_{TH} = 90k||180k = \frac{(90k)(180k)}{(90k + 180k)} = 60k \, \Omega$$

The equivalent bias circuit is then shown in Figure 11.34c. KVL for the base–emitter circuit is

$$-4 + 60k \, I_B + 0.7 + 2.2k \, I_E = 0$$

In addition,

$$I_B = I_E / (\beta + 1)$$

Combining the equations and solving for I_E and I_B yields

$$I_E = 1.28 \, mA$$
$$I_B = 7.95 \, \mu A$$
$$I_C = \beta I_B = 1.27 \, mA$$

KVL for the collector–emitter loop yields

$$V_{CE} = 12 - 3.6k \, I_C - 2.2k \, I_E$$
$$= 4.61 \, V$$

Therefore, the Q-point data is $I_B = 7.95 \, \mu A$, $I_C = 1.27$ mA, and $V_{CE} = 4.61$ V. The small-signal resistance of the forward-biased base to emitter diode is

$$r_{ib} = \frac{0.026}{I_B} = \frac{0.026}{7.95 \times 10^{-6}} = 3.27k \, \Omega$$

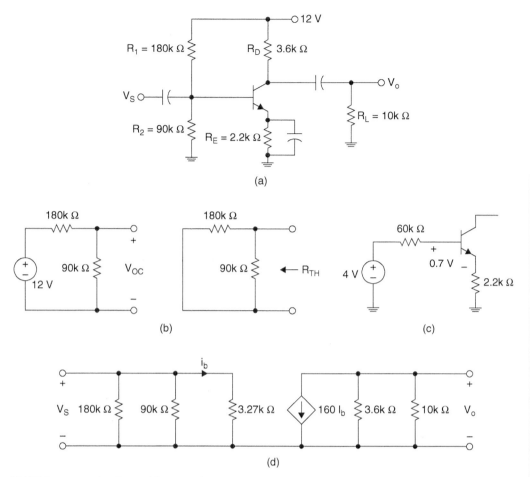

FIGURE 11.34   Circuits used in Example 11.11

The small-signal equivalent circuit is shown in Figure 11.34d, where we can note that a dc source appears as an ac short. The input voltage is

$$v_s = i_b\, r_{ib} = (3.27\ k)i_b$$

The output voltage is

$$v_o = -\beta\, i_b(3.6k\ ||\ 10k) = -i_b\, \beta\, (2.65k) = -160\, i_b\, (2.65k) \text{ and recall } v_s = i_b\, r_{ib}.$$

Then the voltage gain of the amplifier is

$$A_v = \frac{v_o}{v_s} = -(160)(2.65k)/3.27k = -129.5$$

Consider the npn common emitter amplifier circuit in Figure 11.35a. We wish to determine the small-signal gain of this network under the following conditions. $\beta = 100$, $V_{BE} = 0.7\ V$, r_o is infinite, and the base current is negligible in comparison with the current in the 12k Ω and 4k Ω resistors.

Example 11.12

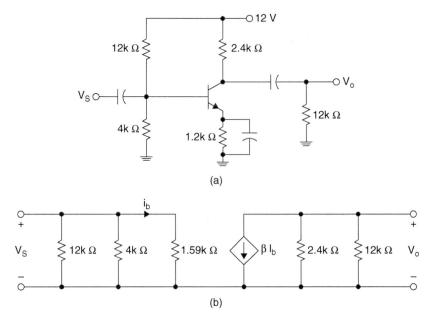

(a)

(b)

FIGURE 11.35 Circuits used in Example 11.12

Given the stated conditions, the base voltage is

$$V_B = 12 \left(\frac{4k}{16k} \right) = 3 \text{ V}$$

Then

$$V_E = V_B - 0.7 = 2.3 \text{ V}$$

And

$$I_E = \frac{V_E}{1.2k} = 1.92 \text{ mA}$$

$$I_B = \frac{I_E}{(\beta + 1)} = \frac{1.92 \times 10^{-3}}{101} = 19 \text{ } \mu\text{A}$$

Now the small-signal resistance of the forward-biased base-to-emitter diode is

$$r_{ib} = \frac{0.026}{I_B} = \frac{0.026}{19 \times 10^{-6}} = 1.39k \text{ } \Omega$$

The small-signal equivalent circuit for this amplifier is shown in Figure 11.35b. The input voltage is

$$v_S = i_b \, r_{ib} = 1.39k \, i_b$$

The output voltage is

$$v_o = -\beta \, i_b (2.4k \, || \, 12k) = -i_b 100 \, (2k)$$

Then, the voltage gain of the amplifier is

$$A_v = \frac{v_o}{v_S} = -\frac{100(2k)}{1.39k} = -144$$

11.1 Describe the difference between an analog circuit and a digital circuit.

11.2 (a) What are the two primary types of transistors? (b) What is the goal or purpose of a transistor in analog circuits?

11.3 Explain Moore's law and its impact on modern electronics.

11.4 (a) Sketch a cross-section drawing of an n-channel enhancement mode MOSFET. (b) Draw two common circuit symbols for this device.

11.5 The device of Problem 11.4 requires the gate-to-source voltage to reach a critical value to initiate current conduction through the device. (a) What is the name of this critical voltage and its common notation. (b) If V_{GS} is less than this critical voltage, in what mode is the transistor biased?

11.6 (a) What are the three important regions (or modes) of operation for a MOSFET? (b) Sketch a hypothetical set of output characteristic curves for an n-channel MOSFET with a threshold voltage of 1.0 V, and a drain current of 6 mA in the active region when V_{GS} is 4 V. (c) Label the three regions on this sketch identified in part (a).

11.7 Given the circuit of Figure P11.7a, the output characteristic curves for the common source n-channel MOSFET shown in Figure P11.7a are shown in Figure P11.7b, (a) draw the load line for the amplifier and (b) determine the Q-point.

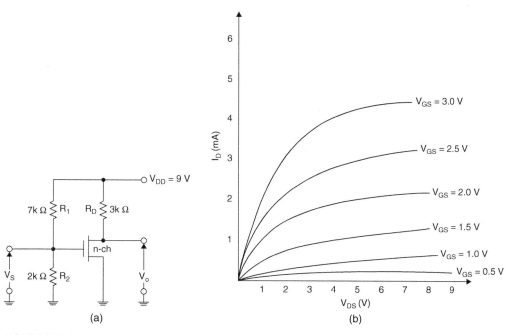

FIGURE P11.7

11.8 Repeat Problem 11.7 if R_D is changed to 1.8k Ω, and (a) determine the new load line and (b) determine the new Q-point.

11.9 Given the circuit of Figure P11.9a with the characteristic output curves shown in Figure P11.9b, (a) draw the load line of the amplifier and (b) determine the Q-point.

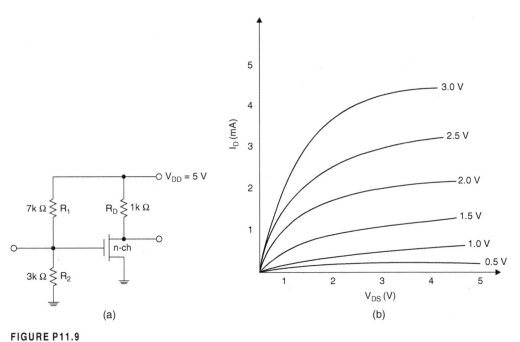

(a)   (b)

FIGURE P11.9

11.10 In Problem 11.9, determine the value of R_2 required to set the value of $V_{GS} = 2$ V

11.11 For the circuit shown in Figure P11.11 and assuming the MOSFET has the output characteristic curves of Figure P11.9b, (a) what is the required voltage V_1 to place the Q-point at $I_D = 2$ mA? (b) what is the value of V_{DS} at this Q-point?

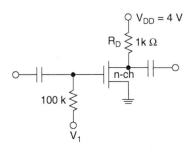

FIGURE P11.11

11.12 For the transistor output characteristic curves and load line shown in Figure P11.12, and the circuit of Figure P11.7a, determine new values for V_{DD} and R_D that would produce this load line.

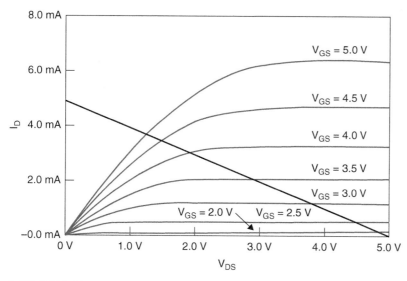

FIGURE P11.12

11.13 For the transistor with output characteristic curves shown in Figure P11.13 operating in the circuit of Figure P11.7a, but with $R_1 = 100k\ \Omega$, $R_2 = 30k\ \Omega$, $R_D = 1.25k\ \Omega$ and $V_{DD} = 5V$, (a) construct the load line for this circuit, (b) determine the Q-point, (c) if a sinusoidal signal is applied with an amplitude of 0.5 V (peak-to-peak voltage of 1.0 V), sketch the variation in output voltage about the Q-point (using arrows along the load line), and (d) determine the ac voltage gain of this circuit.

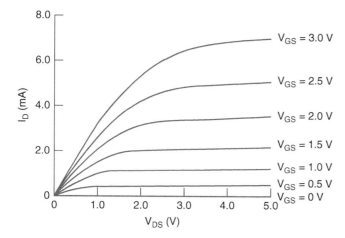

FIGURE P11.13

11.14 For the circuit shown in Figure P11.14a and the MOSFET output characteristic curves shown in Figure P11.14b, (a) draw the dc load line, (b) if we assume the Q-point falls in the approximate middle of the load line (generally desired), what value of R_2 is required? (c) draw and identify the Q-point, (d) draw the ac load line, what is the ac voltage gain of the circuit? (e) what is the voltage gain of the circuit if C_s is removed, and (f) what is the purpose of C_s?

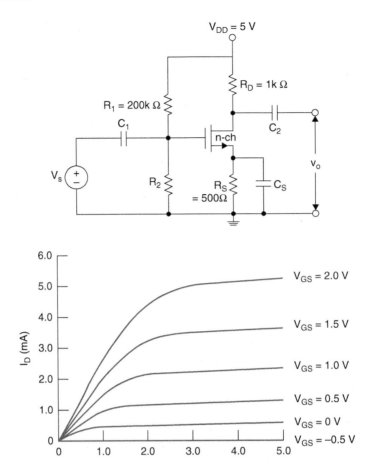

FIGURE P11.14

11.15 The circuit shown in Figure P11.15a has a MOSFET with output characteristic curves shown in Figure P11.15(b). (a) Draw the dc load line. (b) If the Q-point is at $I_D = 1.2$ mA, what is the required value of V_{GS}? (c) What is the required value of V_1 to establish this Q-point? (d) Draw the ac load line. (e) What is the ac voltage gain, calculated around the Q-point?

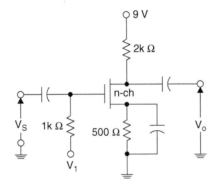

FIGURE P11.15

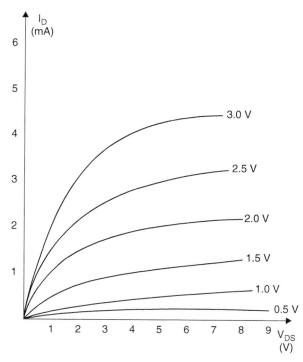

FIGURE P11.15   *(Continued)*

11.16 Measurements at the Q-point of a common source n-channel MOSFET indicate that at a fixed value of V_{DS}, I_D changes from 1.2 to 2.7 mA, while V_{GS} changes from 1.3 to 2.4 V. Determine the value of g_m for the device.

11.17 Measurements at the Q-point of a common source n-channel MOSFET indicate that a change in I_D from 2.4 to 2.7 mA corresponds to a change in V_{DS} from 3.0 to 5.6 V. (a) Determine the value of g_o for the device. (b) What is the value of r_o?

11.18 Measurements at the Q-point of a common source n-channel MOSFET indicate that at a fixed value of V_{DS}, a change in I_D of 1.8 mA corresponds to a change in V_{GS} of 0.8 V. Determine the value of g_m for the device.

11.19 Measurements at the Q-point of a common source n-channel MOSFET indicate that at a fixed value of V_{DS}, a change in I_D of 0.16 mA corresponds to a change in V_{DS} of 3.2 V. (a) Determine the value of g_o for the device. (b) What is the value of r_o?

11.20 If the output characteristic curves for a common source n-channel MOSFET are flat at the Q-point, what does this indicate about the value of g_m and g_o?

11.21 Measurements at the Q-point of a common source n-channel MOSFET indicate that a change in I_D of 0.22 mA corresponds to a change in V_{DS} of 2.8 V. In addition, a change in I_D of 2.1 mA corresponds to a change in V_{GS} of 1.2 V with V_{DS} constant. Determine (a) the value of g_m and (b) the value of g_o for the device.

11.22 An amplifier with a common source n-channel MOSFET is shown in Figure P11.22. Assuming the amplifier is operating in the mid-band frequency range and $g_m = 1.8$ mS and $g_o = 64\mu S$, determine (a) the small-signal equivalent circuit and (b) the small-signal voltage gain.

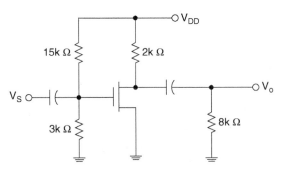

FIGURE P11.22

11.23 Determine the input and output resistances of the amplifier in Figure P11.22.

11.24 An amplifier with a common source n-channel MOSFET is shown in Figure P11.24. Assuming the amplifier is operating in the mid-band frequency range and g_m = 1.4 mS and g_o = 45 μS determine (a) the small-signal equivalent circuit, (b) the small-signal voltage gain, and (c) the input resistance of the amplifier.

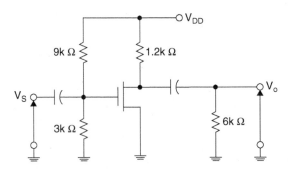

FIGURE P11.24

11.25 An amplifier with a common source n-channel MOSFET is shown in Figure P11.25. Assuming the amplifier is operating in the mid-band frequency range and g_m = 2.6 mS and g_o = 25 μS, determine (a) the small-signal equivalent circuit and (b) the small-signal voltage gain.

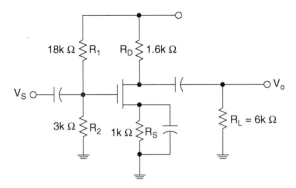

FIGURE P11.25

11.26   Determine the input and output resistances of the amplifier in Figure P11.25.

11.27   An amplifier with a common source n-channel MOSFET is shown in Figure P11.27. Assuming the amplifier is operating in the mid-band frequency range and $g_m = 2.8$ mS and $g_0 = 36$ μS, determine the small-signal voltage gain if $R_L = 4$k Ω

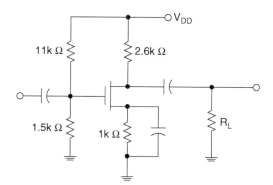

FIGURE P11.27

Note: In all BJT problems, assume $V_{BE} = 0.7$ V, unless specified otherwise.

11.28   (a) Sketch the cross section of a planar npn bipolar junction transistor (BJT) and label the three terminals. (b) Identify the emitter junction and the collector junction.

11.29   For a p–n junction which is forward biased (a) is this junction conducting current? (b) Is the p or the n region more positive in voltage?

11.30   For a p-n junction which is reverse biased, (a) is this junction conducting current? (b) Is the p or the n region more positive in voltage?

11.31   In order to assure a BJT is in the active mode (or region), (a) is the emitter junction forward or reverse biased? (b) same for the collector junction?

11.32   In an npn BJT, the dominant component of collector current comes from what source?

11.33   If a BJT has $\beta = 50$, what percent of the electrons entering the base are collected by the collector?

11.34   A BJT with $\beta = 120$ is operated in the active mode such that $I_C = 3$ mA. Determine the value of I_B and I_E.

11.35   Repeat Problem 11.34 if $\beta = 200$.

11.36   Repeat Problem 11.34 if $I_C = 6$ mA and $\beta = 150$.

11.37   For Problem 11.36, sketch the common emitter equivalent circuit with $\beta = 75$.

11.38   The BJT in Figure P11.38 has $\beta = 100$ and $V_{BE} = 0.7$ V. (a) What mode is the device operating in? (b) Calculate the Q-point (i.e. the values of I_B, I_E, and I_C).

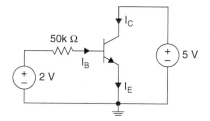

FIGURE P11.38

11.39 Given the transistor circuit in Figure P11.39, determine the Q-point, i.e. I_C, I_B, and V_{CE}. The β of the transistor is 120.

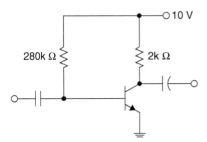

FIGURE P11.39

11.40 If the β of the transistor in the network in Figure P11.40 is 100, calculate the Q-point.

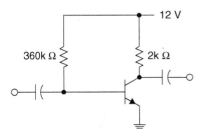

FIGURE P11.40

11.41 Determine the Q-point data for the circuit in Figure P11.41, if the transistor has a β of 80.

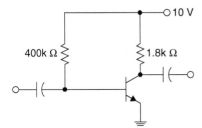

FIGURE P11.41

11.42 Determine the Q-point for the transistor circuit in Figure P11.42 if the transistor has a β of 100.

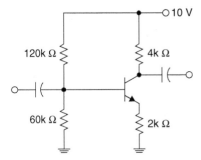

FIGURE P11.42

11.43   Given the transistor circuit in Figure P11.43 determine the Q-point, i.e. I_C, I_B, and V_{CE}. The β of the transistor is 160.

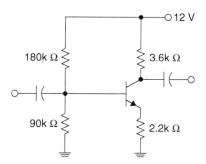

FIGURE P11.43

11.44   Find the Q-point data, i.e. I_C, I_B, and V_{CE} for the network shown in Figure P11.44 assuming a β value of 200.

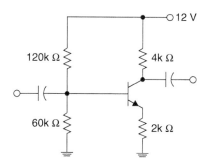

FIGURE P11.44

11.45   Determine the Q-point for the network in Figure P11.45 assuming a β= 100. In addition, use the approximation technique to solve the problem.

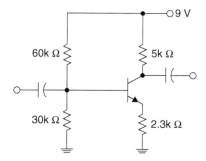

FIGURE P11.45

11.46   The output characteristic curves for the transistor in the network in Figure P11.46a are shown in Figure P11.46b. Assuming $V_{BE} = 0.7$ V. and the base current is much less than the current in the 12k Ω and 6k Ω resistors, determine (a) the load line and (b) the Q-point, (c) the β of the transistor.

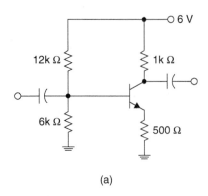

(a)

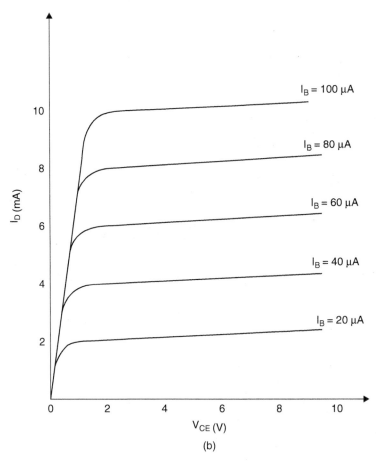

(b)

FIGURE P11.46

11.47 The Q-point for the transistor in the circuit in Figure P11.47a is shown in Figure P11.47b. (a) Construct the load line, (b) find the value of R_C, and (c) determine R_B, and (d) determine the voltage gain, v_0/v_s.

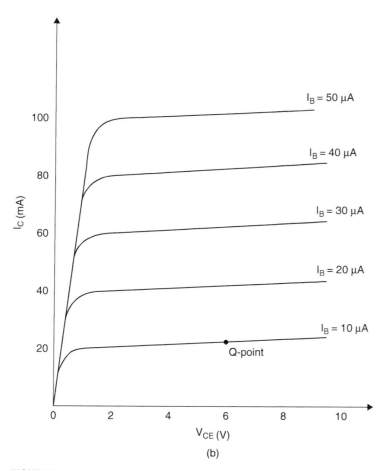

FIGURE P11.47

11.48 For the circuit shown in Figure P11.48a using an npn BJT with output characteristic curves shown in Figure P11.48b, (a) draw the dc load line, (b) determine the Q-point, (c) at the Q-point what is the value of V_{CE} and IC? (d) Determine the transistor's β. (e) What is the voltage gain of the circuit?

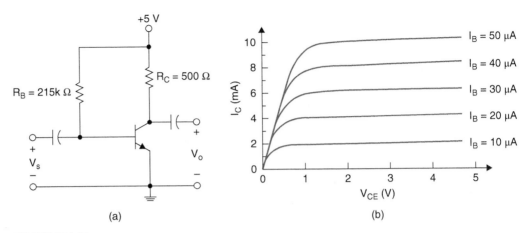

(a)   (b)

FIGURE P11.48

11.49 Draw a small-signal equivalent circuit of a BJT and clearly label r_{ib}, r_o ,and the dependent current source.

11.50 A BJT is connected in a common emitter configuration and has a β of 150. If $I_C = 4.4$ mA, determine the value of r_{ib}.

11.51 A BJT is connected in a common emitter configuration and has a β of 180. If $I_C = 2.6$ mA, determine the value of r_{ib}.

11.52 The output characteristic curves of a BJT at the Q-point show a change in I_C of 1 mA for a change in I_B of 15 μA; also I_C changes by 0.1 mA if V_{CE} is changed by 2 V. (a) What is the β of the transistor, (b) what is the output resistance, r_o?

11.53 Given the BJT output characteristic curves of Figure 11.47b, at the given Q-point, (a) what is the β of the transistor, (b) what is the value of the output resistance, r_o?

11.54 For the circuit shown in Figure P11.54, (a) determine the Q-point by calculating the values of I_B, I_C, and I_E, (b) construct and draw a small-signal equivalent circuit, being careful to label all circuit elements, (c) from the equivalent circuit, calculate the small-signal voltage gain.

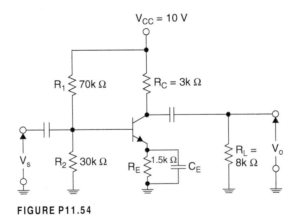

FIGURE P11.54

Digital Electronics and Logic Circuits

CHAPTER 12

LEARNING OBJECTIVES

- To understand the binary number system
- To learn to use Boolean algebra and its role in logic function minimization
- To understand the types and operations of basic logic gates
- To learn to realize NAND gates with both NMOS and CMOS devices
- To learn to analyze and design combinational logic circuits
- To learn to analyze and design sequential logic circuits

INTRODUCTION

Digital electronics is having, and will continue to have, a profound effect on vast areas of technological development. In communications alone, the tentacles of this technology have permeated essentially every possible facet of this area. Only a cursory examination of the growth of cell phones around the world is sufficient to see the effect this technology is having on the lives of everyone. The Internet, which is a high-speed digital communication pipe, has made us aware of events all around the world in seconds of the time in which they have occurred. The processing speed of our computers, which is directly related to the advances in digital electronics, continues to increase at a phenomenal rate.

Digital logic circuits, which form the backbone of the digital communication and processing systems, are driven by electronics that operate in a discrete mode. We saw in the last chapter that two of the transistor's operating states are saturation and cutoff. While these operating states are not used in analog amplifiers, they are the building blocks for digital systems. In saturation, the output voltage of the transistor is low, and in cutoff the output voltage is high. We can then associate the high voltage with a logic state of 1 and the low voltage with a logic state of 0. The blazing speed of transistors permits us to shift from one state to another in the design of high-speed digital circuits.

THE BINARY NUMBER SYSTEM

The number of digits employed in any number system is called the base or radix. The decimal system, with which we are all familiar and use on a regular basis, is base 10 and has 10 digits, i.e. 0, 1, ..., 9. In contrast, the binary system is base 2 and has 2 digits, i.e. 0 and 1. A conversion table that relates these two number systems is listed as follows:

Base 10	Base 2
0	0
1	1
2	10
3	11
4	100
5	101
6	110
7	111
8	1000
9	1001

Addition and multiplication in base 2 is performed as outlined in the following two tables.

+	0	1
0	0	1
1	1	10

X	0	1
0	0	0
1	0	1

Note carefully that in binary, $1 + 1 = 0$ and 1 to carry.

It is often convenient to be able to convert between these two number systems. A general conversion technique useful in converting between base x and base y is known as the series substitution technique. We use the fact that a number in base x can be expressed as

$$N_x = a_{n-1} x^{n-1} + a_{n-2} x^{n-2} + \cdots + a_0 x^0 + a_{-1} x^{-1} + a_{-2} x^{-2} + \cdots$$

Given this format, the terms of a series are expressed in base x, each term is converted to base y, and finally each term converted to base y is evaluated with arithmetic in base y. Examples 12.1–12.3 illustrate the addition, multiplication, and base conversion processes.

Example 12.1

Let us add the decimal numbers 6 and 11 in binary.

The addition is performed as follows, where decimal 11 is equal to binary 1011 and decimal 6 is equal to 110.

```
 1011
+ 110
--------
10001
```

The decimal number is then

$$1(2)^4 + 0(2)^3 + 0(2)^2 + 0(2)^1 + 1(2)^0 = 17$$

Example 12.2

Let us multiply the decimal numbers 6 and 11 in binary.

Multiplication is performed as follows:

```
   1011
  ×110
--------
   0000
  1011
 1011
------------
1000010
```

The decimal number is then

$$1(2)^6 + 0(2)^5 + 0(2)^4 + 0(2)^3 + 0(2)^2 + 1(2)^1 + 0(2)^0 = 66$$

Let us convert the decimal number 24 to binary.

The number 24 can be expressed as

$$24 = 2(10)^1 + 4(10)^0$$

And since 2 in decimal is 10 in binary, 4 in decimal is 100 in binary and 10 in decimal is 1010 in binary.

$$24 = 10(1010) + 100(1010) = 11000$$

Example 12.3

Long before digital systems came into existence, the English mathematician George Boole formulated the mathematics that forms the basis for the analysis and design of logic systems. This mathematical formulation is based upon a number of postulates and theorems developed from them that form the basis for what has come to be known as Boolean algebra. The postulates and theorems are listed in Tables 12.1 and 12.2.

BOOLEAN ALGEBRA

It is important to note at the outset there are several issues concerning this mathematics. First of all, this algebra is in many ways quite different from the real variable analysis we are conditioned to using, and therefore the reader must be careful in applying the rules that govern this algebra. Second, the postulates and theorems are listed in a dual format in which + operators are replaced with · operators, · operators are replaced with + operators, 0s are replaced with 1s, and 1s are replaced with 0s. Finally, each appearance of a logic variable, whether in complemented or uncomplemented form, is referred to as a literal. For example, the function $f(A, B, C) = A\overline{B} + A\overline{C} + BC$ has six literals. As we will indicate, these postulates and theorems are employed with

Table 12.1 Boolean Algebra Postulates

P1: Boolean algebra is a closed system containing two or more elements and the operators + (OR) and · (AND).

P2: Within the closed system, two expressions are considered to be equal (=) if one can be replaced by the other.

P3: There are two unique elements in the system: 1 (one) and 0 (zero) such that for every A

$A + 0 = A$

$A \cdot 1 = A$

P4: The commutative law

$A + B = B + A$

$A \cdot B = B \cdot A$

P5: The associative law

$A + (B + C) = (A + B) + C$

$A \cdot (B \cdot C) = (A \cdot B) \cdot C$

P6: The distributive law

$A + (B \cdot C) = (A + B) \cdot (A + C)$

$A \cdot (B + C) = (A \cdot B) + (A \cdot C)$

P7: The complement of A, i.e. $\overline{A}$, exists such that

$A + \overline{A} = 1$

$A \, \overline{A} = 0$

Table 12.2 Boolean Algebra Theorems

Theorem#	Expression	Dual
1	$A + A = A$	$A \cdot A = A$
2	$A + 1 + A$	$A \cdot 0 = 0$
3	$A + AB = A$	$A(A + B) = AB$
4	$A + \overline{A}B = A + B$	$A(\overline{A} + B) = AB$
5	$AB + \overline{A}C + BC = AB + \overline{A}C$	$(A + B)(\overline{A} + C)(B + C) = (A + B)(\overline{A} + C)$
6	$\overline{A + B} = \overline{A}\,\overline{B}$	$\overline{AB} = \overline{A} + \overline{B}$
7	$\overline{A}B + AB = B$	$(\overline{A} + B)(A + B) = B$

one goal in mind: to minimize the number of literals that exist in a logic function. The reason for this minimization is simple: the fewer the number of literals, the less electronics needed to realize the function.

The following simple example illustrates the use of the postulates and provides a glimpse into the manner in which we can minimize these functions using a visual approach.

Example 12.4

Let us minimize the function $f(A, B, C) = \overline{A}B\overline{C} + A\overline{B}\overline{C} + AB\overline{C} + ABC$.

Using postulate P7, the function can be written as

$$f(A, B, C) = \overline{A}\,\overline{B}\,\overline{C} + A\overline{B}\,\overline{C} + AB(C + \overline{C})$$

Then using postulate P4, the function is reduced to

$$f(A, B, C) = \overline{A}\,\overline{B}\,\overline{C} + A\overline{B}\,\overline{C} + AB$$

By repeating this process, the function can be written as

$$f(A, B, C) = (A + \overline{A})\,\overline{B}\,\overline{C} + AB$$

and

$$f(A, B, C) = \overline{B}\,\overline{C} + AB$$

BOOLEAN FUNCTIONS IN CANONICAL FORM

Boolean functions can be expressed in a number of ways; however, two forms are of particular interest. These two forms are a sum of products (SOP) and a product of sums (POS). For example, $f_1(A, B, C) = AB + AC + BC$ is in SOP form and $f_2(A, B, C) = (A + B)(A + C)(B + C)$ is in POS form. If we restrict each term to contain every variable in either complemented or uncomplemented form, then the functions are said to be in canonical SOP or canonical POS form. Under this condition, each term in canonical SOP form is called a minterm, and each term in canonical POS form is called a maxterm. For example, $f_3(A, B, C) = ABC + A\overline{B}\,\overline{C} + \overline{A}BC$ is in canonical SOP form and $f_4(A, BC) = (A + B + \overline{C})(A + \overline{B} + C)$ is in canonical maxterm form. Although either form can be employed to represent a Boolean function, we will restrict our discussion in the material that follows to canonical SOP form, where each term in the function is a minterm.

It is interesting to note that a function can be easily converted to canonical form. Example 12.5 illustrates the simplicity of the conversion from SOP form to canonical SOP form.

Let us convert the function $f(A, B, C) = A\overline{B} + B\overline{C}$ to canonical SOP form.

Example 12.5

Using the fact that $A + \overline{A} = 1$, we can write the function in the following manner:

$$f(A, B, C) = A\overline{B}(C + \overline{C}) + (A + \overline{A})B\overline{C}$$
$$= A\overline{B}C + A\overline{B}\,\overline{C} + AB\overline{C} + \overline{A}B\overline{C}$$

The functional description can be simplified by coding the minterms. For example, if the variables in uncomplemented form are coded as 1 and complemented variables are coded as 0, then the function $A\overline{B}C$ would be coded as 101, which corresponds to the decimal number 5 in binary and thus is labeled as minterm 5 or m_5.

Let us express the function in Example 12.5 as a sum of minterms.

Example 12.6

The function is written as

$$f(A, B, C) = A\overline{B}C + A\overline{B}\,\overline{C} + AB\overline{C} + \overline{A}B\overline{C}$$
$$= 101 + 100 + 110 + 010$$
$$= m_5 + m_4 + m_6 + m_2$$
$$= \sum m(2, 4, 5, 6)$$

Another technique that can be employed to describe a Boolean function is a *truth table*. Truth tables display all possible combinations of the variables and the corresponding value of the function. The importance of the truth table results from the fact that although we can express a Boolean function in a wide variety of ways, there is one and only one truth table for the function.

Let us construct the truth table for the Boolean function in Example 12.6.

Example 12.7

We begin by noting that there are three variables, A, B, and C and thus there are only eight combinations that range from 000, 001, 010, ..., 111. Furthermore, from the list of Boolean properties, we note that $0 \cdot 0 = 0$, $0 \cdot 1 = 0$, $1 \cdot 1 = 1$, $0 + 0 = 0$, $0 + 1 = 1$, $1 + 1 = 1$, $\overline{1} = 0$, and $\overline{0} = 1$. Therefore,

$$f(A, B, C) = \overline{A}\,\overline{B}\,\overline{C} + \overline{A}BC + \overline{A}\,\overline{B}C + A\overline{B}C$$

and

$$f(0, 0, 0) = 0 \cdot 1 \cdot 0 + 0 \cdot 1 \cdot 1 + 0 \cdot 0 \cdot 1 + 1 \cdot 0 \cdot 1$$
$$= 0$$

The truth table that lists the values for the variables, the value of the function for each combination of variables, and the corresponding minterms is listed as follows:

ABC	f(A,B,C)	m minterm
000	0	m_0
001	0	m_1
010	1	m_2
011	0	m_3
100	1	m_4
101	1	m_5
110	1	m_6
111	0	m_7

If we replace the 1s with True and the 0s with False, we can easily see the combination of variables under which the function is True, and this is, in essence, the genesis of the name truth table. In addition, note that the function can be written directly in canonical form given the truth table.

The mathematical operations involving Boolean functions are governed by the postulates and theorems stated earlier. However, there is a better way to deal with the Boolean functions than this algebraic approach. The use of Venn diagrams is a graphical approach that is, in essence, a visual analysis of the various operations taking place in the algebraic manipulation of the Boolean functions. In this format, the elements of the Boolean function correspond to sets and the set operations of union and intersection correspond to Boolean operations of + and ·. The validity of this approach stems from the fact that the algebra of sets is a Boolean algebra. Not only do the Venn diagrams produce a visual application of the various postulates and theorems, they also form the basis for the minimization techniques employed to reduce the Boolean function to the smallest number of literals.

The set operations displayed in Figure 12.1 are fundamental. Once these fundamental operations are understood, the Venn diagram can be used to verify all the postulates and theorems that govern the operations in Boolean algebra.

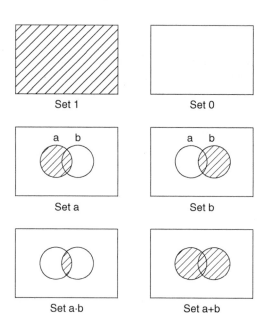

FIGURE 12.1 Venn diagrams

Example 12.8

Let us use the Venn diagram to verify the Boolean identity $A + BC = (A + B)(A + C)$.

The set operations used to obtain the function $A + BC$ are shown together with the operations employed to derive the function $(A + B)(A + C)$ in Figure 12.2. As indicated, the two sets form two representations of the same area, which, of course, are equal.

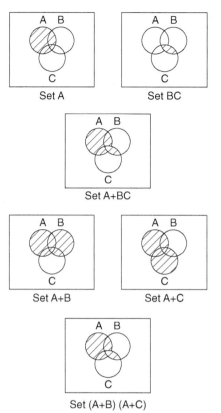

Set A   Set BC

Set A+BC

Set A+B   Set A+C

Set (A+B) (A+C)   **FIGURE 12.2**   Venn diagrams for equivalent functions

BOOLEAN FUNCTION MINIMIZATION

While the Venn diagrams provide a visual approach to the postulates and theorems, which is certainly easier to deal with than the mathematics involved in their use, the real power of the Venn diagrams lies in their use in minimizing the Boolean function in order to obtain an equivalent function with the smallest number of literals. We accomplish this minimization of the Boolean function by transforming the Venn diagram into what is called a Karnaugh map, or K-map for short. The process by which we morph the Venn diagram into the K-map is illustrated in the sequence of diagrams shown in Figure 12.3. The block in Figure 12.3a corresponds to the universal set, and since there are three variables, each area within the diagram corresponds to one of the $2^3 = 8$ minterms as indicated, i.e. $m_0 = \overline{A}\,\overline{B}\,\overline{C}$, $m_1 = \overline{A}\,\overline{B}C$, etc. The next step in the transformation from the Venn diagram to K-map is a little tricky, and it is shown in Figure 12.3c. Note, however, that the minterm 3 is adjacent to minterms 1, 2, and 7 on the Venn diagram in Figure 12.3b and that is also the case in the K-map in Figure 12.3c. Similarly, minterm 6 is adjacent to minterms 2, 4, and 7 on both diagrams. The Venn diagram in Figure 12.3b also indicates that minterm 0 is adjacent to minterms, 1, 2, and 4. In order to satisfy this condition on the K-map, the vertical edges on the K-map become the same edge, i.e. the map is folded into a cylinder. In this configuration, all the minterm adjacencies on the Venn diagram are repeated on the K-map. It is also important to note that blocks 4, 5, 6, and 7 comprise the area of the map where A is uncomplemented, and blocks 0, 1, 2, and 3 comprise the area in which A is complemented. Similar statements can be made about the variables B and C. Therefore, we can immediately identify the variable sequence associated with each minterm. As an example, minterm 2 is outside the area of A, inside the area of B, and outside the area of C. Hence, minterm 2 is $\overline{A}B\overline{C}$. Similarly, m 6 is inside A and B and

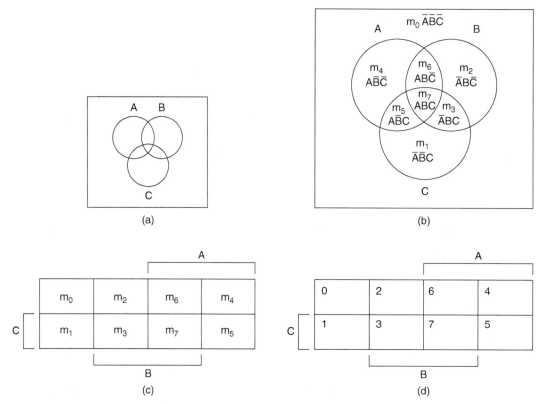

FIGURE 12.3 Venn diagram to K-map development

outside C, i.e. $A\overline{B}\overline{C}$. As a final simplification of the map, we simply drop the m designation and label the minterms with only their number as shown in Figure 12.3d.

As we indicated, our goal is to minimize the Boolean function so that it can be physically realized with a minimum of electronics. The power of the K-map stems from the fact that terms in the function that are logically adjacent are also physically adjacent on the map. Thus, the map provides a visual picture of the logic function, and we can identify immediately the terms that can be combined to eliminate a literal, thereby simplifying the function.

Example 12.9

Let us determine the minimum form for the logic function

$$f(A, B, C) = \Sigma \text{ minterms } (0, 3, 4, 7)$$
$$= \overline{A}\overline{B}\overline{C} + \overline{A}BC + A\overline{B}\overline{C} + ABC$$

This function is plotted on the three-variable map as shown in Figure 12.4a. As was done on the truth table, we have placed a 1 in the block for each of the minterms in the function, but we have left the remaining blocks blank, essentially ignoring the 0s. Once in this format, we see that minterms 0 and 4 are physically adjacent as are minterms 3 and 7. On the K-map terms that are physically adjacent are also logically adjacent and thus can be combined to eliminate the literal that differs in the two terms. This process is accomplished as follows. For minterms 0 and 4, the mathematical minimization is performed as

$$m_0 + m_4 = \overline{A}\overline{B}\overline{C} + A\overline{B}\overline{C} = (A + \overline{A})\overline{B}\overline{C} = \overline{B}\overline{C}$$

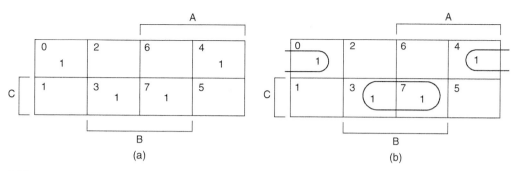

FIGURE 12.4 K-maps for Example 12.9

On the K-map in Figure 12.4b we note that minterms 0 and 4 are logically adjacent and on the map the terms are outside B, outside C and it is the variable A that appears in both the uncomplemented and complemented form. Hence, combining these terms yields $\overline{B}\,\overline{C}$. In a similar manner combining the minterms 3 and 7 yields BC since the combination is inside B and C and A is the variable that differs between the two terms.

The four-variable map is shown in Figure 12.5. In a manner similar to that used in the three-variable map, the horizontal edges in this map are the same as well as the vertical edges, which creates a toroid figure, or a map in the shape of a donut, i.e. minterm 0 is adjacent to minterms 2 and 8 as well as minterms 1 and 4.

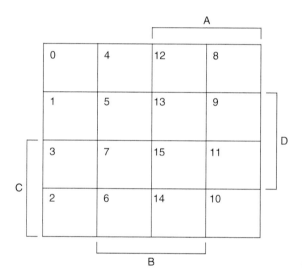

FIGURE 12.5 A four-variable K-map

Example 12.10

Let us determine the minimum form of the logic function

f(A, B, C, D) = Σ minterms (2, 4, 5, 6, 7, 9, 11, 12, 14)

This function is plotted on the four-variable map as shown in Figure 12.6, where the terms are grouped together by drawing a loop around them. Note that the terms are grouped in powers of 2, since combining two terms will eliminate one variable, combining four terms will eliminate two variables, combining eight terms will eliminate three variables, etc. In addition, note that we have encircled several minterms more than once, e.g. minterms 4 and 6. The use of a minterm more than once is permitted since in Boolean algebra $A = A + A + A + \cdots$. The combinations are as follows:

Minterms 2 and 6 yield the function $\overline{A}C\overline{D}$.
Minterms 4, 5, 6, and 7 yield the function $\overline{A}B$.
Minterms 4, 12, 6, and 14 yield the function $B\overline{D}$.
Minterms 9 and 11 yield the function $A\overline{B}D$.
Therefore, the minimum function is

$$f(A, B, C, D) = \overline{A}C\overline{D} + \overline{A}B + B\overline{D} + A\overline{B}D$$

It is important to note a couple of issues concerning the minimization. Note that we cannot group minterms 5 and 7 with 9 and 11. The grouping of 5 and 7 is not logically adjacent to minterms 9 and 11. In addition, we cannot group minterms 2, 6, and 14 because we need a grouping of four to eliminate two variables.

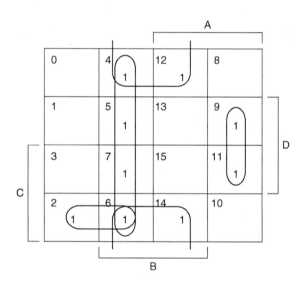

FIGURE 12.6 K-map for Example 12.10

We wish to determine the minimum form of the logic function

$$f(A, B, C, D) = \overline{A}\overline{B}D + AB\overline{C} + A\overline{B}D + \overline{A}BCD.$$

Although we can employ the postulates and theorems to reduce the function to its minimum form, use of the K-map is also a viable alternative. In order to determine the function in minterm form, we simply expand the terms, using the fact that $A + \overline{A} = 1$, in order to write the function as a sum of minterms.

Therefore, the function can be expressed as

$$f(A, B, C, D) = \overline{A}\overline{B}D(C + \overline{C}) + AB\overline{C}(D + \overline{D}) + A\overline{B}D(C + \overline{C}) + \overline{A}BCD$$
$$= \overline{A}\overline{B}CD + \overline{A}\overline{B}\overline{C}D + AB\overline{C}D + AB\overline{C}\overline{D} + A\overline{B}CD + A\overline{B}\overline{C}D + \overline{A}BCD$$
$$= \Sigma \text{ minterms } (1, 3, 5, 9, 11, 12, \text{ and } 13)$$

The K-map for this function is shown in Figure 12.7. The minterm combinations are as follows.

Minterms 1, 3, 9, and 11 combine to yield $\overline{B}D$.
Minterms 1, 5, 9, and 13 combine to yield $\overline{C}D$.
Minterms 12 and 13 combine to yield $AB\overline{C}$.
Therefore, the minimum form of the logic function is

$$f(A, B, C, D) = \overline{B}D + \overline{C}D + AB\overline{C}.$$

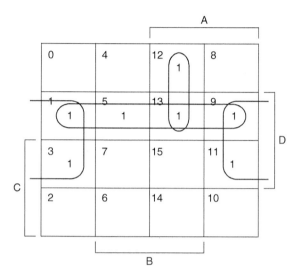

FIGURE 12.7   K-map for Example 12.11

Once we have determined the minimum form of the Boolean function, it is time to realize this function in hardware. For example, suppose the logic function is

$$f(A, B, C) = AB + B\overline{C}$$

LOGIC GATES FOR FUNCTION REALIZATION

The devices employed to build an electronic circuit to realize this function are logic gates. These gates are capable of realizing the functions AND, OR, NOT, NAND, and NOR. Table 12.3 is a complete listing of the different gates, their symbols, I/O relationships, and truth tables. Note that this logic function can be realized by an OR operation performed on two components consisting of an AND operation on both A and B as well as B and the complement of C. Thus, the circuit in Figure 12.8 will realize this function.

The gates AND, OR, and NOT represent a complete set, and any logic function can be realized with these three gates. However, both NAND and NOR are also complete as well, and, therefore, we can realize any logic function by employing only NAND or only NOR gates. This latter point is critical and the reason for it is simple. When manufacturers fabricate an electronic chip, it is easier to produce a chip with only one type of device rather than one with multiple devices. Furthermore, field programmable gate arrays (FPGAs) are popular and sold to companies that program the chip to produce the specific circuit they want. If the gate contained AND, OR, and NOT, the logical question would be how many of each and where do we put them on the chip. However, this is not an issue when using only NAND or NOR gates to populate the chip.

It is easy to demonstrate that NAND and NOR each represent a complete set for realizing any logic function. Figure 12.9 shows how to generate the functions AND, OR, and NOT using only NAND gates.

Table 12.3 Logic Gates

AND			OR			NOT	
A —[AND]→ f(A,B)			A —[OR]→ f(A,B)			A —[NOT]→ f(A)	

f(A, B) = AB			**f(A, B) = A + B**			**f(A) = A**	
A	B	f(A,B)	A	B	f(A,B)	A	f(A)
0	0	0	0	0	0	0	1
0	1	0	0	1	1	1	0
1	0	0	1	0	1		
1	1	1	1	1	1		

NAND				NOR			
A —[NAND]→ f(A,B)				A —[NOR]→ f(A,B)			

f(A, B) = AB				**f(A, B) = A + B**			
A	B	AB	f(A,B)	A	B	A + B	f(A,B)
0	0	0	1	0	0	0	1
0	1	0	1	0	1	1	0
1	0	0	1	1	0	1	0
1	1	1	0	1	1	1	0

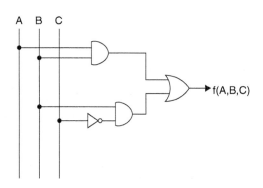

FIGURE 12.8 Logic gate realization of the junction

$$f(A, B, C) = AB + B\overline{C}$$

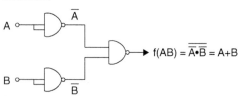

AND GATE

$$f(A,B) = \overline{\overline{AB}} = \overline{\overline{AB}} = AB$$

NOT GATE

$$f(A) = \overline{A \cdot A} = \overline{A}$$

OR GATE

$$f(AB) = \overline{\overline{A} \cdot \overline{B}} = A + B$$

FIGURE 12.9 NAND gate realization of AND, OR, and NOT

Let us generate the logic function $f(A, B, C) = AB + B\overline{C}$ using only NAND gates.

Example 12.12

The circuit shown in Figure 12.10 will generate this function as indicated.

The gates used to realize the logic functions are constructed with transistors, and while both BJTs and MOS devices can be employed, MOS devices are perhaps the most popular, and thus we will confine our discussion to them in the material that follows.

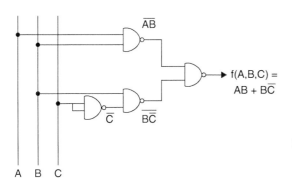

FIGURE 12.10   NAND gate realization of the function

$$f(A, B, C) = AB + B\overline{C}$$

The logic gates described in previous sections can be implemented using circuit networks involving transistors, similar to those discussed in Chapter 11. In Chapter 11, the n-channel MOSFET was discussed in detail and is revisited in this section.

Virtually, all digital circuits operate using the binary logic system. This implies there are two possible states of any input or output, referred to generally as "1" or a "0" (the logic state) or equivalently as a "high" or a "low" (a reference to the relative voltages in an actual circuit). This is in contrast to the amplifier of Chapter 11 where the output voltage varies in proportion to the input; in binary logic circuits, the output voltage has only one of two possible values.

One of the fundamental building blocks of digital circuits is the inverter. To construct a simple inverter circuit, refer to Figure 11.11a – the circuit, and Figure 11.11b – the output characteristic curves of the n-channel MOSFET utilized. These figures are repeated here for easy reference and labeled as Figure 12.11a and 12.11b with some added features to this figure.

The first observation is that if the dc gate voltage is set by the output of a previous stage, resistors R_1 and R_2 can be removed. The input dc voltage to this circuit is provided entirely by the output of the previous stage and will either be a "high" voltage (which we will see is V_{DD}) or a "low" voltage (which we will see is close to zero, but definitely below V_T). The transistor in this circuit will switch from the ohmic region (providing a "low" output voltage) to cutoff (providing a "high" output voltage).

This circuit on the right functions as a digital inverter.

In the previous figure, note that when the input to the circuit is "high" ($V_{GS} = V_{DD}$), the transistor is in saturation (conducting current), and the value of $V_{DS} = V_{LOW}$, where $V_{LOW} < V_T$;

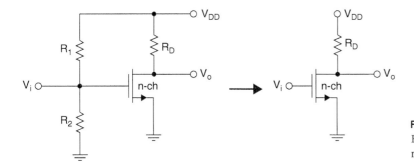

FIGURE 12.11a   Repeat of the circuit of Figure 11.11a and the same circuit with resistors R_1 and R_2 removed

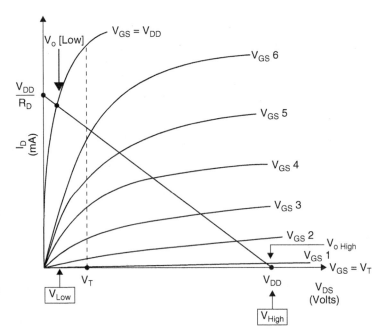

FIGURE 12.11b Repeat of output characteristic curves of Figure 11.11b illustrating that in the inverter circuit of the previous figure, the output voltage exists only at one of the two values, V_{LOW} (below V_T) or V_{HIGH} (V_{DD})

this is a logic "low"; similarly, when the input voltage is "low," the transistor is in cutoff (open circuit) and the value of $V_{DS} = V_o$ is "high" as R_D pulls v_o to V_{DD}. Thus, this inverter circuit *inverts* the logic state (where "1" is defined as V_{HIGH} and "0" is defined as V_{LOW}):

$$V_i = 1 \text{ yields } V_o = 0; \text{ and } V_i = 0 \text{ yields } V_o = 1.$$

NMOS

It can be shown (and it is a good exercise easily done from the output characteristic curves) that if an n-channel MOSFET has its gate connected to its drain so that V_{DS} is always equal to V_{GS}, the device exhibits the V–I curve of a nonlinear resistor. Therefore, since a transistor takes less area on a chip than a resistor, the inverter circuit shown in Figure 12.12a with logic notation and the logic function can be implemented as shown in Figure 12.12b. This is termed NMOS logic. This logic was popular in commercial circuits in the past, because only one type of transistor is required. However, it has a significant disadvantage: High Power Dissipation. When the output is LOW, the circuit is constantly consuming current from V_{DD} to ground.

Using the same approach, a *two-input NMOS NAND gate* is shown in Figure 12.13. The circuit consists of two NMOS transistors in series at the inputs, together with a pull-up "resistor" implemented by biasing an NMOS transistor to act like a resistor.

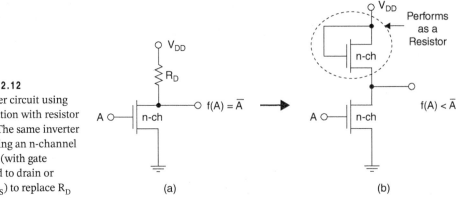

FIGURE 12.12
(a) Inverter circuit using logic notation with resistor load. (b) The same inverter circuit using an n-channel MOSFET (with gate connected to drain or $V_{GS} = V_{DS}$) to replace R_D

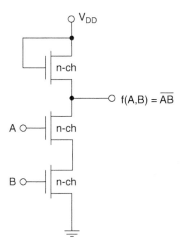

FIGURE 12.13   Circuit for a two-input NMOS NAND gate

This circuit performs as a NAND gate because BOTH input transistors have to be conducting (inputs high) for the output to be connected to ground, pulling the output LOW; otherwise, the connection to ground is broken and the output is HIGH. Stated in logic terms, for A = 1, B = 1 yields an output of 0; otherwise the output is 1; i.e. $f(A, B) = \overline{AB}$.

A truth table expressing this is:

A	B	$f(A, B) = \overline{AB}$
0	0	1
0	1	1
1	0	1
1	1	0

A two-input NMOS NOR gate can be designed using a similar approach as follows. The truth table for a NOR gate, where f(A, B) is the output, is given as follows:

A	B	$f(A, B) = \overline{(A + B)}$
0	0	1
0	1	0
1	0	0
1	1	0

The only set of inputs in which the output is not 0 is the case of A = B = 0. An NMOS circuit that implements this is shown in Figure 12.14 by putting the two input transistors in parallel. In

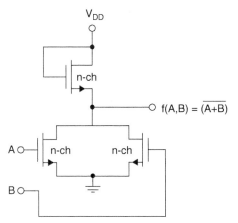

FIGURE 12.14   Circuit for a two-input NMOS NOR gate

the case where EITHER or BOTH of the inputs is "high" at least one transistor will be conducting and pull the output "low"; the only case where the output is "high" occurs when BOTH inputs are "low" and their respective transistors are not conducting. This allows the output node to be pulled "high" by the device biased as a resistor and connected to V_{DD}.

CMOS (COMPLEMENTARY METAL–OXIDE–SEMICONDUCTOR)

CMOS technology dominates most sectors of digital integrated circuits (ICs). It has the potential advantage that the gates do not consume power except when switching states. Power and thermal management are critical in large, dense chips such as microprocessors, controllers, and application-specific ICs (ASICs). Also CMOS can operate faster, and significant technology advances have reduced the area per gate.

CMOS logic gates contain both n-channel MOSFETs and p-channel MOSFETs. The n-channel MOSFET has been discussed in detail in both Chapters 11 and 12. The p-channel MOSFET works on the same basic principle but the polarities are reversed. A p-channel transistor is fabricated by placing a p-type source and drain into an n-type substrate; similar to the n-channel device, an insulating gate oxide is placed between the source and drain, and a conducting gate electrode placed over the oxide spanning the gap between source and drain.

The cross section of a p-channel enhancement MOSFET is shown in Figure 12.15. For the p-channel device to invert the surface and form a p-type conducting channel between the source and drain, negatively charged electrons must be pushed away from the surface region and positive holes attracted to the surface region to form a p-type channel. This requires that the gate voltage be negative with respect to the body and the source (the opposite of an n-channel device). Also, the drain bias is complementary, and the drain is biased at a more negative voltage than the source.

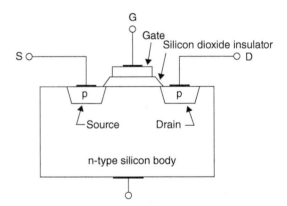

FIGURE 12.15 Cross section of p-channel enhancement mode MOSFET

Therefore, for a p-channel device if $V_{GS} = 0$, the device does not conduct; when the gate is more *negative* than the source (by a voltage exceeding the threshold voltage, $-V_T$), the device conducts current.

The circuit symbols used for a p-channel device mirror that of the n-channel device as illustrated in Figure 11.6 and are illustrated in Figure 12.16(a–c).

Figure 12.17 shows a cross section of how an NMOS and a PMOS transistor are integrated on the same chip. The NMOS device is fabricated directly in the p-substrate as previously described. The PMOS device must be placed in an n-type region, therefore an n-well is fabricated in the substrate, and an MOS device with p-type source and drain can be constructed.

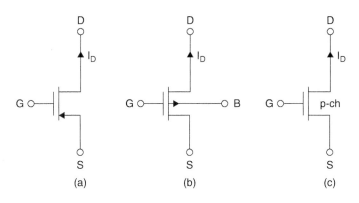

FIGURE 12.16 (a–c) Circuit symbols most commonly used for a p-channel enhancement mode MOSFET

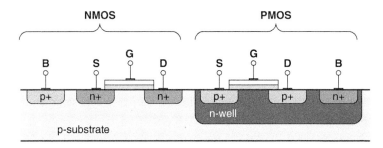

FIGURE 12.17 Cross section of NMOS and PMOS transistors integrated on the same chip

THE CMOS INVERTER

The CMOS inverter is a basic building block of CMOS technology. This section helps explain the multiple advantages of this technology. The ability to fabricate reliably n-channel and p-channel MOSFETs on the same chip was the impetus to giving CMOS a dominant role in modern digital ICs; as noted earlier, this circuit draws no dc current from the power supply source, V_{DD}, except when switching.

Consider the following circuit diagram for a CMOS inverter, as illustrated in Figure 12.18. The circuit contains an n-channel and a p-channel device in series; the input gates of both devices are connected to the input, and the output is at the node where the drains of the two different transistors are connected.

Consider the following conditions:

1. If the input to this circuit A is 0 V (V_{GS} of the n-channel device is 0 V, "low"), this device is not conducting. However, the V_{GS} of the p-channel device equals V_{DD}; therefore it is fully conducting.

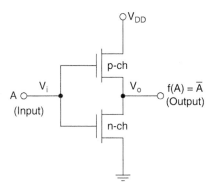

FIGURE 12.18 Schematic diagram of a CMOS inverter circuit

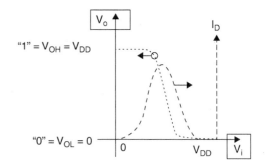

FIGURE 12.19 Voltage transfer characteristics of a CMOS inverter on the left-side scale and current flow on the right-side scale

The result is that the output is connected directly to the supply voltage, V_{DD}, through the conducting p-channel device and the output is "high" at V_{DD}; and there is NO current flow from the source V_{DD} to ground because the n-channel device is not conducting.

2. If the input to this circuit A is V_{DD} volts, "high" (V_{GS} of the p-channel device is 0 V), this device is not conducting. However, the V_{GS} of the n-channel device equals V_{DD}; therefore it is fully conducting.

   The result is that the output is connected directly to ground, through the conducting n-channel device; the p-channel device is not conducting, and the output is "low"; and again there is NO current flow from the source V_{DD} to ground.

Therefore, this circuit operates as an inverter, and in the steady state, where the input is not switching, there is no dc current from the supply, V_{DD} (except for a small amount of leakage current ignored here). The logic levels are V_{DD} and 0 V.

Further insight into the operation of the CMOS inverter can be obtained from the voltage transfer curve, which shows on the horizontal axis the input, v_1, and the output voltage on the vertical axis, v_0.

The voltage transfer characteristics for the CMOS inverter are shown in Figure 12.19. Note that at the extremes or steady state, where the input is either at a "1" or a "0" state, no current flows. The current flow only occurs during the short time interval when the inverter is in transition, in which for a brief period of time both devices are on. The current profile is plotted on the right side of this same figure. This small current pulse averaged over the entire chip is much less total current than if all the gates were all consuming some current.

CMOS NAND GATES AND NOR GATES

The uniqueness of CMOS is that there is always a transistor in the "off" condition in the steady state, which results in no dc current required to sustain the logic states. In this section, we examine the CMOS NAND gate and the CMOS NOR gate, and by comparison with the truth tables for these gates presented in the section on NMOS circuit comparisons, the operation of these circuits can be ascertained.

Note that in the CMOS NAND gate, n-channel devices are in series, analogous to the NMOS circuits.

In the CMOS NOR gate, n-channel devices are placed in parallel, again analogous to the NMOS circuits. The difference is the addition of p-channel devices in positions to replace the load resistances of NMOS; by turning either the p-channel or the n-channel "off" in the static case eliminates the constant need for dc current from the power supply.

Consider the schematic drawing of a two-input CMOS NAND gate, shown in Figure 12.20. For the output to be in the logic "high" state, both n-channel devices must be off or both inputs A and B must be "low" (0 V). In this case, both p-channel devices are "on," pulling the output voltage "high" to V_{DD}.

The truth table for this NAND gate is given on the left side of Table 12.4, and the "on" or "off" state of each transistor in the circuit is shown on the right side. It should be observed that there is no dc path for current in either static logic state; a current pulse only occurs during switching.

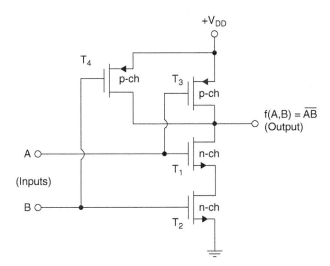

FIGURE 12.20   Schematic drawing for two-input CMOS NAND gate

Table 12.4   Truth Table for CMOS NAND Gate and Status of Each Transistor (on = conducting; off = not conducting)

Input state		f(A,B)	Transistors			
A	B	= $\overline{AB}$	T_1	T_2	T_3	T_4
0	0	1	off	off	on	on
0	1	0	off	on	on	off
1	0	0	on	off	off	on
1	1	0	on	on	off	off

The CMOS NOR gate can be analyzed by a similar process. The schematic of a CMOS NOR gate is shown in Figure 12.21. Generating a truth table for the NOR gate as done above is an excellent exercise to understand the operation of CMOS and verify that this circuit performs as desired.

Now, by combining the basic CMOS logic blocks into more complex forms any logic function can be created. For example, as shown in Figure 12.22, a NAND gate followed by an Inverter, creates the logic AND function. It would be a good exercise to work through this circuit, noting

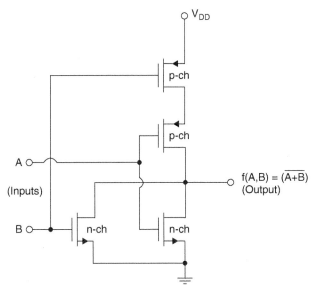

FIGURE 12.21   Schematic drawing of two-input CMOS NOR gate

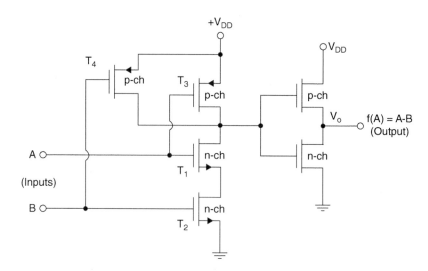

FIGURE 12.22 Schematic drawing for two-input CMOS AND gate.

which transistors are "on" and which are "off" for all the possible input connections; this should result in confirmation that the output is the AND of A and B.

The function $f(A, B, C) = AB + B\overline{C}$ can now be implemented using real hardware, such as CMOS logic. The NAND inverter and three NAND gates shown in Figure 12.10 can be constructed using the CMOS Inverter shown in Figure 12.18 and three CMOS NAND gates shown in Figure 12.20, respectively.

Now we can use all the concepts that we have learned to analyze and design logic circuits. We first examine *combinational logic circuits*, i.e. circuits in which the output is a function of only the current input. Then we examine sequential logic circuits, i.e. circuits in which the output is a function of not only the current input but also prior inputs, and thus sequential logic circuits, in contrast to combinational logic circuits, require the use of memory.

COMBINATIONAL LOGIC CIRCUITS

We now illustrate the techniques involved in designing a combinational logic circuit via some typical examples. The process will normally unfold in the following manner. First a description of the problem is used to develop a truth table to define the input–output relationship; the outputs are then expressed in minterm form, which can be minimized using a K-map to yield a minimum sum of products form, which is finally implemented using NAND gates.

Example 12.13

The input to a logic circuit is a 4-bit binary coded decimal (BCD) number. The circuit has one output line, and the output should be a 1 if the input is either a decimal number 1, 2, 3, or 9. We wish to use NAND gates to design a network that will detect these decimal numbers.

The code representing the relationship between the binary numbers and the decimal equivalent is listed as follows:

Decimal	BCD Code
0	0000
1	0001
2	0010
3	0011
4	0100
5	0101
6	0110
7	0111
8	1000
9	1001

The truth table indicating that the output is a 1 if the input is either a 1, 2, 3, or 9 is shown in Table 12.5. Although we have listed all the decimal numbers and the equivalent code numbers, the four binary digits are also capable of representing the additional numbers 10 through 15. However, these numbers will never occur in a BCD code. Since there is no possibility of the numbers 10 through 15 ever occurring, we don't care whether these numbers are 1 or 0. To indicate that we don't care, we list them as a "d" in the table and we will assign them as a 1 if they aid us in minimizing the function or as a 0 otherwise.

Table 12.5 Truth Table Used in Example 12.13

Input	Output	Minterm Number
ABCD		
0000	0	0
0001	1	1
0010	1	2
0011	1	3
0100	0	4
0101	0	5
0110	0	6
0111	0	7
1000	0	8
1001	1	9
1010	d	10
1011	d	11
1100	d	12
1101	d	13
1110	d	14
1111	d	15

The output function resulting from the truth table is

$$f(A, B, C, D) = \Sigma \text{ minterms } (1, 2, 3, 9)$$

The K-map for this function is shown in Figure 12.23a, where the minterms and don't cares populate the map. Note that we can simplify the function if we assume that minterms 10 and 11 are 1.

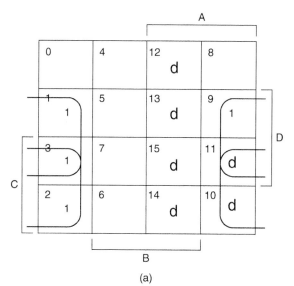

FIGURE 12.23 K-map minimization and realization of the function in Example 12.13

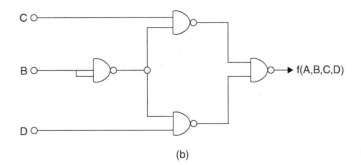

FIGURE 12.23 *(Continued)* (b)

Under this condition, the function reduces to

$$f(A, B, C, D) = \overline{B}C + \overline{B}D$$

The NAND gate realization of this function is shown in Figure 12.23b.

Example 12.14

An alarm system in an industrial plant monitors four features of a process line in which the product ends up in a tank. Line A monitors the flow rate into a tank, line B monitors the pressure in the tank, line C monitors the temperature of the tank, and line D monitors the fluid level in the tank. The system produces a logic value of 1 under the following conditions:

A – the flow rate into the tank exceeds 50 gallons/min

B – the pressure exceeds 500 lb/in²

C – the temperature is above 60°C

D – the fluid level exceeds ¾ of the total tank volume

We wish to design an alarm system that produces a logic 1, to set off an alarm, when either of the following conditions occurs: the flow rate is too fast and the fluid level exceeds ¾ of the total tank volume, or the temperature is below 60°C and the pressure exceeds 500 lb/in².

Given the alarm requirements, the alarm will ring if

$$f(A, B, C, D) = AD + \overline{C}D$$

The NAND gate realization for this alarm circuit is shown in Figure 12.24.

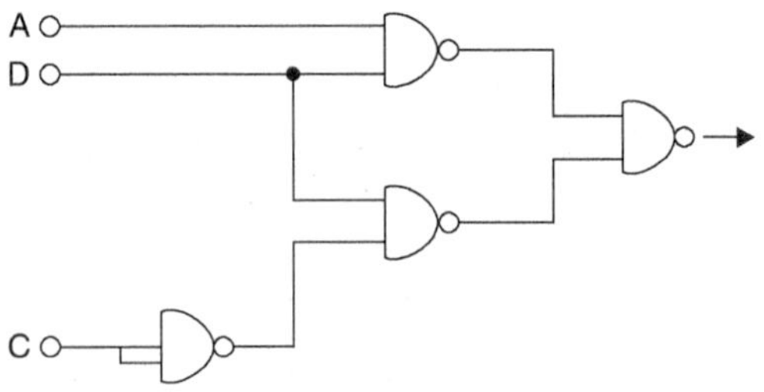

FIGURE 12.24 NAND gate realization of the function
$$f(A, B, C, D) = AD + \overline{C}D$$

We wish to design a multiple-output logic circuit with BCD inputs that (1) detects input digits that are less than 4 and (2) detects input digits greater than 2 and divisible by 2.

Example 12.15

The two logic functions that satisfy the design criteria are as follows:

$$f_1(A, B, C, D) = \text{minterms}(0,1,2,3) + d(10 - 15)$$

$$f_2(A, B, C, D) = \text{minterms}(4,6,8) + d(10 - 15)$$

The K-maps for these functions are shown in Figure 12.25. The minimum forms for these functions are

$$f_1(A, B, C, D) = \overline{A}\,\overline{B}$$

$$f_2(A, B, C, D) = B\overline{D} + A\overline{D}$$

The NAND gate realizations for these two functions are shown in Figure 12.26.

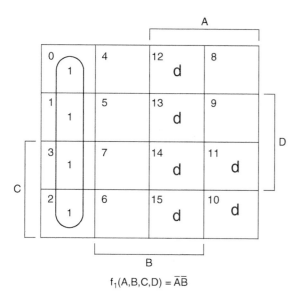

$$f_1(A,B,C,D) = \overline{A}\,\overline{B}$$

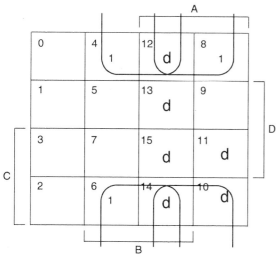

$$f_2(A,B,C,D) = B\overline{D} + A\overline{D}$$

FIGURE 12.25   Functions derived in Example 12.15

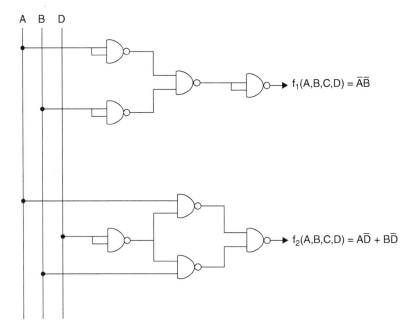

FIGURE 12.26 NAND gate realization for the functions in Example 12.15

We now consider logic circuits that employ memory. These circuits are much more capable than combinational logic circuits because the output is a function of not only the current input but also the current state of the system. For example, an elevator must remember which floor it is on when an input comes in, i.e. does the elevator go up or down in response to the input. With this simple example in mind, we model the sequential circuits using the block diagram shown in Figure 12.27, which clearly indicates the manner in which sequential logic circuits differ from their combinational logic counterpart.

In the model, x_i corresponds to the input, z_i corresponds to the output, y_i corresponds to the present state, and Y_i corresponds to the next state. In essence, the circuit is in a present state when an input occurs. The output is then a function of the input and the present state. In addition, the input and the present state determine the transition that occurs to the next state. In the case of the elevator analogy, the elevator is in its present state on floor A. An input is received requesting the elevator on floor B. The elevator moves to floor B, which then becomes the new present state.

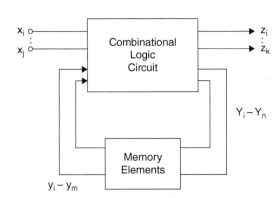

FIGURE 12.27 Block diagram for a sequential circuit

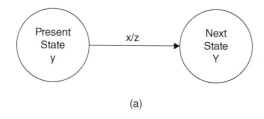

(a)

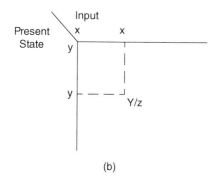

(b)

FIGURE 12.28   State diagram and state table equivalent forms

STATE DIAGRAMS AND STATE TABLES

The two techniques commonly employed to represent the behavior of sequential logic circuits are the state diagram and state table. These two equivalent forms illustrate the relationship among the input, present state, next state, and output in graphical and tabular form. Both diagrams, shown in Figure 12.28, indicate that a circuit in present state y with input x will proceed to next state Y with an output of z.

Let us examine the operation of the sequential circuit shown in both graphical and tabular form in Figure 12.29. Note that the circuit has the following parameters:

Example 12.16

  Inputs: $x = 0$ and $x = 1$
  States: $A = 00$, $B = 01$, $C = 10$, and $D = 11$
  Outputs: $z = 0$ and $z = 1$

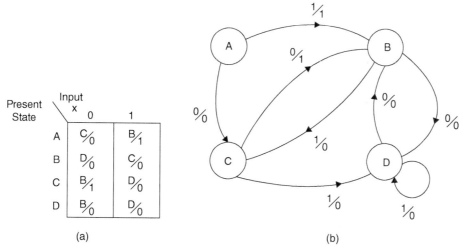

(a)

(b)

FIGURE 12.29   Sequential circuit used in Example 12.16

If we assume that the circuit is initially in state A, then an input of x = 1 will transition the circuit to state B with an output of z = 1. Given an input sequence of x = 011010, the circuit would respond as follows:

Time	Present state	Input	Next state	Output
1	A	0	C	0
2	C	1	D	0
3	D	1	D	0
4	D	0	B	0
5	B	1	C	0
6	C	0	B	1

Therefore, if the circuit is in a present state of A and receives the input string x = 011010, the output would be z = 000001 and the final state would be B.

MEMORY DEVICES

It is important to realize at the outset that sequential circuits operate in a variety of modes. For example, the inputs may be pulses or levels, these pulses or levels may be synchronous or asynchronous, and the memory devices may be clocked or unclocked. We will deal only with the case in which the circuit is under the control of a synchronous clock pulse, which means that the transitions that take place do so only in response to the clock.

The memory devices we will employ are called flip-flops (FFs). There are a variety of these devices, e.g. D or delay FFs, S-R or set–reset FFs, T or trigger FFs, and J-K FFs. We will analyze and design all synchronous sequential circuits using J-K FFs.

The operation of the J-K FF is described in Figure 12.30. Figure 12.30a illustrates the symbol used for the device, its inputs (J and K), its outputs (Q and $\overline{Q}$), and clock signal C. Figure 12.30b, which is a state table, describes the manner in which the device transitions from one state to another. The device is said to be *reset* if the present state is 0 and *set* if the present state is 1. Therefore, if the FF is reset and the input is J = 0 and K = 0, on the clock pulse the FF will reset. Similarly, if the FF is reset and the input is J = 1 and K = 0, on the clock pulse the FF will set. Note that J = 1 tries to set the FF and K = 1 tries to reset the FF and J = 1 and K = 1 toggles the FF, i.e. if it is set, this input will reset it and if it is reset, this input will set it.

Our understanding of combinational logic and the use of memory will now permit us to analyze and design synchronous sequential circuits. Our approach to these subjects will be to illustrate the techniques and salient features via a number of examples.

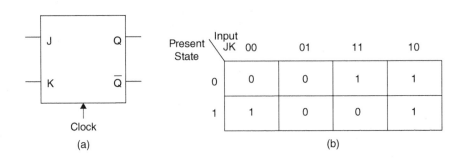

FIGURE 12.30 Symbol and K-map for a J-K FF

ANALYZING SYNCHRONOUS SEQUENTIAL CIRCUITS

There are two approaches to the analysis of synchronous sequential circuits, and we illustrate them both using Example 12.17.

Let us determine the state table that describes the operation of the synchronous sequential circuit shown in Figure 12.31.

Example 12.17

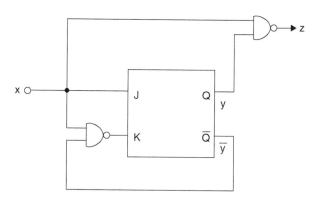

FIGURE 12.31   Synchronous sequential circuit used in Example 12.17

The network has inputs of $x = 0$, 1 and outputs of $z = 0$, 1, and since there is one J-K FF, there are two states, $y = 0$, 1. The state table is shown in Figure 12.32a. The elements in the state table can be determined using two different approaches: (1) an analysis of the next state and output obtained by tracing the signals through the network and determining the next state and output, and (2) using the logic equations for the inputs to the FF and the output.

1. Assuming that the present state is $y = 0$ and the input is $x = 0$, i.e. the upper-left block in the state table, tracing through the circuit we find that $J = 0$, $K = 1$, and $z = 1$. Therefore, the entry in the state table for $y = 0$ and $x = 0$ is $y/z = 0/1$ as indicated in Figure 12.32b. When $y = 0$ and $x = 1$, i.e. the block in the lower left of the state table, we find that $J = 1$, $K = 0$, and $z = 1$.

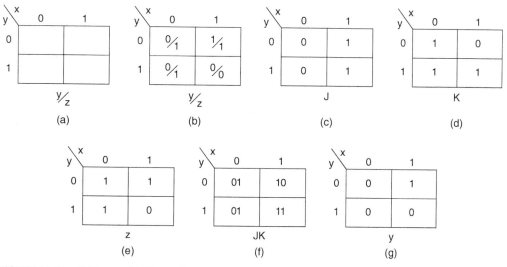

FIGURE 12.32   Tables used in Example 12.17

This J-K combination resets the FF so the entry is 0/1. The two remaining portions of the state table are determined in the same manner. The completed state table in Figure 12.32b describes the operation of the circuit. Thus, this state table describes the input/output sequence for any input string given an initial state.

2. The logic equations that describe the inputs to the FF and the output are

$$J = x$$
$$Y = xy$$
$$z = xy$$

The K-maps for the logic functions are shown in Figure 12.32c–e. The K-maps in Figure12.32c and d can be combined to yield the K-map in Figure 12.32f. Note that this latter table is a listing of the control signals for J and K; therefore they specify the transitions that take place from the present state to next state as a function of the inputs. These transitions are shown in Figure 12.32g. If we now combine the table in Figure 12.32g with that for the output in Figure 12.32e, we will obtain the table shown in Figure 12.32b.

Example 12.18

Let us determine the state table that describes the operation of a synchronous sequential circuit shown in Figure 12.33.

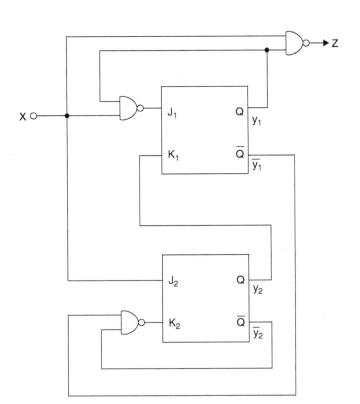

FIGURE 12.33 Synchronous sequential circuit used in Example 12.18

The network has inputs of $x = 0, 1$ and outputs of $z = 0, 1$ and since there are two J-K FFs, there are four states, $y_1 y_2 = 00, 01, 11,$ and 10. The logic equations that describe the inputs to the FFs and the output are

$$J_1 = \overline{x y_1} = \overline{x} + \overline{y_1}$$
$$K_1 = y_2$$
$$J_2 = x$$
$$K_2 = \overline{y_1 y_2} = \overline{y_1} + \overline{y_2}$$
$$z = \overline{x y_1} = \overline{x} + \overline{y_1}$$

The K-maps for these logic functions are shown in Figure 12.34a–e. Combining the maps for J_1 and K_1 and the maps for J_2 and K_2 yields the maps in Figure 12.34f and g, respectively. These two

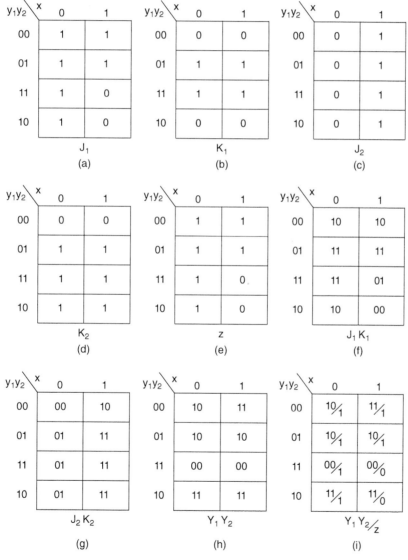

FIGURE 12.34   K-maps for Example 12.18

maps specify the state transition for the two FFs, which results in the table shown in Figure 12.34h. For example, J_1 K_1 control the transition for y_1. In the first row of the table in Figure 12.34h, $y_1 = 0$. The corresponding values for J_1 and K_1 in the block in the table in Figure 12.34f where $x = 0$ and $y_1 y_2 = 00$, are J_1 $K_1 = 10$ and thus y_1 transitions from 0 to 1. In a similar manner, J_2 K_2 control the transition of y_2. In the second row of the table in Figure 12.34h, $y_2 = 1$. The corresponding values for J_2 and K_2 in the block in the table in Figure 12.34g where $x = 0$ and $y_1 y_2 = 01$ are J_2 $K_2 = 01$ and thus y_2 transitions from 1 to 0. The remaining blocks in the table in Figure 12.34h are populated in a similar manner. Then, if the tables in Figure 12.34e and h are combined, the result is the final state table shown in Figure 12.34i, which defines the transitions and the corresponding output for each value of the input given the present state.

DESIGNING SYNCHRONOUS SEQUENTIAL CIRCUITS

The design of synchronous sequential circuits, like most other design problems, begins typically with a specification of the product, i.e. what do you want the resulting circuit to do? In the case of synchronous sequential circuits, such specifications normally result in the development of a state diagram or, equivalently, a state table. Once the specification has been clearly defined in this manner, the design involves transitioning this state diagram/table into an electronic circuit with the smallest number of components. Therefore, the first example on this topic will assume that a state table has been derived and our problem is reduced to turning this state table description into an electronic circuit. Although there are a wide range of problems, the solutions of which are defined by a state diagram, one of the simplest is the detection of a specific bit stream. Thus, our second example will use this problem as an aid in explaining the design process.

Example 12.19

Let us derive the synchronous sequential circuit that will realize the state table shown in Figure 12.35a using clocked J-K FFs and the following state assignment: $A = 00$, $B = 01$, $C = 11$, and $D = 10$.

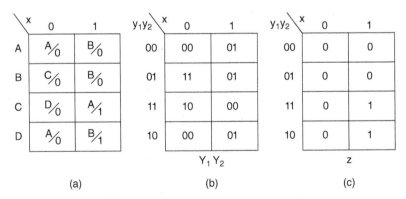

FIGURE 12.35　K-maps for Example 12.19

Since there are four states, two clocked J-K FFs will be required. Using the specified state assignment transforms the state table in Figure 12.35a to that in Figure 12.35b. Figure 12.35b specifies the state transitions, i.e. given a present state y_1 y_2 and the input x, the next state will be Y_1 Y_2. The K-map for the output, z, is shown in Figure 12.35c.

The problem is now reduced to determining the signals on the J and K input lines to effect the state transitions specified in the table in Figure 12.35b. The tables for J_1, K_1, J_2, and K_2 are shown in Figure 12.36. The transition from y_1 to Y_1 for a specified input x is controlled by the J_1 and K_1 lines. In a similar manner, the transition from y_2 to Y_2 for a specified input x is controlled by the J_2 and K_2 lines.

To understand the manner in which the control signals on J and K effect the state transitions, let us consider the first row in the state table in Figure 12.35b. Note that $y_1 = 0$, with both inputs $x = 0$ and $x = 1$, will transition to $Y_1 = 0$. Under this condition, J_1 must be 0 to ensure that we do not transition to 1, but K_1 can be either 0 or 1, i.e. $K_1 = d$ (don't care). Again, consider the first row of the state table in Figure 12.35b and examine the transition of y_2, which is controlled by J_2 and K_2. With $x = 0$, the transition of y_2 from 0 to $Y_2 = 0$ will require $J_2 = 0$, and K_2 can be either 0 or 1, i.e. d. The transition from y_2 to Y_2 with $x = 1$ requires that $J_2 = 1$, but K_2 can be either 0 or 1, i.e. d. The remaining entries in the J and K tables are determined in the same manner.

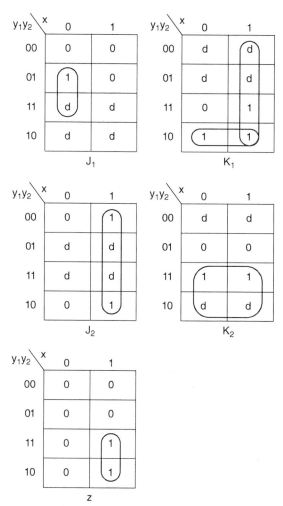

FIGURE 12.36   K-maps for Example 12.19

The K-maps for the FF inputs and the output yield the following logic equations:

$$J_1 = xy_2$$
$$K_1 = x + y_1y_2$$
$$J_2 = x$$
$$K_2 = y_1$$
$$z = xy_1$$

The NAND gate realization of the circuit using clocked J-K FFs is shown in Figure 12.37.

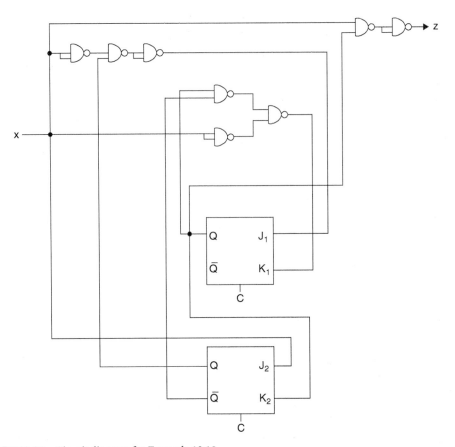

FIGURE 12.37   Circuit diagram for Example 12.19

Example 12.20

In many digital systems, there is a need to detect a specific string of digits. Therefore, let us design a synchronous sequential circuit using clocked J-K FFs with one input and one output that detects the input bit stream 1111 with overlap, i.e. if

$$x = 01111101111$$

then

$$z = 00001100001$$

A state diagram or state table that satisfies this input/output behavior must be developed. A state diagram provides an excellent visual tool for this development. The diagram is constructed as indicated in Figure 12.38. We first assume the circuit is in some starting state A as shown in Figure 12.38a. If the input is a 0, this is not the first element in the desired input stream, so we go back to state A with an output of 0 as we wait for the first element in the desired stream. If the input is a 1, which is the first element in the desired stream, we move to state B and produce an output of 0, as shown in Figure 12.38b. In state B, if the input is a 0, we must return to state A and once again wait for the desired input stream to begin again. However, if the input while in state B is a 1, we move to state C and produce an output of 0, as shown in Figure 12.38c. We repeat this process again in state C as indicated in Figure 12.38d. Now in state D we have received three consecutive 1s. In this state D if the next input is a 0, the string of 1s is not completed, we must move back to state A with an output of 0 and wait for the desired input stream to start again. However, if the input is a 1, this completes the stream of four 1s and we remain in state D and produce an output of 1 as indicated in Figure 12.38e. Note that we remain in state D until an input of 0 occurs in order to satisfy the overlap requirement.

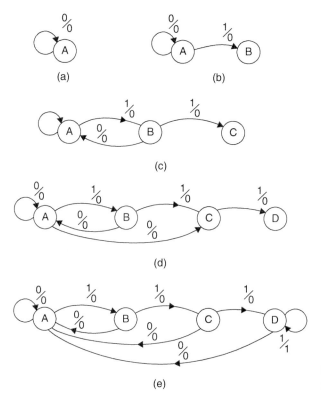

FIGURE 12.38   Diagram development for Example 12.20

Given this state diagram, we can immediately transform this diagram into the state table shown in Figure 12.39a. This table is transformed into the table in Figure 12.39b using the state assignment

$$A = 00$$
$$B = 01$$
$$C = 11$$
$$D = 10$$

x	0	1
A	A/0	B/0
B	A/0	C/0
C	A/0	D/0
D	A/0	D/1

(a)

$y_1 y_2$ \ x	0	1
00	00	01
01	00	11
11	00	10
10	00	10

$Y_1 Y_2$

(b)

FIGURE 12.39   K-maps diagram state assignment for circuit in Example 12.20

Although we have simply assumed that this state assignment did not make any difference, there are procedures for deciding how to make this assignment to minimize the hardware required.

Since the table has four states, two J-K FFs are required. Following the procedure outlined in the previous example, we can determine the K-maps for the J-K inputs and the output as shown in Figure 12.40. The logic equations for the FF inputs and the output are

$$J_1 = x y_2$$
$$K_1 = x$$
$$J_2 = x y_1$$
$$K_2 = x + y_1$$
$$z = x y_1 y_2$$

The actual circuit derived from the logic equations is shown in Figure 12.41.

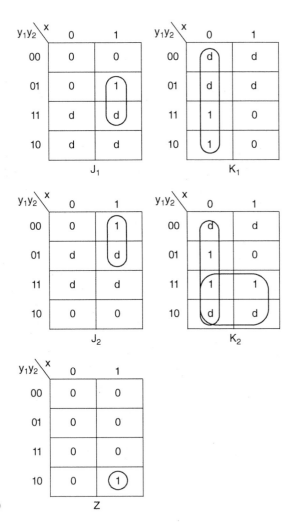

FIGURE 12.40 K-maps used in Example 12.20

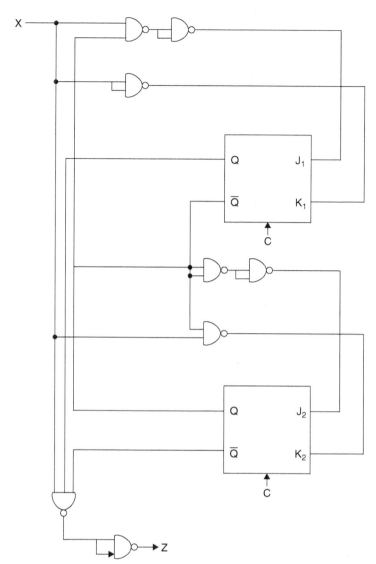

FIGURE 12.41 Circuit developed in Example 12.20

12.1   If A = 1011 and B = 0111, find A + B.

12.2   If A = 1100 and B = 0101, find A + B.

12.3   If A = 1001 and B = 1010, find A + B.

12.4   If A = 1111 and B = 1010, find A + B.

12.5   If A = 10101 and B = 1101, find A + B.

12.6   If A = 1011 and B = 111, find A × B.

12.7   If A = 1100 and B = 0101, find A × B.

12.8 If A = 1001 and B = 1010, find A × B.

12.9 If A = 1111 and B = 1010, find A × B.

12.10 If A = 10101 and B = 1101, find A × B.

12.11 Convert the following numbers in base 2 to base 10:
(a) A = 1011
(b) B = 0111

12.12 Convert the following numbers in base 2 to base 10:
(a) 1100
(b) 101

12.13 Convert the following numbers in base 2 to base 10:
(a) 1001
(b) 1010

12.14 Convert the following numbers in base 2 to base 10:
(a) 1111
(b) 1001

12.15 Convert the following numbers in base 2 to base 10:
(a) 10101
(b) 1101

12.16 Convert the following numbers in base 2 to base 10:
(a) 101011
(b) 110110111

12.17 Convert the following numbers in base 10 to base 2:
(a) 11
(b) 15

12.18 Convert the following numbers in base 10 to base 2:
(a) 13
(b) 21

12.19 Convert the following numbers in base 10 to base 2:
(a) 27
(b) 43

12.20 Convert the following numbers in base 10 to base 2:
(a) 25
(b) 57

12.21 Compute the truth table for the following functions:
(a) $\overline{A} + BC$
(b) $\overline{B} + AC$

12.22 Compute the truth table for the following functions:
(a) $AB + B\overline{C}$
(b) $A\overline{B} + ABC$

12.23 For the NMOS circuit given in Figure P12.23, with one input, A, what is the logic function of the output?

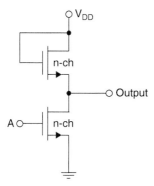

FIGURE P12.23

12.24 For the NMOS circuit in Figure P12.24, with inputs A, B, and C, (a) construct a truth table for this circuit and (b) what is the logic function of the output?

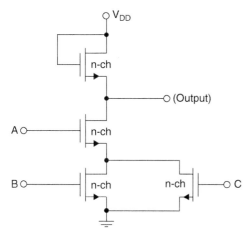

FIGURE P12.24

12.25 (a) Construct the truth table for the NMOS circuit shown in Figure P12.25. (b) What is the name of this logic gate and its logic function?

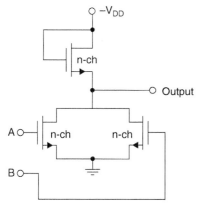

FIGURE P12.25

12.26   (a) Construct the truth table of the four-input circuit shown in Figure P12.26. (b) Using logic gate nomenclature, construct a logic gate configuration that implements the function of this circuit.

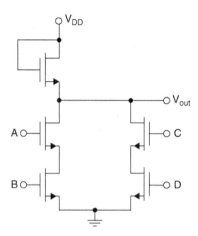

FIGURE P12.26

12.27   Draw the complete circuit diagram, clearly labeling n-channel and p-channel transistors of a CMOS two-input NAND gate.

12.28   Draw the complete circuit diagram, clearly labeling n-channel and p-channel transistors of a CMOS two-input NOR gate.

12.29   Draw a complete circuit diagram, clearly labeling n-channel and p-channel transistors of a three-input CMOS NAND gate.

12.30   (a) Construct a truth table for the circuit shown in Figure P12.30. (b) What logic function does this circuit perform?

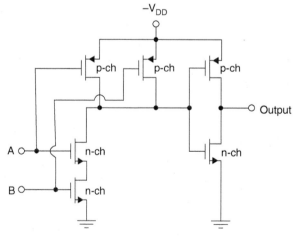

FIGURE P12.30

12.31 Determine the minimum form for the following Boolean functions:
  (a) f(A, B, C) = Sum of minterms (2, 3, 5, 7)
  (b) f(A, B, C) = Sum of minterms (2, 3, 5, 6)

12.32 Determine the minimum form for the following Boolean functions:
  (a) f(A, B, C) = Sum of minterms (1, 2, 5, 6)
  (b) f(A, B, C) = Sum of minterms (0, 2, 4)

12.33 Determine the minimum form for the following Boolean functions:
  (a) f(A, B, C) = Sum of minterms (1, 3, 7)
  (b) f(A, B, C) = Sum of minterms (1, 2, 3, 4, 5)

12.34 Determine the minimum form for the following Boolean functions:
  (a) f(A, B, C, D) = Sum of minterms (0, 4, 5, 6, 7, 14)
  (b) f(A, B, C, D) = Sum of minterms (1, 5, 7, 9, 13, 15)

12.35 Determine the minimum form for the following Boolean functions:
  (a) f(A, B, C, D) = Sum of minterms (1, 3, 4, 6, 9, 11, 12, 14)
  (b) f(A, B, C, C) = Sum of minterms (4, 5, 10, 11, 13, 15)

12.36 Determine the minimum form for the following Boolean functions:
  (a) f(A, B, C, D) = Sum of minterms (0, 2, 6, 7, 8, 10)
  (b) f(A, B, C, D) = Sum of minterms (5, 7, 9, 11, 12, 14)

12.37 Determine the minimum form for the following Boolean functions:
  (a) f(A, B, C, D) = Sum of minterms (1, 7, 9, 13, 15)
  (b) f(A, B, C, D) = Sum of minterms (1, 6, 7, 12, 14, 15)

12.38 Determine the minimum form for the following Boolean functions:
  (a) f(A, B, C, D) = Sum of minterms (3, 6, 7, 11, 13, 15)
  (b) f(A, B, C, D) = Sum of minterms (3, 7, 9, 11, 12, 14)

12.39 Expand the function $f(A, B, C) = \overline{A}C + AC + AB\overline{C}$ into a set of minterms and use the K-map to derive a minimum SOP form for the function.

12.40 Expand the function $f(A, B, C) = \overline{B}CD + \overline{A}BC + ABC$ into a set of minterms and use the K-map to derive a minimum SOP form for the function.

12.41 Design a logic circuit with a BCD input that will detect the decimal numbers 3, 5, and 7. Use NAND gates to produce the design.

12.42 Design a logic circuit with a BCD input that will detect the decimal numbers 3, 4, 6, and 8. Use NAND gates to produce the design.

12.43 Design a logic circuit with a BCD input that will detect the decimal numbers 1, 3, 5, 7 and 9. Use NAND gates to produce the design.

12.44 Design a logic circuit with a BCD input that will detect the decimal numbers 1, 2, 5, and 6. Use NAND gates to produce the design.

12.45 Design a logic circuit with four input lines and a single output line such that the output will be high anytime an even number of inputs greater than 2 are high. Use NAND gates to produce the design.

12.46 Design a logic circuit with a BCD input that produces a logic 1 only when the input decimal number is divisible by 2.

12.47 Design a logic circuit with a BCD input that produces a logic 1 only when the input decimal number is divisible by 4.

12.48 A port on an industrial plant has three output lines that carry information in three parallel bits. The bit pattern should never contain exactly two 1s, which would indicate an error signal. Design a circuit that produces a 1 at the output if this forbidden bit pattern ever occurs.

12.49 Determine the state table for the synchronous sequential circuit shown in Figure P12.49.

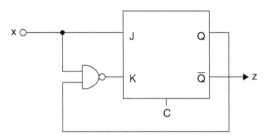

FIGURE P12.49

12.50 Determine the state table for the synchronous sequential circuit shown in Figure P12.50.

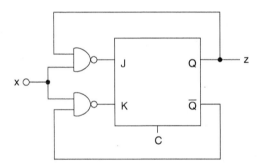

FIGURE P12.50

12.51 Determine the state table for the synchronous sequential circuit shown in Figure P12.51.

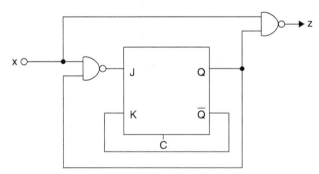

FIGURE P12.51

12.52   Determine the state table for the synchronous sequential circuit shown in Figure P12.52.

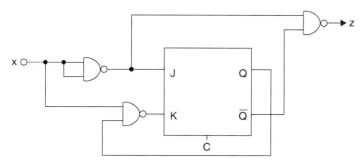

FIGURE P12.52

12.53   Determine the state table for the synchronous sequential circuit shown in Figure P12.53.

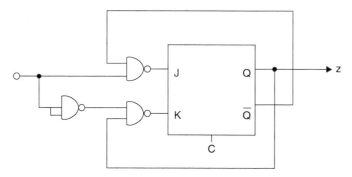

FIGURE P12.53

12.54   Determine the state table for the synchronous sequential circuit shown in Figure P12.54.

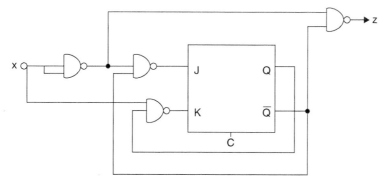

FIGURE P12.54

12.55   Determine the state table for the synchronous sequential circuit shown in Figure P12.55.

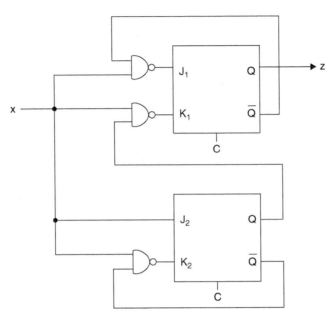

FIGURE P12.55   Clock signal

12.56   Determine the state table for the synchronous sequential circuit shown in Figure P12.56.

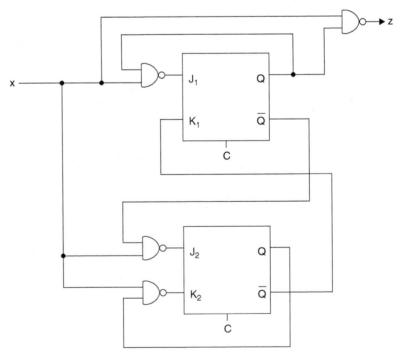

FIGURE P12.56

12.57 Determine the logic equations for a clocked J-K FF circuit that realizes the state table in Figure P12.57, using the state assignment A = 00, B = 01, C = 11, and D = 10.

x	0	1
A	B/0	C/1
B	A/1	C/1
C	D/1	C/1
D	B/0	A/1

FIGURE P12.57

12.58 Determine the logic equations for a clocked J-K FF circuit that realizes the state table in Figure P12.58, using the state assignment A = 00, B = 01, C = 11, and D = 10.

x	0	1
A	A/0	B/0
B	A/0	D/0
C	A/0	C/1
D	A/0	C/0

FIGURE P12.58

12.59 Design a synchronous sequential circuit with clocked J-K FF memory, one input and one output, using NAND gates that detects the input stream 01, i.e.

if
$$x = 01010001$$

then
$$z = 01010001$$

12.60 Design a synchronous sequential circuit with clocked J-K FF memory, one input and one output, using NAND gates that detects the input stream 10, i.e. if

$$x = 0100010$$

then
$$z = 0010001$$

12.61 Design a synchronous sequential circuit with clocked J-K FF memory, one input and one output, using NAND gates that detects the input stream 1001, with overlap i.e.

if
$$x = 1000100100$$
then
$$z = 000100100$$

12.62 Design a synchronous sequential circuit with clocked J-K FF memory, one input and one output, using NAND gates that detects the input stream 0110, with overlap i.e.

if
$$x = 0110110001$$

then
$$z = 0001001000$$

Electrical Measurements and Instrumentation

CHAPTER 13

LEARNING OBJECTIVES

- To learn the different types of devices used to measure voltage, current, and power

- To understand the capability and limitations of measurement devices

- To learn how to condition a signal with amplifiers and filters

- To understand the operation of process control requiring both analog-to-digital (A/D) and digital-to-analog (D/A) conversion

- To be able to understand the basic architecture of a measurement system

DIGITAL MULTIMETERS

BASIC
MEASUREMENT
DEVICES

The very basic measurement quantities are *current, voltage, resistance,* and *power.* Although we studied these quantities earlier, we did not discuss the means by which they are measured. It is this topic that we address in this chapter.

While in the distant past, these measurements were performed by separate instruments, over the years this measurement technology has not only become more sophisticated and smaller through the use of microelectronics technology but now a single instrument performs the job of an ammeter, voltmeter, and Ohmmeter, eliminating the need for multiple devices. For example, the Volt-Ohmmeter (VOM), shown in Figure 13.1, which is a permanent magnet moving coil (PMMC) or D'Arsonval instrument, measures voltage, current, and resistance. All these measurements can be done with a single, handheld digital instrument called a digital multimeter (DMM). A photo of one such instrument is shown in Figure 13.2. A close-up view of the meter dial in Figure 13.3

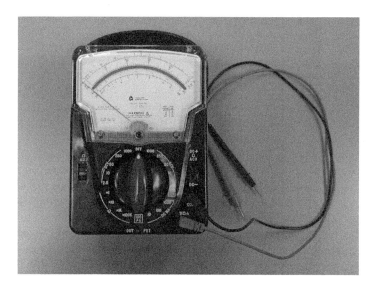

FIGURE 13.1 A Volt-Ohmmeter (VOM). Courtesy Elizabeth Devorie

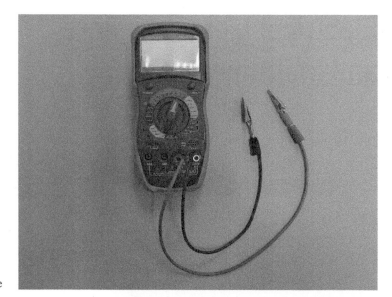

FIGURE 13.2 A digital multimeter (DMM). Courtesy Elizabeth Devorie

FIGURE 13.3 A close-up view of a DMM showing the meters and capability. Courtesy Elizabeth Devorie

indicates the meter's range of capability, e.g. dc and ac currents and voltages, resistance, capacitance, and even a check on npn and pnp transistors.

Although we address this measurement technology at this point in a dc format, we see that the meters are capable of making ac measurements as well. Furthermore, we examine the measurement of ac power later when electric power circuits are addressed.

It is instructive to understand the proper manner in which these measurements should be used. We measure the **voltage** that exists *across* an element as indicated in Figure 13.4. The terminals of the meter are also color coded for polarity identification. The positive terminal is typically in red and the negative terminal in black. Therefore, if the meter reads a positive voltage, then the potential at the red terminal is positive with respect to the black terminal and vice versa.

We measure the **current** *through* an element as shown in Figure 13.5. Note that with this configuration, the current through the meter is the same as that in the element. Once again, if the current enters the red terminal of the meter and exits the black terminal, the meter reading will be positive. A negative meter reading simply means the positive current is entering the black terminal.

Resistance is typically measured as follows. When a resistor is connected into the network, an accurate reading cannot be obtained without essentially disconnecting it from the remainder

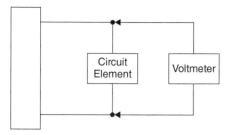

FIGURE 13.4   A voltage measurement

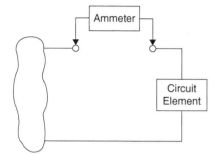

FIGURE 13.5   An ammeter measurement

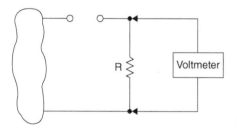

FIGURE 13.6   Resistance measurement

of the circuit and performing the measurement as shown in Figure 13.6. Note that in this measurement situation, the sign (positive/negative) is not an issue.

When we make measurements of voltage and current, we typically assume that our measurements are exact. For this to be the case, the insertion of a meter into the network should be done in such a manner that it does not impact the network in any manner. This implies that the voltmeter has infinite internal resistance (appears as an open circuit) and the ammeter has zero internal resistance (and appears as short). Otherwise, their insertion in the circuit will *load* the network in some manner. The following simple example illustrates this loading effect.

Consider the network shown in Figure 13.7a. Let us insert both an ammeter and voltmeter into the network to illustrate the effect these elements can have on measurements. We assume that the internal resistance of the voltmeter is 1.2 MΩ and the internal resistance of the ammeter is 40 Ω. With neither meter in the network, the current I_{AB} is

$$I_{AB} = 12/(6k + 12k) = 0.6666 \text{ mA}$$

And the voltage V_{CD} is

$$V_{CD} = (12)(12k)/(6k + 12k) = 8.0000 \text{ V}$$

Example 13.1

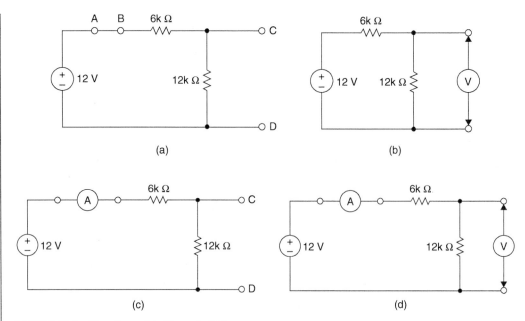

FIGURE 13.7 Circuits used in Example 13.1

When the voltmeter is inserted in the network as shown in Figure 13.7b, then the equivalent resistance R_{CD} is

$$R_{CD} = (12k)(1.2M)/(12k + 1.2M) = 11881.188 \ \Omega$$

Then the voltage V_{CD} is

$$V_{CD} = (12)(11881.188)/(6000 + 11881.188) = 7.973 \ V$$

Therefore, the percent error in the voltmeter reading is

$$\%Error = [(7.973 - 8.000)/8.000](100) = -0.338\%$$

When the ammeter is inserted in the circuit as shown in Figure 13.7c, then the current I_{AB} is

$$I_{AB} = 12/(6000 + 40 + 12000) = 0.6652 \ mA$$

Thus, the percent error in the ammeter reading is

$$\%Error = [(0.6652 - 0.6666)/0.6666](100) = -0.21\%$$

Now, if we insert both the ammeter and the voltmeter in the network as shown in Figure 13.7d, then the current is

$$I_{AB} = 12/(6000 + 40 + 11881.188) = 0.6696 \ mA$$

And thus the percent error in the ammeter reading is

$$\%Error = [(0.6666 - 0.6696)/0.6666](100) = -0.45\%$$

The voltage V_{CD} is

$$V_{CD} = (12)(11881.188)/(6000 + 40 + 11881.188) = 7.956 \text{ V}$$

And the percent error in the voltmeter reading is

$$\%Error = [(7.956 - 8.000)/8.000](100) = -0.55\%$$

There are a number of manufacturers of digital multimeters. The meters have extensive capabilities and can be made small and compact because of the extensive use of microelectronic circuits. For purposes of illustration, we have specified an internal resistance for a multimeter operating as an ammeter in the previous example. However, the manufacturer will typically specify what is called a burden voltage – a typical value of which is 0.3 V. This term represents the maximum voltage developed by the ammeter in the circuit.

Ideally, this burden voltage would be zero so insertion of the ammeter has no effect on the network.

Example 13.2

Consider the network shown in Figure 13.8a, constructed on a breadboard shown in Figure 13.8b. Let us measure the resistors, voltages, and current using a DMM, and then verify the voltage and current measurements using the voltage and resistor values.

The 9 V battery has a measured voltage of 9.51 V (Figure 13.9a).

Resistor R_1 has a measured resistance of 1.002k Ω (Figure 13.9b); resistor R_2 has a measured resistance of 0.996k Ω (Figure 13.9c).

The measured voltages and current defined in Figure 13.8a are as follows:

$$V_{R_1} = 4.72 \text{ V}$$
$$V_{R_2} = -4.67 \text{ V}$$
$$I_S = 4.71 \text{ mA}$$

Measurements for each voltage and current are shown in Figure 13.10.

Note how the terminal on the left of the DMM is connected to the positive terminal and the terminal on the right of the DMM is connected to the negative terminal in Figure 13.10a and Figure 13.10b according to the defined voltages for V_{R1} and V_{R2} in Figure 13.8a. Further, the circuit is broken in Figure 13.10c to place the DMM in series with the circuit, between resistors R_1 and R_2, with the connector in the top of the circuit denotes where the current will flow into the DMM based on the defined clockwise notation of I_S in Figure 13.8a.

Note the circuit can be broken between any two elements in the single-loop circuit to measure the single current flowing.

Using the measured V_S, R_1, and R_2,

$$V_{R_1} = V_S(R_1/(R_1 + R_2)) = 4.77 \text{ V}$$
$$V_{R_2} = -V_S(R_2/(R_1 + R_2)) = -4.74 \text{ V}$$
$$I_S = V_S/(R_1 + R_2) = 4.76 \text{ mA}$$

Although the calculated voltages and current are not equal to the measured quantities, calculations based on the measured V_S, R_1, and R_2 will have less error than calculations based on the ideal circuit values in Figure 13.8a. Further, the measured V_S (Figure 13.9a) neglects any loading effect since the battery was measured before being connected to the breadboard, and losses in the wires are neglected from calculations.

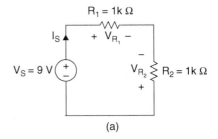

(a)

FIGURE 13.8 Circuit diagram and constructed circuit for Example 13.2. Courtesy Elizabeth Devorie

(b)

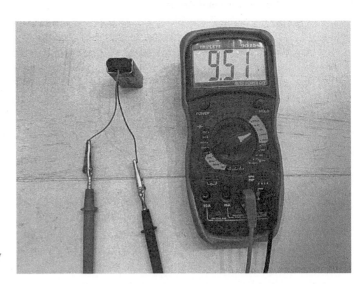

FIGURE 13.9a Measurement of V_S for Example 13.2. Courtesy Elizabeth Devorie

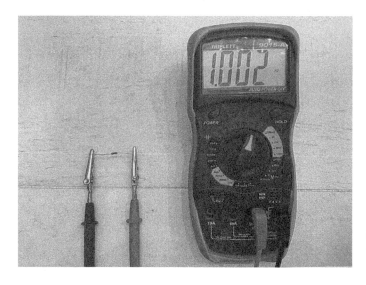

FIGURE 13.9b Measurement of R_1 for Example 13.2. Courtesy Elizabeth Devorie

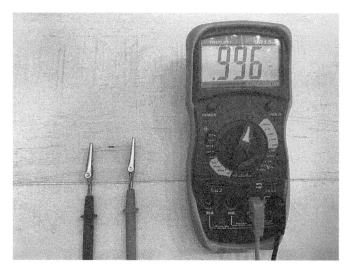

FIGURE 13.9c Measurement of R_2 for Example 13.2. Courtesy Elizabeth Devorie

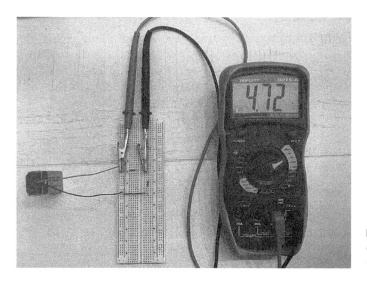

FIGURE 13.10a Measurement of V_{R1} for Example 13.2. Courtesy Elizabeth Devorie

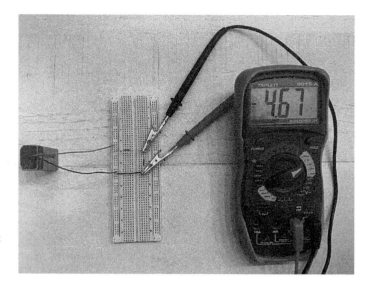

FIGURE 13.10b Measurement of V_{R2} for Example 13.2. Courtesy Elizabeth Devorie

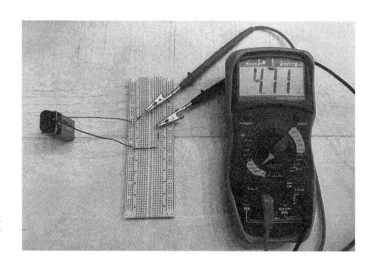

FIGURE 13.10c Measurement of I_S for Example 13.2. Courtesy Elizabeth Devorie

As shown in Example 13.2, multimeters can also be used to measure resistance. These measurements can be made as indicated in Figure 13.9b where a pair of alligator clips are connected to the ends of the resistor. This device provides a good measurement, but it is not very accurate. Since at this point we are very familiar with Ohm's law, it appears that another viable approach would be to simply use a voltmeter and ammeter and use their values to compute the resistance from the expression resistance = voltmeter reading/ammeter reading. If this approach is used, there are two configurations for the measurement (Figure 13.11a and b). However, based on our previous discussion in which we indicated that the internal resistance of the meters will have an effect on the measurements, we note that in Figure 13.11a the voltmeter measurement will include the voltage across the ammeter's internal resistance, and in Figure 13.11b the ammeter measurement will be affected by the current through the voltmeter's internal resistance.

For very accurate resistance measurements, the *Wheatstone Bridge* can be used. This device (see Figure 13.12) employs three precision resistors, R_1, R_2, and a variable resistor, R_3. The unknown resistor is R, and the galvanometer is a very sensitive device used as a null detector. In

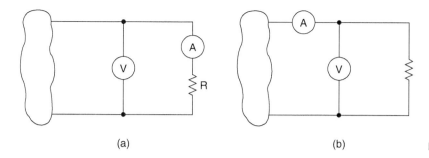

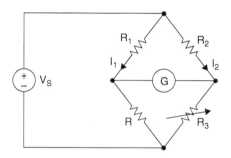

(a)   (b)   **FIGURE 13.11**   Alternative measurements

FIGURE 13.12   A Wheatstone bridge circuit

this configuration, the variable resistor is adjusted until there is no current in the galvanometer, indicating that the bridge is balanced. In this balanced condition, the current I_1 is through R_1 and R, the current I_2 is through R_2 and R_3, the voltage across the galvanometer is zero and there is no current in the device. Therefore, $I_1 R_1 = I_2 R_2$ and $I_1 R_1 = I_2 R_3$. Then,

$$I_1 R_1 / I_1 R = I_2 R_2 / I_2 R_3$$

and

$$R = (R_1 / R_2) R_3$$

It is often convenient to select the ratio R_1 / R_2 to be 0.1, 1.0, 10.0, etc. and in this case the ratio becomes a multiplier.

A Wheatstone bridge is in balance when $R_1 = 2k\ \Omega$, $R_2 = 4k\ \Omega$, and $R_3 = 3k\ \Omega$. Let us determine (a) the value of the unknown resistance, R and (b) the bridge's measurement range if R_3 is adjustable from 1k Ω to 10k Ω.

Example 13.3

(a) $R = (R_1 / R_2) R_3 = (2k/4k)3k = 1.5k\ \Omega$

(b) $R = (R_1 / R_2) R_3 = (2k/4k)1k = 500\ \Omega$

$R = (R_1 / R_2) R_3 = (2k/4k)10k = 5k\ \Omega$

Therefore, the measurement range for the bridge is from 500 to 5k Ω.

To make power measurements, we could employ the multimeter we have already discussed to make ac measurements of current, I rms, and voltage, V rms, the product of which yields the apparent power in kVA. However, to determine the real or average power in watts, we must multiply this apparent power by the power factor as illustrated in Chapter 7. However, this average power can be experimentally measured directly with a device called a wattmeter, an example of which is shown in Figure 13.13 for ac measurements only. As one might expect, the meter contains both current-sensing and voltage-sensing coils, and the meter is designed to time average the product of v(t) and i(t), which yields the average power P = V rms·I rms·cos θ.

FIGURE 13.13   A vintage wattmeter

The circuit symbol for the wattmeter is shown in Figure 13.14. The + − mark on each coil is for polarity identification. The instrument will read upscale when it is connected in the circuit in such a manner that the current enters the + − mark on the current coil, and the + − mark on the voltage coil is connected to the opposite end of the current coil, as shown. As we have indicated earlier when discussing the multimeter, ideally the current coil should have zero impedance and the impedance of the voltage coil should be infinite.

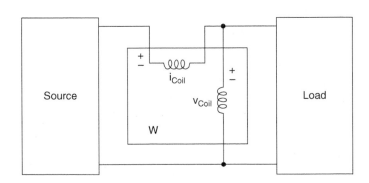

FIGURE 13.14   Use of a wattmeter to measure power

Example 13.4

Consider the circuit shown in Figure 13.15a. We wish to use a wattmeter to determine the average power absorbed by the load consisting of a 10 Ω resistor in parallel with a 25 mH inductor. The wattmeter will be connected in the network as shown in Figure 13.15b. The wattmeter reading is determined as follows.

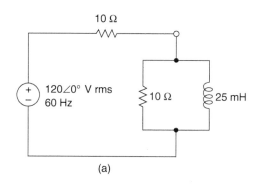

(a)

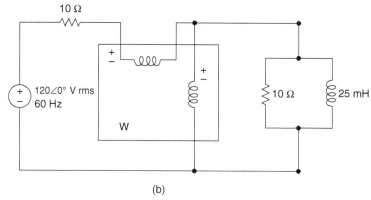

(b)

FIGURE 13.15   A power measurement

The load impedance is

$$\mathbf{Z_{Load}} = 10 // j2\pi(60)(0.025)$$
$$= 94.25\angle 90° / 13.742\angle 43.304°$$
$$= 6.859\angle 46.69° \, \Omega$$

And the total impedance seen by the source is

$$\mathbf{Z_{Total}} = 10 + \mathbf{Z_{Load}}$$
$$= 15.528\angle +18.75° \, \Omega$$

Therefore, the current is

$$\mathbf{I} = 120\angle 0° / 15.528\angle -18.75°$$
$$= 7.728\angle -18.75° \, \text{A rms}$$

The load voltage is then

$$\mathbf{V_{Load}} = \mathbf{I} \, \mathbf{Z_{Load}}$$
$$= (7.728\angle -18.75°)(6.859\angle 46.69°)$$
$$= 53\angle 27.94° \, \text{V rms}$$

The average power, and thus the wattmeter reading, is

$$P = (53)(7.728)\cos(46.69°) = 280.95 \, \text{W}$$

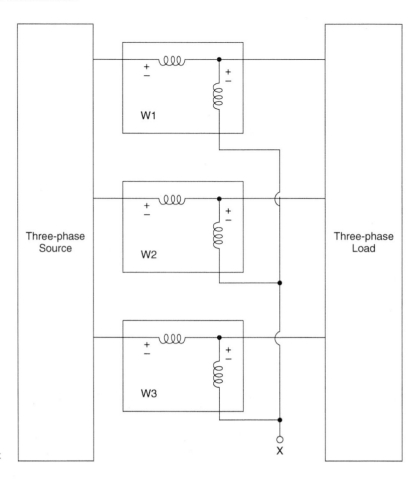

FIGURE 13.16   Three-phase power measurement

These power measurements can be extended to three-phase systems. In a balanced three-phase system, the total power is equal to three times the reading of one wattmeter, and, in a general case, three wattmeters are needed whether the load is connected in wye or delta. The connections for using three wattmeters are shown in Figure 13.16. If we assume an abc sequence of voltages connected in a Y–Y system, the X terminal would be connected to the neutral line. However, the most commonly used technique for three-phase power measurement is the *two-wattmeter method*. In this case, the X point is connected to the b-line as shown in Figure 13.17. When this connection is made, the voltage coil on W2 will read zero, and thus W2 is not needed, i.e. Wl and W3 will measure the total three-phase power. Note that the polarity markings on the current and voltage coils are the same as those used in the single-phase case. Clearly, this two-wattmeter method does not measure the power absorbed by a specific phase but does measure the total average power absorbed by the load, i.e.

$$P_T = P_1 + P_2$$

We can demonstrate the validity of the two-wattmeter method by considering as an example the Y–Y system shown in Figure 13.17. The power absorbed by a single phase will be

$$P_1 = V_{an}I_a \cos(\theta) = V_P I_L \cos(\theta)$$

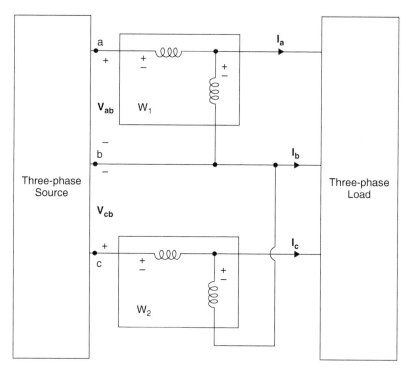

FIGURE 13.17 The two-wattmeter method for power measurement

However, in the two-wattmeter method, the voltage coil measures line voltage. Since $\mathbf{V_{ab}} = \sqrt{3}\,V_P\angle 30°$,

$$P_1 = \sqrt{3}\,V_P I_L \cos(\theta + 30°)$$

and

$$P_2 = \sqrt{3}\,V_P I_L \cos(\theta - 30°)$$

Therefore,

$$P_1 + P_2 = \sqrt{3}\,V_P I_L [\cos(\theta + 30°) + \cos(\theta - 30°)]$$

Then, employing the trigonometric identities

$$\cos(A + B) = \cos A \cos B - \sin A \sin B$$
$$\cos(A - B) = \cos A \cos B + \sin A \sin B$$

yields the expression

$$P_1 + P_2 = 2\sqrt{3}\,V_P I_L \cos(\theta)\cos 30°$$

Since $\cos(30°) = \sqrt{3}/2$

$$P_1 + P_2 = 3 V_P I_L \cos(\theta)$$

This equation is typically written in the form

$$P_T = P_1 + P_2 = \sqrt{3}\,V_L I_L \cos(\theta)$$

since $V_P = V_L / \sqrt{3}$, and the fact that it is the line voltage and line current that are accessible for measurement.

Example 13.5 serves to illustrate the use of the two-wattmeter method for measuring power.

Example 13.5

Let us use the two-wattmeter method to calculate the power absorbed by the load in a balanced three-phase system shown in Figure 13.18. The line voltage and the impedance of the delta are

$$\mathbf{V}_{ab} = 208\angle 0°\text{V rms}$$

$$\mathbf{Z} = 20 + j10\ \Omega$$

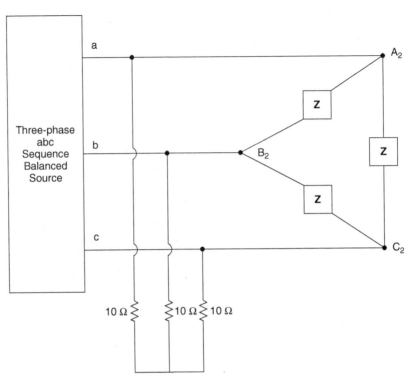

FIGURE 13.18 A three-phase circuit

Given the line voltage, the phase voltage is

$$\mathbf{V}_{an} = [208/\sqrt{3}]\angle -30°\text{V rms}$$

and

$$\mathbf{I}_{aA1} = 120\angle -30°/10 = 12\angle -30°\text{A rms}$$

Since $\mathbf{V}_{ab} = \mathbf{V}_{A2B2}$

$$\mathbf{I}_{A2B2} = 208\angle 0°/(20 + j10)$$
$$= 9.3\angle -26.565°\text{A rms}$$

Then

$$\mathbf{I}_{C2A2} = \mathbf{I}_{A2B2}\angle -240° = 9.3\angle -266.565°\text{A rms}$$

and

$$\mathbf{I}_{aA2} = \mathbf{I}_{A2B2} - \mathbf{I}_{C2A2}$$
$$= 16.11\angle -56.565°\text{A rms}$$

Then, the total line current is

$$\mathbf{I_a} = \mathbf{I_{aA1}} + \mathbf{I_{aA2}}$$
$$= 12\angle-30° + 16.11\angle-56.5650$$
$$= 27.37\angle-45.25°\text{A rms}$$

We now have the data necessary to determine the readings of the two wattmeters.

$$P_1 = \mathbf{V_{ab}I_a}\cos[\theta_v - \theta_i]$$
$$= (208)(27.37)\cos(0 + 45.25°)$$
$$= 4007.93\text{ W}$$

Note that since $\mathbf{V_{BC}} = 208\angle-120°$, then $\mathbf{V_{CB}} = 208\angle-60°$ and therefore

$$P_2 = \mathbf{V_{CB}I_C}\cos[\theta_v - \theta_i]$$
$$= (208)(27.37)\cos[(60° - (-45.25° - 240°))]$$
$$= 5505.35\text{ W}$$

and

$$P_T = P_1 + P_2 = 9513.28\text{ W}$$

Let us compare this result with that obtained via the expression

$$P_T = \sqrt{3}\,V_L I_L\cos[\theta_v - \theta_i]$$
$$= \sqrt{3}\,(208)(27.37)\cos[-30° - (-45.25°)]$$
$$= 9513.28\text{ W}$$

OSCILLOSCOPES

When the signal under investigation varies with time, the oscilloscope is an important instrument for analysis and essentially operates as a voltmeter. The oscilloscope permits us to plot the amplitude of the signal as a function of time. Thus, the waveform can be analyzed to determine its characteristics, such as average value, peak value, and the like. The front panel controls can be adjusted to make the waveform not only fit the screen but also to provide measurements on the raster scale in volts/division for the vertical axis and seconds/division on the horizontal axis.

When the oscilloscope is employed as a measuring device, it is connected in parallel with the element under test in exactly the same mode as that used by a voltmeter. As our earlier example indicated, when connected in this manner loading errors can be introduced. For this reason, the oscilloscope, like the voltmeter, typically has an internal resistance of 1 MΩ or more. When it is necessary to use the device to measure current, a small resistor is inserted in the line and the voltage across this resistor is used with Ohm's law to calculate the current.

A series of screenshots taken from a National Instruments NI ELVIS oscilloscope can be used to illustrate some of the basic features. Figure 13.19 shows that each block on the raster is 1 V and therefore the waveform displayed has a dc level of 2 V. In Figure 13.20, an ac sine wave is shown. Once again, each block in the raster is 1 V. Note that the frequency of the ac signal is 15.46 Hz and the peak-to-peak value is 2.68 V. In Figure 13.21, the scale is changed and each block in the raster is $\frac{1}{2}$ V or 500 mV. Figure 13.22 employs the same ac wave but adds a dc level of 2 V. Figure 13.23 illustrates the same ac signal, but the frequency has been doubled

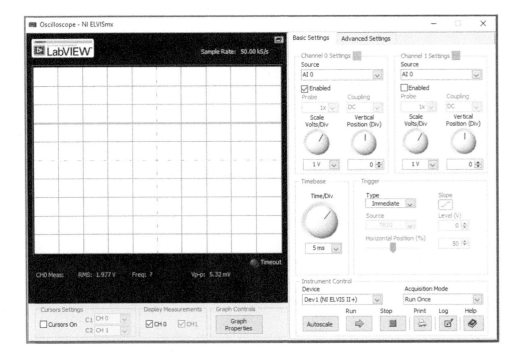

FIGURE 13.19 Display of a 2 V dc signal. Courtesy Elizabeth Devorie

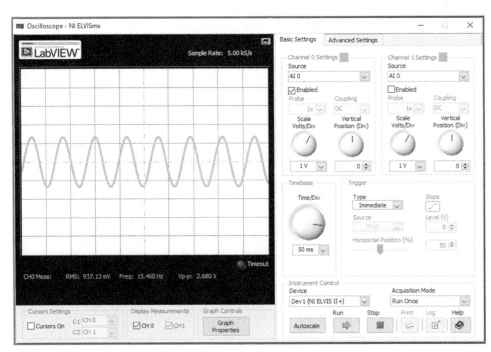

FIGURE 13.20 Display of an ac sine wave with a peak-to-peak value of 2.68 V. Courtesy Elizabeth Devorie

to 30.92 Hz. Figure 13.24 shows the ac signal when the frequency is approximately 10 times the original frequency. Finally, note that the time/division was not changed for any of these figures.

While digital multimeters and oscilloscopes are sufficient for a number of simple measurement applications, as a general rule measurement problems are considerably more complicated and involve a wide spectrum of devices and instruments to not only attain the necessary data but also process the data for a particular application at hand. For these applications, a much more robust system is required.

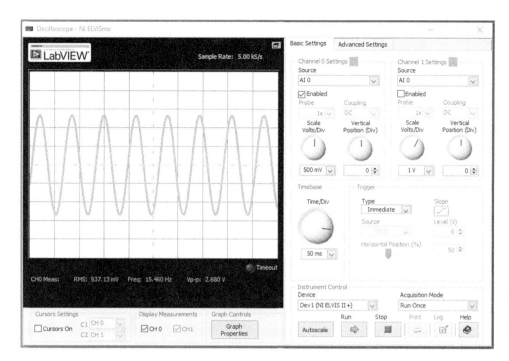

FIGURE 13.21 Display of the ac sine wave in Figure 13.16 with a raster change to $1/2$ V. Courtesy Elizabeth Devorie

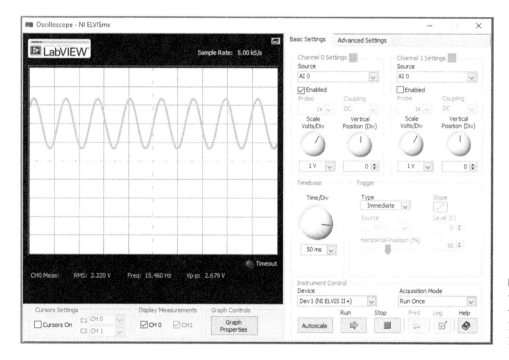

FIGURE 13.22 The ac sine wave in Figures 13.16 and 13.17 with the addition of a 2 V dc level. Courtesy Elizabeth Devorie

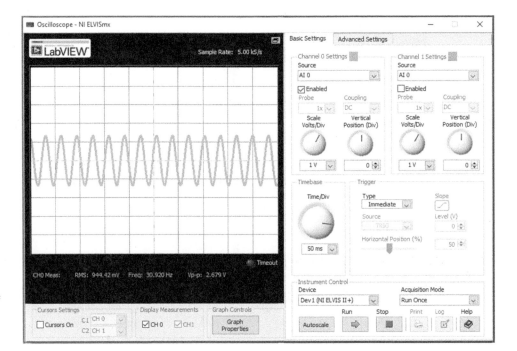

FIGURE 13.23 AC sine wave in Figure 13.20 at double frequency. Courtesy Elizabeth Devorie

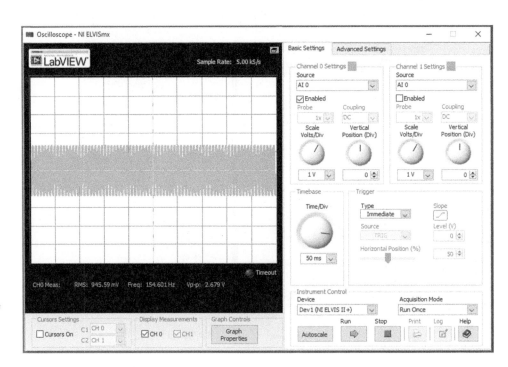

FIGURE 13.24 AC sine wave in Figure 13.20 at 10 times the frequency. Courtesy Elizabeth Devorie

In the development of a properly configured measurement system, there are a whole host of problems that must be considered, e.g. system noise, grounding, capacitive/inductive coupling, to name a few. We ignore these in the following material and assume that the system is operating properly.

A general measurement system is shown in Figure 13.25. The process under investigation could be any type of industrial plant, e.g. chemical, mechanical, etc.

Measurement systems are constructed to obtain data that can be used for adjustment, control and to generally provide the data necessary to make decisions. The adjustment and control are implemented via the feedback path.

SENSORS/TRANSDUCERS

The device that performs the measurement is called a sensor/transducer. The distinction that is typically made between these terms is the following. Sensors convert some physical property into an electrical signal. Transducers convert one type of energy into another. Active sensors normally require a power source, such as a strain gage while passive sensors need no external power source, e.g. a photodiode. Once the distinction is understood, we will simply refer to sensors in the material that follows, and note that their output is typically, although not always, analog. Some of the more common sensors are those that measure acceleration, flow rate, position, pressure, strain, temperature, etc. Many of these sensors have one thing in common – they employ a resistor whose value changes as the quantity being measured changes. For example, a strain gage is essentially a resistor that is attached, perhaps bonded, to a mechanical element, e.g. a beam, and the resistance changes as the beam is flexed and elongated. A thermistor is a resistor whose value changes with temperature. These sensors then become a part of a Wheatstone bridge, and a change in resistance is converted into a change in output voltage.

The Wheatstone bridge circuit is shown in Figure 13.12. It is essentially nothing more than two simple series–parallel paths supplied by a voltage source. The sensor element may consist of one or more of the resistor elements, and balanced bridge circuits are used to measure changes in light intensity, pressure, strain, and the like. Some of the typical sensors found in a wide variety of industrial applications are photo-resistive sensors, e.g. light-dependent resistors (LDRs), position sensors, e.g. potentiometers, thermistors to measure temperature, and piezoelectric sensors to measure strain. Once the sensor has converted the process variable into an electrical signal, then signal conditioning is used to manipulate the signal into a form that is appropriate for display, recording, process control, etc.

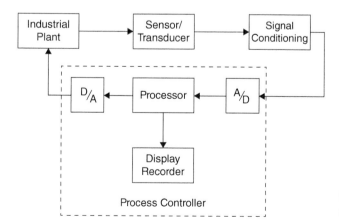

FIGURE 13.25 Measurement/control system

SIGNAL CONDITIONING	Some of the typical signal conditioning functions are amplification, filtering, differentiation, and integration.

AMPLIFICATION

One of the most popular amplifiers used in measurement systems is known as an instrumentation amplifier, which is simply a more sophisticated version of the differential amplifier analyzed in the previous chapter. This amplifier, shown in Figure 13.26, has some important features. The amplifier has a high input resistance, and is used effectively in the measurement of small voltage differences between two points. In addition, since any stray noise will normally be picked up on both inputs, this noise will automatically be canceled since it is common to both inputs. As indicated in the previous chapter, a differential amplifier's ability to cancel common-mode unwanted signals is measured by a term called the common-mode rejection ratio (CMRR), where

$$CMRR = \text{differential-mode gain/common-mode gain}$$

The output of the amplifier can be derived using the techniques employed in the previous chapter. Recall that

$$i_+ = i_- = 0$$
$$v_+ = v_-$$

Therefore, the nodes along the resistor stack indicate that the input voltage v_1 is the same as the voltage between resistor R_1 on top and R_2, etc. Then applying KCL at nodes v_1 and v_2 yield the equations

$$(v_1 - v_0)/R_1 + (v_1 - v_3)/R_2 + (v_1 - v_2)/R_X = 0$$
$$(v_2 - v_3)/R_2 + v_2/R_1 + (v_2 - v_1)/R_X = 0$$

Eliminating v_3 from the two equations and solving for v_0 yields

$$v_0 = [1 + R_1/R_2 + 2R_1/R_X](v_1 - v_2)$$

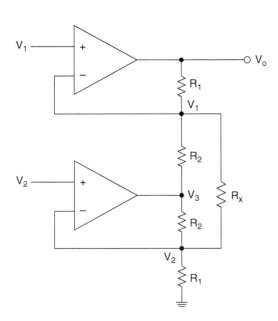

FIGURE 13.26 Instrumentation amplifier

Example 13.6

Let us determine (a) the output voltage V_0 and (b) the voltage V_3 in the network in Figure 13.26 given the following network parameters: $V_1 = 2$ V, $V_2 = 1.8$ V, $R_1 = 120k\ \Omega$, $R_2 = 40k\ \Omega$, and $R_X = 30k\ \Omega$.

(a) The output voltage is

$$V_0 = (1 + 120k/40k + 240k/30k)(2.0 - 1.8)$$
$$= (1 + 3 + 8)(0.2)$$
$$= 2.4\ V$$

(b) The KCL equation at node labeled V_3 is

$$(V_3 - V_1)/R_2 + (V_3 - V_2)/R_2 = 0$$

or

$$V_3 = (V_1 + V_2)/2$$
$$= 1.9\ V$$

FILTERING

There are a wide range of filters that are useful, and often required, in conditioning the signal. Perhaps the signal is corrupted with noise or other unwanted signals are present that provide interference. Regardless of the origin of the problem, filters can, and do, play a fundamental role in measurement systems to eliminate these problems.

Before learning about op amps, we discussed *passive filters* in some detail and showed that with only a few circuit elements we could construct low-pass, high-pass, and bandpass filters. However, at this point, we now have the advantage of knowing about op amps and their salient features. Hence, we are now in a position to consider their use in the design and construction of *active filters*. Although there are many designs for filters that employ op amps, we discuss their use in filter design by presenting a circuit for each of the three types of filters.

The circuit shown in Figure 13.27 is an *active low-pass filter*. One of the interesting properties of this filter is that it exhibits both positive and negative feedback. Rather than the two components used in a simple passive low-pass filter, this filter configuration has four circuit elements and a unity-gain buffer. Applying the ideal op-amp rules to this network, i.e. $v_+ = v_- = v_0$ and $i_+ = 0$, permits us to write the following node equations:

$$[\mathbf{V_i}(j\omega) - \mathbf{V_1}(j\omega)]/R_1 + [\mathbf{V_1}(j\omega) - \mathbf{V_0}(j\omega)]/R_2 + [\mathbf{V_1}(j\omega) - \mathbf{V_0}(j\omega)]/(1/j\omega\ C_1) = 0$$
$$[\mathbf{V_0}(j\omega) - \mathbf{V_1}(j\omega)]/R_2 + \mathbf{V_0}(j\omega)]/(1/j\omega\ C_2) = 0$$

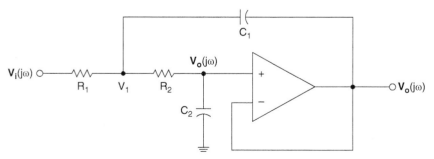

FIGURE 13.27 An active low-pass filter

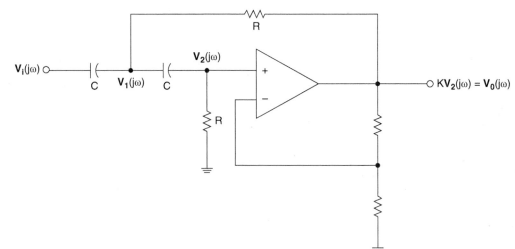

FIGURE 13.28 An active high-pass filter

Solving these equations to obtain the voltage transfer function yields

$$\mathbf{V_0}(j\omega)/\mathbf{V_i}(j\omega) = [1/R_1 R_2 C_1 C_2]/\{(j\omega)^2 + (j\omega)/C_1[1/R_1 + 1/R_2] + 1/R_1 R_2 C_1 C_2\}$$

The circuit configuration shown in Figure 13.28 is an *active high-pass filter*. Once again, we have four filter circuit elements that work in conjunction with a noninverting op amp of gain K. In an effort to simplify the analysis, the filter portion of the circuit uses one value for R and one value for C. Using the properties of the ideal op amp, i.e. $i_+ = 0$, the two node equations for the network are

$$[\mathbf{V_1}(j\omega) - \mathbf{V_i}(j\omega)]/(1/j\omega C) + [\mathbf{V_1}(j\omega) - \mathbf{V_2}(j\omega)]/(1/j\omega C)[\mathbf{V_1}(j\omega) - K\mathbf{V_2}(j\omega)]/R = 0$$
$$[\mathbf{V_2}(j\omega) - \mathbf{V_1}(j\omega)]/(1/j\omega\, C) + \mathbf{V_2}(j\omega)/R = 0$$

Wading through the mathematics yields the transfer function

$$\mathbf{V_0}(j\omega)/\mathbf{V_1}(j\omega) = K(j\omega)^2/[(j\omega)^2 + j\omega(3 - K)/RC + 1/R^2C^2]$$

The quadratic in the denominator indicates that this is a second-order filter. Note that the gain, K, has a dramatic influence on the roots of the denominator polynomial. If K = 3, the filter will oscillate (the response is sinusoidal), and if K > 3, the filter is unstable (the roots lead to a response of the form e^{+xt}). Therefore, in order to have a viable filter, the range for K is between 1 and 3.

One version of an *active bandpass filter* is shown in Figure 13.29, Using the ideal op-amp rules, i.e. $v_+ = v_- = 0$ and $i_- = 0$, we can write the following equations. At the negative input terminal of the op amp,

$$\mathbf{V_1}/(1/j\omega C_1) = -\mathbf{V_0}/R_2$$

or

$$\mathbf{V_1}(j\omega) = -\mathbf{V_0}/j\omega\, CR_2$$

Applying KCL at the node labeled $\mathbf{V_1}$ yields

$$[\mathbf{V_1}(j\omega) - \mathbf{V_i}(j\omega)]/R_1 + [\mathbf{V_1}(j\omega) - \mathbf{V_0}(j\omega)]/(1/j\omega C_2) + \mathbf{V_1}(j\omega)/(1/j\omega C_1) = 0$$

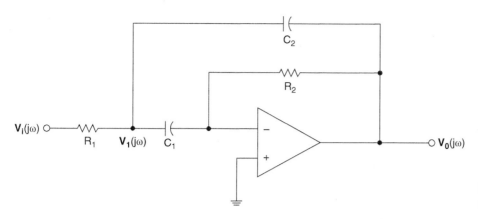

FIGURE 13.29 An active bandpass filter

Combining these two equations yields the transfer function

$$\mathbf{V_0}(j\omega)/\mathbf{V_i}(j\omega) = -(j\omega/R_1C_2)/\{(j\omega)^2 + j\omega(1/R_2C_2 + 1/R_2C_1) + 1/R_1R_2C_1C_2\}$$

Figures 13.30, 13.31, and 13.32 illustrate the advantages of using an op-amp second-order filter rather than a simple passive filter for low-pass, high-pass, and bandpass applications, respectively.

In comparison to the passive filters shown in Chapter 6, these frequency response plots obtained via MATLAB demonstrate tighter control of the response curves, which is achieved with the active filters.

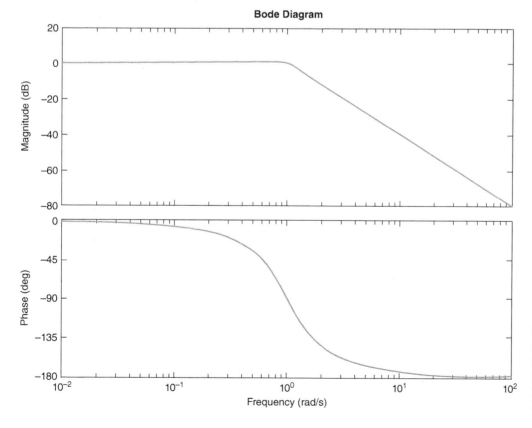

FIGURE 13.30 Op-amp second-order low-pass filter frequency response plot (magnitude and phase). Courtesy of Elizabeth Devore

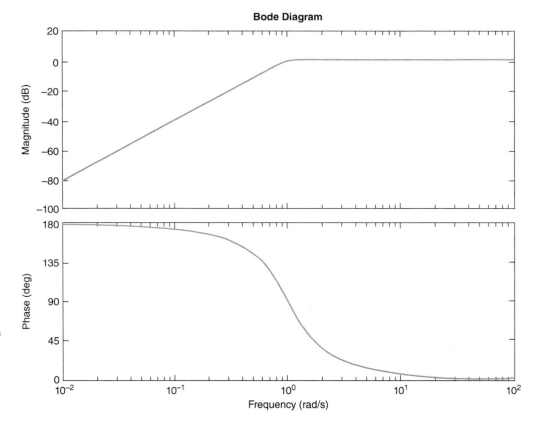

FIGURE 13.31 Op-amp second-order high-pass filter frequency response plot (magnitude and phase). Courtesy of Elizabeth Devore

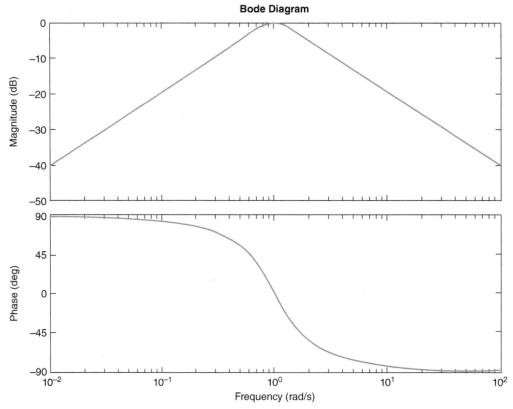

FIGURE 13.32 Op-amp second-order bandpass filter frequency response plot (magnitude and phase). Courtesy of Elizabeth Devore

ANALOG-TO-DIGITAL (A/D) CONVERSION

Given the ubiquitous nature of digital computers and their inherent power for processing signals, it seems only natural to convert any analog signal to digital form so that this power can be brought to bear. Thus, an A/D converter bridges the gap between the analog inputs and the digital processing world, and in doing so it transforms analog information in the form of electrical signals into digital data. Specifically, a signal that is normally a voltage is converted into an n-bit binary number. For example, consider the signal in Figure 13.33 – a continuously varying analog signal with a range from 0 to 3.5 V. A 3-bit A/D converter is used to convert the signal to digital form by quantizing the signal at each time interval into one of the eight quantization levels as illustrated in the figure, i.e. at t = 2 s, the A/D output is 010 and at t = 6 s, the output is 110. As the A/D underestimates and overestimates the actual signal, it creates errors. Note that in this example the 3 bits provides 2^3 or 8 levels of quantization. However, if instead of using 3 bits we had used an 8-bit A/D converter, the range from 0 to 3.5 V would be divided into 2^8 or 256 levels. In this case, the signal could be represented digitally with essentially no quantization error.

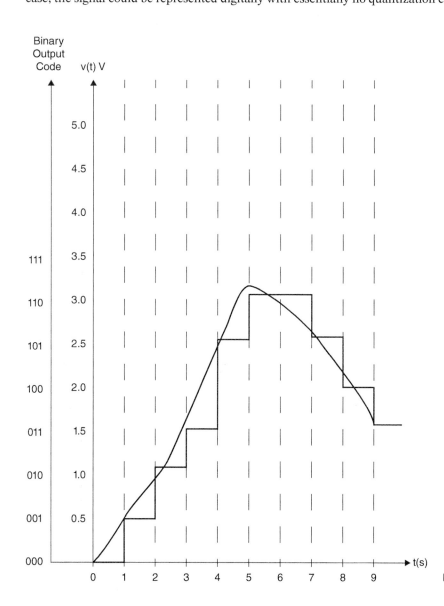

FIGURE 13.33   A/D Converter operation

Example 13.7

If a signal has a range of values from 0 to 6 V, let us determine the resolution that is achieved with 8 bits of quantization.

The number of zones that are achieved with an 8-bit A/D converter is 2^8 or 256 zones. If the signal ranges from 0 to 6 V, then the resolution of the A/D output is

$$\text{Resolution} = 6/256 = 0.02344 \text{ V/zone}$$

An additional issue that comes into play here is the speed at which the signal is sampled for digital encoding. To illustrate the point, consider the signal in Figure 13.34. Note that if the signal is sampled at 1-s intervals, the output of the sampler would indicate that there is no signal. Clearly, this is not the case, and we need a rule that tells us how fast we must sample to ensure that we have completely captured the signal. The Nyquist criterion or theorem provides us with the answer.

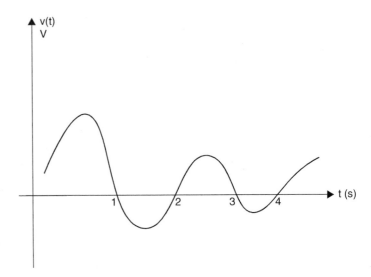

FIGURE 13.34 A poorly sampled signal

Given a complex analog signal, which is typically composed of components of various frequencies, the sampling rate or sampling frequency, i.e. the number of samples per second, must be fast enough to achieve faithful reproduction of the signal. The Nyquist theorem states that if the highest frequency component (in Hertz) of the signal is f_{max}, then the sampling rate, which is typically under the control of a clock, must be at least $2f_{max}$. Thus, we are assured that if we sample the original signal at this rate we can recover this signal when the digitized version is converted back to an analog signal. Clearly, failure to sample fast enough can cause distortion.

Example 13.8

It is estimated that the highest frequency in a control signal is 1 kHz. If the A/D employs 8 bits of quantization, let us determine the sampling interval and the output data rate of the A/D.

Since the highest frequency in the signal is 1 kHz, we must sample at a rate of 2k samples/s. Thus, the sampling interval is $1/2k = 500 \,\mu s$. The output data rate is

$$\text{Data rate} = (2k \text{ samples/s}) (8 \text{ bits/sample}) = 16k \text{ bits/s}$$

Although our purpose here is to introduce the concept of A/D conversion, in practice there are four important types of A/D converters: integrating ADC, successive-approximation ADC, parallel or flash ADC, and switched capacitor converter. Further understanding of this area can be achieved through a search of these specific topics.

PROCESSOR

A processor does the number crunching. The input to the processor is a digital signal derived from the A/D. The processor will be programmed to perform one or more functions that implement the control strategy and perhaps provide for the display and storage of information.

A processor may be a standard digital computer or may be a microprocessor or microcontroller. Although the lines may often blur between microprocessors and microcontrollers, normally fundamental differences exist between them. In general, microprocessors integrate a CPU on a single chip to perform general-purpose applications as opposed to microcontrollers that are employed in dedicated applications. The difference in the manner in which they are used results from the fact that a microprocessor can be expanded at the board level because it typically does not contain RAM, ROM, and I/O connections. A microcontroller, on the other hand, is essentially a minicomputer with a processor, RAM, and I/O all residing on a single chip and, therefore, is essentially a complete system on a chip to perform specialized tasks. For example, modern automobiles use a number of these devices embedded within the automobile's various systems to control a wide spectrum of functions, e.g. engine control and displays.

A typical microcontroller development board for IoT (Internet of Things) applications is shown in Figure 13.35.

The processed data can now be used for control and/or storage. If the data generated, i.e. the control signal, is to be fed back to the industrial process and used for control, its form is normally converted from digital back to analog.

DIGITAL-TO-ANALOG CONVERSION

The device that converts the binary data to an analog voltage (or current) is the D/A converter or DAC. A typical DAC converts binary numbers into a piecewise constant function that is constant over the sampling interval as shown Figure 13.36. This function is then passed through a reconstruction, i.e. low-pass, filter to smooth the staircase-type signal and generate the continuously varying output signal. Once again, while the situation depicted in Figure 13.36 displays a very coarse example to explain the process, note the effect that a much faster sampling rate combined with more bits would produce.

FIGURE 13.35 A typical microcontroller development board for IoT applications. Courtesy Dr. Victor P. Nelson

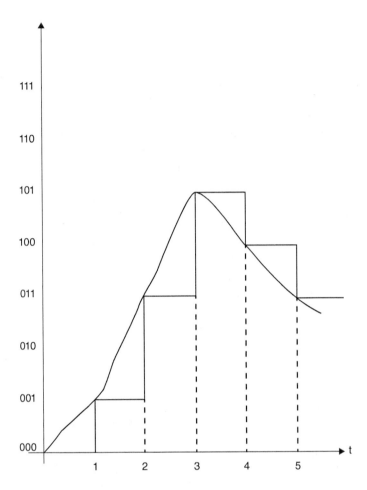

FIGURE 13.36   DAC operation

The actual resolution obtained by the DAC is the number of possible output levels, which is typically defined as the number of bits the DAC employs, i.e. an 8-bit DAC uses 256 levels. The maximum speed at which the DAC can operate and produce the correct output is the maximum sampling rate, and this value is related to the bandwidth of the sampled signal. Since the highest frequency in the signal defines the signal's bandwidth (B), the Nyquist criterion states that the sampling frequency, $f_s > 2B$, where 2B is called the Nyquist rate. If the sampling rate is less than the Nyquist rate, then a phenomenon called *aliasing* occurs, causing distortion, which represents the difference between the signal and its reconstructed function.

The standard approach that is implemented in a DAC is to generate a current, the magnitude of which is proportional to the value of each bit in the digital word and then sum all the currents emanating from the bits that have a logic value of 1. Although many modern DACs are very sophisticated and complicated, the network in Figure 13.37, which consists of binary-weighted resistors connected to a summing op amp, illustrates the essential features that are fundamental to the digital-to-analog conversion process. V_R is a reference voltage. 0 represents an open switch and 1 represents a closed switch. The resistors R_1, R_2, R_3, and R_4, all of which are precision resistors, are binary weighted, and thus the resistance is doubled in the progression from most significant bit (MSB) to least significant bit (LSB) as indicated in the figure, i.e.

$$R_K = 2^n R$$

where R_K is the resistance of the Kth bit and R is the feedback resistance in the summing op amp.

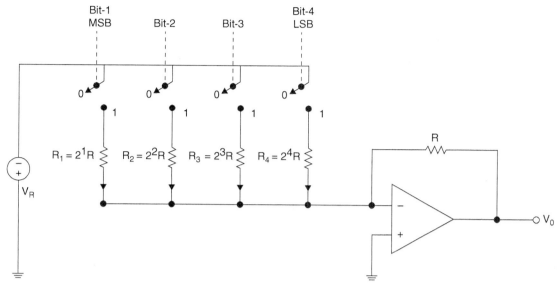

FIGURE 13.37   A simple DAC configuration

When the Kth switch is closed, indicating that the particular bit is logic 1, the current via that path is

$$I_K = V_R/R_K = V_R/2^K R$$

The op-amp output is then

$$V_0 = -R \sum_{K=1}^{n} I_K$$

where the Kth current is summed only if the switch is closed, i.e. logic 1 on the Kth line.

For example, if the digital word in Figure 13.37 was 1111, then the op-amp output would be

$$V_0 = -RV_R[1/2^1 R + 1/2^2 R + 1/2^3 R + 1/2^4 R]$$

And if the digital word was 1010, the output would be

$$V_0 = -RV_R[1/2^1 R + 1/2^3 R]$$

Let us determine the full-scale output voltage for the 4-bit DAC shown in Figure 13.38.

Full-scale output voltage will occur when the input digital signal is 1111. Therefore, under this condition, the output voltage is

$$V_0 = (1k)(5V)[1/2k + 1/4k + 1/8k + 1/16k]$$
$$= 4.69 \text{ V}$$

The output of the DAC, which is an analog signal, can now be used in a feedback loop to correct or adjust the industrial plant/process.

Example 13.9

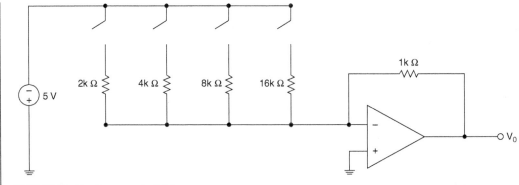

FIGURE 13.38 An example DAC

APPLICATION CIRCUITS

While there are myriad circuits employed in measurement and instrumentation systems, the network shown in Figure 13.39 represents one common configuration. Note that the resistors R_1, R_2, R_3, and R_4 form a bridge circuit. In this format, R_3 is a variable resistor used to balance the bridge. In many cases, the resistor R_1 is the sensor, while in others all the resistors are a part of the sensor. The difference signal obtained as an output of the bridge is then amplified and used as input to the controller.

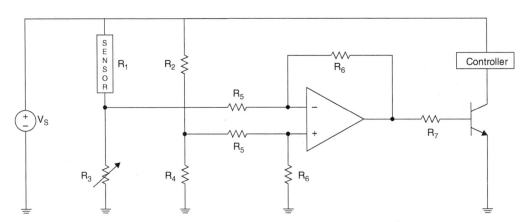

FIGURE 13.39
A common measurement system

Some of the uses of this circuit involve the following. The sensor, R_1, may be a thermistor and the controller could be a heater; the sensor might be an LDR and the controller may be a switch or relay to turn on/off lights, or the sensor might be a pressure-sensing device and the controller may be a pump.

Example 13.10

The pressure sensor bridge circuit, shown in Figure 13.40, uses resistors that are nominally 2k Ω. At maximum pressure, $R_1 = 2.02k \Omega$ and $R_2 = 1.98k \Omega$, i.e. a sensitivity of 10 mV/V. We wish to determine the value of R so the output of the amplifier will read 1 V at maximum pressure.

Using a simple voltage divider

$$V_A = 5[2.02k/(2.02k + 1.98k)] = 2.525 \text{ V}$$
$$V_B = 5[1.98k/(2.02k + 1.98k)] = 2.475 \text{ V}$$

Then $V_A - V_B = 50$ mV

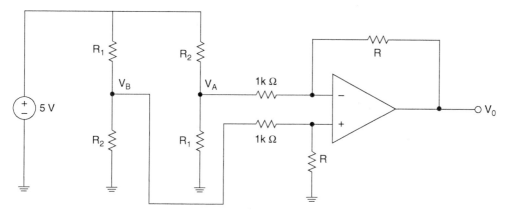

FIGURE 13.40   An example measurement system

The output voltage is

$$V_0 = (R/1k)(0.05) = 1$$

And hence

$$R = 20k\ \Omega$$

Two additional circuits that are often useful are the current-to-voltage converter and the voltage-to-current converter. Once again, there are a variety of configurations for these circuits, but we present only a simple configuration for each.

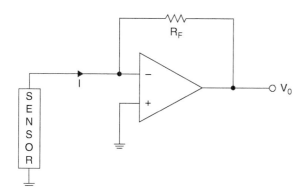

FIGURE 13.41   A current-to-voltage converter

The circuit in Figure 13.41 is a *current-to-voltage converter,* or equivalently a trans-resistance amplifier. Note that KCL at the negative input terminal of the op amp is

$$I + V_0/R_F = 0$$

or

$$V_0 = -R_F I$$

As the equation indicates, R_F is the gain of this amplifier.

Example 13.11

Suppose that the sensor in the network in Figure 13.41 is a photodiode that produces an output in response to light intensity. If it is desired to have a circuit that has a sensitivity of 10 mV/mA, determine the value of R.

The gain of the circuit is a measure of sensitivity; therefore

$$R = V_0/I = 10(10^{-3})/1(10^{-6}) = 10k \; \Omega$$

One possible circuit that implements a *voltage-to-current converter* is shown in Figure 13.42. The output of the unity-gain buffer is V_S, which produces a current I in the transistor circuit, which operates as a high current gain amplifier.

$$V_s = V_0 \text{ and } I = (V_s - V_{BE})/R_E$$

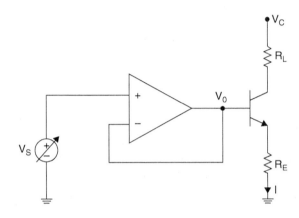

FIGURE 13.42 A voltage-to-current converter

Problems

13.1 If a voltmeter with an internal resistance of 1 MegΩ is connected at the terminals A–B in the network in Figure P13.1 to measure V_0, determine the voltmeter reading.

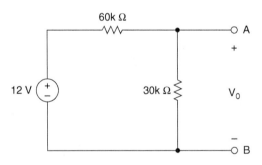

FIGURE P13.1

13.2 Given the data in Problem 13.1, determine the voltmeter reading if the instrument is connected in parallel with the 60k Ω resistor.

13.3 If an ammeter with an internal resistance of 1k Ω is inserted in the circuit in Figure P13.1, determine the meter reading. How does this reading compare with the actual value of the current?

13.4   Given the network in Figure P13.1, with the voltmeter connected across the 30k Ω resistor, determine the reading of an ammeter inserted in series with the 60k Ω resistor if the ammeter's internal resistance is 1k Ω.

13.5   An ammeter and voltmeter are inserted in the circuit as shown in Figure P13.5. If the internal resistance of the ammeter and voltmeter are 2k Ω and 1 Meg Ω, respectively, determine (a) the ammeter reading, (b) the voltmeter reading, and (c) the theoretical values.

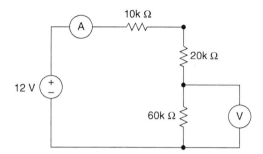

FIGURE P13.5

13.6   If an ammeter with an internal resistance of 100 Ω is inserted in series with the 6k Ω resistor in the network in Figure P13.6, determine the meter reading. How does this value compare to the actual value?

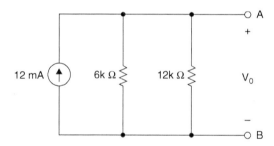

FIGURE P13.6

13.7   If a voltmeter with an internal resistance of 1 MegΩ is connected at terminals A–B in the circuit in Figure P13.6, determine the ammeter reading.

13.8   An ammeter and voltmeter are inserted in a circuit as shown in Figure P13.8. If the internal resistance of the ammeter and voltmeter are 1k Ω and 1 MegΩ, respectively, find (a) the ammeter reading and (b) the voltmeter reading. Which reading yields the largest error?

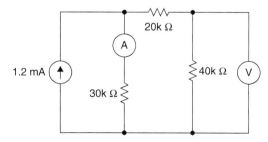

FIGURE P13.8

13.9 If a wattmeter is inserted in the network in Figure P13.9 to measure the average power absorbed by the load, determine the wattmeter reading.

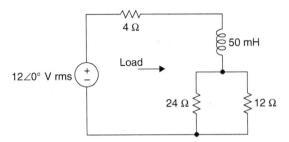

FIGURE P13.9

13.10 If a wattmeter is inserted in the network in Figure P13.10 to measure the average power absorbed by the load, determine the wattmeter reading.

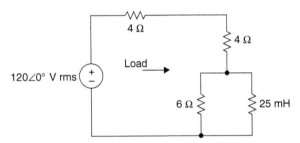

FIGURE P13.10

13.11 Given the three-phase network in Figure P13.11 use two wattmeters to measure the power absorbed by the load. $\mathbf{V_{ab}} = 208\angle30°$V rms and $\mathbf{Z} = 16 + j12\ \Omega$.

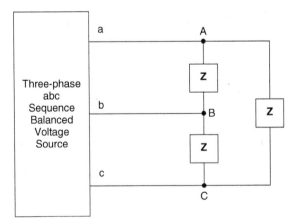

FIGURE P13.11

13.12   Given the three-phase network in Figure P13.12, use two wattmeters to measure the power absorbed by the load. $\mathbf{V}_{ab} = 208\angle0°\,\text{V}$ rms.

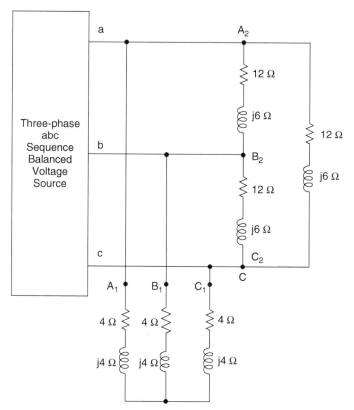

FIGURE P13.12

13.13   Find V_0 in the network in Figure P13.13.

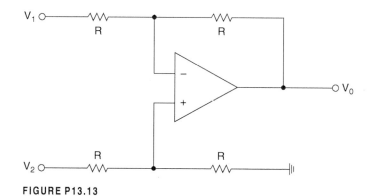

FIGURE P13.13

13.14   Given the amplifier in Figure 13.26, calculate the output voltage if $V_1 = 3$ V, $V_2 = 2.5$ V, $R_1 = 100\text{k}\,\Omega$, $R_2 = 20\text{k}\,\Omega$, and $R_X = 10\text{k}\,\Omega$.

13.15 Find the value of V_3 in the network described in Problem 13.14.

13.16 Determine the equation for V_0 in the network in Figure P13.16.

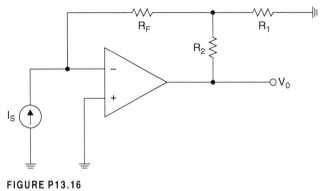

FIGURE P13.16

13.17 Determine the equation for V_0 in the network in Figure P13.17.

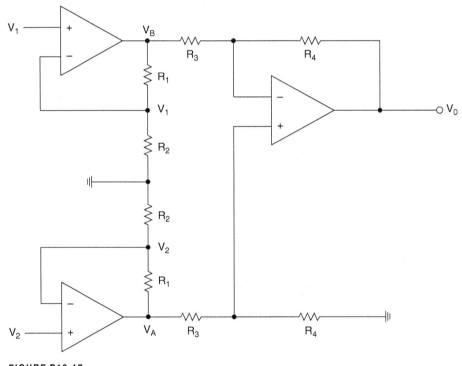

FIGURE P13.17

13.18 Given the instrumentation amplifier in Figure P13.18, determine the equation for V_0.

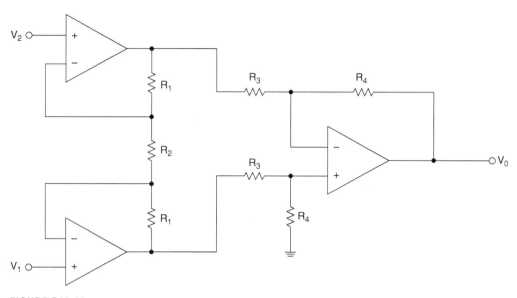

FIGURE P13.18

13.19 Determine the output voltage of the instrumentation amplifier in Figure P13.19.

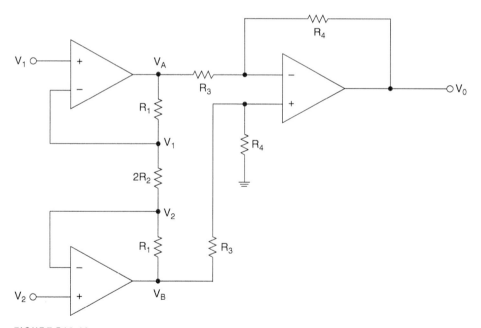

FIGURE P13.19

13.20 The network in Figure P13.20 is an active filter. Determine the transfer function for the circuit and state the type of filter the network represents.

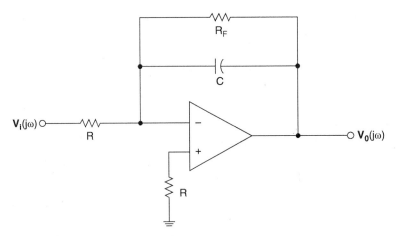

FIGURE P13.20

13.21 The network in Figure P13.21 is an active filter. Determine the transfer function for the circuit and state the type of filter the network represents.

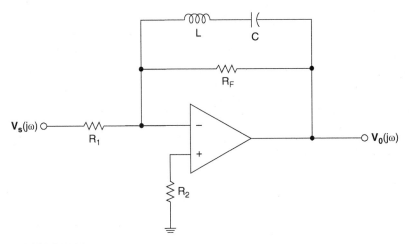

FIGURE P13.21

13.22 An analog signal has a range of 0–2 V. If 10 bits are used to quantize the signal, determine (a) the number of zones of quantization and (b) the resolution achieved.

13.23 An analog signal has a range of 0–3 V. If 6 bits are used to quantize the signal, determine (a) the number of zones of quantization and (b) the resolution achieved.

13.24 The input of an A/D converter is a control signal, the highest frequency of which is 1500 rad/s. If the A/D converter uses 10 bits of quantization, determine (a) the proper sampling rate and (b) the A/D converter's output data rate.

13.25 An A/D converter's input control signal has a frequency range of 0–240 Hz. If the A/D converter uses an 8-bit quantizer, determine (a) the proper sampling frequency, (b) the sampling interval, and (c) the number of zones used to represent the signal.

13.26 If the sinusoidal control signal A cos(2000t) V is the input to an A/D converter that employs 8 bits of quantization, determine (a) the proper sampling rate, (b) the sampling interval, (c) the number of zones employed by the quantizer, and (d) the output data rate of the A/D converter.

13.27 A single-element varying active bridge circuit shown in Figure P13.27 provides a low impedance output for bridge measurement. Determine the equation for the output voltage.

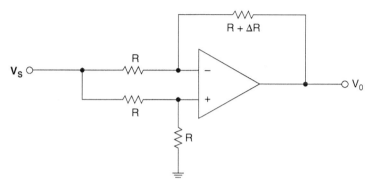

FIGURE P13.27

13.28 A single-element varying bridge circuit used in measurement systems is shown in Figure P13.28. Determine the equation for the output voltage.

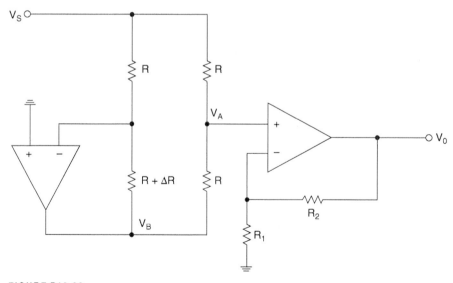

FIGURE P13.28

13.29 A 4-bit DAC is shown in Figure P13.29. Determine the output voltage if the input digital word is 1010.

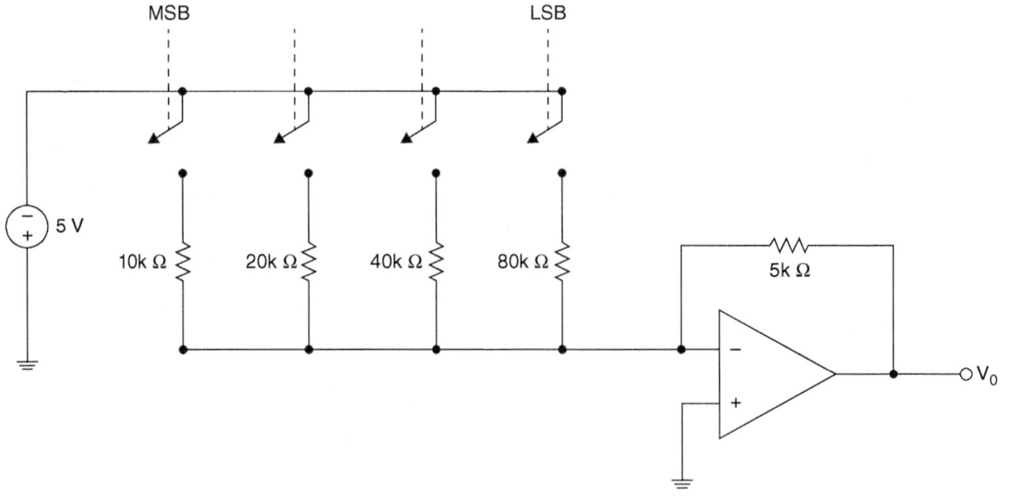

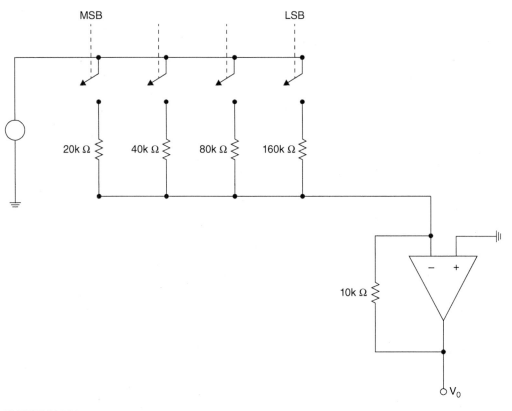

FIGURE P13.29

13.30   A 4-bit DAC is shown in Figure P13.30. Determine the output voltage if the input digital word is 1100.

FIGURE P13.30

DC Machines

CHAPTER 14

LEARNING OBJECTIVES

- To learn that when the machine is operated as a motor, the input is electrical and the output is mechanical

- To learn that when the machine is operated as a generator, the input is mechanical and the output is electrical

- To understand that motor operation is based upon the fact that a force is produced on a current-carrying conductor when moving in a magnetic field

- To understand that generator operation is based upon the fact that a voltage is induced in a conductor when moving in a magnetic field

- To explore the various components of a dc machine and learn their function in machine operation

- To learn how to model dc machine operation and various machine configurations

---

INTRODUCTION

In this chapter, we discuss the fundamentals and some applications of dc machines. First, we describe the basic physical principles that govern their operation. We then show how these concepts can be employed to construct a dc machine. The equivalent circuits for dc motors and generators are presented and analyzed to exhibit some of their operating characteristics. Finally, we describe some applications demonstrating the use of dc machines in industry.

A LINEAR MACHINE

Perhaps the easiest method of describing the fundamentals that govern the operation of a dc machine is to first examine what is called a linear machine. A simple linear machine is shown in Figure 14.1. In this figure, a voltage source is connected through a switch to a pair of electrical conducting rails. A conducting bar, which makes electrical contact with the rails, is free to move along the rails in the x direction. The rails and bar are present in a constant magnetic **B** field that is directed into the page, that is, in the negative z direction. Let us now examine the operation of this machine in three separate time intervals, that is, $t < t_0$, $t = t_0$, and $t > t_0$.

During the time period $t < t_0$, the switch is open. Thus, no current exists in the rails and nothing is happening.

The basic equations that describe the action of a linear machine are as follows.

According to the Lorentz force equation, the vector force on the sliding bar is

$$\mathbf{F} = (\mathbf{i} \times \mathbf{B})\ell \tag{14.1a}$$

where $\times$ represents the *vector cross product,* **F** is measured in the positive x direction, and the vector **i** is measured in the direction of the positive current flow. Since there is no force acting on the bar, the velocity **u** of the bar is zero. Therefore, in view of Faraday's law, we find that

$$\mathbf{v_B} = |(\mathbf{u} \times \mathbf{B})\ell| = 0 \tag{14.1b}$$

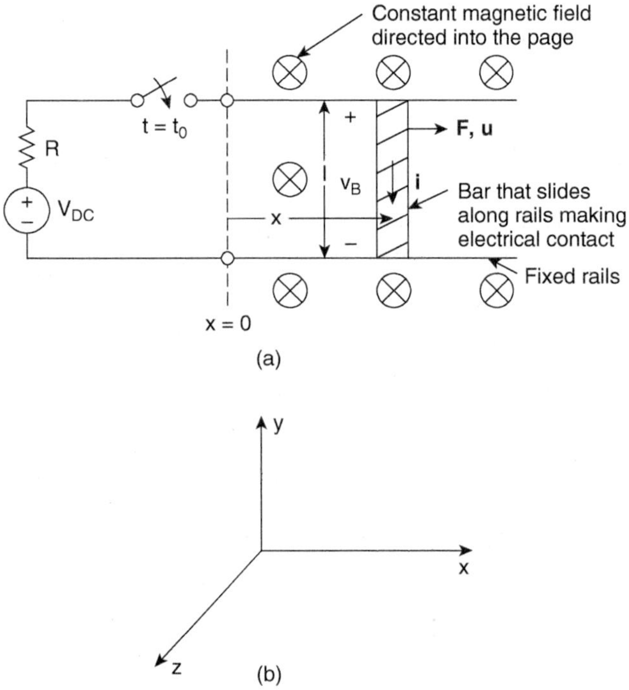

FIGURE 14.1 (a) Linear machine
(b) Coordinates used in discussing
the linear machine

Since **F**, **B**, and **i** (and correspondingly, **u** and **B**) are perpendicular, the scalar versions of
Eqs. (14.1a) and (14.1b) are

$$F = iB\ell \tag{14.2a}$$

and

$$v_B = uB\ell \tag{14.2b}$$

At time $t = t_0$, the switch closes as indicated in Figure 14.2. At that instant, current flows and
$i(t_0) = v_S/R$ and $F = iB\ell$. The bar is not moving, and thus $u = 0$.

This current produces a force (**F**) on the bar. The direction of the force defined by the vector
cross product is obtained using the *right-hand rule,* as illustrated in Figure 14.3. If we rotate the

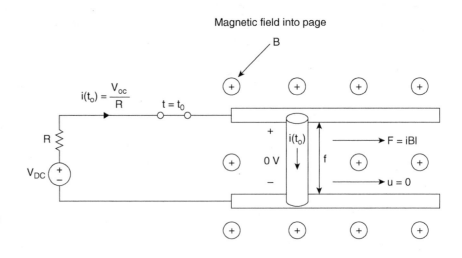

FIGURE 14.2 Linear machine operation
at $t = t_0$

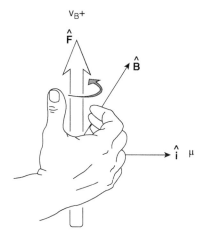

FIGURE 14.3   Illustration of the right-hand rule for determining the direction of **F** and V_B+ (perpendicular to the **i, u,** and **B** plane)

vector **i** into the vector **B**, the force is in the direction as shown. Note that this is the direction of motion of a right-hand screw. The force on the bar causes the bar to accelerate in the +x direction. This is actually the principle behind the rail gun. As the bar gains speed, the voltage across the bar begins to increase in accordance with the expression in Eq. (14.2). The polarity of the induced voltage V_B is obtained by the right-hand rule according to which the vector cross product points to the positive terminal.

The time interval from t_0 to steady state, i.e. $t_0 < t < t_{SS}$, is illustrated in Figure 14.4. In this time interval, the magnitude of the current is given by the expression

$$i(t) = [v_S - v_B(t)]/R \qquad (14.3)$$

and the bar continues to accelerate until

$$v_B(t) = uB\ell = v_S \quad \text{and} \quad u = u_0 = \frac{v_S}{B\ell}$$

When the operation reaches steady state, i.e. $t = t_{SS}, v_B(t) = v_S$ and $u = v_S/(Bl)$. At this point, $i(t) = 0$ and $F = 0$ N as shown in Figure 14.5. Since the current is zero, the force is zero, the bar moves at a constant speed and the machine is in an equilibrium state. In this analysis, it is assumed that the mechanical losses, e.g. friction, are negligible. Otherwise, a nonzero current

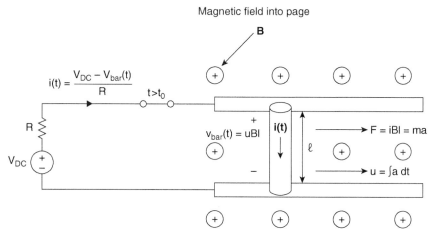

FIGURE 14.4   Machine operation $t_0 < t < t_{SS}$

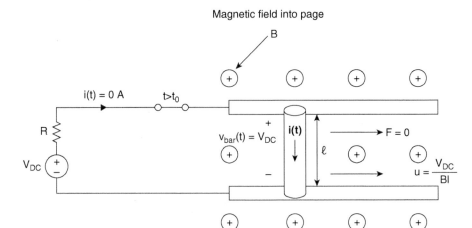

FIGURE 14.5 Machine operation at $t = t_{ss}$

would have to flow in order to produce the force necessary to overcome the mechanical losses. This conversion of energy from electrical to mechanical is the action of a *motor*.

Now if $v_B(t)$ is greater than v_S, the direction of the current is reversed. Using the Lorentz force equation, we find that reversing the direction of the current also reverses the direction of the force on the bar. Since the bar tries to move in the negative x direction, we must apply force in the positive x direction in order to keep the bar moving in this direction at a constant speed, which is greater than the equilibrium speed. The application of this external force produces a voltage at the input terminals, and, therefore, in this mode the linear machine acts like a *generator*.

Note that the key factor that determines whether the machine operates as a motor or generator is the velocity of the bar with respect to the equilibrium speed.

That is,

$$u < u_0 - \text{motor operation}$$
$$u > u_0 - \text{generator operation}$$

A SIMPLE ROTATING MACHINE

Consider the rotating loop of wire shown in Figure 14.6a. The loop rotates in a counterclockwise direction around the z axis and is immersed in a constant magnetic **B** field that is directed along the negative x axis. θ is used to measure the angular position of the loop and is positive in the counterclockwise direction. In addition, we define $\theta = 0$ when the rotating loop lies in the xz plane.

With reference to Figure 14.6a, let us consider the conductor ab, that is, the top side of the rectangular loop abcd. A two-dimensional "free body diagram" of the conductor immersed in the **B** field is shown in Figure 14.6b. The magnitude of the tangential velocity of the conductor $\mathbf{u}_{tan}$ is $r\omega$, where r is the radius of the loop and ω is the angular velocity. The induced voltage along the conductor ab, which we will call e_{ab}, is then

$$e_{ab} = |(\mathbf{u}_{tan} \times \mathbf{B})\ell| \tag{14.4}$$

The velocity $\mathbf{u}_{tan}$ can be split into two components: one tangential to the **B** field and one perpendicular to it. The cross product of the component of $\mathbf{u}_{tan}$ along the **B** field, with the **B** field, is zero. However, the cross product of the velocity component perpendicular to the **B** field with the **B** field produces an induced voltage (out of the page), as shown in Figure 14.6c. If the **B** field is constant, then, as shown in Figure 14.6b, Eq. (14.4) can be expanded as

$$e_{ab} = (r\omega \cos\theta)B\ell \tag{14.5}$$

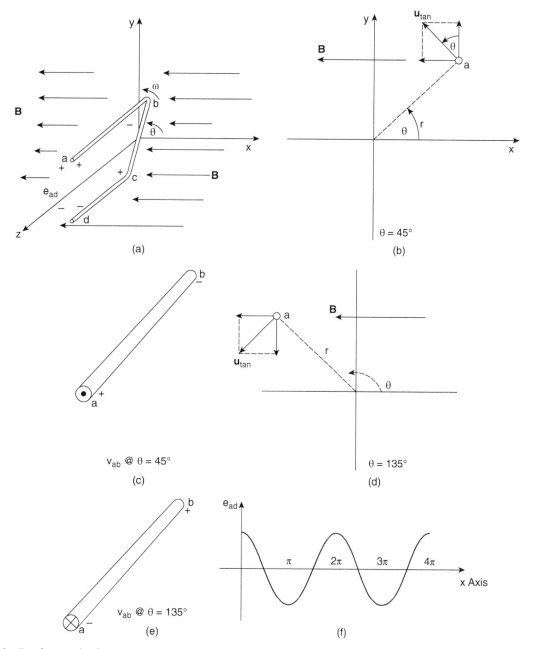

FIGURE 14.6   Fundamentals of a simple rotating machine

Suppose now that the conductor ab is in the position shown in Figure 14.6d. Once again, only the velocity component perpendicular to the **B** field yields a nonzero cross product. However, in this case, the cross product produces an induced voltage (into the page), as shown in Figure 14.6e. A similar argument follows for the conductor cd and hence

$$e_{ad} = e_{ab} + e_{cd}$$
$$= 2Br\ell\omega\,\cos\theta \qquad (14.6)$$

Note that the voltage e_{ad} is a maximum at $\theta = 0°$. Furthermore, the analysis illustrates that the induced voltage as a function of the angle θ is of the form shown in Figure 14.6f.

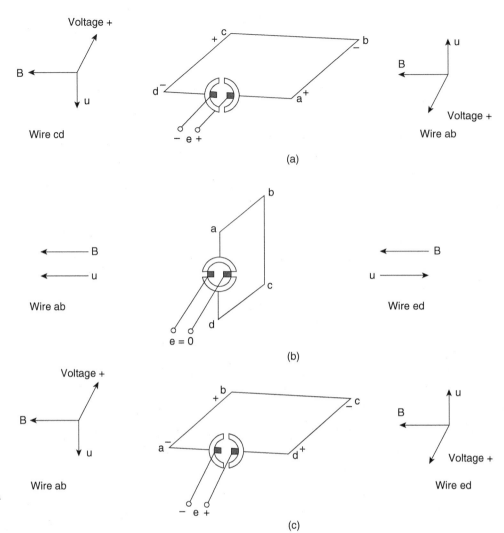

FIGURE 14.7   Demonstration of commutator action for a single loop

Now suppose that our loop of wire abcd in Figure 14.6a is connected to what is called a segmented ring, which is composed of two semicircular pieces of a metal, as shown in Figure 14.7. These segments are in constant contact with *brushes*, which are the connection points for the loop voltage. As the loop rotates, the segments slide under the brushes. This mechanism is called a *commutator*.

This commutator is essentially a mechanical switch that reverses the direction of the currents and fluxes so that the magnetic field of the armature currents is stationary in space while the armature is rotating. The result is the production of a net torque in one direction.

When the loop is in the position shown in Figure 14.7a, the voltage e is positive and decreases as the loop rotates to the position shown in Figure 14.7b. When the loop is in the position shown in Figure 14.7b, note that the loop voltage is zero. As the loop rotates beyond the position shown in Figure 14.7b, the voltage e is positive and increases as the loop rotates to the position shown in Figure 14.7c. Therefore, while the voltage between the commutator segments, e_{ad}, is as shown in Figure 14.8a, the voltage at the brushes, e, is as shown in Figure 14.8b. Note that this voltage shown in Figure 14.8b is a rectified version of the voltage shown in Figure 14.8a.

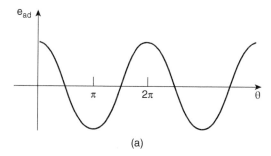

(a)

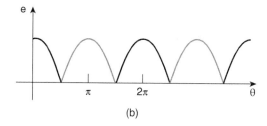

(b)

FIGURE 14.8 (a) Loop voltage and (b) brush voltage for the rotating wire in Figure 14.7

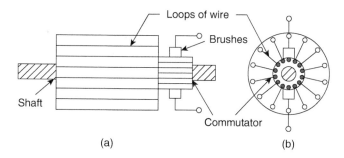

(a)   (b)

FIGURE 14.9 Multiple loops and commutator sections built on a shaft

The previous analysis illustrates the basic principles of a rotating machine. However, in an actual machine, there are numerous coils of wire and commutator sections, as shown in Figure 14.9.

Also, the windings are interconnected in a much more complicated manner and are referred to as the armature windings. Both the armature winding and the commutator are mounted on a structure called the *armature* or *rotor*, as shown in Figure 14.9. The brushes are mounted on a stationary (*stator*) frame, which encloses this rotating structure and contains the items necessary to construct the B field. A cutaway version of a dc generator, which illustrates the internal components inside the physical device, case is shown in Figure 14.10.

The terminal voltage for a generator will resemble that shown in Figure 14.11, which when smoothed will yield a constant dc voltage. It is important to note that while the geometry of the coils and commutator are represented as shown in Figure 14.9, the actual electrical connections are more complex.

At this point, let us try to relate the concepts we have just discussed to an actual machine. The diagram in Figure 14.12a illustrates the basic design of a *dc machine*. For simplicity, we assume that the rotor has a single coil (loop), as shown in Figure 14.12a and b. The rotor and the two field poles that surround it are made of iron. The voltage V_f establishes the current I_f. Because of Ampere's

THE BASIC DC MACHINE

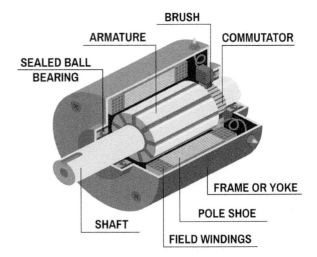

FIGURE 14.10 Cutaway illustration of a dc generator (sivvector/Adobe Stock Photos)

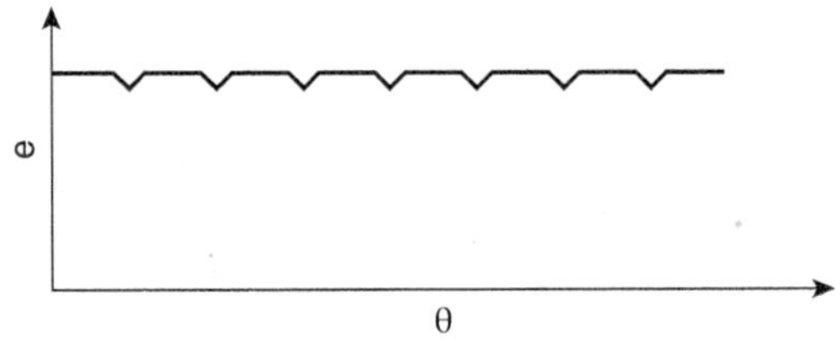

FIGURE 14.11 Terminal voltage of a rotating machine with multiple loops and commutator sections

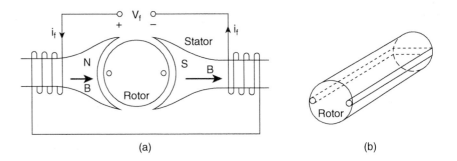

FIGURE 14.12 (a) A basic dc machine (b) Rotor displaying a single coil

rule, this current creates a constant magnetic field, as shown in Figure 14.12a. Figure 14.13 indicates that flux lines of the magnetic field are perpendicular to the rotor at every point except in the two small gaps where the rotor is not covered by a field pole. The flux will follow the path of least reluctance, crossing the air gap approximately radially. This path is the shortest possible distance from one piece of iron to another through the least amount of air. Therefore, the B field is essentially always perpendicular to the velocity vectors of the loop of wire except in the interpolar regions.

Note that the basic dc machine we have described satisfies the conditions that the conducting loop rotates in a constant magnetic field in such a way that the conductor's velocity vector is always perpendicular to the field except in the interpolar regions. The use of multiple conducting loops and commutator sections will then generate a voltage at the brushes, which is of the form shown in Figure 14.11.

Thus far we have described the basics features of a *dc machine*. As noted, the machine can be operated either as a motor or a generator. In the *motor mode*, the input is electrical power and

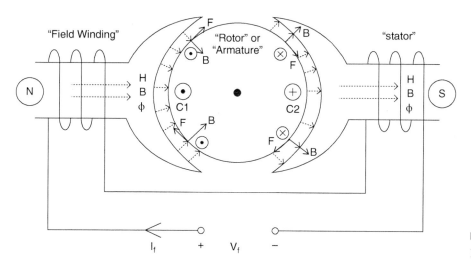

FIGURE 14.13   Illustration of the flux paths in a dc machine

the output is mechanical power. When operated in the *generator mode*, mechanical power is the input and electrical power is the output. Example 14.1 illustrates the dual modes of a dc machine.

A permanent magnet field dc machine is connected as shown in Figure 14.14, and may be assumed to be 100% efficient, that is, $P_{in} = P_{out} = 40$ kW. The speed is $\omega = 100$ rad/s. We wish to find the directions and magnitude of the current and torques if the dc machine is operating in (a) the motor mode and (b) the generator mode.

Example 14.1

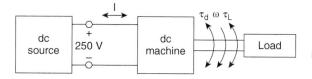

FIGURE 14.14   Schematic diagram used in Example 14.1

(a) In the motor operating mode the current I shown in Figure 14.14 is

$$I = \frac{P_{in}}{250}$$

$$= 160 \text{ A}$$

and is directed *into* the machine.

The developed torque, τ_d, is given by the fundamental relationship

$$\tau_d = \frac{P_{out}}{\omega}$$

$$= \frac{40,000}{100}$$

$$= 400 \text{ N-m}$$

and is *in* the direction of rotation. τ_L, the load torque, is always equal and opposite to τ_d for steady-state operation.

(b) In the generator mode, the current is I = 160 A, as calculated in part (a); however, the current is directed *out of* the machine. In addition, the torque τ_d = 400 N-m is in the direction *opposite to* that of rotation.

In a more general case, we can illustrate the motoring action of a dc machine via Figure 14.15. The voltage V_1 causes a current I to exist in the loops, which are embedded in the rotor. The current enters the upper brush and through commutator action is directed into the loops under the S pole. The current goes around the loops on the rotor and out of the loops under the N pole. The dashed line in the figure illustrates the current path for a single loop. Applying the Lorentz force equation to the single loop, we find that for the portion of the single loop under the S pole, F = (BℓI) yields a downward force producing a clockwise rotation. For the portion of the loop under the N pole, F = (BℓI) yields a force in the upward direction, which also produces a clockwise rotation. The force produced by all loops results in a torque. This torque is proportional to the force:

$$\tau \alpha F$$
$$\tau \alpha \ell B$$

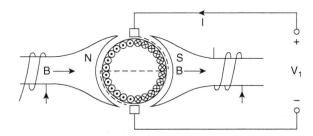

FIGURE 14.15 Illustration of the current path in a dc motor

Thus, we find that the current produced by V_1 produces a torque that causes the rotor to rotate. The rotor speed will continue to increase until the induced voltage (i.e. (u × B)ℓ) is equal to the applied voltage V_1. This equality defines the stable operating speed of the motor.

Our previous discussion has employed a boldface notation for the variables because our description of the physical phenomena required the use of vectors. At this point in our analysis, however, we recognize that the machine is designed in such a way that all quantities are mutually perpendicular and hence the same equations hold for scalar magnitudes. Thus, we can simplify the analysis by the subsequent use of scalar notation.

EQUIVALENT CIRCUITS AND ANALYSIS

Direct current machines can be connected to operate as either a generator or a motor. However, solid-state rectifiers have essentially replaced dc generators in most applications. Thus, dc machines are typically used in industrial drives requiring accurate speed control. For example, their applications include things such as rolling mills, cranes, and electric trains. Because of their universal utility, we concentrate our discussion primarily on the operation of a dc machine as a motor.

A dc machine has several field windings and the exciting-field circuit connections determine the type of machine. Machines may be either *separately excited* or *self-excited*. Consider the circuit representation shown in Figure 14.16 for a separately excited machine. The equations for the circuits in steady state are

$$V_f = I_f R_f$$
$$V_t = E_a \pm I_a R_a \tag{14.7}$$

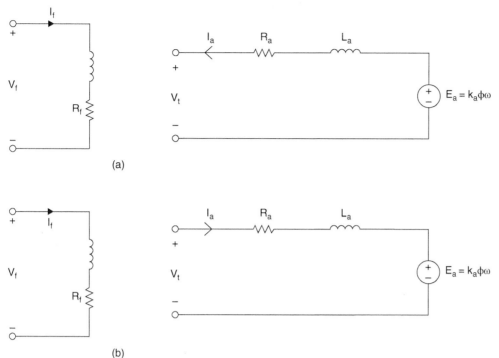

(a)

(b)

FIGURE 14.16
(a) Generator and (b) motor
circuit representation

In these equations, V_f and I_f represent the field voltage and current and R_f represents the winding resistance of the field circuit that establishes the magnetic **B** field of the machine. V_t is the terminal voltage at the commutator terminals (also called V_a), E_a is the generated electromotive force (also known as the back emf) and is the total voltage induced between brushes, I_a is the armature current, and R_a is the armature resistance.

It is important to note that the inductors in the following circuits are commonly ignored, i.e. shorted. The electrical time constants are usually much shorter than the mechanical time constants and therefore the simplified steady-state equations may be used instead of more involved differential equations containing inductances. As such, our focus is spent on investigating the steady-state equations with the inductors modeled as short circuits.

In the second expression in Eq. (14.7), the + sign is used for a motor and the − sign is used for a generator. In other words, the input to the motor is electric power and the output is shaft power, and the input to a generator is shaft power and the output is electric power. Since the focus of our discussion is primarily confined to the operation of the dc machine as a motor, we employ the + sign in Eq. (14.7). In addition to the above equations, from Faraday's law we know that the generated electromotive force is given by the expression

$$E_a = K_a \phi \omega \tag{14.8}$$

where K_a is an armature constant, ϕ is the flux per pole due to the field current, and ω is the rotational speed.

Information on $K_a \phi$ versus I_f is available from the manufacturer in the form of a *magnetization curve* such as that shown in Figure 14.17. The curve is generated by running the machine at some reference rated speed (ω_0) under open-circuit armature conditions ($I_a = 0$), and measuring $V_t = E_a$ versus I_f. The relationship exhibited in the figure occurs because ϕ is proportional to the **B** field and, in turn, the **B** field is created by I_f. Therefore, E_a is "caused by" I_f.

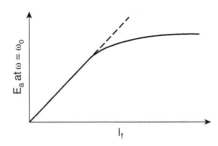

FIGURE 14.17 dc machine magnetization curve

It is desirable to operate close to the knee of the magnetization curve for maximum utilization of the iron. Note that machine weight depends on the size and density of the field poles, which determine the **B** field.

The electromagnetic torque is given by the equation

$$\tau_d = K_a \phi I_a \tag{14.9}$$

And the electromagnetic/mechanical power balance can be expressed as

$$P_d = E_a I_a = \tau_d \omega \tag{14.10}$$

where this developed power, that is, the power converted from the electrical to mechanical form, is shown in Figure 14.18.

Given these general equations, let us now consider two self-excited dc motor arrangements: the *shunt* motor and the *series* motor. A dc machine is called a shunt motor when the field winding is connected in shunt, or parallel, with the armature, as shown in Figure 14.19. For this configuration, the defining equations are

$$V_t = I_f R_f$$
$$V_t = E_a + I_a R_a$$
$$I_t = I_a + I_f \tag{14.11}$$

Since the electromotive force can be expressed as

$$E_a = K_a \phi \omega \tag{14.12}$$

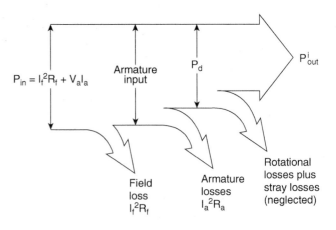

FIGURE 14.18 dc machine power flow analysis

$P_{in} = I_f^2 R_f + V_a I_a$

Armature input

P_d

P_{out}^i

Field loss $I_f^2 R_f$

Armature losses $I_a^2 R_a$

Rotational losses plus stray losses (neglected)

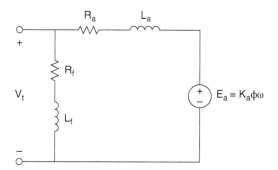

FIGURE 14.19   Shunt-connected motor

The angular velocity can be written as

$$\omega = \frac{V_t - I_a R_a}{K_a \phi} \tag{14.13}$$

This equation indicates that the speed is inversely proportional to flux in the field. If the field flux is very small, the speed can be very high. Furthermore, it is dangerous to open-circuit the field since the speed would theoretically become infinite. This fact is well-known and machines are designed with small stabilizing winding to prevent problems of this type.

Since the armature current is related to the torque by Eq. (14.9), Eq. (14.13) can be rewritten in the form

$$\omega = \frac{V_t}{K_a \phi} - \frac{R_a \tau_d}{(K_a \phi)^2} \tag{14.14}$$

This equation describes the steady-state torque–speed characteristic for a shunt-connected motor.

The series motor configuration is shown in Figure 14.20. Since the field is in series with the armature, the armature current determines the field flux. If we assume that the motor operates in the linear region of the magnetization curve, then the relationship between the flux and the armature current is of the form

$$\phi = K_S I_a \tag{14.15}$$

Then the pertinent equations for this motor become

$$E_a = K_a \phi \omega = K_a K_S I_a \omega$$
$$\tau_d = K_a \phi I_a = K_a K_S I_a^2$$
$$V_t = E_a + I_a (R_a + R_S) = (K_a K_S \omega + R_a + R_S) I_a \tag{14.16}$$

where R_s is the series field winding resistance (similar to R_f).

In a situation similar to that exhibited by the shunt motor, we note that the speed of a series motor can be quite large if the motor is operated at no load. This is why this motor is designed

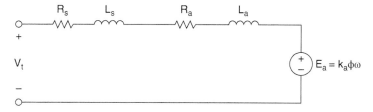

FIGURE 14.20
Series-connected motor

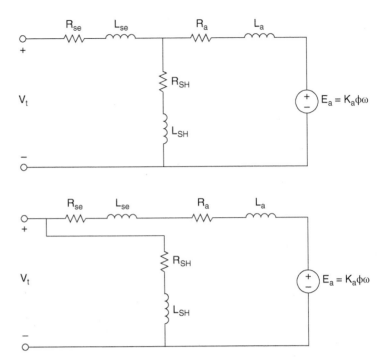

FIGURE 14.21
Compounded-connected machines: (a) short shunt and (b) long shunt

with a shunt field winding, and/or is mechanically coupled to the load, to limit the no-load speed. This motor is typically used in situations where large torques at low speed are required.

Finally, another type of dc machine is the *compound-connected* machine. Its name is derived from the fact that it is a combination of the shunt and series configurations; that is, it has both series and shunt windings. Figure 14.21 illustrates the four types of compound-connected machines.

The machines may be either *long shunt* or *short shunt*, and each of those types can be either *cumulative-compounded* or *differential-compounded*. The latter designation indicates whether the fields add or subtract, respectively. The circuit equations for these machines are straightforward and written in the same manner as those for the shunt and series machines.

Example 14.2

A dc machine with the following parameters has the schematic diagram shown in Figure 14.22a and the magnetization curve shown in Figure 14.22b.

dc Machine Parameters

Ratings

Arm. voltage = 400.0 V	Horsepower = 60.0 hp
Arm. current = 119.7 A	No. of poles = 4
Field current = 4.27 A	Rated speed· = 1800 rpm = 188.5 rad/s
Base speed = 1200 rpm	J motor = 0.581 kg-m²

Equivalent Circuit Values

$R_a = 0.0669\ \Omega$	$R_f = 93.60\ \Omega$

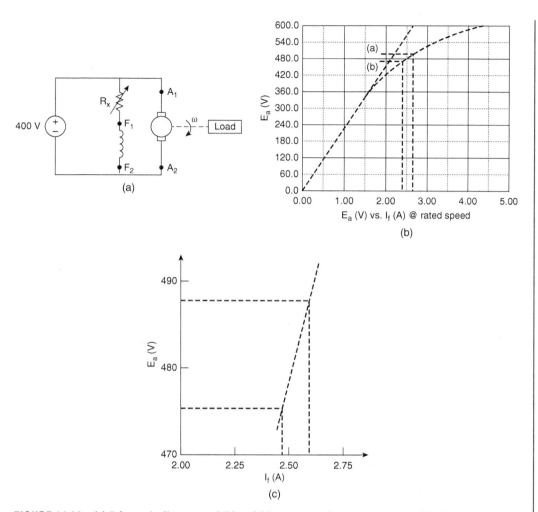

FIGURE 14.22   (a) Schematic diagram and (b) and (c) magnetization curves employed in Example 14.2

We wish to find the field current, the armature current, the operating mode, and the developed torque and power if the shaft speed is 1500 rpm and the field rheostat (variable resistor) is set to (a) 60.4 Ω and (b) 68.4 Ω.

(a) If the field rheostat is set to 60.4 Ω, then by Ohm's law,

$$I_f = \frac{400}{93.6 + 60.4}$$
$$= 2.597 \text{ A}$$

From the expanded version of the magnetization curve in the region of interest (Figure 14.22c), Eq. (14.8) yields

$$K_a\phi = \frac{488.2}{188.5}$$
$$= 2.590 \text{ Wb}$$

Since

$$\omega = \frac{2\pi \times 1500}{60}$$
$$= 157.1 \text{ rad/s}$$

Then

$$E_a = K_a \phi \omega$$
$$= 406.9 \text{ V}$$

Since $E_a > V_a$, current is directed *out of* the machine.

And the value of the current, calculated by Ohm's law, is

$$I_a = \frac{E_a - V_t}{R_a}$$
$$= 103.5 \text{ A}$$

and the machine operates as a generator. Using Eq. (14.9), the developed torque and power are then determined as

$$\tau_d = K_a \phi I_a$$
$$= 268.1 \text{ N-m}$$

and

$$P_d = \tau_d \omega$$
$$= 42.12 \text{ kW}$$

and since 746 W = 1 hp

$$P_d = 56.46 \text{ hp}$$

(b) If the field rheostat is set to 68.4 Ω, then

$$I_f = \frac{400}{93.6 + 68.4}$$
$$= 2.469 \text{ A}$$

From the magnetization curve (Figure 14.22), we find that

$$K_a \phi = \frac{475.6}{188.5}$$
$$= 2.523 \text{ Wb}$$

And since $\omega = 157.1$ rad/s,

$$E_a = K_a \phi \omega$$
$$= 396.3 \text{ V}$$

In this case, $E_a < V_a$, and hence current is directed *into* the machine and

$$I_a = \frac{V_t - E_a}{R_a}$$
$$= 54.7 \text{ A}$$

and the machine operates as a *motor*.

The developed torque and power are

$$\tau_d = K_a \phi I_a$$
$$= 137.9 \text{ N-m}$$

and

$$P_d = \tau_d \omega$$
$$= 21.66 \text{ kW}$$
$$= 29.03 \text{ hp}$$

A separately excited dc generator supplies 120 kW at 600 V. If the armature resistance is 0.2 Ω and the field current is fixed to provide a $K_a \phi = 1.3$ Wb, determine the shaft speed of the generator in rpm and the mechanical torque required to turn the generator. Assume all losses are negligible.

Example 14.3

The generator is modeled as shown in Figure 14.23.

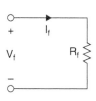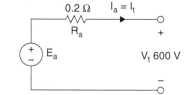

FIGURE 14.23   Circuit used in Example 14.3

The power developed is expressed as

$$P_d = V_t I_a$$
$$120,000 = 600 \, I_a$$
$$I_a = 200 \text{ A}$$

Then from KVL,

$$E_a = V_t + I_a R_a$$
$$= 600 + (200)(0.2)$$
$$= 640 \text{ V}$$

Since

$$E_a = K_a \phi \omega$$
$$\omega = \frac{640}{1.3}$$
$$= 492.31 \text{ rad/s}$$

or

$$\omega = (492.31) \left(\frac{60}{2\pi} \right)$$
$$= 480.19 \text{ rpm}$$

where the factor $\frac{60}{2\pi}$ converts rad/s to rpm. Finally,

$$\tau_d = K_a \phi I_a$$
$$= (1.3)(200)$$
$$= 260 \text{ N-m}$$

Example 14.4

A dc shunt motor develops 13.41 hp. Under this condition, $E_a = 250$ V and the armature resistance is $R_a = 0.1\ \Omega$. We wish to determine the motor's terminal voltage.

    The circuit diagram for the motor is shown in Figure 14.24. The power developed is 13.41 hp or $(13.41)(746)$ W, where the factor 746 converts horsepower to watts. The armature current can be found from the expression

$$P_d = E_a I_a$$

or

$$(13.41)(746) = 250\ I_a$$
$$I_a = 40.015\ \text{A}$$

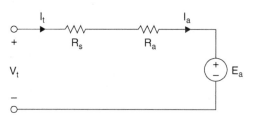

FIGURE 14.24 Circuit used in Example 14.4

    Then applying KVL to the circuit in Figure 14.24 yields

$$V_t = I_a R_a + E_a$$
$$= (40.015)(0.1) + 250$$
$$= 254\ \text{V}$$

Example 14.5

A 250 V, 25 hp dc series motor operates at full load at 750 rpm. The armature resistance is 0.11 Ω and the series field resistance is 0.03 Ω. If the motor draws 80 A at full load, find (a) the back emf at full load, (b) the developed power and torque, and (c) the new speed if the load change causes the line current to drop to 60 A.

(a) The circuit diagram for the machine is shown in Figure 14.25.

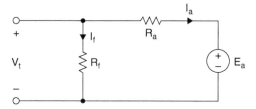

FIGURE 14.25 Circuit used in Example 14.5

    The KVL equations for the circuit are

$$E_a = V_t - I_a(R_S + R_a)$$
$$= 250 - 80(0.03 + 0.11)$$
$$= 238.8\ \text{V}$$

(b) The developed power is obtained by the expression

$$P_d = E_a I_a$$
$$= (238.8)(80)$$
$$= 19.104 \text{ kW}$$

Then

$$\tau_d = \frac{P_d}{\omega}$$
$$= \frac{19104}{(750)\left(\dfrac{2\pi}{60}\right)}$$
$$= 243.24 \text{ N-m}$$

(c) The new value of the back emf corresponding to the new line current is

$$E_{a2} = 250 - 60(0.03 + 0.11)$$
$$= 241.6 \text{ V}$$

Then since $E_a = K_a \phi \omega$, we can form the ratio

$$\frac{E_{a1}}{E_{a2}} = \frac{K_a K_s I_{a1} \omega_1}{K_a K_s I_{a2} \omega_2}$$

And thus

$$\omega_2 = \frac{E_{a2} I_{a1} \omega_1}{E_{a1} I_{a2}}$$
$$= \frac{(241.6)(80)(750)}{(238.8)(60)}$$
$$= 1011.73 \text{ rpm}$$

The paper product produced by a paper mill is to be wound on a 10-in. diameter core at a constant speed of 60 ft/s with a tension of 75 lb. The finished roll is 60 in. in diameter. A 220 V shunt dc motor with a no-load speed of 1750 rpm, an armature resistance of 0.4 Ω, and a field resistance of 100 Ω is utilized in the application. Let us determine (a) the current and torque when starting if rated voltage is applied to the motor terminals and (b) the necessary source voltage to ensure that the starting torque produces the desired tension of 75 lb on the paper. Finally, if the thickness of the paper is 1 mm, plot the source voltage, developed torque, and rated speed of the machine with respect to the roll diameter.

Example 14.6

(a) The equivalent circuit at starting is shown in Figure 14.26a. The armature current is

$$I_a = 220/0.4 = 550 \text{ A}$$
$$K\phi = 220/(1750)(2\pi/60) = 1.2005 \text{ Wb}$$
$$\tau_d = K\phi I_a = (1.2005)(550) = 660.28 \text{ N-m}$$

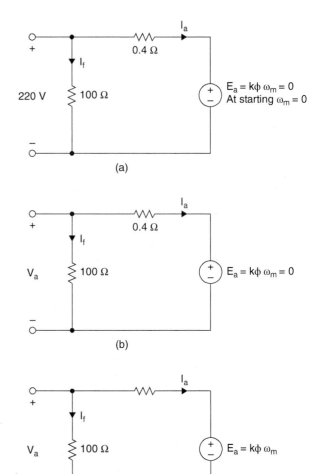

FIGURE 14.26 Equivalent circuits used in Example 14.6

(b) The voltage V_a, shown in Figure 14.26b, is obtained from the developed torque

$$\tau_d = [(75 \text{ lb-ft})(4.448222 \text{ N/lb-ft})] \, [(10/2) \text{ in. } (0.00254) \text{ m/in.}]$$
$$= 42.369 \text{ N-m}$$

Then,

$$K\phi/I_f = K\phi_{rated}/I_{frated}$$

and

$$K\phi_{rated} = 1.2005 \text{ Wb}$$
$$I_{frated} = 220/100 = 2.2 \text{ A}$$

Therefore,

$$K\phi = (1.2005) \, [(V_a/100)/2.2]$$

Since

$$\tau_d = K\phi I_a$$
$$42.369 \text{ N-m} = (1.2005) \, [(V_a/100)/2.2] \, (V_a/0.4)$$

or

$$V^2_a = [(42.369)(2.2)(100)(0.4)]/1.2005$$
$$V_a = 55.73 \text{ V}$$

The plots for the source voltage, developed torque, and rated speed of the machine with respect to the roll diameter are based upon the equivalent circuit in Figure 14.26c.

The defining equations are

$$E_a = K\phi\omega_m$$
$$\tau_d = K\phi I_a$$
$$I_a = (V_a - E_a)/R_a$$

In addition, it is important to note that the torque is equal to the force on the paper times the radius:

$$\tau_d = (\text{Force on pager})(\text{radius})$$

and the force is constant.

The angular speed is

$$\omega_m = \frac{\text{Paper speed}}{\text{Radius}}$$

and the paper speed is constant.

Recall from part (b) that

$$K\phi/I_f = K\phi_{\text{ rated}}/I_{f\text{rated}}$$

and therefore

$$K\phi = (K\phi_{\text{rated}}/I_{f\text{rated}})(I_f)$$
$$= (K\phi_{\text{rated}}/I_{f\text{rated}})(V_a/R_f)$$

Let us define

$$C = K\phi_{\text{rated}}/I_{f\text{rated}}$$

Then

$$K\phi = C \, (V_a/R_f)$$

Since

$$V_a = E_a + I_a R_a$$
$$= K\phi\omega_m + (\tau_d/K\phi)R_a$$
$$= C(V_a/R_f)\omega_m + [\tau_d/C(V_a/R_f)] \, R_a$$

This equation is a quadratic in V_a. Solving for V_a yields the expression

$$V_a = \{ \, [(-\tau_d)(R_a)(R^2_f)]/[(C^2)(\omega_m) \, - \, R_f C] \, \}^{1/2}$$

which can be expressed as

$$V_a = \{ [(-F_{paper})(radius)\, R_a\, R^2_f]/[C^2(paper\ speed/radius) - R_f\, C] \}^{1/2}$$

The plots for the rotor speed, developed torque, and source voltage are shown in Figure 14.27a–c.

It is important to note that this example does not consider the machine dynamics to transition from part (b) to the final analysis.

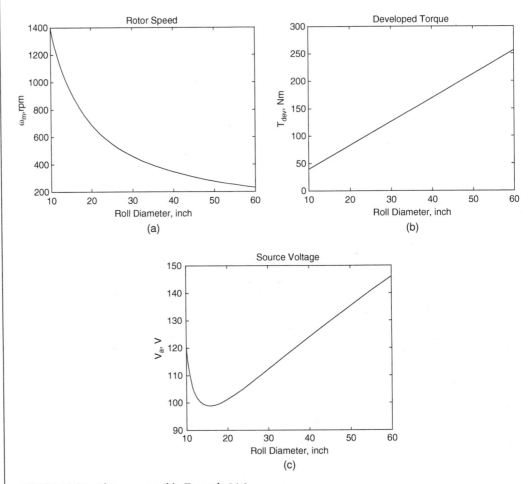

FIGURE 14.27 Plots generated in Example 14.6

At this point, let us investigate speed control under varying load conditions. To do this, we need a relationship between the output torque and the shaft speed. From the equation

$$\tau_d = K_a \phi I_a$$

recall that the circuit equation for the armature is

$$V_t = I_a R_a + E_a$$

Therefore, the armature current can be written as

$$I_a = (V_t - E_a)/R_a$$

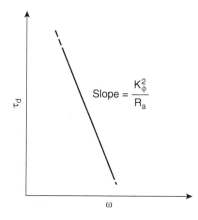

FIGURE 14.28   Torque–speed curve for a dc machine

and since

$$E_a = K_a \phi \omega$$

I_a can be expressed as

$$I_a = [V_t - K_a \phi \omega]/R_a$$

and then the developed torque is

$$\tau_d = \frac{V_t K_a \phi}{R_a} - \frac{(K_a \phi)^2}{R_a}\omega \qquad (14.17)$$

The torque/speed curve represented by this equation is shown in Figure 14.28. Note that V_t and R_a are known constants, and $K_a \phi$ for the separately excited machine is dependent only upon the field current. Note that this torque/speed characteristic permits us to determine the changes that will occur in speed as a result of varying load conditions, that is, changes in torque.

Machine manufacturers may provide multiple windings, which can be employed to create the constant magnetic field. The different methods in which these windings are used lead to machines operating as motors or generators with different torque–speed characteristics.

The steady-state performance of a dc machine can be modeled with reasonable accuracy using the simple circuits, graphs, and equations summarized earlier. Hence, at least in part, dc machine analysis reduces to dc circuit analysis. The key point to note is that the machine is an electrical–magnetic–mechanical (EMM) device, and its operation can only be understood when the interaction between these EMM phenomena is properly accounted for.

In addition to the machines described above, there also exists a *brushless dc machine*. However, this device is discussed in the following chapter on ac machines, since it employs what is traditionally called a three-phase synchronous machine.

The theory behind the EMM phenomena for dc machines has been introduced in the previous sections. While the previous discussion is necessary to have an understanding of the interaction between the EMM aspects of the device, it is also appropriate to consider where the dc machine is used in industry. There are two advantages of a dc machine that make the device very suitable for specific applications. The first advantage of a dc machine is that the maximum torque of the machine occurs when it is stalled. Another advantage is that it is easy to control the linear torque–speed relationship by using a rheostat (potentiometer) to control the terminal voltage for the machine. In addition to these advantages, a dc machine has lower inertia and a smaller physical footprint than an ac machine of comparable power rating, it is easy to repair, often they are

DC MACHINE APPLICATIONS

the cheaper option, and they are very familiar to electrical technicians because of their wide use and simplicity.

Some common industrial applications that utilize dc machines are rolling mills, cranes, electric locomotives, conveyors, elevators, hoists, lifts, lathes, and vacuum cleaners. Cranes, electric locomotives, rolling mills, hoists, lifts, and other applications that involve heavy loads take advantage of the fact that a series-connected dc machine has high, maximum torque when it is stalled (not moving). For example, a crane is used to lift and lower objects that weigh tens or hundreds of tons or more. The high torque at stalled and low speeds of a series-connected dc machine allows the crane to lift and move these heavy objects. Ultimately, heavy loads require large amounts of torque to move and a properly sized series-connected dc machine is able to meet the requirement. Other loads such as conveyors, elevators, lathes, vacuum cleaners, and other similar applications require higher and sometimes constant operational speeds. For example, a lathe needs to be able to reach high speeds and hold those speeds constant while turning the material. In addition, different materials and the physical size of the material require different operating speeds for turning. Thus, the lathe needs a motor that is variable speed and can operate at high speeds. A shunt-connected dc machine is commonly used to meet the operational requirements of the lathe and other similar applications because of easy speed control via a rheostat.

Comprehension of the previous sections allows one to understand why a dc machine is able to convert electrical energy to mechanical energy and vice versa. Common applications of dc machines have also been presented to give examples of why and how these devices are used for specific applications. The combination of dc machine theory and examples of practical applications will aid one in determining the type of dc machine that is suitable for the needs of their specific application.

Problems

14.1 A separately excited dc generator develops 100 N-m of torque. Find the terminal voltage V_a if $E_a = 320$ V, $R_a = 0.3$ Ω, and $K_a\phi = 1.5$ Wb.

14.2 A separately excited dc generator develops 90 N-m of torque and 18 kW of power. Compute the generator speed.

14.3 A separately excited dc generator develops 100 N-m of torque, 20 kW of power, and has an armature resistance of 0.25 Ω. If $K_a\phi = 1.5$ Wb, calculate the terminal voltage.

14.4 If the generator described in Problem 14.1 is operated as a self-excited generator, determine the field resistance R_f if the field current $I_f = 3.0$ A.

14.5 A separately excited dc generator has the following characteristics: $\tau_d = 120$ N-m, $P_d = 24$ kW, $R_a = 0.12$ Ω, and $K_a\phi = 1.5$ Wb. Calculate the terminal voltage.

14.6 A separately excited dc generator has a terminal voltage at no load of 360 V with the shaft rotating at 1600 rpm. If both I_a and I_f remain unchanged, what is the new terminal voltage if the shaft speed drops to 1400 rpm?

14.7 A 300 V self-excited dc generator is used to supply power to a 300 V dc power distribution grid in an underground coal mine. Note that this application requires a constant terminal voltage of 300 V. If the torque developed by the machine is 100.4 N-m, $R_a = 1$ Ω, $R_f = 85$ Ω, and $\omega = 1800$ rpm, find the machine's terminal output power.

14.8 Find the armature current in a dc shunt motor if $E_a = 300$ V and the motor develops 4 kW of power.

14.9 If $K_a\phi = 1.1$ Wb, determine the speed of the motor in Problem 14.8.

14.10 Determine the torque that is developed by the motor described in Problems 14.8 and 14.9.

14.11 A dc shunt motor develops 30 N-m of torque with $K_a\phi = 1.4$ Wb. Find E_a if $V_t = 280$ V and $R_a = 0.16\ \Omega$.

14.12 Determine the speed of the motor in Problem 14.11.

14.13 A dc shunt motor develops 30 hp with $V_a = 350$ V and $E_a = 340$ V. Find the value of the armature resistance R_a.

14.14 If the motor in Problem 14.13 operates at 1423 rpm, find the values of $K_a\phi$ and τ_d.

14.15 A dc shunt motor has the following characteristics: $I_a = 180$ A, $R_a = 0.14\ \Omega$, and $E_a = 340$ V. Find the terminal voltage of the motor.

14.16 A shunt-connected dc motor has the following characteristics: $V_t = 240$ V, $R_a = 0.22\ \Omega$, and $I_a = 40$ A. Determine the induced voltage.

14.17 Determine the armature and field currents in a dc motor if $V_t = 380$ V, $E_a = 330$ V, $R_a = 0.1\ \Omega$, and $R_f = 120\ \Omega$.

14.18 A separately excited dc shunt motor is operated at constant terminal voltage and constant developed power. Assuming the armature resistance is zero, if the field current (and therefore $K_a\phi$) is decreased, will the speed of the machine increase or decrease, and why?

14.19 Given the motor and operating conditions described in Problem 14.18, will the armature current increase, decrease, or remain the same, and why?

14.20 Find the terminal current supplied by the source in a dc shunt motor if $V_a = 250$ V, $R_f = 100\ \Omega$, $R_a = 0.1\ \Omega$, $K_a\phi = 1.25$ Wb, and the shaft speed is 1800 rpm.

14.21 A dc shunt motor has the following characteristics: $V_a = 400$ V, $R_f = 110\ \Omega$, and $R_a = 0.3\ \Omega$. The magnetization curve for the machine running at a speed of $\omega = 3476$ rpm is shown in Figure P14.21. Find the machine's armature current and developed shaft torque at $\omega = 3476$ rpm.

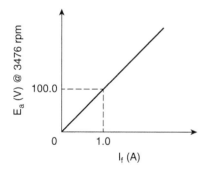

FIGURE P14.21

14.22 Determine the input power that must be supplied to the machine in Problem 14.21.

14.23 If shaft rotational losses are neglected, determine the efficiency of the dc motor described in Problem 14.21.

14.24 A dc shunt motor has the following characteristics: $V_a = 250$ V, $R_a = 0.2\ \Omega$, $R_f = 100\ \Omega$, and $\omega = 1800$ rpm. Use the magnetization curve in Figure P14.24 to find the torque developed by the machine.

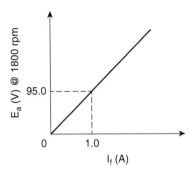

FIGURE P14.24

14.25 Given all the data for the machine in Problem 14.24, derive a torque/speed curve for this motor and use it to find the developed torque if the shaft speed drops to 1200 rpm.

14.26 A shunt dc motor has the following characteristics: $V_t = 640$ V, $R_a = 0.6\ \Omega$, $R_f = 120\ \Omega$, and $K_a\phi = 0.46\ I_f$. If the motor is used to drive the wheels of a subway train, find the torque available for starting if a 20 Ohm resistor is connected in series with the armature.

14.27 A dc series motor operates at full load at a speed of 640 rpm with a terminal voltage of 280 V. $E_a = 236.4$ V at an I_t of 36 A. If $R_S = 0.24\ \Omega$, find R_a. In addition, if $I_t = 1.2$ A at no load, find the no-load speed.

14.28 A 480 V, 120 hp dc series motor has an armature plus field resistance of $0.12\ \Omega$ and operates at 600 rpm. If the full-load current is 180 A, determine E_a, P_d, and τ_d at full load.

14.29 A 20 hp, 230 V dc series motor draws 64 A when the speed is 56 rad/s. If $R_a = 0.12\ \Omega$ and $R_S = 0.06\ \Omega$, determine the speed when the line current is 84 A.

14.30 A 230 V dc series motor draws a line current of 60 A when running at a rated speed of 600 rpm. $R_a = 0.12\ \Omega$ and $R_S = 0.08\ \Omega$. Determine the speed of the motor when the line current drops to 30 A and the no-load speed of the machine for a line current of 3.2 A.

AC Machines

CHAPTER 15

LEARNING OBJECTIVES

- To learn that induction and synchronous machines are two important types of polyphase machines

- To understand that the basis for all ac polyphase machines is a revolving magnetic field

- To learn that both the stator and rotor fields rotate in three-phase induction machines and torque is produced by the interaction of the two fields

- To learn that a balanced constant speed induction machine can be modeled by a per-phase wye equivalent circuit

- To learn that there are two types of rotors used in synchronous machines: salient and nonsalient

- To know that the rotor design is the difference between induction and synchronous machines

- To understand that both induction and synchronous machines can be operated in both the motor and generator modes

- To learn that equivalent circuits for both machines can be employed to analyze performance

- To learn that three-phase induction motors are the overwhelming choice for industrial motor applications

- To learn that three-phase synchronous machines operating in the generator mode are the primary choice for bulk energy production in the world

---

INTRODUCTION

In this chapter, we examine the two most important types of ac polyphase machines: induction and synchronous. In each case, we examine the basic characteristics, present the equivalent circuits for the machines, and discuss the operational modes through a number of examples.

THE REVOLVING MAGNETIC FIELD

Consider a stator structure on which are mounted two identical N-turn sinusoidally distributed windings (a-a′ and b-b′), as illustrated in Figure 15.1a. Suppose that we supply two balanced currents to the windings, so that

$$i_a = I_m \cos(\omega t)$$
$$i_b = I_m \sin(\omega t) \tag{15.1}$$

and

$$\omega = 2\pi f$$

which is the stator radian frequency in rad/s. These currents are plotted in Figure 15.1b. Note that the spatial angle θ, measured positive CCW, is referenced from the winding a-a′ magnetic axis, which is coincident with the positive x axis. The mmf's produced by these windings are

$$\mathscr{F}_a(\theta, t) = Ni_a \cos(\theta) = NI_m \cos(\omega t) \cos(\theta)$$
$$\mathscr{F}_b(\theta, t) = Ni_b \sin(\theta) = NI_m \sin(\omega t) \sin(\theta) \tag{15.2}$$

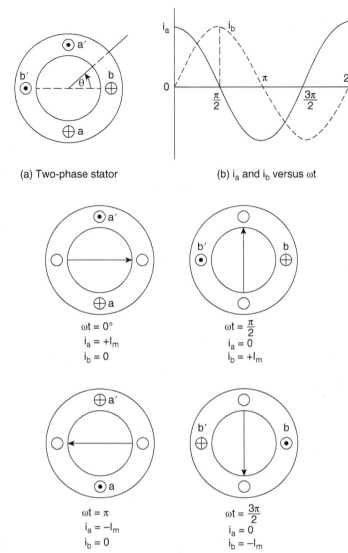

(a) Two-phase stator

(b) i_a and i_b versus ωt

$\omega t = 0°$
$i_a = +I_m$
$i_b = 0$

$\omega t = \dfrac{\pi}{2}$
$i_a = 0$
$i_b = +I_m$

$\omega t = \pi$
$i_a = -I_m$
$i_b = 0$

$\omega t = \dfrac{3\pi}{2}$
$i_a = 0$
$i_b = -I_m$

FIGURE 15.1 Figures used to describe a revolving magnetic field

(c)

Hence, the total mmf, $\mathscr{F}(\theta, t)$, inside the stator is

$$\begin{aligned}
\mathscr{F}(\theta, t) &= \mathscr{F}_a(\theta, t) + \mathscr{F}_b(\theta, t) \\
&= NI_m[\cos(\omega t)\cos(\theta) + \sin(\omega t)\sin(\theta)] \\
&= NI_m \cos(\omega t - \theta)
\end{aligned} \tag{15.3}$$

This mmf varies sinusoidally in space and time and may be visualized as follows. Suppose we draw an arrow in the direction of maximum field intensity with magnetic flux lines flowing in the direction of the arrow. From Eq. (15.3), this orients the arrow such that

$$\omega t - \theta = 0$$

or equivalently

$$\theta = \omega t$$

Figure 15.1c shows the spatial orientation of the mmf at four different ωt values ($0, \pi/2, \pi,$ $3\pi/2$). The overall effect is that $\mathscr{F}(\theta, t)$ appears to be revolving, or spatially rotating, at angular velocity ω, which is also the radian frequency of the currents. This angular velocity is called the *synchronous speed* and is given the symbol ω_s.

We have investigated the mmf $\mathscr{F}(\theta, t)$ produced by two balanced ac currents, 90° apart in *phase*, in two sinusoidally distributed windings, positioned 90° apart in *space*. In general, "n" balanced ac currents, 360°/n apart in phase, which exist in n sinusoidally distributed windings, positioned 360°/n apart in space, will also produce a rotating mmf $\mathscr{F}(\theta, t)$, for all integers n ≥ 3. For this more general case,

> ## AC POLYPHASE MACHINES

$$\mathscr{F}(\theta, t) = (nNI_m/2)\cos(\omega t - \theta) \tag{15.4}$$

In machine terminology, these "windings" are also called "phases" and collectively the "n-windings" configuration, the "n-phase" case. Commonly n = 3 produces a "three-phase" stator winding configuration, and we shall limit our discussion to this case. Also, the foregoing discussion is relevant to the so-called "two-pole" field geometry. The winding locations may be modified to form, in general, a "P-pole" field, where P is any even integer. To deal with the P-pole situation, it is convenient to define two different units of angular measure. We define

$$\theta_e = \text{electrical angle} \tag{15.5}$$

where electrical radian is equal to one electrical cycle/2 π and electrical degree is equal to one electrical cycle/360.

Then

$$\theta_m = \text{mechanical angle} \tag{15.6}$$

where 2π mechanical radians are equivalent to one mechanical revolution or 360 mechanical degrees. Thus,

$$\theta_m = \frac{2}{P}\theta_e \tag{15.7}$$

Given this definition, if we now differentiate Eq. (15.7), we obtain

$$\omega_m = \frac{2}{P}\omega_e \tag{15.8}$$

And thus the synchronous speed in mechanical rad/s is

$$\omega_s = \frac{2}{P}(2\pi f) \tag{15.9}$$

Finally, three balanced ac currents, 120 electrical degrees apart in phase, in three sinusoidally distributed P-pole windings, will produce a rotating mmf $\mathscr{F}(\theta_m, t)$ of the form

$$\mathscr{F}(\theta_m, t) = (3NI_m/2)\cos(\omega_s t - \theta_m) \tag{15.10}$$

This revolving magnetic field, produced by balanced three-phase stator currents, is called the *stator field*, and is fundamental to the operation of all ac three-phase machines. The two- and four-pole cases are illustrated in Figure 15.2a and b, respectively.

Figure 15.3 provides cutaway versions of the machine. Figure 15.3a illustrates the cage rotor design and Figure 15.3b illustrates the wound rotor design.

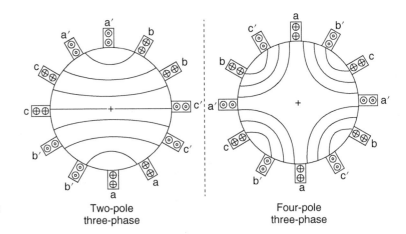

FIGURE 15.2 Field patterns in ac polyphase machine stators

Two-pole
three-phase

Four-pole
three-phase

Cage rotor design

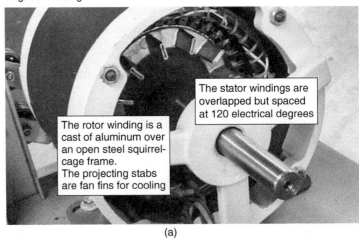

The stator windings are overlapped but spaced at 120 electrical degrees

The rotor winding is a cast of aluminum over an open steel squirrel-cage frame.
The projecting stabs are fan fins for cooling

(a)

Wound rotor design

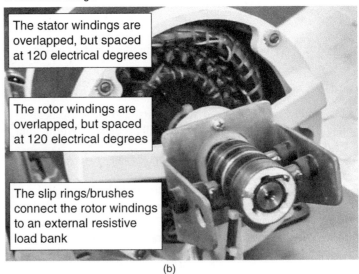

The stator windings are overlapped, but spaced at 120 electrical degrees

The rotor windings are overlapped, but spaced at 120 electrical degrees

The slip rings/brushes connect the rotor windings to an external resistive load bank

FIGURE 15.3 AC Machines
Reference: https:// electronics360.globalspec .com/article/15490/how-to -connect-three-phase-ac -motors (Courtesy of Ahmed Faizan Sheikh)

(b)

BASIC PRINCIPLES OF OPERATION

We shall next discuss the first of the two basic types of ac machines, namely the *three-phase induction machine* operating at constant speed under balanced three-phase conditions. The stator is designed as discussed in previous sections, and produces a sinusoidally distributed P-pole revolving field, revolving at speed ω_s. To simplify things, all further diagrams and discussion will be restricted to the two-pole case; however, the mathematics will be valid for the P-pole case unless specifically stated otherwise.

Consider a cylindrical rotor structure on which are mounted three sinusoidally distributed windings (A-A′, B-B′, C-C′), separated 120° (electrical) apart, which for the moment we consider to be open-circuited. We further consider this *wound rotor* to be rotating at speed ω_r, which we assume is less than ω_s. The situation is illustrated in Figure 15.4a.

From the rotor's perspective, the *stator field* sweeps over the rotor surface at a speed of $(\omega_s - \omega_r)$. If we define s = slip as follows:

$$s = slip = \frac{\omega_s - \omega_r}{\omega_s} \qquad (15.11a)$$

then the stator field rotates at speed $s\omega_s$ (in *mechanical* rad/s) relative to the rotor.

The stator Eq. (15.11a) indicates that the rotor speed in mechanical rad/s is

$$\omega_r = \omega_s(1 - s) \qquad (15.11b)$$

This field will induce balanced three-phase voltages in the rotor windings at radian frequency $s\omega_s$ (in *electrical* rad/s); similarly, the rotor cyclic frequency in Hertz is $f_r = sf$, where f = stator frequency, in Hertz.

If we now connect the rotor windings in a balanced three-phase passive termination, a balanced pattern of ac three-phase currents will flow in the rotor with frequency f_r. Therefore, the rotor currents will produce a second sinusoidally distributed P-pole revolving field, revolving at

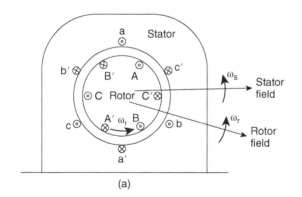

(a)

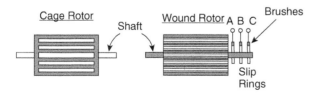

Both behave as "P" pole 3-phase wye-connected ac windings.

(b)

FIGURE 15.4   Induction machine details

speed $s\omega_s = (\omega_s - \omega_r)$. This *rotor field* rotates at $(\omega_s - \omega_r) + \omega_r = \omega_s$, and thus turns synchronously with the stator field. It is the interaction of these two synchronized fields that is the mechanism of torque production, and thus power conversion, in the polyphase induction machine.

It is important to note that the values of slip are related to the mode of machine operation as follows:

Motor mode: $0 < s < 1$

Synchronous speed: $s = 0$

Generator mode: $s < 0$

The above discussion is valid for all conceivable balanced rotor terminations, including a short circuit. In fact, a short circuit is the best possible termination for many operating conditions, since it maximizes the rotor current, and hence the rotor field and torque. Since the number of rotor winding turns is irrelevant, consider a one-turn case. A short circuit would, in effect, short out each rotor conductor. For this case, we don't need a rotor winding at all, simply provision for appropriate conducting paths on the rotor structure. Such a rotor design is called a *squirrel cage or cage rotor*, because of the conductor arrangement resemblance to the exercise cage used for pet gerbils, hamsters, or other small rodents. The two rotor designs are illustrated in Figure 15.3b.

THE EQUIVALENT CIRCUIT

Balanced constant speed operation of the induction machine may be modeled by the ac per-phase wye equivalent circuit shown in Figure 15.5. The parameters shown on the circuit are defined as follows:

V_S = Line-to-neutral stator phase-a phasor voltage applied at the terminals, usually used as phase reference in volts

I_S = Stator phase-a current in amperes

R_S = Phase-a winding resistance of the stator in Ω

X_S = Leakage reactance associated with the stator flux that does not link rotor windings in Ω

X_m = Magnetizing reactance in Ω

I'_r = Rotor phase-a current reflected into the stator in amperes

X'_r = Leakage rotor reactance, reflected into the stator, associated with the rotor flux that does not link stator windings in Ω

R'_r = Rotor resistance reflected into stator, in Ω

s = Refers to the slip, which is a measure of rotor speed. It is defined as

$$s = \frac{\omega_s - \omega_r}{\omega_s}$$

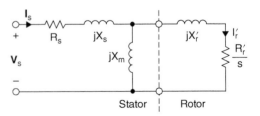

FIGURE 15.5 Per-phase wye equivalent circuit for an induction machine

Note that it is common to see the following notation used because it relates to the nonideal transformer model. While the nonideal transformer model is beyond the scope of this book, the following notation should be familiar to the reader.

$$R_1 = R_s; \ X_1 = X_s; \ R_2' = R_r'; \ X_2' = X_r'$$

It is important to note that the rotor components are reflected to the stator circuit in the same manner in which the secondary circuit of a transformer is reflected to the primary, and are indicated by primes.

The power flow diagram for an induction motor is shown in Figure 15.6a. The per-phase circuit diagram can be redrawn as shown in Figure 15.6b in order to account for some of these terms. In this new circuit, R_s represents the element that accounts for the stator copper losses, R_r the rotor copper losses, and $R_r' = (1 - s)/s$ accounts for the mechanical power developed. Other losses noted in Figure 15.6a will be neglected in our calculations.

Since the circuit in Figure 15.6b is a per-phase equivalent circuit, and the induction motor is a three-phase machine, the three-phase power developed is

$$P_d = 3(I_r')^2 R_r' \left(\frac{1 - s}{s} \right) \tag{15.12}$$

where $I_r' = |\mathbf{I_r'}|$. The torque developed is

$$\tau_d = \frac{P_d}{\omega_r} \tag{15.13}$$

which after some algebraic manipulation can be expressed as

$$\tau_d = \frac{3(I_r')^2 (R_r'/s)}{\omega_s} \tag{15.14}$$

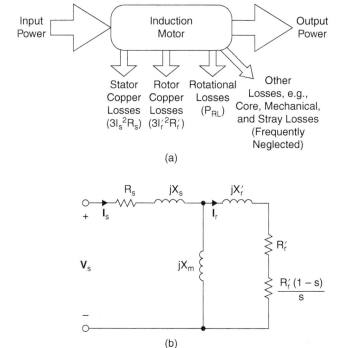

(a)

(b)

FIGURE 15.6 Induction motor diagrams

Given the equivalent circuit and the equations that have been developed, many induction motor problems may be reduced to circuit problems.

Example 15.1

An induction motor is to be used to drive a conveyer belt by turning the main drive roller at an angular velocity of 120 rad/s. We wish to determine (a) the maximum number of pole pairs that the motor can possess and (b) the slip at which the motor is running when operating under the conditions in (a).

Table 15.1, calculated from Eq. (15.9), indicates the relationship between the number of poles and the speed of the stator magnetic field, where 377 rad/s corresponds to the standard power frequency of 60 Hz. The table indicates that the machine should have six poles. Note that eight poles would result in a speed that is too slow. Since $\omega_s = 125.67$ rad/s and $\omega_r = 120$ rad/s, the slip is

$$s = \frac{125.67 - 120}{125.67}$$

$$= 0.0451$$

Table 15.1 Data for Example 15.1

# of Poles	ω_s
4	377/2 = 188.5 mechanical rad/s
6	377/3 = 125.67 mechanical rad/s
8	377/4 = 94.25 mechanical rad/s

Example 15.2

Consider the three-phase wound rotor induction machine described by Table 15.2.

Table 15.2 Three-phase Induction Motor Data

Ratings	
Line voltage = 460 V	Horsepower = 75 hp
Stator frequency = 60 Hz	No. of poles = 4
Rotor type: Wound	Synchronous speed = 1800.0 rpm

Equivalent Circuit Values (in stator Ω)	
Phase voltage = 460/square root of 3 = 265.58 V	
$R_s = 0.0564\ \Omega$	$jX_s = 0.2334\ \Omega;\ jX_m = 9.875\ \Omega$
$R'_r = 0.0564\ \Omega$	$jX'_r = 0.2334\ \Omega$
Rotational loss torque = $\tau_{RL} = 0.03149\ \omega_r$ N-m	

For a shorted rotor termination, and a slip of 0.015, compute rotor speed in rpm and rad/s; rotor frequency; currents (I_s, I'_r); developed, rotational, and output torques; stator copper, rotor copper, and rotational losses; input and output powers; power factor (PF); and efficiency.

The synchronous speed in mechanical rad/s is

$$\omega_s = 2\pi(60)/2$$

$$= 188.5\ \text{rad/s}$$

$$= 1800\ \text{rpm}$$

The rotor speed in mechanical rad/s is

$$\begin{aligned}\omega_r &= (1-s)1800\\ &= 1773.0 \text{ rpm}\\ &= (0.985)188.5\\ &= 185.7 \text{ rad/s}\end{aligned}$$

The a-phase equivalent circuit is shown in Figure 15.7. The mesh currents for the circuit are

$$\mathbf{V_s} = (0.0564 + j10.1289)\mathbf{I_s} + (0.000 + j9.875)\mathbf{I'_r}$$
$$0 = (0.000 - j9.875)\mathbf{I_s} + (3.76 + j10.1289)\mathbf{I'_r}$$

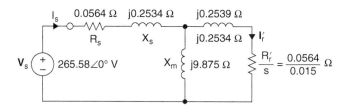

FIGURE 15.7   Circuit for the machine in Example 15.2

Solving these equations yields

$$\mathbf{I_s} = 73.65\angle{-27.54°} \text{ A}$$
$$\mathbf{I'_r} = 67.31\angle{-7.18°} \text{ A}$$

The developed torque is

$$\begin{aligned}\tau_d &= 3(I'_r)^2(R'_r/s)/\omega_s\\ &= \frac{3(67.31)^2(0.0564/0.015)}{188.5}\\ &= 271.14 \text{ N-m}\end{aligned}$$

The rotational loss torque is

$$\begin{aligned}\tau_{RL} &= 0.03149(185.7)\\ &= 5.85 \text{ N-m}\end{aligned}$$

And the load torque is

$$\begin{aligned}\tau_{load} &= \tau_d - \tau_{RL}\\ &= 271.14 - 5.85\\ &= 265.29 \text{ N-m}\end{aligned}$$

The input power to the machine is

$$\begin{aligned}P_{in} &= 3V_sI_s \cos\theta\\ &= 3(265.58)(73.65)\cos[0-(-27.59°)]\\ &= 52.03 \text{ kW}\end{aligned}$$

The stator copper loss (SCL) is

$$SCL = 3I_S^2 R_S$$
$$= 0.917 \text{ kW}$$

The rotor copper loss (RCL) is

$$RCL = 3(I_r')^2 R_r'$$
$$= 0.767 \text{ kW}$$

The power developed by the machine is

$$P_d = P_{in} - SCL - RCL$$
$$= 50.34 \text{ kW}$$

And the rotational losses are

$$P_{RL} = \tau_{RL}\omega_r$$
$$= 5.85(185.7)$$
$$= 1.086 \text{ kW}$$

The total losses are then

$$\text{Total loss} = SCL + RCL + P_{RL}$$
$$= 2.759 \text{ kW}$$

Hence, the output power is

$$P_{out} = P_{in} - \text{Total loss}$$
$$= 49.26 \text{ kW}$$
$$= 66.00 \text{ hp}$$

The machine's PF is

$$= \cos(-27.55°)$$
$$= 0.8867 \text{ lagging}$$

Hence, the efficiency is

$$= P_{out} / P_{in}$$
$$= 94.68\%$$

| **Example 15.3** | Given the machine described in Example 15.2, let us determine the complex power supplied by the source and the output power of the machine when the rotor is spinning at 1825 rpm. |

Once again with reference to Figure 15.7, we find that

$$s = \frac{1800 - 1825}{1800} = -0.0139$$

$$\frac{R_r'}{s} = \frac{0.0564}{-0.0139} = -4.0608 \ \Omega$$

$$\mathbf{V_s} = (0.0569 + j10.1289)\mathbf{I_s} + (0.000 + j9.875)\mathbf{I_r'}$$
$$0 = (0.000 - j9.875)\mathbf{I_s} + (-4.0608 + j10.129)\mathbf{I_r'}$$

$$\bar{I}_s = 70.85\angle{-}150.7°\,A$$
$$\bar{I}'_r = 64.11\angle{-}172.54°\,A$$

The complex power is then

$$\mathbf{S}_{3\phi} = 3(265.58\angle0°)(70.85\angle{-}150.7°\,A) = -49226 + j27627\ V$$

and

$$\tau_d = \frac{3(I'_r)^2\left(\dfrac{R'_r}{s}\right)}{\omega_S} = \frac{3(64.11)^2(-4.0608)}{188.5} = -265.66\ \text{N-m}$$

$$\tau_{RL} = 0.03149\,\omega_r = (0.03149)\,(191.11) = 6.02\ \text{N-m}$$

$$\tau_{load} = \tau_d - \tau_{RL} = -271.68\ \text{N-m}$$

The output power is then determined as

$$P_d = 3(I'_r)^2\left(\frac{1-s}{s}\right)R'_r = 3(64.11)^2\left(\frac{1-(-0.0139)}{-0.0139}\right)0.0564 = -50771\ W$$

$$P_{RL} = \tau_{RL}\omega_r = 6.02(191.114) = 1150.2\ W$$

$$P_{out} = -P_m = P_d - P_{RL} = \tau_{load}\omega_r = -51921\ W$$

BASIC PRINCIPLES OF OPERATION

THE POLYPHASE SYNCHRONOUS MACHINE: BALANCED OPERATION

The second major type of ac machine is the *three-phase synchronous machine*. Note that the stator structure is essentially identical to the three-phase induction machine, that is, a cylindrical ferromagnetic structure inside upon which are mounted balanced three-phase P-pole windings as discussed in Section "The Revolving Magnetic Field." Like the induction device, the fundamental purpose of the stator is to produce a revolving P-pole magnetic field, revolving at speed ω_s. Recall that

$$\omega_s = \frac{2}{P}(2\pi f)\ \text{Mechanical rad/s}$$

Like the three-phase induction machine, the synchronous machine can operate in both the generator and motor modes and has important applications when used both ways.

The difference between synchronous and induction machines is in the design of the rotor. There are two types: *salient* and *nonsalient*, as illustrated in Figure 15.8. The number of stator and rotor poles must always be the same; that is, a P-pole stator always requires a P-pole rotor for proper operation. Another basic difference is that the synchronous machine rotor is always synchronized with the stator field in the steady state. That is,

$$\omega_r = \omega_s$$

Hence

$$s = 0$$

Because there is no relative motion between the rotor and stator field, there are no induced rotor voltages and currents, and hence the rotor field cannot be produced by induction processes.

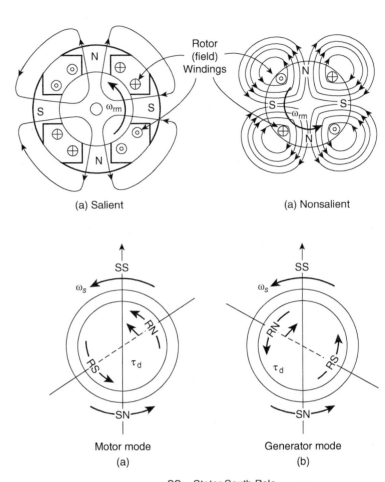

FIGURE 15.8 Two four-pole synchronous machine rotor types

(a) Salient

(a) Nonsalient

FIGURE 15.9 Basic synchronous machine operation

Motor mode
(a)

Generator mode
(b)

SS = Stator South Pole
SN = Stator North Pole
RN = Rotor North Pole
RS = Rotor South Pole

The rotor field is produced by dc currents in windings provided for that purpose, called the "field" windings, as shown in Figure 15.8.

The mechanism of torque production is illustrated in Figure 15.9. In Figure 15.9a, note that the stator field south pole ("SS") would attract the rotor north pole ("RN"), producing a torque in the direction of rotor rotation. In a similar manner, "SN" attracts "RS." We observed earlier that developed electromagnetic torque on the rotor in the direction of motion was a positive indication of *motor* operation. Now consider the situation in Figure 15.9b. Again, the stator field south pole ("SS") would attract the rotor north pole ("RN"), and likewise, "SN" attracts "RS." However, this time the torque on the rotor *opposes* rotation, a sure sign of *generator* operation. Thus, it appears that the relative angular *position* of the stator and rotor fields determines the machine operating mode. Remember that both fields rotate at the same speed $\omega_r = \omega_s$.

THE NONSALIENT SYNCHRONOUS MACHINE EQUIVALENT CIRCUIT

Figure 15.10 shows an actual picture of a nonsalient synchronous machine. The operation of a balanced three-phase ac constant speed nonsalient synchronous machine can be predicted with reasonable accuracy using the equivalent circuits shown in Figure 15.11.

Nonsalient Synchronous Machine

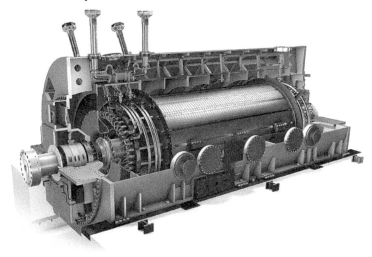

FIGURE 15.10   A nonsalient synchronous machine (Siemens Energy)

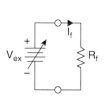

(a) Rotor equivalent circuit

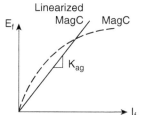

(b) Magnetization characteristic

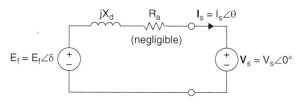

(c) Stator equivalent circuit

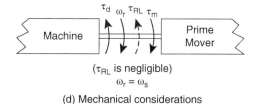

$(\tau_{RL}$ is negligible)

$\omega_r = \omega_s$

(d) Mechanical considerations

FIGURE 15.11   Synchronous machine equivalent circuits generator convention

Consider the rotor field circuit illustrated in Figure 15.11a. The adjustable dc source, called the *exciter*, provides the dc field current I_f needed to create the rotor field. The rotor field circuit may be modeled electrically by its resistance R_f. The ac stator voltage E_f is created by the rotor field sweeping over the stator conductors at $\omega_r = \omega_s$, which also determines the frequency of E_f. Since E_f is directly proportional to the rotor field, E_f is functionally related to I_f. This function is called the *magnetization characteristic* of the machine, and is shown in Figure 15.11b. It will be sufficiently accurate for our purposes to use a linearized approximation to the magnetization characteristic in our calculations. The key equations are

$$I_f = V_{ex}/R_f$$
$$E_f = K_{ag}I_f$$

where K_{ag} is the slope of the magnetization characteristic. The per-phase stator ac wye-equivalent circuit is shown in Figure 15.11c. The source E_f models rotor field effects. The reactance X_d accounts for two basic phenomena: "armature reaction," that is, the voltages induced into the stator windings caused by the rotating stator magnetic field, which is produced by the balanced three-phase stator currents, and the "leakage field," that is, the portion of the stator field that does not cross the air gap. The circuit also has resistance R_a, which we shall neglect since $X_d \gg R_a$. We shall limit our study to the case where the machine is always connected to a large external balanced three-phase ac system, modeled with an ideal voltage source $\mathbf{V_s}$, which shall always be our phase reference; that is, $\mathbf{V_S} = |\mathbf{V_S}| \angle 0°$. The stator current $\mathbf{I_s}$ represents the a-phase line current. The angle δ is the phase angle of $\mathbf{E_f}$ relative to $\mathbf{V_s}$; the angle θ is the phase angle of $\mathbf{I_s}$, relative to $\mathbf{V_s}$, and hence, θ is the PF angle. The key equations are

$$\mathbf{E_f} = \mathbf{V_S} + jX_d\mathbf{I_S} \tag{15.15}$$
$$P_{1\phi} = V_s I_s \cos(\theta) = E_f I_s \cos(\delta - \theta) \tag{15.16}$$
$$= PF = \cos(\theta) \tag{15.17}$$

An alternative expression for $P_{1\phi}$ is

$$P_{1\phi} = (E_f V_s / X_d) \sin(\delta) \tag{15.18}$$

Furthermore, remember that

$$P_{3\phi} = 3P_{1\phi} \tag{15.19}$$

Finally, consider the mechanical issues at the shaft, as shown in Figure 15.11d. Neglecting rotational losses, and for constant speed operation, the torque, τ_m, of the prime mover (for example, a steam turbine) is equal to the electromagnetic torque:

$$\tau_m = \tau_d \tag{15.20}$$

Similarly, the prime mover power is equal to the electromagnetic power:

$$P_m = P_d$$

or

$$P_m = \tau_m \omega_r$$
$$= \tau_d \omega_r$$
$$= P_d \tag{15.21}$$

such that

$$P_d = P_{3\phi} = 3 \left(\frac{E_f V_s}{X_d} \right) \sin(\delta)$$

and

$$\omega_r = \omega_s \tag{15.22}$$

Consider the following example.

A three-phase 2300 V four-pole 1000 kVA 60 Hz synchronous machine has $jX_d = 5\,\Omega$, $R_f = 10\,\Omega$, and $K_{ag} = 200\,\Omega$; it is to be used as a generator connected to a balanced three-phase ac system.

Example 15.4

We wish to find (a) the rated stator current, (b) the exciter setting, V_{ex}, for operation at rated conditions for a PF of 0.866 lagging, (c) V_{ex} in part (b) if the PF is 0.866 leading, (d) V_{ex} in part (b) for unity PF and the same real power output as in parts (b) and (c), and (e) the complex power delivered by the generator to the system for parts (b) and (c).

(a) The rated stator current is found from the complex power as follows:

$$S_{1f\ rated} = 1000k/3$$
$$= 333.3\ kVA$$

and

$$V_{s\ rated} = 2.3k/\sqrt{3}$$
$$= 1.328\ kV$$

then

$$I_{s\ rated} = S_{1\phi\ rated}/V_{s\ rated}$$
$$= 333.3k/1.328k$$
$$= 251.0\ A$$

(b) To find the exciter setting V_{ex} for operation at rated conditions for a PF of 0.866 lagging, we first determine

$$\theta = \cos^{-1}(0.866)$$
$$= -30°$$

then

$$\mathbf{E_f} = 1328\angle0° + j5(251\angle{-30°})$$
$$= 2495\angle14.6°\ V$$

and since

$$I_f = E_f/K_{ag}$$
$$= 2495/200$$
$$= 12.48\ A$$

Therefore,

$$V_{ex} = I_f R_f$$
$$= 12.48(10)$$
$$= 124.8\ V$$

(c) For a PF of 0.866 leading, we find that

$$\theta = \cos^{-1}(0.866)$$
$$= +30°$$

Then

$$\mathbf{E_f} = 1328\angle0° + j5(251\angle{+30°})$$
$$= 1293\angle57.2°\ V$$

Since

$$I_f = E_f/K_{ag}$$
$$= 1293/200$$
$$= 6.465 \text{ A}$$

Then

$$V_{ex} = I_f R_f$$
$$= 6.465(10)$$
$$= 64.65 \text{ V}$$

(d) V_{ex} for operation at rated voltage and unity PF, for the same real power output as in parts (b) and (c), is derived as follows:

From parts (b) and (c),

$$P_{1\phi} = V_s I_s \cos(\theta)$$
$$= 1328(251)(0.866)$$
$$= 288.7 \text{ kW}$$

Therefore, at unity PF,

$$I_s = P_{1\phi}/V_s$$
$$= 288.7k/1.328k$$
$$= 217.4 \text{ A}$$

Since

$$\theta = \cos^{-1}(1.000)$$
$$= 0°$$

Then

$$\mathbf{E_f} = 1328\angle 0° + j5(217.4\angle 0°)$$
$$= 1716\angle 39.3° \text{ V}$$

And

$$I_f = E_f/K_{ag}$$
$$= 1716/200$$
$$= 8.580 \text{ A}$$

Therefore,

$$V_{ex} = I_f/R_f$$
$$= 8.580(10)$$
$$= 85.80 \text{ V}$$

(e) For parts (b), (c), and (d), the complex power delivered by the generator to the system is derived from the equation

$$\mathbf{S_{3\phi}} = 3\mathbf{V_s I_s^*}$$

Thus, for part (b),

$$\mathbf{S_{3\phi}} = 3(1.328)(251\angle +30°)$$
$$= 866 \text{ kW} + j500 \text{ kVAR}$$

For part (c),

$$\mathbf{S_{3\phi}} = 3(1.328)(251\angle-30°)$$
$$= 866 \text{ kW} - j500 \text{ kVAR}$$

And for part (d),

$$\mathbf{S_{3\phi}} = 3(1.328 \text{ k})(217.4)$$
$$= 866 \text{ kW} + j0 \text{ kVAR}$$

Example 15.4 demonstrates some general points about synchronous generator operation. Lagging, unity, and leading generator PF operation is associated with high, medium, and low excitation levels called "over, normal, and under" excitation. Note that the *generator lagging* mode is associated with reactive power Q *delivery,* and *generator leading* operation means that Q is *absorbed* by the machine. The point is that field control can be used to control Q flow into and out of the machine regardless of motor or generator operation.

For the machine operating in the motor mode, the current $\mathbf{I_s}$ would be phase-positioned in the second or third quadrants. Similarly, the powers $P_{1\phi}$ and $P_{3\phi}$ would be negative. To avoid this correct, but awkward, situation, we reverse the positive definition of $\mathbf{I_s}$ and δ, as shown in Figure 15.12, that is, $\mathbf{I_s}$ is now defined positive *into* the machine, and δ is defined positive when E_f lags V_s.

This is because the rotor magnetic field now physically lags the stator magnetic field and so the actual angle δ is negative in the circuit model as seen in Example 15.5

The *motor convention* machine equations are

$$\mathbf{V_s} = \mathbf{E_f} + jX_d\mathbf{I_s} \tag{15.23}$$

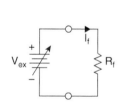

(a) Rotor equivalent circuit

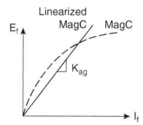

(b) Magnetization characteristic

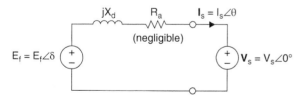

(c) Stator equivalent circuit

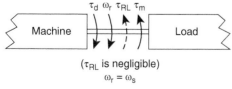

(τ_{RL} is negligible)
$\omega_r = \omega_s$

(d) Mechanical considerations

FIGURE 15.12 Synchronous machine equivalent circuits *motor convention*

Power flow into the machine is

$$P_{1\phi} = V_s I_s \cos(\theta)$$
$$= E_f I_s \cos(\delta - \theta) \qquad (15.24)$$

The PF is

$$PF = \cos(\theta) \qquad (15.25)$$

And

$$P_{1\phi} = (E_f V_s / X_d) \sin(\delta) \qquad (15.26)$$

Example 15.5

A three-phase 2300 V four-pole 1000 kVA 60 Hz synchronous machine has $jX_d = 5\ \Omega$, $R_f = 10\ \Omega$; and $K_{ag} = 200\ \Omega$, that is, the machine in Example 15.3 and is to be used as a motor.

We wish to find (a) the exciter setting, V_{ex}, for operation at rated conditions for a PF of 0.866 lagging, (b) V_{ex} in part (a) if the PF is 0.866 leading, (c) V_{ex} in part (a) for unity PF and the same real power as in parts (a) and (b), and (d) the complex power absorbed by the machine in parts (a), (b), and (c).

(a) To find the exciter setting V_{ex} for operation at rated conditions for a PF of 0.866 lagging, we first determine

$$\theta = \cos^{-1}(0.866) = -30°$$

Then

$$\mathbf{E_f} = 1328\angle 0° - j5(251\angle{-30°})$$
$$= 1293\angle{-57.2°}\ V$$

And since

$$I_f = E_f / K_{ag}$$
$$= 1293/200$$
$$= 6.465\ A$$

Therefore,

$$V_{ex} = I_f R_f$$
$$= 6.465(10)$$
$$= 64.65\ V$$

(b) For a PF of 0.866 leading, we find that

$$\theta = \cos^{-1}(0.866)$$
$$= +30°$$

Then

$$\mathbf{E_f} = 1328\angle 0° - j5(251\angle{+30°})$$
$$= 2237\angle{-29.1°}\ V$$

Since

$$I_f = E_f / K_{ag}$$
$$= 2237/200$$
$$= 11.19\ A$$

Hence

$$V_{ex} = I_f R_f$$
$$= 11.19(10)$$
$$= 111.9 \text{ V}$$

(c) V_{ex} for operation at rated voltage, unity PF, and the same real power input as in parts (a) and (b) is delivered as follows:

From parts (a) and (b)

$$P_{1\phi} = V_s I_s \cos(\theta)$$
$$= 1328(251)(0.866)$$
$$= 288.7 \text{ kW}$$

Therefore, at unity PF,

$$I_s = P_{1\phi} / V_s$$
$$= 288.7k / 1.328k$$
$$= 217.4 \text{ A}$$

Since

$$\theta = \cos^{-1}(1.000) = 0°$$

Then

$$\mathbf{E_f} = 1328\angle 0° - j5(217.4\angle 0°)$$
$$= 1716\angle -39.3° \text{ V}$$

And

$$I_f = E_f / K_{ag}$$
$$= 1716/200$$
$$= 8.580 \text{ A}$$

Therefore,

$$V_{ex} = I_f R_f$$
$$= 8.580(10)$$
$$= 85.80 \text{ V}$$

(d) For parts (a), (b), and (c), the complex power absorbed by the machine is as follows: For part (a),

$$\mathbf{S_{3\phi}} = 3(1.328 \text{ k})(251\angle +30°)$$
$$= 866 \text{ kW} + j500 \text{ kvar}$$

For part (b),

$$\mathbf{S_{3\phi}} = 3(1.328 \text{ k})(251\angle -30°)$$
$$= 866 \text{ kW} - j500 \text{ kvar}$$

And for part (c),

$$\mathbf{S_{3\phi}} = 3(1.328 \text{ k})(217.4)$$
$$= 866 \text{ kW} + j0 \text{ kvar}$$

Example 15.5 demonstrates some general points about synchronous motor operation. Leading, unity, and lagging motor PF operation is associated with high, medium, and low excitation levels called "over, normal, and under" excitation. Note that the *motor leading* mode is associated with reactive power Q flow from motor to system; *motor lagging* operation means that Q is absorbed by the machine.

| **AC MACHINE APPLICATIONS** | The overwhelming majority of industrial motor applications utilize ac three-phase cage rotor induction motors, particularly where speed control is noncritical. Included are pumps, fans, compressors, and drives for industrial processes. Where speed control is important, both induction and synchronous machines, with electronic controllers, called *drives*, compete with dc machines. The speed is controlled by varying stator applied voltage magnitude and frequency such that V/f = constant. As ac drive technology advances, dc machines are becoming less common. |

Applications that utilize ac three-phase wound induction motors are less common because of their much greater cost; however, a significant number are still being used in situations that demand unusually large starting torque and moderate speed control. Very few induction devices are used as generators.

The overwhelming majority of bulk electric energy production in the world utilizes the ac three-phase synchronous machine as the generator. The two main types of electric energy-producing plants, that is, power plants, are thermal and hydro, where the former accounts for better than 80% of the US production and most of the balance is produced by the latter. Thermal plants use either fossil fuels such as coal, oil, gas, and biomass, or nuclear fuels such as enriched uranium. Emerging technologies, such as wind energy, solar thermal, and solar electric, also show promise for making significant contributions. The nonsalient rotor design is typically used for thermal plant generators, whereas the salient pole type is used in slower speed hydro applications. For applications that require constant speed and few starts, synchronous motors are ideal. As we have observed, the ac three-phase synchronous machine also provides the capability of reactive power control in both motor and generator modes.

Another machine that oddly enough falls into the category of machines described in this chapter is the *brushless dc machine*. Recall that ac three-phase synchronous machines operate at a speed determined by the applied stator voltage frequency; indeed, the term *synchronous* means that the stator and rotor permanent magnet fields, and the rotor structure, are synchronized, that is, turn at the same speed. Hence, if you control the frequency, you control the speed. Suppose we start from a constant voltage constant frequency-balanced three-phase ac source. This three-phase ac source can be rectified to dc, and inverted back to variable voltage magnitude and frequency, balanced three-phase ac, which serves as the input stator voltage to a three-phase synchronous machine. This integrated system-rectifier, inverter, synchronous machine, is called a "brushless dc" machine, since its speed controllability is comparable to the dc machine.

Finally, the most common type of electric motor is the ac single-phase type, which, although more complicated, can be analyzed using the same principles. These are the motors found in household appliances, including mixers, dryers, washing machines, refrigerators, blenders, rotisseries, garage door openers, and many other low-power applications.

| **Problems** | **15.1** A three-phase 6 hp induction motor is rated at 220 V, 50 Hz, and 1410 rpm. Find the number of poles, the slip, and the frequency of the rotor currents. |

15.2 A three-phase 4 hp induction motor is rated at 120 V, 400 Hz, and 3840 rpm. Find the number of poles, the slip, and the frequency of the rotor currents.

15.3 A 50 Hz induction motor has a full-load speed of 460 rpm. If the no-load speed is 476 rpm, determine the slip at full load.

15.4 A three-phase, 440 V, 60 Hz, eight-pole, Y-connected induction motor has the following parameters: $R_s = 0.29\ \Omega, jX_s = 1.25\ \Omega, X'_r = 1.25\ \Omega, R'_r = 0.1\ \Omega$, and $jX_m = 18.5\ \Omega$. Find the terminal current for a slip of 10%.

15.5 An often-used simplified equivalent circuit for an induction motor is shown in Figure P15.5, where the shunt branch has been moved to the voltage source side.

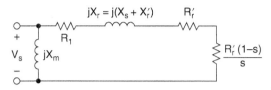

FIGURE P15.5

Using this simplified equivalent circuit, determine the rotor speed and torque of a 40 hp, 440 V, three-phase, 60 Hz, four-pole, Y-connected induction motor with the following parameters: $R'_r = 0.13\ \Omega, R_i = 0.12\ \Omega, X_i = 0.7\ \Omega, jX_m = \infty$, and a slip of 4%.

15.6 A three-phase, 20 hp, 220 V, 60 Hz, six-pole, Y-connected induction motor has the following parameters: $R_1 = 0.15\ \Omega, R_2 = 0.1\ \Omega, X_1 = 0.2\ \Omega, X_2 = 0.3\ \Omega$, and $jX_m = j10\ \Omega$. Using the approximate equivalent circuit in Problem 15.5, determine the input line current and the input PF if the slip is 3%.

15.7 A three-phase, six-pole, 60 Hz, Y-connected induction motor has the following parameters: $R_s = 0.21\ \Omega, jX_s = 1.01\ \Omega, jX'_r = 1.01\ \Omega, R'_r = 0.11\ \Omega$, and $jX_m = \infty$. The motor is used to drive a fan. The fan must turn at 1145 rpm and 10 hp of shaft power is required to run the fan at this speed. Find the magnitude of the terminal voltage required to achieve this operating condition.

15.8 A three-phase, four-pole, 60 Hz, Y-connected induction motor rated at 440 V and 1750 rpm has the following per-phase model parameters: $R_s = 0.35\ \Omega, jX_s = 1.1\ \Omega, jX'_r = 1.1\ \Omega, R'_r = 0.15\ \Omega$, and $jX_m >> |R'_r/s + jX'_r|$, which can, therefore, be neglected. If the motor is operated at rated voltage and shaft speed, find the magnitude of the line current if the motor is used in a hoist that requires a torque of 146.29 N-m to drive a load.

15.9 A three-phase, four-pole, 230 V, 60 Hz induction motor has the following parameters: $R_1 = 0.2\ \Omega, R_2 = 0.1\ \Omega, (X_1 + X_2) = 0.3\ \Omega$, and $jX_m = \infty$. Find the output power and torque for a slip of 4%.

15.10 A three-phase, four-pole, 440 V, 60 Hz, Y-connected induction motor has the following parameters: $R_s = 0.22\ \Omega, jX_s = 1.3\ \Omega, jX'_r = 1.0\ \Omega, R'_r = 0.1\ \Omega$, and it is assumed that $jX_m = \infty$. Find the torque developed at starting if rated voltage is applied to the machine terminals.

15.11 A three-phase, four-pole, 60 Hz, 550 V, Y-connected induction motor has the following parameters: $R_s = 1.0\ \Omega, jX_s = 3.0\ \Omega, jX'_r = 4.5\ \Omega, R'_r = 0.9\ \Omega$, and $jX_m = 35\ \Omega$. When the motor is running at rated speed, the frequency of the rotor currents is measured to be 5 Hz. (a) Find the rated speed. (b) Find the torque developed.

15.12 A three-phase, 50 hp, 440 V, four-pole, 60 Hz induction motor has a stator resistance of 0.05 Ω, a rotor resistance of 0.072 Ω, and a combined $(X_1 + X_2)$ reactance of 0.06 Ω. Find the horsepower and output torque for a speed of 1746 rpm.

15.13 A three-phase, two-pole, 60 Hz, 550 V, Y-connected induction motor has the following parameters: $R_s = 0.3\ \Omega, jX_s = 0.75\ \Omega, jX'_r = 0.75\ \Omega, R'_r = 0.17\ \Omega$, and $jX_m = \infty$. The motor is used to drive a centrifugal pump. When the pump is primed and running, the motor slip is 0.1. Neglecting rotational and stray losses, find the efficiency of the motor at this slip.

15.14 A three-phase, eight-pole, 60 Hz, 440 V, Y-connected induction machine has the following parameters: $R_s = 0.5\ \Omega$, $jX_s = 1.0\ \Omega$, $jX_r' = 1.0\ \Omega$, $R_r' = 0.4\ \Omega$, and $jX_m = \infty$. If the motor draws a line current of 29.09 A, find the shaft speed.

15.15 A local power company charges $0.08 per kW-hr of energy used and pays $0.02 kW-hr that a customer supplies back to the power company's system. A three-phase, four-pole, 60 Hz, 440 V, Y-connected motor with the following parameters: $R_s = 0.8\ \Omega$, $jX_s = 1.9\ \Omega$, $jX_r' = 1.9\ \Omega$, $R_r' = 0.45\ \Omega$, and $jX_m = \infty$, is employed at a local construction site to raise and lower a hoist. The motor speed in the "raise" mode is 1600 rpm and the speed in the "lower" mode is 2000 rpm, and the shaft always turns in the same direction because of a mechanical gearbox. If it takes 10 s to raise the loaded hoist and 5 s to lower the hoist, find the total cost to operate the hoist through one complete raise-and-lower cycle. Neglect rotational losses.

15.16 A three-phase, 220 V, 60 Hz, six-pole induction motor has the following parameters: $R_1 = 0.18\ \Omega$, $R_2 = 0.1\ \Omega$, $X_1 = 0.4\ \Omega$, $X_2 = 0.24\ \Omega$, and $jX_m = j20\ \Omega$. Find the input power and output power and the efficiency if the fixed losses are 300 W and the slip is 2%.

15.17 In parts of South America, the frequency of the power system is 50 Hz. If a three-phase, eight-pole synchronous machine is used as a generator, determine the speed of the rotor.

15.18 A 1000 kVA, three-phase, Y-connected, 4160 V, 60 Hz synchronous generator has an armature resistance and synchronous reactance of 0.14 Ω and 2.5 Ω per phase, respectively. If the PF is 0.77 lagging, determine the full load generated voltage per phase.

15.19 A 960 hp synchronous motor is fed by a 2300 V, three-phase supply at 0.75 PF lagging. If the rotational losses are known to be 20 kW, the armature resistance is negligible and the synchronous reactance is 2.2 Ω, determine the excitation voltage at full load.

15.20 A three-phase, six-pole, Y-connected synchronous machine is operating as a motor. The machine is rated at 2080 V and $jX_s = 4.0\ \Omega$. If the magnitude of the induced voltage $\mathbf{E_f}$ is 1500 V, find the maximum three-phase power that the motor can develop without losing synchronism.

15.21 A three-phase, 4160 V synchronous motor has an jX_s value of 6 Ω. If the motor supplies 600 kW of shaft power and 360 kVAR of reactive power, determine the induced voltage E_f.

15.22 A three-phase, four-pole, Y-connected synchronous motor is operating at a rated voltage of 550 V and the input current is $\mathbf{I_s} = 45\angle{-25°}$ A. Find the three-phase power developed by the machine.

15.23 A 10,000 kVA, three-phase, Y-connected, 60 Hz synchronous generator is fed by a 13.8 kV line. If the armature resistance and synchronous reactance are 0.8 Ω and 2 Ω, respectively, find the full-load generated voltage if the PF is (a) 0.85 lagging and (b) 0.85 leading.

15.24 A three-phase, six-pole, Y-connected synchronous generator is rated at 550 V and has a synchronous reactance of $X_d = 2.0\ \Omega$. If the generator supplies 50 kVA at a rated voltage and a PF of 0.95 lagging, find $\mathbf{I_s}$ and $\mathbf{E_f}$ and sketch the phasor diagram for $\mathbf{V_s}$, $\mathbf{I_s}$, and $\mathbf{E_f}$.

15.25 A three-phase, six-pole, Y-connected synchronous generator with a synchronous reactance of $X_d = 12\ \Omega$ is rated at 4160 V. If the dc field current is adjusted to produce an induced voltage of 5000 V and the rotor angle delta is known to be 35°, find the three-phase complex power output at the generator terminals.

15.26 For the machine in Problem 15.25, if the three-phase real power output does not change, find the new rotor angle if the field current is adjusted to produce an $E_f = 4000\,V$ while the terminal voltage is held constant.

15.27 A three-phase, eight-pole, 4160 V, Y-connected synchronous generator is operated at a rated terminal voltage to supply a terminal current of 100 A at 0.9 PF lagging. If $X_d = 12.0\,\Omega$ and the dc field current in the rotor is related to E_f by the equation $I_f = 0.15\,E_f$, find the dc field current required to operate the generator.

15.28 Repeat Problem 15.27 if the machine is operated as a motor and draws a current of $75.0\angle 15°\,A$.

15.29 A three-phase, six-pole, 2080 V, Y-connected synchronous machine is operated as a generator. The generator delivers 300 kVA at a PF of 0.75 lagging. Find the induced voltage, E_f, and rotor angle, δ, if the per-phase stator impedance is $\mathbf{Z_s} = 0.1 + j8\,\Omega$. Note that in this case we are simply including the effects of stator winding resistance.

Complex Numbers

Complex numbers are typically represented in three forms: exponential, polar, or rectangular. In the exponential form, a complex number **A** is written as

$$\mathbf{A} = Ae^{j\theta}$$

The real quantity A is known as the amplitude or magnitude, the real quantity θ is called the *angle*, and j is the imaginary operator $j = \sqrt{-1}$. θ is expressed in radians or degrees. The polar form of a complex number **A**, which is symbolically equivalent to the exponential form, is written as

$$\mathbf{A} = A\angle\theta$$

and the rectangular representation of a complex number is written as

$$\mathbf{A} = x + jy$$

where x is the real part of **A** and y is the imaginary part of **A**.

The connection between the various representations of **A** can be seen via Euler's identity, which is

$$e^{j\theta} = \cos\theta + j\sin\theta$$

Using this identity, the complex number **A** can be written as

$$\mathbf{A} = Ae^{j\theta} = A\cos\theta + jA\sin\theta$$

which can be written as

$$\mathbf{A} = x + jy$$

Equating the real and imaginary parts of these two equations yields

$$x = A\cos\theta$$
$$y = A\sin\theta$$

From these equations, we obtain

$$x^2 + y^2 = A^2\cos^2\theta + A^2\sin^2\theta = A^2$$

Therefore,

$$\mathbf{A} = \sqrt{x^2 + y^2}$$

Furthermore,

$$\frac{A\sin\theta}{A\cos\theta} = \tan\theta = \frac{y}{x}$$

and hence

$$\theta = \tan^{-1} \frac{y}{x}$$

The interrelationships among the three representations of a complex number are as follows.

Exponential	Polar	Rectangular
$Ae^{j\theta}$	$A\angle\theta$	$x + jy$
$\theta = \tan^{-1} y/x$	$\theta = \tan^{-1} y/x$	$x = A\cos\theta$
$A = \sqrt{x^2 + y^2}$	$A = \sqrt{x^2 + y^2}$	$y = A\sin\theta$

We will now show that the operations of addition, subtraction, multiplication, and division apply to complex numbers in the same manner that they apply to real numbers. The sum of two complex numbers $\mathbf{A} = x_1 + jy_1$ and $\mathbf{B} = x_2 + jy_2$ is

$$\mathbf{A} + \mathbf{B} = x_1 + jy_1 + x_2 + jy_2$$
$$= (x_1 + x_2) + j(y_1 + y_2)$$

that is, we simply add the individual real parts, and we add the individual imaginary parts to obtain the components of the resultant complex number.

Suppose we wish to calculate the sum $\mathbf{A} + \mathbf{B}$ if $\mathbf{A} = 5\angle 36.9°$ and $\mathbf{B} = 5\angle 53.1°$. We must first convert from polar to rectangular form.

$$\mathbf{A} = 5\angle 36.9° = 4 + j3$$
$$\mathbf{B} = 5\angle 53.1° = 3 + j4$$

Therefore,

$$\mathbf{A} + \mathbf{B} = 4 + j3 + 3 + j4 = 7 + j7$$
$$= 9.9\angle 45°$$

The difference of two complex numbers $\mathbf{A} = x_1 + jy_1$ and $\mathbf{B} = x_2 + jy_2$ is

$$\mathbf{A} - \mathbf{B} = (x_1 + jy_1) - (x_2 + jy_2)$$
$$= (x_1 - x_2) + j(y_1 - y_2)$$

that is, we simply subtract the individual real parts and we subtract the individual imaginary parts to obtain the components of the resultant complex number.

Let us calculate the difference $\mathbf{A} - \mathbf{B}$ if $\mathbf{A} = 5\angle 36.9°$ and $\mathbf{B} = 5\angle 53.1°$. Converting both numbers from polar to rectangular form

$$\mathbf{A} = 5\angle 36.9° = 4 + j3$$
$$\mathbf{B} = 5\angle 53.1° = 3 + j4$$

then

$$\mathbf{A} - \mathbf{B} = (4 + j3) - (3 + j4) = 1 - j1 = \sqrt{2}\angle -45°$$

The product of two complex numbers $\mathbf{A} = A_1\angle\theta_1 = x_1 + jy_1$ and $\mathbf{B} = B_2\angle\theta_2 = x_2 + jy_2$ is

$$\mathbf{AB} = (A_1 e^{j\theta_1})(B_2 e^{j\theta_2}) = A_1 B_2 \angle\theta_1 + \theta_2$$

Given $\mathbf{A} = 5\angle 36.9°$ and $\mathbf{B} = 5\angle 53.1°$, we wish to calculate the product in both polar and rectangular forms.

$$\mathbf{AB} = (5\angle 36.9°)(5\angle 53.1°) = 25\angle 90°$$
$$= (4 + j3)(3 + j4)$$
$$= (12 + j16 + j9 + j^2 12)$$
$$= 25j$$
$$= 25\angle 90°$$

The quotient of two complex numbers $\mathbf{A} = A_1\angle\theta_1 = x_1 + jy_1$ and $\mathbf{B} = B_2\angle\theta_2 = x_2 + jy_2$ is

$$\frac{\mathbf{A}}{\mathbf{B}} = \frac{A_1 e^{j\theta_1}}{B_2 e^{j\theta_2}} = \frac{A_1}{B_2} e^{j(\theta_1 - \theta_2)} = \frac{A_1}{B_2}\angle\theta_1 - \theta_2$$

If $\mathbf{A} = 10\angle 30°$ and $\mathbf{B} = 5\angle 53.1°$, we wish to determine the quotient $\mathbf{A/B}$ in both polar and rectangular forms.

$$\frac{\mathbf{A}}{\mathbf{B}} = \frac{10\angle 30°}{5\angle 53.1°}$$
$$= 2\angle -23.1°$$
$$= 1.84 - j0.79$$

Load Line Analysis

A load line analysis is a graphical technique that can be effectively applied when analyzing non-linear circuits. Consider for example the circuit in Figure B.1. The circuit element in the block may be either linear or nonlinear. In either case, the KVL equation for the circuit is

$$v_S = iR + v_L$$

and if $v_S = 12$ V and $R = 2\ \Omega$, the circuit would be as that shown in Figure B.2, and the KVL equation reduces to

$$12 = 2i + v_L$$

Since the source and resistor values are known, the single linearly independent equation has two unknowns, the current and voltage across the circuit element, which are at present unspecified. To determine the unknowns in this equation, we need one additional equation that specifies the voltage–current relationship for the circuit element. If we plot the voltage–current relationships for the equation

$$12 = 2i + v_L$$

together with that of the circuit element on the same graph, the intersection of the two curves will yield the solution, and this process is equivalent to solving two linearly independent equations with two unknowns.

Since the equation $12 = 2i + v_L$ is linear, we need only two points to completely define the line, i.e.

$$\text{If } v_L = 0, \text{then } i = 12/2 = 6$$
$$\text{If } i = 0, \text{then } v_L = 12$$

These two points define the load line shown on the I–V curve in Figure B.3. Now let us assume that the circuit element in Figure B.2 is a $4\ \Omega$ resistor, in which case the voltage–current relationship for this element is

$$v_L = 4i$$

This equation is also specified by a straight line as shown in Figure B.3. Any two points will define the curve, e.g. $i = 0, v_L = 0$ and $i = 1, v_L = 4$. Note that the intersection of the two curves, i.e. the *operating point*, quiescent point, or Q-point is $i = 2$A and $v_L = 8$ V. Clearly, this would be the same result obtained from a series circuit in which the 12 V source is connected to two resistors in series, a $2\ \Omega$ resistor and a $4\ \Omega$ resistor, in which we are determining the current as

$$i = 12/(2 + 4)$$
$$= 2 \text{ A}$$

and

$$v_L = 4i$$
$$= 8V$$

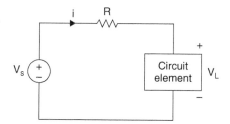

FIGURE B.1 Linear circuit with undefined circuit element

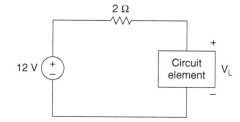

FIGURE B.2 Specific example of Figure B.1

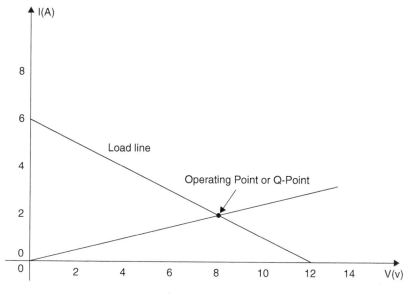

FIGURE B.3 Load line, 4Ω resistor (circuit element) line, and Q-Point for example of Figure B.2

This identical procedure is employed when dealing with a nonlinear element; however, in this case, the curve representing the nonlinear element is not a straight line.

In the general case, the equation for the load line

$$v_S = iR + v_L$$

and that of the diode characteristic are plotted on the same graph and the intersection of the diode characteristic with the load line defines the operating point or Q-point as shown in Figure B.4. Example B.1 serves to illustrate the technique.

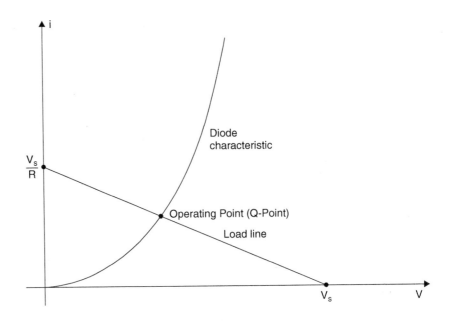

FIGURE B.4 Illustration of determining Q-point of diode in a linear network

---

Example B.1

Given the circuit in Figure B.5 containing a diode with the characteristic shown in Figure B.6, let us determine the current in the circuit and the voltage across the diode.

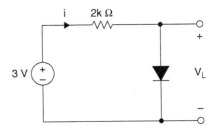

FIGURE B.5 Circuit for Example B.1

SOLUTION:

The load line is defined by the two points $(i, v_L) = (3/2k = 1.5$ mA if $v_L = 0)$, i.e. $(1.5$ mA, 0) and if $i = 0, v_L = 3$, i.e. $(0,3)$. The point $(1.5$ mA, 0) is plotted on the vertical axis, but the point $(0, 3)$ is off the graph. However, the load line is linear and so we can assume a value of $v_D = 1$ V and solve the equation

$$-v_S + iR + v_D = 0$$
$$-3 + i(2k) + 1 = 0$$

which yields the corresponding value for $i = 1$ mA. Therefore, the two points $(1.5$ mA, 0) and $(1$ mA, 1 V) define the load line. When this load line is superimposed on the diode characteristic, the operating point is shown to be the intersection point or the point at which the voltage across the diode is 0.7 V and the current is 1.1 mA.

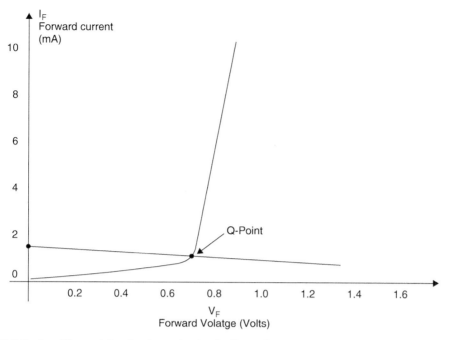

FIGURE B.6   Load line and Q-point determination for Example B.1

Of course, most circuits involving diodes are not as simple as the one in Figure B.5. However, we can approach these situations in the same way in which we dealt with the problem of maximum power transfer previously. In that case, we simply replaced the circuit, exclusive of the load with a Thevenin equivalent circuit that was equivalent at the load terminals to the remainder of the circuit. When this is done, the general circuit in Figure B.7 is reduced to that in Figure B.8. Then the analysis of more complicated circuits can proceed in the same manner as outlined above. Example B.2 illustrates the procedure.

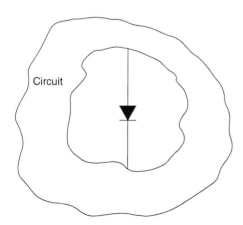

FIGURE B.7   General linear circuit (Thevenin equivalent circuit) and diode

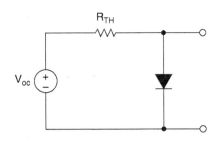

FIGURE B.8 Thevenin equivalent circuit and diode

| Example B.2 |

Given the circuit in Figure B.9 containing a diode with the characteristic shown in Figure B.6, let us determine all currents and voltages in the circuit.

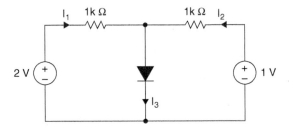

FIGURE B.9 Circuit for Example B.2

To begin, we form a Thevenin equivalent circuit at the terminals of the diode. This circuit is shown in Figure B.10a. Applying KVL to the loop yields

$$-2 + i(1k) + i(1k) + 1 = 0$$

Solving for i yields

$$i = 0.5\,\text{mA}$$

Then, the open-circuit voltage V_{OC} is

$$V_{OC} = i(1k) + 1$$
$$= 1.5\,\text{V}$$

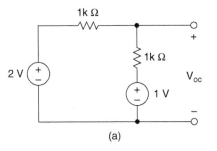

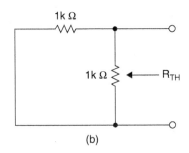

(a)   (b)

FIGURE B.10 Derivation of Thevenin equivalent circuit

The Thevenin equivalent resistance, R_{TH}, is found by looking into the open-circuit terminals with the two sources made zero as shown in Figure B.10b. The Thevenin equivalent resistance is

$$R_{TH} = 1k//1k$$
$$= (1k)(1k)/[1k + 1k]$$
$$= 0.5k\Omega$$

Therefore, the circuit in Figure B.11 is equivalent to that in Figure B.9 at the terminals of the diode. Now, the KVL equation for the network in Figure B.11 is

$$-1.5 + i(1k/2) + v_D = 0$$

The load line is defined by the two points: $(i, v_D) = (0, 1.5 \text{ V})$ and $(3 \text{ mA}, 0)$. A plot of this line together with the diode characteristic is shown in Figure B.12. The intersection of the curves defines the operating point, which is $i = 1.6$ mA and $v_D = 0.72$ V. Given this information, the remaining currents and voltages in the circuit can be obtained. For example,

$$i_1 = (2 - 0.72)/1k$$
$$= 1.28 \text{ mA}$$
$$i_2 = (1 - 0.72)/1k$$
$$= 0.28 \text{ mA}$$

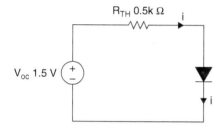

FIGURE B.11   Replacement of original circuit with Thevenin equivalent circuit

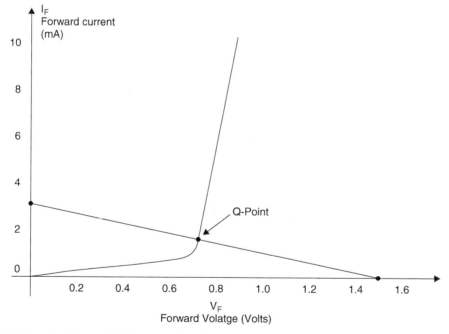

FIGURE B.12   Load line and diode curve plotted to determine Q-point

The Zener or Avalanche Diode and Problems

Zener diodes are a special class of diodes used primarily in voltage regulator circuits in power supplies or in the filters of power supplies, and in clamping circuits to establish a constant voltage. Zener diodes are unique in that they are designed to be normally operated only in *reverse* bias and at a reverse bias that causes Zener breakdown. (All the other diodes we have discussed use the property that the diodes conduct in forward bias and we have assumed they do not conduct in reverse bias.)

For real semiconductor diodes, *in the reverse bias region*, the reverse current remains essentially constant and extremely small until the reverse bias voltage reaches the *breakdown voltage*, usually called the *avalanche* or *Zener breakdown voltage*, V_Z. (Note: Avalanche and Zener breakdown involve different internal mechanisms, but the circuit models are similar.)

At this value of applied reverse voltage, the diode is said to break down and it conducts a large current in the reverse direction with the voltage across the diode essentially clamped at the voltage, V_Z. As reverse bias is increased further, the increasing negative current plotted as a function of reverse voltage shows a finite slope. The inverse of this slope is a small resistance called the equivalent Zener resistance, r_Z. Figure C.1 shows a typical diode voltage–current curve including the region of Zener breakdown.

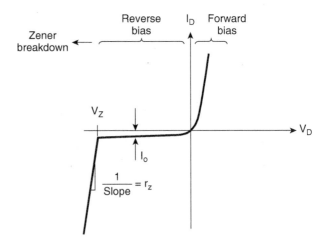

FIGURE C.1   V–I curve for Zener diode

CIRCUIT MODEL OF ZENER DIODE

In Figure C.2a, the circuit symbol for a Zener diode is shown. In Figure C.2b, a circuit model is shown that performs as the device after it is in Zener breakdown; the ideal diode is a short and it appears in the circuit as a voltage source, V_Z and a series resistance r_Z.

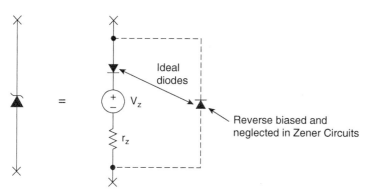

FIGURE C.2   (a) Circuit symbol of Zener diode and (b) circuit model of Zener diode (Note this device would conduct as a normal diode in the forward direction, but since it is never intentionally biased that way, the forward conduction is modeled with a dotted line.)

If a Zener diode with a Zener breakdown voltage, $V_Z = 0.5$ V and $r_Z = 100\ \Omega$, is connected as shown in Figure C.3a, let us find the voltage from A to B and the current through the Zener diode.

Example C.1

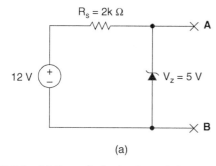
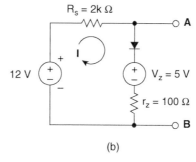

(a)	(b)

FIGURE C.3   (a) Zener diode circuit symbol and (b) circuit model of the circuit

If we replace the Zener diode with its equivalent circuit, we can write the loop equation,

$$12 - V_Z = (12 - 5) = I(2k + 100)$$

and therefore,

$$I = \frac{7}{2.1k} = 3.33\ \text{mA}$$

The current, I, is positive and in the direction that would cause the diode to be in Zener breakdown. The ideal diode in the Zener diode model acts as a closed switch.

The voltage from A to B is the sum of the voltage across r_Z and V_Z:

$$V_{AB} = I(r_Z) + V_Z$$

hence

$$V_{AB} = (3.33 \times 10^{-3})100 + 5 = 5.33\ \text{V}$$

LOAD LINE ANALYSIS OF ZENER DIODE CIRCUITS

As described previously, when the Zener diode is connected to a voltage that applies reverse bias, very little current flows up to a point; as the magnitude of the reverse voltage is increased, Zener breakdown occurs at a particular voltage V_Z (the Zener breakdown voltage), and significant current can flow, while the voltage is essentially clamped at V_Z. A typical V–I curve of a Zener diode is shown in Figure C.4.

Zener diode circuits always use some element or combination of elements to limit the current through the Zener diode after breakdown. Usually, this is a resistor R_S in series with the Zener diode, and this resistance limits the possible current to a value that does not destroy the diode. Such a circuit is shown in Figure C.5.

One very important circuit that takes advantage of the Zener diode's ability to stabilize a voltage is what is commonly known as a *voltage regulator*, which provides a constant voltage through variations in the supply and/or load voltage.

Consider the circuit shown in Figure C.6. This circuit is a Zener diode regulator structured to compensate for variations in the supply voltage or load current. In this circuit, the Zener diode

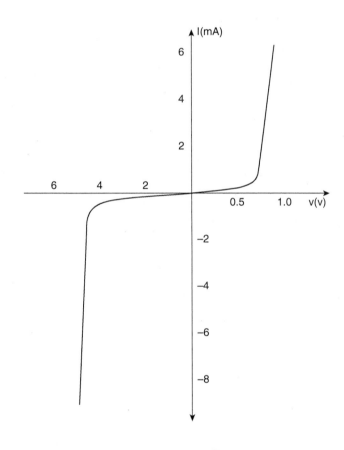

FIGURE C.4 Typical V–I curve of Zener diode

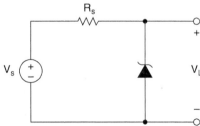

FIGURE C.5 Simple Zener diode voltage regulation circuit

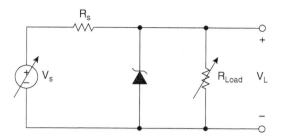

FIGURE C.6   Zener diode voltage regulator with load

operates in the reverse bias mode. As described, the current-limiting resistor, R_S, ensures that the Zener diode never exceeds its maximum power rating. The supply voltage must exceed the breakdown voltage, V_Z. Since the load is connected in parallel with the Zener diode, the voltage across them is the same. And finally, the stabilized voltage desired at the output must be equal to the breakdown voltage, V_Z.

Zener diodes are designed and fabricated by varying the materials used and their doping levels to break down (in reverse bias) at a particular voltage which range over a wide range of voltages. From the manufacturer, you can purchase a Zener diode with virtually any Zener breakdown voltage, V_Z, you choose.

Consider the Zener diode regulator circuit shown in Figure C.7. Let us examine this circuit to determine the output voltage. In addition, let us determine the impact if the source voltage dropped by 10%. Assume the Zener diode characteristic is as shown in Figure C.4.

Example C.2

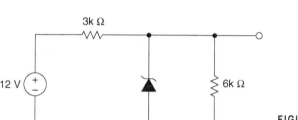

FIGURE C.7   Example of Zener diode regulator circuit

First, the circuit is simplified by determining the Thevenin equivalent circuit of everything except the diode. As shown in Figure C.8a, the open-circuit voltage is

$$V_{OC} = (12)(6k)/[3k + 6k]$$
$$= 8 \text{ V}$$

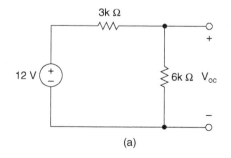
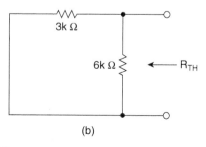

(a)   (b)

FIGURE C.8   Thevenin equivalent resistance of Figure C.7

The Thevenin equivalent resistance is calculated from the circuit in Figure C.8b as

$$R_{TH} = (3k)(6k)/[3k + 6k]$$
$$= 2k\,\Omega$$

Now, the circuit in Figure C.7 is represented by the network in Figure C.9. The KVL equation for this circuit is

$$-8 + i(2k) + v_L = 0$$

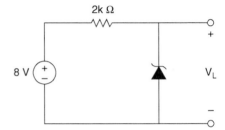

FIGURE C.9   Regulator circuit of Figure C.7 simplified by using Thevenin's equivalent circuit

The load line is defined by the two points $(I, V) = (0, 8V)$ and $(4\ mA, 0)$. The load line is shown in Figure C.10. The operating point indicates that the voltage across the Zener diode and load is -4.6 V.

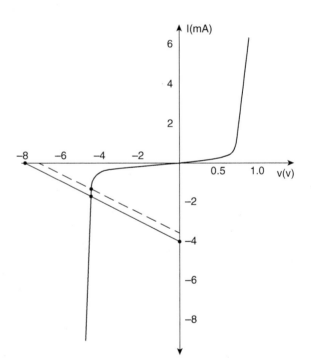

FIGURE C.10   Load line analysis of regulator circuit

If the source voltage drops by 10%, to a value of 10.8 V, then the open-circuit voltage would drop to a value of 7.2 V. The load line in this case would be defined by the two points $(I, V) = (0, 7.2\ V)$ and $(3.6\ mA, 0)$. This curve is also shown dotted in Figure C.10. Note that the change in output voltage is almost imperceptible with a 10% change in supply voltage, which is, of course, the purpose of the voltage regulator.

C.1   Figure PC.1a shows a Zener diode voltage regulator circuit. Using the Zener diode with the V–I curve shown in Figure PC.1b, (a) determine the Zener diode model parameters, V_Z and r_Z, (b) obtain the voltage transfer characteristics of the circuit for $0 < v_i < 15$ V, (c) determine the power dissipated in the Zener diode if $v_i = 10$ V, and (d) determine the output voltage in (c).

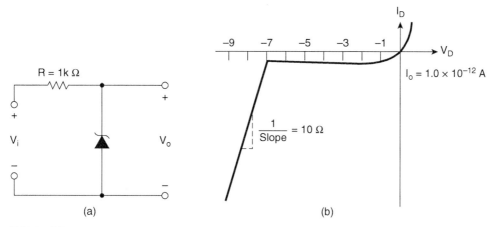

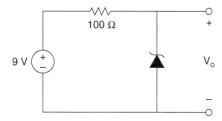

(a)   (b)

FIGURE PC.1

C.2   In the circuit in Figure PC.2, determine the value of the output voltage, v_0. Use the Zener diode characteristics given in Figure PC.1b.

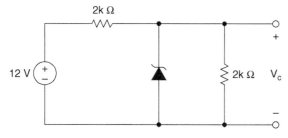

FIGURE PC.2

C.3   A Zener diode with $V_Z = 12$ V and $r_Z = 0$ is placed in the circuit in Figure PC.1a. If v_i is 20 V dc, (a) what is the current through the Zener diode? and (b) if a 6k Ω load resistance is attached at the output, what is the current through the Zener diode?

C.4   Given the circuit in Figure PC.4, determine the voltage across the diode and the current in the circuit if the diode characteristic is represented by the graph in Figure C.10.

FIGURE PC.4

Implementation of Practical Electronic Circuits

IC PACKAGES AND BUILDING REAL CIRCUITS

To produce working circuits, various integrated circuit (IC) chips in their respective packages must be electrically connected. Links to the Data Sheets, as examples of various ICs used in this appendix, are provided. For purposes of small-volume testing, laboratory evaluation or small quantity production, typically ICs are obtained in DIP (Dual-In-Line) packages; see Figure D.1a in which the DIP is secured and electrically connected to points on a protoboard for evaluation (typical protoboards were shown in Chapter 13 (Example 13.2). Typical DIP packages are either 0.3 or 0.6 in. wide (Example 13.2, Figure 13.8).

An alternative and increasingly popular mounting scheme is the surface mounted device; one of the most common of them is identified as an SOP (Small Outline Package), which occupies significantly less area on a circuit board. Type II SOP packages have a width of 5.3 mm (0.21 in.). See Figure D.1b, in which an SOP device is soldered to a circuit board. Connecting an SOP device requires fabrication of a custom circuit board and soldering, which is a more complex process than breadboarding a circuit with a DIP in a protoboard.

However, this approach is not as difficult as it may seem. There are multiple commercial suppliers of custom-made circuit boards that provide design software for layout and placement of these devices, and at nominal prices. There is a popular US-based multiproject organization, OSH Park (https://oshpark.com) that consolidates small boards from many students, hobbyists, and prototype engineers and groups the designs for production on large panels for economy, and then cuts them apart after fabrication to distribute to each board designer.

OSH Park contracts with a high-quality US-based PC Board fabrication company certified for military and high-quality industrial boards; however, the multiproject grouping of designs keeps the cost low for small quantity or prototype work ($5–$10/sq in. for two- and four-layer boards as of this writing).

The utilization of surface mount technology can enable very small, completed circuit boards, as illustrated in Figure D.2.

Another source for low-cost board layout is Easy EDA (https://easyeda.com). This company provides a browser-based platform combining schematic input, SPICE circuit simulation, a PC Board layout tool, component libraries, and online storage for collaborating with a team on circuit projects. Numerous public boards of existing shared designs are available, although private designs can be produced if the user contributes some designs for public sharing. The design and layout tools are free to use, and PC Boards can be manufactured easily at low cost by this company.

OPERATIONAL AMPLIFIERS (OP AMPS)

The selection of which op-amp IC to use depends greatly on the particular application. Historically, the most common op amp, which is made by many manufacturers, is the 741 or LM741. Each manufacturer may have slightly varying characteristics, and, therefore, examination and analysis of the data sheet is important. While this device has been used for many years (considered obsolete by some), it remains an excellent choice for many applications.

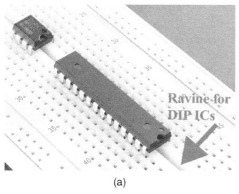
(a)

(b)

FIGURE D.1   (a) DIP packages in a protoboard (STMicroelectronics) (b) SOP package soldered to circuit board

FIGURE D.2   SOP technology enabling very small circuits (Predictable Designs LLC.)

LM741 is a general-purpose operational amplifier. This device has protection against short circuits, and if needed it has the capability of null-offset adjustment through two pins. Also, this op amp is stable with maximum feedback (unity gain); therefore very suitable for voltage-follower (unity-gain) circuits. For the Texas Instruments data sheet, see https://www.ti.com/lit/ds/symlink/lm741.pdf.

Another example is the Fairchild (now part of ON Semiconductor) LM741 (see https://datasheet.octopart.com/LM741CN.-Fairchild-datasheet-7561151.pdf). This shows the device is

FIGURE D.3   Analog Devices quad op amp.

Most manufacturers provide a chip with multiple op amps in a single package. For example, the Analog Devices AD713 contains four op amps (Quad) in a 14-pin package (Figure D.3), each of which offers high-performance equivalent to or better than the basic 741 (see Data Sheet: https://www.analog.com/media/en/technical-documentation/data-sheets/AD713.pdf).

available in an eight-pin DIP package and also a "surface mount" package, which is designed to be soldered directly to a circuit board.

A more recent op-amp design with FET inputs (assuring no current into the inputs) and rail-to-rail output (meaning the output voltage can swing all the way up to the positive voltage supply and likewise down to the value of the negative voltage supply is the Analog Devices AD820 (see https://www.analog.com/media/en/technical-documentation/data-sheets/AD820.pdf).

| INSTRUMENTA-TION AND DIFFERENTIAL AMPLIFIERS | An instrumentation differential amplifier circuit can be implemented using separate op amps as shown in Figure 13.26. There are also single chips available that contain all the elements of this circuit integrated into a single device. Such a circuit is useful in measuring the output of a Wheatstone bridge configuration, as commonly used for mechanical strain measurements.

Consider the Analog Devices Instrumentation Amplifier, AD8227. This device contains, internal to the chip, three op amps as shown in Figure 13.26 and the resistor networks as well. The gain of the entire circuit can be set by one external resistor. The utilization of this device in a strain gauge sensing bridge circuit is shown in Figure D.4. |

| OSCILLATORS (SIGNAL GENERATORS) | A quite common method of generating a precise time delay, or a continuous square wave output is the 555-timer integrated circuit. The continuous generation of a square or rectangular wave output is termed "a-stable" operation. A typical version of this device from Texas Instruments. (See https://www.circuitbasics.com/wp-content/uploads/2015/01/555-Timer-Datasheet.pdf.)

Depending on selection of a capacitor value and two resistors, rectangular or triangular waveforms can be generated of varying frequency and duty cycle.

Another approach for generating a continuous periodic signal utilizes several op amps. For example, in the following circuit (see Figure D.5) there are three stages. (1) The first stage generates a square wave output, as now described. Assume the circuit starts with the output high, that is, at its highest value (near the positive supply voltage) because of the high gain (V_- is lower than V_+), the output is high, and the 1 µF capacitor is being charged. When the voltage at V_- reaches/exceeds the value of V_+, set by the simple voltage divider of 100k Ω and 22k Ω, the output switches to its most negative value and the capacitor is discharged at the same rate, until the output switches again. The net result is a square wave determined by the time constant of the capacitor and the feedback resistor, which is shown as 100k Ω, but variable to adjust the frequency of the oscillation.

The second stage integrates the square wave to obtain a triangle waveform.

The third stage integrates the triangle wave (acts as low-pass filter) to produce a sine wave output. |

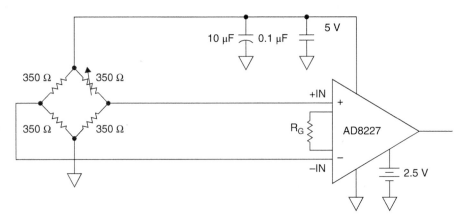

FIGURE D.4 Analog Devices AD8227 in instrumentation circuit with strain gauge sensing bridge (From AD data sheet; see https://www.mouser.com/datasheet/2/609/AD8227-1502262.pdf)

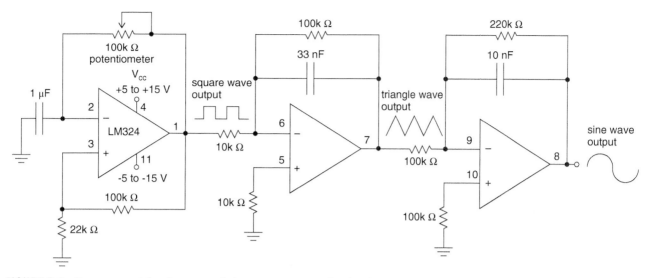

FIGURE D.5   Square wave, triangle wave, and sine wave generator circuit using op amps

As illustrated in Chapter 13, Figure 13.5, the measurement of current normally requires breaking the circuit at some point and placing an ammeter in the circuit. There are a wide variety of current-measuring ICs from IC suppliers. Often, these ICs have a low-value resistor on the chip and provide an output voltage proportional to the measured current.

For example, the Texas Instruments INA family (see https://www.ti.com/product/INA250) contains an internal resistor of only 2 milliohms, and an amplifier to convert the measured current to a proportional voltage output.

Another method of measuring current using semiconductor technology is the use of the Hall effect, an effect that can measure intensity of a magnetic field. The Hall effect results in a voltage difference produced perpendicular to the flow of current through a conductor or semiconductor in the presence of a magnetic field. Some manufactures integrate an extremely low-value current conducting path internal to the chip and calibrate it so that an integrated Hall effect sensor can determine the magnitude of current flow by the magnitude of the magnetic field produced outside the conductor. For example, Texas Instruments produces a family of Hall Effect Current Sensors (The TCMS series; see https://www.ti.com/product/TMCS1100).

Another useful current-measuring technique for ac currents without breaking the circuit is the Rogowski coil (see Figure D.6); it is an electrical device for measuring ac or high-speed

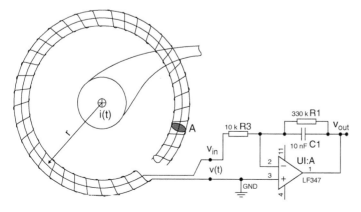

FIGURE D.6   Model of Rogowski coil and measuring circuit (from Wikipedia).

FIGURE D.7   FLUKE-324 clamp-on digital meter

current pulses, which can be clipped around the conductor. It often consists of a helical coil of wire with the lead from one end returning through the center of the coil to the other end so that both terminals are at the same end of the coil. This configuration enables measurement of ac current, without breaking the circuit.

An example of a commonly used instrument using this approach is shown in Figure D.7. This is the FLUKE-324. The jaws open and can clamp around a wire and measure the ac current flowing without breaking the wire (see https://www.fluke.com/en-us/product/electrical-testing/clamp-meters/fluke-324).

As another example, the company GMW Associates produces a small clip on current sensor, the EM AC Current Probe (see https://gmw.com/product/cwt-ultra-mini/).

POWER MEASUREMENTS

There are ICs that can measure current and also contain circuitry to measure voltage, multiply the two measurements, and provide a direct output signal proportional to measured power.

A variety of manufacturers make ICs for power measurement using the technologies previously described (see, for example, the TI INA237series https://www.ti.com/product/INA237). This chip has pins for current "in" and "out," and a voltage measurement, which are multiplexed, digitized, processed and provides outputs of current, bus voltage, power, temperature, and so on. And all on one chip.

PROGRAMMA- BLE LOGIC CONTROLLERS (PLCS)

An additional step-up in capability and ease of use for industrial sensing and control applications is the programmable logic controller (PLC).

IC manufacturers now produce a variety of more complex chips that integrate many of the functions previously described, as well as other functions into IC devices; these devices are programmable with software. The PLC is a compact modular and ruggedized industrial computer having typically tens of inputs and outputs, some digital and some analog for reading conditions from sensors and sending commands to motors and actuators. Program storage is nonvolatile, and units contain a power supply with noise immunity to operate in a harsh industrial environment.

Additionally, most PLCs include digital communication interfaces such as Ethernet, and serial communication allowing them to be networked. The PLC manufacturers include software libraries and programming software to customize and ease setup of a control sequencer for a user's specific application.

These small but powerful systems were initially developed for monitoring and control of industrial manufacturing facilities. They are now used in many applications including the process control of chemical plants, production assembly lines such as in the automotive and other mechanical and electrical fabrication industries as well as many other commercial applications.

Data logging (easily done by the PLC) can provide historical context for maintenance decisions and process improvements. This is in contrast with earlier generations of instrumentation, which were simple gauges or monitors that were read manually by a human operator.

PLCs are available from a variety of manufacturers including Automation Direct, Allen-Bradley, Siemens, Eaton, Honeywell Process, ABB, and others. Cost ranges from a few hundred to a few thousand dollars. The data sheet for the BRX PLC gives significant information on the general capabilities and range of models and cost available (see https://cdn.automationdirect.com/static/catalog/images/product-pdf/BRX-BRXPLC-Overview.pdf).

Index